EXAMPLES & EXPLANATIONS

Constitutional Law
National Power and Federalism

Constitutional Law National Power and Federalism

Sixth Edition

Christopher N. May
Professor Emeritus of Law
Loyola Law School, Los Angeles

Allan Ides
Christopher N. May Professor of Law
Loyola Law School, Los Angeles

Wolters Kluwer
Law & Business

Printed in the United States of America.

1 2 3 4 5 6 7 8 9 0

ISBN 978-1-4548-0524-3

Library of Congress Cataloging-in-Publication Data

May, Christopher N.
    Constitutional law : national power and federalism/Christopher N. May, Professor Emeritus of Law Loyola Law School, Los Angeles; Allan Ides, Christopher N. May Professor of Law, Loyola Law School, Los Angeles. — Sixth edition.
        pages cm. — (Examples & explanations.)
    Includes index.
    ISBN 978-1-4548-0524-3
    1. Constitutional law — United States. 2. Judicial review — United States. 3. Federal government — United States. I. Ides, Allan, 1949- II. Title.

KF4550.M29 2012
342.73 — dc23

                                                2012041900

About Wolters Kluwer Law & Business

Wolters Kluwer Law & Business is a leading global provider of intelligent information and digital solutions for legal and business professionals in key specialty areas, and respected educational resources for professors and law students. Wolters Kluwer Law & Business connects legal and business professionals as well as those in the education market with timely, specialized authoritative content and information-enabled solutions to support success through productivity, accuracy and mobility.

Serving customers worldwide, Wolters Kluwer Law & Business products include those under the Aspen Publishers, CCH, Kluwer Law International, Loislaw, Best Case, ftwilliam.com and MediRegs family of products.

CCH products have been a trusted resource since 1913, and are highly regarded resources for legal, securities, antitrust and trade regulation, government contracting, banking, pension, payroll, employment and labor, and healthcare reimbursement and compliance professionals.

Aspen Publishers products provide essential information to attorneys, business professionals and law students. Written by preeminent authorities, the product line offers analytical and practical information in a range of specialty practice areas from securities law and intellectual property to mergers and acquisitions and pension/benefits. Aspen's trusted legal education resources provide professors and students with high-quality, up-to-date and effective resources for successful instruction and study in all areas of the law.

Kluwer Law International products provide the global business community with reliable international legal information in English. Legal practitioners, corporate counsel and business executives around the world rely on Kluwer Law journals, looseleafs, books, and electronic products for comprehensive information in many areas of international legal practice.

Loislaw is a comprehensive online legal research product providing legal content to law firm practitioners of various specializations. Loislaw provides attorneys with the ability to quickly and efficiently find the necessary legal information they need, when and where they need it, by facilitating access to primary law as well as state-specific law, records, forms and treatises.

Best Case Solutions is the leading bankruptcy software product to the bankruptcy industry. It provides software and workflow tools to flawlessly streamline petition preparation and the electronic filing process, while timely incorporating ever-changing court requirements.

ftwilliam.com offers employee benefits professionals the highest quality plan documents (retirement, welfare and non-qualified) and government forms (5500/PBGC, 1099 and IRS) software at highly competitive prices.

MediRegs products provide integrated health care compliance content and software solutions for professionals in healthcare, higher education and life sciences, including professionals in accounting, law and consulting.

Wolters Kluwer Law & Business, a division of Wolters Kluwer, is headquartered in New York. Wolters Kluwer is a market-leading global information services company focused on professionals.

For our parents
Virginia and Robert May
Frances and Albert Ides

Summary of Contents

Contents

Chapter 3   Justiciability   99

Chapter 4   Special Limitations on Judicial Review of State Laws   163

Chapter 5   The Powers of the National Government   219

Chapter 8   The Dormant Commerce Clause   373

Chapter 9 The Privileges and Immunities Clause of Article IV

Contents

Preface

Most of us arrive at law school with at least a minimal awareness of our constitutional system of government. We know generally that the national government is divided into three branches and that the Bill of Rights protects our fundamental freedoms. That awareness probably began with elementary school Thanksgiving Day pageants, developed substance through various American history and government classes in high school, and finally, for some of us, is topped by an undergraduate course in constitutional law. Outside the educational setting, constitutional law issues ripple through the popular media with frequent references to abortion, free speech, religion, racial and gender discrimination, gay rights, and so forth.

As law students, however, we learn very quickly that the study of constitutional law is anything but a meditation on the commonplace. And therein lies the treachery. The familiar quickly blends with the arcane, and we are forced to grapple with a tumult of doctrines, distinctions, and qualifications. Indeed, the familiar may soon disappear as we trek through justiciability, the commerce power, state action, and various other subjects that never seem to make the headlines. Even those topics that strike a common chord are presented with a treatment that is most uncommon. Add to this a bevy of wavering doctrines, concurring or opposing opinions, and the changing personnel of the Supreme Court, and the complexity can become overwhelming.

We're here to help. We have written two volumes designed to give you a foundation in the doctrines and methods of constitutional law and constitutional argument. This volume, *National Power and Federalism*, covers the powers of the federal courts, Congress, and the President; the doctrines of separation of powers and federalism; and some of the limitations that the Constitution imposes on state power. The second volume, *Individual Rights*, covers the provisions of the Constitution that protect us against the government, including the Takings and Contracts Clauses; the Due Process and Equal Protection Clauses; and the Speech, Press, and Religion Clauses of the First Amendment.

These books try to provoke you into thinking about the larger issues of constitutional law with some depth and perception. They are not outlines. Nor are they research treatises on all the nuances of constitutional law. Rather, they present a problem-oriented guide through the principal doctrines of constitutional law — those covered in typical constitutional law courses — with an emphasis on how one might think about issues that arise within the various contexts in which these doctrines operate. Lawyers, after all, are problem solvers. These books are tools for constitutional law problem solvers (and students confronted with the reality of final exams).

We must include the usual caveat. Our books are not a substitute for your constitutional law class or for a basic casebook. Nor are they a substitute for reading those cases. We hope, however, that they will make the classroom experience richer and more accessible. In fact, our experience is that students who have read these materials along with traditional cases have found the cases more understandable and more easily digested. They have also found that class participation is less threatening and more fruitful. We are confident that you will have the same experience.

The approach we suggest is quite simple. As you begin a new topic in your constitutional law course, read the related chapter in either *National Power and Federalism* or *Individual Rights*. This will give you an overview of the area and a preliminary sense of how doctrines are applied within the area. In reading the chapters, however, don't just *read* the problems — *do them!* In other words, consider the problem and try to anticipate how it will be solved before you read the accompanying explanation. This will develop your analytical skills. Next, as you read your cases, refer back to the related chapters and chapter sections and assess how each case fits into the overall framework developed by the Court. See if the case comports with the problems and explanations. Be critical. Finally, when you complete the coverage of a topic, review the chapter again. This will give you confidence that you know the material. Students have also found these materials useful as study aids when preparing for their final exams. After all, finals are simply problems to be solved. In any event, don't just read these books; use them to develop your understanding and your skills.

Good luck in your studies and in your careers as problem-solving students of the Constitution.

Christopher N. May
Allan Ides

November 2012

Acknowledgments

We would like to express our appreciation to several people who provided assistance in the preparation of these books, beginning with a special thanks to our student research assistants at Loyola Law School and Washington and Lee University: Lilly Kim (LLS '98), Lauren Raskin (LLS '98), Eric Enson (LLS '99), James V. DeRossitt IV (W&L '96), Ashley DeMoss (W&L '97), Lawrence Striley (W&L '95), Kristen Strain (LLS '01), Kasha Arianne Harshaw (LLS '02), Jessica Levinson (LLS '05), Daniel Costa (UCLA '11), Mario Grimm (LLS '11), Mashashi Kawaguchi (LLS '11), Vanda Long (UNC '11), and Jacquelyn Mohr (LLS '11). Thanks also to our secretaries, Ruth Busch and Diane Cochran. In addition, we gratefully acknowledge the financial support provided by Washington and Lee University and by Loyola Law School.

Constitutional Law
National Power and Federalism

CHAPTER 1

Judicial Review

§1.1 INTRODUCTION AND OVERVIEW

In the constitutional law course, we study the United States Constitution as it has been interpreted and explained by the federal courts for more than 200 years. The Constitution itself is an amazingly short document. Stripped of its amendments, the Constitution occupies fewer than a dozen pages in your casebook. Even with its amendments, the document is barely 20 pages long. Yet while the Constitution itself is extremely brief, the interpretation of it can be exceedingly complex. The bulk of your constitutional law textbook consists of cases in which a court — usually the U.S. Supreme Court — has been asked to decide whether certain government decisions or practices are invalid because they violate the requirements of the Constitution. This process by which courts rule on the constitutionality of actions taken by federal and state officials is known as judicial review.

Judicial review is the fountain of constitutional law. This is true for several reasons. First, the process of judicial review has created the body of reported decisions that we think of as the *law of the Constitution*. When we wish to know whether or not the Constitution allows a particular governmental practice, we usually look first to previous court decisions that have interpreted the constitutional provisions in question. Without this steadily accumulating body of case law, we would have little definitive guidance as to the meaning of the Constitution.

Second, it is the process of judicial review that renders the Constitution binding and enforceable *as law*. In the absence of judicial review, the Constitution would be little more than a statement of normative principles and

1

ideals — similar to the Golden Rule or to the Universal Declaration of Human Rights. Public officials would find it much easier to ignore the Constitution, and statutes that were contrary to the Constitution might still be enforced. Judicial review serves as a mechanism by which public officials may be compelled to perform their duties in accordance with the Constitution.

This chapter examines the doctrine of judicial review as it was developed by the Supreme Court in the early nineteenth century. In reviewing the debate surrounding the legitimacy of this doctrine, we will see that nothing in the Constitution's text specifically authorizes the federal courts to pass on the validity of actions taken by the other branches of the federal government or by the states. Yet the historical backdrop against which judicial review emerged makes clear that the doctrine is fully consistent with the Founders' conception of a balanced democracy in which abuses of power by one branch may be checked or prevented by actions of the coordinate branches. In this chapter we will also explore the question of what sources and techniques courts may properly use when they undertake to interpret the Constitution. Finally, we will consider the extent to which the Supreme Court's interpretations of the Constitution are binding on other branches of the federal government, on state governments, and on other courts.

§1.2 THE BACKGROUND OF *MARBURY v. MADISON*

In the case of *Marbury v. Madison*, 5 U.S. (1 Cranch) 137 (1803), Chief Justice John Marshall, writing for a unanimous Supreme Court, ruled that the federal judiciary may review the constitutionality of actions taken by the legislative and executive branches of the national government. If those actions are found to be in violation of the Constitution, federal courts may refuse to honor or enforce them. *Marbury* thus established that federal courts possess the power of judicial review.

Before examining the *Marbury* decision itself, we will take a look at the historical and political backdrop against which the case was decided. The developments that occurred between the signing of the Declaration of Independence in 1776 and the framing of the Constitution in 1787 were critical to the emergence of judicial review as a part of our democratic scheme of government. Equally important were some of the events that transpired during the early years of the new federal government. Only with this setting in mind can we fully appreciate the significance of *Marbury v. Madison*.

§1.2.1 Independence and the Articles of Confederation

When the American colonies jointly issued the Declaration of Independence, thereby severing their ties with Great Britain, the colonists' goal was not to create one new nation. Rather, their aim was to transform these former British colonies into 13 "free and independent states," each possessed of all the sovereignty and nationhood that Great Britain herself enjoyed. At the same time, it was clear to these newly independent states that they would need to cooperate in certain matters. It was especially important that they band together in conducting the War of Independence with England. To this end, the Continental Congress approved the Articles of Confederation in 1777, and sent them to the states for ratification. Though the Articles were not fully ratified until 1781, they were nonetheless implemented in the interim.

The Articles of Confederation did not establish a new national government. Instead, the Articles merely created an alliance or confederation to which the 13 former colonies belonged. Under that system, "the States retained most of their sovereignty, like independent nations bound together only by treaties." *Wesberry v. Sanders*, 376 U.S. 1, 9 (1964). The confederation in some ways resembled today's United Nations: It possessed no independent power of its own and relied for its success on the acquiescence of its member states. While the Articles provided for a Congress of the Confederation, there was no executive or judicial branch. The Congress possessed only limited powers. It had authority to conduct the war, but could not impose taxes to finance the effort. The Congress had limited power to enact laws, but had no means of enforcing them; instead, compliance depended entirely on the voluntary cooperation of the states — cooperation that was not always forthcoming. In short, under the system created by the Articles of Confederation, the states retained virtually all the powers of government.

§1.2.2 The First State Constitutions

How did these 13 fully sovereign states govern themselves after 1776?[1] Once they formally severed their ties with England through the Declaration of Independence, most of the former colonies had to replace their old colonial charters with new state constitutions. These new instruments of government were a direct reaction to the type of government that had existed during the period of English colonial rule.

The form of government in each of the colonies had been determined by the royal charter issued by the King of England to the corporation that had settled the colony. The typical charter provided for a government consisting of an assembly chosen by the people, a governor and council appointed by

---

1. For a more thorough discussion of the ideas presented in this and the following two sections, see Gordon S. Wood's superb study, *The Creation of the American Republic, 1776-1787* (Norton Library ed., 1972).

the King, and a judiciary selected by the King. On its face, this scheme reflects a separation of powers into three distinct branches — legislative, executive, and judicial. In fact, governing power resided with the governor and council who, in addition to their executive duties, exercised both legislative and judicial functions. In most of the colonies, the governor's council sat as the upper house of the legislature, enabling it to block measures passed by the popular assembly. The governor and his council also served as a court of appeals in civil cases, thereby giving them effective control over the judiciary. Thus, during the colonial era, the legislative assembly was the only part of government that was directly accountable to the people.

When the former colonies created new constitutions in the period after 1776, they responded to their experience under the royal charters by making the legislature dominant while radically curtailing the executive and judicial branches. Under most of the new constitutions, the office of governor or president was stripped of its independence and authority. The governor was typically chosen by the legislature for a term of only one year, and governors usually were no longer allowed to veto legislation. The judiciary was likewise made subservient to the legislature. Judges in most states were now appointed by the legislature, rather than by the governor, and typically served for a term of years instead of for life. Even when judges held their positions "during good behavior," the legislature could remove them at will or adjust their salaries and fees.

Through these new constitutions under which the legislative branch was made supreme, the people of the newly sovereign states hoped to create democratic governments that would be free of the tyranny and injustice that had characterized the colonial system. Yet within a few years it was widely felt that these initial experiments in self-governance had proved a failure. As James Madison later wrote, "[e]xperience in all the States had evinced a powerful tendency in the Legislature to absorb all power into its vortex." 2 Farrand, *The Records of the Federal Convention of 1787*, at 74 (1911). This should not have been surprising since the people had deliberately elevated the legislature at the expense of the other branches. Less expected perhaps was what Madison described as the lack of "wisdom and steadiness" on the part of the new state legislatures. In particular, these popularly elected bodies had enacted a host of laws for the relief of debtors, often in patent disregard of the rights of creditors. Laws were enacted suspending the means of collecting debts, closing the courts to creditors, or forcing creditors to accept payment in badly depreciated currency. In addition, property was confiscated without payment of just compensation, statutes were adopted for the benefit of specific individuals, and ex post facto laws were passed. Needless to say, dissatisfaction with this state of affairs was particularly acute among the propertied and creditor classes against whom many of these measures were aimed.

This widespread "corruption" of the legislative process revealed the unsettling truth that power could be as easily abused by a popularly elected government as it had been by the English Crown. During the colonial era it had been assumed that the evils of government stemmed from the fact that the colonial governments did not represent the people. Yet in the period after 1776 it soon became evident that even governments that reflected the wishes of the community could act in a tyrannical and oppressive manner.

§1.2.3 The Emergence of Judicial Review

In an effort to correct this democratic tyranny, the states embarked upon a second round of constitution making. By the early 1780s, New York, Massachusetts, and New Hampshire had amended their initial constitutions to increase significantly the power of the executive and judicial branches at the expense of the once-omnipotent state legislatures. By more completely separating the functions and powers of government among the three branches it was hoped that the pattern of legislative abuse might be checked.

This effort to bring about a true separation of powers was made possible by a new understanding about the nature of sovereignty. The colonists had originally inherited the English conception that sovereignty resided with Parliament, for in England it was only in Parliament that the nation's three estates or social orders — the monarchy, the nobility, and the people — were all represented. When the colonists severed their ties with Britain, the new state constitutions reflected the English practice of making the legislative branch supreme. However, the English concept of sovereignty did not fit the American social landscape where there was neither a monarchy nor a nobility, but only the people. It gradually became clear that sovereign power resided with the people themselves and not with any other body. This being the case, there was no reason why the legislative branch had to be supreme. Since each branch of the government, including the legislature, was composed of the people's agents or servants, the people could grant their agents in each branch as much or as little power as they wished. If the first state constitutions had concentrated too much power in the hands of the legislature, then the solution was to more evenly allocate the powers of government among three branches.

Aided by this conceptual breakthrough concerning the locus of sovereignty, the states amended their constitutions to enhance the executive and judicial branches while reducing the authority of the legislature. The power and independence of the executive was enhanced by giving the governor veto power over legislation, by having the governor elected by the people instead of by the legislature, and by lengthening the governor's term of office. Moreover, state judiciaries began to assert themselves as a check against legislative abuse. With growing frequency, state courts declared that there were judicially enforceable limits to the kinds of laws the legislature could enact. If lawmakers enacted measures that were unconstitutional, courts might declare them null and void. As Elbridge Gerry noted at the Constitutional Convention, "[i]n some States the Judges had actually set aside laws as being ag[ainst] the Constitution. This was done too with general approbation." 1 Farrand, *The Records of the Federal Convention of 1787*, at 97 (1911). In this way, judicial review made its appearance on the American scene. This device was unknown to England, for since the Parliament there was supreme and sovereign, the common law courts lacked authority to review the validity of parliamentary acts. In America, on the other hand, by the time the federal Constitution was adopted in 1787, judicial review was viewed by many as an indispensable tool for curbing legislative abuse and maintaining the principle of separation of powers.

§1.2.4 Creating a New National Government

Despite these structural changes in state governments, the dissatisfaction with American politics only worsened. The amended state constitutions, however perfect in form, were unsatisfactory in practice. Those elected to state office tended to be incompetent and corrupt. They pursued narrow self-interests instead of the republican ideal of "civic virtue" by promoting the common good. In short, it appeared that the people were unable to select those who were best suited to be their leaders.

In response to this failure of self-government, two quite different solutions were proposed. Some critics believed that through religion and education, men and women could acquire the civic virtue necessary to make republican government a success. Others were less sanguine about the ability of mankind to perfect itself and believed that an institutional remedy was necessary. They recommended that the Articles of Confederation be replaced with a true national government that would partially supplant the authority of the states. Federalists, like Alexander Hamilton, had long been urging that the confederation should be given more power, particularly in the areas of finance, war, and commerce. The Federalists' ranks were now swelled by those who believed that creating a new national government was the only way to redress the apparent failure of self-government in the states.

The efforts of the Federalists led to the Constitutional Convention that assembled at Philadelphia in 1787. The draft Constitution that emerged from the Convention in September 1787 benefited greatly from the experiments in constitution making conducted by the states during the previous decade. In fact, the structure of the proposed national government was similar to that of New Hampshire and Massachusetts, states that had amended their constitutions in the early 1780s to incorporate the principle of separation of powers as a check against legislative supremacy.

Though the form of the national government would resemble that of a number of states, the Framers expected it to function with greater virtue than its state counterparts. This was based on the hope that a different kind of people would be chosen for federal office than were typically elected at the state level. Since members of Congress would be elected from much larger geographic areas than were state legislators, they would need to appeal to broader, less parochial concerns. For this reason it would be more difficult for a narrow faction or interest to capture a majority in Congress, thereby reducing the likelihood that unjust measures would be enacted at the expense of the public good. The people's apparent inability to select good leaders would be minimized further by the fact that neither the Senate nor the President would be elected directly by the people. Instead, under Article I, §3, senators would be chosen by the state legislatures, while Article II, §1 provided that the President was to be picked by special electors. The Framers thus envisioned that the new national government "would act as a kind of sieve, extracting 'from the mass of the society the purest and noblest characters which it contains.'" Gordon Wood, *The Creation of the American Republic, 1776-1787*, at 512 (Norton Library ed., 1972).

§1.2.5 The Federalist Era, 1789-1801

Congress submitted the proposed Constitution to the states in September 1787. By the terms of Article VII, the Constitution would take effect upon "[t]he Ratification of the Conventions of nine States. . . ." In every state except Rhode Island, where opposition to the Constitution was quite strong, constitutional conventions were elected to vote on the question of ratification. By June 1788, the requisite nine states had approved the Constitution, and by November 1789, every state but Rhode Island had done so. Rhode Island initially rejected the Constitution by a popular vote of town meetings, but the state ultimately called a convention that ratified the Constitution in May 1790.

The first government under the Constitution took office in April 1789. The Federalists had won control of both houses of Congress, and George Washington, a Federalist, was elected as the first president of the United States. The Federalists controlled Congress and the presidency for the next 12 years. Their downfall was hastened by the passage and enforcement of the Sedition Act of 1798. This Act, inspired by fears that the French Revolution would spread to the United States, made it a crime to "write, print, utter, or publish . . . any false, scandalous and malicious writing . . . against the government of the United States, or either house of the Congress . . . or the President . . . with intent . . . to bring them . . . into contempt or disrepute. . . ." Under President John Adams, the Federalists used this statute to send approximately 25 people to jail — most of them Republican opponents of the Adams administration, including a Republican member of Congress.

The Republicans swept the elections of 1800. When Thomas Jefferson was sworn in as President on March 4, 1801, the Republicans for the first time controlled both the presidency and the Congress. However, the federal judiciary remained in Federalist hands. Indeed, in the waning hours of the Adams administration, the Federalists had taken a number of steps to strengthen their hold on the judicial branch. First, it was known that Oliver Ellsworth, the incumbent Chief Justice of the Supreme Court, would soon resign because of ill health. Ellsworth, a Federalist, decided to step down on December 15, 1800, shortly after the election returns made it clear that the next President would be a Republican. This allowed John Adams to appoint John Marshall, his secretary of state, as the new Chief Justice. Marshall, who was a staunch Federalist, was confirmed by the outgoing Senate on January 31, 1801. This move robbed Thomas Jefferson of the chance to appoint the new Chief Justice.

Second, to further solidify their control over the national judiciary, the Federalists adopted the Circuit Court Act of February 13, 1801. Also known as the "Midnight Judges Act," this law created 16 new federal circuit court judgeships. President Adams immediately filled the positions and the Senate confirmed the last of the nominees, most of whom were Federalists, on March 2, 1801, two days before Adams left office. The Circuit Court Act also reduced the size of the Supreme Court from six Justices to five, effective with the next vacancy. This was a transparent attempt to prevent President Jefferson from filling a new vacancy on the Court, should one occur.

Finally, on February 27, 1801, the Federalist-controlled Congress approved the Organic Act of the District of Columbia. Among other things, this Act authorized President Adams to name as many justices of the peace for the District of Columbia as he "shall, from time to time, think expedient." Adams thought 42 a good number. The Senate confirmed these appointees on March 3, 1801, Adams's last day as President. One of these new justices of the peace was a fellow named William Marbury.

§1.2.6 The Republican Assault on the Judiciary

These measures taken during the closing days of the Adams administration gave the Republicans good cause to resent the national judiciary. It was the Federalist-controlled judiciary that also had enforced the Sedition Act, most of whose victims were Republicans. It is therefore no surprise that once Jefferson and the Republicans were in office, they launched a broad-based attack on the federal judiciary. This offensive was of major significance, for it was largely in response to it that *Marbury v. Madison* became the vehicle for establishing the principle of judicial review. See 3 Albert J. Beveridge, *The Life of John Marshall* 50-100 (1919).

The Republican assault on the judiciary consisted of four measures. First, immediately following his inauguration, Jefferson ordered his secretary of state, James Madison, to withhold the commissions from 17 of the 42 justices of the peace whom Adams had appointed for the District of Columbia. One of the commissions withheld was William Marbury's.

Second, on March 3, 1802, Congress at Jefferson's request repealed the Circuit Court Act of 1801. This had the effect of restoring the size of the Supreme Court to 6 justices and of abolishing the 16 circuit court judgeships that President Adams had filled only a year earlier. In the congressional debates on the Repeal Act, it was noted that since Article III, §1 of the Constitution provides that federal judges shall "hold their Offices during good Behaviour," the Supreme Court might declare the Repeal Act unconstitutional to the extent that it had removed the circuit judges from office. In response, the Republicans denied that the federal courts had authority to strike down an act of Congress. This was the first time the right of the federal courts to review the validity of an act of Congress had been seriously challenged.

The third prong of the Republican attack on the judiciary was designed to make it more difficult for the Supreme Court to declare the Repeal Act unconstitutional. In April 1802, a month after the Repeal Act was adopted, the Republican Congress passed a law canceling the June 1802 and December 1802 Terms of the Supreme Court. The Court, which had been in recess since December 1801, did not meet again until February 1803. This explains the long delay in *Marbury v. Madison* being heard by the Court. An order to show cause was issued to Secretary of State Madison in December 1801, but the matter was not heard until the Court met again on February 9, 1803.

The final weapon in the Republican arsenal was a threat to impeach all six Supreme Court Justices. During the debates on the Repeal Act in 1802, some members of Congress warned that if the Court declared an act of Congress unconstitutional, this would be grounds for impeachment. The Republicans also warned that if the Justices, as expected, ordered the Secretary of State to give Marbury his commission, this judicial interference with the executive branch would likewise lead to impeachment.

While the Republicans now claimed that the federal courts had no power to review the constitutionality of actions taken by Congress or the executive, the Republicans earlier had supported the principle of judicial review. They had urged the Supreme Court in *Hylton v. United States*, 3 U.S. (3 Dall.) 171 (1796), to declare a federal carriage tax unconstitutional. A few years later they castigated the federal courts for not striking down the Sedition Act of 1798. Yet despite their clear political motivation, the Republicans had now placed a cloud over the legitimacy of judicial review.

§1.3 *MARBURY v. MADISON:* JUDICIAL REVIEW OF THE COORDINATE BRANCHES

According to his biographer, Chief Justice Marshall was determined that these doubts be quickly put to rest. The problem was finding a vehicle the Court could use to establish the principle of judicial review. The ideal case would have been a challenge filed by the circuit court judges who had been dismissed under the Repeal Act, but none of them challenged the constitutionality of the act. Marshall eventually realized that the vehicle he was searching for had been pending on the Court's docket since December 1801. In *Marbury v. Madison,* Marshall would persuade the rest of the Court that §13 of the Judiciary Act of 1789, which gave the Supreme Court jurisdiction over Marbury's case, was unconstitutional. Until then, no one had questioned the validity of that statute. The Court had even heard several earlier cases brought under §13. It appears that the issue of §13's validity was not raised by counsel but by the Chief Justice himself. See 3 Albert J. Beveridge, *The Life of John Marshall* 104-133 (1919).

§1.3.1 Judicial Review of Acts of Congress

When William Marbury sued Secretary of State Madison in December 1801 to obtain his commission as justice of the peace, Marbury began his suit in the Supreme Court rather than in a state or lower federal court. In taking this unusual step, Marbury relied on §13 of the Judiciary Act of 1789. Section 13 gave the Supreme Court the "power to issue . . . writs of mandamus . . . to any . . . persons holding office, under the authority of the United States." Since Marbury was seeking a writ of mandamus against an officer of the United States, §13 seemed to apply to his case. Yet it was not clear that the statute gave the Supreme Court *original* jurisdiction in mandamus cases, for the quoted language appeared in a sentence that began: "The Supreme Court shall also have *appellate* jurisdiction from the circuit courts and courts of the several states. . . ." If §13 were read as dealing only with the Supreme Court's power in cases heard on appeal, Marbury's action would have to be dismissed on the ground that no law authorized him to sue originally in the Supreme Court. However, such a reading would have deprived the Court of the opportunity to declare an act of Congress unconstitutional. Instead, the Justices agreed with Marbury that §13 authorized the Supreme Court to take original jurisdiction over his mandamus action but then proceeded to declare §13 unconstitutional. Under the modern Court's practices, the constitutional issue should never have been addressed in *Marbury,* for "'[I]t is a cardinal principle' of statutory interpretation . . . that when an Act of Congress raises "a serious doubt" as to its constitutionality, 'this

Court will first ascertain whether a construction of the statute is fairly possible by which the question may be avoided.' *Crowell v. Benson*, 285 U.S. 22, 62 (1932); . . . ." *Zadvydas v. Davis*, 533 U.S. 678, 689 (2001) (construing Immigration and Nationality Act so as not to authorize government conduct that would raise serious constitutional concerns).

To understand why §13 was invalid, it is necessary to look carefully at Article III, §2 of the Constitution. Clause 1 of this section carefully defines the types of cases that federal courts may hear. No federal court, including the Supreme Court, may hear a case or controversy that does not fall within the scope of the federal "judicial power" defined by Article III, §2, cl. 1. This requirement posed no obstacle in Marbury's case, for his suit came within Article III, §2, as one "arising under . . . the Laws of the United States" — namely the Organic Act of the District of Columbia, under which he had been appointed to a five-year term as justice of the peace. As the Court noted, the federal judicial power extended to Marbury's case "because the right claimed is given by a law of the United States." 5 U.S. (1 Cranch) at 173-174.

The problem arose from the second clause of Article III, §2, which specifies how the judicial power is to be exercised by the Supreme Court. The judicial power defined by Article III, §2, cl. 1 may be thought of as a deck of cards. Article III, §2, cl. 2 divides these cards into two separate piles. The first consists of those cases the Supreme Court may hear in its original jurisdiction — i.e., that may be filed directly in the Supreme Court without having to be initiated in a state or lower federal court. The second pile consists of those cases the Supreme Court can hear only in its appellate jurisdiction — i.e., that must be initiated in a state or lower federal court and work their way up the appellate ladder to the Supreme Court. Article III, §2, cl. 2 assigns only a handful of cases to the Supreme Court's original jurisdiction: those "affecting Ambassadors, other public Ministers and Consuls, and those in which a State shall be a Party. . . ." All of the other cases within the federal judicial power — including diversity cases, federal question cases, and suits to which the United States is a party — may be heard by the Supreme Court only in its appellate capacity.

Into which of these two categories did Marbury's case fall? The federal judicial power extended to Marbury's suit because it arose under a law of the United States. As such, Article III, §2, cl. 2 assigned his case exclusively to the Court's appellate jurisdiction. Though Marbury was suing the secretary of state, his action did not fall within the Court's original jurisdiction as a suit "affecting Ambassadors, *public Ministers* and Consuls," for these terms refer to representatives of foreign governments. Since Article II, §2, cl. 2 thus allowed the Supreme Court to hear Marbury's case under its appellate rather than its original jurisdiction, §13 was seemingly unconstitutional.

However, the Exceptions Clause of Article III, §2 appeared to permit the transfer of cases between the Court's original and appellate jurisdictions. After specifying which cases the Supreme Court may hear as an original matter, Article III, §2, cl. 2 states that "[i]n all the other Cases . . . the supreme Court shall have appellate Jurisdiction, both as to Law and Fact, with such Exceptions, and under such Regulations as the Congress shall make" (emphasis supplied). This clause seemingly permits Congress to redeal the cards so that cases that the Constitution assigned to the Court's original jurisdiction could be moved to the appellate pile, while other cases, such as Marbury's suit for a writ of mandamus, might be shifted from the Court's appellate to original jurisdiction. Under this interpretation of the Exceptions Clause, §13 would have been constitutional. However, Chief Justice Marshall rejected such a reading of the clause, suggesting that the Framers would not have bothered to define the Supreme Court's original and appellate jurisdictions if these categories were subject to alteration at the will of Congress. Instead, said Marshall, the Exceptions Clause allows Congress to remove cases entirely from the Court's appellate jurisdiction, but it does not permit cases to be moved from the appellate to the original jurisdiction category. Because this is exactly what §13 of the Judiciary Act was deemed to do, the Court held the statute to be unconstitutional and dismissed William Marbury's suit for lack of jurisdiction. In so doing, the Chief Justice had established the principle that the federal judiciary may review the constitutionality of acts of Congress.

§1.3.2 Judicial Review of Executive Conduct

In addition to establishing the principle of judicial review over acts of Congress, the Court's opinion in Marbury declared that the judiciary possesses a similar power to review actions taken by members of the executive branch. The Court explained that by withholding Marbury's commission, the secretary of state had committed "an act deemed by the court not warranted by law, but violative of a vested legal right." 5 U.S. (1 Cranch) at 162. Since Marbury's legal rights had been violated, "the laws of his country afford him a remedy" in the form of a writ of mandamus. Id. at 168. Nor would the judiciary's issuance of such a writ constitute "an attempt to intrude into the cabinet, and to intermeddle with the prerogatives of the executive." Id. at 170. Instead, said Marshall, there could be no objection if the courts order an executive officer to perform a nondiscretionary duty that was imposed by law. Though the Justices thus found that the executive had violated a federal statute rather than the U.S. Constitution, the critical point was that the Court had claimed the authority to review and determine the legality of executive conduct.

Having found that the executive branch had acted illegally, the Court proceeded to dismiss Marbury's case for lack of jurisdiction. This was certainly an unorthodox way to proceed. It is well recognized that a court must first determine whether it has jurisdiction over the case; only if jurisdiction is found to exist may the court proceed to the merits. Yet had the issue of jurisdiction been addressed first, Marbury's case would have been dismissed without an opportunity for the Court to address the legality of the executive's conduct. By reversing the usual sequence, the Chief Justice was able to use *Marbury* as a vehicle for establishing the principle of judicial review with respect to Congress as well as the executive branch.

§1.3.3 The Constitution as Paramount Law in Court

The principle of judicial review announced in *Marbury* rests upon the crucial assumption that when a court is asked to apply a particular law to the case before it, the court may also look behind the law to determine whether the legislature had the constitutional authority to enact it. We are so accustomed to the notion of judicial review that it is difficult to imagine a system in which courts lack this authority. Yet at the time the Constitution was framed, courts in England had no authority to invalidate an act of Parliament. In some European countries today, ordinary courts cannot assess the validity of laws; such issues may be heard only by special constitutional courts. Chief Justice John Gibson of the Pennsylvania Supreme Court, in rejecting the doctrine of judicial review, urged that "[i]t is the business of the judiciary to interpret the laws, not scan the authority of the lawgiver; and without the latter, it cannot take cognizance of a collision between a law and the constitution. So that to affirm that the judiciary has a right to judge of the existence of such collision, is to take for granted the very thing to be proved. . . ." *Eakin v. Raub*, 12 Serg. & Rawle 330, 347 (Pa. 1825) (Gibson, J., dissenting).

Yet this is precisely what the Court did in *Marbury*. Chief Justice Marshall's analysis flowed from the fundamental premise that "the constitution is to be considered, in court, as a paramount law. . . ." 5 U.S. (1 Cranch) at 178. From this it followed that since it is "the province and duty of the judicial department to say what the law is," courts may interpret the Constitution just as they interpret ordinary laws. Moreover, said Marshall, if in a particular case "a law be in opposition to the constitution . . . the court must determine which of these conflicting rules governs the case." However, since "an act of the legislature, repugnant to the constitution, is void," it results that "the constitution, and not such ordinary act, must govern the case to which they both apply." 5 U.S. (1 Cranch) at 177-178.

Marbury's critical assumption that the Constitution is to be considered by the courts as a "paramount law" has given birth to that vast body of case law that we think of as "constitutional law." Constitutional law in this sense is the collective product of generations of judges who, in order to resolve cases in the judicial arena, have had to interpret and apply the Constitution. This is not to suggest that the judiciary is the only branch of government that interprets the Constitution. As we will see later in this chapter, Congress and the executive must also construe the Constitution in performing their assigned functions. Yet these interpretations are not enforceable as constitutional law unless they comport with the Court's constitutional interpretations.

§1.3.4 Marshall's Textual Defense of Judicial Review

The Chief Justice's opinion in *Marbury* was sharply criticized at the time for its lengthy and gratuitous dictum concerning the illegality of Jefferson and Madison's conduct. There was little immediate reaction to that part of the decision invalidating §13 of the Judiciary Act. The Republicans had no cause to mourn §13's demise. The provision had been enacted by the Federalists; moreover, by declaring it unconstitutional, the Court had narrowed its original jurisdiction. Yet in the process of curtailing its jurisdiction, the Court had also greatly expanded its authority by claiming the power of judicial review. As Robert McCloskey observed, the Court was "in the delightful position . . . of rejecting and assuming power in a single breath." Robert G. McCloskey, *The American Supreme Court* 42 (1960).

In later years, the decision in *Marbury* would come under attack from legal scholars who questioned the soundness of the Chief Justice's defense of the doctrine of judicial review. Nothing in the text of the Constitution explicitly gives the federal courts the authority to invalidate actions taken by the other branches. Chief Justice Marshall's opinion in *Marbury* sought to justify the doctrine through a series of arguments, most of them based on "the peculiar expressions" and "particular phraseology of the constitution. . . ." 5 U.S. (1 Cranch) at 178, 180. Yet none of these arguments is entirely satisfactory. See, e.g., Alexander M. Bickel, *The Least Dangerous Branch: The Supreme Court at the Bar of Politics* 1-14 (1962).

Marshall's first argument was based on the tripartite structure of the federal government rather than on any specific textual provision. The Chief Justice suggested that without judicial review, Congress could "at pleasure" ignore the limits that the Constitution places upon it, "giving to the legislature a practical and real omnipotence. . . ." 5 U.S. (1 Cranch) at 178. Yet the Constitution defines and limits the powers of all three branches, including the judiciary. The fact that Congress's powers are limited by the Constitution gives the Court no special license to assume the role of constitutional policeman. The federal courts have no greater claim to monitor the actions of the other branches than those branches would have to oversee the conduct of the courts. If Marshall's argument were a sound one, Congress would be entitled to respond to *Marbury* by passing a law overturning the decision on the ground that the Court had exceeded its constitutional authority in invalidating an act of the legislature.

Chief Justice Marshall also offered four textually based arguments in support of the principle of judicial review. The first and probably the strongest of these is found in Article III, §2, which states that the federal judicial power, including the Supreme Court's appellate jurisdiction, extends to cases arising under the Constitution. Yet this language does not conclusively prove that federal courts are entitled to review the constitutionality of actions taken by Congress and the President. The Founders may simply have intended that the federal courts should be able to hear challenges to the validity of *state* laws and practices. There is nothing specifically indicating that the federal judiciary was authorized to review the validity of conduct undertaken by the coequal federal branches.

Second, Marshall observed that certain provisions of the Constitution are "addressed especially to the courts." For example, Article III, §3, cl. 1 states that no one may be convicted of treason except on the testimony of at least two witnesses. "If the legislature should change that rule," asked Marshall, "must the constitutional principle yield to the legislative act?" 5 U.S. (1 Cranch) at 179. Yet this argument supports only a narrow principle of judicial review. It suggests that each branch of the federal government is charged with interpreting those provisions of the Constitution that are addressed specifically to it. If, for example, Congress were to pass a law authorizing the federal courts to convict a person of treason on the testimony of one witness, a federal court would be justified in ignoring the statute on the ground that it is unconstitutional. But this limited principle of judicial review would not permit a federal court to invalidate a statute on the basis that it exceeded the scope of Congress's Article I, §8 power to regulate interstate commerce, for the latter provision is addressed to Congress, not to the courts. Judicial review under these limited circumstances was accepted by some critics who otherwise rejected Marshall's broad claim that courts may invalidate legislation under virtually any provision of the Constitution. See *Eakin v. Raub*, 12 Serg. & Rawle 330, 352 (Pa. 1825) (Gibson, J., dissenting).

Marbury's invalidation of §13 of the Judiciary Act was defensible under this narrow principle of judicial review. The constitutional provision at issue in the case, Article III, §2, cl. 2, addressed itself to the federal judiciary by restricting the types of cases that the Supreme Court could hear in its original jurisdiction. To the extent that §13 of the Judiciary Act directed the Court to ignore these limits on its original jurisdiction, the Court was justified in declaring the act unconstitutional. However, the Chief Justice was not content to establish only a limited doctrine of judicial review. Instead, *Marbury* proclaimed the sweeping principle that federal courts may review and invalidate acts of Congress under any provision of the Constitution, including provisions that are not specifically addressed to the courts.

Third, the Chief Justice urged that the federal judiciary's authority to review actions taken by the other branches is supported by Article VI, cl. 3, which requires that judges take an oath "to support this Constitution. . . ." Judges would violate this oath, said Marshall, if they were to honor an unconstitutional law. Yet the oath provision is perhaps the strongest argument *against* the propriety of judicial review. Since the Constitution imposes the same oath on members of Congress and officers of the executive branch, the Oath Clause seems to contemplate a system in which each branch assesses the constitutionality of its own actions. When a member of Congress considers whether or not to support a bill, or when the President decides whether to sign or veto a measure, they are obliged by their oath to ensure that their action comports with the Constitution. By enacting a law, the political branches have signaled their solemn belief that it is constitutional. The oath taken by federal judges gives them no license to review the constitutionality of actions taken by other branches. To the contrary, the oath requirement suggests that each branch is to monitor its own (and only its own) compliance with the Constitution.

Finally, Marshall relied on the Supremacy Clause of Article VI, cl. 2, which advises state judges that "[t]his Constitution, and the Laws of the United States *which shall be made in Pursuance thereof* . . . shall be the supreme Law of the Land . . ." (emphasis supplied). This Clause suggests that state judges may decide whether or not a federal statute comports with the Constitution. Since the Founders presumably did not intend to give state judges the last word as to the validity of federal laws, the Founders must have expected the Supreme Court in its appellate capacity to review a state court's ruling as to the constitutionality of federal laws. However, this argument rests on the key assumption that the "in Pursuance" language of the Supremacy Clause authorizes state judges to assess the substantive validity of federal laws. The language may instead have meant simply that a federal law is valid as long as it was adopted pursuant to the procedural formalities of Article I — i.e., that it was approved by both Houses of Congress and presented to the President. Under this reading of the Supremacy Clause, a federal law that was so enacted is "the supreme Law of the Land" and neither a state court nor the Supreme Court could decline to enforce it just because the judges might think the measure unconstitutional.

Thus, despite the arguments advanced by the Chief Justice in *Marbury*, the text of the Constitution offers no definitive support for the doctrine of judicial review. From the text, it is equally plausible to infer that each branch of the government should be able to construe the Constitution concerning its own functions. These interpretations would not be subject to review or revision by any other branch. Under such an approach, Congress would be the final arbiter of whether a statute falls within the scope of Congress's Article I, §8 power to regulate interstate commerce, or of whether a federal law is consistent with the free speech guarantee of the First Amendment. Similarly, the President would have the last word as to whether Article II allows the executive to seize private industries in time of war, or of whether the President enjoys an executive privilege to withhold information sought by the courts. Likewise, the federal courts would have the ultimate say as to whether the Seventh Amendment right to jury trial may be satisfied by a jury of less than 12, or of whether a talking parrot counts as one of the two witnesses required to convict a person of treason.

While the text of the Constitution does not foreclose a scheme in which each branch would have the final word as to those constitutional provisions that pertain to it, such a scheme would render the Constitution no longer enforceable as law. Instead, the requirements and limitations set forth in the Constitution would amount merely to moral and political norms that each branch could honor or ignore as it chose. If federal officials violated the Constitution, the only recourse would lie with the political process — a process that is likely to offer little protection when those whose rights have been violated constitute a minority of the electorate.

§1.3.5 The Legitimacy of Judicial Review

From a purely textual standpoint, the Court's reading of the Constitution in *Marbury* was a permissible one, though as we have seen, other readings were also possible. Yet the lack of clear textual support for the principle of judicial review does not necessarily mean that the doctrine is illegitimate or that its enunciation by the Court amounted to a judicial usurpation of power. Indeed, other evidence suggests that while the Founders failed to provide textually for the doctrine, they in fact expected that the federal courts would perform the very function of judicial review that Marshall established in *Marbury*.

At one point during the Constitutional Convention, it was proposed that a Council of Revision, composed of the President and a number of Supreme Court Justices, be given authority to veto acts of Congress. One of the delegates, Luther Martin, objected to the proposal on the ground that since questions "as to the Constitutionality of laws . . . will come before the Judges in their proper official character," the Justices would have a "double negative" if they also sat on the Council. In response, Colonel Mason noted that while the federal courts "could declare an unconstitutional law void," they could not refuse to honor laws that were merely "unjust, oppressive or pernicious"; Mason therefore favored including the Justices on the Council. 2 Farrand, *The Records of the Federal Convention of 1787*, at 76, 78 (1911). Martin and Mason thus operated on the explicit assumption, not contradicted by anyone during the Convention, that the federal courts would possess the power of judicial review.

The Federalist Papers also make clear that at the time of the Founding it was generally accepted that federal courts would have the power to declare acts of Congress unconstitutional. *The Federalist* is a collection of letters that appeared in New York newspapers in 1787 and 1788. They were written by Alexander Hamilton, James Madison, and John Jay for the purpose of persuading the people of New York to ratify the Constitution. Despite their unofficial character and the fact that they were written as propaganda, the papers reveal a great deal about what those who ratified the Constitution thought the document meant.

In one of the papers, Hamilton acknowledged that "there is not a syllable in the plan under consideration which *directly* empowers the national courts to construe the laws according to the spirit of the Constitution"; yet, he said, the principle "that wherever there is an evident opposition, the laws ought to give place to the Constitution" is "deducible . . . from the general theory of a limited Constitution. . . ." *The Federalist No. 81*, at 482 (Clinton Rossiter ed., 1961). In another paper Hamilton noted that the life tenure given federal judges would enhance their ability to engage in judicial review:

> The complete independence of the courts of justice is peculiarly essential in a limited Constitution. By a limited Constitution, I understand one which contains certain specified exceptions to the legislative authority; such, for instance, as that it shall pass no bills of attainder, no *ex post facto* laws, and the like. *Limitations of this kind can be preserved in practice no other way than through the medium of courts of justice, whose duty it must be to declare all acts contrary to the manifest tenor of the Constitution void.* Without this, all the reservations of particular rights or privileges would amount to nothing.

The Federalist No. 78, at 466 (Clinton Rossiter ed., 1961) (emphasis supplied). The authors of *The Federalist Papers* and their readers thus understood that the federal judiciary would have the power to review the constitutionality of acts of Congress.

Given the evidence as to the Founders' intent, few people today question the legitimacy of the doctrine of judicial review. As one leading commentator concluded, "It is as clear as such matters can be that the Framers of the Constitution specifically, if tacitly, expected that the federal courts would assume a power . . . to pass on the constitutionality of actions of the Congress and the President. . . . Moreover, not even a colorable showing of decisive historical evidence to the contrary can be made." Alexander M. Bickel, *The Least Dangerous Branch: The Supreme Court at the Bar of Politics* 15 (1962).

§1.4 FEDERAL JUDICIAL REVIEW OF STATE CONDUCT

In addition to being able to review the constitutionality of actions taken by Congress and the executive, the federal courts may also review the constitutionality of conduct engaged in by the states. Included in this authority is the power of the Supreme Court to review state court judgments in cases that raise federal constitutional issues.

§1.4.1 Challenges Initiated in Federal Court

In *Fletcher v. Peck*, 10 U.S. (6 Cranch) 87 (1810), the federal judiciary for the first time struck down a state law on the ground that it violated the Constitution. The suit, which was filed in federal court based on diversity of citizenship, involved a parcel of land that had originally belonged to the state of Georgia. The case turned on the validity of a Georgia statute that attempted to rescind the original sale of the land. The Supreme Court held that the statute rescinding the sale was unconstitutional because it violated the Contracts Clause of Article I, §10, which bars states from passing any "Law impairing the Obligation of Contracts. . . ."

The exercise of judicial review in *Fletcher v. Peck* followed from the reasoning employed by the Court seven years earlier in *Marbury*. There, Chief Justice Marshall had explained that whenever a federal court is presented with a conflict between a law and the Constitution, "the court must determine which of these conflicting rules governs the case." 5 U.S. (1 Cranch) at 178. It should make no difference whether the law at issue is federal or state. In either case, the court must rule on the law's constitutionality to resolve the dispute at hand.

§1.4.2 Supreme Court Review of State Judgments

Section 25 of the Judiciary Act of 1789 gave the Supreme Court authority to hear appeals from state courts in cases involving questions of federal law. In the early years, the Court's exercise of this appellate jurisdiction met with little opposition. However, with the rise of states' rights agitation during and after the War of 1812, the Court's right to review such state rulings was challenged. In response, the Supreme Court was forced to defend the authority conferred by §25. The Court did so in *Martin v. Hunter's Lessee*, 14 U.S. (1 Wheat.) 304 (1816), and again in *Cohens v. Virginia*, 19 U.S. (6 Wheat.) 264 (1821).

Martin v. Hunter's Lessee was an ejectment action filed in a Virginia state court by Denny Martin, a descendant of Lord Fairfax, claiming title to land that Virginia had confiscated from Lord Fairfax during the Revolutionary War and later conveyed to David Hunter. Martin contended that under a treaty between the United States and Great Britain title remained with Fairfax and his heirs. After the Virginia Court of Appeals in 1810 rejected Martin's claim, he appealed to the U.S. Supreme Court under §25 of the Judiciary Act, which allowed such appeals in cases where a state court had rejected a claim made under the Constitution, laws, or treaties of the United States. The Supreme Court reversed the Virginia Court of Appeals, holding that the federal treaty confirmed the title of Fairfax and his heirs. On remand, the Virginia Court of Appeals "declined" to comply with the Supreme Court's mandate, on the ground that §25 was unconstitutional. According to the state court, Virginia was a sovereign state whose judgments were not subject to review by any other sovereignty. Martin again appealed to the Supreme Court under §25. The Court for the second time reversed the Virginia high court and held that §25 was constitutional.

Justice Story's opinion for the Court in *Martin* relied on the text of Articles III and VI in concluding that the Supreme Court may review state judgments involving issues of federal law. Story noted that Article III was a compromise between those who wished to create a complete system of lower federal courts and those who feared that the federal judiciary would undermine the existing state judicial systems. The result was that the Constitution created a Supreme Court but left it up to Congress to create any inferior federal courts. See Art. I, §8, cl. 9; Art. III, §1. Yet, said Story, since the Framers knew that there might be no lower federal courts, they must have envisioned that the Supreme Court's appellate jurisdiction in cases arising under the Constitution might extend to cases decided by state courts. While the Supremacy Clause directs state judges to honor the Constitution over conflicting state laws, the Framers nonetheless provided for Supreme Court review in such cases to ensure the supremacy and the uniformity of federal law. As Story put it, "state attachments, state prejudices, state jealousies, and state interests" might cause state judges to shirk their duty under the Supremacy Clause. Moreover, since "[j]udges of equal learning and integrity, in different states, might differently interpret a statute, or a treaty of the United States, or even the constitution itself," without Supreme Court appellate review to "control these jarring and discordant judgments, and harmonize them into uniformity, the laws, the treaties, and the constitution of the United States . . . might, perhaps, never have precisely the same construction . . . in any two States." 14 U.S. (1 Wheat.) at 347-348.

Five years later, in *Cohens v. Virginia*, 19 U.S. (6 Wheat.) 264 (1821), the Court again upheld the constitutionality of §25 of the Judiciary Act. *Cohens* was an appeal from a conviction under a Virginia law banning the sale of lottery tickets. The Virginia courts had rejected the defendant's contention that because he was selling tickets for a lottery authorized by federal law, the prosecution was barred by the Supremacy Clause. In holding that the Supreme Court could hear Cohens's appeal under §25, Chief Justice Marshall rejected Virginia's argument "that the constitution of the United States has provided no tribunal for the final construction of itself, or of the laws or treaties of the nation; but that this power may be exercised in the last resort by the courts of every State in the Union." 19 U.S. (6 Wheat.) at 377. Nor did it matter, said Marshall, that here in contrast to *Martin* the state itself was a party to the suit, for Article III, §2 gives the Supreme Court appellate jurisdiction in all cases arising under the Constitution, laws, or treaties of the United States — "whoever may be the parties." Id. at 392.

In *Cohens*, the Chief Justice pointedly observed that the Framers provided for Supreme Court review of state decisions partly because state court judges could not always be trusted to honor the supremacy of federal law. "It would be hazarding too much to assert that the judicatures of the States will be exempt from the prejudices by which the legislatures and people are influenced, and will constitute perfectly impartial tribunals." Id. at 386. "There is certainly nothing in the circumstances under which our constitution was formed," wrote Marshall, "which would justify the opinion that the confidence reposed in the States was so implicit as to leave in them and their tribunals the power of resisting or defeating, in the form of law, the legitimate measures of the Union." Id. at 388.

The holdings in *Martin* and *Cohens* that the Supreme Court may review state court decisions involving questions of federal law is supported by what we now know of the Framers' intent. The delegates to the Convention recognized that there had to be some mechanism for ensuring that the states respected the supremacy of federal law. The Convention at first considered having Congress perform this monitoring function in conjunction with the Council of Revision. This procedure was later abandoned in favor of having the federal courts perform this oversight duty. State judges would be allowed to rule in the first instance on the constitutionality of state laws, but their rulings would be subject to appellate review by the Supreme Court. Even delegates who opposed the creation of any lower federal courts agreed that state court decisions involving questions of federal law should be subject to Supreme Court review. For example, John Rutledge of South Carolina urged that the "clause for establishing *inferior* tribunals under the national authority . . . be expunged: arguing that the State Tribunals might and ought to be left in all cases to decide in the first instance[,] the right of appeal to the supreme national tribunal being sufficient to secure the national rights & uniformity of Judgments. . . ." 1 Farrand, *The Records of the Federal Convention of 1787*, at 124 (1911).

The Federalist Papers reflect the same assumption that the Supreme Court could review state court decisions involving federal constitutional issues. As Hamilton explained, "The Constitution in direct terms gives an appellate jurisdiction to the Supreme Court in all the enumerated cases of federal cognizance in which it is not to have an original one, without a single expression to confine its operation to the inferior federal courts." Consequently, if a case presenting a federal constitutional issue is decided by a state court, "an appeal would certainly lie from the latter to the Supreme Court of the United States." *The Federalist No. 82*, at 493-494 (Clinton Rossiter ed., 1961).

The principle established in *Martin* and *Cohens* has endured to the present day. Section 25 of the Judiciary Act of 1789 exists in modern form as 28 U.S.C. §1257. In contrast to the original Judiciary Act, which gave an absolute right of review by petition for writ of error anytime a state court had rejected a claim made under the Constitution, laws, or treaties of the United States, review under §1257 is by petition for writ of certiorari, the grant of which is discretionary with the Court. To invoke §1257, however, the federal issue on which Supreme Court review is being sought must have been addressed by, or at least properly presented to, the state court whose decision is now being appealed. Otherwise, the Supreme Court will almost invariably deny the petition, or if granted, dismiss the writ of certiorari as improvidently granted. See *Howell v. Mississippi*, 543 U.S. 440 (2005) (dismissing writ of certiorari after concluding that petitioner, who sought Supreme Court review under §1257, never raised his federal constitutional claim in state court).

§1.4.3 Adequate and Independent State Grounds

In §25 of the Judiciary Act of 1789, Congress expressly limited the Supreme Court's review of state court judgments to questions of federal law. If a state court had also decided questions of state law, the Supreme Court could not review the correctness of those state law rulings. Though Congress later dropped this limitation on the scope of review, the Supreme Court has adhered to the principle that it will not review state court rulings on issues of state law.

As a result of this limitation, if a state court's judgment rests on two alternative grounds — one state and the other federal — the Supreme Court's inability to review the state ground of decision may mean that any decision the Court rendered would have no effect on the outcome of the case. In other words, even if the Justices were to disagree adamantly with the state court's resolution of the federal issue, the judgment might still stand, based on the unreviewable state ground of decision. Such a state court judgment is said to rest on an adequate and independent state ground of decision.

For the Supreme Court to grant certiorari and issue an opinion when its ruling could have no possible effect on the rights or duties of the parties would amount to an unconstitutional advisory opinion. Article III, §2 limits the judicial power of the United States to the resolution of actual "cases and controversies." See Chapter 3. If nothing more is at stake than an abstract question of law, the Supreme Court cannot hear the matter. As Justice Jackson wrote for the Court, "our power is to correct wrong judgments, not to revise opinions. We are not permitted to render an advisory opinion, and if the same judgment would be rendered by the state court after we corrected its views of federal laws, our review could amount to nothing more than an advisory opinion." *Herb v. Pitcairn*, 324 U.S. 117, 126 (1945). Yet as the Supreme Court has stressed, the fact that a state court "might" have rested its decision on such grounds is of no consequence if it in fact failed to do so; "'a *possible* adequate and independent state ground' for a decision does not 'bar our reaching the federal questions' where ... a 'State Supreme

Court quite clearly rested its decision solely on the Federal Constitution.'" *Oregon v. Guzek*, 546 U.S. 517, 523 (2006).

When the requirements of the adequate and independent state ground doctrine are met, the state court's decision is absolutely shielded from Supreme Court review, no matter how erroneous the state court's handling of federal law. It is therefore critical to understand when a state ground of decision will be deemed "adequate" and when it will be deemed "independent"; unless both of these elements are satisfied, the Supreme Court will be able to review the case.

What Constitutes an "Adequate" State Ground?

An adequate state ground fully sustains the result and does not itself violate any provision of the Constitution or federal law. Under such circumstances, the resolution of any purported federal issue would be "advisory" since, by definition, a decision on that issue could not alter the result in the case.

In considering whether a judgment rests on adequate state grounds, the Court has drawn a distinction between procedural grounds of decision and substantive grounds of decision. An example of a procedural ground of decision would be a contemporaneous objection rule that prevents litigants from raising a federal constitutional claim because it was not asserted in a timely manner.

State procedural grounds are usually deemed adequate if:

1. The procedure does not deny due process or violate any other constitutional provision;
2. The procedure advances a legitimate state interest; and
3. The procedure is applied in a consistent fashion.

In general, while some procedural defaults may be so trivial or contrived as to be inadequate — e.g., a plaintiff's complaint alleging a federal constitutional claim was dismissed because it contained two misspelled words — the Court is likely to uphold a procedural forfeiture unless it appears that the state court has seized on a pretext to avoid hearing the merits of the federal claim. See *Sanchez-Llamas v. Oregon*, 548 U.S. 331 (2006) (upholding a state procedural forfeiture as "adequate" in the context of a noncitizen criminal defendant's failure to make a timely objection to a violation of his rights under a treaty ratified by the United States). On the other hand, even if a state procedure is otherwise deemed adequate, a litigant may be able to overcome a procedural default by showing cause and prejudice — i.e., that there was good reason for its failure to follow the procedure, and there was a resulting harm. As applied, this is a difficult standard to satisfy.

Example 1-A

Suppose that at his criminal trial in state court, Charles requested the judge to admonish the jury that no adverse inference could be drawn from Charles's failure to take the witness stand. The U.S. Supreme Court has held that if requested, such an instruction must be given to protect a defendant's Fifth and Fourteenth Amendment right to remain silent. However, the trial judge failed to so instruct the jury and Charles was convicted. The state supreme court affirmed, ruling that by requesting an "admonition" rather than an "instruction," Charles had failed to comply with required state procedures. Does the state court decision rest on an adequate state ground so as to preclude Supreme Court review?

Explanation

The state procedural rule requiring that defendants request the judge to deliver desired instructions does not itself violate the Due Process Clause or any other constitutional provision. However, a good argument can be made that no legitimate state interest is served by insisting that such requests be made through the use of specific magic words. Alternatively, Charles might be able to show that the state has not applied the rule on a consistent basis because in other cases judges have given the desired instructions even though a defendant asked only for an "admonition." Or, Charles might demonstrate that he had good cause for failing to follow the state rule since the distinction between "admonitions" and "instructions" is highly ambiguous and difficult to comply with; if the Court also agreed that Charles was prejudiced by the judge's failure to give the requested instruction, the state decision would not rest on an adequate procedural ground. See *James v. Kentucky*, 466 U.S. 341 (1984).

The adequacy issue also arises where a state court decision rests on a substantive state ground of decision. For example, suppose a state court dismisses plaintiff's suit for injunctive relief on the merits, finding that the challenged state statute violates neither the U.S. Constitution nor the state constitution. When will such a substantive state ground be deemed adequate so as to insulate the state court's judgment from Supreme Court review? The answer to this question is straightforward: A state ground of decision is adequate if it fully supports the result *and* does not conflict with the U.S. Constitution, with a federal statute, or with a federal treaty.

Example 1-B

Abbey Jones was convicted by a state court of second-degree murder and was sentenced to death under a state death penalty statute. On appeal Jones argued that imposing the death penalty constitutes "cruel and unusual punishment," in violation of the state constitution and the Eighth and Fourteenth Amendments to the U.S. Constitution. The state supreme court rules in Jones's favor, holding that imposing the death penalty violated both the state and federal constitutions. The state petitions the Supreme Court for review under 28 U.S.C. §1257. Is the state ground of decision adequate?

Explanation

First, the state ground of decision fully sustains the result. Regardless of what is said about the Eighth and Fourteenth Amendments, under the state constitution Jones cannot be executed. And, since the state court has the last word as to the meaning of its own constitution, the Supreme Court cannot review the *correctness* of that ruling. Instead, the Supreme Court could reverse the state constitutional ruling only if it were *invalid* because it conflicted with the Constitution, laws, or treaties of the United States. That is not the case here. States are free to give people more rights under state law than they enjoy under federal law. While second-degree murderers may possess no federal right not to be put to death, the state may give them this right under its own constitution or laws. The state ground of decision is therefore adequate.

By contrast, a state ground of decision will not be deemed adequate if a state court has attempted through state law to take away rights protected by the Constitution, laws, or treaties of the United States.

Example 1-C

Suppose that in the previous example the state supreme court had affirmed the defendant's sentence, holding that imposition of the death penalty for second-degree murder does not violate either the U.S. or the state constitution. The defendant has filed a petition for certiorari under 28 U.S.C. §1257. May the Supreme Court, if it wishes, grant the petition?

Explanation

The state ground of decision is not adequate to insulate the state judgment from Supreme Court review. If the Supreme Court were to take the case and find that imposition of the death penalty under these circumstances violated the federal Constitution, the state ground of decision purporting to authorize use of the death penalty would be invalid under the Supremacy Clause. A state may not use its constitution or laws to take away rights that a person enjoys under federal law. The Supreme Court could therefore grant the petition for certiorari.

What Constitutes an "Independent" State Ground?

If a state ground of decision is adequate because it fully sustains the result and does not conflict with any provision of federal law, that state ground will serve to insulate the state judgment from Supreme Court review only if it is also "independent." An independent state ground of decision is one that is not based on the state court's understanding of federal law. See *Hawaii v. Office of Hawaiian Affairs*, 563 U.S. 163, 171 (2009) (state ground not independent when state court describes its decision as "dictated" by federal law). For example, a state court may have interpreted the state constitution as it did out of a desire to mirror a comparable provision of federal law. In that event, the state ground of decision is not independent of federal law. Any mistake by the state court in its understanding of federal law would undermine both the federal and state grounds of decision. If the Supreme Court were to review the case and conclude that the state court was wrong in its handling of the federal ground, the state ground of decision would fall as well, thereby allowing the Supreme Court to reverse the state court's judgment. *Ohio v. Reiner*, 532 U.S. 17 (2001) (taking jurisdiction when state court's interpretation of state law was influenced by its interpretation of the Fifth Amendment).

Example 1-D

In Example 1-B above, the state supreme court held that imposition of the death penalty violated both the federal and state constitutions. The federal ground of decision was based on the state court's reading of the Cruel and Unusual Punishment Clause of the Eighth Amendment. Suppose that the state ground of decision was based on a similar provision of the state constitution. The state court's opinion relied primarily on prior decisions of the U.S. Supreme Court interpreting the Eighth Amendment, although the state court cited a few state cases dealing with the death penalty. The opinion concluded, "We find that imposition of the death penalty on Abbey Jones violated both the federal and state constitutions." The state has sought review in the Supreme Court. Does the decision rest on an adequate and independent state ground so as to bar the Supreme Court from hearing the case?

Explanation

While we saw earlier that the state ground of decision was adequate, the facts here suggest that it was not independent of federal law. The state court's heavy reliance on federal cases dealing with the Eighth Amendment implies that it read the state constitution in light of its understanding of federal law. If so, and if the Supreme Court were to find that the Eighth Amendment allows imposition of the death penalty on Jones, the state ground of decision would likewise fall since the two were inextricably linked. Under these circumstances, the state ground of decision would not be independent.

Yet it is also possible that the state court cited the federal cases only because it thought they reinforced the state court's reading of the state constitution and not because it sought to read the state constitution as mirroring the federal Constitution. In this event, the state court presumably would have reached the same conclusion under the state constitution even if it was mistaken about the Eighth Amendment. The state ground of decision would then be independent and, since it was also adequate, the Supreme Court could not review the case.

In Case of Doubt: Michigan v. Long

As the last example suggests, it may at times be difficult to determine whether or not a state court judgment rests on an independent state ground. Prior to 1983, the Supreme Court often dealt with these doubtful cases by vacating the state judgment and remanding the case to the state court for clarification as to the basis of the decision. If the state court indicated that the judgment was intended to rest on an independent state ground, no further Supreme Court review occurred. However, in *Michigan v. Long*, 463 U.S. 1032 (1983), the Supreme Court announced that in the future, unless it is absolutely clear from the face of the state court opinion that the decision rests on an independent state ground, the Court will assume that the state and federal grounds are not independent, thereby allowing Supreme Court review of the case.

The effect of the presumption created by *Michigan v. Long* is to make it easier for the Supreme Court to review and reverse decisions in which a state court attempted to give a person more rights against the state than they possess under federal law. For, if the only question is the *independence* of the state ground of decision, that ground is presumably *adequate* in the sense that the state is adding to — rather than taking away — rights conferred by federal law. This was true in *Long* itself, where the Michigan Supreme Court's decision gave motorists more rights against police searches than motorists enjoyed under the Fourth and Fourteenth Amendments. By employing a presumption against the existence of independent state grounds, the Court was able to overturn the state court's attempt to enhance motorists' rights against warrantless vehicle searches. While a state court can usually avoid the consequences of *Long* by including "a plain statement in its judgment or opinion" that "indicates clearly and expressly that [the decision] is alternatively based on bona fide separate, adequate, and independent grounds," 463 U.S. at 1041, the Supreme Court might still ignore such a statement if the Court concludes that the asserted adequate and independent state grounds are not "bona fide."

Michigan v. Long rests on the principle that a state court's interpretation of the *federal* Constitution must exactly match that of the Supreme Court. State courts are prohibited from construing the federal Constitution to give individuals fewer rights — or more rights — than the Supreme Court has prescribed. *Arkansas v. Sullivan*, 532 U.S. 769, 771-772 (2001) (state supreme court may not grant greater protections under the United States Constitution than would be provided by the United States Supreme Court). Thus, once the Court in *Long* concluded that there were no independent state grounds of decision, it went on to hold that the state court had erred in reading the Fourth Amendment to give Michigan residents more protections against the state than the Supreme Court had prescribed. As the Court said in another case, "a State is free *as a matter of its own law* to impose greater restrictions on police activity than those this Court holds to be necessary upon federal constitutional standards. . . . [A] State may not impose such greater restrictions as a matter of *federal constitutional law* when this Court specifically refrains from imposing them." *Oregon v. Hass*, 420 U.S. 714, 719 (1975). If a state court wishes to give people more rights than they possess under the U.S. Constitution, it is therefore imperative that the court do so under the state constitution and laws, and that the court's interpretation of these provisions be entirely independent of federal law.

The *Michigan v. Long* presumption that a state court decision does not rest on adequate and independent state grounds can in some cases result in the Supreme Court's rendering what amounts to an advisory opinion. This may occur if the Court grants review in such a case and reverses the state court decision, on the basis that it incorrectly decided a question of federal law. When the case is then remanded to state court for further proceedings, that court is free to reinstate its prior decision by making clear — clearer than it may have been before — that its decision in fact rests on independent state grounds. Indeed, the Supreme Court may expressly invite such a state court response. *Florida v. Powell*, 130 S. Ct. 1195, 1203 (2010) ("Nothing in our decision today, we emphasize, trenches on the Florida Supreme Court's authority to impose, based on the State's Constitution, any additional protections against coerced confessions it deems appropriate."); see also, *Marmet Health Care Center, Inc. v. Brown*, 132 S. Ct. 1201, 1204 (2012) (inviting state court on remand to consider whether its decision can be based on purely state contract law principles). As long as those newly-clarified grounds are also adequate, in that they do not conflict with federal law, the state court's action will in effect render the Supreme Court's opinion one that is purely advisory, for it will have no effect on the rights or obligations of the parties. See *Washington v. Recuenco*, 548 U.S. 212, 223 (2006) (Stevens, J., dissenting) (objecting to Court's having decided case, noting that "[t]he Washington Supreme Court can, of course, reinstate the same judgment on remand . . . because that court chooses, as a matter of state law, to adhere to its view" that state law gives petitioner more rights against the state than what the majority held he was entitled to as a matter of federal law). Nor have state courts hesitated to take this route following a Supreme Court reversal of an earlier state decision. See, e.g., *Racing Association of Central Iowa v. Fitzgerald*, 675 N.W.2d 1 (Iowa), cert. denied, 541 U.S. 1086 (2004); *People v. P.J. Video, Inc.*, 68 N.Y.2d 296, 508 N.Y.S.2d 907 (1986), cert. denied, 479 U.S. 1091 (1987); and see *State v. Powell*, 66 So.3d 905 (Fla. 2011) (Florida Supreme Court, on remand in *Florida v. Powell*, supra, accepts invitation to reconsider state law ground and concludes that Florida's constitution conferred no rights beyond those afforded by the U.S. Constitution).

Example 1-E

George and Al were the Republican and Democratic candidates for President of the United States in the 2000 election. That election was a very close one. Its outcome hinged on which candidate was deemed to have won the popular vote in Florida so as to be entitled to that state's 25 electoral college votes. The initial Florida vote count showed Al trailing George by fewer than 1,800 votes out of 6 million votes cast. As a result, Al was entitled to a recount under Florida law. Al raised several challenges to the recount process, but Florida's secretary of state rejected each of them and, after a partial recount, certified George as having won the popular vote in Florida. Al sued the secretary in state court. Florida's high court ruled in Al's favor and held that under state law, counties had an extended but limited amount of time to submit their recount returns. The deadline set by the court was such that Florida would still be able to benefit from a federal "safe harbor" provision, 3 U.S.C. §5, under which Congress would accept the state's designation of its presidential electors. George then sought review in the U.S. Supreme Court, even though the Florida decision was based solely on state law. His petition argued that the Florida court's decision rested on principles derived from the state constitution, whereas Article II, §1 of the U.S. Constitution provides that the manner for choosing presidential electors must be determined by a state's "Legislature." George also claimed that the Florida court had relied on a novel interpretation of state law, thus altering the procedure for choosing presidential electors after the election occurred, in violation of 3 U.S.C. §5, which requires Congress to accept a state's timely designation of its presidential electors if they were chosen in accord with laws enacted prior to election day. Al urged the Court to deny the petition, arguing that the state court decision simply reflected "a narrow reading and clarification of state statutes that were enacted long before the present election took place." May the U.S. Supreme Court review this case if it wishes to do so?

Explanation

Unlike cases in which there are both federal and state grounds for a decision, the Florida court's decision rests entirely on state grounds. Yet such a decision is insulated from Supreme Court review only if those state grounds are adequate and independent. As to adequacy, George contends that the state grounds are contrary to two federal provisions. Even if his arguments may appear strained — e.g., 3 U.S.C. §5 seems only to address when Congress will accept a state's designation of its presidential electors, not when a designation is invalid as a matter of law — each is such that, if *accepted by the Court*, it would render the state ground contrary to federal law and hence inadequate. The possibility of such a ruling is itself enough to defeat the adequacy of a state ground.

As to independence, the state court's grounds of decision satisfy this requirement if they were based solely on the court's interpretation of state law. However, if the state court's reading of state law was influenced by its understanding of what Florida needed to do to satisfy the federal "safe harbor" provision, that ground would not be independent of federal law, since a misreading of the federal statute might have affected the court's reading of state law. Thus, the state court's decision arguably did not rest on adequate state grounds; nor is it clear that those grounds were independent. See *Bush v. Palm Beach County Canvassing Board*, 531 U.S. 70 (2000).

In the actual case, the Supreme Court did not address the adequate and independent state ground doctrine as such. However, its opinion noted that the Florida court's decision may have violated Article II, §1 (i.e., no *adequate* state ground) and may have been shaped by that court's reading of 3 U.S.C. §5 (i.e., no *independent* state ground). Yet, it was unclear from the state court's opinion whether either of these federal questions was present. The Florida court may have relied solely on state statutes rather than on the state constitution, and while 3 U.S.C. §5 was cited in a footnote, it may have played no role in the decision. Given this uncertainty, *Michigan v. Long* would have allowed the Supreme Court to review the case. Instead, the Court remanded the case so the Florida high court could clarify the bases for its decision. As the Court explained, "After reviewing the opinion of the Florida Supreme Court, we find that there is considerable uncertainty as to the precise grounds for the decision. This is sufficient reason for us to decline at this time to review the federal questions *asserted* to be present." 531 U.S. at 78 (emphasis supplied). By reversing and remanding on this basis, the Supreme Court was able to halt the vote recount in Florida without having to address the merits of the case. A day after Florida's high court clarified its decision, the Supreme Court in another case held Florida's recount procedure to be unconstitutional and barred the state from continuing with the process. See *Bush v. Gore*, 531 U.S. 98 (2000).

Cases Filed in the Federal Courts

Before leaving the adequate and independent state grounds doctrine, it is important to note that the doctrine applies only to Supreme Court review of state court decisions. As we saw, the doctrine stems from the principle that state courts have the last word as to what state law means. When the Supreme Court is reviewing a case that originated in state court, the state courts have necessarily spoken on any issues of state law contained in the case. The Supreme Court will therefore accept these state law rulings as being correct.

By contrast, when the Supreme Court is reviewing a lower federal court decision that involves questions of state law, the Supreme Court is presented only with lower federal court judges' reading of state law, not with a definitive interpretation from the state court. For this reason, 28 U.S.C. §1254 allows the Supreme Court to review all issues involved in cases appealed from the lower federal courts, including any state grounds of decision on which the lower court's ruling may rest. If the Supreme Court believes that federal judges have misinterpreted state law, the Court is free to correct the error.

§1.5 THE ROLE OF JUDICIAL REVIEW IN A DEMOCRATIC SOCIETY

Judicial review is an inherently antimajoritarian doctrine. When a federal court overturns action taken by Congress, by the executive branch, or by one of the states, the court may be acting contrary to the wishes of the majority, as expressed through their elected representatives. The same is true when the Supreme Court overturns the decision of a state court, for state judges are more likely to reflect majoritarian sentiments since most of them remain accountable to the people through periodic elections.

Because judicial review poses this "counter-majoritarian difficulty," it may seem to be "a deviant institution in the American democracy." Alexander M. Bickel, *The Least Dangerous Branch: The Supreme Court at the Bar of Politics* 17-18 (1962). Yet it is precisely because judicial review is counter-majoritarian that it represents such an indispensable part of our constitutional system of government. Contrary to popular myth, our system of government is not purely democratic nor was it designed to be. We saw earlier that the experience with state government during the years from 1776 to 1787 left many of the Framers fearful of democratic politics in which majoritarian power was essentially unchecked. In fact, the federal government came into being largely as a response to the perceived tyranny of popular democracy. To safeguard individual rights against an unrestrained majority, the Constitution and the Bill of Rights placed an array of restrictions on the authority of the federal and state governments. By carefully separating the powers of the national government among three branches, and by further dividing authority between the federal government and the states, the Framers hoped, in the words of the Preamble, to "secure the Blessings of Liberty to ourselves and our Posterity. . . ." Even with these built-in structural safeguards, few were so naive as to believe that elected representatives would always respect the limitations the Constitution places on their exercise of power. It was through the mechanism of judicial review that government actors could, where necessary, be forced to honor the Constitution, even if this was contrary to the wishes of those who elected them to office.

Judicial review is based on the reality that our elected representatives may at times ignore values that "We the People" care about. See Bruce Ackerman, *We the People: Foundations* 3-33 (1991). In the rough and tumble of daily politics where expediency and pragmatism are the order of the day, the Constitution may easily become obscured from view. Against this backdrop, judicial review affords us an opportunity for a sober second thought. When a court invalidates action taken by the legislature or the executive, it initiates a dialogue with the political branches and with the people by suggesting that an important value or principle has been overlooked. Judicial review forces us to reexamine what we or our representatives have done and to decide whether or not we agree with the Court.

In this dialogue, the Justices do not necessarily have the last word. If the Supreme Court employs judicial review in a manner contrary to values that are deeply shared by the majority, the Court's interpretation of the Constitution may, in the end, be rejected. As Alexis de Tocqueville (a French visitor to the United States in the early nineteenth century) observed, federal judges "must be statesmen, wise to discern the signs of the times, not afraid to brave the obstacles that can be subdued, nor slow to turn away from the current when it threatens to sweep them off. . . ." 1 Alexis de Tocqueville, *Democracy in America* 157 (Phillips Bradley ed., Vintage Books 1945) (1862 ed.). If the Supreme Court should seriously misgauge the current, its reading of the Constitution may be rejected by the people in a number of different ways.

First, the people may register their disagreement with the Court by amending the Constitution. While this is a difficult feat to accomplish, it has occurred four times in our history. The Eleventh Amendment overturned *Chisholm v. Georgia*, 2 U.S. (2 Dall.) 419 (1793), which had allowed a state to be sued in federal court without its consent. The Fourteenth Amendment reversed *Dred Scott v. Sandford*, 60 U.S. (19 How.) 393 (1857) and its holding that former slaves and their descendants could not be citizens of the United States. The Sixteenth Amendment overturned *Pollock v. Farmers' Loan & Trust Co.*, 157 U.S. 601 (1895), which had barred the federal government from collecting an income tax that was not apportioned among the states. And the Twenty-Sixth Amendment rejected *Oregon v. Mitchell*, 400 U.S. 112 (1970), which had held that states could deny persons 18 to 21 years old the right to vote in state elections.

A second means by which the political majority may register its disagreement with the Court's reading of the Constitution is through the appointment process. Because Supreme Court Justices and all lower federal court judges are appointed by the President with the advice and consent of the Senate (Art. II, §2, cl. 2), the process of filling judicial vacancies may be used to bring the federal courts more closely into line with popular thinking. This form of "court packing" may produce dramatic changes in the meaning of the Constitution without resort to the formal amendment process. For example, after *Roe v. Wade*, 410 U.S. 113 (1973), held that women have a liberty interest in the abortion decision, the 1980, 1984, and 1988 Republican Party platforms expressed opposition to *Roe* and pledged that the President would appoint federal judges who "respect . . . the sanctity of innocent human life." 1980 *Cong. Q. Almanac* 62B, 74B; 1984 *Cong. Q. Almanac* 55B-56B; 1988 *Cong. Q. Almanac* 54A. During the 1980s and early 1990s, Senate confirmation hearings focused closely on a nominee's stance toward certain key Supreme Court decisions. Such "court packing" efforts may so alter the Court's makeup as to allow a controversial precedent to be overruled or substantially altered. This is what happened to *Roe* in *Planned Parenthood of Southeastern Pennsylvania v. Casey*, 505 U.S. 833 (1992). At the time *Casey* was decided, only three Justices who participated in *Roe* remained on the Court. The five new appointees named by Presidents Reagan and Bush all voted either to overrule *Roe* or to substantially weaken it.

Third, popular opposition to the Supreme Court's interpretation of the Constitution may cause individual Justices to change their views. If a significant segment of the public does not agree with one of the Court's rulings, the chances are good that laws of the type the Court declared invalid will continue to be enacted and enforced, triggering further legal challenges. This pattern of continuing litigation may cause individual Justices to reconsider a matter and to ultimately change their minds. Chief Justice Burger, for example, concurred in *Roe v. Wade*, 410 U.S. 113, 207 (1973), but after confronting the abortion issue in a series of later cases, Burger concluded that the decision in *Roe* should be reexamined. *Thornburgh v. American College of*

Obstetricians and Gynecologists, 476 U.S. 747, 782-785 (1986) (Burger, C.J., dissenting).

Finally, members of the Court might be impeached if their views are strongly at odds with popular thinking. In 1970, 110 members of Congress introduced a resolution to impeach Justice William O. Douglas. The resolution, which died in committee, stemmed from conservative opposition to Douglas's interpretation of the Constitution. Fortunately, impeachment has never been employed successfully to remove a federal judge because of public disagreement with the judge's constitutional decisions. Such use of the impeachment power could cripple the independence of the federal judiciary and virtually destroy judicial review's check against the misuse of power by the political branches.

Despite the existence of these avenues to override the Supreme Court's interpretation of the Constitution, judicial review nevertheless remains a counter-majoritarian institution. None of these democratic checks is easily executed. Moreover, even if one of them should succeed, it may take decades for it to do so. In the interim, generations have had to live with the consequences of the Court's decision. Thus, while judicial review plays an indispensable role in preserving our system of constitutional government, courts wield an awesome power when they undertake that function.

§1.6 THE DEBATE OVER CONSTITUTIONAL INTERPRETATION

In light of the inherently counter-majoritarian nature of judicial review, it is no surprise that one of the debates that still surrounds the doctrine concerns the amount of discretion judges should have when interpreting the Constitution. The more leeway judges possess, the greater the courts' ability to block measures desired by the democratic majority. The debate has largely centered on what sources federal judges may look to in seeking to interpret the Constitution. Should they be limited to the letter of the Constitution's text, or should they be allowed also to take into account the intent of the Framers? May judges give even broader meaning to the Constitution's text by considering sources such as history, tradition, political theory, moral philosophy, or social policy? And finally, to what extent may judges use the Constitution as a vehicle for enforcing values that are in no way tied to the text or the intent of the Framers?

The debate over what sources are relevant to constitutional interpretation has involved two main issues. The first involves the role of the constitutional text, while the second concerns the extent to which the Framers' understanding is binding on the courts. We will examine each of these in turn.

§1.6.1 Interpretivism versus Noninterpretivism

One of the first issues to emerge in the debate over the proper method of interpreting the Constitution was the relevance of the document's text. So-called interpretivists insisted that when courts engage in judicial review, their only legitimate task is to interpret the Constitution. Courts may therefore not strike down actions of the people's elected representatives on the basis of norms that lie wholly outside the Constitution and that are discovered through judicial forays into the realms of natural law, political science, and moral philosophy.

Noninterpretivists, on the other hand, took the position that courts are not limited to interpreting the words of the Constitution. Instead, courts in appropriate cases may enforce unwritten norms that derive entirely from extraconstitutional sources such as natural law or moral philosophy, without tying or tracing them to any specific provision of the document's text. Noninterpretivists relied for support on the Ninth Amendment, which provides that: "The enumeration in the Constitution of certain rights shall not be construed to deny or disparage others retained by the people." A noninterpretivist judge might thus decide, based on principles of natural law, that people have a constitutional right to an education, even though no particular provision of the Constitution purports to confer such a right.

The debate between interpretivists and noninterpretivists has largely run its course. Most people today subscribe to some form of interpretivism, agreeing that the text of the Constitution must be the starting point for any exercise in constitutional interpretation. The demise of noninterpretivism stemmed from a number of serious difficulties posed by such an approach to judicial review. First, because a noninterpretivist sees no need to tie constitutional interpretation to the written Constitution, noninterpretivism raises the counter-majoritarian difficulty to a level that most found to be unacceptable. It is one thing for judges to strike down laws on the basis of principles and values that are fairly traceable to the Constitution. It is quite another for courts to thwart the democratic majority by invoking nothing more than a judge's own notions of what is desirable in terms of morality, ethics, or social policy. While ours is not a true democracy, judicially imposed restraints that have their foundation in the Constitution are at least democratic in the sense that they were ratified by an earlier majority and passively accepted by today's majority through its failure to amend the Constitution.

Second, noninterpretivism is in conflict with the idea of a *written* Constitution. *Marbury v. Madison* defended judicial review on the theory that because we have a "written constitution," federal courts must "expound and interpret" it "as a paramount law," just as courts construe and apply other laws that govern a case. 5 U.S. (1 Cranch) at 176-178. The process of interpreting laws has always been based on the text of the law and the intent of those who drafted it. To free constitutional law entirely from these interpretive moorings would leave judges rudderless in an ocean of values and principles that may have no apparent connection to the written Constitution they are purporting to construe. To this extent, noninterpretivism seems to violate the axiom that "[t]he government of the United States has been emphatically termed a government of laws, and not of men." *Marbury*, supra, 5 U.S. (1 Cranch) at 163.

Finally, noninterpretivism increases the likelihood that judicial review will be discordant and incoherent in the sense that individual judges would construe the Constitution based on widely varying sources and standards of interpretation. Some judges might rely on history and tradition, others on natural law, others on moral philosophy, and still others on social policy. It is deeply unsatisfying to know that the outcome of a case may hinge on the chance makeup of the court rather than on the principled application of a shared set of principles.

The collapse of noninterpretivism by no means ended the constitutional interpretation debate. Instead, the debate over how courts should go about interpreting the Constitution has continued within the interpretivist camp. Three competing theories of interpretation have emerged: textualism, originalism, and nonoriginalism. The theories form a spectrum, with the degree of interpretive discretion given to the courts increasing as one moves from textualism towards nonoriginalism. Because each of these theories contains a range of views, the distinctions between them tend to blur at the margins. As we will see, each of the approaches poses certain difficulties of its own.

§1.6.2 Textualism

Some have argued that judges must zealously follow the text of the Constitution without consulting any source other than the words themselves. This position is known as textualism, though it is also sometimes referred to as strict constructionism, clause-bound interpretivism, or absolute literalism. However designated, textualists take a literal approach to the task of constitutional interpretation, thereby seeking to limit the amount of discretion available to judges.

Textualism is at times an adequate approach to construing the Constitution. Some provisions in the Constitution can be construed literally without consulting other sources and without producing results that are difficult to accept. This is true, for example, of Article I, §3, which makes it clear that a 25-year-old is too young to serve in the Senate, and of Article II, §1, which stipulates that the President is elected to serve a term of four, not six, years.

However, textualism is often problematic. For one thing, few of the constitutional issues that end up in court involve provisions as simple to apply as the minimum age for senators or the number of years in a presidential term. Instead, courts must frequently interpret constitutional clauses that are so vague and open textured that it is impossible to construe them without consulting other sources, such as the Framers' understanding, history, tradition, political theory, or the like. Examples include such constitutional terms as "privileges and immunities," "cruel and unusual punishments," "liberty," "due process of law," "equal protection," and "involuntary servitude." It is simply not possible to construe clauses of this type by consulting nothing more than a dictionary.

Textualism may also be unsatisfactory because it produces results that are "unacceptable" in the sense that they are illogical or absurd, contrary to the intent of the Framers, or violative of fundamental moral, social, or political values. Under a textualist reading of the Constitution, no woman could serve as a member of Congress or as President, since Articles I and III both employ the masculine pronoun to describe these officials. A strict textualist approach to Article I, §9 would allow the President to accept a Lordship from the Queen — but not the King — of England. A literalist approach to the Thirteenth Amendment, which provides that "[n]either slavery nor involuntary servitude, except as punishment for crime whereof the party shall have been duly convicted, shall exist within the United States," would permit slavery as a punishment for crime even though we know that those who adopted this Amendment sought to abolish slavery entirely.

Because of these difficulties, few people today seriously espouse textualism as a viable *general theory* of constitutional interpretation. While there are cases in which it may prove satisfactory, textualism as an across-the-board approach simply does not work. It is unavoidable that in the process of constitutional interpretation courts must look to sources outside the text to give meaning to the document's words. One obvious place to look is to the intent or understanding of those who adopted the provision in question, a move that brings us to originalism.

For an interesting and recent clash over constitutional text, see *Utah v. Evans*, 536 U.S. 452 (2002), where the majority interpreted the text of the Census Clause ("actual Enumeration"), Art. I, §2, cl. 3, as permitting the Census Bureau to impute numbers of persons where no actual count is available, id. at 473-479, while the dissent focused on the language of the text and insisted that an actual counting of persons is required. Id. at 488-496 (Thomas, J., dissenting, joined by Kennedy, J.).

§1.6.3 Originalism

Originalists contend that in construing the Constitution, a court may properly look to the text of the document itself and, where the text is unclear, to the original intent of the constitutional Framers as well. However, if these two sources are not sufficient to give meaning to a clause of the Constitution, judges cannot invoke that provision to block actions taken by the political branches. According to originalism, the power of judicial review may be invoked only when it is absolutely clear from the text of the Constitution or from the Framers' intent that the *specific practice or conduct* in question is unconstitutional. Originalism seeks to curtail judicial discretion, although less severely than does textualism. The goal of originalism is to prevent judges from imposing their own personal beliefs on society under the guise of interpreting the Constitution.

There are a number of problems with originalism as an interpretive theory. First, since few of the issues that are presented to the courts involve unambiguous textual provisions, it is frequently necessary for an originalist judge to ascertain the intent of the Framers. One issue that immediately arises is who should count as the Framers? Are they limited to the roughly 75 delegates who attended the Constitutional Convention in Philadelphia, or does the term also embrace the hundreds of delegates who participated in the various state ratifying conventions? Whichever the case, since only a handful of these delegates left any record of their intentions, how are we to ascertain the intent of the others? Moreover, many of the issues that arise in the courts were never discussed by the Federal Convention or the state ratifying bodies, so there is no original intent in the matter. Originalism fails as a serviceable tool for interpreting the Constitution because it often provides no means of resolving the question at hand.

A second but related objection to an originalist approach tied to the specific intentions of the Framers is that it would render the Constitution a static document incapable of dealing with an array of contemporary issues. Since originalism insists that courts employ judicial review only when the text or intent of the Framers unequivocally reveals that the specific government action is unconstitutional, the Constitution would rapidly become an anachronism. The Bill of Rights would become increasingly irrelevant since it could be invoked only against the particular evils that threatened Americans in 1791. The First Amendment's protection of speech, for example, would not extend to radio, television, or other forms of communication that were not within the Framers' notion of protected speech, nor would the Fourth Amendment's Search and Seizure Clause apply to electronic eavesdropping.

Third, originalism would require that many of the Supreme Court's landmark cases be overruled because they were not based on the strict text of the Constitution or on the demonstrable intent of the Framers. Even *Marbury v. Madison* and the principle of judicial review might face extinction, for, as we saw earlier, the proposition that federal courts may review actions taken by the other federal branches is unsupported by the text of the Constitution and only inferentially supported by evidence of the Framers' intent. Equally vulnerable would be the line of decisions that have used the

Fourteenth Amendment to extend the Bill of Rights to the states, for it is far from clear that the drafters of the Fourteenth Amendment intended this result. *Brown v. Board of Education*, 347 U.S. 483 (1954) might also have to be overruled since it is highly debatable whether those who drafted the Fourteenth Amendment intended the Equal Protection Clause to bar racial segregation of the public schools. In recognition of the chaos that would follow if the Court were to adopt an originalist approach, most originalists add the caveat that they would respect stare decisis by applying their interpretive theory only to constitutional issues that are still open, not to matters that have long been settled and resolved.

§1.6.4 Nonoriginalism

Nonoriginalists, by contrast, reject the binding effect of original understanding. Nonoriginalists are of two types. Some are textualists who believe that the only legitimate basis for constitutional interpretation is the words of the document itself. Indeed, since textualists are by definition also nonoriginalists, they are sometimes referred to as nonoriginalist-textualists. Yet other nonoriginalists reject textualism. Instead, they take the position that while courts may consider the text of the Constitution, as well as the intent of the Framers, courts are not limited to these sources. According to these nonoriginalists, judges may interpret the Constitution in light of all potentially relevant sources, including history and tradition, logic, natural law, moral philosophy, political theory, and social policy. In doing so, courts may reach results that conflict with the understanding of the Framers. Though nonoriginalists usually agree that it would be improper to construe the Constitution in a manner that contradicts the text, not all of them accept this limitation.

In contrast to textualism and originalism, both of which seek to limit judges' interpretive freedom, nonoriginalism allows courts virtually unfettered discretion in construing the Constitution. Indeed, nonoriginalists of this persuasion closely resemble noninterpretivists, with the important distinction that nonoriginalists are still seeking to interpret some provision of the Constitution whereas noninterpretivists might regard the text as being entirely irrelevant. Nonoriginalists defend their flexible approach to constitutional interpretation as necessary to preserving a "living Constitution" that can be adapted to the evolving needs of succeeding generations.

The problems posed by nonoriginalism are similar to those raised by noninterpretivism (see §1.6.1). When judges construe the Constitution in ways that are neither apparent from the text nor supported by the Framers' intent, judicial review is most vulnerable to the charge of illegitimacy. To the extent that individual judges rely on widely varying extraconstitutional sources of meaning, the outcome of a case may depend more on the composition of the court than on the application of settled principles of law. Finally, though nonoriginalism is designed to ensure that the Constitution does not become outdated, it may actually offer less protection for individual rights than does originalism. For while originalism is criticized for its time-bound inability to *expand* the scope of the Bill of Rights, nonoriginalism arguably poses the greater danger that courts, freed of the constraints of the text and the intent of the Framers, may *reduce* the scope of these protections. If, as some nonoriginalists contend, judges are not bound by either the text or the Framers' intent when it comes to adding to one's rights against government, it is hard to see why judges would not be equally free to ignore text and original intent so as to reduce the scope of individual liberty. Thus, while the guiding purpose of nonoriginalism has been to allow for the continued expansion of rights, the theory carries the risk that it could be employed to yield the very opposite results.

§1.6.5 Approaching Consensus

As a result of the difficulties posed by both originalism and nonoriginalism, the polarized versions of these theories have been abandoned by many participants in the interpretation debate in favor of more moderate positions closer to the middle of the spectrum. By shedding some of their more extreme views and by borrowing ideas from each other, the two camps share a great deal of common ground. As a result, the distance that now separates many originalists and nonoriginalists is so slight as to suggest that the debate between them may have run its course.

Thus, in response to the charge that originalism is so rigid as to render the Constitution incapable of adaptation, many originalists have abandoned the early version of this doctrine, which interpreted the Constitution in light of the Framers' views about *specific practices*. In place of such specific practices originalism, these "sophisticated originalists" seek to implement the *general principles or concepts* the Framers endorsed, even if doing so means extending constitutional protection to practices the Framers may never have envisioned. This general principles originalism in effect asks how the Framers, if they were alive today, would apply a particular constitutional provision even in settings that were unknown in their time. By seeking to implement the Framers' general concepts, the values that the Framers sought to constitutionalize remain relevant to a changing world.

Example 1-F

Suppose that a court is presented with the question of whether the First Amendment's prohibition against laws "abridging the freedom of speech" applies to government censorship of radio broadcasts. How might different judges approach this question?

Explanation

A judge who adhered to *specific practices originalism* would conclude that the First Amendment does not protect such expression since it was unknown in 1791 and was not a form of speech that the First Amendment's proponents intended to shield from government interference.

A *general principles originalist*, on the other hand, would not look to the specific types of speech or practices the Framers had in mind, but would seek to apply the general principle that the Framers sought to protect — i.e., the principle of freedom of expression. Because that concept is broad enough to embrace radio broadcasts, a sophisticated originalist would find them protected by the First Amendment.

In this example, a *textualist* would probably reach the same conclusion as a general principles originalist. A textualist might reason that the Constitution protects "speech," that radio broadcasts are a form of "speech," and that since the First Amendment makes no exception for speech that is broadcast electronically, such broadcasts are therefore protected.

By seeking to implement the general principles that are embodied in the Constitution, sophisticated originalists engage in a process of interpretation that is almost indistinguishable from that which nonoriginalists would employ. For example, to decide what is embraced by the term "liberty" in the Fifth Amendment Due Process Clause, a general principles originalist and a nonoriginalist would both look beyond the liberties that were envisioned in 1791 by considering such sources as history, tradition, political theory, and moral philosophy. Each might thus arrive at the conclusion that the Due Process Clause protects the freedoms to marry, to beget children, to acquire education, and to pursue a trade — whether or not the Framers had any of these specific liberties in mind when they adopted the Fifth Amendment.

The shift in focus by many originalists from specific practices to general principles has been matched by a tempering in the views of many nonoriginalists. Whereas some early nonoriginalists deemed the Framers' intent to be largely irrelevant, moderate nonoriginalists accept original intent as an important starting point and deserving of great weight, even though it is not always binding. Because general principles originalists are also willing to ignore the Framers' intent at least as to specific practices, the two schools of constitutional interpretation have largely converged to a point where it is often difficult to tell them apart. While both consider original intent to be important, both may be willing to depart from that intent to shape the Constitution to contemporary circumstances. As Justice Scalia has written, since most judges today are either general principles originalists or moderate nonoriginalists, "the sharp divergence between the two philosophies does not produce an equivalently sharp divergence in judicial opinions." Antonin Scalia, "Originalism: The Lesser Evil," 57 U. Cin. L. Rev. 849, 862 (1989).

§1.6.6 Sources and Levels of Generality

Even if judges tend to agree that the task of interpreting the Constitution requires courts to implement the general principles that underlie a particular constitutional provision rather than the Framers' beliefs concerning specific practices, judges may still disagree as to how these general principles should apply in a given case. These differences stem partly from disagreements about what sources judges ought to consult in giving meaning to the general principle in question.

Example 1-G

Tom was suspended from public school for refusing to wear the school uniform. The lower federal courts rejected Tom's claim that his right to express himself by the way he dresses is a protected form of speech under the First Amendment. How might individual Justices approach this question?

Explanation

A Justice who subscribes to either textualism or specific practices originalism would probably reject Tom's claim since neither the text of the Constitution nor the Framers' intent indicates that conduct of this type is protected speech.

On the other hand, Justices who are either general principles originalists or moderate nonoriginalists would seek to implement the general principle of freedom of expression embodied in the First Amendment. Yet even these Justices might not reach the same result. One such Justice might interpret freedom of expression by looking to history and tradition and on that basis reject the claimed right because custom and law have long restricted the way people may appear in public. A second Justice might look to precedent to see whether a similar right has been recognized in other contexts; this Justice might find a protected right by analogizing the wearing of clothes to wearing an armband or displaying a flag, both of which are recognized forms of expression under prior case law. A third Justice might adopt a philosophical view that focuses not on clothing as such but rather on the notion that people have the liberty to express themselves in any manner they choose, so long as they do not risk causing serious harm to others; this approach would also find that Tom's First Amendment rights were implicated.

Thus, disparities in the sources that judges are willing to consider when implementing a general constitutional principle may lead to divergent results in a particular case.

Judges may also disagree with one another in the application of a constitutional principle because they define that principle at differing levels of generality. Whereas one judge may state the principle in broad and abstract terms, another may phrase it narrowly to cover only a limited range of circumstances. The level of generality or abstraction at which a constitutional norm is phrased may be decisive of whether the principle controls a particular case.

Example 1-H

A court is asked to determine whether the Due Process Clause of the Fourteenth Amendment bars a state from criminalizing private sexual conduct between consenting homosexual adults. In previous cases the Supreme Court recognized that one of the liberties protected by the Due Process Clause is a privacy right to make certain personal decisions involving sex and procreation without interference from the government. The level at which this privacy right is articulated will determine whether or not it covers the case before the court.

Explanation

One judge might phrase the constitutional privacy protection narrowly as encompassing only "a fundamental individual right to decide whether or not to beget or bear a child"; under this formulation, the basic principles underlying the Due Process Clause would not protect relations between two homosexuals. Another judge, however, might articulate the right or privacy at a more general level of abstraction, as involving "the fundamental interest of all individuals . . . in controlling the nature of their intimate associations with others"; under the latter formulation, the right of privacy would apply to the case before the court. Compare *Bowers v. Hardwick*, 478 U.S. 186 (1986) (upholding criminal ban on homosexual sodomy) with *Lawrence v. Texas*, 539 U.S. 558 (2003) (reversing *Bowers*).

There are no legally correct rules as to which sources a judge should consult or how abstractly a constitutional norm should be articulated. As a result, the differences that exist among judges in these matters may reflect the fact that judges are human beings. Regardless of how assiduously a judge strives to decide constitutional cases based on a good faith understanding of the text, its history, and relevant case law, it is almost certain that a judge's own moral, philosophical, and social views will to some degree influence both the selection of sources and the level at which constitutional principles are generalized.

§1.7 THE TECHNIQUES OF CONSTITUTIONAL INTERPRETATION

Whatever a judge's theoretical approach in terms of sources and levels of generality, she is likely to employ a variety of techniques in interpreting the Constitution. The specific techniques employed will vary, depending on the nature of the case and the result the judge is trying to reach. Frequently, several different devices will be used in the same opinion. In *U.S. Term Limits, Inc. v. Thornton*, 514 U.S. 779, 806 (1995), Justice Stevens's majority opinion construed the Qualifications Clauses of Article I by relying on "the text and structure of the Constitution, the relevant historical materials, and . . . the 'basic principles of our democratic system.' . . ." And in *Printz v. United States*, 521 U.S. 898, 905 (1997), which posed the issue of whether Congress may force state officials to implement a federal firearms law, the Court observed that "the answer . . . must be sought in historical understanding and practice, in the structure of the Constitution, and in the jurisprudence of this Court." We will briefly explore a few of the principal devices that courts may employ to give meaning to the Constitution.

§1.7.1 Constitutional Text

As we saw above, originalists and nonoriginalists of all stripes usually begin their interpretive analysis with an examination of the Constitution's text. In some cases, a careful examination of the textual provision itself may prove to be highly illuminating. For example, *Gibbons v. Ogden*, 22 U.S. (9 Wheat.) 1 (1824), struck down New York's steamboat monopoly on the ground that it conflicted with a federal licensing statute. The issue before the Court was whether the Commerce Clause (Art. I, §8, cl. 3) gave Congress the power to adopt the licensing act. One approach Chief Justice Marshall took in answering this question was to closely examine the key words of the clause — "commerce"; "among"; "the several states"; and "regulate." While Marshall buttressed the conclusions provided by this textual analysis with other types of arguments, the words of the Constitution played a central role in the Court's analysis.

§1.7.2 Original Intent

Just as the text is a common starting point for most judges, if the intent of those who drafted the constitutional provision is discernible, many judges will at least take this original intent into account, whether or not they feel absolutely bound by it. As we noted earlier, one problem posed by pure originalism is that the Framers may never have considered the issue confronting the court, or if they did, the evidence may not indicate what a majority of the Framers thought about the matter. Nevertheless, judges often look to evidence of the Framers' intent. In *Cohens v. Virginia*, 19 U.S. (6 Wheat.) 264 (1821), the Court quoted from *The Federalist Papers* to demonstrate that those adopting the Constitution expected the Supreme Court to review state court decisions involving federal constitutional issues. Many years later, Justice Black relied on his own exhaustive "study of the historical events that culminated in the Fourteenth Amendment, and the expressions of those who sponsored and favored, as well as those who opposed its submission and passage" to support his conclusion that the Fourteenth Amendment was "intended . . . to make the Bill of Rights applicable to the states." *Adamson v. California*, 332 U.S. 46, 71-72 (1947) (Black, J., dissenting). Yet, as we have suggested, the Court today rarely feels bound by original intent, even to the extent that it is discernible. This is particularly true with respect to those constitutional provisions that are designed to protect individual rights against governmental interference. As the Court said in *Lawrence v. Texas*, 539 U.S. 558, 578-579 (2003):

> Had those who drew and ratified the Due Process Clauses of the Fifth Amendment or the Fourteenth Amendment known the components of liberty in its manifold possibilities, they might have been more specific. They did not presume to have this insight. They knew times can blind us to certain truths and later generations can see that laws once thought necessary and proper in fact serve only to oppress. As the Constitution endures, persons in every generation can invoke its principles in their own search for greater freedom.

Another objection to original intent, at least as a definitive purveyor of constitutional meaning, is that it asks the wrong question by focusing the interpretive inquiry on the subjective intent of the Framers rather than on the more democratically relevant understanding of the ratifying public. In other words, according to this objection, the critical question should not be what the Framers intended, but what the public understood them to have intended. Some commentators and some members of the Court, therefore, have endorsed a variation of originalism that focuses less on the intent of the Framers and more on the contemporaneous public understanding of the proposed constitutional text. See *District of Columbia v. Heller*, 554 U.S. 570 (2008) (interpreting the Second Amendment from the perspective of the public understanding of the text at the time the Amendment was adopted). This approach is referred to as *original understanding*. Its virtue is that it emphasizes what the people who ratified the Constitution thought they were ratifying and not what the Framers may have intended the text to accomplish, though in most cases one would expect that the public understanding and the subjective intent of the Framers would be roughly the same. See id. at 640-662 (Stevens, J., dissenting) (intermingling the questions of "intent" and "public understanding" in interpreting the Second Amendment). The vice of an original understanding approach is that it runs the risk of exaggerating our ability to determine definitively the actual and singular understanding of an ambiguous text. See id. at 681-687 (Breyer, J., dissenting) (arriving at a different "original understanding" of the Second Amendment than the majority).

§1.7.3 Constitutional Structure

The Supreme Court has often derived meaning from the structure of the Constitution itself. Two structural principles that have often been used for such interpretive purposes are the division of the federal government into three distinct branches (i.e., separation of powers), and the division of power between the federal government and the states (i.e., federalism). Structural arguments may be used to add meaning to a textual provision that is otherwise ambiguous, or they may be employed independent of any textual provision as a source of meaning of their own.

An example of a structural argument based on separation of powers is found in *Plaut v. Spendthrift Farm, Inc.*, 514 U.S. 211 (1995), where the Court relied on the tripartite structure of the federal government and the need to maintain separation of powers between the legislative and judicial branches to strike down an act of Congress that would have required the federal courts to reopen a case that had already been decided. The Court's structural analysis in *Plaut* was used to lend meaning to the text by suggesting that inherent in the "judicial power" conferred by Article III is the limitation that Congress may not compel the courts to reopen final judgments.

A structural argument based on federalism was employed in *New York v. United States*, 505 U.S. 144 (1992), which held that the framework of the Constitution bars Congress from impairing the states' sovereignty by forcing them to enact and administer a federal radioactive waste disposal program. The Court's structural analysis was independent of any textual provision. Though the Court mentioned the Tenth Amendment, which reserves to the states those powers not delegated to the United States, the Court noted that the Tenth Amendment itself places no limits on the federal government. Rather, the Amendment simply recognizes that the effect of *other limits* on the national government — such as those that derive from the structure of the Constitution — may be to reserve powers to the states.

§1.7.4 History and Tradition

A court may use history as an interpretive device in any number of different ways; we will consider a few of them here. First, history may serve as an indirect means of determining the original intent or understanding. By examining the historical backdrop against which a particular constitutional provision was adopted, a court may be able to identify the kinds of practices or conduct the provision was intended to deal with. In *Cummings v. Missouri*, 71 U.S. (4 Wall.) 277 (1867), for example, the Court looked to English law to define the term "bill of attainder" in Article I, §10. The Court also relied on history in the *Slaughter-House Cases*, 83 U.S. (16 Wall.) 36 (1872), to determine whether the Fourteenth Amendment barred Louisiana from granting a monopoly on butchering in the City of New Orleans to a state-chartered corporation. The excluded butchers alleged that the monopoly violated their rights under the Fourteenth Amendment Equal Protection Clause. The Court, after carefully reviewing the "history of the times" preceding adoption of the Fourteenth Amendment, rejected the butchers' claim on the ground that the Equal Protection Clause, despite its universal language, was limited to "discrimination against the negroes as a class, or on account of their race. . . ." Id. at 67, 80-81. More recently, in *Nevada Commission on Ethics v. Carrigan*, 131 S. Ct. 2343, 2347-2350 (2011), the Court rejected a First Amendment challenge to a state law that required legislators to refrain from voting on matters in which they have a specified conflict of interest. In doing so, the Court noted that generally applicable conflict-of-interest recusal rules had been in effect for over 200 years at both the federal and state levels, without a single court decision invalidating any of them.

Besides offering indirect insight into the original intent or understanding, a court may rely upon history as a basis for extending the reach of a constitutional provision. In *Frontiero v. Richardson*, 411 U.S. 677, 684 (1973), Justice Brennan thus cited the country's "long and unfortunate history of sex discrimination" as reason to give laws that discriminate against women the same strict scrutiny that courts give to racial classifications. Note, however, that this use of history may lead to a result that is directly contrary to that seen above, where a long practice of denying a claimed right — such as that of equal treatment — provided a justification for continuing to deny it.

Judges may also utilize history to decide whether certain conduct deserves constitutional protection because it is part of an established American tradition. In *Moore v. City of East Cleveland*, 431 U.S. 494, 503 (1977), the Court cited the fact that "the institution of the family is deeply rooted in this Nation's history and tradition" to support its conclusion that families have a due process right to live together as a unit. On the other hand, the absence of such a tradition may lead a judge to deny the existence of a claimed right. In *Planned Parenthood of Southeastern Pennsylvania v. Casey*, 505 U.S. 833 (1992), Chief Justice Rehnquist, after reviewing the history of anti-abortion legislation in this country, remarked that "it can scarcely be said that any deeply rooted tradition of relatively unrestricted abortion in our history supported the classification of the right to abortion as 'fundamental' under the Due Process Clause of the Fourteenth Amendment." Id. at 952-953 (Rehnquist, C.J., concurring and dissenting). And in *Lawrence v. Texas*, 539 U.S. 558, 567-568 (2003), the Court, in holding that the Due Process Clause protects the liberty of adults to engage in private consensual sexual conduct with members of the same sex, was able to show that state proscriptions against such conduct had no "ancient roots" and were not part of a "longstanding history in this country of laws directed at homosexual conduct as a distinct matter."

§1.7.5 Fairness and Justice

Courts will at times interpret a constitutional provision in accordance with principles of fairness and justice. For example, the Supreme Court has construed the Fifth and Fourteenth Amendments as commanding special scrutiny of laws that discriminate against illegitimate children, on the ground that "visiting condemnation upon the child in order to express society's disapproval of the parents' liaisons 'is illogical and unjust. Moreover, imposing disabilities on the illegitimate child is contrary to the basic concept of our system that legal burdens should bear some relationship to individual responsibility or wrongdoing.'" *Mathews v. Lucas*, 427 U.S. 495, 505 (1976) (quoting *Weber v. Aetna Casualty & Surety Co.*, 406 U.S. 164, 175 (1972)).

§1.7.6 Political Theory

Judges may interpret the Constitution in light of basic principles of political theory. In *Powell v. McCormack*, 395 U.S. 486 (1969), the issue was whether

Article I, §5, which authorizes the House of Representatives to judge the qualifications of its members, permits the House to impose qualifications in addition to the age, citizenship, and residency requirements specified by Article I, §2. In ruling that the House lacked the power to exclude a member who met the three Article I, §2 qualifications, the Supreme Court relied upon "basic principles of our democratic system," one of which is "that the people should choose whom they please to govern them." Id. at 547-548.

§1.7.7 Social Policy

Judges sometimes construe the Constitution in light of what they consider to be sound social policy. In *West Coast Hotel Co. v. Parrish*, 300 U.S. 379 (1937), the Court upheld a state minimum wage law in the face of an employer's claim that the law violated the Fourteenth Amendment's Due Process Clause. Chief Justice Hughes's opinion for the Court relied on

> an additional and compelling consideration which recent economic experience has brought into a strong light. The exploitation of a class of workers who are in an unequal position with respect to bargaining power and are thus relatively defenceless against the denial of a living wage is not only detrimental to their health and well being but casts a direct burden for their support upon the community. . . . We may take judicial notice of the unparalleled demands for relief which arose during the recent period of depression and still continue to an alarming extent despite the degree of economic recovery which has been achieved.

Id. at 399.

More recently in *Plyler v. Doe*, 457 U.S. 202 (1982), the Court ruled that Texas had violated the Fourteenth Amendment's Equal Protection Clause by denying a free public education to undocumented alien children. The Court considered the social consequences of the Texas law, noting that "education provides the basic tools by which individuals might lead economically productive lives to the benefit of us all. In sum, education has a fundamental role in maintaining the fabric of our society. We cannot ignore the significant social costs borne by our Nation when select groups are denied the means to absorb the values and skills upon which our social order rests." Id. at 221.

§1.7.8 Foreign, International, and State Law

In construing the Constitution, the Court has at times gained insight from how other sovereignties construe similar provisions in their own constitutions or charters. While such rulings are obviously not binding on the

Supreme Court as a matter of federal constitutional law, they may offer valuable insight, especially when the Court is being asked to recognize a new federal constitutional right. The Court drew upon such sources in *Lawrence v. Texas,* 539 U.S. 558 (2003), where it held that the Due Process Clause bars a state from criminalizing the private sexual conduct of consenting adults even if it involves members of the same sex. In reaching this conclusion, the Court cited with approval the British Parliament's repeal of laws punishing homosexual conduct and a decision by the European Court of Human Rights that is binding on the Council of Europe's 45 member nations. Id. at 573. In addition, and perhaps most surprisingly, the Court took note of how "[t]he courts of five different States have [proceeded] in interpreting provisions in their own state constitutions parallel to the Due Process Clause of the Fourteenth Amendment. . . ." Id. at 576. Similarly, in *Roper v. Simmons,* 543 U.S. 551 (2005), the Court in ruling that the Eighth Amendment's Cruel and Unusual Punishment Clause bars imposition of the death penalty on those under 18, looked at the United Nations Covenant on the Rights of the Child, other international covenants, and other nations' practices. After doing so, the Court acknowledged "the overwhelming weight of international opinion against the juvenile death penalty," and "the stark reality that the United States is the only country in the world that continues to give official sanction to the juvenile death penalty." Id. at 575, 578. And in *Graham v. Florida,* 130 S. Ct. 2011, 2033 (2010), the Court looked to the law of other nations in reaching the conclusion that it was cruel and unusual punishment to impose a sentence of life without possibility of parole on juveniles who did not commit homicide. The Court found that "the United States adheres to a sentencing practice rejected the world over. This observation does not control our decision. . . . But the climate of international opinion concerning the acceptability of a particular punishment is also not irrelevant" (internal citations omitted).

§1.7.9 Supreme Court Precedent

As in other areas of the law, a judge's ruling as to the meaning of the Constitution may rest on the doctrine of stare decisis. Out of respect for precedent, a Supreme Court Justice may interpret the Constitution in accord with prior case law even though the Justice would otherwise be inclined to construe the Constitution differently. In *Pennsylvania v. Union Gas Co.,* 491 U.S. 1 (1989), Justice Scalia invoked stare decisis in concluding that the Court should not overrule *Hans v. Louisiana,* 134 U.S. 1 (1890), a case that had given a broad reading to the states' Eleventh Amendment immunity from being sued in federal court. Because the question of whether *Hans* was correctly decided "is at least close," said Scalia, "the mere venerability of an answer consistently adhered to for almost a century, and the difficulty of changing, or even clearly identifying, the intervening law that has been based on that answer, strongly argue against a change." 491 U.S. at 34 (Scalia, J., concurring and dissenting). A similar reluctance to overrule precedent appears to have caused several Justices in *Planned Parenthood of Southeastern Pennsylvania v. Casey*, 505 U.S. 833 (1992), not to overrule the holding of *Roe v. Wade*, 410 U.S. 113 (1973), that women have a constitutional right to choose an abortion. 505 U.S. at 854-869 (O'Connor, J., Kennedy, J., and Souter, J.).

Just as respect for precedent may cause the Court not to retreat from a prior ruling, adherence to precedent may be the basis for extending an earlier constitutional ruling. For example, *Powell v. McCormack*, 395 U.S. 486 (1969), held that the House of Representatives cannot exclude a member except on the basis of the age, citizenship, and residency qualifications set forth in Article I, §2. Twenty-six years later, the Court relied on *Powell* in concluding that the states are likewise barred from imposing additional qualifications on those running for Congress. *U.S. Term Limits, Inc. v. Thornton*, 514 U.S. 779 (1995) (invalidating an Arkansas constitutional amendment that excluded from the ballot any congressional candidate who had served three terms in the House or two terms in the Senate).

On the other hand, while the Court has suggested that even "in constitutional cases, any departure from the doctrine of *stare decisis* demands special justification," *Arizona v. Rumsey*, 467 U.S. 203, 212 (1984), a Supreme Court Justice who wishes to ignore precedent is freer to do so in the field of constitutional law than in other areas. As Justice Brandeis explained:

> Stare decisis is usually the wise policy, because in most matters it is more important that the applicable rule of law be settled than that it be settled right. This is commonly true even where the error is a matter of serious concern, provided correction can be had by legislation. But in cases involving the federal Constitution, where correction through legislative action is practically impossible, this Court has often overruled its earlier decisions. The Court bows to the lessons of experience and the force of better reasoning, recognizing that the process of trial and error, so fruitful in the physical sciences, is appropriate also in the judicial function.

Burnet v. Coronado Oil & Gas Co., 285 U.S. 393, 406-408 (1932) (Brandeis, J., dissenting) (footnotes and internal citations omitted). In the seminal case of *Citizens United v. Federal Election Commission*, 130 S. Ct. 876, 911-913 (2010), holding that the First Amendment protects corporate political speech, the Court noted that "[o]ur precedent is to be respected unless the most convincing of reasons demonstrates that adherence to it puts us on a course that is sure error," but then proceeded to overrule two of its recent prior decisions based upon their lack of antiquity, the absence of serious reliance interests, a belief that they were not well reasoned, and intervening changes in technology. As Chief Justice Roberts candidly said in a concurring opinion, "[w]hen considering whether to reexamine a prior erroneous holding, we must balance the importance of having constitutional questions *decided* against the importance of having them *decided right*." Id. at 920. And "right," of course, means "right" in the eyes of the Court's current beholders.

§1.8 AUTHORITATIVENESS OF JUDICIAL INTERPRETATIONS

As we will see in more detail in Chapter 3 ("Justiciability"), the Supreme Court may interpret the Constitution only in the context of an actual case pending before it. When the Court does so, the parties to the case are bound by whatever constitutional interpretation the Court adopts. For them, the interpretation is part of the Court's binding judgment. Yet what of persons or institutions who are not parties to the case; are they also bound by the Court's constitutional interpretations? Specifically, are state governments or the other branches of the federal government bound by the "constitutional law" that is developed in cases to which they were not parties and in which they did not participate? Indeed, are the people of the United States somehow bound by the Court's pronouncements on constitutional law? One is tempted to answer these questions with a resounding negative. After all, it is fundamental to our system of justice that only the parties to a lawsuit are legally bound by anything decided within that suit. Thus, if the Supreme Court decides that a specific school district's policy of racial segregation violates the Equal Protection Clause, that ruling legally binds only that school district. Certainly, other school districts with identical policies cannot be held in contempt for failure to comply with the Court's order to desegregate for the simple reason that they were not parties to the case.

But suppose we use the word "bound" in a looser sense that connotes a general obligation to obey, just as one must obey a duly enacted statute. In this sense, do nonparties to a lawsuit have a general obligation to obey constitutional law as enunciated by the Supreme Court? In other words, if the Court says that racial discrimination in public education is unconstitutional, must nonparty school districts conform to that ruling as a matter of obligation to the principles of constitutional law? And if the answer to these questions is "yes," does it follow that the Supreme Court has the exclusive authority to interpret the Constitution in the sense that it has the final word on the meaning of our constitutional text? If the answer is "no," then can we truly describe the body of constitutional principles developed by the Supreme Court as constitutional *law*? Or do these principles reflect no more than the law of the case in which they arise? We will explore these questions in the sections that follow.

§1.8.1 The Supreme Court's Interpretations as Law

In 1954, the Supreme Court held that public school districts in the States of Kansas, South Carolina, Virginia, and Delaware had violated the Equal Protection Clause of the Fourteenth Amendment by racially segregating their public schools. *Brown v. Board of Education*, 347 U.S. 483 (1954) (*Brown I*). The following term, the Court ordered these school districts to begin immediately the process of dismantling their systems of enforced segregation. *Brown v. Board of Education*, 349 U.S. 294, 300-301 (1955) (*Brown II*). Of course, many other school districts throughout the nation were racially segregated at the time *Brown I* and *Brown II* were decided. Those districts were not, however, parties to the *Brown* litigation. Were these nonparty school districts free to remain segregated until sued and judicially compelled to desegregate, or were they subject to a duty to adhere to the Court's interpretation of the equal protection guaranty? In other words, did the *Brown* Court's constitutional interpretation of the Equal Protection Clause become the law of the Constitution, binding on the nation as a whole, or was it merely the rule to be followed in the *Brown* litigation and perhaps in subsequent cases raising the same issue?

The Supreme Court addressed these questions in *Cooper v. Aaron*, 358 U.S. 1 (1958), a case that arose out of the infamous efforts by the governor and state legislature of Arkansas to thwart a federal district court order mandating the desegregation of public schools in Little Rock, Arkansas. These state officials claimed a sovereign authority to resist *Brown* as an unconstitutional usurpation of power by the Supreme Court. In a unanimous opinion signed by each of the Justices, the Court emphatically rejected the notion that government officials who were not parties to the *Brown* litigation were free to ignore the Court's constitutional interpretation of the Equal Protection Clause. The Supreme Court's response not only held that the state had no authority to resist a federal judicial order in a case to which it was a party—a narrow and obvious principle of federal supremacy—but seemed to assert as well that the state was under a general duty to comply with the constitutional mandate of *Brown* regardless of any pending litigation or judicial orders. In the Court's words:

> Article VI of the Constitution makes the Constitution the "supreme Law of the Land." In 1803, Chief Justice Marshall, speaking for a unanimous Court, referring to the Constitution as "the fundamental and paramount law of the nation," declared in the notable case of *Marbury v. Madison*, 1 Cranch 137, 177, that "It is emphatically the province and duty of the judicial department to say what the law is." This decision declared the basic principle that the federal judiciary is supreme in the exposition of the law of the Constitution, and that principle has ever since been respected by this Court and the Country as a permanent and indispensable feature of our constitutional system. It follows that the interpretation of the Fourteenth Amendment enunciated by this Court

> in the Brown case is the supreme law of the land, and Art. VI of the Constitution
> makes it of binding effect on the States "any Thing in the Constitution or Laws
> of any State to the Contrary notwithstanding."

358 U.S. at 18. In essence, the Court equated its interpretations of the Constitution with the Constitution itself. All government officials, therefore, were bound by oath to conform their conduct to the Court's constitutional interpretations. Thus when the Court held that separate was not equal in the field of public education, that ruling established a legal principle requiring compliance by all public school districts, including those that were not parties to the Brown suit. The Court reiterated this position in *Dayton Board of Education v. Brinkman*, 443 U.S. 526, 537-540 (1979), where it held that once Brown I was decided in 1954, the Dayton, Ohio, Board of Education, though not a party to the Brown litigation, was under an affirmative constitutional duty to dismantle its segregated schools, even in the absence of any lawsuit filed against the Dayton Board.

At first blush, the *Cooper* Court's description of its own authority may seem like an arrogation of power, and some have so argued. To claim supremacy in the exposition of the law of the Constitution and to equate the Court's constitutional interpretations with the document itself is to place the judiciary over the Constitution and over all other institutions of government. But in truth the Court's constitutional interpretations are, for all practical purposes, the law of the Constitution. If one defines laws as enforceable regulations of human conduct stemming from an authoritative source, it would seem that the law of the Constitution consists largely of the Court's applied interpretations of that document. After all, the judiciary, over which the Supreme Court presides, is the vehicle through which the provisions of the Constitution are enforced, and quite obviously the judicial enforcement of a constitutional provision is wholly dependent on the judicial interpretation of that provision. Moreover, within this system of enforcement, the Supreme Court's constitutional interpretations are unreviewable by any other body. So to say that the Court is supreme in the exposition of the law of the Constitution and that the Court's constitutional interpretations are the supreme law of the land states but a truism of our legal system.

None of this means that the Court has the absolute final say as to the content of constitutional law. We have already noted in §1.5 the various means through which a constitutional interpretation can be altered: by amendment, through the appointment process, by individual Justices reconsidering their views, and through impeachment. In this larger sense, all branches of the federal government, every state government, and the public at large are involved in an ongoing process of constitutional lawmaking. This broader framework does not, however, alter the simple reality that the Court defines what the law of the Constitution is at a given point in time, and that its judgment on this score is definitive until altered by amendment or reconsideration by the Court. The question to be resolved is how other institutions of government must respond to this practical reality.

§1.8.2 Binding Effect on Other Courts

Given the foregoing, it should not be surprising that the Supreme Court's constitutional interpretations are binding on the lower federal courts and on all state courts. This conclusion is based on the fact that in a hierarchical judicial system such as ours, an inferior court must follow the law as announced by any higher court that has authority to revise or reverse the lower court's rulings. Since the Supreme Court may review all lower federal and state court decisions where constitutional questions are involved, the judges of these courts must adhere to the Supreme Court's reading of the Constitution. The Supreme Court articulated this principle in *Hutto v. Davis*, 454 U.S. 370 (1982). After finding that a U.S. Court of Appeals had "failed to heed our decision" in an earlier case, id. at 372, the Justices chastised the appellate court for "having ignored, consciously or unconsciously, the hierarchy of the federal court system created by the Constitution and Congress" and warned that "unless we wish anarchy to prevail within the federal judicial system, a precedent of this Court must be followed by the lower federal courts no matter how misguided the judges of those courts may think it to be." Id. at 374-375. State courts are subject to this same principle when adjudicating questions of federal constitutional law. See *Lockhart v. Fretwell*, 506 U.S. 364, 376 (1993) (Thomas, J., concurring) (noting that state courts are bound by Supreme Court interpretations of federal law).

Of course, this does not mean that Supreme Court precedent rigidly controls the disposition of all constitutional cases decided by lower federal courts and state courts. For one thing, the Supreme Court's constitutional interpretations are sometimes ambiguous, leaving these lower courts ample latitude to interpret and distinguish what may or may not be a binding precedent. If the Supreme Court precedent is not quite on point, the lower court may try to predict the direction the Supreme Court will take or may simply forge new constitutional territory. Or the issue presented may be completely novel, in which case the lower court must interpret the constitutional provision as a matter of first impression. Finally, there are cases, albeit quite rare, in which a lower court overtly departs from one of the Supreme Court's constitutional rulings. In such cases, if the adversely affected party appeals, the remedy is a virtually automatic reversal. See, e.g., *Jaffree v. Board of School Commrs.*, 554 F. Supp. 1104 (S.D. Ala.), *rev'd in part*, 705 F.2d 1526 (11th Cir. 1983), *aff'd*, 472 U.S. 38 (1985) (refusing to follow Supreme Court's reading of the First Amendment's Establishment Clause). Yet despite these modest wrinkles in the system, the general principle holds true. Lower federal courts and all state courts are under a duty to adhere to the Supreme Court's constitutional interpretations. This is both the rule and the firmly established practice.

§1.8.3 Binding Effect on Nonjudicial Officials

In *Cooper v. Aaron*, supra, the Court did not claim for itself an exclusive right to interpret the Constitution. Rather, the Court's interpretive power exists only as a product of the judicial function of deciding cases. As the Court explained in *Marbury v. Madison*, supra, "if a law be in opposition to the constitution; if both the law and the constitution apply to a particular case, . . . the court must determine which of these conflicting rules *governs the case*." 5 U.S. at 178 (emphasis supplied). Yet, the practical effect of this specific interpretive role, especially given the Supreme Court's position in the judicial hierarchy, is to define the enforceable principles of constitutional law. Hence, the *Cooper* Court's conclusion that its constitutional interpretations are the supreme law of the land. This is not, however, a claim of exclusivity, but one of prerogative within a constitutionally assigned sphere. Thus, each of the other branches of government may interpret the Constitution for itself within its own assigned sphere.

It was on this understanding that President Jefferson, upon taking office in 1801, pardoned those who had been convicted under the Sedition Act, a measure he believed was unconstitutional. Jefferson explained that although the federal courts had upheld the validity of the act, "nothing in the Constitution has given them a right to decide for the Executive, more than to the Executive to decide for them. Both magistrates are equally independent in the sphere of action assigned to them. . . . [T]he opinion which gives to the judges the right to decide what laws are constitutional, and what not, not only for themselves in their own sphere of action, but for the legislature and executive also, in their spheres, would make the judiciary a despotic branch." Letter from Thomas Jefferson to Abigail Adams (Sept. 11, 1804), in 11 *The Writings of Thomas Jefferson* 50-51 (Andrew A. Lipscomb ed., 1905).

Notice that by pardoning individuals convicted under the Sedition Act, Jefferson did not take any action that was either expressly or implicitly precluded to him by the federal judiciary's interpretation of the Constitution. The federal judiciary had upheld the Sedition Act. It had not held, however, that persons convicted under the act could not be pardoned. The pardon power is expressly vested in the President and is designed to be exercised even when a conviction has been affirmed by the judicial branch. Moreover, any exercise of the pardon power is completely discretionary with the President. The President may exercise the pardon power for any reason or for no reason at all. Thus, while Jefferson's opinion as to the constitutionality of the Sedition Act may explain why he took the action he did, that opinion was not necessary to his exercising the pardon power. In short, the federal judiciary's opinion on the constitutionality of the Sedition Act simply had no bearing on the scope of Jefferson's power to pardon. In this context, both branches were entitled to their different interpretations of the Constitution when operating within their separate "spheres of action." Similarly, and perhaps more to the point at hand, the President is free to nominate and, with the advice and consent of the Senate, to appoint Justices who reject the current Court's constitutional interpretations. Again, the President is entitled to promote his preferred interpretation of the Constitution since doing so does not in any manner transgress any known constitutional principle.

Example 1-1

A bill has been introduced in Congress to require all children who attend school on U.S. military bases to recite the Lord's Prayer at the start of each school day. Suppose that two years ago, the Supreme Court invalidated a state law requiring school children to recite the same prayer at the beginning of each school day, on the ground that it violated the First Amendment Establishment Clause. Are members of Congress required to vote against this bill because of the Supreme Court's ruling? If the bill passes Congress, would the President be obligated to veto the measure?

Explanation

The members of Congress and the President are not required to adhere to the Supreme Court's interpretation of the Constitution when exercising functions over which the Constitution grants them complete discretion. Both a member's power to vote for or against a pending bill and the President's power to veto a bill are discretionary and not subject to judicial review. Therefore, if members of Congress and the President believe the statutory prayer requirement does not violate the Establishment Clause, they are free to support the bill regardless of the Court's view on this subject. Indeed, members of Congress and the President may support or reject the bill even if they have no opinion on the potential applicability of the Establishment Clause. Like Jefferson's exercise of the pardon power, their opinion merely operates as a potential motivating factor in their exercise of discretion. Of course, in reaching their decision, members of Congress and the President may well take the Supreme Court's opinion into account, just as they might consider other influential views on the bill's constitutionality. They might also assess the likelihood that the Court would reject its earlier decision. Yet in the final analysis the Court's interpretation is not binding on Congress or the President in their exercise of constitutionally vested discretion.

State or local legislative and executive branch officials enjoy this same type of interpretive freedom when enacting laws or when taking action that does not itself violate any principle of constitutional law. Under such circumstances, they are equally free to entertain contrary constitutional interpretations and to offer those interpretations as a motivation for the action they plan to undertake.

This realm of interpretive freedom in which contrary constitutional interpretations peacefully coexist is, however, quite limited. When the assigned "spheres of action" overlap and a conflict develops between a political and a judicial interpretation of the Constitution, the latter will always trump the former. Thus, as the Court recently observed, "Congress may not legislatively supersede our decisions interpreting and applying the Constitution." *Dickerson v. United States*, 530 U.S. 428, 436-437 (2000) (rejecting congressional effort to modify the *Miranda* rule); *City of Boerne v. Flores*, 521 U.S. 507, 517-521 (1997) (rejecting congressional effort to expand scope of the Free Exercise Clause). Nor may the executive branch take action that contravenes the Court's constitutional interpretations. *Youngstown Sheet & Tube Co. v. Sawyer*, 343 U.S. 579 (1952) (enjoining executive officer from taking action in violation of the separation of powers). And, of course, these same restrictions apply to action undertaken by state government officials.

Example 1-J

In the previous example, suppose that Congress passes and the President signs the bill requiring schools on military bases to begin each day with a recitation of the Lord's Prayer. The parents of several children sue the secretary of defense in federal district court to enjoin implementation of the law. The court, after finding that the statute is unconstitutional under the Supreme Court's interpretation of the Establishment Clause, issues an injunction barring the secretary from carrying out the law. May the secretary ignore the judgment, or may the President order the secretary not to comply with it on the good-faith belief that the law is constitutional?

Explanation

Neither of these options would be constitutional. While the executive branch is free to disagree with the court's reading of the Establishment Clause, the court's judgment is nevertheless binding on the parties to the case, including the secretary of defense. And, though the President was not a party to the suit, the President may not act to thwart the implementation of a federal court judgment. For the secretary or the President to do so would violate separation of powers by undermining the judiciary's Article III authority to decide cases and controversies. If the executive branch is displeased with the decision, it may appeal the ruling. However, unless the

Court of Appeals or the Supreme Court reverses the trial court's ruling, the executive branch must honor the trial court's judgment.

To this point we've established a few important propositions with respect to nonjudicial government officials. First, such government officials are free to entertain and act on interpretations of the Constitution that differ from the Supreme Court's constitutional interpretations when these officials are acting solely within their constitutionally assigned spheres. Second, a government official who is a party to a lawsuit filed in federal court must adhere to the judgment of the court unless that judgment is reversed on appeal. Third, a government official who is not a party to such a suit is nonetheless precluded from taking action that would thwart the execution of the court's judgment.

That brings us to the final question. Must governmental officials conform their conduct to the norms of the Supreme Court's constitutional interpretations when doing otherwise would transgress the principles emanating from those interpretations? To phrase the question in terms of the hypothetical we began with, were racially segregated school districts that were not parties to the litigation in *Brown v. Board of Education* under a constitutional obligation to begin the process of desegregation once the rule of *Brown* was announced? This scenario would appear to raise the same problem of conflicting "spheres of action" that arises when a government official attempts to thwart a federal court judgment that is based on a constitutional interpretation with which the official disagrees. In both cases, the official wishes to take action that in itself conflicts with a judicially recognized principle of constitutional law. The only difference between these scenarios is the pendency of litigation in the latter context. The question is whether that pendency should make any difference in terms of the obligation to comply with a Supreme Court constitutional interpretation.

Notice that the problem presented here is quite different from the example of Jefferson's pardoning individuals convicted of violating the Sedition Act. Although Jefferson's opinion as to the constitutionality of the Sedition Act differed from that of the federal judiciary, his act of pardoning did not itself violate any principle of constitutional law as articulated by the Court. He was, therefore, free to entertain that opinion as a motivating factor in his exercise of the pardon power. The judicial and presidential "spheres of action" did not collide because nothing the Court had said precluded the President from exercising the pardon power. Post-*Brown*, however, a school district's blanket refusal to desegregate violated the Court's interpretation of the Equal Protection Clause because that Clause restrains the conduct of all state and local public officials. A refusal to desegregate operated as more than a difference of opinions on constitutional interpretation. Rather, the action itself transgressed applicable and judicially articulated principles of constitutional law. Here, the spheres of action truly collided. The Court had stated what the law is and the school district failed to comply.

Yet some argue that such nonparty government officials are free to act on their own independent interpretations of the Constitution. See, e.g., Edwin Meese, "The Law of the Constitution," 61 Tul. L. Rev. 979 (1987). This view derives from the notion that the Supreme Court's constitutional interpretations bind only the parties to the cases in which those interpretations are applied. From this perspective, constitutional law is not "law" as that term is commonly used, but merely the rule to be applied in a specific case pending before the Court. Hence, nonparty government officials may ignore the judicially announced principle with impunity since it reflects no more than an opinion of the Court. Under this view, racial segregation in public schools was not outlawed by Brown, but merely declared to be unconstitutional in those school districts involved in the Brown litigation. All other school districts remained free to continue to discriminate until sued. Such an approach would seem to invite a type of constitutional anarchy, rendering the meaning of the Constitution variable throughout the nation. It also does not fully comport with practice under our Constitution. Indeed, in Cooper the Little Rock School Board itself thought it had a duty to desegregate based on the rulings in Brown I and Brown II. It was the governor and state legislature that attempted to prevent the board from undertaking that constitutional responsibility.

The contrary view, the one declared in Cooper, presumes that the principles of constitutional law bind the nation's government bodies in the same manner that other provisions of the law bind us as individuals. Just as we do not think of a person as being "free" to engage in negligent conduct until sued or to violate criminal proscriptions until prosecuted, a government official is not free to ignore applicable principles of constitutional law until haled into court. In all of these situations, the expected overall conduct is one of conformity to the law. Judicial enforcement arises only when aberrant behavior requires the sanction of the law to enforce conformity with its provisions. This is certainly the way constitutional law actually operates. If a government official takes action that violates a judicially recognized principle of constitutional law, the judiciary, in a properly filed suit, may enjoin that action, and if the violation is willful, in the sense that the official knew or should have known of the applicable precedent, then in most cases monetary damages may be assessed as well. To say that the official is free to act on his own interpretation of the Constitution despite the availability of these enforcement remedies seems to be nothing more than clever wordplay, tantamount to saying we are free to commit larceny or murder unless caught. The important thing from a legal perspective, however, is what happens once we are caught. See Allan Ides, "Judicial Supremacy and the Law of the Constitution," 47 UCLA L. Rev. 491

(1999); Daniel A. Farber, "The Supreme Court and the Rule of Law: *Cooper v. Aaron* Revisited," 1982 *U. Ill. L. Rev.* 387.

Adopting this broader view of the Court's constitutional interpretations does not mean that once the Supreme Court articulates a principle of constitutional law all governmental officials automatically comply with that principle. A dangerous and embarrassing resistance to *Brown* was overcome only by years of persistent litigation, not to mention the support of federal troops. The decision in *Cooper* arose out of that resistance. But the usual practice is one of good-faith compliance. Of course there are subtle ways in which government officials may seek to distinguish Supreme Court precedent. That's all part of accepted practice. Certainly, good-faith efforts to challenge or distinguish a judicial precedent are part of the method through which constitutional doctrine is refined or even altered. For example, a prosecutor may attempt to enforce a statute that is similar to one that was held unconstitutional in the hope of distinguishing the statute he is enforcing from the one struck down. Or he may have reason to believe that the Court is amenable to altering its earlier view. In both situations, however, the prosecutor is not defying the Court's constitutional interpretation, but attempting to convince the Court to either limit or alter that interpretation.

This brings us back to *Cooper* and the Court's assertion that its interpretations of the Constitution are the supreme law of the land. Despite the surface boldness of this statement, the assertion appears to comport with the way in which constitutional law is applied and enforced within our system of government. Again, the Court's power to interpret is not exclusive or final. Yet, until revised by amendment or by the Court itself, that interpretation is for all practical purposes the law of the Constitution. Whether this involves the normatively best approach to constitutional lawmaking presents a question well beyond the scope of this discussion. What is essential at this point is that we understand how judicially driven constitutional law operates within our legal system. That reality can be captured by returning to our school desegregation hypothetical. Whether the nonparty school districts were automatically obligated to comply with the doctrine enunciated in *Brown* is perhaps less important than the simple fact that they were eventually compelled by the judiciary to do so. It is difficult to think of a stronger form of authoritativeness.

Congressional Power to Limit the Jurisdiction of the Supreme Court and Inferior Federal Courts

§2.1 INTRODUCTION AND OVERVIEW

Article III, §1 provides that "[t]he judicial Power of the United States, shall be vested in one supreme Court, and in such inferior Courts as the Congress may from time to time ordain and establish." Section 2 of the same Article describes nine subject matters over which the "judicial Power shall extend," vesting two of those subject matters in the Supreme Court's original jurisdiction, and with respect to the remaining seven providing, "the supreme Court shall have appellate Jurisdiction, both as to Law and Fact, with such Exceptions, and under such Regulations as the Congress shall make."

Thus, in two brief sections consisting of three somewhat cryptic paragraphs, Article III establishes the judicial branch. It will consist of a Supreme Court and those lower federal courts Congress decides to create. The Constitution's only other textual references to the composition of the Supreme Court are indirect — most notably, a description of the role of the "Chief Justice" in the impeachment process, and the inclusion of "Judges of the supreme Court" within the President's appointment power. Art. I, §3, cl. 6; Art. II, §2, cl. 2. There is also one other textual reference to inferior federal courts, but that reference merely provides the source of the power to create those courts — a grant of authority to Congress "To constitute Tribunals inferior to the supreme Court." Art. I, §8, cl. 9.

Quite clearly, the Constitution, both expressly and impliedly, presumes that Congress will supply much of the design and most of the detail for the newly created third branch. Presumably the Framers expected Congress to create a working structure for the Supreme Court pursuant to the Necessary and Proper Clause, Art. I, §8, cl. 18 (see §5.2), and pursuant to the power to regulate and make exceptions to the Court's appellate jurisdiction. Art. III, §2, cl. 2. Thus such matters as the number of Justices, the length of the Court's term, the extent of support personnel, etc., would be determined by Congress. In fact, this has been the historical practice. Similarly, the express grant of authority to "constitute" courts inferior to the Supreme Court certainly contemplated congressional involvement in the creation and design of this component of the judicial branch.

But what is the scope of these powers granted to Congress? Are they simply meant to implement the constitutional vision of three branches, vesting Congress with a somewhat limited "design" authority, or are they meant to provide Congress with a substantive check on the judicial branch and its power of judicial review? For example, may Congress use its exceptions power to adopt jurisdiction-stripping measures that preclude the Supreme Court from exercising appellate jurisdiction over specific categories of constitutional disputes, such as those involving school prayer, abortion, or school desegregation? Or may Congress, relying on its power to constitute inferior federal courts, deny those courts the authority to hear such matters? More generally, are there any constitutional limits to these implied and express powers of Congress?

The simple answer to these questions is that there are limits on all powers conferred by the Constitution. Indeed, as we will learn, limitation is the very essence of constitutional law. These limitations come in three forms. First, any purported exercise of constitutional power must come within the defined scope of that power. Thus the power to make exceptions to the appellate jurisdiction of the Supreme Court cannot be used to make exceptions to the Court's original jurisdiction. Such an exercise of authority is beyond the defined scope of the power granted. Second, the purported exercise of power may not violate limitations inherent in the structure of the Constitution, particularly those principles embodied in the separation of powers. Congress cannot, therefore, use its exceptions power to vacate a decision by the Supreme Court. To do so would usurp a judicial prerogative. Finally, an exercise of constitutional power may not transgress any external limits or guarantees imposed by the Constitution, such as those found in the Bill of Rights. Thus a jurisdictional statute that excepted from the Supreme Court's jurisdiction all cases brought by members of a particular religious denomination would run afoul of the First Amendment religion clauses.

The foregoing paragraph should not be read as suggesting that solutions to questions regarding the scope of congressional power over the federal judiciary are simple. In fact, at all three steps of the inquiry — definitional, structural, and external — there are significant unresolved ambiguities and controversies. Neither the Court nor commentators have devised a universally accepted solution. Yet even though this three-part inquiry will not provide definite solutions for any but the simplest of problems, it will provide a structure through which to ask the correct questions and to consider the relevant possibilities.

In this chapter we will examine the congressional power to impose limits on the jurisdiction of the Supreme Court and inferior federal courts. Consistent with the above discussion, the chapter is organized around the definitional, structural, and external limits on that power. In addition, in exploring the scope of congressional authority over the judicial branch, we will also examine the related topic of the congressional power to create courts that are not subject to the strictures of Article III — i.e., the power to create non-Article III courts.

§2.2 THE POWER TO MAKE EXCEPTIONS TO THE JURISDICTION OF THE SUPREME COURT

As noted above, Article III grants the Supreme Court both original and appellate jurisdiction. Congress can neither add to nor subtract from the Court's original jurisdiction. The first proposition was established in *Marbury v. Madison*, 5 U.S. (1 Cranch) 137 (1803). The second proposition, although never dispositively established by the Court, has been generally accepted by both the Court and commentators. In essence, the Court's original jurisdiction is completely self-executing, and jurisdictional statutes that purport to ignore this fact will not be followed. Congress may, however, grant lower federal courts and state courts concurrent jurisdiction over matters otherwise within the Supreme Court's original jurisdiction. Beyond this, however, the power of Congress over the Supreme Court's original jurisdiction is limited to the regulation of procedural matters that do not impinge upon the jurisdictional authority of the Court.

Congressional power over the Supreme Court's appellate jurisdiction is more complicated and more controversial. After describing the two subject matters that fall within the Court's original jurisdiction, Article III provides, "In all the other Cases before mentioned, the supreme Court shall have appellate Jurisdiction, both as to Law and Fact, with such Exceptions, and under such Regulations as the Congress shall make." This language vests the Supreme Court with appellate jurisdiction over seven subject matters, including cases arising under the Constitution or laws of the United States. But the exercise of that jurisdiction is expressly subject to the power conferred on Congress by the Exceptions Clause. Our first task, therefore, is to *define* the scope of the power invested by that clause.

§2.2.1 Defining the Scope of the Exceptions Power

The Traditional or Plenary Power View

The language of the Exceptions Clause, read in isolation, may appear to grant Congress a virtually unlimited discretion to make exceptions to the Court's appellate jurisdiction — "with such Exceptions . . . as the Congress shall make." See §1.3.1 (exceptions power does not apply to Court's original jurisdiction). From this narrow textual perspective, the only question is whether a particular jurisdictional limitation imposed by Congress constitutes an "exception" to the Court's appellate jurisdiction. If it does, then imposition of that exception comes within the power of Congress. In essence, Congress is granted plenary power to withdraw subject matters from the Court's appellate jurisdiction. Thus, if Congress were to provide that the Supreme Court could not exercise appellate jurisdiction over cases arising under the First Amendment to the Constitution, the Exceptions Clause would provide a textual basis for the congressional action. A jurisdictional limitation excluding First Amendment cases is, quite literally, an exception to the Court's appellate jurisdiction. This interpretation of the Exceptions Clause is sometimes referred to as the "traditional view."

Mandatory Interpretations

But the Exceptions Clause is part of the more comprehensive text of Article III, and perhaps our interpretation should take that larger perspective into consideration. For example, in describing the various subject matters to which the federal judicial power "shall extend," Article III uses the modifier "all" with respect to three of those subject matters. Thus Article III provides that the judicial power "shall extend to *all* Cases . . . arising under this Constitution [and] the laws of the United States. . . ." Some have argued that this language requires that some Article III court — either the Supreme Court or an inferior federal court — must be available to hear such cases; i.e., the federal judicial power must extend to *all* cases arising under the Constitution or federal laws.

Under this view, which we will label a "mandatory" interpretation, Congress may not use its exceptions power to eliminate the Supreme Court's appellate jurisdiction over cases arising under the Constitution unless, at a minimum, Congress vests jurisdiction over such cases in an inferior federal court created pursuant to Article III. In other words, the Exceptions Clause is inherently limited by the requirement that for any case arising under the Constitution there must be at least one Article III court with jurisdiction to hear that case. Other mandatory interpretations rely on the "shall be vested" language of Article III, §1, or on the perceived intent of the Framers to establish a national judiciary with the full range of authority described in Article III. Under the latter views, the exceptions power is limited to merely regulating administrative detail and cannot be used to strip the Supreme Court of any of its constitutionally vested jurisdiction.

Example 2-A

Suppose Congress passes the following statute: "The Supreme Court shall not have jurisdiction to review, by appeal, writ of certiorari, or otherwise, any case arising out of any State statute, ordinance, rule, regulation, or practice, which relates to voluntary prayer, Bible reading, or religious meetings in public schools. The district courts shall not have jurisdiction of any case or question which the Supreme Court does not have jurisdiction to review under this title."

Explanation

If Article III grants Congress plenary authority to make exceptions to the Supreme Court's appellate jurisdiction, then, in terms of raw congressional power, the above statute would be well within the defined power granted by the Exceptions Clause. The statute explicitly and literally creates an exception to the Court's appellate jurisdiction. If, however, one interprets the Exceptions Clause as a component of an Article III requirement that the judicial power must in some manner extend to "all" cases arising under the Constitution, then this statute would be beyond the exceptions power since it completely eliminates Article III jurisdiction over a specified category of cases arising under the Constitution. A similar result will follow from the application of other mandatory theories.

In short, from a purely textual perspective, the resolution of the question presented by Example 2-A depends on how one defines the scope of the Exceptions Clause. The traditional view posits that the power of Congress is plenary, while a mandatory interpretation holds that Article III requires the availability of at least one federal court for all cases arising under the Constitution or laws of the United States. One thing is certain. Regardless of which interpretation one finds most amenable, the Court will not lightly assume that Congress intended to limit the Court's jurisdictional authority (or that of lower federal courts) to hear constitutional claims. "[W]here Congress intends to preclude judicial review of constitutional claims its intent to do so must be clear." *Demore v. Hyung Joon Kim*, 538 U.S. 510, 517 (2003) (quoting *Webster v. Doe*, 486 U.S. 592, 603 (1988)). The consequence of this principle is that the need to choose between the traditional and mandatory interpretations is often avoided by resort to statutory construction.

Historical Practice

Historical practice also sheds some light on the meaning of the Exceptions Clause, but like the text, historical practice is far from conclusive. Congress first exercised its exceptions power when it passed the Judiciary Act of 1789. Although the act did not expressly prohibit the Court from exercising jurisdiction over any of the subject matters listed in Article III, it did not affirmatively include the complete range of those subject matters within its description of the Court's appellate jurisdiction. That failure to include was interpreted as an intent to exclude — i.e., as an intent to make an exception to the Court's appellate jurisdiction. More specifically, under the Judiciary Act of 1789, Congress affirmatively provided the Court with appellate jurisdiction over cases decided by state courts in which claims arising under the Constitution had been denied. By inference, Congress *excepted* from the Court's appellate jurisdiction those state-court cases in which a federal constitutional claim had been upheld. Since the Judiciary Act of 1789 did not vest inferior federal courts with federal question jurisdiction, the federal judicial power did not, therefore, extend to "all" cases arising under the Constitution, but only to those in which state courts had denied federal claims. Thus the prestigious authors of the Judiciary Act — many of whom participated in the drafting of the Constitution — would seem to have adopted, at least by inference, the traditional or plenary power interpretation of the Exceptions Clause. Congress could except from the Court's appellate jurisdiction any subject matter Congress deemed appropriate, including cases arising under the Constitution.

Significantly, the model adopted by the Judiciary Act set the pattern followed throughout our history. The Court will exercise appellate jurisdiction only if Article III permits it, and only if Congress affirmatively authorizes it. A failure to authorize a particular instance of Article III appellate jurisdiction operates as an affirmative denial of that jurisdiction. And at no time has Congress provided the Supreme Court with the full range of appellate authority described in Article III. For example, although Article III grants the Court appellate jurisdiction over controversies between citizens of different states, Congress has never provided the Court with appellate jurisdiction over diversity suits decided by state courts. This historical practice of providing the Court less than the full range of its Article III appellate jurisdiction would seem to support an interpretation of the Exceptions Clause that vests Congress with plenary authority over the scope of the Court's appellate jurisdiction.

On the other hand, the Judiciary Act's failure to provide the federal judiciary with jurisdiction over *all* cases arising under the Constitution has never been directly challenged before the Court, and as we saw in *Marbury v. Madison*, despite the prestige of the authors of the Judiciary Act of 1789, the act was not without constitutional defect. So although the text of the Judiciary Act may shed *some* light on how *some* of the Framers interpreted the Exceptions Clause, the illumination is at best a distant glimmer and far from dispositive as an interpretive tool. Moreover, current jurisdictional statutes come very close to granting the Supreme Court the full range of its Article III jurisdiction, particularly in the context of federal question cases. The modern exceptions are largely trivial and arise in "non-mandatory" subject matters — e.g., the diversity exception noted in the previous paragraph. This evolution toward full inclusion of "mandatory" subject matters may be seen as evidence of the validity of the mandatory interpretation of the Exceptions Clause, specifically, a recognition by Congress of its duty to provide the federal judiciary with the full range of its Article III jurisdiction in cases arising under the Constitution or laws of the United States.

Precedent

Precedent leaves us with the same ambiguity. The leading case construing the exceptions power is Ex parte McCardle, 74 U.S. (7 Wall.) 506 (1868). In that Reconstruction-era case, a civilian, McCardle, was arrested by military authorities and scheduled to be put on trial for the publication of "incendiary and libelous" articles. He sought a writ of habeas corpus in federal circuit court, claiming he was being held in violation of his constitutional rights. The writ was denied. McCardle lodged an appeal directly with the Supreme Court pursuant to an 1867 statute that specifically provided the Court with jurisdiction over such appeals from the circuit courts. After McCardle's case was argued on the merits, but before a decision was issued, Congress repealed the specific jurisdictional provision upon which McCardle had relied. The Court dismissed the suit, holding that the repeal divested it of jurisdiction over the case.

In so ruling, the Court took the text of the Exceptions Clause at face value. "[T]he power to make exceptions to the appellate jurisdiction of this court is given by express words." Id. at 514. Therefore, once Congress exercised its exceptions power to divest the Court of jurisdiction, there was nothing for the Court to do but to dismiss the case: "Without jurisdiction the court cannot proceed at all in any cause. Jurisdiction is power to declare the law, and when it ceases to exist, the only function remaining to the court is that of announcing the fact and dismissing the cause." Id. From this perspective, McCardle lends strong support to the traditional or plenary power interpretation of the Exceptions Clause. Under this interpretation, the statute described in Example 2-A falls squarely within the defined sphere of congressional authority. It divests the Court of appellate jurisdiction over school prayer cases. And, taking McCardle at face value, if Congress wishes to prevent the Supreme Court from hearing cases involving any particular topic, it may do so by the simple expedient of excluding such cases from the Court's appellate jurisdiction. The statute in Example 2-A does exactly that.

There is, however, an important caveat. First, the repeal of the jurisdictional statute upon which McCardle relied did not divest the Supreme Court of appellate jurisdiction over all cases of habeas corpus. At the end of its opinion, the *McCardle* Court noted that the repeal affected only the specific jurisdictional statute upon which McCardle had relied. Id. at 515. The Judiciary Act of 1789 continued to provide the Court with appellate jurisdiction over habeas corpus petitions, and the Court exercised that jurisdiction one year later in *Ex parte Yerger*, 75 U.S. (8 Wall.) 85 (1869). Whether the availability of this alternate vehicle for appellate review of habeas petitions was essential to the holding in *McCardle* remains unclear. But given the availability of that alternative, one must be careful not to read too much into the *McCardle* decision. Under a more circumspect reading, one cannot say with certainty that the decision in *McCardle* validates the statute described in Example 2-A, since the statute described there leaves no jurisdictional basis for the exercise of any federal judicial power — whether by lower federal courts or the Supreme Court — in the context of school prayer cases. Cf. *Immigration and Naturalization Service v. St. Cyr*, 533 U.S. 289 (2001), and *Calcano-Martinez v. Immigration and Naturalization Service*, 533 U.S. 348 (2001) (jurisdiction-stripping measure pertaining to deportation proceedings construed so as to leave open the possibility of federal court habeas review).

Although no text, history, or precedent reveals a definitive interpretation of the Exceptions Clause, let us err on the side of tradition and assume for present purposes that the power of Congress as defined by the Exceptions Clause is plenary and unmodified by other Article III considerations. (A student must, of course, be prepared to argue from a mandatory perspective as well.) In short, for our purposes, from a *definitional* perspective, the Constitution grants Congress plenary power to make exceptions to the Supreme Court's appellate jurisdiction. That assumption merely opens the door for the larger and somewhat more difficult debate over potential structural and external limits upon the exercise of that power.

§2.2.2 Structural Limits on Exercises of the Exceptions Power

Even if we interpret the Exceptions Clause as granting Congress plenary power to make exceptions to the Supreme Court's appellate jurisdiction, it does not follow that every exercise of that power will comport with the Constitution. As was mentioned previously, all purported exercises of constitutional power are subject to three restraints: definitional, structural, and external. We have already assumed that from a definitional perspective, the exceptions power of Congress is, in essence, limited only by the judgment of Congress as to which exceptions are appropriate. We must now consider whether anything in the *structure* of our constitutional system restrains the exercise of that power. More particularly, to what extent, if at all, does the principle of separation of powers limit potential applications of the exceptions power?

The doctrine of separation of powers is built upon the constitutionally mandated division of governmental power among three branches: the legislative, the executive, and the judicial. See Chapter 7 ("The Separation of Powers"). This tripartite division of power was designed as a bulwark against tyranny, and from this design a basic principle emerges: No branch may usurp or encroach on the constitutionally vested functions of another branch. In terms of the exceptions power, we must therefore ask whether any particular exercise of that power usurps or encroaches on the constitutionally vested authority of another branch. Thus, while we might easily conclude that a statute divesting the Supreme Court of appellate jurisdiction over school prayer cases falls within the *definitional* scope of the exceptions power, we would still have to consider whether that statute either usurped or encroached on a judicial function.

The leading case in this context is *United States v. Klein*, 80 U.S. (13 Wall.) 128 (1871). During the Civil War, Congress passed a series of statutes that empowered the United States government to confiscate property used in "promoting the insurrection." The statutes also provided for the return of any confiscated property upon proof that the owner had "never given any aid or comfort to the present rebellion." V. F. Wilson had voluntarily given aid to the Confederacy. As a consequence, his property was confiscated. After the war, however, Wilson received a presidential pardon that granted him a restoration of all property rights. He filed suit in federal court seeking a return of his property. The Court of Claims, relying on the presidential pardon and a recent Supreme Court precedent, ordered the return of Wilson's confiscated property. In the prior case, the Supreme Court had held that the effect of such a pardon was to relieve the party of the consequences of any offense that may have been committed, including any penalty he may have incurred. Despite this precedent, the government appealed Wilson's case to the Supreme Court.

While the appeal was pending, Congress enacted a law that made evidence of a pardon inadmissible in any case seeking a return of confiscated property. Moreover, with respect to pending cases, the statute divested the Supreme Court of jurisdiction over any case in which proof of such a pardon had been submitted. In practical effect, the new statute divested the Court of jurisdiction when, under settled principles of law, the Court was prepared to rule against the government. The question for the Court was whether this was a proper exercise of the exceptions power. The Court held that it was not. Although on its face, the statute technically created an "exception" to the Court's appellate jurisdiction, the operation of the statute passed "the limit which separates the legislative from the judicial power." Id. at

147. In essence, Congress was using its exceptions power to manipulate the result in a pending case. As such, the statute usurped the judicial function of deciding cases and controversies. In addition, this purported exercise of the exceptions power encroached on the constitutional prerogative of the President to issue pardons. Id. at 147-148. In short, the jurisdictional "exception" at issue in *United States v. Klein* violated the principle of separation of powers in two ways: by usurping a judicial function and by encroaching on a presidential prerogative.

Of course, whenever Congress enacts a law, it instructs the federal judiciary how it must decide cases arising under that law. For example, a statute that establishes the standards of illegal employment discrimination "instructs" the federal judiciary to decide employment discrimination cases in accord with those standards. *Klein* provides no barrier to such laws. The critical flaw in *Klein* was the effort by Congress to do more than create the standards under which a case should be adjudicated; rather, in *Klein* Congress attempted to manipulate the Court's jurisdiction to achieve a particular result in a pending case.

Example 2-B

An environmental group, claiming violations of various federal environmental statutes and regulations, files a lawsuit against the United States Forest Service challenging timber harvesting in certain forests managed by the government. While the suit is pending, Congress passes a statute changing the standards pertaining to timber harvesting. The new statute specifically refers to the pending case and provides that compliance with the newly enacted standards will satisfy all applicable statutory and regulatory requirements. Does this latter provision violate the principles of *Klein*?

Explanation

The answer depends on how one characterizes the new statute. If the new statute instructs the trial court to make specific findings of fact or conclusions of law in a pending case, then Congress has invaded the province of the judiciary. But if the statute merely changes the legal standards under which a pending case is to be judged, there is no violation of separation of powers. Congress has simply exercised its lawmaking authority. The latter seems to be the more likely interpretation since Congress did not order a particular result, but merely altered the standards the court must apply to the pending controversy. The fact that these new standards may lead to a different result is irrelevant. See *Robertson v. Seattle Audubon Society*, 503 U.S. 429 (1992) (arriving at a similar conclusion under similar facts).

In short, *Klein* does not preclude Congress from enacting laws that affect pending cases. As long as the congressional action does not invade the judicial authority to decide cases in accord with the law, the principle of *Klein* is not violated.

Some further refinement of this principle is necessary. Reconsider Example 2-A, in which Congress passed a statute that stripped the Supreme Court and lower federal courts of jurisdiction over school prayer cases. Does that statute violate the principle of separation of powers as applied in the *Klein* case? Probably not — at least not if one limits *Klein* to its precise circumstances. By merely stripping the Supreme Court of appellate jurisdiction over school prayer cases, Congress has not usurped a judicial function. Stated somewhat differently, the jurisdiction-stripping measure does not inject Congress into the resolution of a case or controversy. The Court's jurisdiction over school prayer cases is simply removed, regardless of the potential outcome. To more closely parallel the *Klein* case, our statute would have to premise the "stripping" on the achievement of a particular result. For example, the specific principles of *Klein* would be implicated if the stripping measure only applied after the Court found a potential violation of the Establishment Clause.

Yet *Klein* and its underlying principles can be read more broadly. Some commentators have argued that the Supreme Court, either as envisioned by the Constitution or as a product of our modern constitutional democracy, performs an "essential function" within our governmental system, namely, exercising the power of judicial review as a constitutional check on the coordinate branches and the states. As a consequence, the Supreme Court's jurisdiction must be sufficiently inclusive to ensure governmental compliance with the Constitution. Although in *Klein* the Court was addressing an example of congressional usurpation of a particular judicial function, namely, the resolution of cases or controversies, the larger principle at stake in *Klein* was not that particular judicial function, but the more general principle of the Court's mandate to protect the integrity of the Constitution. Read from this perspective, *Klein* stands for the proposition that Congress may not use its exceptions power to undermine the Supreme Court's ability to carry out its essential function of judicial review.

Under this more expansive reading of *Klein*, one can certainly argue that a jurisdiction-stripping measure such as that described in Example 2-A violates the principle of separation of powers because it undermines the Court's ability to carry out its essential function. In particular, the measure disables the Court from exercising the power of judicial review over school prayer cases — i.e., cases in which it is alleged that public schools have violated the Establishment Clause through the inclusion of prayer in the school curriculum. Certainly if one of the Court's essential functions is to enforce the provisions of the Bill of Rights and the Fourteenth Amendment, then this jurisdiction-stripping measure prevents the Court from engaging in that function in the context of school prayer.

If one accepts this expansive reading of *Klein*, it would seem to follow that the separation of powers problem becomes even more acute if Congress attempts to insulate its own actions from judicial review. Thus, if Congress were to pass a statute stripping the Supreme Court and all lower federal courts of jurisdiction over cases involving exercises of the congressional power over interstate commerce, a serious separation of powers problem would emerge. Such a device would directly undermine constitutional structure by permitting Congress to define the scope of its own powers without any potential check by the federal judicial branch.

Example 2-C

A proposed immigration reform measure provides for expedited procedures for the deportation of undocumented aliens who have been arrested while attempting to enter the United States. Among other things the measure describes the specific standards to be used by the Immigration and Customs Enforcement (ICE) for assessing "immediate deportability," and precludes "any Court of the United States" from exercising jurisdiction over any case involving an application of the "immediate deportability" standard. If enacted, would this measure violate the separation of powers?

Explanation

First, the measure does not implicate the precise type of problem at issue in *Klein*. The federal courts' jurisdiction is not predicated on potential outcomes, but merely on the subject matter of the lawsuit. Regardless of the outcome of the ICE administrative proceedings, judicial review is precluded. On the other hand, the measure does appear to prevent the federal judiciary from reviewing the constitutionality of the overall congressional scheme as well as specific administrative applications of that scheme. Congress has, therefore, insulated from judicial scrutiny potentially unconstitutional exercises of its power and that of the executive branch. As such, this jurisdiction-stripping measure can be seen as undermining the federal judiciary's ability to carry out its essential function of judicial review, and from that perspective, the measure may well be unconstitutional.

Of course, we have no way of knowing which reading of *Klein* the Supreme Court will adopt. Fortunately, although Congress often threatens to pass jurisdiction-stripping measures, the threats almost never come to fruition. Yet this much we do know: It is certain that Congress cannot use its exceptions power in a manner that violates the principle of separation of powers. And the closer a particular measure comes to creating a parallel with the *Klein* case by injecting Congress into the judicial process, the more likely it is that the Court will find a violation of the *Klein* principle. But to the extent the measure only interferes with what is perceived as the Court's "essential function" of providing a check on the federal political branches and on the states, the potential constitutional outcome becomes much less certain. In this context, as in so many others, the composition of the Court that considers such a question will be of paramount importance.

§2.2.3 External Limits on Exercises of the Exceptions Power

Just as Congress may not use its exceptions power in a manner that violates the separation of powers, Congress may not use that power, or any other power, in a manner that violates specific limitations imposed by the Constitution, such as those found in the Bill of Rights. At one end of the spectrum, potential transgressions of constitutional limitations are so obvious as to warrant little comment. For example, an exception to the Court's appellate jurisdiction that discriminated on the basis of religious belief or affiliation would run afoul of the religion clauses of the First Amendment. The Court would have no difficulty in finding such a measure unconstitutional. The problem becomes more complex, however, when the exception limits the Court's jurisdiction over a particular topic without directly violating the underlying constitutional rights.

Example 2-D

Compare two statutes. The first provides that "[t]he Supreme Court shall not have jurisdiction to review, by appeal, writ of certiorari, or otherwise, any case arising out of any State statute, ordinance, rule, regulation, or practice, which relates to voluntary prayer, Bible reading, or religious meetings in public schools *when such case is brought by a person who does not profess a belief in God.*" The second statute excludes the italicized language.

Explanation

The first statute violates a basic principle of the First Amendment by using a person's beliefs as a measure of the law. Notice that the constitutional defect is on the face of the statute itself—a discrimination against those who do not profess a belief in God. Since the right to believe what one chooses is absolute, this exception is unconstitutional.

The constitutionality of the second statute is not so easily resolved. At first reading, it appears that the second statute merely insulates certain constitutional claims from Supreme Court review, namely, Establishment Clause claims challenging public school prayer or Bible reading. If this characterization is accepted, then this statute does not transgress the *external limitations* component of our analysis. Assuming we have found no definitional or structural defects in the statute, it reflects a proper exercise of the exceptions power. One can plausibly argue, however, that this seemingly neutral jurisdictional exception does violate the Establishment Clause by in effect insulating public school prayer from constitutional scrutiny and thereby indirectly promoting the practice of public school prayer. If this argument is accepted, the second statute is equally as defective as the first.

We do not know how the Court would rule in such a case. A Justice with a broad conception of the exceptions power could easily interpret the second statute as a legitimate exercise of the power, free of any structural or external defects. The exception is not premised on the violation of anyone's rights. It is simply this: an exception to the Court's appellate jurisdiction. On the other hand, a Justice with a less expansive view of the exceptions power may well perceive both structural and external defects in such a statute. The statute undermines the Court's ability to carry out its essential function, and it violates the Establishment Clause by promoting a religious practice. Of course, one might also want to factor in the Justice's perception of the underlying constitutional rights. A Justice particularly concerned with protecting the underlying right may be more likely to discover a violation of that right in a jurisdiction-stripping measure than would a Justice less favorably disposed to the right. Consider another example.

Example 2-E

Suppose that a federal statute provides that "[t]he Supreme Court shall not have jurisdiction to review, by appeal, writ of certiorari, or otherwise, any case arising out of any State statute, ordinance, rule, regulation, or practice, which proscribes or regulates abortions."

Explanation

The Supreme Court has interpreted the Fourteenth Amendment as protecting a woman's right to procure an abortion free from "undue burdens" imposed by the government. The quoted statute does not in itself impose any direct restriction on the right to procure an abortion. Thus, unlike the statute that discriminated against persons not professing a belief in God, this statute does not directly violate any constitutional proscription against government action. On the other hand, by insulating abortion challenges from Supreme Court review, the statute may well impose an undue burden on a woman's right to procure an abortion by making it significantly more difficult to challenge state laws that themselves impose such burdens. As you can imagine, a Justice's perception of abortion rights could be a major factor in that Justice's determination of whether this jurisdiction-stripping measure violated the "undue burdens" test.

The general rule is easy to state. Congress may not use its exceptions power in a manner that violates constitutional limitations on government power. Application of this rule, however, is only simple in the most obvious cases. While it is quite likely that the Court will strike down an exception to its jurisdiction that directly and unequivocally violates a provision of the Bill of Rights, it is far from clear that the Court would take similar action when the claimed violation is indirect, as in Examples 2-D and 2-E.

§2.2.4 A Comment on Ambiguities in the Jurisprudence of the Exceptions Clause

Our effort to discover the scope of the Exceptions Clause has revealed significant ambiguities at three key points: definitional, structural, and external. These ambiguities are a good thing. They create a constitutional tension that tempers both Congress and the Court. If it were absolutely clear that Congress could limit the Court's appellate jurisdiction at will, without concern for any competing constitutional principles, the authority of the Court would be severely undermined. Similarly, if it were equally certain that the Court could trump every attempt by Congress to create an exception to the Court's appellate jurisdiction, the hubris of unrestrained judicial review might well damage the delicate balance between constitutional oversight and the ideals of a republican democracy. The ambiguity requires good judgment from both branches. The practical result has been a history of very few conflicts in this sphere.

§2.3 THE POWER TO CREATE ARTICLE III COURTS INFERIOR TO THE SUPREME COURT

Article I, §8, cl. 9 expressly grants Congress the power to "constitute Tribunals inferior to the supreme Court." This power is referenced in Article III, which defines the federal judicial power as being vested in one Supreme Court and in such inferior courts "as the Congress may from time to time ordain and establish." Art. III, §1, cl. 1. In other words, the judicial power described in Article III is vested in the Supreme Court as well as in those inferior courts created by Congress pursuant to Article I, §8, cl. 9. Both the Supreme Court and these inferior federal courts, therefore, are referred to as Article III courts, and, as we will discuss below, the limits and protections of Article III apply to both.

§2.3.1 Defining the Power to Constitute Inferior Tribunals

The power to constitute tribunals inferior to the Supreme Court is, simply stated, the power to create Article III courts other than the Supreme Court. The scope of the power is thus dependent on our definition of the phrase "Article III court," and the meaning to be assigned to the adjective "inferior." As to the first part of our definition, all Article III courts share at least three characteristics. First, they are federal courts created either by the Constitution (the Supreme Court) or by Congress (inferior courts). Second, they are vested with jurisdiction to decide some or all of the cases and controversies described in Article III, such as cases arising under the Constitution or laws of the United States, or controversies between citizens from different states. And third, they are presided over by judges who are vested with two important rights of office, namely, life tenure "during good Behaviour," and a compensation that will not be diminished "during their Continuance in Office." Art. III, §1; see *United States v. Hatter*, 532 U.S. 557 (2001) (holding that discriminatory imposition of Social Security taxes on federal judges who had not been subject to such taxes at the time of their appointment violates Compensation Clause). A court that possesses each of these characteristics is an Article III court; a court that lacks any one of these characteristics is not.

The second part of our definition involves the judicial status of these courts — they must, according to the text, be "inferior" to the Supreme Court. As such these Article III courts cannot review decisions of the Supreme Court. It is also probably true, although not definitively established, that the decisions of these courts must be subject to review by the Supreme Court or some other court whose judgments are themselves reviewable by the Supreme Court.

Given the above definition of inferior Article III courts, it follows that Congress may, pursuant to Article I, §8, cl. 9, create courts that exercise jurisdiction over subject matters described in Article III as long as the judges of those courts are granted life tenure during good behavior and salary protection while in office, and as long as the status of those courts can be described as inferior in the sense noted above.

Example 2-F

Congress created the system of United States district courts pursuant to its power to constitute tribunals inferior to the Supreme Court. District courts exercise jurisdiction over specified Article III subject matters including federal question and diversity cases. The judges of these courts are vested with life tenure and salary protection. Furthermore, the decisions of U.S. district courts are reviewable by the Supreme Court (though usually through the intermediary of the circuit courts of appeals).

Explanation

Given the above facts, United States district courts are, by definition, inferior Article III courts, and their creation comes within the defined power of Congress to constitute tribunals inferior to the Supreme Court.

One further question must be considered to complete our definition of this power. Is the power mandatory — i.e., must Congress create inferior tribunals? According to the commonly accepted view, the power vested in Congress is completely discretionary in that Congress may either exercise the power or choose to leave it dormant. The plausibility of this interpretation is difficult to deny. The power to constitute inferior tribunals is, after all, included within the general list of powers granted to Congress in Article I, §8, none of which expressly imposes a duty to act. Nor have any of those powers been so interpreted by the Court. The text of Article III is to a similar effect — "The judicial Power of the United States, shall be vested in one supreme Court, and in such inferior Courts *as the Congress may from time to time ordain and establish.*" The permissive texture of this language supports the view that Congress is free to either exercise the power or ignore it. Finally, the records of the Federal Convention of 1787 indicate that the authors of the text intentionally drew a distinction between constitutionally established courts (the Supreme Court) and courts that could be created in the discretion of Congress (inferior tribunals) to strike a compromise between those who supported the creation of a system of inferior federal courts and those who opposed such a system. In essence, the controversy over the creation of inferior courts was removed from the convention and deflected to Congress.

The above interpretation, although widely accepted, has not met with universal approbation. Justice Joseph Story suggested the possibility of a mandatory model in *Martin v. Hunter's Lessee*, 14 U.S. (1 Wheat.) 304, 328-333 (1816). Story argued in dictum that the entire range of jurisdiction described in Article III must be vested in the federal judiciary, and that to accomplish this, Congress was required to create a system of inferior federal courts. His argument was premised on the text of the Constitution, which uses the phrases "shall be vested" and "shall extend" with reference to the judicial power and to the enumerated categories of cases and controversies described in Article III. Both phrases were, in Story's reckoning, imperative. Furthermore, since the Supreme Court's original jurisdiction is textually limited to two subject matters, and since state courts are not competent to hear certain "exclusively" federal matters described in Article III, the Supreme Court's exercise of its appellate jurisdiction over those matters requires the existence of a system of federal tribunals capable of exercising original jurisdiction over them. Only in this fashion will the entire judicial power *extend* to all subject matters *vested* in the federal judiciary by Article III.

There are several modern variations of Story's argument. One posits that given the scope and complexity of our modern legal system, coupled with the essential role of judicial review as a check upon congressional and presidential action, a system of lower federal courts is a constitutional and pragmatic necessity. The Supreme Court, working alone, cannot possibly satisfy this constitutional mission. As a consequence, Congress must create tribunals inferior to the Supreme Court with a capability of fully executing the power of judicial review. Another variation premises the constitutional necessity for federal courts upon the inadequacy of state tribunals to adjudicate claims of unconstitutional state action. Still other arguments reassert Story's reliance on the text of the Constitution and argue that at least with respect to the "mandatory" subject matters described in Article III (see §2.2.1), tribunals inferior to the Supreme Court are a constitutional necessity.

The mandatory arguments are intellectually attractive; moreover, they serve the important function of emphasizing the critical role that the federal judiciary plays within our system of government, a perception that is not lost on Congress or the executive branch. Whether these arguments are "correct" in some measurable sense or, perhaps more importantly, whether they will ever dominate the jurisprudence in this realm, remains an open question. Quite likely, however, this debate over discretion and duty is not likely to be resolved in any doctrinal sense. The First Congress exercised the power to constitute inferior courts when it passed the Judiciary Act of 1789. The act created a system of district and circuit courts, both with a relatively modest range of jurisdiction. Since that time, Congress has consistently provided for a system of Article III courts "inferior to the supreme Court," although both the jurisdiction and structure of that system have evolved significantly over the past 200 years. Today the congressionally created federal judiciary consists of an extensive system of trial and appellate courts, exercising a broad range of jurisdiction, although at no time has the range of jurisdiction been as extensive as that described in Article III. In short, Congress has exercised its authority to constitute tribunals inferior to the Supreme Court, and given practical realities it is quite unlikely that Congress will dismantle that system to a degree that requires a resolution of the tension between unfettered discretion and constitutional duty. Let us assume, therefore, that the power conferred on Congress is discretionary, but that the discretion conferred carries the weight of careful judgment, tempered by our system of checks and balances.

§2.3.2 The Implicit Authority to Regulate Jurisdiction

An important corollary to the power to constitute inferior tribunals is the implicit authority to define the jurisdiction of any court created pursuant to this power. Although Justice Story and others have argued that to some extent and in various fashions the jurisdiction of inferior tribunals is mandatory, the widely accepted view is that although Congress may not extend the jurisdiction of inferior tribunals (or the Supreme Court) beyond the jurisdictional categories provided in Article III, Congress may provide inferior courts with less jurisdiction than would be permitted by Article III. Thus Congress is free to grant or withhold any aspect of Article III jurisdiction that it deems appropriate.

Significantly, at no time in our history has Congress granted lower federal courts the full range of jurisdiction provided in Article III. For example, although Article III provides that the judicial power "shall extend" to controversies "between Citizens of different States," Congress has consistently limited the scope of diversity jurisdiction by imposing an amount in controversy requirement. Thus, despite the language of Article III, not all controversies between citizens of different states may be filed in federal court. Similarly, Congress did not grant lower federal courts general federal question jurisdiction until 1875, and until 1980, general federal question jurisdiction was further limited by an amount in controversy requirement. In short, once Congress decides to create an Article III court, Congress may define the jurisdiction of that court in any manner it chooses so long as that jurisdiction does not exceed the limits of Article III. This congressional practice of limiting the jurisdiction of lower federal courts has been consistently upheld by the Supreme Court. In *Sheldon v. Sill*, 49 U.S. (8 How.) 441, 448-449 (1850), the Court observed, "Congress, having the power to establish the courts, must define their respective jurisdictions . . . [and] Congress may withhold from any court of its creation jurisdiction of any of the enumerated controversies [in Article III]. Courts created by statute can have no jurisdiction but such as the statute confers."

In short, implicit in the constitutional grant of discretion to create lower federal courts is an authority to define and limit the jurisdiction of those courts, so long as the jurisdiction conferred does not include powers not enumerated in Article III. In other words, Congress may grant lower courts it chooses to create the full range of Article III judicial power or some portion of that power. It may not, however, vest an Article III court with authority over a subject matter not enumerated in Article III. For example, Congress cannot vest an Article III court with the power to hear a suit between private parties that arises wholly under state law unless the parties to the suit are diverse from one another. This is so because Article III does not provide jurisdiction for such cases.

Under its power to define and limit federal jurisdiction, Congress may require that certain cases that would otherwise fall within a federal district court's subject matter jurisdiction instead be heard by some other tribunal. See, e.g., *Elgin v. Department of the Treasury*, 132 S. Ct. 2126 (2012) (Congress could give the federal Merit System Protection Board exclusive jurisdiction over certain federal employee claims that would otherwise fall within a district court's "federal question" jurisdiction (28 U.S.C. §1331), with Board decisions then reviewable by the U.S. Court of Appeals for the Federal Circuit). In federal question cases, however, there is a presumption in favor of federal jurisdiction, a presumption that is not overcome simply by the fact that Congress has expressly provided that a certain type of federal question case may be brought in an appropriate state court. *Mims v. Arrow Financial Services, LLC*, 132 S. Ct. 740, 749 (2012) (federal district court retains §1331 jurisdiction over federal question claims unless a federal statute "expressly or by fair implication, excludes federal-court adjudication." Congress's power to limit the scope of federal jurisdiction also includes the authority to limit the remedial powers of lower federal courts. *Lauf v. E. G. Shinner & Co.*, 303 U.S. 323, 329-330 (1938) (federal district court has no jurisdiction to issue injunction in a labor dispute except as provided by Congress); *Kline v. Burke Construction Co.*, 260 U.S. 226 (1922) (federal district court has no jurisdiction to enjoin parallel state proceeding).

§2.3.3 Structural Limits on the Power to Create Inferior Tribunals

Both the express power to constitute inferior tribunals and the implied power to define the jurisdiction of those tribunals are subject to the separation of powers doctrine in the same fashion as is the power to make exceptions to the Supreme Court's appellate jurisdiction. As a consequence, Congress may not manipulate inferior court jurisdiction in a manner designed to achieve a particular result in a pending case. *United States v. Klein*, 80 U.S. (13 Wall.) 128 (1871). Nor, more generally, may Congress take any action that encroaches upon or usurps a judicial function.

Example 2-G

In a case involving the Securities and Exchange Act, the Supreme Court decided that certain actions for monetary relief filed under the act are subject to a one-year statute of limitations. In accord with that decision, several inferior federal courts dismissed pending securities cases and entered final judgments against the plaintiffs. No appeals were taken. Subsequently Congress adopted legislation that permitted a longer statute of limitations for such cases. This same legislation also provided for the reopening of the final judgments described above, with instructions to apply the longer statute of limitations to cases that were pending the day before the Supreme Court decision was announced. Does this action violate the separation of powers?

Explanation

Yes. Although Congress is free to alter the limitations period for all pending and future cases, Congress may not require a federal court to reopen a final judgment. The federal judiciary is vested with the power to decide cases and controversies. That power includes the authority to issue dispositive judgments in pending cases. "By retroactively commanding the federal courts to reopen final judgments, Congress has violated this fundamental principle." *Plaut v. Spendthrift Farm, Inc.*, 514 U.S. 211, 219 (1995) (so holding on similar facts).

Similarly, Congress may not subject decisions of inferior courts to review by officers of the executive branch.

Example 2-H

Congress has adopted legislation to provide pensions for military personnel injured while in the service of the United States. A petition for such a pension must be filed in a U.S. district court by the individual who claims the entitlement. Upon the receipt of such a petition, the district court is required to hold a hearing to determine if the facts warrant the granting of a petition under applicable legal standards. A decision to grant or deny a petition for a pension may be reviewed by the secretary of defense. The secretary's decision is final.

Explanation

This scheme violates the separation of powers by subjecting a judicial decision to review by the executive branch. By exercising such a review power, the executive branch is usurping the judicial function of deciding cases. See *Hayburn's Case*, 2 U.S. (2 Dall.) 409 (1792).

Of course not all interferences with the judicial function will amount to a separation of powers violation. We have previously noted that Congress is free to establish the substantive legal standards to be applied in the resolution of cases and controversies.

Example 2-I

Prior to 1984, sentencing in federal criminal cases vested federal district court judges with broad discretion to determine the length of sentence to be imposed in any particular case. In essence, sentencing judges exercised almost unfettered discretion to determine the length of a sentence within a customarily wide range of options. In 1984, Congress adopted legislation that largely eliminated that discretion by requiring the sentencing judge to impose a sentence in accord with relatively fixed guidelines. Did imposition of this determinate sentencing scheme violate the separation of powers by limiting judicial discretion in the imposition of sentences?

Explanation

No. Although Congress has clearly limited the ability of federal judges to impose individualized sentences, Congress has not encroached upon or usurped a judicial function. Congress has merely set the legal standards within which the judicial function is to operate. The fact that the new guidelines are rigid as opposed to flexible makes no difference. The sentencing judge will still apply the law to the facts in determining the length of sentence within the ranges established by law, thus preserving the judicial function of deciding cases. See *Mistretta v. United States*, 488 U.S. 361, 364 (1989).

Example 2-J

In 1975, in a class action suit filed by state prison inmates, a federal district court entered a permanent injunction to remedy violations of the Eighth Amendment regarding conditions of confinement at the prison in which the inmates were housed. While the injunction was still in effect and long after the court's final judgment had been entered, Congress passed the Prison Litigation Reform Act, which sets specific standards for the entry and termination of injunctive relief in civil actions challenging prison conditions. The act applies to all pending and future "prison condition" injunctions. Essentially, the act requires that any such injunction be narrowly tailored to remedy the violation of federal law. In addition, §3626(e)(2) of the act provides for an automatic stay of any previously issued prison condition injunction if a defendant moves to terminate the injunction under the terms of the act. The defendant in the class action litigation described above has moved to terminate the injunction under the terms of the act. Would the imposition of the new standards for injunctive relief violate the separation of powers? Does imposition of the automatic stay violate the separation of powers?

Explanation

At first blush it would appear that this case is indistinguishable from *Plaut v. Spendthrift Farm, Inc.*, Example 2-G. In both cases a district court entered a final judgment, and in both cases Congress passed legislation that appears to require the respective district court to reopen its judgment to apply new legal standards. But there is a distinction. *Plaut* involved a suit for monetary relief. In such suits a final judgment represents the district court's final resolution of the case. Any interference with that resolution undermines the district court's judicial authority to decide the case. The immediate problem involves prospective relief in which, despite the technical entry of a final judgment, the district court retains ongoing supervisory authority over the case. There has been no final decision. In essence, the case remains pending as long as the injunction is in effect. Hence, Congress is free to alter the legal standards to be applied to it. See Example 2-B. Nor does §3626(e)(2)'s automatic stay provision violate the separation of powers. The automatic stay does not transgress the principle of *Klein* by directing a particular outcome in the case. Rather, it places a temporary hold on a previously issued injunction while the district court determines whether the standards of the act have been satisfied. The ultimate determination of whether those standards are satisfied remains with the district court. See *Miller v. French*, 530 U.S. 327 (2000).

One final separation of powers issue must be considered. To what extent, if at all, does the separation of powers doctrine require Congress to maintain either the current system of inferior federal courts or a system of similar magnitude? Some commentators have argued that given the complexity of our modern legal system, inferior federal courts play an essential role in the delivery of justice and in the protection of constitutional values. Since, as a practical matter, the Supreme Court would be incapable of carrying out that mission on its own, a system of inferior federal courts is a constitutional necessity. To eliminate that system would be to undermine the essential function of the federal judiciary, or so the argument goes. As was true with the essential function argument in the context of Supreme Court appellate jurisdiction, the validity of this argument turns on whether one accepts the basic premise that there is a constitutionally mandated "essential function" for inferior federal courts and, if so, how broadly one defines that term. Law on this point is virtually nonexistent, largely because Congress has seen fit to create an extensive system of inferior federal courts, thus obviating any need to resolve this theoretical argument. But see *Stuart v. Laird*, 5 U.S. (1 Cranch) 299, 309 (1803) (cryptically observing that Congress's power to create inferior courts is "unrestrained" by anything in the Constitution). One can safely conclude, however, that the proponents of this view have a relatively difficult burden of persuasion, at least if one accepts the view that the Constitution vests Congress with discretion regarding the creation and jurisdictional composition of such courts.

§2.3.4 External Limits on the Power to Create Inferior Tribunals

The principles discussed in §2.2.3 regarding external limits on the exceptions power are fully applicable to the congressional power over the creation and regulation of inferior tribunals. Congress may not exercise its power over these tribunals in a manner that violates constitutional limits such as those found in Article I, §9 (e.g., proscriptions against the suspension of habeas corpus or the enactment of ex post facto laws) or in the Bill of Rights. See *Boumediene v. Bush*, 553 U.S. 723, 792 (2008) (provision of Military Commissions Act of 2006 effected an unconstitutional suspension of the writ of habeas corpus). The examples used in §2.2.3 are fully applicable in this context. Thus if Congress were to pass a jurisdictional statute applicable to inferior courts that discriminated on the basis of religious belief, the measure would be struck down under the Establishment Clause. On the other hand, if Congress merely stripped inferior courts of jurisdiction over public school prayer cases, the potential Establishment Clause violation would be at best indirect. As was true in the context of Supreme Court appellate jurisdiction (see Example 2-D), the constitutionality of such a measure would depend on one's perception of the scope of the underlying right and of the scope of the power exercised.

§2.4 THE POWER TO CREATE NON-ARTICLE III COURTS

§2.4.1 The Argument Against Non-Article III Courts

As was noted above, Congress's power to constitute Article III tribunals inferior to the Supreme Court is limited by Article III's substantive description of the judicial branch. The subject matter jurisdiction, tenure, and compensation requirements contained in that description must therefore attach to any tribunal created pursuant to this power. The judges of any court so constituted must be granted Article III's guarantees of office, and the court's jurisdiction must be limited to the types of cases and controversies defined in Article III. Courts created in accord with these principles are sometimes referred to as constitutional courts.

Given these postulates of power and limitation, one is tempted to assume that Congress is without authority to create judicial tribunals other than constitutional courts. That is, Congress would seemingly be barred from creating courts that could hear non-Article III cases, or that were staffed by judges who do not enjoy life tenure and guaranteed compensation. Both the text of Article III and the structure of the Constitution support this assumption. Indeed, the language of Article III, §1 appears to provide a relatively rigid framework within which Congress must operate whenever it exercises the power to constitute inferior tribunals: "The judicial Power of the United States, *shall be vested* in one supreme Court, and in such inferior Courts as the Congress may from time to time ordain and establish. The Judges, both of the supreme and inferior Courts, shall hold their Offices during good Behaviour, and shall, at stated Times, receive for their Services, a Compensation, which shall not be diminished during their Continuance in Office." There is little room for compromise within this language. The judicial power shall reside in the Supreme Court and in the inferior courts established by Congress. The judges of all such courts will have life tenure and salary protection. And there is no provision for courts other than Article III courts.

Arguments from constitutional structure are to the same effect. The basic idea is that an independent judiciary is essential to the system of checks and balances created by the Constitution. In the words of Alexander Hamilton, "The complete independence of the courts of justice is peculiarly essential in a limited constitution." *The Federalist No. 78*, at 466 (Clinton Rossiter ed., 1961). That independence requires that the judiciary remain distinct from the other branches, and that all judicial officers be vested with the guarantees of office provided by Article III. Again in Hamilton's words, "That inflexible and uniform adherence to the rights of the constitution and of individuals, which we perceive to be indispensable in the courts of justice, can certainly not be expected from judges who hold their offices by a temporary commission." Id. Stated somewhat differently, the structural function of the federal judiciary, namely, the effective preservation of constitutional rights and principles, can be maintained only through strict adherence to the requirements of Article III and the principle of separation of powers.

§2.4.2 The Justification for Non-Article III Courts

Both text and structure provide powerful arguments for the proposition that Congress can create Article III or constitutional courts and no others. This proposition is, however, incorrect, at least as a matter of practical reality. Congress has, pursuant to a variety of legislative powers, created judicial tribunals that function outside the context of Article III — usually within the executive branch — and whose presiding officers lack either life tenure or salary protection or both. And on a number of occasions, and under a variety of theories, the Supreme Court has upheld the constitutional validity of these "non-constitutional" courts. Such courts are sometimes referred to as Article I or legislative courts since they are not part of the Article III judicial branch, and since they are created pursuant to the legislative prerogatives of Congress. Yet the nomenclature is somewhat misleading. Not all such courts are created pursuant to Article I powers. Nor are these courts usually part of the legislative branch; rather, more typically, they are part of the Article II executive branch. Yet the distinction drawn by the nomenclature is significant. Article III or constitutional courts must satisfy the requirements of Article III; Article I or legislative courts — i.e., non-Article III courts — need not.

The power to create non-Article III courts is not, however, unconstrained by Article III concerns. Indeed, that power is best understood as an exception to the general principle and strong presumption that the judicial power of the United States "shall be vested" in the Article III judiciary. Although the jurisprudence in this realm can sometimes appear somewhat serpentine, the circumstances under which the Supreme Court has been willing to validate non-Article III courts can be divided into four relatively discrete categories. The techniques used to explore the scope of the fourth category can also be seen as providing a more general method for validating the three other categories. We will examine each category in turn.

§2.4.3 Territorial Courts

The first category establishes an exception to Article III for territorial courts. This exception is premised on Article IV, §3, cl. 2, which provides, "The Congress shall have Power to dispose of and make all needful Rules and Regulations respecting the Territory or other Property belonging to the United States. . . ." The Court has interpreted this grant of power as encompassing an implicit authority to create non-Article III courts for United States territories. *American Insurance Co. v. Canter*, 26 U.S. (1 Pet.) 511 (1828). These courts function within the territories of the United States in much the same fashion as do state courts within their respective jurisdictions, and when a territory becomes a state, the territorial courts may then be dissolved, there being no Article III tenure and compensation limitations imposed. In essence, Article IV — by interpretation — grants Congress the authority to exercise the general powers of government over the territories, thus vesting Congress with a broad discretion to design the structure and composition of territorial courts. This same approach and leniency have been adopted with respect to the congressional creation of local courts for the District of Columbia. *Palmore v. United States*, 411 U.S. 389 (1973). Obviously, only a narrow category of courts fit within this exception, namely, courts for the territories or local courts for the District of Columbia. A judge who has been properly appointed to a territorial court may not, however, participate in hearing matters before an Article III court. See *Nguyen v. United States*, 539 U.S. 69 (2003) (vacating, on statutory grounds, judgment of U.S. Court of Appeals for the Ninth Circuit where the three-judge panel, at a special sitting in the Northern Mariana Islands, included the chief judge of the District Court for the Northern Mariana Islands, an Article IV territorial court judge appointed by the President and confirmed by the Senate for a ten-year term and who was removable by the President for cause).

§2.4.4 Military Courts

Article I, §8, cls. 12, 13, and 14 grant Congress the power "To raise and support Armies . . . ; To provide and maintain a Navy; [and] To make Rules for the Government and Regulation of the land and naval Forces. . . ." These provisions have been construed as vesting Congress with power to create two types of non-Article III courts: courts-martial and military commissions. With respect to courts-martial, pursuant to the above Article I powers, Congress may "provide for the trial and punishment of military and naval offences . . . without any connection between it and the 3rd article of the Constitution defining the judicial powers of the United States." *Dynes v. Hoover*, 61 U.S. (20 How.) 65, 79 (1858). The jurisdiction of courts-martial is limited to the trial of U.S. military personnel. *Kinsella v. United States ex rel. Singleton*, 361 U.S. 234 (1960); *Reid v. Covert*, 354 U.S. 1 (1957); *Ex parte Milligan*, 7 U.S. (4 Wall.) 2 (1867). Military commissions, on the other hand, are designed to try offenses against the law of war. As such, the jurisdictional reach of a military commission may extend beyond U.S. military personnel. *In re Yamashita*, 327 U.S. 1 (1946); *Ex parte Quirin*, 317 U.S. 1 (1942). The Military Commissions Act of 2006 (MCA) provides a recent example. The MCA established a system of military tribunals to try "unlawful enemy combatants" captured during the so-called War on Terror and held at the U.S. naval station at Guantanamo Bay in Cuba. But see *Boumediene v. Bush*, 553 U.S. 723 (2008) (holding unconstitutional those provisions of the MCA that denied detainees held at Guantanamo the right to petition for habeas corpus in an Article III court).

§2.4.5 Adjunct Courts

The third categorical exception involves the use of non-Article III judges as adjuncts to Article III courts. Simply put, the purpose of an adjunct is to assist an Article III court in carrying out its constitutional and statutory duties. For example, the Supreme Court often appoints a special master — who may or may not be an Article III judge — to assist it in the adjudication of border disputes between states. The special master may hold a hearing, make findings, and submit a recommendation to the Court. The Court, however, has the ultimate authority to resolve the dispute by either accepting or rejecting the special master's findings and recommendations. As such, the special master operates as a mere adjunct to the Court. She assists the Court, but does not decide for the Court.

The constitutionality of an adjunct court depends on balancing the scope of the jurisdiction vested in that court against the residual supervisory authority remaining in the Article III court served by the adjunct. The nature of the rights being adjudicated may affect the level of supervision that must be retained. Thus, in the civil context, Congress will have a freer hand to assign the initial adjudication of federal statutory rights to an adjunct than it would the adjudication of constitutional or even common law rights. This is because federal statutory rights are, by definition, created by Congress.

The two leading cases in this category are *Crowell v. Benson*, 285 U.S. 22 (1932), and *United States v. Raddatz*, 447 U.S. 667 (1980). In *Crowell*, the Court upheld the use of an administrative agency as an adjunct to a federal district court. The agency was empowered to make factual determinations under a federal statute that required employers to compensate their employees for work-related injuries occurring on the navigable waters of the United States. The agency performed the limited role of determining "questions of fact as to the circumstances, nature, extent and consequences of the injuries sustained." 285 U.S. at 54. Based on its findings, the agency could enter a compensation order — the amount being derived from a fixed schedule — but had no power to enforce the order. Only the federal district court having jurisdiction over the case could do so, and enforcement of the agency's order would follow only if the district court found that the order was in accord with the law and supported by the evidence of record. Id. at 44-45, 48. The *Crowell* Court found that this scheme did not violate the principles of Article III because the scope of the agency's power was limited to a specific aspect of fact-finding in a narrow class of cases, and the district court was vested with substantial oversight over any agency decision.

United States v. Raddatz involved the use of a United States magistrate for the initial determination of a pretrial motion to suppress evidence in a criminal case. Magistrates serve a term of years, and are appointed by the district court under which they serve. The general function of a magistrate is to assist the district court in the processing and disposition of pretrial matters. 28 U.S.C. §636. In *Raddatz*, a district court referred a pretrial suppression motion to a magistrate for an evidentiary hearing. The magistrate held the hearing, and submitted proposed findings of fact as well as a recommendation to deny the motion. Although the district court could have done so, it declined to hold a second evidentiary hearing. Instead, the court examined the transcript of the magistrate's hearing, considered the parties' proposed findings and memoranda, and heard oral arguments by counsel. Having done so, the court accepted the recommendation of the magistrate and denied the motion to suppress. The Supreme Court held that this "de novo determination" by the court adequately preserved the Article III values at stake. The Court's reasoning was straightforward. The ultimate decision on the suppression motion remained at all times in the district court. Therefore, the role of the magistrate was clearly subsidiary to the district judge and could be properly characterized as that of an adjunct.

Notice that the level of retained authority (virtually complete authority to accept or reject the magistrate's findings and recommendations) in *Raddatz* was greater than that provided in *Crowell*, which was something akin to appellate review. Some commentators have placed significance in this distinction, suggesting that the scope of the retained authority in *Raddatz* was a necessary product of the *constitutional* right being adjudicated. *Crowell*, on the other hand, involved only the adjudication of a federal *statutory* claim.

Example 2-K

The Federal Magistrates Act describes a laundry list of duties that may be assigned to a magistrate. It then provides that district courts may also assign magistrates "such additional duties as are not inconsistent with the Constitution and laws of the United States." Pursuant to this authority, a district court, with the consent of all parties, assigned a magistrate the duty of selecting a jury for a felony trial. The district court retained authority to decide whether to empanel the jury selected. Does this delegation of judicial authority violate the principles of Article III?

Explanation

The key factor from a structural perspective is the control retained by the district court. The entire process, from the initial decision to delegate, to the ultimate decision to empanel, remained under the control of the district court. The district court was fully free to reject the magistrate's recommendation. As a consequence, the process in no way undermined the values of Article III. See *Peretz v. United States*, 501 U.S. 923 (1991).

Of course, the above example might have been resolved against the process employed. Indeed, the dissenters in *Peretz* argued that the district court's "control" was inadequately established since there was no indication that "meaningful judicial review" of the jury selection could be accomplished. 501 U.S. at 951-952. Cf. *Gomez v. United States*, 490 U.S. 858 (1989) (Federal Magistrates Act does not allow district court to assign jury selection function to a magistrate in a felony case in the absence of the defendant's consent).

Example 2-L

The Bankruptcy Act of 1978, as amended, established a system of United States Bankruptcy Courts to serve as adjuncts to district courts. The bankruptcy judges are appointed by the Court of Appeals of the federal circuit in which they sit. They serve 14-year terms and may be removed from office by the Judicial Council for good cause. 28 U.S.C. §152. In short, they are not Article III judges. The act grants bankruptcy courts jurisdiction over all civil proceedings arising under the act or "related to" cases arising under the act. The latter clause permits bankruptcy courts to adjudicate a wide array of claims, including common law claims arising in contract or tort that did not necessarily fall within the scope of the federal judicial power as defined by Article III (e.g., due to a lack of diversity). The act also vests bankruptcy judges with a broad range of legal and equitable powers in all "core" bankruptcy proceedings, including the power to hold jury trials, to issue declaratory judgments, to issue final judgments, to issue writs of habeas corpus, to issue writs in aid of jurisdiction, and to issue any order necessary to carry out the provisions of the act. The only Article III review of "core" proceedings is by appeal to either the district court or the court of appeals. In "non-core" proceedings, however, a bankruptcy judge may only issue proposed findings of fact and conclusions of law which must then be submitted for approval to a federal district court.

Vickie filed a bankruptcy petition in the U.S. District Court for the Central District of California. In that proceeding, she also filed a common law tort defamation claim against Pierce, one of the bankruptcy claimants. The bankruptcy court, after ruling that Vickie's tort claim was part of the "core" bankruptcy proceeding, conducted a bench trial at the conclusion of which it issued a judgment awarding Vicki $425 million in compensatory and punitive damages. Pierce has appealed the bankruptcy judgment, arguing that the bankruptcy court was not acting as an adjunct to the district court and that its judgment on this state law tort claim therefore violated the principles of Article III. How should the court rule on Pierce's appeal?

Explanation

The bankruptcy court appears to have violated Article III even if Vickie's tort claim were somehow deemed to be part of the "core" bankruptcy proceedings. The bankruptcy judge exercised complete authority to adjudicate her state law claim and then entered a final judgment. The only role of the district court is appellate, with but limited authority to reverse the bankruptcy court's judgment. The extensive nature of the powers vested in the bankruptcy judge here, and the limited retained authority of the district court, distinguish this problem from both *Crowell* and *Raddatz*. In *Crowell*, although the review by the district court was "appellate" in nature, the scope of the delegation to the agency was comparatively minuscule. The scope of the agency's fact-finding power was confined to a specific category of facts involving a narrow range of workers' compensation cases; moreover, the agency had no independent enforcement power. Similarly, although the duties of the magistrate in *Raddatz* were somewhat broader, they were also subject to substantial oversight by the district court. The bankruptcy court, by contrast, combines a substantial delegation of decisional and enforcement power with very light Article III review authority. As such, it is difficult to characterize the bankruptcy court as a mere adjunct of the district court. It would therefore appear that the bankruptcy court, whose judges do not meet the appointment or life tenure provisions of Article III, was here exercising judicial power that Congress could not constitutionally assign to it. See *Stern v. Marshall*, 131 S. Ct. 2594 (2011) (bankruptcy court could not hear and enter a final judgment on a common law tort claim); see also *Northern Pipeline Co. v. Marathon Pipe Line Co.*, 458 U.S. 50, 76-87 (1982) (plurality opinion).

§2.4.6 The Public Rights Exception: Original Form

The final and most difficult category, often referred to as the public rights exception, involves the creation of non-Article III tribunals — typically administrative law courts — authorized to adjudicate civil disputes arising in the context of federal regulatory schemes. In its original form, this exception applies only to civil disputes between the *government* and *private parties*, and only when such disputes involve the enforcement of *congressionally created rights and obligations*. Typically the decisions of these administrative law courts are subject to review by Article III courts, either under the terms of the Administrative Procedure Act or under the organic act creating the relevant administrative tribunal. However, the constitutionality of this non-Article III tribunal does not depend on the availability of Article III review, for the matters being adjudicated are such that they could be conclusively resolved by the legislative or executive branch without any resort to Article III oversight.

Importantly, the public rights exception does not authorize Congress to insulate statutory programs from *constitutional* oversight. *Crowell v. Benson*, 285 U.S. 22 (1932). Rather, the exception merely permits Congress to determine if an Article III court will be involved in assessing the scope and application of the *statutory* rights and obligations created by Congress. The constitutionality of the underlying scheme and of the manner in which it is implemented is presumptively subject to judicial review regardless of the public rights exception. Thus if Congress were to adopt statutory criteria that violated a provision of the Bill of Rights, the public rights exception would not prevent an Article III court from striking down those criteria. Similarly, if an administrator assigned to award benefits under a congressionally created program awarded those benefits in a manner that discriminated on the basis of race or gender, the public rights exception would not prevent an Article III court from enjoining that behavior. The public rights exception simply recognizes that matters that can be conclusively resolved by the political branches may be so resolved without resort to the Article III judiciary.

The genesis for the public rights exception is found in *Murray's Lessee v. Hoboken Land and Improvement Co.*, 59 U.S. (18 How.) 272, 284 (1855), a case involving the power of the solicitor of the treasury to seize and sell property of a customs collector who failed to deliver customs duties collected on behalf of the United States. The Court upheld the solicitor's action as consistent with both due process and Article III. As to the latter, the Court observed (by way of dicta),

> [W]e do not consider congress can either withdraw from judicial cognizance any matter which, from its nature, is the subject of a suit at the common law, or in equity, or admiralty; nor, on the other hand, can it bring under the judicial power a matter which, from its nature, is not a subject for judicial determination. At the same time there are matters, involving public rights, which may be presented in such form that the judicial power is capable of acting on them, and which are susceptible of judicial determination, but which congress may or may not bring within the cognizance of the courts of the United States, as it may deem proper.

Id. at 284. Later decisions have construed this language to permit the quasi-judicial resolution of "public rights" — i.e., disputes between "the government and others" that arise in the context of congressionally created rights and obligations. *Crowell v. Benson*, 285 U.S. 22, 50 (1932); *Ex parte Bakelite Corp.*, 279 U.S. 438, 451 (1929).

In accord with this interpretation, the disposal of the property of the United States would involve a public right, as would the granting of government benefits such as welfare or Social Security; so too with respect to the collection of taxes. In each of these examples, the dispute is between the government and a private party, and the nature of the dispute involves a right or obligation created by Congress. Under the public rights exception, disputes arising in these areas can, if Congress so provides, be fully resolved by resort to non-Article III adjudication. However, in actual practice, Congress has opted to make the decisions of most such non-Article III tribunals subject to some form of review by an Article III court.

Example 2-M

Suppose Congress is considering a proposal to grant "educational stipends" to all veterans who have been honorably discharged and who meet certain specified criteria. Congress has several options in determining how to implement this plan. Congress can pass legislation that lists by name each veteran who is eligible for the proposed stipends — a daunting task to be sure. Or, more realistically, Congress can specify the criteria for eligibility and delegate to an administrative agency or officer the authority to award the stipends to those veterans who satisfy the specified criteria. Does either option violate Article III?

Explanation

Under the first option, Congress has conclusively resolved the matter, while under the second, Congress has vested the executive branch with the authority to do so. Neither option violates Article III, and this is so regardless of the availability of Article III oversight. Nor would Article III be violated if Congress were to choose the second option and at the same time vest an administrative law court with the nonreviewable power to assess the correctness of the administrator's decision with respect to statutory eligibility.

§2.4.7 The Public Rights Exception: Modern Form

At one time, the public rights exception, as its name suggests, was thought by some to be limited to cases in which a party asserted a statutory right against the government, such as a claim for Social Security benefits. *Northern Pipeline Construction Co. v. Marathon Pipe Line Co.*, 458 U.S. 50 (1982) (plurality opinion). Under this formal view, although administrative law courts were permitted to adjudicate private rights, such adjudications were constitutional only if sufficient review was available in an Article III court. *Crowell v. Benson*, 285 U.S. at 51-65. In other words, in adjudicating private rights, agencies operated as adjuncts. More recent cases, however, have abandoned the formal distinction between public and private rights and have assessed the constitutionality of all jurisdictional grants to administrative law courts — including those involving private rights — by weighing the interests Congress seeks to advance by use of these non-Article III courts against the potential intrusion upon Article III values. The net effect of this more flexible approach has been to broaden the public rights exception into a more generalized principle that may allow for the administrative adjudication of public and private matters related to the administration of federal regulatory schemes.

In *Commodity Futures Trading Commn. v. Schor*, 478 U.S. 833, 851 (1986), the Court described the appropriate inquiry as follows:

> In determining the extent to which a given congressional decision to authorize the adjudication of Article III business in a non-Article III tribunal impermissibly threatens the institutional integrity of the Judicial Branch, the Court has declined to adopt formalistic and unbending rules. Although such rules might lend a greater degree of coherence to this area of the law, they might also unduly constrict Congress' ability to take needed and innovative action pursuant to its Article I powers. Thus, in reviewing Article III challenges, we have weighed a number of factors, none of which has been deemed determinative, with an eye to the practical effect that the congressional action will have on the constitutionally assigned role of the federal judiciary. Among the factors upon which we have focused are the extent to which the "essential attributes of judicial power" are reserved to Article III courts, and, conversely, the extent to which the non-Article III forum exercises the range of jurisdiction and powers normally vested only in Article III courts, the origins and importance of the right to be adjudicated, and the concerns that drove Congress to depart from the requirements of Article III.

Resort to this balancing formula has permitted the Court to validate non-Article III jurisdiction over purely private disputes and over common law claims, thus deviating from both elements of the public rights exception. In *Schor*, for example, the Court allowed an administrative agency to exercise jurisdiction over a state-law counterclaim in a reparation proceeding under the Commodity Exchange Act. The Court noted that the agency dealt only with a "particularized area of the law," and that the orders of the agency were enforceable only by the district court. Id. at 852. The fact that the claim involved a private right did trigger some Article III concerns, but those concerns were allayed by the Court's conclusion that the overall scheme did not "create a substantial threat to the separation of powers." Id. at 854.

Example 2-N

A federal statute requires manufacturers of pesticides, as a precondition to registering a pesticide, to submit research data to the Environmental Protection Agency (EPA) concerning the pesticide's health, safety, and environmental effects. The statute permits the EPA to use previously submitted data on similar products by other registrants, but only if the "follow-on" registrant has compensated the original registrant for the use of the data. If the parties fail to agree on the amount of compensation, the statute provides for binding arbitration by a non-Article III judge, subject to Article III review only for "fraud, misrepresentation, or other misconduct." The statute was passed in response to a logjam of litigation in federal courts over the proper amount of compensation in such cases. Does this statutory scheme violate Article III?

Explanation

From a "pure public rights" perspective, the scheme does violate Article III. Although the arbitration may involve a right created by Congress, the dispute is between private parties; i.e., the dispute is not between the government and others as required by the public rights exception. Nor would this scheme satisfy any of the other categorical exceptions. Clearly the arbitrator is not a territorial court or a military court, and given the very limited scope of Article III review, the arbitrator cannot be considered an adjunct. From the perspective of the balancing test employed in *Schor*, however, the scheme may well be constitutional. The right of compensation created by Congress is closely related to a complex federal regulatory scheme, the intrusion upon Article III values is limited when one considers the narrow scope of authority vested in the arbitrator, and the need for an efficient and uniform approach was manifest. See *Thomas v. Union Carbide Agricultural Products Co.*, 473 U.S. 568, 589-593 (1985).

The balancing approach adopted by the Court in *Schor* and *Thomas* has permitted small but significant expansions of the public rights exception, altering that exception to one that is premised less on public rights than it is on the needs of the administrative state. More importantly, the balancing test provides a general, noncategorical model for the constitutional assessment of all non-Article III courts. Thus one can use this test to justify the three other categorical exceptions. For example, from the perspective of the balancing test, territorial courts are permitted because they serve an important function in the context of congressional regulation of the territories, while posing little or no threat to the integrity of the Article III judiciary. Similar arguments can be made for military courts and adjuncts. And although the

Court does not appear inclined to revisit these well-established exceptions, nothing in the Court's recent cases indicates a reluctance to consider new possibilities through the lens of this balancing test. Dissenters from the Court's approach in *Schor* and *Thomas* see this potential for the incremental expansion of the non-Article III concept as a serious, albeit subtle, threat to the independence of the judicial branch. See *Commodity Futures Trading Commn. v. Schor,* supra, 478 U.S. at 859-867 (Brennan, J., dissenting); see also *Granfinanciera, S.A. v. Nordberg,* 492 U.S. 33, 65-71 (1989) (Scalia, J., concurring) (calling for a more rigid adherence to the public rights model). Others welcome the balancing test as a reasonable accommodation of the growing administrative state.

Justiciability

§3.1 INTRODUCTION AND OVERVIEW

The term *justiciability* refers to a body of judicially created doctrines that define and limit the circumstances under which an Article III federal court may exercise its constitutional authority, including its authority to engage in judicial review. These doctrines are derived in part from an interpretation of Article III's case or controversy requirement, and in part from prudential policy considerations involving perceptions of the proper role of the federal judiciary within the constitutional structure of government.

Stated very broadly, a matter is deemed justiciable—i.e., one over which an Article III court may exercise authority—if it possesses a sufficient number of those characteristics historically associated with the judicial function of dispute resolution. *Flast v. Cohen*, 392 U.S. 83, 94 (1968). Thus justiciability defines the limits of Article III judicial power by focusing on our expectations of the types of matters judges commonly decide. *Lujan v. Defenders of Wildlife*, 504 U.S. 555, 560 (1992). Those expectations are applied and developed through the lens of four specific doctrines—the doctrines of standing, ripeness, mootness, and political questions—each of which is designed, at least in part, to ensure that Article III courts do not become embroiled in matters of a nonjusticiable nature—i.e., matters that would take a federal court beyond the sphere of activity commonly associated with judging.

The limitations imposed by the justiciability doctrines apply not only to the federal district courts, but to the federal appellate tribunals as well. Thus, a case that was sufficiently "live" to have been properly decided by a federal district court may, due to intervening events, become moot while the case is on appeal, thereby stripping the federal courts of their ability to proceed in the matter. Similarly, even if a plaintiff had standing to bring a case and seek relief from a district court, this does not automatically mean that a dissatisfied defendant has standing to pursue the matter on appeal. Instead, the Court of Appeals or the Supreme Court may need to first determine whether, in light of the relief sought on appeal, the appellate proceeding itself qualifies as an Article III case or controversy. See *Monsanto Co. v. Geertson Seed Farms*, 130 S. Ct. 2743, 2752-2754 (2010) (a defendant seeking Supreme Court review of an adverse lower federal court ruling must show that the injury defendant complains of and the relief sought on appeal qualify the matter as an Article III "case" that the Court is allowed to hear).

Example 3-A

Jean received severe burns as the result of the explosion of the gas tank in a car in which she was a passenger. The explosion was triggered by a 10 mph rear-end collision. Jean files suit against the manufacturer of the car, claiming that the explosion was caused by a design defect in the gas tank. She seeks compensatory damages.

Explanation

Regardless of whether Jean will prevail on the merits, her claim is justiciable. It presents precisely the type of controversy judges have historically decided. An injured party seeks relief against the entity she claims is legally responsible for her injuries.

By way of contrast, suppose Jean was not injured in an automobile accident, but that she has studied a series of accidents involving exploding gas tanks. On the basis of this study she concludes that the current state of product liability law is insufficiently protective of consumers; among other things, it has allowed several manufacturers to escape liability. Jean files suit against those manufacturers, seeking to establish that stricter standards of liability ought to be applied to their defective products. Her claim is not justiciable. Although Jean may well have a dispute with certain automobile manufacturers over the scope of their liability, the dispute is not of the nature usually resolved through the judicial process. In particular, Jean has suffered no judicially cognizable injury.

Because the justiciability doctrines derive in large part from Article III, they operate as limitations on *federal* judicial power. While states may if they wish impose similar limitations on their own courts, nothing in the federal

Constitution requires them to do so. As a result, state courts are often able to hear matters that would not qualify as "cases" or "controversies" within the meaning of Article III. Thus, even though certain types of suits filed in state court may be removed by defendants to federal court, including those that "arise under" the Constitution (see 28 U.S.C. §1441), if the suit does not meet federal justiciability standards, the federal court will have no choice but to remand the action to state court or dismiss it. See *DaimlerChrysler Corp. v. Cuno*, 547 U.S. 332 (2006) (suit by taxpayers in state court, alleging that state tax violated the federal Constitution, was improperly removed to federal court because plaintiffs did not meet federal standing requirements and their suit thus did not qualify as an Article III case or controversy).

The materials that follow begin with a general examination of the basic elements of a justiciable case or controversy. Following this general examination is a more specific discussion of the doctrines of standing, ripeness, mootness, and political questions. As you read these materials, keep the basic premise in mind. Article III courts are, by constitutional definition, vested with the power to exercise a specific and limited type of authority, namely, the authority to function as decision makers in the context of disputes commonly understood to be susceptible to a judicial resolution.

§3.2 THE ELEMENTS OF A CASE OR CONTROVERSY

Article III, §2 provides that the "judicial Power shall extend to" certain enumerated categories of "cases" and "controversies." These words have been interpreted as not merely descriptive of the business of Article III federal courts, but as imposing a specific constitutional limitation on the circumstances under which an Article III court may exercise its judicial authority. The essence of that limitation is that an Article III court may only exercise jurisdiction over those matters:

- In which there is an actual dispute involving the legal relations of adverse parties, and
- For which the judiciary can provide some type of effective relief.

Aetna Life Ins. Co. v. Haworth, 300 U.S. 227, 240-241 (1937). In the words of the *Haworth* Court, "A justiciable controversy is thus distinguished from a difference or dispute of a hypothetical or abstract character; from one that is academic or moot." Id. at 240. The elements of this constitutional minimum must be satisfied in every matter pending before an Article III federal court.

Returning to Example 3-A, Jean, as an accident victim, has satisfied the elements of a case or controversy in her suit against the manufacturer of the allegedly defective automobile. She and the manufacturer are adverse parties involved in an actual dispute regarding their respective legal rights and obligations — one seeks to establish the very liability that the other resists. In addition, the judiciary is in a position to provide effective relief by awarding compensatory damages if liability is established. On the other hand, when Jean, as a consumer advocate, sues automobile manufacturers to establish stricter standards of liability, the elements of a case or controversy are lacking. Although Jean and the manufacturers may well disagree over the appropriate legal standards to be applied in product liability cases, the dispute between them does not involve their legal relations. At most, Jean's suit involves an abstract disagreement about matters of policy. She has not stated a justiciable case or controversy.

§3.2.1 Constitutional Minimum Applied: Advisory Opinions and Collusive Suits

An important corollary to the case or controversy requirement is that an Article III court may not issue an advisory opinion — i.e., an opinion issued outside the context of a justiciable case or controversy. *Hayburn's Case*, 2 U.S. (2 Dall.) 409 (1792). Consistent with this corollary, Congress may not ask the Supreme Court to comment upon the constitutionality of proposed legislation; nor may the President ask the Court to render an opinion on the legality of pending executive action. In neither situation is there an actual dispute between adverse parties involving the legal relations of those parties; similarly, in neither situation is there any suggestion that the Court's opinion would be anything more than a nonbinding recital of the views of the Court. In short, there is no case or controversy.

Example 3-B

The President is considering issuing an executive order that would dramatically reduce the federal government's share of welfare payments for temporary assistance for needy families (TANF). The net effect of the order will be to require states to shoulder a larger percentage of the costs of TANF. The President is uncertain whether the proposed executive order is consistent with a number of arguably relevant statutes and congressional funding mandates. She instructs the secretary of state to ask the Justices of the Supreme Court to render an opinion on that issue. Why will the Court decline to do so?

Explanation

The President's request does not arise out of an actual dispute between adverse parties — at least not in the sense that one normally associates with the judicial process; nor does the request ask for any type of binding or conclusive relief. In sum, the President is asking for an advisory opinion, and the Court may not issue such an opinion consistent with the case or controversy requirement of Article III.

On the other hand, if the executive order is issued, a party affected by the order — e.g., a state that will now have to shoulder a larger percentage of TANF payments — may file a suit against the appropriate executive officer and seek to enjoin implementation of the order. Under these circumstances, an Article III federal court, including the Supreme Court, could render an opinion on the legality of the executive action. There is an actual dispute between the state and the executive branch involving their legal relations, and any relief ordered by the court will be binding on the parties. In other words, the court's opinion will not be merely "advisory."

Although the circumstances under which an Article III court will be asked to issue an advisory opinion are rare, the underlying principles of this proscription provide the foundation for all other justiciability doctrines. Those doctrines — standing, ripeness, mootness, and political questions — are designed, at least in part, to ensure that Article III courts will not exercise authority under circumstances in which the basic elements of a constitutional case or controversy are lacking — i.e., in which a party is requesting nothing more than an advisory opinion.

Just as an Article III court will not entertain requests for advisory opinions, an Article III court will not entertain a collusive suit — i.e., a suit in which the parties attempt to fabricate an actual case or controversy.

Example 3-C

An owner of rental property wishes to challenge the constitutionality of a federal statute that regulates the amount of rent he can charge. To this end, he provides one of his tenants with a lawyer and asks the tenant to file a "friendly suit" against him in which the tenant will allege that the rents charged by the landlord are in violation of the federal statute. The suit is filed in federal district court. May the district court adjudicate this claim?

Explanation

No. The absence of an actual dispute between adverse parties is fatal to this lawsuit. There being no case or controversy, the court must dismiss. See *United States v. Johnson*, 319 U.S. 302 (1943) (dismissing a suit as collusive under similar facts).

§3.2.2 Constitutional Minimum Applied: Declaratory Relief

The proscription against advisory opinions does not preclude an Article III court from providing declaratory relief when requested to do so in the context of an actual case or controversy. *Aetna Life Ins. Co. v. Haworth*, 300 U.S. 227 (1937). In an actual dispute between adverse parties involving their legal rights and obligations, declaratory relief is not merely advisory; it is legally binding upon the parties, and may be enforced through the application of other judicially imposed forms of relief. Thus both elements of the constitutional minimum are satisfied. There is an actual dispute between adverse parties involving their legal relations, and the relief issued by the Court will have a binding or conclusive effect upon that dispute.

Example 3-D

In Example 3-B, we concluded that the President could not ask the Supreme Court to advise her as to the legality of the contemplated executive order. Suppose, however, that after the order is promulgated, a state refuses to comply with various provisions of the order on the ground that the order violates a number of applicable statutes. Does this conflict create a justiciable case or controversy?

Explanation

Yes. The appropriate officer of the executive branch may file a suit in federal court seeking a declaratory judgment with respect to the legality of the President's action and the obligations of the recalcitrant state. There is an actual controversy between the executive branch and the state, and the relief sought, a declaratory judgment, will be binding on the parties and enforceable if necessary.

§3.2.3 Constitutional Minimum Applied: Supreme Court Review of State Decisions

State courts are not constrained by the limitations of Article III, §2. As a result, they may issue decisions in settings that do not qualify as a "case" or "controversy" within the meaning of Article III. For example, a state court might allow a person like Jean, suing simply as a consumer advocate, to bring a suit to force automobile manufacturers to comply with a federal statute imposing certain safety design standards. If the state courts were to rule against Jean on the basis that the federal statute did not impose any such duty on the manufacturers, she could not obtain review in the U.S. Supreme Court, for even though the case involves a federal question, there is no actual dispute involving the legal relations of adverse parties. However, if the state court had instead ruled in Jean's favor and enjoined the defendants from continuing to produce vehicles that do not comply with federal law, the dispute would now qualify as a "case" or "controversy" within the meaning of Article III, §2. For as a result of the state court's decision, the defendants are now under a legal duty to undertake the expense of altering their manufacturing operations, which duty may be enforced by the state court through its power to hold defendants in contempt. Thus, what may have begun in state court as something that was not a "case" or "controversy" may become one, depending on how the state court rules in the matter. See, e.g., *ASARCO Inc. v. Kadish*, 490 U.S. 605, 617-619 (1989).

§3.3 PRUDENTIAL CONSIDERATIONS: BEYOND THE CONSTITUTIONAL MINIMUM

While the case or controversy requirement establishes the constitutional minimum for the exercise of Article III authority, the mere satisfaction of that constitutional minimum is not always sufficient to establish justiciability. Prudential considerations sometimes operate to divest an otherwise constitutional case of its justiciable character. These prudential considerations are premised on a combination of concerns derived from principles of separation of powers, federalism, and sound judicial administration. At the heart of "prudence" is the Court's perception of the federal judiciary's proper function within the structure of government, and the Court's desire to avoid unnecessary clashes with other government institutions. These are essentially the same principles that inform the Court's interpretation of the case or controversy requirement. The prudential overlay, however, allows the Court to expand the application of those principles somewhat beyond the established minimum requirements of constitutional justiciability.

Example 3-E

The City of Freedonia has adopted a Sunday-closing law that bans the operation of retail businesses on Sundays. Chico, the owner of a local sub shop, files suit against the city claiming that the law deprives him of property without due process of law. He also claims that the ordinance violates the First Amendment free exercise rights of other shop owners who, unlike himself, worship on Saturdays because of the economic burden it imposes on them by in effect forcing them to close on both Saturday and Sunday. May Chico assert this latter claim in federal court?

Explanation

Chico's lawsuit against the city satisfies the constitutional minimum established by the case or controversy requirement — there is an actual dispute between adverse parties that can be resolved through the judicial process. Nonetheless, prudential considerations dictate that Chico's effort to raise the free exercise claims of Saturday worshipers be dismissed. Until such time as those parties see fit to press their own claims, there is no need to determine whether the city has violated the constitutional rights of these individuals. See §3.4.5 ("The Rule Against Third-Party Standing").

Prudential considerations are not usually applied in an ad hoc fashion. Rather, such considerations are folded into various aspects of the specific justiciability doctrines that will be discussed below. For example, the dismissal of Chico's free exercise argument is based on a prudential component of standing analysis that precludes Article III courts from entertaining "third-party claims." This more structured approach to prudence means that a lower federal court is not generally free to dismiss an otherwise justiciable case merely to avoid deciding a controversial or difficult issue. It also means, however, that once the Supreme Court identifies a prudential limitation on the exercise of jurisdiction, lower courts are bound to follow that limitation as fully as they must follow Article III's case or controversy requirements.

Since prudential limitations are not constitutionally required, the Supreme Court can (and does) develop exceptions to its prudential rules. An exception to the rule against third-party claims, for example, allows plaintiffs standing to raise such claims if there are substantial obstacles that prevent the absent third party from doing so itself. Similarly, Congress can mandate exceptions to the Court's prudential rules. However, as we will see, since the line between what is constitutionally required and what prudence dictates has become increasingly blurred, the actual scope of congressional authority in this sphere is somewhat less than clear.

§3.4 THE STANDING DOCTRINE

As noted above, the elements of a case or controversy require the presence of an actual dispute between adverse parties that is capable of judicial resolution. The standing doctrine examines that constitutional minimum from the perspective of the individual seeking to invoke the court's authority, typically a plaintiff in a civil suit. The basic question is whether the plaintiff has established a personal stake in the outcome of an otherwise justiciable controversy. For example, did Jean, as an accident victim, have standing to seek compensatory damages from the automobile manufacturer alleged to have caused her injuries? The answer is found by examining the basic components of Jean's claim against the manufacturer — Jean was injured, the defendant manufacturer allegedly caused those injuries, and Jean seeks damages to compensate for those injuries. See *Horne v. Flores*, 557 U.S. 433, 445-447 (2009) (party subject to an injunction has "personal stake" in outcome of proceeding seeking relief from the underlying judgment).

The components of Jean's claim expose the basic elements of a case or controversy. Injury and causation ensure the existence of an actual dispute between adverse parties by pitting the injured party against the entity or individual alleged to have caused the injury; the availability of redress through damages ensures that the case is subject to judicial resolution and is not merely a hypothetical dispute. All three elements, taken together, ensure that Jean has a personal stake in the outcome of the litigation.

From this simple hypothetical, we can discern what the Court has described as Article III's "irreducible constitutional minimum" for standing. *McConnell v. Federal Election Commn.*, 540 U.S. 93, 225 (2003). To establish standing, a plaintiff must show three things:

- Injury-in-fact,
- Causation, and
- Redressability.

See *Department of Commerce v. United States House of Representatives*, 525 U.S. 316, 329-330 (1999); *Bennett v. Spear*, 520 U.S. 154, 162 (1997). With respect to each of these elements, the party invoking federal court jurisdiction — i.e., ordinarily the plaintiff — bears the burden of pleading and proof. *Lujan v. Defenders of Wildlife*, 504 U.S. 555, 561 (1992); *Warth v. Seldin*, 422 U.S. 490, 500-502 (1975); and see *DaimlerChrysler Corp. v. Cuno*, 547 U.S. 332, 342 & n.3 (2006) (when a case is removed from state to federal court, defendant has the initial burden of showing that the case meets federal justiciability requirements).

It is also important to note that where a plaintiff's complaint seeks several different forms of relief, or asserts a number of different claims, plaintiff must separately establish standing as to each of these claims. This may mean, for example, that while a plaintiff has suffered a sufficient past injury to give her standing on a claim for damages, any threatened future injury may be too speculative or remote to give plaintiff standing to seek prospective injunctive relief. *City of Los Angeles v. Lyons*, 461 U.S. 95, 102 (1983) ("[P]ast exposure to illegal conduct does not in itself show a present case or controversy regarding injunctive relief. . . ."); and see *Gratz v. Bollinger*, 539 U.S. 244, 267 (2003) (plaintiffs seeking damages and injunctive relief had standing to assert both claims); *DaimlerChrysler Corp. v. Cuno*, supra, 547 U.S. at 349-353 (rejecting theory of "ancillary standing" and holding that plaintiff must separately satisfy standing as to each claim asserted).

Finally, because Article III's "case or controversy" requirement limits the authority of all federal courts, a party seeking relief at the federal appellate level — whether from a Court of Appeals or from the U.S. Supreme Court — must show that a ruling in their favor would redress whatever injury they suffered from the adverse lower court ruling. If a favorable appellate court ruling would not correct a cognizable injury, then such a ruling would be purely advisory and beyond the authority conferred by Article III. Thus, standing must be satisfied not only in the federal district court but at the federal appellate levels as well. At each stage it is incumbent upon the party invoking a federal court's jurisdiction to demonstrate that standing exists. See *Monsanto Co. v. Geertson Seed Farms*, 130 S. Ct. 2743, 2752 (2010) (petitioner satisfied requirement that a defendant seeking Supreme Court review of an adverse district court judgment that was affirmed by the court of appeals must show a cognizable injury caused by the lower federal court decisions that "would be redressed by a favorable ruling from this Court").

§3.4.1 Injury-in-Fact

To satisfy the injury-in-fact requirement, the plaintiff must establish that he or she has suffered a perceptible and recognized harm. Jean's allegations of personal injury easily satisfy this requirement. Basic tort law recognizes a right to be free from bodily harm, and Jean claims a concrete invasion of that interest. The typical individual rights case is also easily resolved. For example, suppose a public school fires a teacher because of her religious beliefs. The teacher's First Amendment claim against the public school satisfies the injury-in-fact requirement since her dismissal constitutes an abridgment of her religious freedom as protected by the First Amendment. Her loss of employment also qualifies as an economic harm sufficient to satisfy the injury-in-fact requirement.

The invasion of any right recognized under the Constitution, statutes, or the common law is sufficient, although not necessary, to establish an injury-in-fact. More generally, any type of perceptible harm to the individual will suffice so long as a court does not believe the interest invaded is too abstract to satisfy Article III's case or controversy requirement. Included within the realm of recognized interests are such things as the quality of the environment, the character of one's neighborhood, consumer choice, and a wide variety of economic and personal interests. The injury may be either a present injury or a threatened injury, so long as the threat is not too speculative or remote.

Example 3-F

The American Israel Public Affairs Committee (AIPAC) describes itself as an issue-oriented organization that seeks to promote goodwill between the United States and Israel. A group of voters (Voters) who are often opposed to the views of AIPAC filed a complaint with the Federal Election Commission (FEC) seeking to have AIPAC declared a "political committee" within the meaning of the Federal Election Campaign Act (FECA). The consequence of such a declaration would be that AIPAC would be required to make a public disclosure of the amount of any disbursement it made in support of any candidate for federal elective office. The Voters claim that this information would assist them in evaluating candidates who had received assistance from AIPAC and in determining the role that AIPAC contributions may play in any particular election. The FEC concluded that AIPAC was not a political committee and dismissed the claim. The Voters then filed suit in federal district court under a provision of FECA that grants any "party aggrieved" by an order of the FEC the right to file a petition in federal district court seeking review of that action. Can the Voters allege a sufficient injury to satisfy the injury-in-fact requirement?

Explanation

Yes. The Voters claim that under FECA they are entitled to specific information regarding AIPAC's contributions to candidates for federal elective office. The injury to the Voters stems from their inability to obtain this information. Moreover, the information sought would be valuable to them because it would assist them in evaluating candidates who had received AIPAC support. In short, FECA creates a statutory right to certain information that would be useful to Voters, and if the facts are as Voters allege, the refusal by the FEC to declare AIPAC a political committee and to require disclosure operates as an injury to that right. See *Federal Election Campaign Commn. v. Aikens*, 524 U.S. 11, 21 (1998).

There is no test to determine whether an asserted interest or harm is adequate to satisfy the injury-in-fact requirement. The basic principle, however, is that when the interest or harm is either conceptually or factually too abstract or speculative, it will not trigger an Article III court's authority to adjudicate. With respect to conceptual infirmities, as the allegations of harm become more creative in the sense that they are premised on less familiar legal turf, courts become increasingly reluctant to conclude that an invasion of the underlying interest satisfies the injury-in-fact requirement. For example, in *Lujan v. Defenders of Wildlife*, 504 U.S. 555 (1992), the Court rejected three creative theories of harm (ecosystem nexus, animal nexus, and vocational nexus) by noting that "standing is not 'an ingenious academic exercise in the conceivable,' but as we have said requires . . . a factual showing of perceptible harm." Id. at 566. Thus the Court was unwilling to credit as constitutionally sufficient the supposed harm a person interested in an endangered species would experience whenever government action threatened that species' chances for survival, a so-called animal nexus. The Court did concede, somewhat grudgingly, that it was plausible "that a person who observes or works with animals of a particular species in the very area of the world where that species is threatened by a federal decision is facing [constitutionally sufficient] harm, since some animals that might have been the subject of his interest will no longer exist." Id. at 566-567. But regardless of that more concrete possibility, the claims of a generalized "animal nexus" were inadequate to satisfy Article III, ingenious though the theory may have been.

Compare the injuries alleged in *Lujan* with the injury described in Example 3-F. In that example, the plaintiffs relied on the violation of an informational right created by the Federal Election Campaign Act. Simply put, their injury was the violation of that right. Such a claimed injury is not conceptually speculative, especially given the fact that the injured right was specifically defined by Congress. Thus, confronted with similar facts, the Court easily found that the plaintiffs had adequately alleged an injury-in-fact. See *Federal Election Campaign Commn. v. Aikens*, 524 U.S. 11, 21 (1998).

Next, and similarly, as the factual premise for the invasion of a recognized interest becomes more speculative, the less likely it is that a court will find that an injury-in-fact has occurred. The decision in *Lujan* is again instructive. In that case, environmental organizations challenged a federal regulation that rendered the Endangered Species Act inapplicable to the federal funding of projects in foreign nations. To establish standing, the plaintiff organizations relied on injuries claimed by two of their members. See §3.4.7 ("Organizational Standing"). One member claimed that she had visited the habitat of the Nile crocodile and that federal support for the rehabilitation of the Aswan High Dam threatened to destroy that habitat. She also alleged that she hoped to return to that habitat at some unspecified future date. The claimed injury of the second member was essentially identical but with respect to a different species' habitat. Although the Court agreed that aesthetic or environmental harm could be sufficient to establish standing, the Court found that the facts as asserted by the two members were inadequate to do so. In the Court's words, "affiants' profession of an 'inten[t]' to return to the places they had visited before — where they will presumably, this time, be deprived of the opportunity to observe animals of the endangered species — is simply not enough. Such 'some day' intentions — without any description of concrete plans, or indeed even any specification of *when* the some day will be — do not support a finding of the 'actual or imminent' injury our cases require." 504 U.S. at 564. By contrast, threatened injury might have sufficed here if that injury were less speculative and remote — e.g., if plaintiff had already purchased her ticket or had made specific arrangements to visit the area at a definite point in the future.

Again, contrast the factually speculative nature of the injury alleged in *Lujan* with the relatively more concrete basis for the claimed injury in Example 3-F. There the plaintiffs alleged that they often opposed the views of AIPAC and that access to AIPAC's contribution records would provide them with specific information needed to evaluate candidates for federal office who had received contributions from AIPAC. While these facts may be somewhat general, they are at least more concrete than the "some day" allegations the Court disparaged in *Lujan*.

In short, although satisfaction of the injury-in-fact requirement usually involves a relatively low threshold, as the claimed harm becomes increasingly creative and unfamiliar, or as the factual premise for the harm becomes increasingly speculative, the odds of satisfying the requirement diminish. Of course, the opposite is true as well. As the claimed harm becomes more familiar and the facts to establish that harm more concrete, the odds of satisfying the requirement increase.

Example 3-G

Alice regularly hikes through an area of a national forest that the U.S. Forest Service has approved for development as a ski resort. The resort will destroy the trails on which Alice hikes. She files suit to enjoin the development, claiming a failure by the service to comply with the National Environmental Policy Act. The act specifically provides a cause of action for "any person adversely affected or aggrieved" by agency action inconsistent with the act. Does Alice's claim satisfy the injury-in-fact requirement for standing?

Explanation

Yes. Courts have consistently concluded that harm to one's enjoyment of the environment is sufficient to satisfy Article III. Moreover, Congress appears to have created a legally protected interest in environmental quality for those who are specifically harmed by incidents of environmental degradation. Alice claims a concrete invasion of that interest by alleging that the proposed development will adversely affect her regular use of the national forest. See *Friends of the Earth, Inc. v. Laidlaw Environmental Services, Inc.*, 528 U.S. 167, 181-183 (2000); *United States v. Students Challenging Regulatory Agency Procedures*, 412 U.S. 669 (1973); *Sierra Club v. Morton*, 405 U.S. 727 (1972).

Example 3-H

A well-documented rise in global temperatures has coincided with a significant increase in the concentration of carbon dioxide in the atmosphere. Respected scientists believe the two trends are related. For when carbon dioxide is released into the atmosphere, it acts like the ceiling of a greenhouse, trapping solar energy and retarding the escape of reflected heat. Calling global warming "the most pressing environmental challenge of our time," the State of Massachusetts joined a suit against the Environmental Protection Agency (EPA) arguing that the EPA had abdicated its responsibility under the Clean Air Act to regulate the emissions of four greenhouse gases, including carbon dioxide. Specifically, Massachusetts sought to force the EPA to regulate greenhouse gas emissions from new motor vehicles. The harms associated with climate change, which the EPA itself recognized as credible, include the global retreat of mountain glaciers, reduction in snow-cover extent, the earlier spring melting of rivers and lakes, and the accelerated rate of the rise of sea levels. The rising seas have already begun to impact the Massachusetts coastline, much of which is state-owned property. If sea levels continue to rise as predicted, the state alleges that a significant fraction of the coastline and its coastal property will be "either permanently lost through inundation or temporarily lost through periodic storm surge and flooding events." Has Massachusetts alleged a cognizable injury sufficient for purposes of standing?

Explanation

As Example 3-G establishes, harm to a plaintiff's interest in the environment is a well-recognized and constitutionally sufficient type of injury for purposes of standing. The harm to the Massachusetts coastline alleged by the state would appear to fall well within this broad and presumptively sufficient category of environmental harm. In this sense, the claimed injury is not *conceptually* speculative. On the other hand, one could certainly argue that the alleged harm is *factually* speculative since no one actually knows whether, when, or how much the sea level will rise. Yet, on similar allegations, the Court held that the injuries alleged by the state were sufficiently concrete to sustain standing. See *Massachusetts v. Environmental Protection Agency*, 549 U.S. 497, 521-523 (2007) (so holding on similar facts). The four-person dissent disagreed, concluding that the allegations of injury were inadequate given that the alleged injury was not "certainly impending." Id. at 542 (Roberts, C.J., dissenting).

Example 3-I

The Internal Revenue Service grants tax exemptions to private schools. Bill claims that because of the IRS's failure to follow its own internal guidelines, some of these tax exemptions are awarded to schools that discriminate on the basis of race, thereby helping these schools to stay in business. He claims that as a result of this government action he feels stigmatized because he is a member of the race excluded from those schools. Has Bill satisfied the injury-in-fact requirement?

Explanation

No. Neither the Constitution, statutes, nor the common law recognizes a right to be free from "stigmatic" harm. Nor is the Court likely to recognize stigmatic harm as a sufficient basis for invoking the authority of an Article III court. Unless Bill can demonstrate that his traditional equal protection rights have been violated by the IRS policy, he will not likely be granted standing to challenge that policy. See *Allen v. Wright*, 468 U.S. 737 (1984). This does not mean that Bill is not harmed by the IRS policy, it merely means that the Court is unwilling to accept stigmatization as constitutionally sufficient for standing purposes.

The primary distinction between Examples 3-G and 3-H, on the one hand, and Example 3-I, on the other, is that the former examples involve a familiar type of environmental injury, long recognized by federal courts, while the latter involves a creative effort to establish a novel way of characterizing the harm generated by a governmental policy that assists private acts of racial discrimination. Of course, this is not meant to discourage creative characterizations of injury, especially when the old forms will not work. One merely needs to recognize that the federal judiciary is more likely to accept those allegations of injury that can be described in more-or-less traditional terms. Compare *Shaw v. Reno*, 509 U.S. 630 (1993) (white voters who constitute a minority of voters in a legislative district, the composition of which they claim to have been a product of racial gerrymandering, have alleged a cognizable injury), with *Sinkfield v. Kelley*, 531 U.S. 28, 30 (2000) (white voters who constitute a majority of voters in a legislative district, the composition of which they claim to have been a product of racial gerrymandering, have not alleged a cognizable injury).

Example 3-J

Jeff, an African American, was pulled over by the city police in a routine traffic stop. One of the officers subjected Jeff to a "choke hold," which caused him to lose consciousness. Several months later, Jeff filed suit against the city seeking an injunction to prevent further use of the choke hold under similar circumstances. The facts establish that the city police use this maneuver frequently, particularly against African-American males, and under circumstances when the maneuver is completely unwarranted. The facts also establish that the choke hold is dangerous, having caused 15 recent fatalities. The basis on which Jeff seeks an injunction is his fear that he will again be stopped by a city police officer who will illegally choke him into unconsciousness without any provocation or resistance on his part. Has Jeff satisfied the injury-in-fact requirement?

Explanation

Under the current view, Jeff's claimed injury involves a well-recognized harm, but it is *factually* too speculative to satisfy the injury-in-fact requirement. In a similar case, the Court explained, "There was no finding that [the plaintiff] faced a real and immediate threat of again being illegally choked." *City of Los Angeles v. Lyons*, 461 U.S. 95, 110 (1983). In essence, the *Lyons* Court insisted on a concrete factual showing that the plaintiff *would likely be* stopped by the police in the future, and that regardless of the circumstances surrounding the stop he *would likely be* subjected to a choke hold. This seeming rigidity was in part a product of the Court's perception that the circumstances of the case provided an inadequate basis upon which to invoke the equitable powers of the federal judiciary. The result would have been no different had Jeff's complaint sought damages as well as injunctive relief. Because standing must be separately established as to each form of relief sought, the fact that Jeff clearly had suffered a sufficient injury to give him standing to seek monetary relief would in no way alter the conclusion that he lacked standing to seek injunctive relief against a threatened future harm that was deemed too speculative. By contrast, if it is clear from plaintiff's past conduct that but for a challenged law they would engage in statutorily prohibited activity, and if it is clear that the government will enforce that law against those who do violate it, the injury requirement is satisfied. See *Holder v. Humanitarian Law Project*, 130 S. Ct. 2705 (2010) (so holding with respect to pre-enforcement challenge to federal statute barring provision of "material support" to designated "foreign terrorist organizations, in suit by plaintiffs who had previously given "material support" to these groups and wished to continue doing so).

Example 3-K

Public School District No. 1 (PSD) operates ten public high schools. In 1998, it adopted a pupil assignment plan that allowed incoming ninth graders to choose from among any of the district's high schools, ranking as many schools as they wish in order of preference. If too many students list the same school as their first choice, the district employs a series of "tiebreakers" to determine who will fill the open slots at the oversubscribed school. The first tiebreaker selects for admission students who have a sibling currently enrolled in the chosen school. The next tiebreaker depends upon the racial composition of the particular school and the race of the individual student. In the district's public schools, approximately 41 percent of enrolled students are white; the remaining 59 percent, comprising all other racial groups, are classified for assignment purposes as nonwhite. If an oversubscribed school is not within 10 percentage points of the district's overall white/nonwhite racial balance, it is what the district calls "integration positive," and the district employs a tiebreaker that selects for assignment students whose race will serve to bring the school into balance. The parents of white children enrolled in the district's middle schools brought a suit in a U.S. district court seeking to enjoin the plan, arguing that their children "might be denied admission to the high schools of their choice when they apply to those schools in the future," in violation of the Equal Protection Clause. PSD has filed a motion to dismiss for lack of standing, arguing that the children have not suffered an injury-in-fact since there is no claim that any specific child will apply to an oversubscribed school or be denied admission to any such school on the basis of race. How should the district court rule? (Assume the parents have standing to sue on behalf of their children if their children would have standing; assume also that the parents' claimed violation of the Equal Protection Clause is conceptually valid.)

Explanation

As was the case in Example 3-J, the plaintiffs here seek an injunction against future possible injuries. Hence, there is a potential argument that the claimed injury is too speculative or conjectural. Therefore, the district court must determine whether the children face "a real and immediate threat" of being subjected to racial discrimination as alleged. Clearly, the children *could* be denied enrollment at the school of their choice on the basis of race if they applied to an oversubscribed school that was "integration positive." There is, however, no showing that such an occurrence is definite or even likely. On the other hand, given the relatively small size of the PSD — ten high schools — and the fact that the middle school students are on the verge of enrolling in high school, the possibility that race will be a factor in a particular student's enrollment is certainly not as speculative as the claimed possibility of a future choke hold in Example 3-J.

In a case based on similar facts, the Supreme Court ruled that the parents — actually an organization of parents — had alleged a sufficiently concrete injury. The Court stated, "The fact that it is possible that children of group members will not be denied admission to a school based on their race — because they choose an undersubscribed school or an oversubscribed school in which their race is an advantage — does not eliminate the injury claimed." *Parents Involved in Community Schools v. Seattle School District No. 1*, 551 U.S. 701, 718-719 (2007). It was sufficient for the Court that the children would be required to compete in a system that used race (or potentially used race) as a criterion for pupil assignment. Id.

The different conclusions reached in Examples 3-J and 3-K can be explained as a product of the relative degree of speculation involved in each respective plaintiff's allegations of future harm. They can also be explained by the fact that the Court has adopted a somewhat more lenient approach to injury-in-fact in the context of claims premised on affirmative action and other forms of reverse discrimination. See Allan Ides and Christopher N. May, *Constitutional Law: Individual Rights*, §6.4.7 (affirmative action); §7.3.5 (nondilutional race-based districting) (6th ed. 2013). With respect to such claims, the injury is the *fact* of discrimination without regard to any tangible *consequence* of that discrimination. See *Northeastern Florida Chapter of Assoc. Gen. Contractors of America v. City Jacksonville, Fla.*, 508 U.S. 656, 666 (1993) (plaintiff challenging barrier created by affirmative action plan "need not allege that he would have obtained the benefit but for the barrier in order to establish standing").

In sum, Article III requires that a plaintiff establish injury-in-fact. To do so, the plaintiff must claim the invasion of an interest deemed adequate for Article III purposes and must produce facts adequate to convince a court that the harm alleged is sufficiently concrete to satisfy Article III's case or controversy requirement. The standards for measuring that sufficiency are at least somewhat malleable.

§3.4.2 Causation

Article III also requires that the injured plaintiff establish a causal link between the claimed injury and the conduct of the defendant. As the Court has often phrased it, the injury must be "fairly traceable" to defendant's conduct. *Department of Commerce v. United States House of Representatives*, supra, 525 U.S. at 329-330; *Bennett v. Spear*, supra, 520 U.S. at 162; *Allen v. Wright*, supra, 468 U.S. at 757. The causation requirement is essentially identical to the concept of proximate cause in torts. The more direct the link between the plaintiff's injury and the defendant's conduct, the more likely it is that a court will find this element satisfied.

In Jean's case of the exploding gas tank (see Example 3-A), she claims that her injuries were sustained because of the defective vehicle manufactured by the defendant. In other words, she claims that the defendant's defective product "caused" her injuries. Since for purposes of determining standing the allegations of her complaint are deemed to be true, the element of causation is satisfied; so too with respect to the teacher allegedly fired for her religious beliefs. See §3.4.1. The injury to her First Amendment rights emanates directly from the action of the defendant school in firing her. Both colloquially and legally, the school *caused* the teacher's injury.

The more difficult causation cases involve causal links that are less obvious than those described in the preceding paragraph. And as was the case with injury-in-fact, one can expect the current Court to be somewhat reluctant to accept what may be characterized as speculative or elongated chains of causation, particularly so when the actions of absent third parties are a factor in that causal chain.

For example, in *Warth v. Seldin*, 422 U.S. 490 (1975), several low-income individuals filed suit challenging the constitutionality of a town's zoning ordinance that, according to their allegations, had the purpose and effect of excluding persons of low income from residing within the town. Even though the Court accepted plaintiffs' allegation that the zoning ordinance had the above exclusionary effect, the Court concluded that plaintiffs had not established causation with respect to their personal injuries. There were no facts establishing that any builder had specific plans to develop low-cost housing within the town that plaintiffs could afford. According to the Court, in the absence of such a showing, the "cause" of plaintiffs' injuries — the inability to purchase low-cost housing within the town — was not the zoning ordinance, but "the economics of the area housing market." Id. at 506. Of course, one could certainly argue that "the economics of the area housing market" were, in part, a product of the exclusionary zoning ordinance. But regardless of the merits of this argument, the Court's attitude was clear. Causation, like injury-in-fact, may not be established through conjecture, but must be premised on specific and plausible allegations of fact establishing a tangible causal link between plaintiff's injury and the defendant's conduct.

Example 3-L

Same facts as Example 3-I — IRS regulations provide tax exemptions to schools that discriminate on the basis of race, and a suit is filed challenging those regulations. Instead of claiming "stigmatization," however, the plaintiffs claim that the IRS policy diminishes the chances of their children receiving an integrated public school education. Assume the plaintiffs have now stated a cognizable injury for purposes of standing. But did the IRS policy cause this injury?

Explanation

Arguably it did. In the absence of these valuable tax exemptions, the racially discriminatory private schools would not continue to exist and at least some of the children attending those schools would attend local public schools, thereby promoting integration. The Court in *Allen v. Wright*, however, held to the contrary. The injury was not "fairly traceable to the government," but was a product of the independent action of third parties whose actions were not motivated by the government policy. In short, the role of the IRS in the chain of causation was too tenuous.

Example 3-M

Same facts as Example 3-H — the challenge by the State of Massachusetts to the EPA's refusal to regulate greenhouse gas emissions from new motor vehicles. The EPA does not dispute the existence of a causal connection between man-made greenhouse gas emissions and global warming. It does, however, dispute the causal connection between the injury alleged by the state — rising sea levels and coastal damage — and the EPA's refusal to regulate emissions from new motor vehicles. Thus, although the EPA agrees that greenhouse gases must be reduced to combat global warming, the agency argues that the impact of its refusal to regulate emissions from new motor vehicles is insubstantial given the worldwide scope of greenhouse gas emissions. Any decrease in such emissions by the regulation of new motor vehicles would, according to the EPA, be more than offset by major new contributions of greenhouse gases by developing countries. The state counters that motor vehicle emissions in the United States constitute

6 percent of worldwide carbon dioxide emissions. Has the state demonstrated a sufficient causal connection between its injury and the challenged EPA refusal to regulate?

Explanation

Taking the facts asserted by both parties as true, one could certainly argue that the state has met its burden of establishing causation. If, as the EPA agrees, man-made greenhouse gas emissions contribute to global warming, then it would seem to follow that a refusal to regulate such emissions domestically would contribute in some degree to that warming. Moreover, the claimed 6 percent U.S. transportation contribution to emissions, though relatively small compared with all other sources, cannot be seen as inconsequential. That domestic contribution presumably has some effect on the pace and intensity of global warming and, therefore, on the consequent damage to the Massachusetts coastline. See *Massachusetts v. Environmental Protection Agency*, 549 U.S. 497, 523-525 (2007) (so holding on similar facts). On the other hand, one could also argue that the actual contribution of new vehicle emissions in the United States, which would be smaller than the overall 6 percent contribution of transportation generally, is simply too small and speculative to warrant standing. See id. at 543-545 (Roberts, C.J., dissenting) (arguing that the "bit-part" contribution to global warming played by new motor vehicle emissions, combined with the complexity of global warming, renders any allegation of causation here too speculative for purposes of establishing standing).

§3.4.3 Redressability

The third standing requirement, redressability, focuses on the relationship between the injury and the relief sought. The relief requested must be designed to alleviate the injury caused by defendant's conduct. In fact, the redressability requirement is quite similar to the causation requirement, and in many cases — particularly those involving injunctions — merely serves as another perspective from which to examine the causal chain. The question now is not, however, whether the defendant caused the plaintiff's injury, but whether the relief sought from the court will alleviate or otherwise redress that injury. However, the mere possibility of redress is not enough. Rather, "it must be 'likely,' as opposed to merely 'speculative,' that the injury will be 'redressed by a favorable decision.'" *Arizona Christian School Tuition Organization v. Winn*, 131 S. Ct. 1436, 1442 (2011) (quoting *Lujan v. Defenders of Wildlife*, 504 U.S. 555, 561 (1992)). Will Jean's personal injuries likely be redressed by the award of money damages against the defendant auto manufacturer? Yes, the award of money damages will compensate Jean for her injuries — that is the very theory behind money damages. Will the fired teacher's injury be redressed by reinstatement and back pay? Yes, both remedies are designed to alleviate the injuries incurred — the loss of job and salary.

As was the case with causation, redressability becomes somewhat more difficult to establish when alleviation of plaintiff's injury depends upon the action of an absent third party. See *Simon v. Eastern Kentucky Welfare Rights Organization*, 426 U.S. 26 (1976). But see *Utah v. Evans*, 536 U.S. 452 (2002) (finding redressable a state's claim that it was deprived of a congressional seat by a census miscount when a correction of the count *could* add a seat to the state's congressional delegation, but only if the President and House of Representatives chose to honor the recount); see also id. at 510-515 (Scalia, J., dissenting).

Example 3-N

Victoria filed suit against the National Highway Traffic Safety Administration (a federal agency), claiming that fuel efficiency standards established by the agency had caused the availability of affordable large automobiles to decrease dramatically. She also claimed that the standards were beyond the scope of the agency's statutory authority. Victoria seeks an injunction to prevent enforcement of these standards. Assuming she has stated a legally recognized injury — a substantial limitation on her ability to purchase a large automobile — has Victoria satisfied the causation and redressability requirements?

Explanation

Resolution of both of these issues depends on actions taken by absent third parties, namely, the automobile manufacturers, and neither requirement will be satisfied unless Victoria can show that the behavior of the automobile manufacturers is dependent on the challenged regulations. As to causation, she must show that because of these regulations, the automobile manufacturers have significantly decreased the production of affordable large cars; as to redressability, she must show that if enforcement of the standards is enjoined, the automobile manufacturers will likely increase their production of affordable large cars to a degree sufficient to alleviate her injury.

Example 3-O

Same facts as Examples 3-H and 3-M — the challenge by the State of Massachusetts to the EPA's refusal to regulate greenhouse gas emissions from new motor vehicles. Given the facts as alleged, including the EPA's agreement that greenhouse gases must be reduced, is the injury alleged by the state likely to be redressed?

Explanation

One could certainly argue that it is. Even though the sought-after regulation will not reverse global warming or eliminate the damage caused by rising sea levels, it may provide a step toward slowing the pace of global warming and may reduce the overall impact of that warming. In other words, with the regulation, the damage caused by global warming may be less sudden and less severe than it would be without the regulation. See *Massachusetts v. Environmental Protection Agency*, 549 U.S. 497, 525-526 (2007) (so holding on similar facts); but see id. at 545-547 (Roberts, C.J., dissenting) (given the very substantial global contributions to carbon dioxide emissions and the relatively insignificant contribution of new motor vehicle emissions in the United States, state's alleged injury not "likely" to be redressed by agency action).

Redressability also becomes problematic when the nature of the underlying injury is not clearly identified. In *Linda R. S. v. Richard D.*, 410 U.S. 614 (1973), an unwed mother challenged the constitutionality of a Texas policy under which the state prosecuted fathers of legitimate children who failed to pay child support but did not prosecute similarly situated fathers of illegitimate children. The mother, suing on behalf of her illegitimate child who needed child support, claimed a denial of equal protection. The Court held that plaintiff had failed to establish redressability. Prosecution of the father would not, according to the Court, ensure the payment of child support. In other words, alleviation of her injury was dependent on the action of an absent third party. Of course, this result depends on how one characterizes the injury. If the injury is the absence of legally required child support, then the Court is at least arguably correct. Redressability is surely not guaranteed since the child's father, even if prosecuted, might not have the ability to pay child support. On the other hand, if the injury is a violation of equal protection rights arising from the state's failure to even prosecute the father, adoption of a policy under which all nonsupporting fathers are prosecuted would clearly alleviate that injury. The decision in *Linda R. S.* demonstrates the importance of precision in discussing redressability. Both the specific nature of the injury and the specific manner in which that injury will be alleviated by the requested relief must be made clear.

Example 3-P

Frank, who is white, applied for admission to a graduate program in counseling psychology at State University (SU). In the year that he applied, the school received 223 applications for the program and offered admission to roughly 20 candidates. As part of its admissions process, SU took the race of the applicants into account. After SU rejected his application, Frank filed suit seeking money damages and injunctive relief. He alleged that, by establishing and maintaining a race-conscious admissions process, the school violated the Equal Protection Clause of the Fourteenth Amendment. Frank does not allege that he would have been admitted but for the use of racial preferences. Is Frank's claim redressable?

Explanation

Yes. Frank's claimed injury is that the SU admissions policy violated his constitutional right to compete with other applicants on a race-neutral basis — i.e., on an equal footing. Assuming a constitutional violation, unless SU can demonstrate that Frank would not have been admitted even in the absence of an affirmative action program, Frank's injury is redressable either through the award of damages or injunctive relief. As to the latter, SU could be required to abandon its racial preferences and to consider Frank's application anew. See *Northeastern Fla. Chapt. of Ass. Gen. Contractors of Am. v. City of Jacksonville,* 508 U.S. 656 (1993) (party challenging racial preference in government contracting need not establish that he would have been awarded contract but for the preference). Frank will not, however, be entitled to relief if SU can prove that he would have been denied admission regardless of any racial preferences granted to other applicants. See *Texas v. Lesage,* 528 U.S. 18, 21 (1999) ("where a plaintiff challenges a discrete governmental decision as being based on an impermissible criterion and it is undisputed that the government would have made the same decision regardless, there is no cognizable injury warranting relief under §1983"). Under such circumstances, SU would have rebutted both the causation and the redressability elements of Frank's standing. For while Frank may have been injured by being denied admission to SU, that injury was neither caused by SU's affirmative action program nor would it be redressed by a court's holding the admissions policy to be unconstitutional. To put it differently, SU would have shown that Frank's right to compete equally on a race-neutral basis was not impaired because he would have been rejected regardless of his race.

Redressability also limits the remedies a plaintiff may request. For example, although Jean in Example 3-A can clearly seek money damages to redress her personal injuries, she is not entitled to seek an injunction against the future production of the defective gas tank because that relief would not redress any recognized injury she has suffered. *City of Los Angeles v. Lyons,* 461 U.S. 95, 105-106, 111-113 (1983). On the other hand, our fired teacher has standing to seek reinstatement and back pay since both remedies are specifically designed to alleviate the injuries caused by her termination.

Example 3-Q

The Emergency Planning and Community Right-to-Know Act (EPCRA) requires users of specified toxic chemicals to file annual "toxic chemical release forms," which contain, among other things, the waste-disposal method employed and the annual quantity of the toxic chemical released into each environmental medium. The purpose is to inform individuals of potentially dangerous toxic disposals in or near their communities. EPCRA also provides that "any person" may commence an enforcement action against any covered facility that fails to file a release form. A person seeking to commence such an action must first notify the alleged violator. Pursuant to these provisions, Chuck notified Steel Company of his intention to file an enforcement action against it based on the company's failure to file any toxic chemical release forms over the previous seven years. Steel Company admitted its failure to comply and immediately filed all past due forms. Nevertheless, Chuck filed suit against the company, alleging past violations of EPCRA. Chuck claimed that the failure of Steel Company to file these release forms had injured him by violating his statutory right to the information EPCRA required Steel Company to disclose. As relief Chuck sought (1) a declaratory judgment as to the past violations, (2) an authorization to inspect periodically Steel Company's facility and records, (3) an order requiring Steel Company to provide Chuck with copies of all future compliance reports, (4) an order to pay civil penalties to the United States Treasury, and (5) an award of Chuck's costs of suit. Assuming an adequate injury has been alleged, has redressability been satisfied?

Explanation

To answer this question, we must examine each form of relief requested by Chuck to determine if any of them redresses the alleged informational injury. First, the declaratory relief goes only to the past conduct over which there is no present controversy. On receiving Chuck's notification, Steel Company admitted its noncompliance and filed all past due release forms. The declaratory relief, therefore, would not resolve any live controversy between the parties. Next, the second and third forms of relief are prospective in nature and do not redress the past injuries; rather, they are premised on a potential for future injuries that Chuck has not alleged. Similarly, the order to pay civil penalties to the U.S. Treasury will not alleviate the harm suffered by Chuck. Although those penalties may deter future misconduct, Chuck's suit is based on a past injury. And finally, to say that the award of the costs of suit satisfies redressability would lead to the conclusion that the mere filing of a lawsuit establishes redressability — a very unlikely conclusion under the current state of the law. In short, Chuck has failed to seek any relief that would redress the injuries he suffered from

Steel Company's past failure to comply with EPCRA. See *Steel Co. v. Citizens for a Better Environment*, 523 U.S. 83, 104-109 (1998).

General Federal and State Taxpayer Standing

The Supreme Court has relied on Article III's case or controversy requirements to reject the notion that a person has standing to challenge a government tax or spending provision simply because he or she is a federal or state taxpayer. We are not dealing here with a person's standing to challenge a tax that is imposed specifically on him or her, for such a case will usually meet normal standing requirements. See *United States v. Butler*, 297 U.S. 1 (1936) (food processor had standing to challenge the constitutionality of a federal tax imposed only on food processors). A female taxpayer would have standing to challenge a tax imposed only on women, just as an African-American taxpayer would have standing to challenge a tax falling only on persons of color. The situation is very different where a person, suing simply as a general taxpayer, seeks to challenge a government tax break provision or spending program on the theory that it affects him or her only indirectly because of its negative effect on the government's revenue. In such cases, Article III's standing requirements will not be met for several reasons.

First, in terms of a cognizable injury, it is often not clear that a challenged tax break provision or spending program will in fact injure taxpayers as a group, for the challenged provision may ultimately increase rather than decrease government revenue as, for example, where it encourages local investment by those who would not otherwise have done business in the state. Moreover, not all tax breaks or spending provisions that reduce net governmental revenue result in increased taxes, for the government may simply make up the loss by reducing other expenditures. Even where it is clear that a challenged tax or spending provision has caused an economic injury to taxpayers in the form of higher taxes, there is no assurance that a favorable judicial decision will redress that injury, for the government may simply decide to spend the funds elsewhere rather than reducing taxes. Thus, due both to "the conjectural nature of the asserted injury" and the fact that "it is pure speculation whether the lawsuit would result in any actual tax relief" for plaintiffs, the Supreme Court has held that federal and state taxpayers "have no standing under Article III to challenge . . . tax or spending decisions simply by virtue of their status as taxpayers." *Daimler-Chrysler Corp. v. Cuno*, 547 U.S. 332, 344-346 (2006). See also *Frothingham v. Mellon*, 262 U.S. 447 (1923) (no federal taxpayer standing to challenge federal spending measure as inconsistent with the Tenth Amendment); *Ex parte Levitt*, 302 U.S. 633 (1937) (no federal citizen standing to challenge judicial appointment alleged to violate the Emoluments Clause); *United States v. Richardson*, 418 U.S. 166 (1974) (no federal citizen standing to challenge secrecy of CIA budget). While the Supreme Court has rejected both *federal* and *state* taxpayer standing as being incompatible with the requirements of

Article III, it has applied a different rule at the municipal government level, on the basis that municipal corporations have a different and arguably more direct relationship to their residents than the federal and state governments have to their citizens. See *DaimlerChrysler Corp. v. Cuno*, supra, 547 U.S. at 349.

§3.4.4 The Prohibition Against Generalized Grievances

In addition to the problems that "citizen" and "taxpayer" suits present in terms of meeting the injury-in-fact, causation, and redress requirements of standing, they also run afoul of the rule against generalized grievances. This rule precludes Article III courts from entertaining lawsuits in which the only injury claimed by the plaintiff is the shared harm experienced by all citizens and taxpayers when the federal government or a state fails to comply with the Constitution or laws of the United States. With one exception (discussed below), unless the plaintiff can show that the challenged government action caused him or her to suffer a particularized injury — e.g., damage to property or a curtailment of personal liberty — standing will be denied. In the Court's view, it is simply inadequate to premise standing on nothing more than a generalized claim that the government must comply with the law. See *Lance v. Coffman*, 549 U.S. 437, 442 (2007) (citizen's undifferentiated interest in Colorado's compliance with the Elections Clause nonjusticiable). To hold otherwise "would interpose the federal courts as 'virtually continuing monitors of the wisdom and soundness' of state [and federal] fiscal administration, contrary to the more modest role Article III envisions for federal courts." *DaimlerChrysler Corp. v. Cuno*, supra, 547 U.S. at 346. Neither would such an expansive judicial role necessarily be accepted by the other branches. "For the federal courts to decide questions of law arising outside of cases and controversies would be inimical to the Constitution's democratic character. And the resulting conflict between the judicial and the political branches would not, 'in the long run, be beneficial to either.'" *Arizona Christian School Tuition Organization v. Winn*, supra, 131 S. Ct. at 1442 (internal citations omitted). Finally, if a grievance is in fact one that is shared by virtually everyone, it can presumably be rectified through the political process — without having to involve the federal judiciary.

Example 3-R

The Gun-Free School Zones Act was passed by Congress to combat violence in the nation's public schools. It prohibits the possession of any firearm within specifically defined "school zones." Marlo believes that the act exceeds the constitutional authority of Congress and infringes upon the reserved powers of the states. She files suit against the attorney general, seeking to enjoin enforcement of the act. Does Marlo have standing?

Explanation

No. The only injury alleged in her complaint is premised on her status as a citizen harmed by the government's failure to comply with the Constitution. Since Marlo alleges no harm beyond that shared with all other citizens, she lacks standing to assert this claim. Her generalized grievance will be dismissed.

Suppose, however, that Marlo owns a gun shop within a "school zone." She is told by the local United States attorney that she must close her shop or face certain prosecution under the Gun-Free School Zones Act. Marlo can now allege a particularized harm to herself. As a consequence, she has standing to challenge the constitutionality of the act, not as a citizen but as an individual who is experiencing or will experience personal injury because of the operation of the act.

A grievance is not "generalized" merely because the harm generated by challenged government action is widely shared. For example, a federal law that made it unlawful to engage in political speech during the week preceding a federal election would infringe on every citizen's right to engage in such speech. Even though this "grievance" is shared by all citizens, the harm to each individual citizen who wishes to exercise free speech rights during the proscribed time frame is *factually* particular to that individual. See *Massachusetts v. Environmental Protection Agency*, 549 U.S. 497, 522 (2007) (fact that effects of global warming are widely shared does not minimize the particularized injuries to the plaintiff state). An individual's suit to challenge the statute does not present a generalized grievance. The rule against generalized grievances is triggered only if the plaintiff's *sole* claim of injury is a share of an undifferentiated and conceptual harm such as that suffered by all citizens when the government does not conform its actions to the law. *Federal Election Campaign Commn. v. Aikens*, 524 U.S. 11, 23-24 (1998). In short, a generalized grievance is one that is both widely shared and abstract. Id.

The Court has been inconsistent on the question of whether the rule against generalized grievances is prudential, and hence waivable by the Court or Congress, or constitutionally mandated, and hence not waivable. In *Warth v. Seldin*, 422 U.S. 490, 499 (1975), the Court suggested that both the Court and Congress can create exceptions to the rule so long as those exceptions otherwise conform to the requirements of Article III. Yet, more recently the Court observed, "[A] plaintiff raising only a generally available grievance about government — claiming only harm to his and every citizen's interest in proper application of the Constitution and laws, and seeking relief that no more directly and tangibly benefits him than it does the public at large — does not state an Article III case or controversy." *Lujan v. Defenders of Wildlife*, 504 U.S. 555, 573-574 (1992).

At issue in *Lujan* was a "citizen-suit" provision of the Endangered Species Act, which provided that "any person may commence a civil suit on his own behalf . . . to enjoin any person, including the United States and any other governmental instrumentality or agency . . . who is alleged to be in violation of any provision of this chapter." Id. at 571-572. There was no requirement of a concrete injury to the person suing. The Court held that Congress could not "convert the undifferentiated public interest in executive officers' compliance with the law into an 'individual right' vindicable in the courts. . . ." Id. at 577. In essence, the purported injury was too abstract to satisfy Article III's injury-in-fact requirement. Nor could Congress use this abstract injury to create an exception to what the Court perceived as Article III's rule against generalized grievances.

Finally, to make matters more challenging, the Court seemed to back away from (or at least to obfuscate) its holding in *Lujan* when, in *Federal Election Commn. v. Aikens*, supra, it cryptically observed that the rule against generalized grievances had been treated as both a prudential and a constitutional limitation on standing. 524 U.S. at 23. The Court provided no guidance as to when one or the other approach would be adopted. Hence, the best one can do is to be prepared for either possibility.

Taxpayer Standing and the Establishment Clause

We have seen that general "taxpayer" and "citizen" standing are typically barred because of their failure to satisfy the injury, causation, redress, and nongeneralized grievance requirements for standing. However, the Court has recognized one limited exception to this prohibition. Stated in its most general terms, a taxpayer will be granted standing to challenge government action if that taxpayer can establish a nexus between his or her status as a taxpayer and the challenged government action, as well as a nexus between that status and the precise nature of the constitutional infringement claimed. In practice, this means that a federal, state, or municipal taxpayer must be challenging the government's expenditure of monies raised through taxes and must be doing so on the ground that the particular expenditure violates the First Amendment's Establishment Clause. *Flast v. Cohen*, 392 U.S. 83 (1968); *Valley Forge Christian College v. Americans United for Separation of Church and State*, 454 U.S. 464 (1982).

To come within this exception, the plaintiff taxpayer must challenge a taxing or spending measure, not a governmental expenditure that is merely incidental to the exercise of some other power. Thus a taxpayer's challenge to a regulatory program passed pursuant to the Commerce Clause will not be permitted even if operating that program requires the expenditure of public funds. However, where a spending measure is involved, the size of the expenditure need not be great to give a taxpayer standing to bring an Establishment Clause case. See, e.g., *Lynch v. Donnelly*, 465 U.S. 668 (1984) (municipal taxpayers had standing to challenge city's $20 per year expense to display Nativity scene) (see *Donnelly v. Lynch*, 525 F. Supp. 1150, 1162 (D.R.I. 1981)).

In *Hein v. Freedom From Religion Foundation, Inc.*, 551 U.S. 587 (2007), a divided Court limited the scope of taxpayer standing to cases in which the taxpayer was challenging an "express congressional mandate and a specific congressional appropriation." Id. at 604. By way of contrast, executive action that potentially runs afoul of the Establishment Clause will be immune from taxpayer suits unless that expenditure is itself mandated by Congress. At issue in *Hein* was an Establishment Clause challenge to the constitutionality of a program created by the executive branch — President George W. Bush's "Faith-Based Initiative" — and funded out of general appropriations, none of which had been mandated or appropriated by Congress for any specific purpose. As a consequence, the Court held that the taxpayers lacked standing to challenge this executive branch expenditure. The five-person Court majority was composed of three Justices who sought to limit *Flast v. Cohen* to cases involving challenges to legislative action and two Justices who would have overruled *Flast* in its entirety. See id. at 591 (plurality opinion by Alito, J., joined by Roberts, C.J., and Kennedy, J.) (limit *Flast*) and id. at 618 (concurring opinion by Scalia, J., joined by Thomas, J.) (overrule *Flast*). Whether this limitation will be applied in taxpayer challenges to state and municipal action remains to be seen.

The dual requirements for taxpayer standing are sometimes referred to as the "double-nexus test." The nexus between one's taxpayer status and taxing and spending measures is self-evident; the nexus with the Establishment Clause derives from the Court's interpretation of that clause as specifically designed to prevent the government from forcing taxpayers to support religion or religious institutions. In such cases, because the injury plaintiff complains of is not the economic harm of having to pay federal taxes, but rather the noneconomic injury of the government's using that tax money to favor one religion or support religion in general, "an injunction against the spending would . . . redress *that* injury, regardless of whether lawmakers would dispose of the savings in a way that would benefit the taxpayer-plaintiffs personally." *DaimlerChrysler Corp. v. Cuno*, 547 U.S. 332, 348-349 (2006). In short, the problems of injury, causation, and redress that defeat general taxpayer standing are simply not present in the Establishment Clause setting. Although there are conceivably other constitutional provisions that are also designed to limit the taxing and spending power, the Court has pointedly noted that "only the Establishment Clause has supported federal taxpayer standing since *Flast*." *DaimlerChrysler Corp. v. Cuno, supra*, 547 U.S. at 347. Thus, any extension of *Flast* to other constitutional provisions would appear to be highly unlikely.

Example 3-S

Congress passes legislation that provides Christian College with a grant of $5 million to construct a new chapel on the college campus. Fred, a federal taxpayer, files suit challenging this expenditure as a violation of the Establishment Clause. Does Fred have standing to bring this suit?

Explanation

Yes. Fred is challenging a taxing or spending measure and he claims that this measure violates the Establishment Clause. In other words, he has satisfied the double-nexus test.

Suppose, however, that the secretary of health and human services decides to dispose of a $5 million parcel of surplus government land by donating it to Christian College. Fred, a taxpayer, sues to challenge this action. He will not have standing since he is not challenging a taxing or spending measure. Rather he is challenging executive (not congressional) action taken pursuant to the power to dispose of property under Article IV, §3. *Valley Forge Christian College v. Americans United for Separation of Church and State*, 454 U.S. 464 (1982). In short, Fred has failed to satisfy the first half of the double-nexus test, which requires a connection between Fred's status as a taxpayer and the challenged government action. That nexus will only be satisfied when Fred challenges a taxing or spending measure.

Instead, suppose Congress passes legislation that gives individuals a tax credit for any money they contribute to groups that arrange for the construction of buildings on public or private college campuses, including classroom buildings, dormitories, athletic facilities, and religious chapels. Fred, a federal taxpayer, challenges this legislation on the ground that it encourages the construction of religious buildings on college campuses, in violation of the Establishment Clause. While Fred clearly satisfies the second requirement of the dual nexus test, does he also meet the first requirement? The answer is no, for Fred is not challenging a law that imposes a tax, but rather one that declines to impose one on certain taxpayer income. If the government imposed a tax that took such dollar amounts from taxpayers for the construction of religious buildings, the first nexus requirement would be met. But here, the money in question is not that of the government (the government expressly declined to take it), and neither is the decision to spend the money for religious purposes that of the government (but rather that of a private individual). While the net effect of this scheme may be the same as if the government itself imposed a tax for the purpose of constructing religious buildings, the critical distinction is that it is ultimately a private party's decision — not the government's — to spend their money in a certain religious way. See *Arizona Christian School Tuition Org. v. Winn*, 131 S. Ct. 1436 (2011).

While the exception for taxpayer standing created in *Flast v. Cohen* has been narrowly construed, and while nothing in the Court's recent decisions suggests that this limited exception will be extended in any fashion, taxpayer standing nevertheless provides an important and frequently invoked means for challenging federal, state, and local laws on First Amendment Establishment Clause grounds.

§3.4.5 The Rule Against Third-Party Standing

Normally a party who has established Article III standing may assert only his or her own rights. *United States v. Raines*, 362 U.S. 17, 21 (1960). Stated somewhat differently, "[O]ne to whom application of a statute is constitutional will not be heard to attack the statute on the ground that impliedly it might also be taken as applying to other persons or other situations in which its application might be unconstitutional." Id. This is known as the rule against third-party standing. It means that a party may not raise the rights of absent or hypothetical parties in challenging the legality of government action. Like other justiciability doctrines, the rule against third-party standing is designed to ensure that Article III courts will not become immersed in unnecessary or abstract disputes. The presumption is that the absent party is fully capable of representing his or her own interests, if he or she wishes to do so. If those to whom the rights belong are not in fact interested in vindicating them in court, then judicial intervention may be unnecessary and the matter is one that would better be left to other governmental institutions.

Example 3-T

Bob is denied admission to a state military school. The denial is premised on what Bob characterizes as arbitrary admissions standards. He sues the school claiming that its arbitrary rejection of his application was a violation of due process. In addition, because the school's admissions policy happens to be "all male," Bob also seeks to raise the equal protection rights of female applicants who have been denied admission as a result of that discriminatory policy. His goal is to establish the complete unconstitutionality of the school's admission guidelines. Does Bob have standing to raise the rights of applicants other than himself?

Explanation

No. Bob meets the first requirement of standing (injury-in-fact) because he has suffered a personal injury, namely, the denial of his application to attend the state military school. His allegations also satisfy the requirements of causation and redressability, since the school caused his injury and since that injury can be redressed by an injunction ordering the school to admit him. Bob has standing to assert his own rights under the Due Process Clause. However, under the rule against third-party standing, he will not be allowed to raise the equal protection rights of the female applicants. Adjudication of that issue is more appropriately left to a case in which a female applicant challenges the all-male admissions policy.

In may not always be clear to whom a particular constitutional right belongs. Thus, until 2011, lower federal courts were divided on the question of whether the principle of federalism, which is embodied in the Tenth Amendment and which limits the national government to certain enumerated powers, was one that could be invoked only by the states or whether it was also designed to protect the rights of individuals. Under the first view, an individual seeking to invoke the principle of federalism would not be asserting their own rights in claiming that a federal law exceeds Congress's powers and invades the domain of the states. Under the second view, the principle could be invoked by an individual on the theory that it is designed to protect them as well as the states by ensuring that governmental powers are dispersed. In *Bond v. United States*, 131 S. Ct. 2355 (2011), the Supreme Court endorsed the second view, with the result that an individual challenging a federal law on Tenth Amendment grounds is asserting their own constitutional rights.

The federal judiciary's reluctance to allow third-party standing is closely related to its general unwillingness to allow so-called *facial challenges* to a law's constitutionality. Thus, a person against whom a law can constitutionally be applied normally cannot attack its validity on the basis that the law, as written or on its face, is overly broad and could conceivably be applied in other settings where doing so might be unconstitutional. Such judicial action may impinge prematurely and unnecessarily on the other federal branches or the states, for there is no assurance that the measure will ever be applied in such a hypothetical situation. Instead, the law might be enforced or construed more narrowly, or amended to narrow its reach before any unconstitutional applications ever occur. Thus, as the Supreme Court has explained, "Facial challenges . . . are especially to be discouraged. Not only do they invite judgments on fact-poor records, but they entail a further departure from the norms of adjudication in federal courts: overbreadth challenges call for relaxing familiar requirements of standing, to allow a determination that the law would be unconstitutionally applied to different parties and different circumstances from those at hand." *Sabri v. United States*, 541 U.S. 600, 609 (2004).

The rule against third-party standing is prudential. It applies *in addition to* the Article III requirements for standing. In Bob's case, for example, although he may have satisfied Article III's constitutional minimum for standing with respect to his own claims, he will nonetheless be prevented from raising the equal protection rights of female applicants. Thus the third-party standing rule operates as an overlay on the minimum requirements for standing. The rule may take on heightened significance if the area of law is one in which the federal courts are otherwise reluctant to become involved. For example, in the domestic relations setting, the Supreme Court has held that "in general it is appropriate for the federal courts to leave delicate issues of domestic relations to the state courts" — even if such a case would otherwise fall within the federal courts' diversity or federal question jurisdiction. *Elk Grove Unified School District v. Newdow*, 542 U.S. 1, 13 (2004). On this basis, the *Newdow* Court held that a divorced father who sought to challenge the constitutionality of a public school policy requiring that the Pledge of Allegiance be recited each day in class failed to meet the third requirement of standing, for the First Amendment rights he sought to invoke belonged to his minor daughter, over whom the child's mother had been awarded sole legal control. And, since it was clear that the mother did not oppose recitation of the Pledge, the effect of the Court's ruling was to keep this family law dispute out of federal court, despite its constitutional dimensions.

On the other hand, since the rule against third-party standing is prudential, it is not required by Article III. Accordingly, the Court has recognized three exceptions to the rule. A party who has satisfied the constitutional minimum for standing (injury-in-fact, causation, and redressability) as to his or her own cause of action will be allowed to raise the claims of an absent third party:

- If, as a practical matter, there is "some hindrance" to the third party's ability to protect his or her own interests, and if the party asserting the right has a "close relationship" with the third party to whom the right belongs, such that he or she will be an effective advocate of the right in question; or
- If the party with Article III standing is challenging a law that requires him or her to take action inconsistent with the rights of the absent third party; or
- If, in the context of freedom of expression, the Article III party's claim involves a law that suffers from overbreadth.

We explore each of these exceptions below. As you will see, the first two exceptions represent slightly different perspectives from which to consider whether the party with Article III standing ought to be permitted to assert the interests of the absent party.

The first exception is premised on the notion that the party before the court is in the best position to protect the rights of the absent third party. This is usually so either because there is no judicial forum within which the third party can personally assert those rights or because for practical reasons that party is in some way hindered from doing so. For example, in *Campbell v. Louisiana*, 523 U.S. 392 (1998), the Court allowed a white criminal defendant to assert the equal protection rights of African Americans who had been systematically excluded from service on a grand jury. The Court permitted third-party standing under these circumstances because the excluded group had an economic disincentive to challenge the practice by filing their own lawsuit. Moreover, a close relationship existed, for "[t]he defendant and the excluded grand juror share a common interest in eradicating discrimination from the grand jury selection process, and the defendant has a vital interest in asserting the excluded juror's rights because his conviction may be overturned as a result." Id. at 400.

Example 3-U

Dorothy owns a house that is subject to a covenant that restricts ownership to "whites only." After Dorothy sold the house to a nonwhite couple, she was sued for money damages by another party to the covenant. Dorothy's defense is premised on the equal protection rights of potential nonwhite purchasers of property subject to such restrictions. May Dorothy raise this defense?

Explanation

Based on the first exception to the rule against third-party standing, Dorothy will be allowed to raise this defense. As a practical matter it is unlikely that nonwhites will have an opportunity to challenge these covenants in court. Among other things, a nonwhite whose offer to purchase was rejected would have difficulty proving that the rejection was based on a racially restrictive covenant, making satisfaction of Article III's causation and redressability requirements difficult at best. Yet if parties to such covenants continue to adhere to them out of fear of being sued under the terms of the covenants, the rights of nonwhites to equal protection of the law will, as a practical matter, be impaired or diluted. There is also a close relationship between Dorothy and the nonwhites adversely affected by such covenants, for they share the same interest in having such covenants declared invalid, and Dorothy has every incentive to be an effective advocate on their behalf since the outcome of her case will turn on how this particular issue is resolved.

Example 3-U is based on the Court's decision in *Barrows v. Jackson*, 346 U.S. 249 (1953). In that case, the Court allowed a white person who owned property subject to a racially restrictive covenant to raise the rights of non-whites in a suit filed against him for breach of that covenant. The Court observed, "[I]t would be difficult if not impossible for the persons whose rights are asserted to present their grievance before any court. Under the peculiar circumstances of this case, we believe the reasons which underlie our rule denying standing to raise another's rights, which is only a rule of practice, are outweighed by the need to protect the fundamental rights which would be denied by permitting the damages action to be maintained." Id. at 257. See *Eisenstadt v. Baird*, 405 U.S. 438, 445-446 (1972) (applying this same principle in the context of the right of privacy).

Example 3-V

Two attorneys who represent indigent criminals filed suit in federal court under 42 U.S.C. §1983, challenging the federal constitutionality of a state law that severely restricts the ability of indigent criminal defendants who have pled guilty to then have appointed counsel in pursuing an appeal. The attorneys contend that the state provision denies indigents their Fourteenth Amendment due process and equal protection rights. Do these attorneys have standing to bring this case in federal court?

Explanation

The attorneys meet the first two requirements of standing insofar as they assert a threatened economic injury from a law that will reduce the instances in which they can be appointed to represent indigent criminal defendants. Their injury is caused by the state law being challenged and will be redressed if the provision is invalidated. However, these plaintiffs are asserting the due process and equal protection rights of their would-be clients, rather than any constitutional rights of their own. The case arguably qualifies for an exception to third-party standing on the basis that indigent criminal defendants are, as a practical matter, hindered from challenging this state law themselves. On the other hand, since state law still allows indigent criminal defendants to appeal *pro se*, and to then ask a state appellate court to review the denial of appointed counsel, they are not being totally precluded from asserting their own rights. As to the close relationship requirement, this is arguably met here by the fact that the attorneys have the same interest as their hypothetical clients in establishing a right to appointed counsel. Yet since the plaintiffs do not currently represent any of the criminal defendants whose rights they seek to invoke, the requisite close relationship is arguably not satisfied. Moreover, to allow third-party standing would permit these attorneys to raise, in federal court, a matter that state criminal defendants, under the so-called *Younger* doctrine (see §4.5), are expected to pursue as part of their ongoing state criminal proceedings. See *Kowalski v. Tesmer*, 543 U.S. 125 (2004) (denying standing to two attorneys on facts similar to these).

The second exception focuses on the relationship between the party before the court and the absent third party. While this exception does not require that the third party be unable to assert his or her own rights, the presumption underlying this exception is that the party before the court is in an ideal position to fully and fairly assert those rights.

Example 3-W

A doctor is charged with violating a state's ban on the use of contraceptives by prescribing a contraceptive device to a married couple. In defense, she attempts to raise the constitutional privacy rights of the married couple. Does she have standing to do so?

Explanation

Yes. Because state law requires the doctor to take action that undermines those privacy rights (i.e., the right to decide whether to bear or beget a child), the court, under the second exception to third-party standing, will permit her to rely on the privacy rights of her patients in challenging the constitutionality of the state law. See *Griswold v. Connecticut*, 381 U.S. 479 (1965) (doctor permitted to assert the privacy rights of his married patients).

The second exception is often described as involving a special relationship between the litigant and the absent third party — e.g., the doctor/patient relationship in *Griswold*. But it is not a relationship in the abstract that triggers the exception. Rather the relationship between the parties must be such that the law being challenged by the plaintiff (or defendant) requires him or her to take action that will dilute the absent party's rights. This was clearly the case in Example 3-W since the doctor's compliance with the state ban on contraceptive use would dilute the privacy rights of the married couple by making it difficult or impossible for them to procure contraceptives.

Another example of this type of relationship is found in *Craig v. Boren*, 429 U.S. 190 (1976), where a bartender was allowed to assert the equal protection rights of her male patrons when she challenged a law that required her to discriminate against them. The key factor was not the "bartender/patron" relationship, but the fact that the bartender was required by law to discriminate against certain of her male customers. Under this exception, she was allowed to raise the rights of those patrons.

Example 3-X

Bob is the admissions officer at a state military school with an all-male admissions policy. In contravention of the policy, Bob admits several women to the incoming class. The school refuses to allow the women to matriculate and Bob is fired for approving their admission. He files suit against the school claiming that the dismissal violated his rights under the Due Process Clause. He also seeks to raise the equal protection rights of the women whose admission he approved. Does Bob have standing to raise the equal protection issue?

Explanation

Bob's equal protection claim probably satisfies the second exception. As an admissions officer, Bob was being required to take action that potentially violated the equal protection rights of female applicants. As a consequence, he should have third-party standing to assert their rights.

The third exception to the rule against third-party standing — the overbreadth doctrine — applies only in the context of freedom of expression. Suppose Joan is charged with violating a city ordinance that makes it unlawful to engage in "any offensive speech" in a public place. The charges stem from an incident in which she spewed a combination of four-letter words and verbal threats at a specific individual under circumstances quite likely to cause an imminent breach of the peace. Assume that Joan's speech would be deemed unprotected under relevant First Amendment principles (e.g., the "fighting words" doctrine). Nonetheless, Joan will be allowed to challenge the constitutionality of this ordinance on the theory that the scope of the ordinance is so broad — "any offensive speech" — that it may well encompass the protected speech of individuals not before the court. This is the basic idea of overbreadth. An individual to whom the application of a law is constitutional will be granted standing to challenge the constitutionality of the law on the theory that, as applied to other persons or in other circumstances, it may be unconstitutional under the First Amendment. The individual is afforded this privilege because of the concern that such overly broad statutes may chill the free speech rights of those not before the court. In our example, such individuals would otherwise be left to ponder exactly what is meant by the phrase, "any offensive speech," with the consequence that much protected speech might go unspoken out of fear of violating the proscription.

The Court has described the overbreadth doctrine as "strong medicine" that should only be applied "sparingly" and "as a last resort." *Broadrick v. Oklahoma*, 413 U.S. 601, 613 (1973). Thus if a statute is subject to a reasonable, limiting construction that avoids the overbreadth problem, a court is likely to adopt that construction in lieu of the strong medicine of overbreadth. Moreover, in the context of expressive activity that includes nonverbal conduct, the Court has required the party attempting to rely upon overbreadth to establish that the challenged law suffers from "substantial" overbreadth, further limiting the circumstances under which the doctrine may be used. Id. at 615.

Example 3-Y

Ed, a state government employee, has accepted the position as campaign manager for the Democratic candidate for city council. In undertaking those duties, Ed has violated a state law that limits state employees from participating in partisan political activities. Although Ed's duties as campaign manager can be characterized as expressive activity within the scope of the First Amendment protections, Ed concedes, based on controlling precedent, that the law may be constitutionality applied under the circumstances presented. He argues, however, that the law at issue is worded such that it may apply to other expressive activity that is constitutionally protected — e.g., the wearing of campaign buttons or the display of bumper stickers. May Ed use the overbreadth exception to his advantage?

Explanation

Given that Ed's expressive activities — the duties of a campaign manager — involve conduct and not simply pure, verbal speech, unless Ed can demonstrate that the breadth of the law is such that its sweeps within its coverage a substantial amount of protected activity, the "strong medicine" of overbreadth will not be applied. That conclusion is particularly true if the state has placed a limiting interpretation on the scope of this law that focuses the proscription on activities such as Ed's. If that is the case, a challenge to the law as it applies to campaign buttons and bumper stickers will have to await a case in which a party has been charged with violating the statute by engaging in such conduct.

§3.4.6 The Zone of Interests Test

The zone of interests test is a prudential standing requirement that most often comes into play when a plaintiff challenges governmental action under a federal regulatory scheme that does not directly regulate the plaintiff's own conduct. For example, a consumer might challenge a federal regulation that mandates certain fuel efficiency standards for automobile manufacturers. The basic question is whether the interest plaintiff seeks to protect is "arguably within the zone of interests to be protected or regulated by the statute" on which plaintiff's claim rests. *Association of Data Processing Service Organizations, Inc. v. Camp*, 397 U.S. 150, 153 (1970). Resolution of this question depends on the intent of Congress as reflected in the language of the statute under which the plaintiff sues. *Bennett v. Spear*, 520 U.S. 154, 162-167 (1997). The zone of interests test will be satisfied where plaintiff seeks to protect several interests as long as one of them falls within the zone served by the federal provision under which relief is sought. See, e.g., *Monsanto Co. v. Geertson Seed Farms*, 130 S. Ct. 2743, 2755-2756 (2010) (plaintiff alfalfa growers seeking injunctive relief under a federal statute designed to address environmental rather than commercial harms met zone of interests test since the relief sought, besides furthering plaintiffs' commercial interests, would also protect their local environment).

The Court has made it clear that the prudential zone of interests test "'is not meant to be especially demanding,'. . . . [W]e have always conspicuously included the word 'arguably' in the test to indicate that the benefit of any doubt goes to the plaintiff." *Match-E-Be-Nash-She-Wish Band of Pottawatomi Indians v. Patchak*, 132 S. Ct. 2199, 2210 (2012) (quoting *Clarke v. Securities Industries Association*, 479 U.S. 388, 399 (1987)). However, a plaintiff challenging government action that does not regulate his or her own conduct must present at least a plausible basis for concluding that the interest he or she asserts falls within the "zone" protected by the statute or regulation upon which the plaintiff relies. *Air Courier Conference of America v. American Postal Workers Union*, 498 U.S. 517, 523-528 (1991). In *Air Courier Conference*, for example, the Court declined to grant postal workers standing to challenge certain postal regulations as being inconsistent with the Private Express Statutes. According to the Court, the federal statutes were designed to promote the government's interest in earning revenues, rather than protect the interests of postal workers. Thus the interests of the postal workers did not come within the zone of interests protected by these statutes.

By contrast, the zone of interests test was satisfied in *Match-E-Be-Nash-She-Wish Band of Pottawatomi Indians v. Patchak*, supra, where a property owner challenged the federal government's acquisition of adjacent land on behalf of an Indian tribe that planned to use it to open a casino. Though plaintiff's legal challenge was to the Secretary of the Interior's statutory right to *acquire* the land, the interests plaintiff sought to protect related solely to the property's *intended use*. Yet there was an arguable connection between the statute authorizing the Secretary to acquire the land and plaintiff's objection to the land's intended use, for "when the Secretary obtains land for Indians under [the statute], she does not do so in a vacuum. Rather, she takes title to properties with at least one eye directed toward how tribes will use those lands to support economic development. . . . And so neighbors to the use . . . are reasonable — indeed predictable — challengers of the Secretary's decisions: Their interests, whether economic, environmental, or aesthetic, come within [the statute's] regulatory ambit." 132 S. Ct. at 2211-2212.

Example 3-Z

Relying on the Endangered Species Act (ESA), the Fish and Wildlife Service issued a biological opinion, the effect of which was to seriously curtail the amount of water available from the Klamath Irrigation Project (KIP) for use by local ranchers. The essence of the opinion was that KIP's water usage was endangering the critical habitat of the shortnose sucker. Several ranchers filed suit claiming that the opinion violated the ESA since it failed to consider the economic consequences of water rationing and since there was no scientific evidence that water rationing would improve the habitat of the shortnose sucker. The ESA provides that "any person may commence a civil suit" to enjoin violations of the act. Assuming the ranchers satisfy Article III's requirements, do they come within the zone of interests protected by the ESA?

Explanation

Yes. The ranchers clearly qualify as persons who may sue under the ESA. The broad language — "any person" — is all-encompassing, and unless there is some clear indication that Congress wished to restrict that language to some particular subgroup — e.g., environmentalists — then the ranchers asserting a violation of the ESA will come within the zone of interests protected by that statute. *Bennett v. Spear*, 520 U.S. at 162-167.

Even though the Court has applied the zone of interests test mainly in cases involving statutory rights, the Court has stated that the test is also potentially applicable in suits arising under the Constitution. *Bennett*, 520 U.S. at 163.

§3.4.7 Organizational Standing

There are two ways in which an organization can establish standing. First, an organization can sue on its own behalf if it can satisfy the same Article III and prudential requirements for standing that an individual must satisfy. Thus an organization that is injured by judicially redressable government action will have standing, assuming prudential considerations are satisfied as well. For example, an organization could sue to challenge an unlawful search of its headquarters. Second, an organization can sue on behalf of its members if "(a) its members would otherwise have standing to sue in their own right;

(b) the interests it seeks to protect are germane to the organization's purpose; and (c) neither the claim asserted nor the relief requested requires the participation of individual members in the lawsuit." *Hunt v. Washington State Apple Advertising Commission*, 432 U.S. 333, 343 (1977); *Friends of the Earth, Inc. v. Laidlaw Environmental Services, Inc.*, 528 U.S. 167, 181 (2000).

Example 3-AA

The Sierra Club files suit challenging a governmentally approved plan to develop a ski resort in a national forest located in the Sierra Nevadas. The suit is premised on the inadequacy of the Environmental Impact Statement (EIS) filed by the government — a violation of the National Environmental Policy Act — and is filed on behalf of several members of the club who actively use the area in question for hiking and camping purposes. Will the Sierra Club be allowed to sue on behalf of these members?

Explanation

First, the members themselves would have standing. See Example 3-G. Second, environmental protection of the Sierra Nevadas is a core function of the Sierra Club and hence germane to the purposes of the club. Third, since the issue in the suit does not involve individualized damages, but rather involves only a legal challenge to the adequacy of the EIS, the participation of the individual members is not required. On the other hand, if none of the Sierra Club's members used the area in question, the organization would lack standing since none of its members would have had standing to sue as individuals.

Suppose, however, that the challenge to the planned development comes from Cattle Barons, an organization designed to protect the rights of ranchers. According to Cattle Barons, several of its members have long-term grazing permits that will be rendered useless by the proposed development. Cattle Barons' suit on behalf of these members seeks money damages for the lost grazing rights. The amount of damages incurred by any specific rancher depends on facts particular to that rancher's permit and scope of operations within the national forest. Given the individual nature of the harm incurred by each rancher and the need to assess monetary damages with respect to each ranger, Cattle Barons would probably not be granted standing to sue on behalf of its members.

§3.4.8 Legislative Standing

Legislators, like all other persons, may sue in federal court whenever they have suffered a personal injury. Thus, in *Powell v. McCormack*, 395 U.S. 486

(1969), the Court recognized that an elected member of Congress had standing to challenge his exclusion from the House of Representatives. The exclusion and consequent loss of salary were personal injuries caused by the allegedly unconstitutional action. His case was, therefore, justiciable. But sometimes legislators sue claiming not a personal injury, but an institutional injury such as a dilution of their legislative prerogatives. It is in these latter circumstances that the doctrine of legislative standing must be considered.

The Supreme Court has accepted the legitimacy of institutional legislative standing in only one case, Coleman v. Miller, 307 U.S. 433 (1939). In that case, 20 of Kansas's 40 state senators voted not to ratify the "Child Labor Amendment," a proposed federal constitutional amendment. The lieutenant governor, however, cast a tie-breaking vote in favor of ratification. The dissenting senators, joined by one other senator and three members of the state house of representatives, filed suit seeking to compel appropriate state officials to recognize that the legislature had not ratified the Amendment. In essence, they claimed that their collective votes had been completely nullified by the lieutenant governor's illegal act. Although the Supreme Court ruled against the plaintiffs on the merits, it implicitly agreed that they had standing to bring this suit.

The Court has subsequently made it clear, however, that the institutional legislative standing recognized in Coleman is quite narrow:

> It is obvious, then, that our holding in Coleman stands (at most . . .) for the proposition that legislators whose votes would have been sufficient to defeat (or enact) a specific legislative act have standing to sue if that legislative action goes into effect (or does not go into effect), on the ground that their votes have been completely nullified.

Raines v. Byrd, 521 U.S. 811, 823 (1997). This means that legislators who cannot establish a personal injury as in Powell will not having standing to challenge government conduct that allegedly undermines the legislative function unless they allege what is tantamount to a complete nullification of their legislative prerogatives. Moreover, in a significant footnote, the Raines Court left open the possibility that other factors, such as the separation of powers, might preclude institutional legislative standing altogether in suits filed by federal legislators. Id. at 824 n.8.

The facts of Raines are instructive. In that case several members of Congress challenged the constitutionality of the Line Item Veto Act, which had been passed over their dissenting votes and signed into law by the President. Unlike the situation in Coleman, there was no argument that the votes of these members had been nullified; rather, they had simply lost the vote on the Line Item Veto Act. In the Court's words,

> They have not alleged that they voted for a specific bill, that there were sufficient votes to pass the bill, and that the bill was nonetheless deemed defeated. Nor can they allege that the Act will nullify their votes in the future in the same way that the votes of the *Coleman* legislators had been nullified. In the future, a majority of Senators and Congressmen can pass or reject appropriations bills; the Act has no effect on this process. In addition, a majority of Senators and Congressmen can vote to repeal the Act, or to except a given appropriations bill (or a given provision in an appropriations bill) from the Act; again, the Act has no effect on this process.

Id. at 824. In addition, further underscoring the narrow ambit given to the *Coleman* decision, the Court rejected the argument that injury-in-fact was established because the Line Item Veto Act diluted the effectiveness of a member's vote on appropriations measures by allowing the President to trump the legislative process. In the Court's view, this "abstract dilution of institutional legislative power" was insufficient to satisfy the case or controversy requirement. Id. at 824-826.

Example 3-BB

The United States House of Representatives filed a lawsuit against the Department of Commerce and the Bureau of the Census challenging defendants' plan to use statistical sampling for the 2000 census. The House claimed that the use of statistical sampling would violate the Census Act by failing to provide the House with a statement of "the whole number of persons in each state . . . as ascertained under the . . . decennial census of the population." The House further claimed that in the absence of such information, it would be unable to fulfill its constitutionally mandated function of determining the proper number of representatives for each state. In essence, the House claimed to have suffered an "informational injury." Is this a proper case for legislative standing?

Explanation

Perhaps. This situation is distinguishable from *Raines v. Byrd*. In *Raines*, the plaintiffs were dissenting members of Congress who had voted against the Line Item Veto Act. They had not suffered a nullification of their votes as in *Coleman v. Miller*, nor, in the Court's view, was their "dilution of effectiveness" claim sufficient to satisfy the injury-in-fact requirement. Here, by way of contrast, the suit is filed not by dissenting members of the House, but by the House as an institution, placing the case more in line with *Coleman*. In essence, the House argues that its statutory right to certain information will be nullified by the challenged action. Moreover, this informational injury is significantly more concrete than the "dilution of effectiveness" injury rejected in *Raines*. Indeed, it is similar to the informational injury recognized by the Court as legally sufficient in *Federal Election Commn. v. Akins*, supra. The House also seems to have satisfied the remaining Article III requirements of causation and redressability. According to the House's allegations, the informational injury will be caused by the use of statistical sampling and can be redressed by enjoining the Bureau from using that technique. The only question remaining is whether the Court will extend the principles of *Coleman* to the context of congressional standing. The Court carefully avoided addressing the question in *Department of Commerce v. United States House of Representatives*, 525 U.S. 316 (1999), a case in which the federal district court had upheld the House's claim of standing. See *United States House of Representatives v. Department of Commerce*, 11 F. Supp. 2d 76, 83-90, 95-97 (D.D.C. 1998), *appeal dismissed*, 525 U.S. 316 (1999).

§3.5 THE TIMELINE OF JUSTICIABILITY: THE RIPENESS AND MOOTNESS DOCTRINES

The ripeness and mootness doctrines examine the problem of justiciability from the perspective of time. Ripeness focuses on the potential prematurity of a lawsuit, while mootness addresses the potential staleness. Both doctrines are premised on the same Article III and prudential considerations that animate the standing doctrine. The Court has not, however, segregated the component parts of ripeness and mootness into constitutional and prudential domains. Rather, both doctrines simply operate to advance the general policy of avoiding judicial involvement in speculative or hypothetical lawsuits. Whether any particular application emanates from Article III or prudential considerations is rarely, if ever, dispositive. But see *Stop the Beach Renourishment, Inc. v. Florida Dept. of Environmental Protection*, 130 S. Ct. 2592, 2610 (2010) (where plaintiff's claim met the Article III aspects of standing and ripeness, defendant waived any prudential, nonjurisdictional ripeness objections by failing to raise them in a timely manner).

To understand the doctrines of ripeness and mootness, one need only place the doctrine of standing in a time frame. Assume that at some point in time there is a controversy between two parties such that one of the parties has established standing to sue the other. Place that point in the middle of a continuum. To the left of that point, the facts giving rise to this controversy are contingent and not yet fully developed. To the right, the facts have developed such that there is no longer a live controversy between the parties. The left side of the continuum represents problems invoking the ripeness doctrine; the right side of the continuum represents problems involving the mootness doctrine.

Example 3-CC

Babette owns a video rental store in which she carries an eclectic selection of videos, including a large number of what she labels "adult videos." Babette learns from a lawyer friend that a city ordinance prohibits the rental of adult videos. As a result, Babette files a suit against the city in federal court, seeking to enjoin enforcement of the ordinance. Is her suit ripe?

Explanation

Babette's suit is most likely not ripe. There is no threatened prosecution; nor is there any evidence that the city ordinance has been applied to videos such as those used by Babette. At most there is a speculative possibility that Babette's rentals may be subject to this ordinance. In the absence of more developed facts indicating a live and justiciable controversy between Babette and the city, it is unlikely that the federal court will entertain Babette's suit. Place this controversy at the left end of our continuum. (One could also describe Babette's suit as one in which the requirements of standing have not been satisfied.)

Suppose, however, that Babette receives a warning from the local prosecutor to the effect that Babette's adult videos are in violation of the ordinance. The warning states that any future rental of these videos will subject her to prosecution. Suppose, too, that another nearby video store owner has been prosecuted for the rental of these same videos. Under these circumstances, although no action has yet been taken against Babette, her claim against the city is most likely ripe. The threatened prosecution creates a real controversy between the parties in which Babette must either comply with the law or run the risk of prosecution. Place this controversy in the middle of our continuum. See *Steffel v. Thompson*, 415 U.S. 452 (1974).

Finally, suppose that during the pendency of her suit, Babette goes out of business for reasons unrelated to the lawsuit. There is no longer a live controversy between Babette and the city. Remember, Babette sought only an injunction. At best there is now only a hypothetical dispute. The suit is therefore moot and must be dismissed; it falls at the right end of our continuum.

§3.6 RIPENESS APPLIED

Ripeness becomes a potential issue in a case when a claimed injury is contingent upon future events. In other words, when all the events necessary to give rise to an injury have not yet happened, the potential lack of ripeness must be considered. Compare two situations. In one, a party seeks money damages for having been subjected to an unlawful search; in the other a party seeks to enjoin a threatened search. In the first situation, there is no ripeness problem. The claimed injury is not contingent on future behavior or events; rather, it is premised on conduct that has already occurred. In the second situation, however, there is a potential ripeness problem. Even if the claimed injury is sufficient to confer standing, the injury is contingent on future events, namely, the actual execution of the threatened search.

The method for determining whether a contingent claim is sufficiently ripe for Article III and prudential purposes requires the consideration of three factors:

- The probability that the predicted harm will take place,
- The hardship to the parties if immediate review is denied, and
- The fitness of the record for resolving the legal issues presented.

See *National Park Hospitality Assn. v. Department of the Interior*, 538 U.S. 803, 808 (2003); *Ohio Forestry Assn., Inc. v. Sierra Club*, 523 U.S. 726, 732-733 (1998).

The first two factors, although separate, are closely related. The first involves an assessment of probability. Will the predicted harm occur? In Example 3-CC, the probability that Babette will be harmed is slight to non-existent when she merely hears of the potentially applicable ordinance, but that probability increases once there is an actual threat of prosecution. The second factor — hardship to the party — measures the degree of harm generated by a denial of immediate review. Here one considers such questions as: Is there an adverse economic impact? Will the party be forced to forgo the exercise of a protected right? Does the party run the risk of criminal prosecution? Combining factors one and two, we arrive at this very subjective formula: The greater the probability of the harm and the more significant that harm, the more likely it is that a court will find the case to be ripe.

The third factor measures the adequacy of the record for judicial resolution. Purely legal issues — e.g., the meaning of a statute — usually require little factual development and may be fairly and fully adjudicated at the early stages of a dispute. Fact-bound issues — e.g., the reasonableness of future action — may require a full development of the facts giving rise to the dispute to provide a sound basis for wise adjudication. Whether an issue is legal or factual will often depend on a judge or justice's perception of the underlying claim. For example, a judge who views the guarantee of freedom of speech as an absolute will be more likely to conclude that free speech claims present purely legal issues than would a judge who applied a balancing of interests to the resolution of free speech claims. The former would need very few facts to resolve the controversy, while the latter would require considerably more factual development.

In short, these factors are not applied mathematically. Rather they are used to explore the conflict between the party's desire for an immediate adjudication and the judiciary's constitutional and prudential interest in avoiding immersion in hypothetical or abstract disputes. Obviously, a certain amount of subjectivity goes into the application of each factor; hence, one should not expect complete consistency in the pattern of results.

Example 3-DD

The Food and Drug Administration (FDA) has promulgated a regulation that requires prescription drug manufacturers to print the generic name of drugs on all labels and printed materials. One potential sanction for failure to comply with this regulation is criminal prosecution. Several drug manufacturers have filed suit against the FDA, seeking pre-enforcement review of the new regulation. They claim that the regulation is beyond the power delegated by Congress to the FDA. They further claim that enforcement will cause them to incur great expense in designing and printing new labels. Since the injury to the manufacturers is premised on future events — namely, enforcement of the regulation — their suit presents a potential ripeness problem, and the three factors listed above must be considered.

Explanation

First, the probability that the predicted harm will take place appears great. The FDA is unlikely to promulgate such a regulation without an intent to enforce it; and, from the plaintiffs' allegations, it appears equally clear that the very existence of the regulation will have a significant, immediate economic impact on their businesses — they will undertake the cost of compliance rather than run the risk of criminal prosecution. Of course, in a real case we would want more facts on both of these points. Second, the hardship to the plaintiffs derives from the dilemma they find themselves in: comply with an expensive and (according to them) illegal regulation or risk criminal prosecution. Finally, since the issue tendered is a purely legal question of statutory construction — does the FDA have authority to issue such a regulation? — the record requires no further factual development to permit a judicial resolution of the controversy. In short, the case is most likely ripe. See *Abbott Laboratories v. Gardner*, 387 U.S. 136 (1967).

Example 3-EE

The Food and Drug Administration has adopted a regulation that requires cosmetic manufacturers to grant the FDA access to all manufacturing facilities, processes, and formulas involved in the manufacture of color additives. The purpose of the regulation is to enforce the FDA's authority to certify and decertify color additives. A refusal to permit access will result in a "decertification" order, meaning that the manufacturer will be prohibited from using whatever color additive is at issue. The decertification order is immediately reviewable through administrative procedures.

Cosmetic manufacturers have filed suit against the FDA, challenging the validity of this regulation. They claim that the regulation transcends the authority granted by Congress. None of these manufacturers has yet been subjected to an access request or a decertification order. As a consequence, any harm to these manufacturers is contingent on the future conduct of the FDA. Is the case ripe?

Explanation

First, it is somewhat difficult to assess the probability that the harm will occur. While it is true that the FDA may request access to the facilities owned by some of these manufacturers, there are no facts indicating the actual likelihood of that happening. Nor are we certain what the response to such a request will be. Compare Example 3-DD, in which all drug manufacturers were required to comply immediately with the FDA's labeling requirement. Here, the speculative nature of the threatened injury might even be enough to preclude standing. Second, the hardship to the cosmetic manufacturers caused by waiting for the case to ripen through actual enforcement is relatively light. A refusal to comply with an FDA request will at most lead to a decertification order, which is immediately reviewable through administrative proceedings. Finally, the issue tendered appears to be purely legal, namely, whether Congress granted the FDA the authority to demand access. However, additional facts and the passage of time may illuminate the FDA's interpretation of the scope of its authority and therefore inform that legal judgment. A court inclined to deny review could easily conclude that this case was not yet ripe. See *Toilet Goods Assn. v. Gardner*, 387 U.S. 158 (1967).

§3.7 MOOTNESS APPLIED, AND VARIATIONS

The requirement that a case satisfy the requisites of justiciability applies from the outset of litigation up through the final stages of appellate review, including Supreme Court review. This means that during the entire federal litigation process, the parties must be and remain adverse to one another in the context of a judicially resolvable controversy. If at any time during the litigation process that adversity ceases, the case will be deemed moot. Stated slightly differently, the requirements of standing must be satisfied during the entire course of litigation. If either the law or the facts change such that any one of the basic standing elements—injury-in-fact, causation, or redressability—is no longer satisfied, the mootness doctrine will be triggered. See *Arizonans for Official English v. Arizona*, 520 U.S. 43 (1997). Once a case becomes moot, not only may it proceed no further, but all prior lower court proceedings will usually be erased as well. Thus, if the events giving rise to mootness occur while a case is on appeal, the case will usually be remanded to the federal district court with instructions to vacate its judgment. Otherwise, a lower court precedent would remain on the books and could bind or affect the parties in future proceedings, even though they lacked a full opportunity to challenge the correctness of the decision in the appellate courts. *Camreta v. Greene*, 131 S. Ct. 2020, 2033-2036 (2011); *United States v. Munsingwear, Inc.*, 340 U.S. 36, 40 (1950).

Example 3-FF

Yxta is an officer in the United States Army. Although she is assigned to an infantry unit, she has been excluded from combat duties solely because of her gender. She files suit in federal district court claiming that this gender-based exclusion violates her right to equal protection under the Due Process Clause of the Fifth Amendment. She seeks an injunction against enforcement of the policy. The district court rules against her, and she files an appeal. During the pendency of the appeal, Yxta retires from the military with no possibility of returning to the service. Is her claim moot?

Explanation

Yes. The *change in facts* eliminates the legal adversity between Yxta and the United States Army. As a consequence, her claim is moot. The court of appeals will dismiss her appeal and remand the case to the district court with instructions to dismiss the action. See *Arizonans for Official English v. Arizona*, supra, 520 U.S. at 66-72.

Suppose, however, that Yxta has not retired. Instead, Congress has adopted legislation eliminating all gender-based restrictions on combat duty and mandates that all female officers in the infantry be given priority in combat assignments if so requested. Yxta is eligible for priority assignment to combat duty. Clearly, an injunction against enforcement of the prior policy would be without practical effect since that policy no longer exists. As a consequence, this *change in the law* renders the controversy between Yxta and the United States Army moot. Again, the case must be dismissed.

There are four situations in which a case that appears to have been rendered moot will not be dismissed. Although these situations are often described as exceptions to the mootness doctrine, they are more appropriately described as doctrines designed to expose the remaining vitality of what only appears to be a moot controversy. These variations can be categorized as follows:

- Collateral consequences,
- Wrongs capable of repetition yet evading review,
- Voluntary cessation of challenged activity, and
- Class actions.

§3.7.1 Collateral Consequences

The collateral consequences doctrine applies when a significant aspect of the controversy between the parties has dissipated because of a change in law or facts, but where there remains at least some residual aspect of the dispute for which a judicial remedy may provide relief. For example, suppose a convicted defendant serves his or her sentence prior to the completion of appellate review. In one sense, the case is moot. A reversal of the conviction will not alter the fact that the defendant has served the sentence imposed. On the other hand, criminal convictions almost always have collateral consequences for the defendant, such as limitations imposed on various civil rights including the right to vote or hold office, the potential for use of the conviction as impeachment evidence, the effect on employment opportunities, and so forth. Thus the fact that a defendant has served the sentence imposed will generally not moot a challenge to an underlying conviction. In *Sibron v. New York*, 392 U.S. 40, 55 (1968), the Court noted "the obvious fact of life that most criminal convictions do in fact entail adverse collateral legal consequences. The mere 'possibility' that this will be the case is enough to preserve a criminal case from ending 'ignominiously in the limbo of mootness.'" Compare *Spencer v. Kemna*, 523 U.S. 1 (1998), where the Court refused to presume that collateral consequences attached to a parole revocation for which the underlying sentence had expired. Unlike the conviction itself, the future consequences of the parole revocation were deemed at best speculative. Since the petitioner alleged no plausible collateral consequences, the Court dismissed his habeas corpus petition as moot. A case that is otherwise moot cannot be saved under the collateral consequences doctrine simply because a favorable ruling might serve as a useful precedent in a "hypothetical" future case. Such a "possible, indirect benefit . . . cannot save this case from mootness," for "'if that were enough to avoid mootness, no case would ever be moot.'" *United States v. Juvenile Male*, 131 S. Ct. 2860, 2864 (2011) (quoting *Commodity Futures Trading Commn. v. Board of Trade of Chicago*, 701 F.2d 653, 656 (7th Cir. 1983) (Posner, J.)).

Similarly, suppose that in Example 3-FF, Yxta had also filed a claim for damages premised on the combat pay she would have received in the absence of the discriminatory policy. Neither her retirement nor a change in the law would alter the controversy on this issue. Thus, although the part of her suit that requested equitable relief would be dismissed as moot, the court would retain jurisdiction over the damages claim. Although the damages claim is not technically a collateral consequence, the idea is the same. So long as some aspect of the dispute remains subject to judicial resolution, the case is not moot. See, e.g., *Alvarez v. Smith*, 130 S. Ct. 576, 580, 583 (2009) (though plaintiffs' claims for declaratory and injunctive relief were moot, the case might still proceed on remand if district court allows plaintiffs to amend their complaint to seek damages).

§3.7.2 Wrongs Capable of Repetition Yet Evading Review

The category of wrongs capable of repetition yet evading review involves those cases in which (1) the challenged action is of such a short duration that full judicial consideration is not, as a practical matter, likely; and (2) there is a reasonable expectation that the same complaining party will be subjected to the same action again. *Turner v. Rogers*, 131 S. Ct. 2507, 2515 (2011). The decision in *Roe v. Wade*, 410 U.S. 113 (1973), presents a classic example. In *Roe*, a pregnant woman challenged the constitutionality of a state law that prohibited most abortions. By the time her case reached the Supreme Court she was no longer pregnant. Yet the Court held that her case was not moot. She could become pregnant again and again find herself subject to this same state law, and, given the duration of a typical pregnancy, the litigation process would likely outlive her claim. Under such circumstances, the controversy remains justiciable based on the assumption that the plaintiff has a continuing, nonhypothetical interest in establishing the legal principles at stake. Id. at 125.

The Court has sometimes ignored the second element of this test. For example, in *Moore v. Ogilvie*, 394 U.S. 814 (1969), independent candidates for the office of presidential elector challenged a state law that imposed substantial ballot access restrictions upon them. By the time the case reached the Supreme Court, the election had been held and a suggestion of mootness was placed before the Court. The Court noted that the challenged rule remained in place and would be applied in future elections. As a consequence, "[t]he problem [was] therefore 'capable of repetition, yet evading review.'" Id. at 816. There was no reference to the plaintiffs' desire to run for this office in the future, a point on which the dissent criticized the majority. Id. at 819 (Stewart, J., dissenting).

Despite the Court's sometimes cavalier attitude toward this second element, the generally accepted view is that both elements must be satisfied. However, given *Moore*, one cannot assume that the second element will always be required—a reality that underscores the elastic nature of justiciability doctrines.

§3.7.3 Voluntary Cessation

The voluntary cessation of challenged activity will not moot a controversy unless it can be established with fair assurance that there is "no reasonable expectation" that the party will "return to his old ways" once the case is dismissed. *United States v. W. T. Grant Co.*, 345 U.S. 629, 632-633 (1953); see also *Parents Involved in Community Schools v. Seattle School District No. 1*, 551 U.S. 701, 718-719 (2007) (recent application of the doctrine). Suppose, for example, that an environmental group has sued to enjoin a paper mill from dumping toxic chemicals into a river. The mere fact that the mill now adopts a moratorium on such dumping will not moot plaintiff's case. This is true even if the mill claims that it has no plans to engage in such dumping in the future. See *Friends of the Earth, Inc. v. Laidlaw Environmental Services, Inc.*, 528 U.S. 167, 189 (2000) (defendant carries a heavy burden to establish that voluntary cessation moots case). On the other hand, if the mill purchases an expensive waste disposal system that completely eliminates the necessity and practicality of dumping in the river, a court may well conclude that there is "no reasonable expectation" that the mill will again dump toxic chemicals into the river. This would be particularly true if the plaintiff agrees that the mill's actions in fact satisfied the concerns that led it to file the lawsuit. In such a case, the suit to prevent future dumping will be moot. However, voluntary cessation that occurs only after the Supreme Court has agreed to review a case is inherently suspect: "Such postcertiorari maneuvers designed to insulate a decision from review by this Court must be viewed with a critical eye." *Knox v. Service Employees Intl. Union, Local 1000*, 132 S. Ct. 2277, 2287 (2012).

An interesting but related question may arise when the Supreme Court is asked to review a state court decision under 28 U.S.C. §1257. While the petitioner is obviously unhappy with the state court ruling, the respondent, who won in state court, may seek to have the Supreme Court decline review by claiming that an intervening event has now rendered the case moot. Yet such a contention, if successful, might leave the state court ruling intact, allowing the victorious state court litigant to then revert to its old ways and invoke the state court decision, after the time for seeking Supreme Court review has lapsed. In *City of Erie v. Pap's A. M.*, 529 U.S. 277 (2000), the Supreme Court noted this concern in rejecting a mootness argument. In that case, plaintiff, who operated Pap's, a nude dancing establishment, won a state high court ruling declaring the city's public nudity ordinance unconstitutional and enjoining its further enforcement. After the Supreme Court granted the city's petition for review, plaintiff filed an affidavit suggesting that the case should be dismissed as moot because plaintiff, who was elderly, had closed his nude dancing club. The Court declined to do so, explaining, "Several Members of this Court can attest . . . that the 'advanced age' of Pap's owner (72) does not make it 'absolutely clear' that a life of quiet retirement is his only reasonable expectation." Id. at 288. Moreover, said the Court, "this is not a run of the mill voluntary cessation case. Here it is the plaintiff, who having prevailed below, now seeks to have the case declared moot," a ruling that would have left the state court injunction in place. "Our interest in preventing litigants from attempting to manipulate the Court's jurisdiction to insulate a favorable decision from review further counsels against a finding of mootness here." Id.

A statutory change that eliminates the controversy between the parties will render a case moot so long as there is no reasonable possibility that the law will be changed back once the case is dismissed. Typically, when the change is rendered by Congress or a state legislature, courts apply the mootness doctrine. See Example 3-FF. However, when the change occurs at the local level, for example by a city council, courts are more likely to be suspicious that the offending law will be reenacted, and hence the mootness doctrine is less likely to be applied. Compare *Kremens v. Bartley*, 431 U.S. 119 (1977) (legislative change renders case moot), with *City of Mesquite v. Aladdin's Castle, Inc.*, 455 U.S. 283 (1982) (repeal of local ordinance does not render case moot).

We saw earlier that if a federal court case becomes moot while it is on appeal, this will ordinarily result in vacating the judgment or judgments below out of fairness to the losing party who might otherwise suffer adverse effects from the judgment's remaining on the books. However, the Supreme Court has recognized an exception to this rule in cases where the losing party who sought appellate review then engages in voluntary action that results in settling the case. In that situation, any unfairness to the appellant of leaving the precedent in place vanishes, for "'[w]here mootness results from settlement' rather than 'happenstance,' the 'losing party has voluntarily forfeited his legal remedy . . . [and] therefore surrender[ed] his claim to the equitable remedy of vacatur.'" *Alvarez v. Smith*, supra, 130 S. Ct. at 581 (quoting *U.S. Bancorp Mortgage Co. v. Bonner Mall Partnership*, 513 U.S. 18, 25 (1994)).

§3.7.4 Class Actions

The Court has developed two special rules for mootness that apply in the context of class actions. First, if a class has been certified and the case becomes moot as to the named representative, the action will not be deemed moot if there remains a live controversy between any member of the plaintiff class and the defendant. *Gerstein v. Pugh*, 420 U.S. 103, 110 n.11 (1975). Second, if the district court refuses to certify the class and the case becomes moot with respect to the named representative, the named representative will nonetheless be allowed to appeal the refusal to certify the class. *United States Parole Commn. v. Geraghty*, 445 U.S. 388 (1980); and see *Alvarez v. Smith*, supra, 130 S. Ct. at 580 (case would not have been moot had plaintiff appealed district court's denial of class certification). In both circumstances, the case or controversy is premised on the interests of the class members and not upon the interests of the named representative. Indeed, the Supreme Court has seemingly welcomed use of the "class action vehicle [as] a mechanism for ensuring that a justiciable claim is before the Court." *Gratz v. Bollinger*, 539 U.S. 244, 267 (2003) (internal quotation marks omitted).

§3.8 THE POLITICAL QUESTION DOCTRINE

Under the political question doctrine, certain constitutional issues are deemed off limits to the federal judiciary. In essence, this means that as to these issues, enforcement of the Constitution is dependent on the will of the executive and legislative branches, the so-called political branches — hence the name, the political question doctrine. This does not mean that federal courts may not hear cases that involve "political" issues; rather, it means that under some circumstances certain provisions of the Constitution may not be judicially enforceable, and that the resolution of the controversy must therefore be referred to the political branches.

Although there is no precise litmus test for determining whether a particular issue presents a political question, the Court has tended to focus on two questions, both of which must be answered in the affirmative:

- Does the issue implicate the separation of powers?
- Does the Constitution commit resolution of this issue to either the President or Congress?

Consideration of these questions, and particularly the second, must be undertaken with a sensitivity to prudential considerations going to the heart of the judicial function. To what extent may the judiciary interfere with what appears to be the primary prerogative of a coordinate branch? In fact, in the context of political questions, prudence is sometimes applied in an ad hoc fashion to insulate a particular issue from judicial review.

The first question provides an important threshold consideration. The Court has held that the "nonjusticiability of a political question is primarily a function of the separation of powers." *Baker v. Carr*, 369 U.S. 186, 210 (1962). This is not to suggest that every separation of powers issue involves a political question. Rather, this simply means that the political question doctrine is potentially applicable when the issue presented implicates a separation of powers concern — i.e., when the issue involved places the

Court in a possible conflict with either the executive branch or Congress. Conversely, the political question doctrine will not come into play where no separation of powers concerns are present. Thus the doctrine does not apply to challenges to state action unless that state action somehow implicates the powers of the political branches of the federal government. Cf. *Gilligan v. Morgan*, 413 U.S. 1 (1973) (challenge to state's training of national guard nonjusticiable since Constitution places the authority to oversee such training in Congress). In short, a negative answer to the first question ends the inquiry.

The second question is premised on the assumption that the controversy presented creates a potential conflict between the Court and one of the coordinate branches. The focus of this question, however, is not on the existence of the conflict, but on how the Constitution resolves it. The Court has begun this inquiry by looking for a textually demonstrable constitutional commitment to one of the coordinate branches. *Baker v. Carr*, supra, 369 U.S. at 217. If there is such a commitment, express or implied, then the Court must stay out of the controversy. This is simply another way of asking which branch of the government has final constitutional authority over the matter presented.

Suppose, for example, that a member of Congress is impeached by the House of Representatives and convicted by the Senate. He seeks to overturn his conviction by filing a lawsuit in federal court challenging the Senate's procedures as inadequate under the Fifth Amendment Due Process Clause. The member's case clearly raises a separation of powers concern that potentially pits the federal judiciary against Congress. The first question having been answered affirmatively, we must determine if the Constitution commits final authority over the impeachment process to the Senate; or, conversely, if the Constitution permits the federal judiciary to review the Senate's action. In *Nixon v. United States*, 506 U.S. 224 (1993), the Court concluded that Article I of the Constitution committed the entire impeachment process to the House and Senate. This conclusion was not based solely on the text of the Constitution. Rather, it derived from the Court's interpretation of that text based upon the language of the text, history, precedent, and policy. In short, a textually demonstrable constitutional commitment involves more than a simple reference to the language of the Constitution; it involves the wide array of factors that courts use in discovering the meaning of that text.

As *Nixon v. United States* suggests, the Court will often consider a number of factors, in addition to the text, in explaining why a particular matter involves (or does not involve) a political question. Here prudence plays a major role.

- Are there judicially discoverable and manageable standards for resolving the controversy?

- Does resolution of the controversy require an initial policy determination of a kind clearly for nonjudicial discretion?
- Will judicial resolution express a lack of respect for a coordinate branch of government?
- Is there an unusual need for unquestioning adherence to a political decision already made?
- Will multifarious pronouncements by various departments cause embarrassment to the government?

While these factors may operate as independent reasons for finding the presence of a political question, they are often used to illuminate the Court's judgment on whether there is or is not a textual constitutional commitment. Thus, a lack of judicially discoverable standards or the necessity of a policy determination involving discretion of a nonjudicial nature would support a conclusion that there is a textually demonstrable constitutional commitment to one of the coordinate branches. In addition, however, these factors give the Court a latitude of discretion within which to apply prudential considerations in deciding whether a particular matter ought to be resolved by the judicial branch.

Luther v. Borden, 48 U.S. (7 How.) 1 (1849), presents a classic example of the political question doctrine applied. There the Court was asked to determine which of two rival factions represented the legitimate government of the State of Rhode Island. The "out" faction argued that the faction in power was a "nonconstitutional" government in violation of Article IV, §4 of the Constitution, which provides, "The United States shall guarantee to every State in this Union a Republican Form of Government." The Court held that resolution of this dispute was nonjusticiable. Under the Constitution, it was for Congress to determine both the legitimacy and the republican character of any purported state government. Those decisions could not be questioned in any judicial tribunal. 48 U.S. (7 How.) at 42. Since the decision in Luther, the Court has consistently held that claims arising under the Guarantee Clause are nonjusticiable. The "guarantee," therefore, is political; it must be enforced, if at all, by Congress.

The decision in Luther fits the pattern of the questions discussed above. First, although the primary dispute involved a state government and a private party challenging the legitimacy of that government, the actual conflict as envisioned by the Court was between the federal judiciary and Congress, namely, which federal branch was empowered to determine the republicanism of a purported state government, a separation of powers question. Next, in essence, the Court concluded that Article IV, §4 operated as a textual constitutional commitment of the "republican" issue to Congress. In part, this conclusion rested on the Court's doubts about the availability of judicial standards to measure republicanism, and in part, it derived from pragmatic concerns regarding the potential instability that would be generated were the Court to rule against the recognized government. 48 U.S. (7 How.) at 43-46.

Other contexts in which the political question doctrine has been applied include the constitutional amendment process, certain aspects of foreign affairs, the determination of when military hostilities begin or end, impeachment, congressional self-governance, etc. The key to understanding the political question doctrine, however, will not be found in memorizing a litany of specific results, but in appreciating the policies and techniques at the heart of the doctrine.

Example 3-GG

State T is divided into 25 legislative districts. Each district elects one representative to serve in the U.S. House of Representatives. There is a relatively large disparity between the populations of the various districts. For example, District One, which is located in a rural section of the state, has a population of 100,000, while District Seven, located in an urban area, has a population of 1 million. Voters from District Seven have filed suit in federal court claiming that the 10-1 disparity in district sizes dilutes the voting strength of voters living in District Seven. They claim that this disparate treatment violates the Equal Protection Clause of the Fourteenth Amendment. Does this claim present a political question?

Explanation

First, this challenge to *state* action does not, on its face, raise separation of powers concerns, for the authority of the federal coordinate branches is simply not at issue. Yet separation of powers might be implicated to the extent it is claimed that Congress, rather than the federal judiciary, should oversee the manner by which states elect representatives to the House. Next, there would appear to be no clear textual constitutional commitment of the plaintiffs' equal protection claim to one of the coordinate branches. Although §5 of the Fourteenth Amendment clearly gives Congress the authority to enforce the provisions of the Fourteenth Amendment, it is well established that the Supreme Court has the final word over the meaning of the Fourteenth Amendment in cases pending before the Court. Similarly, while Article I, §4 gives Congress the authority to regulate the "times, places, and manner of holding elections for . . . Representatives," this clause could be read to address only the election itself rather than the geographic basis of districting. Thus, there is no clear or obvious textual commitment of this issue to Congress.

The Court might go on, however, to consider some of the other factors we have mentioned. One could argue that there are no judicially discoverable standards for the enforcement of equal protection in the context of vote dilution. Certainly, that was true when the first such cases were brought; however, over the years the Court has developed a "one-person, one-vote" standard that can be applied without resort to a nonjudicial policy determination. In other words, equality is judicially measurable. Again it would appear that the issue presented is not a political question. See *Baker v. Carr*, 369 U.S. 186 (1962) (holding that a vote dilution challenge to legislative reapportionment does not present a political question). Compare *Vieth v. Jubelirer*, 541 U.S. 267 (2004) (statewide political gerrymandering claims alleging that a state's districts for the election of congressional representatives, though equally apportioned in terms of population, were drawn to give one political party an unfair advantage by diluting the opposition's voting strength, are nonjusticiable, four Justices invoking the political question doctrine and one Justice relying upon standing).

Example 3-HH

The House of Representatives, exercising its powers under Article I, §5 ("Each House shall be the Judge of the Elections, Returns, and Qualifications of its own Members . . ."), has voted to exclude Eve from membership in the House despite the fact that Eve is the duly elected representative from District Twenty-Seven in her state. The exclusion vote was based on Eve's refusal to fire a member of her staff who had leaked confidential information regarding a congressional hearing. Eve files suit challenging the exclusion as beyond the power of the House of Representatives. Does Eve's challenge present a political question?

Explanation

To resolve Eve's claim, the Court must determine whether it or the House of Representatives has the final word on Eve's "excludability." Thus Eve's challenge clearly implicates the separation of powers. Next, the text of the Constitution appears to commit resolution of this specific issue to the House — "Each House shall be the Judge . . . of the Qualifications of its own Members." However, the question is, "What is the scope of that textual commitment?" In other words, does the text give the House complete discretion to exclude a member, regardless of the basis for that exclusion, or is that discretion somehow limited? In *Powell v. McCormack*, 395 U.S. 486 (1969), under roughly similar facts, the Court held that while the text of Article I, §5 did commit the "qualifications" issue to the House, the scope of the commitment was limited to consideration of three factors listed in the text of a previous section of the Constitution: age, citizenship, and residency. Art. 1, §2. Thus the question of whether Eve could be excluded for refusing to dismiss an employee would not come within the scope of the

Constitution's textual commitment. Nor are any of the other reasons for finding a political question present here.

Examples 3-GG and 3-HH have a surface simplicity. In part, that derives from the fact that both examples are premised on settled applications of the political question doctrine to particular circumstances. Neither result was, however, inevitable. Nor were the solutions simple. The underlying complexity of the inquiry can best be appreciated by considering a context in which the Court has not yet determined the applicability or scope of the political question doctrine.

Example 3-II

Menachem was born in Jerusalem. Because his parents are United States citizens, he is a United States citizen as well. Shortly after his birth, Menachem's mother asked the U.S. State Department to issue him a passport listing "Israel" as his place of birth, in accord with a federal statute that requires the Department to list "Israel" as the place of birth of any U.S. citizen born in Jerusalem if the citizen so requests. The Department refused, citing its policy of listing only "Jerusalem" so as not to take sides in the dispute as to whether the city properly belongs to Israel or to Jordan. Menachem has sued the U.S. Secretary of State in federal district court, seeking an injunction requiring the Department to honor his request that "Israel" be listed as his place of birth. The Secretary has moved to dismiss on the ground that the case presents a political question. How should the court rule on the Secretary's motion?

Explanation

This case clearly involves separation of powers, one of the usual prerequisites to finding a political question. However, as to the second factor, a commitment of the issue to either Congress or the President, the answer turns on how we characterize the issue presented. If the case is viewed as one where federal courts are being asked to decide the political status of Jerusalem, i.e., whether it falls within the sovereignty of Israel or of Jordan, this would likely present a political question because it involves the recognition of foreign governments, an area of foreign affairs that the Constitution has textually assigned to the President. See §§5.5, 5.5.3. However, the issue presented can be viewed more narrowly as being simply whether Menachem has a federal statutory right to have Israel listed on his passport as his place of birth. Viewed this way, the case involves the kind of question federal courts routinely decide. A court would first have to determine whether Menachem's interpretation of the federal statute is correct. If the court agrees that it is, the court would then have to decide whether Congress, by enacting the statute and imposing this duty on the Department, impermissibly invaded the Executive domain. Regardless of how it answers these questions, however, the court would not be resolving the issue of whether Jerusalem belongs to Israel or to Jordan. If the court finds that Congress acted constitutionally, Jerusalem's status will then have been resolved by Congress. If, on the other hand, the court finds that Congress violated separation of powers and invaded the Executive sphere, Jerusalem's status will be governed by the President's policy. Thus, either Congress's or the President's determination as to the status of Jerusalem will in the end control, not any independent determination made by the courts. See *Zivotofsky v. Clinton*, 132 S. Ct. 1421 (2010) (reversing lower courts' conclusion that case presented a political question).

The Supreme Court's two most significant political question cases may have been two that weren't. In December 2000, the Supreme Court twice intervened in the process of determining the winner of the November 2000 presidential election. That election was an extraordinarily close one. Its outcome ultimately turned on who was deemed to have won the popular vote in Florida and was thus entitled to that state's 25 Electoral College votes. If Al Gore had been found the winner there, he would have defeated George Bush for the presidency by an electoral vote of 291 to 246. In the end, of course, Bush was determined to have carried Florida, giving him an electoral margin of 271 to 266, one more vote than the minimum needed to win the office. Because the Florida vote count was so close, with Bush's initial lead less than 1,800 votes out of the roughly 6 million that were cast, Gore was entitled to a manual recount. Time was a critical factor because under 3 U.S.C. §5, Congress was not required to accept Florida's electoral vote results as "conclusive" unless they were submitted by December 12. However, results submitted after that "safe harbor" date would still be considered, because Congress would not meet again until December 18 and would not actually determine the validity of and count the state electoral votes until January 6, 2001. See 3 U.S.C. §§7, 12, 15. Indeed, after the 1960 presidential election, Congress accepted a state's slate of electoral votes that was submitted to it on January 4, 1961, the day on which the electoral votes were finally counted.

The two cases that reached the Supreme Court — *Bush v. Palm Beach County Canvassing Board*, 531 U.S. 70 (Dec. 4, 2000) (*per curiam*) and *Bush v. Gore*, 531 U.S. 98 (Dec. 12, 2000) (*per curiam*) — both originated in Florida state court. While both raised issues as to what recount procedures were mandated by Florida law, both also presented possible federal questions. In *Bush v. Palm Beach County*, the potential federal issue was whether the state's high court had violated Article II, §1 — which provides that the state "legislature" must determine the "manner" for choosing the state's presidential electors — by imposing standards that derived from the state constitution or the courts' inherent equitable powers, neither of which constituted action by the "legislature." However, because the basis for the Florida court's ruling was not entirely clear, the Supreme Court vacated the decision and remanded the case to let Florida's high court clarify its ruling. The Florida Supreme Court promptly issued a new opinion, making clear that its prior decision had rested solely on a construction of state statutes and not on any other body of law. See Example 1-E.

In Bush v. Gore, the federal issue was whether the recount procedures ordered by the Florida high court, which allowed the state's counties to use different recount procedures, violated the Equal Protection Clause. This time, the Supreme Court resolved the constitutional issue. In a 5-4 decision, it held that to allow such variations would be contrary to the Fourteenth Amendment, for "[w]hen a court orders a statewide remedy, there must be at least some assurance that the rudimentary requirements of equal treatment and fundamental fairness are satisfied." 531 U.S. at 109. When the Supreme Court first agreed to hear the case on December 9, it stayed the Florida high court decision, temporarily halting the Florida recount. The Court then issued its decision three days later, but rather than lifting its stay, the Court now ruled that Florida was barred from conducting any further recounts because the "safe harbor" period would lapse that day. Justices Souter, Stevens, Ginsburg, and Breyer strenuously dissented, noting that even without a "safe harbor," Florida was entitled to proceed with a recount as long as it was completed in time for the results to in fact be considered by Congress. As Justice Souter wrote, "I see no warrant for this Court to assume that Florida could not possibly comply with this requirement before the date set for the meeting of electors. . . . To recount these manually would be a tall order, but before this Court stayed the effort to do that the courts of Florida were ready to do their best to get that job done. There is no justification for denying the State the opportunity to try to count all disputed ballots now." Id. at 135.

More importantly, the dissenters in Bush v. Gore urged that the Court should never have become involved in that dispute and that the matter should have been left for Congress to resolve should that become necessary. Justice Souter noted that the equal protection question was "an issue that might well have been dealt with adequately by the Florida courts if the state proceedings had not been interrupted, and if not disposed of at the state level it could have been considered by Congress in any electoral vote dispute." Id. at 133. The same was true of the issue in Bush v. Palm Beach County as to whether the Florida state court applied electoral standards that were judicially rather than legislatively created. For if the Florida court did employ such standards — a matter the Supreme Court never had to address — Congress could have so found and on that basis rejected the state's certification of its electoral vote as not comporting with Article I, §2. Justice Breyer in a separate dissent in *Bush v. Gore* agreed that the case presented a political question. He noted that "the selection of the President is of fundamental national importance. But that importance is political, not legal." Id. at 153. In his view, "[t]he Constitution and federal statutes themselves make clear that restraint is appropriate. They set forth a road-map of how to resolve disputes about electors, even after an election as close as this one. That road-map foresees resolution of electoral disputes by *state* courts. . . . But it nowhere provides for involvement by the United States Supreme Court." Id. Instead, he wrote, "the Twelfth Amendment commits to Congress the authority and responsibility to count electoral votes." Id. Breyer feared that in taking up "this highly politicized matter, the appearance of a split decision runs the risk of undermining the public's confidence in the Court itself." Id. at 157. By doing so, he wrote, "we . . . risk a self-inflicted wound—a wound that may harm not just the Court, but the Nation." Id. at 158.

The *Bush v. Gore* majority never directly responded to the dissent's political question argument. The closest the majority came to discussing the issue was at the end of its per curiam opinion where it stated, "None are more conscious of the vital limits on judicial authority than are the Members of this Court, and none stand more in admiration of the Constitution's design to leave the selection of the President to the people, through their legislatures, and to the political sphere." Id. at 111. Yet the majority then went on to suggest that there is simply no such thing as a political question, and that whenever a case is otherwise properly before it, a federal court has no choice but to decide the matter: "When contending parties invoke the process of the courts . . . it becomes our unsought responsibility to resolve the federal and constitutional issues the judicial system has been *forced* to confront." Id. (emphasis supplied). However, as every student of justiciability knows, a federal court's hands are never so unconditionally and inextricably tied.

The bottom line is that the political question doctrine is driven by more than a mechanical response to a series of questions. Rather, at the heart of the political question doctrine is one's basic notion of justiciability and the role of the Court within our system of government. Previously resolved cases are easy to describe; future possibilities depend upon an exercise of judgment regarding the *proper* scope and timing of judicial review.

Special Limitations on Judicial Review of State Laws

§4.1 INTRODUCTION AND OVERVIEW

In Chapter 3 we saw that the ability of the federal courts to exercise the power of judicial review is constrained by the Article III case or controversy requirement and by the various justiciability doctrines that the Court has created in connection with it. In this chapter we explore five additional limitations that often arise when federal courts — and sometimes state courts — are asked to review the constitutionality of state laws. These limitations are the Eleventh Amendment, the *Pullman* doctrine, the *Siler* doctrine, the *Younger* doctrine, and the immunity of state and local officials from damages liability. While these limitations are distinct from one another, they share a common goal — rooted in principles of comity and federalism — of seeking to reduce or minimize federal judicial interference with the states.

§4.2 THE ELEVENTH AMENDMENT

§4.2.1 The Eleventh Amendment and Sovereign Immunity

Federal courts are courts of limited subject matter jurisdiction. As we have noted, Article III, §2, cl. 1 defines the "judicial power of the United States" as extending to nine enumerated categories of "cases or controversies." No other type of case may enter a federal court. You might think of each of these categories — federal question cases, diversity cases, admiralty and maritime cases, etc. — as a door to the federal courthouse through which only that type of case may pass. Of the nine Article III, §2 categories or doors, seven would allow a suit to be brought against one of the 50 states in federal court. These seven categories of cases are (1) a suit "arising under" the Constitution or laws of the United States; (2) a suit brought by an ambassador, public minister, or consul; (3) a suit to which the United States is a party; (4) a suit between two or more states; (5) a suit filed by a citizen of another state (i.e., the Citizen-State Diversity Clause); (6) a suit brought by a foreign state, its citizens, or subjects (i.e., the Alien-State Diversity Clause); or (7) a suit brought in admiralty or maritime.

Almost immediately after the adoption of the Constitution, cases were brought against states in federal court. One of these was *Chisholm v. Georgia*, 2 U.S. (2 Dall.) 419 (1793), a suit filed in the Supreme Court against the State of Georgia by two citizens of South Carolina to collect on a pre-Revolutionary War debt. This common law action for assumpsit fell within the federal judicial power by virtue of the Citizen-State Diversity Clause since it was "between a State and citizens of another State" (Art. III, §2, cl. 1); moreover, the suit came within the Supreme Court's original jurisdiction as a case "in which a State shall be a Party. . . ." Art. III, §2, cl. 2. Georgia refused to appear in the action, claiming that the federal courts could not entertain a suit against a sovereign state. The Supreme Court disagreed and entered a default judgment on behalf of the plaintiffs.

Chisholm was bitterly received. The reaction stemmed in large part from the fact that the Constitution's supporters had given express assurances that the federal courts would not be employed to enforce the claims of creditors, many of whom were Loyalists, against a recalcitrant state. In *The Federalist*, Alexander Hamilton had written:

> It is inherent in the nature of sovereignty not to be amenable to the suit of an individual *without its consent*. . . . [T]he exemption, as one of the attributes of sovereignty, is now enjoyed by the government of every State in the Union. Unless, therefore, there is a surrender of this immunity in the plan of the convention, it will remain with the States and the danger intimated must be merely ideal. . . . [T]here is no color to pretend that the State governments would, by the adoption of that plan, be divested of the privilege of paying their own debts in their own way. . . . [T]o ascribe to the federal courts, by mere implication, and in destruction of a pre-existing right of the State governments, a power which would involve such a consequence, would be altogether forced and unwarrantable.

The Federalist No. 81, at 487-488 (Clinton Rossiter ed., 1961).

Two years after *Chisholm* was decided, the case was overruled by the Eleventh Amendment. The Amendment narrowed the subject matter jurisdiction of the federal judiciary to ensure that states could no longer be sued in federal court simply because the plaintiff was a citizen of another state or of a foreign country. The Amendment provides that "[t]he Judicial power of the United States shall not be construed to extend to any suit in law or in equity, commenced or prosecuted against one of the United States by Citizens of another State, or by Citizens or Subjects of any Foreign State." The Eleventh Amendment can be read as simply repealing the Citizen-State and Alien-State Diversity Clauses of Article III, §2, in effect closing or boarding up those two doors to the federal courts. The Amendment did not specifically address the other five doors through which actions against a state might enter federal court, including the door for suits "arising under" the Constitution or laws of the United States. Thus, while citizens of other states or countries could no longer bring common law actions against a state in federal court, they, like anyone else, could arguably still sue a state in federal court to redress violations of federal law. In a number of cases decided not long after the Eleventh Amendment was adopted, the Court in fact heard cases in which it was alleged that a state had violated the Constitution or federal laws, despite arguments that the suits were barred by the Eleventh Amendment. *Cohens v. Virginia*, 19 U.S. (6 Wheat.) 264 (1821); *Osborn v. Bank of United States*, 22 U.S. (9 Wheat.) 738 (1824).

Nearly a century after the Eleventh Amendment was adopted, however, the Supreme Court decided a case that resulted in giving the Amendment a very different and far more expansive reading than is suggested by its text. *Hans v. Louisiana*, 134 U.S. 1 (1890), as it has been construed by the Court, ruled that the Eleventh Amendment did not simply repeal the Citizen-State and Alien-State Clauses of Article III; instead, the Amendment was designed to incorporate the principle of sovereign immunity under which a state may not be sued in federal court without its consent.

Hans was a suit initiated in federal court against the State of Louisiana by a Louisiana plaintiff who alleged that the state had violated the Contracts Clause of Article I, §10 by reneging on bonds the state had issued during Reconstruction. Since the case arose under the Constitution, plaintiff had not attempted to enter federal court through either of the doors boarded up by the Eleventh Amendment but rather came in through the federal question door. The Court nevertheless held that the action had to be dismissed. Some have argued that *Hans* did not rest on the Eleventh Amendment and that it instead merely construed the federal question jurisdiction statute as having been intended to preserve the states' sovereign immunity. However, the Court has construed *Hans* as establishing the constitutional principle that states may not be sued in federal court without their consent — regardless of whether the suit is brought against the state by a foreign citizen, by a citizen of another state, or by one of the state's own citizens. The Court today still adheres to *Hans's* reinterpretation of the Eleventh Amendment under which "the principle of sovereign immunity is a constitutional limitation on the federal judicial power established in Art. III. . . ." *Pennhurst State School & Hosp. v. Halderman,* 465 U.S. 89, 98 (1984). As a result, there are in a sense "two Eleventh Amendments, the one ratified in 179[8], the other (so-called) invented by the Court nearly a century later in *Hans v. Louisiana.* . . . " *Seminole Tribe of Florida v. Florida,* 517 U.S. 44, 100 (1996) (Souter, J., dissenting).

In *Hans* and its progeny, the Court reinterpreted the Eleventh Amendment to expand the range of suits that cannot be filed against an unconsenting state in federal court. The Court's expansion of the Eleventh Amendment took another dramatic step in *Alden v. Maine,* 527 U.S. 706 (1999), which held by a vote of five to four that the states' sovereign immunity from suit likewise extends to suits brought against a state in its own courts. In reaching this conclusion, the Court explained that the states' "Eleventh Amendment immunity" is a "convenient shorthand but something of a misnomer, for the sovereign immunity of the States neither derives from nor is limited by the terms of the Eleventh Amendment." Id. at 713. Instead, that immunity stems "from the structure of the original Constitution itself" (id. at 728), which incorporated the traditional understanding that a sovereign was not subject to suit without its consent. The Eleventh Amendment confined itself to the federal judicial power because it was that power *Chisholm* had construed in a manner that departed from the original understanding. Until then, said the Court in *Alden,* "the Constitution was understood, in light of its history and structure, to preserve the States' traditional immunity from private suits. As the Amendment clarified the only provisions of the Constitution that anyone had suggested might support a contrary understanding, there was no reason to draft with a broader brush." Id. at 724. Thus, though the Eleventh Amendment speaks only of states' immunity from suit in federal court, the "original constitutional design" that it acted "to restore" embraced the fundamental structural principle that unconsenting states are shielded from private suits both in their own courts and in the federal courts. Id. at 722-724. On this basis, the *Alden* Court held that the State of Maine could not be sued by its employees in state court for having violated the provisions of the federal Fair Labor Standards Act. See also *Federal Maritime Commission v. S.C. State Ports Auth.,* 535 U.S. 743 (2002) (sovereign immunity bars a private party from instituting an administrative proceeding before the Federal Maritime Commission against a nonconsenting state agency).

If the Eleventh Amendment absolutely barred federal and state courts from hearing suits against a state without the state's consent, the Amendment would be relatively easy to apply. Over the years, however, the Court has carved a series of exceptions to the Eleventh Amendment that allow unconsenting states to be sued under a variety of circumstances. These exceptions cover (1) suits brought by the United States, (2) suits brought by another state, (3) suits in which the Supreme Court is reviewing the decision of a state court, (4) suits filed against state officials under the "stripping doctrine," (5) suits brought against a political subdivision of a state, and (6) suits as to which Congress has abrogated the states' Eleventh Amendment immunity. We will consider each of these exceptions in turn.

§4.2.2 Suits Filed by the United States

The Court has long recognized that despite *Hans*'s reading of the Eleventh Amendment as constitutionalizing the doctrine of state sovereign immunity, a state may be sued in federal or state court without its consent "where there has been 'a surrender of this immunity in the plan of the convention.'" *Monaco v. Mississippi*, 292 U.S. 313, 322-323 (1934) (quoting *Federalist No. 81*). One of the waivers of immunity deemed to have been implicit in the plan of the convention involves suits brought against a state by the United States itself. The United States as a superior sovereign must of necessity at times bring suits against a state; it would be ignominious and perhaps self-defeating if the United States had to do so in the courts of the defendant state. Thus despite the Eleventh Amendment, the United States might, for example, sue a state in federal court for breach of contract or to enjoin a state tax that discriminated against the federal government. And in *Alden v. Maine*, 527 U.S. 706, 759-760 (1999), the Supreme Court noted that even though the state was shielded from a private lawsuit to enforce the Fair Labor Standards Act (FLSA), the act could have been enforced against the state through a suit brought by the United States.

Since it may be impractical, however, for the United States to sue in every instance where a state has violated a federal law such as the FLSA, the question arises of whether the exception to the Eleventh Amendment for suits brought by the United States would still apply if Congress authorized private parties to sue the state on behalf of the federal government. Through so-called *qui tam* actions, Congress has from time to time allowed private parties to bring a civil suit on behalf of the United States. The plaintiff — known as the "relator" — receives a bounty if he or she wins the suit. However, *qui tam* actions usually involve suits against other private parties. In *Vermont Agency of Natural Resources v. United States ex rel. Stevens*, 529 U.S. 765 (2000), the Court held that the federal False Claims Act, which authorizes *qui tam* actions against any person who knowingly presents a false claim for payment to the United States, did not by its terms allow such an action to be brought against a state. Although the Court did not resolve the Eleventh Amendment question, it noted that there is "a serious doubt" as to "whether an action in federal court by a *qui tam* relator against a State" would satisfy the Eleventh Amendment. Id. at 787. It thus seems unlikely that Congress could use *qui tam* actions as a means of circumventing the states' Eleventh Amendment immunity.

§4.2.3 Suits Filed by Another State

The Court has likewise held that under the plan of the convention, the states implicitly waived their immunity from suit in federal court with respect to actions brought by other states. This exception makes sense, for if disputes between the states are to be resolved judicially, it is surely better that the litigation occur in a neutral federal forum rather than in a court operated by one of the interested parties. However, this exception to the Eleventh Amendment does not necessarily apply any time a suit is instituted against a state by another state. It may be invoked only if the plaintiff state is suing to redress either an injury to itself, or an injury suffered by a large proportion of its citizens who would otherwise have no means of obtaining redress. Moreover, the exception applies only to suits brought by one of the United States; suits instituted against a state by a foreign country remain subject to the Eleventh Amendment.

Example 4-A

The State of New Jersey imposes a special income tax on commuters from other states that results in out-of-state commuters paying a higher income tax to New Jersey than is paid by New Jersey's own citizens. The State of Pennsylvania, some of whose citizens pay the commuter tax to New Jersey, has brought an action against New Jersey in federal court, alleging that the discriminatory tax violates the Privileges and Immunities Clause of Article IV. May New Jersey prevent the federal court from hearing this case?

Explanation

The Eleventh Amendment probably bars the suit. While the action is between two states, the exception for suits brought against a state by another state does not apply because Pennsylvania is not suing to redress an injury directly to itself. Even if Pennsylvania may suffer an indirect economic injury in the form of reduced tax revenues if its citizens pay excessive taxes to New Jersey, this is too indirect an injury to permit the state to sue New Jersey in federal court.

Nor is Pennsylvania likely to be able to sue on behalf of its injured citizens. The New Jersey tax probably does not affect a substantial proportion of Pennsylvania's population but rather only those who work in New Jersey. In addition, those Pennsylvania citizens who are injured by the tax may challenge it before the New Jersey tax authorities. See *Pennsylvania v. New Jersey*, 426 U.S. 660 (1976).

By contrast, if Pennsylvania had sued New Jersey in federal court to challenge a New Jersey tax on electricity sold to Pennsylvania consumers and Pennsylvania was itself a buyer of New Jersey electricity, the suit would not necessarily be barred by the Eleventh Amendment since Pennsylvania would now be suing at least in part for an injury suffered directly by the state itself as a consumer. See *Maryland v. Louisiana*, 451 U.S. 725, 735-739 (1981). In general, as long as a state has a direct interest of its own in a legal controversy with another state, it may sue that state in federal court even if the remedy sought includes damages to residents of the suing state. The suing state must, however, be more than a nominal party and it must control the litigation as well as the ultimate disposition of any damages awarded. In other words, in representing its citizens the state must, during the pendency of the lawsuit, retain the authority "to deposit the proceeds of any judgment in the general coffers of the State or to use them to benefit those who were hurt." *Kansas v. Colorado*, 533 U.S. 1, 9 (2001).

§4.2.4 Bankruptcy Proceedings

The Supreme Court has held that in giving Congress the power to enact "uniform Laws on the subject of Bankruptcies throughout the United States," Art. I, §8, cl. 4, it was the Framers' intent that states would be amenable to such proceedings without the necessity for further consent on their part or formal abrogation on Congress's part. Instead, by ratifying the Bankruptcy Clause, the "States agreed in the plan of the Convention not to assert any sovereign immunity defense they might have had in proceedings brought pursuant to 'Laws on the subject of Bankruptcies.'" *Central Virginia Community College v. Katz*, 546 U.S. 356, 377 (2006). A federal court could thus hear a suit brought by a bankruptcy trustee against several Virginia state colleges, seeking to set aside preferential transfers made to the colleges by an insolvent debtor, despite the state's objection that sovereign immunity shielded it from federal court suit without the state's consent.

§4.2.5 Supreme Court Review of State Court Decisions

A state may of course consent to being sued in its own courts (see §4.2.9). Yet that does not necessarily mean that the state also consented to having the case reviewed by the U.S. Supreme Court under 28 U.S.C. §1257 (see §1.4.2). Since the Supreme Court exercises "[t]he Judicial power of the United States," the Eleventh Amendment would appear to shield an unconsenting state from such federal appellate review. However, the Court has long held that the Amendment does not apply to Supreme Court review of state court decisions even though the suit is one that the

Eleventh Amendment would have prevented the federal courts from hearing as an original matter.

Example 4-B

South Central Bell Telephone Company sued the State of Alabama in an Alabama state court seeking a refund of franchise taxes, claiming that the tax discriminated against out-of-state corporations in violation of the Commerce Clause (Art. I, §8, cl. 3). Alabama consented to allowing such actions to be filed against it in state court. The Alabama trial court dismissed the plaintiff's claim and the Alabama Supreme Court affirmed. The company now seeks review in the U.S. Supreme Court under 28 U.S.C. §1257. The State of Alabama has objected that the literal language of the Eleventh Amendment bars appellate jurisdiction because "this case began in state court as a suit brought against one State . . . by citizens of another. . . ." May the Supreme Court hear the case?

Explanation

The Eleventh Amendment poses no obstacle to the Supreme Court's hearing the case. Even though the suit could not have been filed in a state court or in a lower federal court without Alabama's consent, the Eleventh Amendment does not apply to the Supreme Court's exercise of appellate jurisdiction over suits from the state courts. See *South Central Bell Telephone Co. v. Alabama*, 526 U.S. 160, 165-166 (1999) (refusing to overturn the Court's "long-established and uniform practice of reviewing state-court decisions on federal matters, regardless of whether the State was the plaintiff or the defendant in the trial court").

§4.2.6 The Stripping Doctrine

Ex parte Young and the Fiction of Stripping

If the Eleventh Amendment were construed as barring all private suits instituted against unconsenting states, it would be virtually impossible to bring a federal or state court action to force a state to honor the Constitution and laws of the United States.

The Court has therefore recognized an exception to the Eleventh Amendment that allows suit to be brought to enjoin a state official from violating the Constitution or laws of the United States. In Ex parte Young, 209 U.S. 123 (1908), the Court explained this exception through the fiction that when a state official acts contrary to federal law, the official is thereby "stripped" of any state garb and transformed into an ordinary private individual. The stripping doctrine rests on the Supremacy Clause (Art. VI, cl. 2), which prohibits a state from violating the Constitution or laws of the United States. Since the state itself has no authority to violate federal law, it cannot confer such authority on its officials. A state official who acts contrary to federal law is therefore illegally attempting to use the name of the state to engage in conduct that the state is powerless to perform. A suit to enjoin that state official from violating federal law is therefore not a suit against the state for purposes of the Eleventh Amendment. Such suits are authorized by a federal statute, 42 U.S.C. §1983, which, first enacted in 1871, provides a cause of action for legal or equitable relief against any "person" who, while acting "under color of" state law, violates someone's federal constitutional or statutory rights. Those who may be sued as "persons" under this statute include cities, counties, and other political subdivisions of a state, as well as individual state and local governmental officials. However, suit cannot be brought under §1983 against a state itself or against a state-level agency. See §4.2.7.

Example 4-C

Verizon and MCI entered into a reciprocal compensation agreement for carrying the calls of each other's Maryland customers. The agreement was approved by a state agency — the Maryland Public Service Commission ("the Commission"). After the approval, Verizon informed MCI that it would not pay reciprocal compensation for calls made by Verizon's customers to the local access numbers of Internet service providers. In response to a complaint filed by MCI, the Commission ordered Verizon to make the contested payments. Verizon, claiming that the Commission's order violates federal law, has filed a suit against the individual commissioners in federal district court, seeking injunctive and declaratory relief. On the assumption that the State of Maryland has not waived sovereign immunity, is Verizon's suit barred by the Eleventh Amendment?

Explanation

No. This is a classic example of a case to which the stripping doctrine applies. Verizon's suit, naming the commissioners individually as defendants, will be treated as one against the commissioners and not as one against the state. Furthermore, as the Court stated in *Verizon Maryland Inc. v. Public Service Commission of Maryland*, 535 U.S. 635 (2002), "In determining whether the doctrine of *Ex parte Young* avoids an Eleventh Amendment bar to suit, a court need only conduct a straightforward inquiry into whether [the] complaint alleges an ongoing violation of federal law and seeks relief properly characterized as prospective." Id. at 645. Consistent with this statement of principle, Verizon alleges that the Commission's order is an ongoing violation of federal law to the extent that it requires Verizon to continue making the contested payments. As a remedy Verizon seeks the prospective relief of an injunction.

The stripping doctrine is a fiction since in nearly every instance where a state official violates a person's federal rights, the official has acted within the scope of his or her official duties and pursuant to a custom, policy, or law of the state. Whether or not the state in *theory* could authorize such conduct, the state in *fact* authorized or permitted the violation to occur, with the result that someone was injured. It is a fiction to pretend that the injury was caused by an ordinary private individual rather than by an official representative of the state.

Yet if, as the fiction suggests, state officials cease to be representatives of the state the moment they violate federal law, a state could never violate the Constitution. The state itself is a legal abstraction that can act only through its officers, agents, and employees. Unless the conduct of these individuals is deemed to be that of the state, it would be literally impossible for a state ever to violate the Fourteenth Amendment or any other constitutional provision that restrains the state's behavior. The Court has therefore held that the stripping doctrine applies only to the Eleventh Amendment and not to other constitutional provisions. As the Court has noted, there is "the 'well-recognized irony' that an official's unconstitutional conduct constitutes state action under the Fourteenth Amendment but not the Eleventh Amendment." *Pennhurst State School & Hosp. v. Halderman*, 465 U.S. 89, 105 (1984).

While the *Ex parte Young* stripping doctrine is an exception to the Eleventh Amendment's ban on suits against a state, the doctrine is consistent with *Hans*'s view that the Eleventh Amendment incorporated the doctrine of sovereign immunity. The ancient doctrine of sovereign immunity rested on the precept that "the king can do no wrong." The king's officers, however, were not shielded by sovereign immunity and could be sued when they violated the law. The stripping doctrine recognizes a similar distinction. Although the Eleventh Amendment shields the state from suit in federal or state court, the state's officers, agents, and employees enjoy no similar immunity and may be sued if they violate the federal Constitution or laws.

The stripping doctrine sometimes allows a federal court to enforce obligations on state officials that go beyond those specifically imposed by federal law. This may occur in situations where a suit brought against state officials to enforce some provision of federal law results in a settlement that is reduced to a so-called *consent decree*. Under the terms of the decree, state officials may have agreed to provisions that go beyond what the federal statute specifically requires. It might be argued that the stripping doctrine should not allow judicial enforcement of such provisions, on the theory that as to them, the state was not acting contrary to federal law. However, the Supreme Court has rejected this contention, noting that a consent decree "is a federal court order that springs from a federal dispute and furthers the objectives of federal law." *Frew ex rel. Frew v. Hawkins*, 540 U.S. 431, 438 (2004). As such, it "reflects a choice among various ways that a State could implement" federal law; therefore, "enforcing the decree vindicates an agreement that the state officials reached to comply with federal law." Id. at 439.

Designating the Proper Defendant

To invoke the stripping doctrine, plaintiff must be careful to sue a *named state official* rather than the *state* itself, a *state agency*, or a *state office*. This is necessary to preserve the fiction on which the stripping doctrine rests, namely, that the suit is against an individual and not against the state. At the same time, a plaintiff alleging a constitutional violation must also make it clear to the court that the conduct complained of was action of the state and not that of a purely private individual, for otherwise the Constitution would not apply to the challenged action. To satisfy these seemingly contradictory requirements, plaintiffs must sue the defendant state officials *by name*, and must indicate that the officials are being sued both in their "individual capacity" *and* in their "official capacity." The "individual capacity" designation preserves the fiction on which the Eleventh Amendment stripping doctrine rests; the "official capacity" designation reveals that the action complained of was that of the state for purposes of establishing a constitutional violation.

Example 4-D

Jerry is an inmate at an Alabama state prison. He filed suit in an Alabama federal court claiming that conditions at the prison constitute cruel and unusual punishment in violation of the Eighth and Fourteenth Amendments. Jerry named various defendants, including "the State of Alabama; the Alabama Board of Corrections; the Governor of Alabama; and Judson Locke, individually and in his official capacity as Commissioner of the Alabama Board of Corrections." May any of the defendants have the action dismissed on the ground that it is barred by the Eleventh Amendment?

Explanation

The action must be dismissed as to all defendants except Judson Locke. The stripping doctrine cannot be applied to the State of Alabama or to the Board of Corrections since neither of these defendants is an individual. Nor does the doctrine apply to the governor of Alabama since the action has not been filed against the person who occupies this office but only against the office. However, the action is proper against Judson Locke since Jerry was careful to sue this defendant by name both in his individual capacity and in his official capacity as a commissioner, thereby successfully invoking the stripping doctrine. See *Alabama v. Pugh*, 438 U.S. 781 (1978).

Prospective versus Retroactive Relief

The fact that plaintiff is careful to sue a state official rather than the state, a state agency, or a state office will not always guarantee that the suit will survive an Eleventh Amendment challenge. The Court has warned that even if "a State is not named a party to the action, the suit may nonetheless be barred by the Eleventh Amendment. . . . '[W]hen the action is in essence one for the recovery of money from the state, the state is the real, substantial party in interest and is entitled to invoke its sovereign immunity from suit even though individual officials are nominal defendants.'" *Edelman v. Jordan*, 415 U.S. 651, 663 (1974).

The prohibition against suits to recover money from the state is also the basis for the Court's having limited the stripping doctrine to claims for prospective relief — i.e., relief directed toward the future behavior of the defendant, such as an injunction to prevent a continuing violation of federal law. The stripping doctrine thus does not apply to claims for retroactive relief — i.e., relief designed as a remedy for past behavior, such as damages, compensation, or an injunction directed at undoing a completed transaction. The Eleventh Amendment bars claims for retroactive relief. Even if a suit is nominally against a state official, it is still barred by the Eleventh Amendment if the retroactive relief will require payment of funds from the state treasury. On the other hand, a federal court may order state officials to pay money that will come from the state's treasury in connection with the award of prospective relief; this is permitted, for example, when a court awards plaintiff's attorney's fees or costs in a suit for injunctive relief, or where a state official is fined for contempt in violating a federal injunction.

The relief sought in Ex parte Young was consistent with these limitations on use of the stripping doctrine. Plaintiffs there sued the Minnesota attorney general to enjoin continued enforcement of a railroad rate statute that violated the Fourteenth Amendment. Such prospective injunctive relief to bar a state official from violating the Constitution in the future did not run afoul of the Eleventh Amendment. While the defendant official's compliance with the injunction would cost the state money in the form of fines it could no longer collect from railroads that ignored the rate law, this incidental impact on the state treasury was an inevitable consequence of requiring that state officials comply prospectively with federal law. On the other hand, the plaintiffs in Young would have been barred by the Eleventh Amendment from attempting to recoup any fines they may have paid to the state under the challenged rate statute.

Example 4-E

John brought a class action in federal court on behalf of himself and other Illinois welfare recipients and applicants against Robert Smith, the director of the Illinois Department of Welfare, alleging that because the department failed to process welfare applications within the time periods required by federal law, eligible recipients were denied benefits for many months. In his complaint, John sued Smith both individually and in his official capacity as director of the welfare department. John sought an injunction ordering that Smith adhere to the federal timetables and that he release all benefits wrongfully withheld from members of the plaintiff class. Is the suit barred by the Eleventh Amendment?

Explanation

Although the complaint named only a state official rather than the state or a state agency, to the extent John seeks an order requiring Smith to make retroactive payments based on past violations of federal law, the suit is in reality against the state treasury and is barred by the Eleventh Amendment. However, that part of the suit which seeks an injunction against future violations of federal law falls squarely within the stripping doctrine and is deemed to be a suit against Robert Smith rather than against the state. The claim for prospective relief is not barred by the Eleventh Amendment despite the fact that it will probably cost the state millions of dollars to comply with the court's decree. "Such an ancillary effect on the state treasury is a permissible and often an inevitable consequence of the principle announced in Ex parte Young. . . . " Edelman v. Jordan, supra, 415 U.S. at 668.

Even though prospective relief is usually injunctive in nature, ordering governmental officials to take certain specified action, it sometimes takes monetary form. For example, if, under the stripping doctrine, a federal court issues an injunction and the state official to whom it is directed then fails in good faith to comply with the order, a federal court may award attorney's fees to the plaintiff's lawyers, to be paid from the state treasury. Though such an order may have the appearance of a damages award, it is distinguishable in that instead of being based on past behavior, it is ancillary to and an inseparable part of a federal court's authority to enforce a prospective injunction. As the Supreme Court explained, "In exercising their prospective powers under Ex parte Young and Edelman v. Jordan, federal courts are not reduced to issuing injunctions against state officers and hoping for compliance. Once issued, an injunction may be enforced. . . . If a state agency refuses to adhere to a court order, a financial penalty may be the most effective means of insuring compliance." Hutto v. Finney, 437 U.S. 678, 690-691 (1978).

Holding Officials Personally Liable in Damages

Despite the Eleventh Amendment, a plaintiff may be able to obtain retroactive relief against state officials for past violations of federal law if it is clear that the recovery is sought solely from the official's own pocket and not from the state treasury. Under these circumstances, the fiction on which the stripping doctrine rests — i.e., that the suit is against the individual official personally and not against the state — is preserved and the suit is not barred by the Eleventh Amendment. This is true even if the state has agreed to indemnify the official for any damages the official is ordered to pay. While a damages judgment against the official will ultimately result in money being paid from the state treasury, this is a consequence of the state's voluntary decision to indemnify its officials. If the mere existence of an indemnity agreement were sufficient to block a damages claim against a state official under the Eleventh Amendment, every state would make such an agreement since it would cost them nothing. The very fact of the agreement would prevent the official from ever being found liable and the obligation to indemnify would therefore never arise.

Although the Eleventh Amendment will pose no bar to recovering retroactive damages from a state official personally, the official may be shielded by common law immunity. Because the Supreme Court has read this immunity into 42 U.S.C. §1983, the statute that allows state and local officials to be sued for having violated an individual's federal rights, the immunity applies whether the §1983 action is brought in federal or state court. The purpose of common law immunity is to ensure that government officials will not be unduly inhibited in discharging their duties, out of fear that they could be subject to personal monetary liability. It is also designed to free them from the burden of having to defend against lawsuits based on insubstantial claims, a burden that could seriously impair government's ability to function. These common law immunities protect both state and local governmental officials.

The extent of an official's common law immunity from civil liability will depend on the type of function the official was performing when he or she violated the plaintiff's rights. If the function was legislative in nature, the official is absolutely immune from civil suit — including both damages claims and claims for declaratory or injunctive relief. If the function was prosecutorial or judicial in nature, the immunity is likewise absolute, but only as to damages claims; as to the latter, however, the immunity attaches no matter how blatant or willful the violation may have been. The same absolute immunity extends to government officials who appear as witnesses before a grand jury or at trial. *Rehberg v. Paulk*, 132 S. Ct. 1497 (2012). For other types of governmental functions, such as executive and ministerial actions, the official possesses a qualified immunity but solely with respect to claims for damages. Under qualified immunity, a defendant official will not be held liable for damages if a reasonable person in defendant's shoes would not have realized that their conduct was in violation of federal law. This shields an official from damages liability if, in light of preexisting law, the legal rule or right in question was not "clearly established" at the time the violation occurred. *Pearson v. Callahan*, 555 U.S. 223, 232 (2009). The test is one of "objective legal reasonableness." *Harlow v. Fitzgerald*, 457 U.S. 800, 819 (1982). Private individuals who are temporally retained by the government to help carry out its work likewise enjoy a qualified immunity in suits brought against them under §1983. *Filarsky v. Delia*, 132 S. Ct. 1657 (2012).

Similar principles apply to federal government officials — with the exception of the President who enjoys absolute immunity from civil damages liability for all conduct within the outer perimeter of his office. See §§7.7, 7.8.1.

The Supreme Court has not resolved the question of what sources of law are sufficient to "clearly establish" a right for purposes of the qualified immunity doctrine. In the case of a federal statutory right, the statute itself may be sufficiently clear to satisfy the requirement. With respect to constitutional rights, or statutory rights that are facially unclear, the rights must be clarified and refined by case law. The question is, what courts are sufficient for this purpose? Some federal circuits insist on a ruling from the U.S. Supreme Court, from the court of appeals for that circuit, or perhaps from a state supreme court. Other federal circuits are less rigid in their approach. One of the Supreme Court's more recent decisions in this area, *Hope v. Pelzer*, 536 U.S. 730 (2002), discussed below, suggests a more eclectic approach.

In deciding, for qualified immunity purposes, whether a legal right or rule was clearly established at the time defendant acted, the rule must not be described at so abstract a *level of generality* that it ignores the circumstances under which the defendant was acting. Thus, in *Anderson v. Creighton*, 483 U.S. 635 (1987), involving an FBI agent's warrantless search of a home where a bank robber was believed to be hiding, the lower court rejected the agent's qualified immunity defense on the ground that there was a clearly established Fourth Amendment right to be free from warrantless searches of one's home unless probable cause and exigent circumstances exist. The Supreme Court held that this was too general and abstract a level at which to frame the relevant legal rule. Instead, said the Court, the question was whether, under the circumstances that the officer confronted, "a reasonable officer could have believed [the] warrantless search to be lawful, in light of clearly established law *and the information the searching officers possessed*." Id. at 641 (emphasis supplied).

This does not mean that the precedents and legal authorities establishing the principle of law on which the plaintiff relies must involve facts identical to those giving rise to the lawsuit. "We do not require a case directly on point, but existing precedent must have placed the statutory or constitutional question beyond debate." *Ashcroft v. al-Kidd*, 131 S. Ct. 2074,

2083 (2011). The test is one of reasonable notice. "[O]fficials can still be on notice that their conduct violates established law even in novel factual circumstances. . . . Although earlier cases involving 'fundamentally similar' facts can provide especially strong support for a conclusion that the law is clearly established, they are not necessary to such a finding." *Hope v. Pelzer*, 536 U.S. 730, 741 (2002). The question in every case is simply whether "at the time of the challenged conduct, the contours of a right are sufficiently clear that every reasonable official would have understood that what he is doing violates that right," *Ashcroft v. al-Kidd*, supra, 131 S. Ct. at 2083. The answer to this question in *Ashcroft* was an easy one, for the Court unanimously agreed that at the relevant point in time, "not a single judicial opinion" supported al-Kidd's theory as to why his Fourth Amendment rights were violated. Id.

The Court used this same standard in *Hope v. Pelzer*, supra, to conclude that Alabama prison guards, as of 1995, had fair warning that handcuffing a prisoner to a hitching post in the sun for seven hours with his arms extended above his shoulders, and with only one or two opportunities to drink water and no bathroom breaks, was cruel and unusual punishment within the meaning of the Eighth Amendment. That fair warning derived from two circuit precedents, from a regulation of the Alabama Department of Corrections (ADOC), and from a U.S. Department of Justice (DOJ) report issued to the ADOC. As to the circuit precedents, the first, decided in 1974, found a number of violations of constitutional rights in Mississippi prisons, including a finding that the practice of handcuffing inmates to a fence or cell for long periods of time was cruel and unusual punishment. 536 U.S. at 741-742. The other circuit court opinion, albeit in dicta, had explained that withholding water solely as a punishment for a previous refusal to work or when a prisoner's health was at risk would constitute actionable violations of the Eighth Amendment. Id. at 743. The ADOC regulation required water every 15 minutes and the DOJ report notified the ADOC of the "constitutional infirmity" of using the hitching post. Taken together, these materials, along with what the Court described as the "obvious cruelty" of the practice, constituted fair notice to the prison guards. Id. at 742-745.

In *Hope v. Pelzer*, the various authorities relied upon by the Court — several federal court of appeals' decisions, state regulations, and a Department of Justice report — all pointed in the same direction and suggested that the guards' conduct was unconstitutional. However, where none of the relevant authorities "squarely governs the case," and where the closest existing authorities point in different directions depending on the specific facts involved, the conduct in question may then be said to fall on the "hazy border" between constitutional and unconstitutional, with the result that the "clearly established" requirement is not met. *Brosseau v. Haugen*, 543 U.S.

194, 200-201 (2004) (split of lower court authority barred a finding that the right in question was "clearly established"). Similarly, where there is a substantial and credible difference of opinion among lower courts as to the proper interpretation of a controlling Supreme Court precedent, the standard emanating from that precedent will not be treated as "clearly established" in cases falling within the bounds of that interpretive disagreement. See *Safford Unified School District #1 v. Redding*, 557 U.S. 364, 377-379 (2009) (so holding).

The Supreme Court has strongly suggested that in applying the qualified immunity doctrine with respect to both federal and state officials, all doubts are to be resolved in favor of the defendant. As the Court explained, the immunity is designed to "give[] government officials breathing room to make reasonable but mistaken judgments about open legal questions. When properly applied, it protects all but the plainly incompetent or those who knowingly violate the law." *Ashcroft v. al-Kidd*, supra, 131 S. Ct. at 2085 (federal official); and see *Messerschmidt v. Millender*, 132 S. Ct. 1235, 1244-1245 (2012) (state officials).

Example 4-F

In Example 4-E suppose that instead of suing the Illinois welfare director on behalf of a class, John sued only on behalf of himself. Will the Eleventh Amendment bar a federal court from ordering the director to pay John the benefits that were withheld from him in violation of federal law?

Explanation

The Eleventh Amendment compels dismissal of John's claim for monetary relief only if the funds must be paid from the state treasury. If John makes clear in his complaint that retroactive relief is being sought solely from Smith personally and not from the state, the damages claim will not be barred by the Eleventh Amendment.

Yet Smith might still be shielded by common law immunity. Since he was performing an executive (as opposed to a legislative, prosecutorial, or judicial) function, he has only a qualified rather than an absolute immunity. To successfully invoke this immunity, Smith would have to show that a reasonable official in his position would not have realized that federal law required welfare applications to be processed within set time periods.

Even if the statute itself or prior case law from a court of sufficient stature clearly established that welfare applicants have the legal right to have their applications processed within a set time period, Smith might argue that this is too general a level at which to formulate the legal rule.

Instead, he might insist that the legal rule be framed to take into account the particular circumstances with which he was confronted. For example, suppose he had received assurances from federal officials that the time limits would be temporarily suspended. Or suppose the delay had resulted from a lengthy strike by welfare case workers and that Smith believed that this constituted an "emergency exception" under the federal statute. Smith might then successfully argue that even if there were a clearly established legal rule that welfare applications must be processed within a set time, he is entitled to qualified immunity because a reasonable official in his *particular circumstances* would not have thought his conduct to be unlawful.

Example 4-G

Sally, a lawyer, has sued the justices of her state supreme court under 42 U.S.C. §1983, alleging that the Rules of Professional Conduct that the court promulgates and enforces to regulate attorney advertising violate the First Amendment. Her complaint seeks damages for lost business, and an injunction barring enforcement of the rules against her. The justices have moved to dismiss the suit on the basis of common law immunity. How should the court rule on the motion?

Explanation

The motion should be granted in part and denied in part. Though the defendants are judges, the acts for which they are being sued do not involve judicial or adjudicative conduct. Instead, to the extent they promulgated rules governing attorney advertising, the judges were performing a legislative function. As such, they are absolutely immune from civil suit, whether the claim is for damages or for prospective injunctive relief. To the extent that the justices are responsible for enforcing the rules by initiating proceedings against attorneys, they function in a prosecutorial capacity, giving them absolute immunity from damages claims but no immunity from injunctive relief. Thus Sally's claim for damages must be dismissed, but her request to enjoin future enforcement of the rules against her is not barred by common law immunity. See *Supreme Court of Virginia v. Consumers Union of the United States*, 446 U.S. 719 (1980).

Example 4-H

Cookie was released from prison after establishing that his murder conviction depended on the false testimony of a jailhouse informant who had received reduced sentences for providing prosecutors with favorable testimony in previous cases. Cookie claims that prosecutors knew but failed to give his attorney this potential impeachment information and that this failure led to his erroneous conviction. He has now filed a §1983 lawsuit against the district attorney for having failed to properly train and supervise the prosecutors. The district attorney claims she is entitled to absolute immunity. Is she correct?

Explanation

The answer depends on the nature of the activity for which the district attorney is being sued. If the activity is properly characterized as prosecutorial, the district attorney is entitled to absolute immunity. If, on the other hand, the activity is deemed administrative, only qualified immunity is available. At first blush, "training and supervision" appears to be administrative. Such activities fall within the district attorney's duty to run and administer her office. Yet looked at more closely, there is a strong argument that the training and supervision at issue here are functionally prosecutorial. After all, it is the specific prosecutor's failure to disclose that is at the heart of Cookie's claim. Moreover, the choices made by the district attorney in determining how to train and supervise them necessarily required legal knowledge and the exercise of related discretion pertaining to prosecutions. In this sense, the ostensibly administrative chores are intimately and functionally involved with the actual trial process. See *Van de Kamp v. Goldstein*, 555 U.S. 335 (2009) (training and supervision of prosecutorial trial practices are the functional equivalent of specific prosecution for purposes of absolute immunity).

Finally, it should be noted that even in those situations where common law immunity does not pose an obstacle to the recovery of damages, obtaining monetary relief from individual state officials who have violated a plaintiff's federal rights will succeed only where the damages sought are fairly small or where the official happens to be wealthy.

No Stripping for State Law Claims

The stripping doctrine allows federal courts to grant relief against individual state officials because of the need to protect the supremacy of federal law. This supremacy rationale does not apply where a state official is alleged to have violated state law. The Supreme Court has therefore refused to extend the stripping doctrine to state law claims. *Pennhurst State School & Hosp. v. Halderman*, 465 U.S. 89 (1984). Regardless of the type of relief sought, a claim against a state official for violating state law is deemed to be a claim against the state and is barred by the Eleventh Amendment. Such claims are barred even if they would otherwise fall within a federal court's subject matter jurisdiction based on the existence of diversity or supplemental jurisdiction.

Example 4-1

Mary was fired from her job with the Arizona Department of Highways for having criticized the state's governor. She has sued Jim Jones, the director of the department, in federal court, seeking reinstatement and back pay on the ground that the firing violated her free speech rights under the federal and state constitutions. Is Mary's suit barred by the Eleventh Amendment?

Explanation

The stripping doctrine applies to Mary's federal constitutional claim as long as she sued the director both individually and in his official capacity. Under the stripping doctrine her claim for reinstatement is proper since it will prevent the director from continuing to penalize Mary for having exercised her free speech rights. The claim for back pay involves retroactive relief. Under the stripping doctrine, monetary relief may not be awarded from the state treasury, but the court may order the director to pay this money from his own pocket, unless he can show that he is protected by qualified immunity. Mary's federal constitutional claim is therefore not barred by the Eleventh Amendment.

Mary's claim for relief under the state constitution must be dismissed. While she sued the director rather than the state or a state agency, the stripping doctrine does not apply to state law claims. Since that claim is deemed to be against the state, it is barred by the Eleventh Amendment even though it would otherwise fall within the court's supplemental jurisdiction.

The doctrine of sovereign immunity incorporated into the Eleventh Amendment is thus broader than the common law doctrine of sovereign immunity. At common law, the king's officers enjoyed no immunity from suit if they violated people's rights under the law. Under the Eleventh Amendment, by contrast, state officials are shielded from suit for any violations of state law.

Congressional Restriction of the Stripping Doctrine

The stripping doctrine is a judge-made exception to the Eleventh Amendment. When it applies, the doctrine has the consequence of allowing claims that arise under federal law to be brought against state officials. As we saw in Chapter 2, Congress has the power to narrow the lower federal courts' subject matter jurisdiction by excluding certain cases, even those that may arise under federal law. Consistent with these principles Congress may, if it wishes, direct that the stripping doctrine not be employed in selected federal question cases, with the result that these claims against state officials would be barred from federal court. Thus, Congress can in effect expand the states' Eleventh Amendment immunity beyond that established by the Supreme Court.

Congress's intent to limit use of the stripping doctrine may be either express or implied. In *Seminole Tribe of Florida v. Florida*, 517 U.S. 44 (1996), the Court found an implied intent to bar use of the stripping doctrine in a case where plaintiffs sought a federal injunction requiring the governor of Florida to negotiate with local Indian tribes as required by the federal Indian Gaming Regulatory Act. In the Court's view, for a federal judge to issue an injunction that could be enforced through the court's contempt powers would impose a more drastic mode of enforcement than the "modest set of sanctions" provided for under the "carefully crafted and intricate remedial scheme" created by Congress. Id. at 73-76. Since the stripping doctrine could not be used in this particular setting, plaintiffs' case against the governor was barred by the Eleventh Amendment as a suit against the state.

Example 4-J

In Example 4-E above, we concluded that under the stripping doctrine, a federal court could enjoin the Illinois welfare director from continuing to ignore federal time limits for processing welfare applications. Assume now that federal law established a complaint procedure for persons dissatisfied with a state's handling of their welfare application. Under this statutory procedure, an applicant may file a complaint with the regional office of the U.S. Department of Health and Human Services. If the regional office cannot resolve the matter, the complaint will be referred to the secretary of Health and Human Services, who is authorized to withhold funding from the state until compliance is ensured. Can Illinois welfare recipients still obtain a federal injunction ordering the welfare director to comply with the time limits mandated by federal law?

Explanation

While Congress has not expressly barred the federal court from issuing an injunction to enforce the statutory time limits, Congress has provided a remedial scheme that may be sufficiently detailed to create an inference that Congress did not want federal courts enforcing the time limits through injunctive relief backed by the power to impose contempt sanctions against state officials. On this basis, a court might conclude that the stripping doctrine cannot be employed in this case and that the suit for injunctive relief is barred by the Eleventh Amendment as a suit against the state.

In cases involving federal *constitutional* rights, the Court may be less willing to infer a congressional intent to bar use of the stripping doctrine than it was in *Seminole Tribe*, where only a *statutory* right was at stake. Before finding that the stripping doctrine cannot be employed in a case involving constitutional rights, the Court would perhaps insist that Congress's intent be stated expressly, and that the alternative remedies available to plaintiff be adequate. Where these conditions were met, Congress could bar use of the stripping doctrine even in a constitutional case. Although the Court has not addressed this question in terms of the Eleventh Amendment, it has allowed Congress to selectively deny lower federal courts the power to grant injunctive relief in constitutional cases. In such instances plaintiffs must litigate their constitutional claims in state court, with possible review in the Supreme Court.

Example 4-K

In Example 4-A above, suppose that a group of Pennsylvania commuters who worked in New Jersey had challenged the constitutionality of New Jersey's commuter income tax by suing Mia Wolfe, New Jersey's director of revenue, in a New Jersey federal court, seeking an injunction against continued collection of the tax and a refund of taxes already paid. Wolfe was sued in her individual and official capacities. Is the suit barred by the Eleventh Amendment?

Explanation

Even if the stripping doctrine applied here, the refund claim is probably barred by the Eleventh Amendment as a suit against the state. Though plaintiffs have named only a state official, the amounts sought are such that they probably must come from the state treasury. Unless plaintiffs made clear that they were seeking monetary relief solely from Wolfe's personal assets, the refund claim would be dismissed.

The claim for prospective injunctive relief would qualify under the stripping doctrine but for the fact that Congress has barred use of the doctrine in cases of this type. The Tax Injunction Act, 28 U.S.C. §1341, prohibits lower federal courts from enjoining collection of a state tax if "a plain, speedy and efficient remedy" exists in state court. Though the act does not mention the Eleventh Amendment or the stripping doctrine by name, it has the same effect as a law that read, "[T]he stripping doctrine shall not apply in any suit to enjoin collection of a state tax." Assuming New Jersey's courts will hear a challenge to the validity of the state tax, plaintiffs' claim for injunctive relief must be dismissed.

§4.2.7 Suits Against Governmental Entities

The Eleventh Amendment's prohibition against bringing a suit against an unconsenting state does not protect "political subdivisions such as counties and municipalities even though such entities exercise a 'slice of state power.'" *Lake Country Estates, Inc. v. Tahoe Regional Planning Agency*, 440 U.S. 391, 401 (1979). The reason for this is that the states' immunity from suit derives from the sovereignty they possessed prior to ratification of the Constitution, a sovereignty that was not enjoyed by cities, counties, or other political subdivisions of a state. As a result, under the Eleventh Amendment, "only States and arms of the State possess immunity from suits authorized by federal law." *Northern Insurance Company of New York v. Chatham County*, 547 U.S. 189, 193 (2006). The Eleventh Amendment's narrow definition of "state" stands in sharp contrast to many other constitutional provisions such as the Fourteenth Amendment, in which the word "state" is deemed to embrace all of a state's political subdivisions.

Classifying a Governmental Entity

Governmental entities other than cities, counties, and political subdivisions of the state may qualify for Eleventh Amendment immunity if it is determined that they are in effect acting as arms of the state. However, it may at times be difficult to decide whether a particular governmental entity should be treated as being part of the state and therefore shielded by the Eleventh Amendment, or whether it is a political subdivision of the state that enjoys no Eleventh Amendment protection. Some cases are easy. The various departments, offices, and bureaus of the state government are part of the state. These could include such entities as the state Office of Education, the state Department of Highways, and the attorney general's office. At the opposite extreme, cities, counties, mosquito abatement districts, community college districts, and metropolitan water districts are political subdivisions of the state.

The Court has identified a number of factors that may be helpful in determining an entity's status for purposes of the Eleventh Amendment. The most important of these is the source of the entity's funding. If the entity is funded largely or entirely by the state, so that a judgment against the entity will operate against the state treasury, it is very likely the entity will be protected by the Eleventh Amendment. On the other hand, if the entity receives funding from sources other than the state, or if it has been given the power to generate its own funds, such as through taxation or the issuance of bonds, it is more likely to be treated as an independent non-state entity. Other relevant factors, besides funding, include the extent of state control over the entity; the type of functions the entity performs; and how the state has designated the entity. In *Lake Country Estates*, the Court applied these factors in concluding that a bi-state agency created by a compact between California and Nevada enjoyed no Eleventh Amendment immunity. The agency was funded by the counties in which it operated, not by the states; the agency's governing board was controlled by counties and cities rather than by the states; the agency performed land use functions of a type traditionally undertaken by local governments; and the states had identified the agency as being a "separate legal entity" and "a political subdivision." 440 U.S. at 401.

Example 4-L

Florence was fired from her job with the University of California after the university discovered that she was a member of a radical underground group. Florence had been working on a project funded heavily by the federal government. In its contract with the federal government, the university agreed that no one posing a security risk would be allowed to work on the project. Florence has sued the university in federal court under 42 U.S.C. §1983 claiming that the university violated her First Amendment right of free association. She seeks damages of $250,000. May the federal court hear her suit?

Explanation

The suit is barred by the Eleventh Amendment. Courts have found the university to be part of the state for a number of reasons: The university is funded by the State of California; it is controlled by a board of regents appointed by the governor; higher education is a function traditionally assumed by the state rather than by local government; and the state has treated the university as being an arm of the state. See, e.g., *Mascheroni v. Board of Regents*, 28 F.3d 1554, 1559 (10th Cir. 1994).

Once the university is deemed to be part of the state for Eleventh Amendment purposes, Florence's suit will also fail on the ground that she has no cause of action, for neither the state nor a state entity is a "person" who can be sued under §1983. See *Thompson v. City of Los Angeles*, 885 F.2d 1439, 1442-1443 (9th Cir. 1989).

———————————

An entity that is normally not protected by the Eleventh Amendment because it is deemed to be a political subdivision of a state may sometimes be immunized from suit in federal court. If a judgment against the entity would in effect be a judgment against the state treasury, the court will ignore the fact that the suit is nominally against a political subdivision and treat the action as being one against the state or a state officer. Whether or not the suit is barred will then depend on whether any of the exceptions to the Eleventh Amendment applies.

Example 4-M

Suppose that a county administers a state-funded welfare program. A class action is brought in federal court against county officials by program recipients who claim that benefit levels are lower than required by federal law. Plaintiffs seek an injunction ordering the county to raise benefits to the federally mandated levels and pay retroactive benefits to the plaintiff class. Is the suit barred by the Eleventh Amendment?

Explanation

While counties normally are not protected by the Eleventh Amendment since they are political subdivisions of the state, the Amendment applies here since the relief sought runs against the state. The claim for retroactive benefits must be dismissed because it is in effect a suit against the state treasury. The claim for prospective injunctive relief, however, even when treated as being a suit against state officials, is not barred by the Eleventh Amendment, for the stripping doctrine allows the court to enjoin state officials from continuing to violate a federal law.

The fact that cities, counties, and other political subdivisions of the state are usually not shielded by the Eleventh Amendment means that federal and state courts can potentially issue money judgments against these entities. Thus, it is beneficial for a plaintiff to sue, if possible, a political subdivision of the state rather than the state, a state agency, or a state-level official.

Stating a Cause of Action: §1983

However, to sue a political subdivision of the state, the plaintiff must have a cause of action; i.e., the law must afford plaintiff the right to recover for the injury complained of. As we noted earlier, a federal statute, 42 U.S.C. §1983, gives a cause of action against any *"person"* who, while acting *"under color of state law,"* deprives a plaintiff of a federal constitutional or statutory right. Section 1983 is the primary vehicle used for asserting claims against state and local officials who have violated a plaintiff's federal rights.

The Supreme Court has held that neither states nor state-level agencies are "persons" within the meaning of §1983. A plaintiff may therefore only sue the individual state officials or employees who impaired her federal rights; she may not sue the state itself or the state agency or state entity for whom the individual defendant was working.

Cities, counties, and other political subdivisions of the state, on the other hand, are "persons" within the meaning of §1983. Suits for legal or equitable relief may be brought directly against these entities, but only if plaintiff can prove that the conduct causing her injury was taken pursuant to an official policy or custom of the entity. *Monell v. Department of Social Services*, 436 U.S. 658, 694 (1978). Liability may not be imposed on a political subdivision simply on a theory of respondeat superior or vicarious liability. Id. at 691. Absent a proven custom or policy, the entity cannot be held liable in damages or made subject to prospective injunctive relief. *Los Angeles County v. Humphries*, 131 S. Ct. 447 (2010) (absent a proven county custom or policy, court in a §1983 action could not enjoin county based on constitutional wrongs of its employees).

A subdivision's policy or custom need not be a written one in order to trigger §1983 liability. Instead, it may consist of "deliberate indifference" on the entity's part to a pattern or practice of constitutional violations by its employees, where the entity has taken no steps to prevent such violations through the provision of adequate training. *Connick v. Thompson*, 131 S. Ct. 1350, 1359-1360 (2011). If a custom or policy is shown to exist, plaintiff may then seek both damages and prospective relief from the entity and from the individuals who acted on its behalf. Moreover, while the entity's officers or employees may be shielded from damages liability by absolute or qualified common law immunity (see §§4.2.6, 4.6), the entity itself enjoys no common law immunity. This rule encourages cities and counties to respect the people's federal rights, even in areas where the precise scope of these rights may be unclear. Thus, while a lack of clarity will shield an individual defendant from liability through the doctrine of common law immunity, the entity, because it can be held liable even in cases of doubt, is likely to err on the side of over rather than underprotecting an individual's federal rights.

The "under color of state law" requirement of §1983 is satisfied in cases brought against political subdivisions of the state as long as the action complained of was within the scope of the officer's or employee's official duties or responsibilities, as opposed, for example, to action that was taken after hours or while the employee was on vacation. As long as the action was within the scope of the employee's city or county duties, there is no requirement that a state law also have sanctioned the conduct.

Example 4-N

Cecil filed suit in federal court against the City of Los Pulgas and against Ann Mills, director of the city public library, claiming that Ann regularly denies him use of the library because he is a homeless person. Cecil alleged that defendants' conduct violates his Fourteenth Amendment rights to receive information, to obtain an education, and to equal protection of the law. Cecil prayed for injunctive relief and for damages of $50,000. May the federal court hear Cecil's suit?

Explanation

First, Cecil has stated a cause of action under §1983. Ann is a "person" who was acting "under color of state law" since she was acting within the scope of her duties when she excluded Cecil. The city is also a "person" under §1983 if Cecil can prove that in excluding him, Ann was acting pursuant to an official city custom or policy. Second, the suit is not barred by the Eleventh Amendment. The city, as a political subdivision of the state, has no Eleventh Amendment protection, and this is not a case where a judgment against the city would operate against the state treasury. Finally, Ann may be able to invoke a qualified immunity from damages liability, but the city has no immunity. Thus, even if the court agrees that the rights Ann violated were not clearly established at the time, Ann will be shielded from liability but the city will be liable in damages.

Suing Federal Officials

While 42 U.S.C. §1983 provides a cause of action against state and local government officials who violate a person's federal rights, Congress has never enacted a comparable statute authorizing such suits to be brought against federal government officials who violate our constitutional rights. In *Bivens v. Six Unknown Named Federal Narcotics Agents*, 403 U.S. 388 (1971), the Supreme Court finally filled this gap by recognizing a common law cause of action that allows a suit for damages to be brought against a federal agent who violates a person's federal constitutional rights. This so-called "*Bivens* action is the federal analog to suits brought against state officials under . . . 42 U.S.C. §1983." *Hartman v. Moore*, 547 U.S. 250, 254 n.2 (2006). *Bivens* actions are subject to the same common law immunities as are §1983 actions and to the same proscription against vicarious liability.

The Supreme Court will not automatically create a *Bivens* remedy whenever a person claims that federal officials have violated their constitutional rights. Instead, because this involves crafting federal common law, the Court will ask whether a *Bivens* remedy is necessary in such cases and whether there is any "convincing reason for the Judicial Branch to refrain from providing a new and freestanding remedy in damages." *Minneci v. Pollard*, 132 S. Ct. 617, 623 (2012). In making this inquiry, a key question is the extent to which state laws afford a remedy for the kind of wrong involved. "[T]he question is whether, in general, state . . . law remedies provide roughly similar incentives for potential defendants to comply with the [federal constitutional provision] while also providing roughly similar compensation to victims of violations." Id. at 625. If so, an individual "must seek a remedy under state tort law. We cannot imply a *Bivens* remedy in such a case." Id. at 626. The *Minneci* Court thus declined to create a common law cause of action under the Eighth Amendment for a federal prison inmate who claimed that prison officials had denied him adequate medical care. See also *Reichle v. Howards*, 132 S. Ct. 2088, 2093 n.4 (2012) (leaving open the question of whether *Bivens* extends to First Amendment retaliatory arrest claims); *Ashcroft v. Iqbal*, 556 U.S. 662, 665 (2009) (assuming without deciding that First Amendment free exercise claims are actionable under *Bivens*). Because a *Bivens* action is created as a matter of federal common law, it can be extinguished by an act of Congress. See *Hui v. Castaneda*, 130 S. Ct. 1845 (2010) (no *Bivens* action where federal statute barred damages claims against the federal officials being sued).

While the Supreme Court has at times created a common law cause of action against federal officials who violate a person's constitutional rights, no similar implied cause of action lies against the federal government itself or against its agencies. Instead, a cause of action will lie in such cases only if Congress has expressly and unambiguously waived the government's sovereign immunity from suit by authorizing the specific type of relief being sought. See *Federal Aviation Administration v. Cooper*, 132 S. Ct. 1441 (2012) (statute authorizing recovery of "actual damages" against the federal government did not clearly and unmistakably allow recovery for non-pecuniary mental or emotional harm).

§4.2.8 Congressional Abrogation

The final exception to the Eleventh Amendment comes into play where Congress has passed a law abrogating the states' immunity from suit. We saw earlier that Congress may quite easily *expand* the states' Eleventh Amendment immunity by prohibiting the federal courts from using the stripping doctrine. It is more difficult, however, for Congress to *narrow* the states' Eleventh Amendment immunity through abrogation. An attempt by Congress to abolish the states' sovereign immunity from suit will be upheld by the Court only if two requirements are met. First, Congress must have made its intention to abrogate the immunity "unmistakably clear in the language of the statute" (*Atascadero State Hosp. v. Scanlon*, 473 U.S. 234, 242 (1985)); since the intent "must be both unequivocal and textual," any "recourse to legislative history will be unnecessary. . . ." *Dellmuth v. Muth*, 491 U.S. 223, 230 (1989). Second, the law abrogating the states' immunity may not have been enacted under one of Congress's Article I powers, such as the Commerce Clause (Art. I, §8, cl. 3) or the Patent Clause (Art. I, §8, cl. 8), but must have been adopted pursuant to the Fourteenth Amendment. *Seminole Tribe of Florida v. Florida*, 517 U.S. 44, 57-73 (1996) (Indian Commerce Clause); *Florida Prepaid Postsecondary Education Expense Board v. College Savings Bank*, 527 U.S. 627, 635 (1999) (Interstate Commerce Clause and Patent Clause); *Alden v. Maine*, 527 U.S. 706, 755 (1999) (Interstate Commerce Clause).

The first requirement constitutes a "clear statement" rule. It is designed to protect the states by ensuring that they have notice and an opportunity to defend themselves when legislation to abolish their Eleventh Amendment immunity is being debated in Congress. Unless it is clear at the time of enactment that the law will subject the states to suit, the states' representatives in Congress have no chance to oppose the measure on this ground. The Court relied on the clear statement principle in *Raygor v. Regents of the University of Minnesota*, 534 U.S. 533 (2002), where it held that the tolling provision of the supplemental jurisdiction statute, 28 U.S.C. §1367(d), could not be construed to toll the statute of limitations on a federal claim against a state that was first filed in federal court but dismissed on Eleventh Amendment grounds, and then refiled in a state court after the statute of limitations had run out. As the Court noted, the text of §1367 did not specifically refer to claims filed against a state or to dismissals premised on the Eleventh Amendment. As such Congress had not made its intent to abrogate a state's sovereign immunity on such claims unmistakably clear. Id. at 544-545. See also *Nevada Dept. of Human Resources v. Hibbs*, 538 U.S. 721, 724-726 (2003) (statutory provision that allows party to seek money damages against a "State or political subdivision thereof" or "any agency of State" constitutes a clear statement).

The second requirement bars Congress from abrogating the states' Eleventh Amendment immunity under any of its Article I powers. This requirement follows logically from the fact that the Eleventh Amendment is, in part, a constitutional limitation on the subject matter jurisdiction of the federal courts — i.e., it removes certain cases from the federal judicial power defined by Article III, §2. The Court has long held that Congress cannot expand the federal courts' subject matter jurisdiction beyond the limits defined by the Constitution. Just as Congress may not use its commerce power (Art. I, §8, cl. 3) to give federal courts jurisdiction over tort claims between motorists from the same state, it may not use its Article I powers to give the courts jurisdiction over cases that are excluded from the federal judicial power by the Eleventh Amendment. In *Seminole Tribe of Florida v. Florida*, 517 U.S. 44 (1996), the Court on this basis struck down a law enacted by Congress under the Indian Commerce Clause (Art. I, §8, cl. 3), which had allowed Indian tribes to file suit against a state in federal court to enforce the Indian Gaming Regulatory Act. *Seminole Tribe* overruled *Pennsylvania v. Union Gas Co.*, 491 U.S. 1 (1989), a short-lived decision in which a bare majority of the Court ruled that the states' Eleventh Amendment immunity may be abrogated by Congress under any of its lawmaking powers, including those contained in Article I. In *Alden v. Maine*, 527 U.S. at 753-754, the Court held that "the States' immunity from private suits in their own courts" is likewise "an immunity beyond the congressional power to abrogate by Article I legislation." Were the rule otherwise, said the Court, "the National Government would wield greater power in the state courts than in its own judicial instrumentalities." Id. at 752.

Even though Congress may not use its Article I powers to lift the states' Eleventh Amendment immunity, Congress may do so through a law enacted pursuant to the Fourteenth Amendment. The Fourteenth Amendment was ratified in 1868, 70 years after the Eleventh Amendment. Section 5 of the Fourteenth Amendment expressly authorizes Congress to enforce the Amendment "by appropriate legislation"; this may include legislation that allows suit to be brought against a state. In *Fitzpatrick v. Bitzer*, 427 U.S. 445 (1976), the Court thus upheld provisions of Title VII of the 1964 Civil Rights Act to the extent that they authorized state workers to sue the state for gender discrimination in employment. The Court reasoned that the Fourteenth Amendment, which prohibits the states from denying equal protection of the laws, in effect modified the Eleventh Amendment by authorizing Congress to subject the states to suit in federal or state court if Congress believed this was necessary to enforce the Equal Protection Clause. As the Court later explained:

> *Fitzpatrick* was based upon a rationale wholly inapplicable to the Interstate Commerce Clause, viz., that the Fourteenth Amendment, adopted well after the adoption of the Eleventh Amendment and the ratification of the Constitution, operated to alter the pre-existing balance between state and federal power achieved by Article III and the Eleventh Amendment.

Seminole Tribe of Florida, supra, 517 U.S. at 65-66.

If Congress intends to abrogate a state's sovereign immunity pursuant to §5 of the Fourteenth Amendment, the abrogation must be both "congruent" and "proportional" to the actual violation of judicially recognized Fourteenth Amendment §1 rights. See Allan Ides and Christopher N. May, *Constitutional Law: Individual Rights*, §1.5.2 (6th ed. 2013). This means that Congress must identify a pattern of state violations of a judicially recognized constitutional right, create a statute that is plainly designed to ameliorate the violation of those constitutional rights, and devise a remedy that is tailored to the demonstrated pattern of state-induced constitutional violations. In recent years, the Court has applied the congruence and proportionality requirements rather strictly, thus limiting Congress's ability to use its §5 power to abrogate a state's sovereign immunity.

For example, in *Board of Trustees of the University of Alabama v. Garrett*, 531 U.S. 356 (2000), the Court held that the attempted abrogation of state sovereign immunity in Title I of the Americans with Disabilities Act (ADA) was ineffective since the substantive provisions of Title I, prohibiting disability discrimination in public employment, were neither congruent with nor proportional to any established pattern of state violation of constitutional rights of the disabled in the public employment setting. Because Title I in essence sought to create and protect rights that went beyond those guaranteed by §1 of the Fourteenth Amendment, it exceeded Congress's §5 power.

Four years later, in a case involving access to courthouses and court proceedings, the Court upheld Title II of the ADA, which prohibits discrimination against the disabled in the provision of public services. *Tennessee v. Lane*, 541 U.S. 509 (2004). In contrast to Title I, Congress in enacting Title II had amassed a large "volume of evidence demonstrating the nature and extent of unconstitutional discrimination against persons with disabilities in the provision of public services," including specifically their access to the courts. Id. at 526-528. In addition to there being far more evidence of past discrimination in this Title II setting, the Fourteenth Amendment §1 rights at issue in *Lane* were also more fundamental than the Title I right involved in *Garrett*, making it far easier to show that the rights had been violated in the past. As the Court noted in *Lane*, the Title I equal employment right at stake in *Garrett* was one that triggers mere rational basis review under the Equal Protection Clause; by contrast, Title II "seeks to enforce a variety of other basic constitutional guarantees, infringements of which are subject to more searching judicial review" — including the right of access to the courts. Id. at 522-523. Once it concluded that Title II sought to protect a group whose §1 Fourteenth Amendment rights had in fact been violated, the *Lane* Court went on to hold that Congress, in invoking its §5 power, may enact remedial, as well as preventative or prophylactic measures, the latter not being limited to state conduct that would itself violate §1. With adequate findings, Congress may thus invoke its §5 power to prohibit state conduct that might not itself be found unconstitutional, as long as the legislation is congruent and proportional to the past §1 violations. Compare *Nevada Dept. of Human Resources v. Hibbs*, 538 U.S. 721 (2003) (Family and Medical Leave Act (FMLA) provision authorizing state employees to sue their employer for failure to grant spousal or parental leaves, as required by Act, was proper exercise of §5 enforcement powers given history of gender discrimination in public and private employee benefit plans, even though this statutorily prohibited conduct might not itself be unconstitutional), with *Coleman v. Court of Appeals of Maryland*, 132 S. Ct. 1327 (2012) (plurality opinion) (FMLA provision authorizing state employees to sue their employer for failure to grant sick leave, as required by the FMLA, was invalid exercise of §5 enforcement power where there was no evidence that states had discriminatory sick-leave policies and where nothing in the Congressional Record suggested that Congress had reason to believe women were being discriminated against in this respect).

Example 4-O

Daniel works as an accountant for the Florida Department of Corrections. He and some of his fellow employees have brought an action in state court against the department, claiming that its compensation scheme discriminates against older workers, in violation of the federal Age Discrimination in

Employment Act (ADEA). The ADEA makes it unlawful for any employer —
including "a State or . . . any agency or instrumentality of a State" — to
discriminate against any employee "because of such individual's age." Plaintiffs seek back pay, damages, and permanent salary adjustments. The department has moved to dismiss the case as barred by the Eleventh Amendment.
How should the court rule?

Explanation

The suit appears to be one that falls within the Eleventh Amendment,
which, under the ruling in *Alden v. Maine*, protects an unconsenting state
against private suits brought in its own courts or in federal court. Since
the named defendant is an agency of the state, the Amendment comes
into play unless the ADEA is a valid exercise of Congress's power to
abrogate the states' sovereign immunity from suit. The first requirement
for abrogation is met because the ADEA clearly authorizes suits to be filed
against a state in either federal or state court. The act defines "employer"
to include a state or any of its agencies, and provides that an aggrieved
employee may bring suit "in any Federal or State court of competent
jurisdiction. . . ."

The second requirement for abrogation, however, is not satisfied. To
the extent that the ADEA was adopted by Congress under its power to
regulate interstate commerce (Art. I, §8, cl. 3), the abrogation is invalid
under the principles set forth in *Seminole Tribe* and *Alden*. Nor does the ADEA
constitute a valid exercise of Congress's authority under §5 of the Fourteenth Amendment to enforce the Equal Protection Clause contained in §1
of that Amendment. As construed by the Supreme Court, the Equal Protection Clause does not prohibit a state from discriminating on the basis of
age as long as there is some rational basis for doing so. The "rational basis"
test is so easy to satisfy that the Court has never found an age classification
to violate the Fourteenth Amendment. Absent a demonstrated pattern of
state irrationality with respect to age discrimination, the department cannot reasonably claim that the ADEA was a congruent and proportional
remedy to deter or punish state violations of the Equal Protection Clause.
In this respect, *Fitzpatrick v. Bitzer* is distinguishable. There, Congress used its
§5 power to enact Title VII of the 1964 Civil Rights Act, which prohibits
states from discriminating in employment on the basis of race, gender, and
national origin. In contrast to age discrimination, these are types of discrimination that often violate the Equal Protection Clause and which Congress thus has the power to legislate against under §5. Since Congress's
attempt to lift the states' Eleventh Amendment immunity through the
ADEA is invalid, the state court may dismiss Daniel's suit. See *Kimel v. Florida
Board of Regents*, 528 U.S. 62 (2000) (holding, in a case filed in federal court,

that the Eleventh Amendment bars a state from being sued under the ADEA).

The Court's rationale in *Seminole Tribe* would seemingly allow Congress to abrogate the states' Eleventh Amendment immunity through legislation enacted under other, later-adopted amendments that expressly restrict conduct on the part of the states — such as the Thirteenth and Fifteenth Amendments. To date, however, the Court has limited Congress's power to abrogate to legislation passed pursuant to the Fourteenth Amendment.

As we will see in Chapter 5, the Constitution limits the circumstances under which Congress may directly regulate the states. Yet even where Congress has the authority to do so, as it did in the Fair Labor Standards Act, the Eleventh Amendment will frequently make it impossible to enforce these laws against a recalcitrant state other than through a suit for prospective injunctive relief. In such cases, compensation for any harm caused by the state's failure to comply with federal law will come, if at all, solely from the pocket of a state official.

§4.2.9 State Waiver by Consent to Suit

If none of the exceptions to the Eleventh Amendment applies, a suit may nonetheless be brought against a state in federal or state court if the state has waived its Eleventh Amendment immunity by consenting to the suit. The Supreme Court has been highly protective of the states by insisting that any waiver of a state's Eleventh Amendment immunity be "by the most express language or by such overwhelming implications from the text as [will] leave no room for any other reasonable construction." *Edelman v. Jordan*, 415 U.S. 651, 673 (1974) (quoting *Murray v. Wilson Distilling Co.*, 213 U.S. 151, 171 (1909)).

A state's waiver of its Eleventh Amendment immunity from private suit must thus be express, unequivocal, and voluntary. The Court has thus rejected the notion that Congress may exact a "constructive" or "implied" waiver of a state's sovereign immunity through legislation enacted under its Article I powers. In *Parden v. Terminal Railway*, 377 U.S. 184 (1964), Congress did just this by providing that any state that operated a railroad in interstate commerce thereby consented to being sued in federal court, under the Federal Employers' Liability Act, by an injured employee. However, *Parden's* approval of the constructive waiver theory was expressly overruled in *College Savings Bank v. Florida Prepaid Postsecondary Education Expense Board*, 527 U.S. 666, 680 (1999). As the Court explained, "we cannot square *Parden* with our cases requiring that a State's express waiver of sovereign immunity be unequivocal. . . . The whole point of requiring a 'clear declaration' by the State of its waiver is to be certain that the State in fact consents to suit. But there is little reason to assume actual consent based upon the State's mere presence in a field subject to congressional regulation." Id. Moreover, to recognize "a congressional power to exact constructive waivers of sovereign immunity through the exercise of Article I powers would also, as a practical matter, permit Congress to circumvent the antiabrogation holding of *Seminole Tribe*. Forced waiver and abrogation are not even different sides of the same coin — they are the same side of the same coin." Id. at 683.

To the extent that a state has waived its sovereign immunity from suit, such waivers will be read narrowly. Thus, a federal statute that allows a person to bring suit "for appropriate relief against a government" that accepts funds under that statutory program and that defines "government" to include "States," does not "so clearly and unambiguously waive sovereign immunity to private suits for damages that we can 'be certain that the State in fact consents' to such a suit." *Sossamon v. Texas*, 131 S. Ct. 1651, 1658-1659 (2011). Similarly, a state may waive its sovereign immunity from suit in its own courts without necessarily exposing itself to suit in federal court. The fact of "a State's waiver of sovereign immunity in its own courts is not a waiver of the Eleventh Amendment immunity in the federal courts." *Pennhurst State School & Hosp. v. Halderman*, 465 U.S. 89, 99 n.9 (1984). Instead, if the state is being sued in a federal court, it must be unequivocally clear that the state has not only waived its sovereign immunity, but that it has specifically agreed to be sued in *federal court*. If, however, a state expressly waives its sovereign immunity over a state law claim that has been filed in state court and then voluntarily removes that claim to federal court, the removal by the state will constitute a waiver of its sovereign immunity in the federal proceeding. *Lapides v. Board of Regents of the University System of Georgia*, 535 U.S. 613 (2002).

Example 4-P

In Example 4-E, John brought a class action in federal court against Robert Smith, director of the Illinois Department of Welfare, challenging the state's failure to adhere to federal time limits for processing welfare applications. We found that while the federal court could issue an injunction requiring the director to comply with the federal time limits in the future, the Eleventh Amendment barred the court from awarding retroactive benefits from the state treasury. However, assume that an Illinois law provides that "[a] person who is wrongfully denied any benefits provided or administered by this state may bring suit against the state to recover those benefits in a court of competent jurisdiction." In light of this statute, may the federal court grant plaintiffs retroactive monetary relief that will come from the state treasury?

Explanation

Although the state has clearly waived its sovereign immunity from suit by allowing itself to be sued on claims for retroactive benefits, it is not clear that the state intended to waive its Eleventh Amendment from suit in federal court. The federal court is a court of "competent jurisdiction" in the sense that 28 U.S.C. §1331 allows it to hear this case "arising under" federal law, but it is not absolutely clear that the state statute was meant to include federal as well as state courts. In light of this ambiguity, the federal court would probably find that the state had not waived its Eleventh Amendment immunity and that plaintiffs therefore cannot obtain retroactive monetary relief from a federal court.

§4.2.10 The Eleventh Amendment Anomaly

The effect of the Eleventh Amendment may be to make it extremely difficult to hold a state accountable for having violated the Constitution or laws of the United States. Through the stripping doctrine, state officials can usually be enjoined by a federal or state court from engaging in future illegal conduct. Redress for *past* violations, however, is generally impossible other than through whatever remedies a state may have consented to provide. And since Congress's ability to abrogate the states' Eleventh Amendment immunity is essentially limited to enforcing the Fourteenth Amendment, courts can award damages for a state's violation of federal environmental, welfare, and other federal laws only if the state has waived its sovereign immunity, or those damages will come from the pocket of an individual state official — a pocket that will often be either empty or protected by common law immunity. Thus, as the Supreme Court noted in a case where a state withheld welfare benefits in violation of federal law, "whether or not the [plaintiffs] will receive retroactive benefits rests entirely with the State, its agencies, courts and legislature, not with the federal court." *Quern v. Jordan*, 440 U.S. 332, 348 (1979).

To the extent that the Eleventh Amendment deprives plaintiffs of federal redress for harms they suffer at the state's hands, the Amendment may encourage a state to ignore federal law. If a state violates an individual's federal constitutional or statutory rights, the worst that will ordinarily happen *to the state* is that one of its officials will be enjoined by a federal court from continuing to violate the law. While such relief may cost the state money in the future, the state will normally not have to compensate for any of the injuries it has already caused.

In *Alden v. Maine*, 527 U.S. 706 (1999), the Supreme Court rejected the proposition that its broad reading of the Eleventh Amendment "confer[s] upon the State a . . . right to disregard the Constitution or valid federal

197

law. . . . We are unwilling to assume that States will refuse to honor the Constitution or obey the binding laws of the United States. The good faith of the States thus provides an important assurance that '[t]his Constitution, and the Laws of the United States . . . shall be the supreme Law of the Land.'" Id. at 755. The Court also noted that states are not necessarily shielded from damages liability, even in situations like *Alden* where Congress lacks the power to abrogate the state's sovereign immunity because the federal law in question (e.g., the Fair Labor Standards Act (FLSA)) was enacted under Article I. In these situations, said the Court, Congress may authorize a suit to be brought against the state in the name of the United States, thereby invoking one of the recognized exceptions to the Eleventh Amendment. The FLSA, under which the private employees unsuccessfully sued the State of Maine in *Alden*, authorized the United States to sue the state in federal court to recover damages on behalf of aggrieved state workers. Yet as Justice Souter noted in dissent:

> [U]nless Congress plans a significant expansion of the National Government's litigating forces to provide a lawyer whenever private litigation is barred by today's decision and *Seminole Tribe*, the allusion to enforcement of private rights by the National Government is probably not much more than whimsy. Facing reality, Congress specifically found . . . "that the enforcement capability of the Secretary of Labor is not alone sufficient to provide redress in all or even a substantial portion of the situations where compliance is not forthcoming voluntarily." . . . One hopes that such voluntary compliance will prove more popular than it has in Maine, for there is no reason today to suspect that enforcement by the Secretary of Labor alone would likely prove adequate to assure compliance with this federal law in the multifarious circumstances of some 4.7 million employees of the 50 States of the Union.

Id. at 810. While Congress might try to deal with this problem by authorizing private parties to bring a so-called *qui tam* action on behalf of the United States, thereby relieving the U.S. Justice Department of the litigation burden, the Supreme Court has cast doubt on whether a *qui tam* action against a state would qualify as a suit by the United States so as to trigger one of the exceptions to the Eleventh Amendment. *Vermont Agency of Natural Resources v. United States ex rel. Stevens*, 529 U.S. 765, 786-787 (2000). See §4.2.2.

Though the Court in *Alden* asserted that "[t]he principle of sovereign immunity as reflected in our jurisprudence strikes the proper balance between the supremacy of federal law and the separate sovereignty of the States" (id. at 757), the notion that a state is effectively immune from damages — no matter how willful or flagrant its violation of the Constitution or laws of the United States — seems fundamentally at odds with the principle of federal supremacy. This anomaly is a result of the Court's reinterpretation of the Eleventh Amendment in *Hans v. Louisiana* and its progeny. Had the Court adhered to the text of the Eleventh Amendment — which merely bars suits against a state by citizens of another state, or by citizens or subjects of foreign countries — rather than expanding its scope to enshrine a broad doctrine of sovereign immunity, federal and state courts would have been able to entertain damages actions against a state on the basis of the state's violation of federal law. Such actions would not have been affected by the Eleventh Amendment's repeal of the Citizen-State and Alien-State Clauses in Article III, for they could have entered federal court as cases "arising under" federal law. In recent years some Justices have called for rejecting *Hans*'s interpretation of the Eleventh Amendment, but a majority has declined the invitation. See, e.g., *Atascadero State Hosp. v. Scanlon*, 473 U.S. 234, 247-302 (1985) (Brennan, J., Marshall, J., Blackmun, J., and Stevens, J., dissenting).

§4.3 THE *SILER* DOCTRINE

The *Siler* doctrine is a judge-made rule that requires federal courts, where possible, to resolve a case on state law grounds rather than on the basis of the federal Constitution. *Siler v. Louisville & Nashville R.R. Co.*, 213 U.S. 175, 193 (1909). The *Siler* doctrine, which is mandatory rather than discretionary, is one of a series of rules followed by the federal courts to avoid the unnecessary resolution of federal constitutional questions. The doctrine serves several purposes. First, it reduces the burden on the Supreme Court of having to review lower federal court decisions that address the meaning of the Constitution. Every time lower courts decide a federal constitutional issue, they muddy the waters by adding another precedent to the body of constitutional law. That precedent may conflict with rulings reached by other courts, thus creating pressure on the Supreme Court to resolve the conflict through its appellate jurisdiction. The fewer constitutional decisions that are issued by lower federal courts, the lighter the burden on the Supreme Court.

The *Siler* doctrine also furthers the goals of comity and federalism by minimizing the federal judiciary's impact on the states. If a federal court decision is based on state law rather than the Constitution, the state retains the ability to mitigate the effect of that decision by amending or repealing its law so that future cases will be decided differently. On the other hand, a federal decision based on the Constitution leaves the state with few choices, for unless it can get the ruling overturned on appeal, its only recourse is the extraordinarily difficult route of having the Constitution amended.

Example 4-Q

Sheldon applied for a permit to hold a parade in Dodge City. The permit was denied on the ground that Sheldon had not paid the city a $5,000 parade permit fee required under the city charter. Sheldon sued the city in federal court claiming that the permit denial violated his rights under the First and Fourteenth Amendments, and under a state law that bars cities from charging more than a nominal fee for the use of public facilities. Sheldon seeks damages of $10,000. May the federal court decide the case on the basis of the federal Constitution?

Explanation

Under the *Siler* doctrine, the court must attempt to resolve this case on the basis of the state law claim so as not to reach the federal constitutional issues. Thus, the court should first examine the state statute to see if it entitles Sheldon to the full relief that he seeks. If it does, the court should rule for him on that basis without ever reaching the federal constitutional claims. However, if the court decides that the state law was not violated here, or that it was violated but does not allow Sheldon to recover all of the damages he seeks, then and only then would it be appropriate to address the federal constitutional issues.

The *Siler* doctrine presumes the existence of a state law claim and a federal constitutional claim; where both are present, the federal court must resolve the state claim first. Since the Eleventh Amendment bars a federal court from hearing state law claims brought against a state, its agencies, or its officials, the *Siler* doctrine obviously cannot apply in such cases. However, the doctrine will come into play in suits against political subdivisions of the state, as was the case in Example 4-Q. Prior to the Court's ruling in *Pennhurst State School & Hosp. v. Halderman*, 465 U.S. 89 (1984), federal courts routinely heard pendent state law claims against state officials, with the result that the *Siler* doctrine was often invoked in such cases. That is of course no longer true today.

Example 4-R

George is a patient at the state hospital for the developmentally disabled. A suit has been filed on his behalf in federal court alleging that conditions at the hospital violate the Eighth and Fourteenth Amendments, the state constitution, the state Public Facilities Act, and the federal Rehabilitation Act. The suit was filed against the state Department of Public Welfare and four state officials who run the hospital. George seeks damages and injunctive relief. How should the court proceed with the case?

Explanation

The Eleventh Amendment requires dismissal of all claims against the state Department of Public Welfare, for this is a state entity to which the stripping doctrine does not apply. The Eleventh Amendment also compels dismissal of the state constitutional and statutory claims against the state officials, as the stripping doctrine does not apply to state law claims. However, the stripping doctrine allows the court to hear the two federal claims against the state officials. The court may potentially award plaintiff injunctive relief as well as damages from the officials' own pockets.

Since there are no remaining state claims, the *Siler* doctrine does not come into play here. However, under a rule analogous to *Siler*, the court must try to avoid reaching the federal constitutional claim by deciding the federal statutory claim first. If George can obtain all of the relief he seeks under the Rehabilitation Act, the court will not have to resolve the federal constitutional issues presented by this case.

§4.4 THE *PULLMAN* DOCTRINE

The *Pullman* abstention doctrine, like the *Siler* doctrine, is based on principles of comity and federalism. Under the *Pullman* doctrine if, in a case raising a federal constitutional issue, a federal court is confronted with a state law whose meaning is unclear and the state's own courts have not had an opportunity to resolve the ambiguity, the federal judge may stay the action until the state courts have had a chance to clarify the meaning of the state law. The federal court may abstain, however, only if there is a realistic chance the state courts will construe their law to either make it unnecessary for the federal court to ever consider the constitutional issue, or at least reduce the likelihood the state law will be held unconstitutional. *Railroad Commn. of Texas v. Pullman Co.*, 312 U.S. 496 (1941). *Pullman* abstention is often triggered when there is a new state law but the doctrine may also apply with respect to older laws if a novel and unsettled question arises that the state courts have not had a chance to address.

There are a number of procedural avenues for obtaining a clarification from the state courts. In most cases, the federal plaintiff will have to institute a separate action in state court asking the state court to resolve the ambiguity in the state law. However, if there is already a suit pending in state court involving another party and resolution of that case will clarify the meaning of the state law, the federal plaintiff need do nothing but wait for the state suit to conclude. A third means of obtaining clarification of state law exists if the state has adopted a certification procedure through which questions about state law may be submitted to the state supreme court by other state and federal courts. If the state has such a procedure, as many states do, the federal judge may certify the question to the state supreme court and wait for an answer to be received. Once the state law has been clarified by any of these means, the federal court may proceed unless plaintiff has in the interim obtained full relief from the state court. See, e.g., *United States v. Juvenile Male*, 130 S. Ct. 2518 (2010) (certifying to Montana Supreme Court question of state law critical to determining whether a pending federal court challenge to the constitutionality of a state statute was now moot). However, *Stenberg v. Carhart*, 530 U.S. 914, 945 (2000), held that federal courts are not obligated to invoke a state certification procedure. Rather, "[c]ertification of a question (or abstention) is appropriate only where the statute is 'fairly susceptible' to a narrowing construction." The Court there concluded that a Nebraska law banning certain abortions was sufficiently clear on its face to eliminate the need for certification even though the state's courts had not yet had a chance to either interpret or apply the statute.

The *Pullman* doctrine can arise in two different types of situations. First, when a federal plaintiff asserts both federal and state law claims for relief, *Pullman* will sometimes cause the court to send the state claim to state court for clarification or decision.

Example 4-S

In Example 4-Q where the city refused to give Sheldon a parade permit, the *Siler* doctrine required the federal court to consider the state statutory issue first. However, the state statute is arguably ambiguous for it is not clear whether the term "public facilities" includes city streets or whether it applies only to city buildings. If the law were construed to include streets, Sheldon would likely win his case based on the statute, eliminating any need to reach the federal constitutional issue. Should the federal court stay the action under the *Pullman* doctrine?

Explanation

Assuming the state courts have not had a chance to interpret this aspect of the law, *Pullman* abstention would be appropriate here. If the court invoked *Pullman*, Sheldon's case would be put on hold while he filed suit in state court for a clarification of the term "public facilities." If he wished he could also ask the state court to award him damages under state law if it concluded that the city had violated the statute, thus making it unnecessary for the federal court to take any further action in the case. However, should the state court instead rule that the statute does not apply to parades, Sheldon could then return to federal court for a ruling on whether the permit denial violated his federal constitutional rights.

In the previous example, *Siler* and *Pullman* worked in tandem with one another. While *Siler* required the federal court to consider the state law claim first, *Pullman* resulted in sending that state claim to state court because it hinged on an ambiguous state law. In this type of case, the *Pullman* doctrine may result in the federal court's never having to address the federal constitutional claim, for the case may be entirely disposed of on the basis of the state law claim.

The *Pullman* abstention doctrine also comes into play in cases where instead of separate federal and state law claims, there is only a single federal claim asserting that a state law violates the federal Constitution. In such cases, the validity of the state law may turn on how it is construed. "If the state courts would be likely to construe the statute in a fashion that would avoid the need for a federal constitutional ruling or otherwise significantly modify the federal claim, the argument for abstention is strong." *Harris County Commrs. Court v. Moore*, 420 U.S. 77, 84 (1975). Under such circumstances, a federal court might abstain under the *Pullman* doctrine until a state court has had a chance to clarify the statute, thereby perhaps curing any constitutional defects it may contain.

Example 4-T

Emil was fired from his job as city police officer after the city learned that he was more than six months in arrears in paying child support. The city terminated Emil under a new state law that provides that "[a]ny state or local governmental employee who falls more than six months behind in *his* child support payments shall be immediately fired from *his* job" (emphasis supplied). Emil has sued the city in federal court claiming that the statute under which he was fired is unconstitutional because it discriminates on the basis of gender in violation of the Fourteenth Amendment. Should the federal court rule on the merits of Emil's claim?

Explanation

The validity of this state law hinges entirely on how it is construed. If the pronoun "his" is deemed to include females, the statute does not discriminate on the basis of gender. While the law is new, the legislature or the state courts may have already determined that as a general matter, the male pronoun in any state statute is deemed to include females. If this is the case, the federal court need not abstain since state law on this point is not unsettled. Otherwise, since the state courts have probably not had a chance to construe this particular statute for themselves, *Pullman* abstention would be appropriate here. The federal court should stay the suit and either take advantage of any certification procedure the state may have, or direct Emil to file a declaratory judgment action in state court.

If a plaintiff is sent to state court under the *Pullman* doctrine to obtain clarification of a state law, the plaintiff may decide for efficiency's sake to let the state court decide the entire case, including the federal constitutional questions that it presents. A plaintiff who does so, however, does not get two bites at the apple. The state court's ruling on the constitutional issues is binding on the parties as a matter of collateral estoppel. And while the state court's ruling may be reviewed by the Supreme Court on appeal, the issues cannot be relitigated by the parties in federal district court.

A litigant subject to *Pullman* abstention who wishes to ensure that the federal constitutional issues will be decided by a federal court rather than conclusively determined by the state court must expressly "reserve" those issues upon entering state court. *England v. Louisiana State Bd. of Medical Examiners*, 375 U.S. 411 (1964). If, in the face of a so-called *England* reservation the state court nevertheless proceeds to rule on the federal constitutional issues, the parties will be allowed to relitigate those issues in federal court and will not be subject to collateral estoppel.

In contrast to the *Siler* doctrine, which is mandatory, *Pullman* abstention is discretionary with the court. "[B]ecause of the delays inherent in the abstention process and the danger that valuable federal rights might be lost in the absence of expeditious adjudication in the federal court," *Harris County Commrs. Court, supra*, 420 U.S. at 83, a judge may conclude that invoking the *Pullman* doctrine would be too prejudicial to the plaintiff, in which case the federal court would construe the state law for itself.

§4.5 THE *YOUNGER* DOCTRINE

§4.5.1 The Basic Doctrine

The *Younger* abstention doctrine is a judge-made rule that prohibits a federal court from ruling on the constitutionality of a state law if there is a pending state proceeding in which the federal plaintiff could raise that constitutional challenge. The doctrine takes its name from *Younger v. Harris*, 401 U.S. 37 (1971), a §1983 suit that was brought by John Harris in federal court to enjoin enforcement of the California Criminal Syndicalism Act on the ground that it violated the First and Fourteenth Amendments. At the time Harris filed his federal suit, criminal proceedings under the act had already commenced against him in state court. The Supreme Court held that since Harris could raise his constitutional objections as a defense to the state criminal action, it would be improper for a federal court to interfere with the pending state proceeding by enjoining prosecution of the case. In contrast to *Pullman* abstention, where the federal court retains jurisdiction, the *Younger* doctrine requires that the federal action be dismissed.

The *Younger* doctrine rests in part on principles of equity. Under traditional rules of equity jurisprudence, a court may grant injunctive relief only if plaintiff has no adequate remedy at law and will suffer irreparable harm. The Court has held that litigants in Harris's position have an adequate remedy at law as long as the state court allows a criminal defendant to raise the constitutional issue as a defense to the state prosecution. As for the requirement of irreparable injury, the Court has held that "the cost, anxiety, and inconvenience of having to defend against a single criminal prosecution, could not by themselves be considered 'irreparable' in the special legal sense of that term." *Younger v. Harris*, supra, 401 U.S. at 46.

Younger also rests on notions of federalism and "'comity,' that is, a proper respect for state functions. . . ." Id. at 44. For a federal court to interfere with a pending state court proceeding that allegedly involves an unconstitutional state law "'would entail an unseemly failure to give effect to the principle that state courts have the solemn responsibility equally with the federal courts' to safeguard constitutional rights and 'would reflect[] negatively upon the state court's ability' to do so." *Trainor v. Hernandez*, 431 U.S. 434, 443 (1977) (quoting *Steffel v. Thompson*, 415 U.S. 452, 460-461, 462 (1974)). So long as the state affords a litigant an opportunity to raise the constitutional issue in the state court proceeding, the state court will be trusted to adjudicate the issue in a fair and impartial manner. If the state courts ultimately reject a defendant's federal constitutional challenge, the defendant may seek review in the Supreme Court through 28 U.S.C. §1257.

In the *Younger* case itself, Harris asked the federal court for an injunction barring enforcement of the Criminal Syndicalism Act. However, the doctrine is equally applicable where the federal plaintiff seeks only a declaratory judgment that a state statute is unconstitutional "since the intrusive effect of declaratory relief 'will result in precisely the same interference with and disruption of state proceedings that the long-standing policy limiting injunctions was designed to avoid.'" *Steffel v. Thompson*, supra, 415 U.S. at 461 (quoting *Samuels v. Mackell*, 401 U.S. 66, 72 (1971)). This disruption stems from the fact that the declaratory judgment must be given collateral estoppel effect by the state court. Thus, once the federal court declares a state statute unconstitutional, this determination is binding on the parties in the pending state court action with the result that the state proceeding must be dismissed.

The *Younger* doctrine will be triggered if three basic requirements are satisfied:

1. There must be a pending state proceeding;
2. The state proceeding must be judicial in nature and must implicate important state interests; and
3. There must be an adequate opportunity in the state proceeding to raise the federal constitutional challenge.

After examining each of these requirements, we look at a number of possible exceptions to the *Younger* doctrine and at the potential for returning to federal court once the state proceeding is over.

§4.5.2 "Pending" State Proceedings

The *Younger* doctrine bars federal courts from proceeding only when there is a *pending* or *ongoing* state proceeding that involves the federal plaintiff. Otherwise, a federal court may issue declaratory or injunctive relief against the future enforcement of a state law, provided plaintiff is able to show a sufficient threat of future prosecution to satisfy the requirements of standing and ripeness. See §§3.4.1 and 3.6.

Example 4-U

Alex is an activist who often distributes handbills at a local shopping mall. Alex was stopped by a mall security guard who told him to stop handbilling. When Alex ignored the warning, the police arrived and warned him that unless he stopped handbilling he would be arrested and prosecuted under a state trespass statute. Alex left but returned a week later. When the police were called, he again had to leave to avoid arrest. Alex has filed a §1983 suit in federal court against the shopping center owner and the local police seeking a declaratory judgment that application of the state trespass statute to prevent him from handbilling violates his free speech rights under the First and Fourteenth Amendments. Can the federal court hear the case?

Explanation

The *Younger* doctrine poses no bar to Alex's suit since no state court proceeding is pending against him. If the federal court were to issue a judgment declaring that the state trespass law cannot be applied to Alex's handbilling activity, this would not disrupt any ongoing state suit. Nor would that federal judgment reflect negatively on the state's ability to uphold the Constitution as there is no pending state suit in which Alex could present his claim to a state judge. Since Alex has been threatened with arrest twice, the threat of prosecution is sufficiently real to satisfy standing and ripeness requirements. See *Steffel v. Thompson*, 415 U.S. 452 (1974).

Even if there is no pending state suit at the time the federal suit is filed, *Younger* still requires dismissal of the federal action if a state suit is begun "before any proceedings of substance on the merits have taken place in the federal court. . . ." *Hicks v. Miranda*, 422 U.S. 332, 349 (1975). In *Hicks* the

Court ruled that the *Younger* doctrine compelled dismissal of a federal suit where state criminal proceedings were instituted against the federal plaintiff more than six weeks after the federal complaint was filed but a day after service of the complaint — well before the federal court could address the merits of plaintiff's claim. The rule of *Hicks* makes sense; otherwise, a person who violates a state law could defeat *Younger* by racing to the federal court before the state was able to institute proceedings in its own courts.

The *Younger* doctrine poses a dilemma for someone who wishes to test the constitutionality of a state criminal law in federal court. To avoid having his or her federal suit dismissed, a plaintiff must comply with the state law prior to filing suit and must continue to comply until the federal court reaches the merits of the case. Otherwise, the state will be in a position to institute proceedings against the federal plaintiff in its own courts, forcing a dismissal of the federal suit under *Hicks*. Depending on the circumstances, having to honor the state law during this lengthy interim may cause serious harm to the plaintiff.

A possible means of escaping this dilemma is for plaintiff to comply with the state law long enough to obtain a preliminary injunction from a federal court barring enforcement of the state law against plaintiff while the federal suit is pending. The plaintiff may then ignore the state law without fear that the state will trigger *Younger* by initiating a prosecution in state court. If the federal court ultimately declares the state law unconstitutional, the injunction will be dissolved and plaintiff will be protected against prosecution by the federal declaratory judgment, which must be given collateral estoppel effect by the state courts.

Example 4-V

In the previous example, Alex might be severely prejudiced if he must refrain from handbilling until the federal court reaches the merits of his case. Can he obtain a preliminary injunction from the court barring defendants from enforcing the state trespass law against him during the pendency of the federal suit?

Explanation

Since a preliminary injunction is a form of equitable relief, Alex must demonstrate that such relief is necessary to prevent irreparable harm; that there is a strong likelihood he will prevail on the merits of his constitutional challenge; and that he has "clean hands." While Alex may be able to satisfy the first two requirements, the fact that he already twice violated the state law may cause the court to deny him a preliminary injunction on the ground that he has "unclean hands." However, assuming the court grants the injunction, Alex can resume handbilling without fear that the state will file a criminal action against him, forcing dismissal of his federal suit. If the federal court later holds the state law unconstitutional, the injunction will be lifted. Should the state thereafter attempt to prosecute Alex under the trespass statute for handbilling, the state court will be obliged to give collateral estoppel effect to the federal determination that the law is unconstitutional and dismiss the case. See *Doran v. Salem Inn, Inc.*, 422 U.S. 922 (1975).

In those instances where the *Younger* doctrine is triggered, the federal action must be dismissed and may not be refiled until the state proceeding is no longer pending. For these purposes, a state proceeding is "pending" until the would-be federal plaintiff has exhausted all appeals available in the state courts. If a party allows the time for taking such an appeal to lapse, the state proceeding is deemed pending forever and the *Younger* doctrine will stand as a perpetual bar to plaintiff's challenging the state proceeding in federal court.

Example 4-W

Smith operates an adult theater. The city filed an action in state court to declare Smith's operation of the theater a public nuisance. The court ruled for the city and ordered the theater closed for one year. Instead of appealing the judgment to a higher state court, Smith brought a §1983 action against the city in federal district court seeking an injunction reopening the theater. May the federal court entertain the case?

Explanation

Smith's suit must be dismissed under the *Younger* doctrine. Before bringing suit in federal court challenging the constitutionality of the state nuisance statute, Smith was required to exhaust all available appeals in state court. Assuming it is now too late for Smith to file an appeal in state court, the state suit will be deemed pending forever. See *Huffman v. Pursue, Ltd.*, 420 U.S. 592 (1975).

A party's failure to exhaust appeals in the state courts will not preclude the party from seeking federal declaratory or injunctive relief against *future enforcement* of a statute. Such an action is not barred by the *Younger* doctrine so long as the plaintiff does not seek to annul the results of the prior state trial or prevent enforcement of the state judgment.

Example 4-X

In the previous example, suppose that instead of seeking to block enforcement of the state judgment, Smith waited until the one-year closure period had expired. Wishing to reopen his theater but fearful of a second nuisance action by the city, Smith filed a §1983 against the city in federal court seeking a declaratory judgment that application of the nuisance statute to his theater would violate the First Amendment. May the federal court hear Smith's suit?

Explanation

The *Younger* doctrine does not require dismissal of the suit. Smith is not trying to annul the results of the state proceeding or prevent enforcement of the state judgment, for the judgment closed his theater only for one year. Smith's failure to appeal the judgment in the earlier case is therefore no bar to his seeking to enjoin future application of the state law. See *Wooley v. Maynard*, 430 U.S. 705 (1977).

§4.5.3 The Nature of the State Proceedings

Although the *Younger* doctrine originated in the context of pending state criminal actions, the doctrine has been expanded to bar a federal court from interfering with some pending state court civil suits and administrative proceedings, including those in which the state is not a party. In order for these noncriminal state proceedings to trigger *Younger* abstention, however, the proceedings must be both *judicial in nature* and *implicate important state interests*. This dual requirement will always be met if the state proceeding is a criminal action, as it was in the *Younger* case. The requirement may pose a problem if the pending state proceeding is a civil or administrative action.

Proceedings of a Judicial Nature

The *Younger* doctrine requires a federal court to abstain only if the pending state proceedings are judicial — rather than legislative or executive — in nature. A proceeding is judicial if it "investigates, declares and enforces liabilities as they stand on present or past facts and under laws supposed already to exist." *Prentis v. Atlantic Coast Line Co.*, 211 U.S. 210, 226 (1908) (quoted with approval in *New Orleans Public Service, Inc. v. Council of City of New Orleans*, 491 U.S. 350, 370-371 (1989)).

Example 4-Y

Linda was fired from her job as teacher with the Dayton Christian School because she was pregnant. According to the school's religious doctrine, it is a mother's duty to stay home with her young children. Linda notified the state Civil Rights Commission, which instituted administrative proceedings against the school, charging that it had engaged in gender discrimination in violation of a state civil rights law. The school has filed a §1983 action in federal court to enjoin the commission's proceedings on the ground that any interference with the school's hiring process would violate the Religion Clauses of the First Amendment. Does *Younger* require the federal court to dismiss the school's suit?

Explanation

The suit must be dismissed. The commission proceedings are clearly pending. They are judicial in nature since their purpose is to determine whether the school should be sanctioned for violating the state civil rights law. The proceedings implicate the state's important interest in eliminating gender discrimination from the workplace. Therefore, assuming the school has an opportunity to raise its constitutional objection in the commission proceedings, *Younger* abstention applies here. See *Ohio Civil Rights Commn. v. Dayton Christian Schools, Inc.*, 477 U.S. 619 (1986).

Where a state agency or entity performs different types of functions, the fact that the *Younger* doctrine may require a federal court to defer to some proceedings pending before the agency does not mean that federal abstention will always be called for.

Example 4-Z

In the previous example, suppose that Dayton Christian School instead brought a §1983 action in federal court to enjoin the state Civil Rights Commission from promulgating regulations that will have the effect of barring gender discrimination by all employers, including religious institutions whose religious teachings sanction some forms of gender discrimination. Is the school's federal suit barred by the *Younger* doctrine?

Explanation

This suit by the school would not be dismissed under *Younger*. While the commission's proceedings may be pending or ongoing, they are not judicial proceedings. They are instead legislative in nature since they entail "the making of a rule for the future," *Prentis v. Atlantic Coast Line Co.*, supra, 211 U.S. at 226, not the enforcement of an existing rule to specific facts. See *New Orleans Public Service, Inc.*, supra, 491 U.S. at 369-372.

If a state entity's proceedings are legislative or executive in nature and thus not protected from federal interference by the *Younger* doctrine, state judicial proceedings reviewing such legislative or executive action are likewise entitled to no deference under *Younger*. *New Orleans Public Service, Inc.*, supra, 491 U.S. at 367-368. Thus, in the previous example, the federal court could still hear the school's case even if the commission, after issuing its regulations, had sued the school in state court for a declaratory judgment that the regulations were valid.

Implicating Important State Interests

Younger abstention is appropriate only where "the State's interests in the [pending] proceeding are so important that exercise of the federal judicial power would disregard the comity between the States and the National Government." *Pennzoil Co. v. Texaco, Inc.*, 481 U.S. 1, 11 (1987). This requirement is clearly satisfied in cases like *Younger* itself, where the pending action is a criminal proceeding brought by the state itself. Similarly, the requirement is virtually certain to be met where the pending state proceeding is a civil or administrative action brought by the state or one of its agencies. Federal interference with such proceedings will directly interfere with the state's ability to achieve the objectives that caused it to initiate the proceeding in question. It is unlikely the Court would find that the objectives the state itself seeks to accomplish through such judicial or administrative proceedings are too insignificant to trigger federal abstention.

Whether a state proceeding implicates important state interests may be more problematic when the state is not a party to the pending proceedings. In *Pennzoil Co. v. Texaco, Inc.*, the Court expanded the *Younger* doctrine by applying it to a purely civil suit between private parties in which the state was not involved. The Court in *Pennzoil* held that a New York federal court should have dismissed a §1983 action brought by Texaco against Pennzoil to enjoin the enforcement of a prior Texas state court judgment that Pennzoil had obtained against Texaco.

Pennzoil does not necessarily mean that states will always have a sufficient interest in private civil actions to trigger *Younger* abstention. Indeed, the *Pennzoil* Court expressly disavowed such a reading, noting that abstention may not "always [be] appropriate whenever a civil proceeding is pending in a state court. Rather," said the Court, "we rely on the State's interest in protecting 'the authority of the judicial system so that its orders and judgments are not rendered nugatory. . . . '" 481 U.S. at 14 n.12. This suggests that if, in a suit between private parties, the challenged state law does not affect any order or judgment rendered by the state court, the state's interest might not be sufficient to bring *Younger* into play. It remains to be seen, however, whether the Court would refrain from applying *Younger* in such a situation.

Example 4-AA

State C law provides that in products liability cases, punitive damages may not exceed $50,000 if the product was manufactured in state C. Acme manufactures tires in state D. Penny sued the company in a state C court for injuries suffered when an Acme tire exploded; she asked for punitive damages of $1 million. Acme has filed an action in federal court to enjoin Penny from seeking more than $50,000 in punitive damages, claiming that state C's punitive damages law violates the Commerce and Equal Protection Clauses by discriminating against companies that manufacture goods in other states. Does *Younger* require the federal court to dismiss Acme's suit?

Explanation

Acme will argue that the pending state suit is between purely private parties and does not implicate any state interests sufficiently important to require federal abstention. Unlike *Pennzoil*, a federal judgment holding the state's punitive damages law to be unconstitutional would not interfere with the execution of any state court order or judgment. Nor is the state's interest in the recovery of damages between private parties significant enough to warrant dismissal of the federal suit. Penny will respond that the state C law furthers the state's legitimate and important interest in promoting employment by protecting the financial well-being of companies that operate manufacturing plants there. While the answer is unclear, given the Court's willingness to steadily extend the reach of the *Younger* doctrine, the state's interest might be found sufficient to warrant abstention here.

§4.5.4 Opportunity to Raise the Federal Claim in the State Proceeding

The third and final requirement for application of *Younger* abstention is that the would-be federal plaintiff must have an adequate opportunity to raise the federal constitutional issue in the pending state proceeding. The basic premise of the *Younger* doctrine is that since the state is willing and able to entertain this objection, principles of equity and comity require deference on the part of the federal court. If no such opportunity exists, the entire basis for abstention vanishes. Thus, in Example 4-AA, federal abstention would be proper only if Acme can raise its constitutional challenge to the punitive damages cap in the pending state court suit.

The burden is on the party seeking federal relief to show that the state proceeding does not afford an adequate opportunity to raise the federal challenge. In *Trainor v. Hernandez*, 431 U.S. 434 (1977), a suit challenging the constitutionality of an Illinois attachment statute, the federal court plaintiffs were ultimately able to avoid a *Younger* dismissal by proving that it was very unlikely their challenge to the state's attachment law could be raised in the pending state civil suit. See *Hernandez v. Finley*, 471 F. Supp. 516 (N.D. Ill. 1978), *aff'd per curiam sub nom. Quern v. Hernandez*, 440 U.S. 951 (1979). However, this is a difficult showing to make. The Court has held that even if a state administrative proceeding affords a litigant no opportunity to present a federal constitutional challenge, *Younger* abstention is still required if the state courts, in reviewing the administrative proceeding, will entertain the constitutional challenge. *Ohio Civil Rights Commn. v. Dayton Christian Schools, Inc.*, 477 U.S. 619, 629 (1986); *Middlesex County Ethics Commn. v. Garden State Bar Assn.*, 457 U.S. 423, 436 (1982).

§4.5.5 Exceptions to the *Younger* Doctrine

The Court has suggested that there may be exceptional situations in which a federal court could grant declaratory or injunctive relief against a pending state proceeding despite the *Younger* doctrine. These exceptions are (1) the state suit is shown to have been brought in bad faith or for purposes of harassment; (2) the state law is flagrantly and patently violative of express constitutional prohibitions; and (3) extraordinary circumstances exist such that plaintiff would suffer irreparable injury without immediate federal intervention. The Supreme Court has read these exceptions extremely narrowly, to the point where they may exist only in the realm of theory. Nevertheless, we will briefly consider each of the three exceptions.

Bad Faith or Harassment
If it can be proved that state officials instituted a criminal prosecution against the federal plaintiff in bad faith or for the purpose of harassment, an exception to *Younger* might be justified. However, it must also be shown that the prosecution was brought "without hope of obtaining a valid conviction. . . ." *Perez v. Ledesma*, 401 U.S. 82, 85 (1971). In *Dombrowski v. Pfister*, 380 U.S. 479 (1965), this exception was met in a situation where state

prosecutors had filed repeated criminal actions against the plaintiff civil rights workers, causing them to be arrested and indicted but without any intention of bringing them to trial. In other settings, however, even if it can be proved that the state proceeded against the federal plaintiff for illegitimate or evil motives, unless the state case is one that stands no chance of success on the merits, the *Younger* doctrine will seemingly bar federal intervention.

Example 4-BB

In Example 4-U, Alex was warned twice by the local police that he would be arrested and prosecuted if he again distributed handbills at the mall. Alex thereafter complied with the ban and brought a §1983 action in federal court to challenge its constitutionality. Suppose that immediately after Alex's complaint was served on the defendants, he was arrested and charged with trespass based on the earlier two incidents. After instituting this proceeding in state court, defendants asked the federal court to dismiss Alex's suit under the *Younger* doctrine. Does *Younger* require dismissal?

Explanation

Since the federal court has not yet reached the merits of the case, abstention would seem to be required under *Hicks*. However, Alex might argue that the court should make an exception to the *Younger* doctrine because the state prosecution was brought in bad faith and for the sole purpose of forcing a dismissal of his federal suit. However, defendants will note that they never promised not to prosecute Alex for the earlier incidents, nor is this a case where the state lacks all hope of winning a valid conviction. It is therefore unlikely the court would make an exception to *Younger* and Alex's federal suit will probably be dismissed.

Patently Unconstitutional

Just as the bad faith or harassment exception has been severely curtailed by the Court, the exception for patently unconstitutional state laws is so narrow that it is difficult to imagine a case that would satisfy it. In *Younger*, the Court said that to trigger this exception, the challenged statute must be "flagrantly and patently violative of express constitutional prohibitions in every clause, sentence and paragraph, and in whatever manner and against whomever an effort might be made to apply it." 401 U.S. at 53-54. Justice Stevens later complained that the Court has applied this exception so stringently that it will fail "whenever a statute has a legitimate title," even if everything else about the law is unconstitutional. *Trainor v. Hernandez*, 431 U.S. 434, 463 (1977) (Stevens, J., dissenting).

Extraordinary Circumstances

The final exception to the *Younger* doctrine applies where, because of extraordinary circumstances, irreparable harm would occur if the federal court did not intervene. However, this, too, is an empty category. The Court has suggested that this exception might be appropriate in cases where the federal plaintiff lacks an adequate opportunity to raise the constitutional issue in the state proceeding. *Kugler v. Helfant*, 421 U.S. 117, 125 n.4 (1975) (citing *Gibson v. Berryhill*, 411 U.S. 564 (1973)). Yet such a situation would not constitute an *exception* to the *Younger* doctrine but rather an instance where one of the doctrine's basic prerequisites has not been satisfied (see §4.5.4). The Supreme Court has routinely rejected claims that extraordinary circumstances warrant an exception to *Younger*. The lower federal courts have applied the exception almost as sparingly.

§4.5.6 Returning to Federal Court

The *Younger* doctrine itself merely delays a litigant's access to federal court. However, *Younger* often interacts with principles of collateral estoppel to prevent a litigant from ever obtaining a federal court ruling on the constitutionality of a state law. According to *Younger*, once a state proceeding is no longer pending — i.e., once all available appeals have been exhausted — a would-be plaintiff is free to file her constitutional challenge in federal court. Yet collateral estoppel or issue preclusion may now defeat plaintiff's federal suit. The Supreme Court has held that the doctrines of res judicata and collateral estoppel are fully applicable to §1983 actions brought in federal court, for 28 U.S.C. §1738 commands federal courts to give state court judgments "the same full faith and credit" the rendering state court would give them, even if doing so will "deprive plaintiff of the 'right' to have their federal claims relitigated in federal court. . . . This is so even when the plaintiff would have preferred not to litigate in state court, but was required to do so by statute or prudential rules." *San Remo Hotel, L.P. v. City and County of San Francisco*, 545 U.S. 323, 342 (2005). As a result, if in the earlier state proceeding the state court or administrative agency rejected a litigant's challenge to the constitutionality of the state law, that finding is normally binding on the parties in a subsequent §1983 action in federal court and the issue may not be relitigated. Thus, the ultimate effect of the *Younger* abstention doctrine is often to permanently bar — rather than just temporarily delay — a federal court from ruling on the constitutionality of a state law. In these instances, unless a litigant is able to secure Supreme Court review of the state ruling, the state courts will have had the final word as to the constitutionality of the state law.

This is a troubling consequence to the extent that one believes federal courts are sometimes more capable of fairly resolving constitutional challenges to state laws than are politically accountable state judges. Yet whether or not this is a valid concern, it is not shared by the modern Supreme Court. Refusing to entertain such "a general distrust of the capacity of the state courts to render correct decisions on constitutional issues," the Court has instead reaffirmed "the constitutional obligation of the state courts to uphold federal law, and its expression of confidence in their ability to do so." *Allen v. McCurry*, 449 U.S. 90, 105 (1980).

Nevertheless, there are several ways in which litigants may try to obtain a federal court ruling on their constitutional challenges to state laws even though *Younger* initially blocked access to the federal court. Where the state proceeding was a criminal action, a convicted defendant who presented the constitutional issue to the state court and who has exhausted all state appeals may usually challenge the conviction by bringing a habeas corpus action in federal district court. Federal habeas is available if the defendant was sentenced to jail, placed on probation, or released on parole. Because all state appeals have necessarily been pursued, the suit is no longer pending for *Younger* purposes. Nor does collateral estoppel pose an obstacle because in habeas corpus actions, federal courts are not bound by the state courts' findings on constitutional issues. Thus, in the context of many criminal cases, the *Younger* doctrine will not permanently deny a litigant access to the federal court.

Younger also applies with respect to pending state civil and administrative proceedings. Habeas corpus is not available in these settings, nor is it an option in criminal cases that resulted only in the imposition of a fine. Litigants in these situations may try to protect their ability to obtain a federal ruling on their constitutional challenge by not raising the issue in the state proceeding, thus reserving it for later presentation to a federal court. Such attempts to deny state courts a chance to address the constitutional issue would seem to be inconsistent with the rationale of the *Younger* doctrine. As the Court has said, "*Younger v. Harris* contemplates the outright dismissal of the federal suit, and the presentation of all claims, both state and federal, to the state courts." *Gibson v. Berryhill*, 411 U.S. 564, 577 (1973). In *Juidice v. Vail*, 430 U.S. 327 (1977), the Court thus held that plaintiffs' federal action had to be dismissed under *Younger* even though they did not raise their federal constitutional challenge in the state court proceedings. Instead, the plaintiffs "need be accorded only an opportunity to fairly pursue their constitutional claims in the ongoing state proceedings, and their failure to avail themselves of such opportunities does not mean that the state procedures were inadequate." Id. at 337. Lower federal courts have accordingly ruled that "when *Younger* abstention applies, federal plaintiffs cannot reserve their federal claim from state court adjudication for later decision by the federal court." *Beltran v. California*, 871 F.2d 777, 783 n.8 (9th Cir. 1989); accord, *Temple of the Lost Sheep Inc. v. Abrams*, 930 F.2d 178, 181-183 (2d Cir.), cert. denied, 502 U.S. 866 (1991); *Duty Free Shop, Inc. v. Administracion de Terrenos*, 889 F.2d 1181,

1182-1183 (1st Cir. 1989). A litigant who fails to raise the constitutional issue in the state proceeding may be deemed to have waived the objection. Thus, except in the criminal setting, the *Younger* doctrine usually has the effect of permanently foreclosing the lower federal courts from ruling on the constitutionality of the challenged state law.

§4.6 COMMON LAW IMMUNITY

As we noted earlier in discussing the Eleventh Amendment "stripping doctrine," state and local officials who are sued under 42 U.S.C. §1983 for having violated an individual's federal rights may enjoy a common law immunity from civil damages actions. See §4.2.6 ("Holding Officials Personally Liable in Damages"). Because the Supreme Court has read this immunity into §1983, the immunity applies whether the §1983 action is filed in a federal or a state court.

The extent of an official's immunity depends on the nature of the function he or she was performing when he or she violated the plaintiff's rights. If the function was legislative in nature, the official is absolutely immune from civil suit — including both damages claims and claims for declaratory or injunctive relief. If the function was judicial or prosecutorial in nature, the immunity is likewise absolute but only as to damages claims. Finally, if the function was executive or ministerial in nature, the official possesses a qualified immunity but solely with respect to claims for damages. Under qualified immunity, the defendant official will not be held liable for damages if a reasonable person in the defendant's shoes would not have realized that his or her conduct was in violation of federal law. If, however, the federal constitutional or statutory right sued upon was "clearly established" at the time the official acted, qualified immunity will not attach. See §§4.2.6, 7.8.1 (exploring application of qualified immunity). Similar principles apply with respect to civil suits for damages brought against federal officials.

The Powers of the National Government

§5.1 INTRODUCTION AND OVERVIEW

The government created by the Constitution is national in the sense that its authority may be exercised throughout the nation and as a member of the family of nations. But it is also a limited government. This means that it may exercise only those powers granted to it by the Constitution. Powers not granted to the national government are, in the words of the Tenth Amendment, "reserved to the States respectively, or to the people." This principle of federalism embodied in the Constitution serves a dual function. First, by allocating only certain powers to the national government, "the federal system preserves the integrity, dignity, and residual sovereignty of the States." *Bond v. United States*, 131 S. Ct. 2355, 2364 (2011). Second, "[b]y denying any one government complete jurisdiction over all the concerns of public life, federalism protects the liberty of the individual from arbitrary power." Id. Thus, the states as well as individuals are the intended beneficiaries of federalism.

The bulk of the powers granted to the national government, sometimes referred to as enumerated powers, are described in Article I, §8; others are found in various provisions of the Constitution, as well as in certain constitutional amendments. In addition, the Court has recognized that the United States possesses certain inherent powers that place the national government on an equal footing with other nations. These implied powers, although not specifically enumerated, are nonetheless properly characterized as granted powers implicit in the constitutional conferral of nationhood.

The consequence of the related principles of limited government and federalism is that every exercise of national authority must be linked to a constitutionally granted power. Typically the Court is quite deferential when determining whether Congress has acted within the scope of a granted power. From an analytical perspective, the specific power must be identified and its scope defined. The question then becomes whether the exercise of authority at issue comes within that defined scope. For example, suppose Congress passes a statute that regulates the length of trucks engaged in interstate commerce. The most plausible power being exercised is the power over "commerce among the states" granted by Article I, §8, cl. 3. If this regulation comes within the defined scope of that power — a topic we will explore below — the congressional enactment is constitutional. If it does not, either another power must be identified or the law will be invalidated. Congress sometimes identifies the specific power under which a statute is being enacted. Yet Congress's designation is not binding on a reviewing court. A court may thus rule that a federal law involved the improper exercise of a power Congress expressly relied upon, while conversely a court can uphold a law under a power that Congress never in fact invoked. "The 'question of the constitutionality of action taken by Congress does not depend on recitals of the power which it undertakes to exercise.'" *National Federation of Independent Business v. Sebelius*, 132 S. Ct. 2566, 2598 (2012) (quoting *Woods v. Cloyd W. Miller Co.*, 333 U.S. 138, 144 (1948)).

Although analytically there is nothing particularly difficult in this process of identifying possible powers and applying the defined scope of each, underlying the process is a significant philosophic debate regarding the nature of our federal system of government. From a nationalist perspective, the tendency is to give the granted powers a broad sweep, substantially diminishing the realm of powers reserved to the states or to the people. If, for example, the power over commerce among the states embraces every possible commercial transaction conducted within the United States, then what is "reserved" in this context becomes nothing more than a product of congressional inaction. On the other hand, if one adopts a state-oriented perspective, the tendency is to corral the scope of the granted powers in a manner that preserves a perceived principle of federalism or reserved powers, thus leaving more independent authority to the states. The tension between nationalism and states' rights is inherent in every exercise of federal power and is reflected in the analytical models developed by the Court to measure the scope of that power.

This chapter examines three major national powers: the power to regulate interstate commerce, the power to tax and spend, and the power over foreign affairs. This triumvirate of federal powers, although not exclusive, represents the major and most frequently exercised and examined grants of authority found in the body of the Constitution. Moreover, the judicial treatment of these powers also provides a general sense of the Court's approach to assessing the scope of national powers. We begin our discussion, however, with an important prelude—the Necessary and Proper Clause (Art. I, §8, cl. 18)—a provision that has been interpreted to give the national government substantial though not unlimited discretion in the implementation of its granted powers. Overall, one should get the sense from this chapter that at least until recently, the limited nature of the federal government has been more often a theory than a fact.

§5.2 THE NECESSARY AND PROPER CLAUSE

As was noted above, Article I, §8 contains the bulk of the powers granted to the national government. Those granted powers are described in seventeen separate paragraphs or clauses, each focusing on a particular subject matter or cluster of subject matters. For example, one clause grants Congress the power "To establish Post Offices and post Roads," while another grants the power "To declare War, grant Letters of Marque and Reprisal, and make Rules concerning Captures on Land and Water." Art. I, §8, cls. 7 & 11. The final clause of Article I, §8, generally referred to as the Necessary and Proper Clause, is different. It grants Congress the power "To make all Laws which shall be necessary and proper for carrying into Execution the foregoing Powers, and all other Powers vested by this Constitution in the Government of the United States, or in any Department or Officer thereof." This clause does not vest regulatory or supervisory authority over any particular subject matter; rather, it guarantees a latitude of discretion in the exercise of all other granted powers (including those granted in other parts of the Constitution). By so doing, the Necessary and Proper Clause ensures that the particularized grants can be exercised completely and effectively.

Example 5-A

As part of its effort to improve postal services in rural communities, Congress has delegated to the U.S. Postal Service an authority to exercise the power of eminent domain to procure land for new and expanded post office facilities in those communities. The Constitution grants Congress the power to "establish Post Offices and post Roads." It does not, however, mention anything about a power of eminent domain. Does the congressional action represent an appropriate exercise of constitutional power?

Explanation

Yes. Under the Necessary and Proper Clause, the power of eminent domain may be exercised as a means to ensure that the power to establish post offices can be exercised completely and effectively.

The key case interpreting the Necessary and Proper Clause is *McCulloch v. Maryland*, 17 U.S. (4 Wheat.) 316 (1819). The opinion was authored by Chief Justice John Marshall and contains some of his most powerful and creative rhetoric. It is also one of the pillars of modern constitutional law. Specifically at issue in *McCulloch* was the constitutionality of a state law that taxed the activities of the Second Bank of the United States, a federally chartered financial institution. The first question to be resolved was whether the Constitution granted Congress the power to charter the bank. The Court began its discussion of this issue by affirming the principle that the national government may act only pursuant to an enumerated power. Id. at 405-406. Yet despite the absence of any specific constitutional grant of power to charter a bank or a corporation, the Court upheld the authority of Congress to do so.

Marshall premised his conclusion on two lines of reasoning, the first structural and the second textual. The structural argument described the Constitution as a foundational charter that created a system of government designed to address problems of national concern. The specific grants of power marked the outlines of that government's authority, but could not describe the details or the future contingencies to which the granted powers might be applied. Moreover, Marshall assumed that the people would want this national government to be an effective government. He reasoned, therefore, that the Constitution vested Congress with the authority to select reasonable means through which to exercise its constitutional responsibilities. Thus, after outlining several granted powers that implicated monetary concerns — "the great powers to lay and collect taxes; to borrow money; to regulate commerce; to declare and conduct a war; and to raise and support armies and navies," 17 U.S. at 407 — Marshall observed,

> But it may with great reason be contended, that a government, entrusted with such ample powers, on the due execution of which the happiness and prosperity of the nation so vitally depends, must also be entrusted with ample means for their execution. The power being given, it is the interest of the nation to facilitate its execution. It can never be their interest, and cannot be presumed to have been their intention, to clog and embarrass its execution by withholding the most appropriate means.

17 U.S. at 408. He then explained, somewhat elliptically, why the creation of a national bank was a reasonable means to effectuate the previously described granted powers:

> Throughout this vast republic, from the St. Croix to the Gulph of Mexico, from the Atlantic to the Pacific, revenue is to be collected and expended, armies are to be marched and supported. The exigencies of the nation may require that the treasure raised in the north should be transported to the south, *that* raised in the east conveyed to the west, or that this order should be reversed. Is that construction of the constitution to be preferred which would render these operations difficult, hazardous, and expensive? Can we adopt that construction, (unless the words imperiously require it,) which would impute to the framers of that instrument, when granting these powers for the public good, the intention of impeding their exercise by withholding a choice of means?

Id. at 408. Marshall's answer to his rhetorical questions was an emphatic no.

The second component of Marshall's argument focused directly on the Necessary and Proper Clause. "But the constitution of the United States has not left the right of Congress to employ the necessary means, for the execution of the powers conferred on the government, to general reasoning." Id. at 411. The Necessary and Proper Clause was, according to Marshall, a textual affirmation of that general reasoning. In so concluding, he rejected the state's argument that the Necessary and Proper Clause was designed to limit Congress to the choice of those means that were the "most direct and simple." Id. at 413. Necessary did not mean absolutely necessary. "To employ the means necessary to an end, is generally understood as employing any means calculated to produce the end, and not as being confined to those single means, without which the end would be entirely unattainable." Id. at 413-414. He further explained, in terms that echoed his general reasoning:

> It must have been the intention of those who gave these powers, to insure, as far as human prudence could insure, their beneficial execution. This could not be done by confiding the choice of means to such narrow limits as not to leave it in the power of Congress to adopt any which might be appropriate, and which were conducive to the end. This provision is made in a constitution intended to endure for ages to come, and, consequently, to be adapted to the various *crises* of human affairs. . . . To have declared that the best means shall not be used, but those alone without which the power given would be nugatory, would have been to deprive the legislature of the capacity to avail itself of experience, to exercise its reason, and to accommodate its legislation to circumstances.

Id. at 415-416.

Finally, Marshall summed up the combination of his general reasoning and his interpretation of the Necessary and Proper Clause as follows:

> We admit, as all must admit, that the powers of the government are limited, and that its limits are not to be transcended. But we think the sound construction of the constitution must allow to the national legislature that discretion, with respect to the means by which the powers it confers are to be carried into execution, which will enable that body to perform the high duties assigned to it, in the manner most beneficial to the people. Let the end be legitimate, let it be within the scope of the constitution, and all means which are appropriate, which are plainly adapted to that end, which are not prohibited, but consist with the letter and spirit of the constitution, are constitutional.

Id. at 421.

Marshall's interpretation of the Necessary and Proper Clause remains the authoritative interpretation of that clause. Thus, "in determining whether the Necessary and Proper Clause grants Congress the legislative authority to enact a particular federal statute, we look to see whether the statute constitutes a means that is rationally related to the implementation of a constitutionally enumerated power." *United States v. Comstock*, 130 S. Ct. 1949, 1956 (2010). As a consequence, Congress today is vested with broad discretion in choosing the means through which it will exercise its granted powers. Yet that discretion is not unlimited. Nor are the terms "necessary" and "proper" always synonymous. The Court has thus held that even though a particular law may satisfy the requirement of being "necessary" in the rationally related sense, it may still not be "proper" if it would tend to "undermine the structure of government established by the Constitution." *National Federation of Independent Business v. Sebelius*, 132 S. Ct. 2566, 2592 (2012).

The Necessary and Proper Clause applies not only to the powers described in Article I, §8, but also to "all other Powers vested by this Constitution in the Government of the United States, or in any Department or Officer thereof." This means that Congress may rely on the Necessary and Proper Clause as a means to execute all constitutionally granted powers, including those vested in the executive and judicial branches. In other words, the clause empowers Congress to provide the coordinate branches with the means to carry out their respective constitutional responsibilities. Thus, through the creation of administrative agencies, Congress provides a "necessary and proper" means through which the President can exercise his Article II duty to see "that the Laws be faithfully executed." Similarly, by providing support personnel to the federal judiciary, Congress provides a "necessary and proper" means through which the judiciary can effectively exercise the judicial power vested in it by Article III.

§5.3 THE POWER OVER INTERSTATE COMMERCE

The Commerce Clause, Article I, §8, cl. 3, provides that "[t]he Congress shall have Power . . . To regulate Commerce with foreign Nations, and among the several States, and with the Indian Tribes. . . ." The power to regulate commerce among the several states is typically referred to as the interstate commerce power or, more simply, as the commerce power. The modern Court has tended to give the commerce power a broad interpretive sweep, vesting Congress with substantial authority to regulate private economic activity in the domestic sphere. Indeed, the Commerce Clause is the primary tool relied on by Congress to regulate domestic affairs. The sweep of the power is not, however, infinite. In a series of recent decisions, which we will consider below, the Court found that despite the breadth of the commerce power, Congress had exceeded the granted authority by attempting to regulate noneconomic activity that was more properly left to the states. The goal of this section, therefore, is to discover the boundaries of this generally expansive power.

The basic formula for analyzing applications of the commerce power is relatively simple. It begins with the words of the clause—"commerce," "among the states," and "regulate." The word "commerce" embraces any activity involved in the *commercial exchange of goods and services*, including the marketing, purchase, and transportation of those goods. The key phrase is "commercial exchange." Thus the sale of goods is a classic instance of commerce, while the production of those goods is not. Production may affect exchange, but it is not part of the process of exchange. Next, commerce "among the several states"—i.e., interstate commerce—includes those commercial exchanges that involve activity occurring in more than one state. For example, a sale that begins in one state and ends in another is interstate commerce, while a sale that is consummated entirely in one state is not. Finally, the power to "regulate" this interstate commerce is the power to prescribe the rules under which that commerce shall be transacted, including the power to prohibit particular transactions.

Given the above definitions, the Court has recognized three broad categories of activity that Congress may regulate under its commerce power. First, Congress may regulate the use of the *channels* of interstate commerce. This embraces the power to prescribe the rules of conduct to be applied to any activity that can rationally be characterized as constituting interstate commerce. Congress may on this basis regulate the terms and conditions on which goods or services are sold interstate and may restrict the types of goods that can be shipped from one state to another.

Second, Congress may regulate the *instrumentalities* of interstate commerce such as railroads, airlines, and trucking companies, since these activities are the conduits through which interstate commerce occurs. This includes the power to protect these instrumentalities from threats that come from interstate or local activities. Thus, Congress may impose safety standards on local or intrastate carriers that use the same railway tracks, airspace, or highways as interstate carriers to prevent these local carriers from endangering interstate carriers that operate on the same routes.

Third, by using the Necessary and Proper Clause in connection with the Commerce Clause, the commerce power also includes the authority to regulate any economic activity that has a substantial relationship with interstate commerce or that *substantially affects* that commerce. The Court sometimes refers to this extension of the commerce power to activities that are not themselves part of interstate commerce as the "affecting commerce" rationale. (The terms "substantial relationship" and "substantially affects" are treated synonymously; we will refer to them jointly as the substantially affects test.)

Thus, although the production of goods for sale in interstate commerce is not itself interstate commerce, but is rather local activity that precedes interstate commerce, it is an economic activity that substantially affects interstate commerce and may, therefore, be subjected to congressional regulation through a combination of the Commerce Clause and the Necessary and Proper Clause. Given the interdependence of our national economy, few, if any, economic or commercial matters can escape the sweep of the commerce power, particularly the third part of that test. As we shall see, however, the meaning one assigns to the word "substantially" is of key significance, for this will determine the extent to which Congress may reach local activities that exert an effect on interstate commerce. Over the years the Court has taken sharply contradictory approaches under the third part of the test.

Before examining more closely how the Court today applies these concepts to concrete situations, we will first examine briefly the history of the Court's Commerce Clause jurisprudence. The purpose is not academic. The theories and techniques applied to exercises of the commerce power over the last two centuries continue to recur in modern jurisprudence. History, therefore, is a primer for modern practice. In reviewing this history, it is useful to keep in mind the distinction between the Commerce Clause itself and its extension by the Necessary and Proper Clause. Whether or not the Court is careful to point this out, whenever Congress is attempting to regulate an activity that does not itself constitute interstate commerce or an instrumentality of interstate commerce, what is at issue is the reach of the Necessary and Proper Clause as it augments the Commerce Clause.

§5.3.1 A Brief History of Commerce Clause Jurisprudence

One of the principal purposes of the Commerce Clause was to prevent individual states from erecting trade barriers to interstate and foreign trade. *The Federalist No. 11*, at 53-54 (A. Hamilton); *The Federalist No. 42*, at

214-215 (J. Madison) (Clinton Rossiter ed., 1961). From this perspective, the Commerce Clause empowers Congress to wield a negative trump on such state-imposed restraints, the implicit goal being the creation of a common market among the states. Yet the text of the Commerce Clause describes a general power over commerce among the states, not merely an authority to rescind state barriers to that commerce. And in accord with that text, the Court has consistently interpreted the clause as permitting positive exercises of authority — i.e., exercises of authority that promote the positive economic agenda of Congress. In short, the clause has been interpreted as vesting Congress with the authority to adopt legislation designed to promote an interstate economic agenda that transcends the vision of a common market free from state-imposed restraints.

The foundation for the modern interpretation of the commerce power was laid, not too surprisingly, by Chief Justice John Marshall. In *Gibbons v. Ogden*, 22 U.S. (9 Wheat.) 1 (1824), decided only five years after *McCulloch v. Maryland*, the Chief Justice described that power as vesting Congress with a plenary authority over commerce that affected more states than one:

> The genius and character of the whole government seem to be, that its action is to be applied to all the external concerns of the nation, and to those internal concerns which affect the States generally; but not to those which are completely within a particular State, which do not affect other States, and with which it is not necessary to interfere, for the purpose of executing some of the general powers of the government.

Id. at 195. Explicit in Marshall's description of federal power is the notion that Congress may, under the Commerce Clause as augmented by the Necessary and Proper Clause, regulate any commerce that has interstate effects — essentially the same scope assigned to the power by our modern three-part formula. But this nationalist vision is tempered by a potentially important caveat. "The enumeration presupposes something not enumerated; and that something, if we regard the language, or the subject of the sentence, must be the exclusively internal commerce of a State." Id. Congress may not, therefore, rely on the commerce power to regulate matters that are completely internal to a state — i.e., economic matters that do not affect more states than one.

Despite the characteristic confidence with which Chief Justice Marshall wrote, the seemingly simple *Gibbons* formula did not provide an obvious solution for the myriad of commerce problems that confronted the Court in the late nineteenth and early twentieth centuries. In part, this was because of the vast expansion of commercial activity that took place during that period. The consequent state and federal regulation of commerce seemed to create constitutional and conceptual difficulties that caused the Court to retreat from the nationalistic scheme described by Marshall in *Gibbons*.

One problem created by *Gibbons'* broad view of federal power over the nation's commercial affairs concerned the validity of state regulations of local matters that were *potentially* subject to federal regulation under the Commerce and Necessary and Proper Clauses. If the federal government chose not to regulate these matters, could states continue to do so? In *Cooley v. Board of Wardens*, 53 U.S. (12 How.) 299 (1851), the Court resolved this issue in a manner that preserved federal regulatory authority at a maximum, but without seriously impairing the states' ability to exercise their police powers in the interim. *Cooley* held that except in those areas which by their nature require a uniform national rule, the states retained a concurrent power to regulate local activities that affect interstate commerce until such time as Congress might opt to regulate those matters itself. *Cooley* thus allowed for the expansive view of federal power envisioned by *Gibbons v. Ogden*, while preserving state authority to regulate most local activities when the federal commerce power lay dormant.

In the decades following *Cooley*, the Court abandoned the view that there were areas of local economic activity over which the states and the federal government had concurrent authority. Instead, the Court divided the universe into two mutually exclusive realms. Some matters such as interstate commerce itself were reserved for regulation by the federal government. Other activities deemed to be of a local nature were no longer subject to federal regulation, even though they might affect interstate commerce; instead, they were now subject to regulation exclusively by the states. In abandoning *Cooley*'s concurrent power view, the Court greatly expanded the regulatory enclave that was set aside for the states; at the same time, it substantially curtailed the ability of Congress to regulate local economic activity through the Necessary and Proper Clause as it augments the Commerce Clause.

The Court's frequent reluctance during the late nineteenth and early twentieth centuries to validate exercises of the commerce power that interfered with matters perceived to be within the exclusive prerogative of the individual states was, in part, premised on the Tenth Amendment, which provides, "The powers not delegated to the United States by the Constitution, nor prohibited by it to the States, are reserved to the States respectively, or to the people." The underlying assumption was that there existed an enclave of activity, internal to the states, that was virtually insulated from congressional regulation. The definition of this enclave was not premised on a lack of external effects, but on what was perceived to be the inherently local nature of the activity at issue.

For example, in *United States v. Dewitt*, 76 U.S. (9 Wall.) 41 (1870), the Court struck down a congressional enactment that attempted to regulate the retail sale of certain mixed illuminating oils. The Court reasoned that the enactment represented an impermissible regulation of internal trade operating solely within the individual states; in other words, the regulation addressed an exclusively local matter. According to the Court, "this express grant of power to regulate commerce among the States has always been understood as limited by its terms; and as a virtual denial of any power to interfere with the internal trade and business of the separate States. . . ." Id. at 43-44. This, of course, ignores the possibility that the sale of those fuels was a matter that affects more states than one, thus potentially falling within the scope of the Commerce Clause under the more inclusive *Gibbons* model.

Similarly, in *United States v. E. C. Knight Co.*, 156 U.S. 1 (1895), the United States attempted to enforce provisions of the Sherman Act against a company that was alleged to have gained complete control over the manufacture of refined sugar within the United States. The Court held that the power over interstate commerce could not extend into this realm since manufacturing was a local activity, the regulation of which was reserved to the states. The Court suggested that "agriculture, mining, [and] production in all its forms" likewise came within this exclusive state enclave since they all involved local activities that preceded interstate commerce. Id. at 16. In the Court's words,

> Doubtless the power to control the manufacture of a given thing involves in a certain sense the control of its disposition, but this is a secondary and not the primary sense; and although the exercise of that power may result in bringing the operation of commerce into play, it does not control it, and it affects it only incidentally and indirectly. Commerce succeeds to manufacture, and is not a part of it.

Id. at 12. Thus, under the enclave theory of exclusive state power, Congress could not regulate these local activities under the commerce power notwithstanding their potential interstate effects.

Despite its restrictive view as to the reach of the commerce power, the Court was willing to uphold some federal laws that could be said to regulate the stream of interstate commerce itself. In *Swift & Co. v. United States*, 196 U.S. 375 (1905), for example, the government brought suit under the Sherman Act to restrain the practices of certain meat dealers who were alleged to have engaged in a conspiracy to control the prices at which livestock was sold throughout the United States. The conspiracy operated after the livestock had begun their interstate journey and while they remained in transit as part of interstate commerce. The Court, adopting a current or stream of commerce theory, affirmed this application of the act. Even though the activities being challenged took place within a single state, the effect on commerce was "direct" since the object of the conspiracy was to restrain sales of livestock arriving from other states:

> When cattle are sent for sale from a place in one State, with the expectation that they will end their transit, after purchase, in another, and when in effect they do so, with only the interruption necessary to find a purchaser at the stock

yards, and when this is a typical, constantly recurring course, the current thus existing is a current of commerce among the States, and the purchase of the cattle is a part and incident of such commerce.

Id. at 398-399.

In other cases, the Court upheld commercial regulations of admittedly local activities, returning to *Gibbons v. Ogden*'s more expansive view of federal power. In the *Shreveport Rate Cases*, 234 U.S. 342 (1914), the Court sustained a federal statute that authorized the Interstate Commerce Commission to prohibit a railroad from charging a higher rate for interstate services than was charged for similar intrastate services. The Court observed, "Wherever the interstate and intrastate transactions of carriers are so related that the government of the one involves the control of the other, it is Congress, and not the State, that is entitled to prescribe the final and dominant rule, for otherwise Congress would be denied the exercise of its constitutional authority and the State, and not the Nation, would be supreme within the national field." Id. at 351-352.

Yet *Shreveport* and *Swift* did not usher in a period of judicial deference to exercises of the commerce power. In fact, during the period between 1905 and 1936, the Court became even more hostile toward federal economic regulation. Indeed, the Court even curtailed the authority of Congress to regulate the stream of interstate commerce itself, authority that did not depend on a resort to the Necessary and Proper Clause. In doing so, the Court placed renewed reliance on the enclave theory as applied to the commerce power. Thus, in *Hammer v. Dagenhart*, 247 U.S. 251 (1918), the Court held that Congress could not prohibit the interstate transportation of goods manufactured with child labor. Since there was no inherent dangerousness in the shipment of the goods, the Court deemed the regulation not to be of commerce but of the conditions under which the goods were manufactured. In other words, even though the statute literally regulated interstate commerce itself, the Court concluded that the real object and purpose of the law was to regulate manufacturing, a purely local activity that was reserved to the states:

> The grant of power to Congress over the subject of interstate commerce was to enable it to regulate such commerce, and not to give it authority to control the States in their exercise of the police power over local trade and manufacture.
>
> The grant of authority over a purely federal matter was not intended to destroy the local power always existing and carefully reserved to the States in the Tenth Amendment to the Constitution.

Id. at 273-274. Justice Oliver Wendell Holmes wrote a sharp dissent, noting that the regulation here was of interstate transportation and therefore directly within the power of Congress. "The act does not meddle with anything belonging to the States. They may regulate their internal affairs and their domestic commerce as they like. But when they seek to send their products across the state line they are no longer within their rights. . . . Under the Constitution such commerce belongs not to the States but to Congress to regulate." Id. at 281. Nonetheless, from the perspective of the majority, the "enclave" of manufacturing was deemed immune from federal interference.

The Court's less-than-deferential approach to exercises of the commerce power continued through the early years of the New Deal, with the Court invalidating various congressional enactments on the theory that the laws being challenged exceeded the scope of the power. In *Schechter Poultry Corp. v. United States*, 295 U.S. 495 (1935), for example, the Court relied on a formal and evanescent distinction between "direct" and "indirect" effects on interstate commerce in striking down a congressional enactment that regulated the hours and wages of employees in the poultry business. Id. at 548-550. See also *Railroad Retirement Board v. Alton R.R. Co.*, 295 U.S. 330 (1935) (relationship between interstate commerce and railroad pensions too tenuous to permit Congress to regulate the latter); see generally Stern, "The Commerce Clause and the National Economy, 1933-1946," 59 *Harv. L. Rev.* 645 (1946).

These and other cases striking down New Deal legislation eventually led President Franklin Roosevelt to propose his infamous court-packing plan. Although the court-packing plan was never adopted, President Roosevelt did succeed in his ultimate goal of changing the direction of the Court, in part because of the implicit threat of the plan and in part because of the natural course of judicial retirements and new appointments. The result, in the context of the Commerce Clause, was a return to a model akin to that first suggested by Chief Justice Marshall in *Gibbons*, but, as we shall see, in some respects much broader. See *NLRB v. Jones & Laughlin Steel Corp.*, 301 U.S. 1, 37 (1937) (abandoning the direct/indirect test and applying a "close and substantial relationship" formula to uphold the National Labor Relations Act's regulation of local activity that affected interstate commerce).

§5.3.2 The Modern Law of the Commerce Clause

The Court's decision in *United States v. Darby*, 312 U.S. 100 (1941), provides a classic example of *Gibbons* reformulated to advance the goals of a national economy. It also describes the basic framework for the current jurisprudence of the Commerce Clause. At issue in *Darby* was a federal statute, the Fair Labor Standards Act (FLSA), which prohibited the shipment in interstate commerce of certain products manufactured by employees who earned less than the minimum wage or who worked more hours than a specified maximum. The statute also prohibited the employment of workers, at other than the prescribed wages and hours, in the production of goods intended to be shipped in interstate commerce. The *Darby* Court upheld both components of the statute as proper exercises of the commerce power.

With respect to the prohibition of the interstate shipment of goods, the Court found no difficulty in sustaining the law under the Commerce Clause itself, unaided by the Necessary and Proper Clause. "While manufacture is not of itself interstate commerce, the shipment of manufactured goods interstate is such commerce and the prohibition of such shipment by Congress is indubitably a regulation of the commerce." Id. at 113. Regardless of Congress's motive and regardless of any effect upon matters internal to a state, the law was constitutional since it came within the granted authority of Congress as a regulation of the channels of interstate commerce. In contrast with *Hammer v. Dagenhart*, the Court held that even if a prohibition on interstate shipment was designed to compel in-state manufacturers to adopt federal standards and even if the prohibition had that effect, the law was constitutional so long as it actually regulated interstate commerce. Since the interstate transportation of manufactured goods is interstate commerce, the prohibition of any such shipment fell squarely within the authority granted by the Commerce Clause. *Hammer v. Dagenhart*, which had applied an enclave theory to prevent Congress from using the commerce power under such circumstances, was overruled.

The second component of the FLSA did not regulate interstate commerce. Rather, it regulated an aspect of manufacturing, namely, the wages and hours of individuals employed in the production of goods. But this regulation of a local commercial activity was a permissible exercise of the commerce power as augmented by the Necessary and Proper Clause:

> The power of Congress over interstate commerce is not confined to the regulation of commerce among the states. It extends to those activities intrastate which so affect interstate commerce or the exercise of the power of Congress over it as to make regulation of them appropriate means to the attainment of a legitimate end, the exercise of the granted power of Congress to regulate interstate commerce.

Id. at 118. With the aid of the Necessary and Proper Clause, Congress could regulate intrastate activity that had a "substantial effect on interstate commerce." Id. at 119. Indeed, the Court in *Darby* favorably cited *McCulloch v. Maryland*'s broad view of the Necessary and Proper Clause. Id. at 118-119, 124.

The FLSA's regulation of wages and hours satisfied this test. In the Court's view, the regulation was an appropriate means to ensure the effectiveness of the prohibition on the interstate shipment of goods produced under "substandard" labor conditions. Id. at 121. By preventing the production of goods under substandard labor conditions, Congress prevented (or made more difficult) the interstate shipment of those goods as well. In addition, Congress could reasonably conclude that substandard labor conditions adversely affected interstate commerce in two other ways: (1) by making interstate commerce an instrument for the spread of substandard labor conditions and (2) by causing a dislocation of interstate commerce through the unfair destruction of businesses adhering to higher labor standards. Id. at 122. As a consequence of these interstate effects, the regulation of production was constitutional without any reference to the prohibition on interstate shipments.

The *Darby* Court also rejected an argument that the Tenth Amendment prevented Congress from enacting the FLSA: "Our conclusion is unaffected by the Tenth Amendment which provides: 'The powers not delegated to the United States by the Constitution, nor prohibited by it to the States, are reserved to the States respectively, or to the people.' The amendment states but a truism that all is retained which has not been surrendered." Id. at 123-124. Since the power over commerce was "surrendered" to the United States by the Constitution, and since the FLSA came within the scope of that power, the Tenth Amendment had no bearing on the constitutionality of the FLSA.

In terms of Commerce Clause jurisprudence, *Darby* represented two important developments. First, the Court abandoned the view that under the commerce power, Congress could regulate only the "stream of commerce" and those activities that had "direct effects" on interstate commerce; instead, the Court adopted a more inclusive "substantially affects" test that broadened the reach of the commerce power. Second, by treating the Tenth Amendment as a truism, the *Darby* Court essentially destroyed the enclave theory and the notion that certain activities were automatically off-limits to federal regulation. The net effect was a significant expansion of federal power. Post-*Darby*, Congress, pursuant to the Commerce Clause and the Necessary and Proper Clause, may regulate interstate commerce itself as well as any local economic activity that substantially affects interstate commerce.

We will now look at a number of examples dealing with laws enacted pursuant to the commerce power.

Example 5-B

In 1994 Congress enacted the Drivers' Privacy Protection Act (DPPA). The DPPA regulates the disclosure and resale of personal information contained in the records of state motor vehicle departments (DMVs). Congress adopted the measure after finding that many states were selling this information to individuals and businesses who then used it to contact drivers for marketing purposes. The DPPA prohibits DMVs from disclosing this information without a driver's consent unless the disclosure falls within one of the act's enumerated exceptions. Those who receive information from a DMV pursuant to one of the statutory exceptions are likewise subject to strict regulation concerning their resale or redisclosure of the information. Is the DPPA a proper exercise of Congress's commerce power?

Explanation

The DPPA might be justified under two different aspects of the commerce power. See §5.3. First, the act might be viewed as a valid regulation of the channels of interstate commerce to the extent that it prohibits a particular good or thing — i.e., state-collected information about drivers — from being sold or released into the stream of interstate commerce (except under limited conditions). Yet while such information is an article of commerce if used for commercial purposes, the DPPA prohibits all releases of such information, not just those releases that are destined for interstate commerce. In theory, at least, a DMV might release information about a particular driver to someone intending to use it exclusively in that state.

Alternatively, the DPPA might be defended on the ground that it regulates an economic activity — the sale of state-collected drivers' information — that is substantially related to or substantially affects interstate commerce. Under this approach, Congress may use the Necessary and Proper Clause to regulate the entire class of activity, even though not all of the information sold or disclosed by a DMV will necessarily find its way into interstate commerce. See *Reno v. Condon*, 528 U.S. 141 (2000) (upholding the DPPA as being a valid regulation of the channels or stream of interstate commerce without discussing whether it might also be sustained under the Necessary and Proper Clause). See also *Pierce County v. Guillen*, 537 U.S. 129 (2003) (federally created discovery privilege for information compiled and collected by state agencies participating in a federal highway safety program represents permissible exercise of the commerce power).

Example 5-C

The Federal Surface Mining Act (FSMA) regulates the practice of "strip mining," a technique through which the surface of land is stripped away to extract minerals resting below the surface. The FSMA limits the circumstances under which strip mining can be used, and requires that all strip mines be returned to their original contour once a mining operation is complete. In adopting this legislation, Congress found that strip mining creates serious environmental harm by causing erosion and landslides, by polluting rivers, by destroying wildlife habitats, and by counteracting government efforts to preserve soil, water, and other natural resources. Does the regulation of strip mining come within the commerce power? Does it matter that the FSMA regulates land use, an area of law typically left to the states?

Explanation

The practice of strip mining is not itself interstate commerce. Strip mining is a local economic activity much like farming or manufacturing. Yet, although strip mining is not itself interstate commerce, the practice of strip mining may substantially affect interstate commerce. Certainly this is true if the assertions made by the proponents of the FSMA have any basis in fact. The cited harms could affect interstate commerce by imposing substantial economic costs on the affected communities, which in turn could have a dislocating impact on interstate commerce. Similarly, several of the perceived negative impacts are of a type likely to have an interstate spillover (e.g., pollution of rivers, destruction of wildlife habitats, and harm to natural resources), all of which could be rationally described as substantially affecting interstate commerce. If the practice of strip mining does substantially affect interstate commerce, it makes no difference that the FSMA regulates land use. Unless the Court were to return to an enclave theory, the fact that land-use regulation is typically within the province of the states does not limit the scope of the commerce power. See *Hodel v. Virginia Surface Mining & Reclamation Assn., Inc.*, 452 U.S. 264 (1981).

In order for Congress to regulate local activities on the basis that they substantially affect interstate commerce, it is not necessary that each and every person or entity being regulated exert a substantial effect on interstate commerce. Rather, it is enough that Congress is regulating a class or group of activities that in the aggregate exerts this effect, regardless of the effect caused by any individual member.

Example 5-D

The Produce Marketing Act (PMA) is a federal statute that regulates the "marketing" of farm produce throughout the United States. Marketing is defined to include the selling of produce grown on the farm as well as the consumption of produce before it leaves the farm. The act limits the amount of produce that may be grown on a farm regardless of whether the produce is sold or is instead consumed there. Filbert owns a small dairy farm in Alabama. Each year he grows a winter crop of wheat, some of which he sells and some of which he keeps for his own consumption on the farm. Under the act, Filbert is permitted to sow no more than 11 acres of wheat; in violation of the act, however, he sowed 20 acres of wheat. He intends to keep the entire excess for consumption on the farm. Nonetheless, under the act, he must pay a substantial penalty for having grown the excess wheat. Under the commerce power, may Congress regulate the production and consumption of wheat on Filbert's farm?

Explanation

The PMA is not a regulation of interstate commerce. Farming, like manufacturing, is not itself commerce; rather, farming is production, an activity that is at best antecedent to commerce. Nor is the activity in any fashion "interstate." However, growing wheat even if exclusively for home consumption might still be fairly characterized as involving "economic" activity, for it does involve the production and use of a form of wealth. Moreover, as was true with strip mining, farming does substantially affect interstate commerce, and despite the relatively limited farming engaged in by Filbert, Filbert is a member of a group whose activities as a class substantially affect interstate commerce. Under the class of activities rationale or so-called aggregation principle, Congress could rationally conclude that the collective consumption of "excess" wheat on farms has a substantial impact on the interstate market for wheat; Filbert's small contribution to this impact is enough to bring his activity within the regulated whole. If a large number of farmers grow *excess* wheat and consume that wheat on the farm, they will deliver their entire *authorized* allotment of wheat to the market (since they won't need to save any), thus potentially glutting the market and driving prices down. Similarly, farmers who store excess wheat will have no need to resort to the market for the purchase of wheat, again driving the prices down. See *Wickard v. Filburn*, 317 U.S. 111 (1942) (applying a similar analysis under similar facts).

Example 5-E

Tommy grows marijuana on his farm in rural Virginia. He sells a small portion of his crop to neighbors and friends, and keeps the rest for himself. On the basis of these activities, Tommy has been charged with violating the Controlled Substances Act (CSA), a federal statute that makes the sale of marijuana a federal offense. Although the elements of the offense do not require any showing of a nexus with interstate commerce, the CSA includes the following congressional findings: "Controlled substances distributed locally usually have been transported in interstate commerce immediately before their distribution; local distribution and possession of controlled substances contribute to swelling the interstate traffic in such substances; and, federal regulation of the intrastate incidents of the traffic in controlled substances is essential to the effective control of the interstate incidents of such traffic." Consistent with the commerce power, may Tommy be convicted under the CSA for the local sale of marijuana?

Explanation

Yes. Whether Tommy's own activity actually affects interstate commerce is irrelevant. It is enough that Congress has rationally concluded that the intrastate sale of marijuana is sufficiently related to the interstate traffic in marijuana, such that the regulation of intrastate traffic is necessary or appropriate to the effective regulation of interstate traffic. Given the findings made by Congress, it is quite likely that a court will find that Congress has made a rational policy judgment regarding the need to proscribe the intrastate sale of marijuana. In other words, the congressional judgment that there is a substantial relationship between the intrastate marijuana market and the interstate marijuana market is sufficiently rational to permit Congress to regulate the former to more effectively regulate the latter. See *Perez v. United States*, 402 U.S. 146 (1971) (applying similar reasoning to a purely local extortionate credit transaction).

In the preceding examples, the statutes at issue were premised on a congressionally established presumption that a certain type of intrastate economic activity — strip mining, growing and consuming excess wheat, or the local sale of controlled substances — substantially affected interstate commerce. Application of the law required proof only that the individual had engaged in the regulated intrastate activity. No additional proof of a particular interstate nexus was required to establish a violation of the statute. This "generic" approach is constitutional so long as the standards of the Commerce Clause are satisfied.

Sometimes, however, Congress will require proof of a "jurisdictional nexus" with interstate commerce before a regulation can be applied in a particular case. Thus, under the Sherman Act, antitrust plaintiffs must prove that the defendant's activity restrained "commerce among the states." In essence, proof of this element ensures that enforcement of the Sherman Act remains within constitutional bounds. Similarly, many federal criminal statutes include a jurisdictional nexus element. For example, 18 U.S.C. §922 prohibits both the interstate *transportation* of stolen firearms and the *possession* of stolen firearms that have been transported interstate. Note how §922 parallels the statute upheld in *Darby* — the first part of the statute regulates interstate commerce, while the second part regulates a matter that substantially affects interstate commerce.

In general, although a statutory jurisdictional nexus informs constitutional analysis, the presence of such a nexus is neither a necessary nor a sufficient basis on which to validate an exercise of the commerce power. Rather, it is a tool through which Congress attempts to confine federal law to constitutional norms. Whether any particular jurisdictional nexus succeeds at that task requires the same judicial oversight that is applied to other regulations. In other words, with respect to any particular jurisdictional nexus, one must ask whether application of the nexus establishes an adequate constitutional link with interstate commerce by limiting the scope of the law to regulations of interstate commerce or matters that substantially affect interstate commerce. For example, in *Jones v. United States*, 529 U.S. 848 (2000), the Supreme Court reversed a conviction under the federal arson statute. The statute contained a jurisdictional nexus requiring that the property in question be "used in interstate or foreign commerce or in any activity affecting interstate or foreign commerce." The Court, however, refused to read this jurisdictional nexus requirement broadly to include a private residence merely because it received interstate natural gas, was used as security for an interstate mortgage, and was covered by an out-of-state insurance company. The Court noted that such a reading of the statute risked extending the affecting commerce rationale to unconstitutional lengths.

§5.3.3 The Commerce Clause and Civil Rights

Congress has used the commerce power as a source of governmental authority to prohibit various forms of discrimination in the economic marketplace, including discrimination based on race, gender, age, and disability. The two leading cases in this context are *Heart of Atlanta Motel, Inc. v. United States*, 379 U.S. 241 (1964), and *Katzenbach v. McClung*, 379 U.S. 294 (1964). Both cases involved challenges to the Civil Rights Act of 1964; and in both cases, the Court affirmed the use of the Commerce Clause as a means to promote civil rights in a broadly defined marketplace. (In adopting the Civil Rights Act of 1964, Congress also relied on its Fourteenth Amendment enforcement power; the scope of that power is discussed in Allan Ides and Christopher N. May, *Constitutional Law: Individual Rights*, Ch. 1 (6th ed. 2013). See also §4.2.8 (Example 4-O).)

Specifically at issue in *Heart of Atlanta Motel* was a provision of the Civil Rights Act of 1964 that made it unlawful for "any inn, hotel, motel, or other establishment which provides lodging for transient guests" to discriminate on the basis of race, color, religion, or national origin. The act was challenged by a motel that solicited and catered to a largely out-of-state clientele. Among other things, the motel owners claimed that the act exceeded the power of Congress under the Commerce Clause. The Court, however, found that Congress could have reasonably concluded that racial discrimination by motels serving interstate travelers substantially affected interstate commerce. Hearings held by Congress had revealed a pattern of nationwide exclusionary practices that imposed a

> qualitative as well as quantitative effect on interstate travel by Negroes. The former was the obvious impairment of the Negro traveler's pleasure and

convenience that resulted when he continually was uncertain of finding lodging. As for the latter, there was evidence that this uncertainty stemming from racial discrimination had the effect of discouraging travel on the part of a substantial portion of the Negro community.

379 U.S. at 253. The Civil Rights Act of 1964 was designed to ameliorate this burden on interstate commerce, and as such was well within the power of Congress under the Commerce Clause.

The Civil Rights Act of 1964 also prohibited racial discrimination by any restaurant that "serves or offers to serve interstate travelers or a substantial portion of food which it serves . . . has moved in [interstate] commerce." In *Katzenbach v. McClung*, this aspect of the act was challenged by the owner of a restaurant who wished to continue discriminating against customers on the basis of race. The restaurant, Ollie's Barbeque, was a family-owned operation located in Birmingham, Alabama. It catered to a largely local clientele, but 46 percent of the food it served was purchased from a "local supplier who had procured it from outside the State." 379 U.S. at 296. As a consequence of these facts, the act clearly applied to Ollie's Barbeque — in other words, the act's jurisdictional nexus was satisfied; the question was whether, as so applied, the act exceeded the power of Congress. Again the Court turned to the congressional hearings, citing evidence that racial discrimination by restaurants had a depressing effect on the economy by diminishing the amount spent in such restaurants by black customers and by imposing a "depressant effect on general business conditions in the respective communities." Id. at 299-300. This burden on interstate commerce, albeit indirect, was sufficiently substantial to unleash the power of Congress to prohibit such discrimination under the Commerce Clause.

Example 5-F

The Age Discrimination in Employment Act (ADEA) prohibits covered employers from discriminating against their employees on the basis of age. The act defines "employer" as "a person engaged in an industry affecting interstate commerce who has 20 or more employees for each working day in each of 20 or more calendar weeks in the current or preceding calendar year." The Best Seller is a family-owned bookstore located in central Texas. Its primary business is the sale of current titles, especially those on the *New York Times* bestseller list. The store does a large volume of business, and has employed over 20 people on each working day for the past several years. A recently dismissed employee of the Best Seller has filed a claim against the company under the ADEA. Can the ADEA be constitutionally applied to the employment practices of the Best Seller?

Explanation

The sale of current titles surely involves books that have recently moved in interstate commerce, as well as orders that have been placed through interstate channels. Given these facts, it would seem that the Best Seller is engaged in an industry "affecting interstate commerce." The statutory jurisdictional nexus is, therefore, satisfied. In addition, given these facts, one could say that the business of the Best Seller affects interstate commerce, and that when viewed collectively with the activities of other similar businesses, the aggregate effect is substantial.

But this does not answer our constitutional question. Notice that in both *Heart of Atlanta* and *Katzenbach*, the question was not simply whether motels or restaurants affected interstate commerce, but, more precisely, whether *the practice of racial discrimination* by such businesses affected interstate commerce. The inquiry here, therefore, must focus on the particular activity being regulated, namely, *the practice of age discrimination* in employment. Does this practice, when engaged in by an industry affecting commerce, substantially affect interstate commerce? The answer to that question requires an economic assessment of the consequences of age discrimination. If one could reasonably conclude that such discrimination causes a decrease in spending by the protected group or has a "depressant effect" on the overall economy, particularly when engaged in by an industry affecting interstate commerce, then the ADEA is constitutional and can be applied to the business practices of the Best Seller. This is essentially the reasoning followed by the Court in *Katzenbach*. Moreover, given the generally deferential approach applied where as here the regulated activity is economic and commercial in nature, it is likely that the Court would uphold such a "presumed" determination by Congress even in the absence of specific findings.

§5.3.4 Closer Judicial Scrutiny: *Lopez* and *Morrison*

The commerce power as construed by the Supreme Court is unquestionably quite elastic, so much so that some Justices have expressed concern that modern applications of the Commerce Clause run the risk of obliterating the principle that the United States is a limited government. See, e.g., *Hodel v. Virginia Surface Mining & Reclamation Assn., Inc.*, supra, 452 U.S. at 307-313 (Rehnquist, J., concurring). That concern was translated into law in *United States v. Lopez*, 514 U.S. 549 (1995), a case in which the Court held, for the first time since the New Deal, that a congressional regulation of private activity exceeded the authority granted to Congress under the Commerce Clause.

The defendant in *Lopez* was caught carrying a handgun on a public high school campus; he was charged and convicted under a federal statute, the

Gun-Free School Zones Act of 1990, which made it a crime to possess a firearm in a "school zone." The act had been adopted pursuant to the commerce power. Lopez challenged the constitutionality of the statute on the grounds that it exceeded the scope of federal power under the Commerce Clause. The precise question was whether possession of a gun in a school zone was sufficiently related to interstate commerce to justify this exercise of power. The Court held that it was not.

The Court's holding was premised on two related concerns. The first focused on the nature of the activity being regulated, while the second focused on its relationship to interstate commerce. As to the first concern, the Court stated that, "[w]here *economic activity* substantially affects interstate commerce, legislation regulating that activity will be sustained." Id. at 560 (emphasis supplied). The Court's elaboration of this standard suggests that "economic activity" establishes a threshold requirement for regulating conduct under the commerce power. To come within the realm of economic activity one of two standards must be satisfied: either the activity being regulated must itself be properly characterized as economic in nature, or the regulation of the activity must be "an essential part of a larger regulation of economic activity." Id. at 561. As applied to the possession of a gun in a school zone, the Court concluded that the regulated activity — gun possession — was not itself economic, nor was the prohibition part of a larger economic regulatory scheme.

Although the Court did not provide any definition of "economic activity," the tenor of the Court's opinion suggested that creative efforts to expand the phrase beyond what is commonly accepted as commercial in nature would be viewed with a fatal suspicion. Thus, the Court rejected the dissent's argument that Congress could have rationally concluded that schools were commercial in the sense that they contributed to the economic well-being of the nation. Id. at 565-566. Such an expansive application of the term would, in the Court's view, transform the commerce power into a general police power.

However, even if the regulated activity can fairly be characterized as "economic," to fall within the ambit of the commerce power the activity must also have "a substantial relation to interstate commerce" or must "substantially affect interstate commerce." Id. at 558-559. The Court here placed special emphasis on the words "substantial" and "substantially." Thus, a mere effect on interstate commerce will not sustain an exercise of the power. Nor will the Court simply defer to the judgment of Congress in this regard. In assessing a Commerce Clause challenge, the Court's duty is to make an independent evaluation of whether a sufficiently *substantial* relationship or *substantial* effect validates the exercise of power.

The Court explained that in applying the substantial relationship requirement, it would consider whether or not the statute in question contained an "express jurisdictional element" limiting the measure's reach to activities having an explicit connection to interstate commerce.

Id. at 562. In addition, the Court said that it would consider — but not be bound by — any "express congressional findings" concerning the effects of the regulated activity on interstate commerce. Id. at 562-563.

The government in Lopez argued that the effects on interstate commerce were, indeed, substantial: (1) possession of guns in school zones leads to violent crime, the cost of which is spread throughout the nation, thereby imposing a burden on interstate commerce; (2) violent crime reduces the willingness of individuals to travel into areas of the country deemed unsafe, thereby affecting interstate commerce; and (3) the presence of guns in schools undermines the educational process and leads to the creation of a less productive citizenry, which in turn affects interstate commerce.

The Court found none of these connections to be "substantial." In reaching this conclusion, the Court noted that the act contained no jurisdictional element confining its application to gun possession having an explicit link to interstate commerce. Nor had Congress made any prior findings as to the effects of gun possession on interstate commerce. In the Court's words,

> To uphold the Government's contentions here, we would have to pile inference upon inference in a manner that would bid fair to convert congressional authority under the Commerce Clause to a general police power of the sort retained by the States. Admittedly, some of our prior cases have taken long steps down that road, giving great deference to congressional action. The broad language in these opinions has suggested the possibility of additional expansion, but we decline here to proceed any further. To do so would require us to conclude that the Constitution's enumeration of powers does not presuppose something not enumerated, cf. Gibbons v. Ogden. . . .

Id. at 567. As was true with the element of "economic activity," the Court provided no particular test for measuring the substantiality of the necessary relationship with interstate commerce. The Court simply concluded that the regulation of gun possession in a school zone did not satisfy the standard.

Two potential interpretations of Lopez should be considered, each of which finds some basis in the decision. Under the first, no exercise of the commerce power will be validated under the "substantially affects" test unless two independent elements are satisfied: (1) the activity regulated must be *economic activity* — i.e., it must itself be economic in nature or regulation of it must be essential to a larger regulation of economic activity — and (2) the regulated activity must *substantially affect* interstate commerce. Under this interpretation, "economic activity" is a necessary threshold that must be crossed in any exercise of the commerce power.

A second plausible interpretation is that the two elements are not necessarily independent of one another, but merely present different perspectives on the "substantially affects" inquiry, one focusing on the nature of the activity and the other focusing on the actual relationship with interstate commerce. Under this second interpretation, an absence of economic activity merely suggests, but does not definitively determine, the insubstantiality of the relationship with interstate commerce. In other words, if the economic activity prong is not satisfied, a court will be much less deferential to Congress and it will be harder but not necessarily impossible to convince a court that the activity substantially affects interstate commerce. In the wake of *Lopez*, lower courts have applied both interpretations.

Lopez makes it clear that while laws enacted under the commerce power will be upheld if the regulated class of activity exerts a substantial economic effect on interstate commerce, the level of judicial scrutiny will be much stricter (and very likely fatal) if the activity in question is deemed to be noncommercial rather than commercial in nature. However, the decision left two critical questions unanswered: First, what does it take for a class of activity to qualify as being commercial or economic in nature; and second, what standard of judicial review should apply if a law sweeps within its ambit both commercial and noncommercial activity?

The Court addressed each of these questions in *Gonzales v. Raich*, 545 U.S. 1 (2005), where it upheld the constitutionality of the federal Controlled Substances Act (CSA) as applied to the purely intrastate, noncommercial cultivation and possession of marijuana for personal medical purposes. First, with respect to the nature of the regulated activity, earlier cases had suggested that the terms "economic" and "commercial" were to be used synonymously. See Allan Ides, *Economic Activity as a Proxy for Federalism: Intuition and Reason* in United States v. Morrison, 18 Const. Comm. 563 (2001). However, the *Gonzales* Court held that for Commerce Clause purposes, an activity may qualify as being "economic" in nature even though it is "not itself 'commercial,' in that [the goods are] not produced for sale. . . ." 545 U.S. at 18. As the Court explained, "'Economics' refers to 'the production, distribution, and consumption of commodities'" — a definition that clearly embraced respondent's personal cultivation and use of marijuana. To the extent that characterizing an activity as "economic" then allows Congress to regulate it under the Commerce and Necessary and Proper Clauses with only rational basis judicial review, the Court has greatly narrowed the circumstances under which the much stricter standard of *Lopez* will apply. As Justice O'Connor noted in her dissent, "the Court's definition of economic activity is breathtaking," one that "threatens to sweep all of productive human activity into federal regulatory reach." Id. at 49.

Second, *Gonzales* suggested that even if the personal cultivation and use of medical marijuana were deemed to be noneconomic and noncommercial in nature, a court in assessing the reach of Congress's lawmaking power must accept the class of activity as defined by Congress, asking whether it exerts a substantial economic effect on interstate commerce, rather than zooming in to "excise individual applications of a concededly valid statutory scheme." Id. at 23. In *Lopez*, the sole activity being regulated was noneconomic in nature. In *Gonzales*, by contrast, the allegedly noneconomic activity was part of a broader regulatory scheme that embraced what was clearly economic and commercial drug activity. In such circumstances, as long as "Congress acted rationally" in "includ[ing] this narrower 'class of activities' within the larger regulatory scheme," the regulation of that subclass of activity is constitutional. Id. at 26-27. Justice O'Connor's dissent voiced concern that the Court's approach "gives Congress a perverse incentive to legislate broadly pursuant to the Commerce Clause—nestling questionable assertions of its authority into comprehensive regulatory schemes—rather than with precision." Id. at 43. As she explained, "Today's decision suggests that federal regulation of local activity is immune to Commerce Clause challenge because Congress chose to act with an ambitious, all-encompassing statute, rather than piecemeal. In my view, allowing Congress to set the terms of the constitutional debate in this way, i.e., by packaging regulation of local activity in broader schemes, is tantamount to removing meaningful limits on the Commerce Clause." Id. at 45. In response, the majority suggested that such fears were overblown, for "political checks . . . would generally curb Congress' power to enact a broad and comprehensive scheme for the purpose of targeting purely local activity. . . ." Id. at 25 n.34.

The *Gonzales* Court also rejected another subclass argument, namely that Congress's ability to regulate a local activity may hinge on whether the same goals are already being achieved by state law, in which case the federal statute would not be "necessary" and hence could not constitutionally be applied to the subclass of activity in that particular state. The *Gonzales* plaintiffs lived in California, whose Compassionate Use Act allowed, but strictly regulated, the cultivation and possession of marijuana for medicinal purposes. While Justice Thomas accepted this argument, he was alone in doing so. As Justice Stevens wrote for the majority, such a principle "would turn the Supremacy Clause on its head. . . ." Id. at 29 n.38. "Just as state acquiescence to federal regulation cannot expand the bounds of the Commerce Clause, so too state action cannot circumscribe Congress' plenary commerce power" (id. at 29) by in effect shielding that state from an otherwise valid federal law.

Example 5-G

In the wake of *Lopez*, Congress amended the Gun-Free School Zones Act to make it a federal crime to "transfer or possess a firearm within a distance of 1,000 feet from the grounds of a public, parochial or private school." Louis, who was caught carrying a handgun while walking across the street from a public high school, has been criminally charged under the act. Can the act constitutionally be applied to him?

Explanation

In its amended form, the act now reaches both economic and noneconomic activity, for while the mere possession of a gun may be noneconomic in nature, the transfer of a firearm certainly qualifies as economic and commercial activity. It is no doubt rational to conclude that the class of regulated activity, in the aggregate, exerts a substantial economic effect on interstate commerce, for many if not most of the firearms in question will have come from or may be destined for other states. Congress is therefore free to include within that class a subclass of noneconomic activity — i.e., mere gun possession. While there are limits on how far Congress may go in terms of including a subclass of noneconomic activity within a larger regulated class, the Court has insisted merely that there be a rational basis for doing so. Here, it is rational to conclude that enforcing a limitation on the *transfer* of weapons near schools will be enhanced by also prohibiting the *possession* of such weapons, since possession is much easier to detect than a transfer, which takes only seconds to accomplish.

Example 5-H

The Violence Against Women Act (VAWA) creates a federal cause of action against any person who commits a crime of violence motivated by the gender of the victim. Included within this category are such crimes as rape and spousal abuse. In essence, VAWA gives the victim of such a crime a federal civil rights cause of action against the perpetrator. The act was passed pursuant to the Commerce Clause on findings that violence against women imposes severe and substantial economic costs to society including, but not limited to, costs incurred from hospitalization, rehabilitation, and lost productivity. The Senate report accompanying the act specifically found: "Gender-based crimes and fear of gender-based crimes restricts movement, reduces employment opportunities, increases health expenditures, and reduces consumer spending, all of which affect interstate commerce and the national economy." Is VAWA constitutional as an exercise of the commerce power under *Lopez* and *Gonzales?*

Explanation

Since VAWA is not a regulation of either the channels or the instrumentalities of interstate commerce, the specific question is whether gender-based violence, as defined by the act, substantially affects interstate commerce. But before answering that question we must first determine if gender-based violence is properly characterized as economic activity or if its regulation is part of a more comprehensive regulatory scheme directed at economic activity. Quite likely the answer to both preliminary inquiries is no.

Gender-based violence is not commonly understood as economic activity. Nor would gender-based violence satisfy the *Gonzales* Court's broader definition of economic activity as including the "production, distribution, and consumption of commodities." 545 U.S. at 18. It also does not seem that this regulation is part of any larger economic regulatory scheme. Rather, it is quite simply a civil remedy directed at a particular type of reprehensible but noneconomic behavior, and as such is similar to the gun possession prohibition at issue in *Lopez*. If the "economic activity" element of *Lopez* is a constitutional prerequisite to the exercise of the commerce power, VAWA does not represent an appropriate exercise of that power. If, on the other hand, "economic activity" is merely one factor to consider in the application of the "substantially affects" test, then we must proceed to examine the sufficiency of the relationship between gender-based violence and interstate commerce, albeit with the recognition that the activity being regulated does not fall within the sphere of activities generally thought to come within the ambit of the commerce power.

Does gender-based violence substantially affect interstate commerce? One can certainly construct an argument that it does. Given the statistical prevalence of such violence (millions of such crimes are reported each year), there can be little doubt that, collectively, gender-based violence generates enormous economic costs to society, and at some point these costs are reflected in the interstate market in goods and services. The quoted findings by Congress would seem to be at least rational in this regard. Moreover, the connection with interstate commerce under VAWA is at least as substantial as the connection upheld by the Court in *Wickard v. Filburn*, where consumption of wheat on farms was deemed sufficiently related to interstate commerce to trigger the commerce power. (*Wickard* is the case on which Example 5-D is based.)

But *Lopez* strongly suggests that the economic consequences of this "noneconomic" behavior are too tenuous to establish a "substantial" link with interstate commerce. First, the fact that the regulated activity is noneconomic weighs heavily against validation of the act under the "substantially affects" test. Next, aside from the noneconomic nature of the regulated activity, to uphold VAWA, one arguably "would have to pile inference upon inference in a manner that would bid fair to convert congressional authority under the Commerce Clause to a general police power of the sort retained by the States." *Lopez*, 514 U.S. at 567.

In *United States v. Morrison*, 529 U.S. 598 (2000), the Supreme Court ruled five to four that VAWA was not a valid exercise of Congress's commerce power. The Court was unswayed by Congress's findings because they were based on the same "method of reasoning" that was rejected in *Lopez* — i.e., a "but-for causal chain from the initial occurrence of violent crime (the suppression of which has always been the prime object of the States' police power) to every attenuated effect upon interstate commerce." Id. at 615. Such reasoning, said the Court, "would allow Congress to regulate any crime as long as the nationwide, aggregated impact of that crime has substantial effects on employment, production, transit, or consumption." Id. The Court thus rejected "the argument that Congress may regulate non-economic, violent criminal conduct based solely on that conduct's aggregate effect on interstate commerce. . . . The regulation and punishment of intra-state violence that is not directed at the instrumentalities, channels, or goods involved in interstate commerce has always been the province of the States." Id. at 617-618. Though it stopped short of holding that noneconomic activity may *never* be reached under the affecting commerce rationale, the Court pointedly observed that "in those cases where we have sustained federal regulation of interstate activity based upon the activity's substantial effects on interstate commerce, the activity in question has been some sort of economic endeavor." Id. at 611. For a pre-*Gonzales* discussion of the "economic activity" element, see Allan Ides, *Economic Activity as a Proxy for Federalism: Intuition and Reason in* United States v. Morrison, 18 Const. Comm. 563 (2001).

§5.3.5 Regulating Commercial "Inactivity"

All of the Commerce Clause cases we have looked at so far involved legislation through which Congress sought to regulate those who were *engaged in* economic or commercial activity. In *National Federation of Independent Business v. Sebelius*, 132 S. Ct. 2566 (2012), the Court confronted the question of whether the commerce power allows Congress to regulate those who have *refrained from*, or not yet engaged in, a particular economic activity. *Sebelius* involved the 2010 Patient Protection and Affordable Care Act, which, among other things, imposed an "individual mandate" that required people who do not receive health insurance through an employer or a government program to purchase such insurance from a private company. The Court held 5-4 that this individual mandate provision exceeded Congress's power under the Commerce and Necessary and Proper Clauses. Unlike *Wickard*, where the farmer whose activity was being regulated had already engaged in the economic activity of growing wheat, those being regulated in *Sebelius* had refrained from engaging in the economic activity involved. The difference was critical, said the Chief Justice, for "[t]he power to *regulate* commerce presupposes the existence of commercial activity to be regulated." 132 S. Ct. at 2586. By contrast, the Affordable Care Act's

> individual mandate . . . does not regulate existing commercial activity. It instead compels individuals to *become* active in commerce by purchasing a product, on the ground that their failure to do so affects interstate commerce.

> Construing the Commerce Clause to permit Congress to regulate individuals precisely *because* they are doing nothing would open a new and potentially vast domain to congressional authority. Every day individuals do not do an infinite number of things. In some cases they decide not to do something; in others they simply fail to do it. Allowing Congress to justify federal regulation by pointing to the effect of inaction on commerce would bring countless decisions an individual could *potentially* make within the scope of federal regulation, and — under the Government's theory — empower Congress to make those decisions for him.

Id. at 2587. Instead, said the Chief Justice, "The Framers gave Congress the power to *regulate* commerce, not to *compel* it. . . ." Id. at 2589. He was unmoved by the fact that "[e]veryone will eventually need health care," id. at 2585, and that everyone will at some point in their lives therefore enter the health care market. "The proposition that Congress may dictate the conduct of an individual today because of prophesied future activity finds no support in our precedent." Id. at 2590. This position was shared by the four joint dissenters, who agreed that "one does not regulate commerce that does not exist by compelling its existence." Id. at 2644 (Scalia, J., Kennedy, J., Thomas, J., and Alito, J., dissenting).

Neither did the Necessary and Proper Clause save the individual mandate on the theory that regulating this commercial "inactivity" was rationally related to the Government's desire to improve the national health care insurance market. While the Chief Justice agreed that the mandate may have been "necessary" in the sense that it was a convenient and useful means of strengthening the interstate health care insurance market, it was "not a 'proper' means for making those reforms effective." Id. at 2592. To uphold this provision, he said, "would undermine the structure of government established by the Constitution" for it would give Congress "the extraordinary ability to create the necessary predicate" — here commerce — "to the exercise of an enumerated power." Id.

> No longer would Congress be limited to regulating under the Commerce Clause those who by some preexisting activity bring themselves within the sphere of federal regulation. Instead, Congress could reach beyond the natural limit of its authority and draw within its regulatory scope those who otherwise would be outside of it. Even if the individual mandate is "necessary" to the Act's insurance reforms, such an expansion of federal power is not a "proper" means for making those reforms effective.

Id.

The joint dissenters likewise feared that to accept the government's argument that the Commerce Clause may be used to reach commercial inactivity would "extend federal power to virtually everything." Id. at 2648. Such a reading, they said, "threatens our constitutional order . . . because it gives such an expansive meaning to the Commerce Clause that *all* private conduct (including failure to act) becomes subject to federal control, effectively destroying the Constitution's division of governmental powers" between the federal government and the states. Id. at 2649. Instead, said the dissenters, "the scope of the Necessary and Proper Clause is exceeded . . . when it violates the background principle of enumerated (and hence limited) federal power." Id. at 2646.

There was, of course, another way of viewing the case. As Justice Ginsburg wrote in a separate opinion joined by three other Justices, the Chief Justice's attempt to place a categorical limit on the Commerce Clause by confining its reach to commercial "activity" as distinct from "inactivity" was to view "the Clause as a 'technical legal conception,'" id. at 2622, similar to the Court's earlier unsuccessful efforts to limit the reach of the Commerce Clause during the Progressive and New Deal eras. See §5.3.1. Yet, as Justice Ginsburg suggested, even under the Chief Justice's narrow view of the Commerce Clause, "[a]n individual's decision to self-insure . . . is an economic act," id. at 2624, for someone "who self-insures opts against prepayment for a product the person will in time consume. When aggregated, exercise of that option has a substantial impact on the health-care market." Id. at 2622 n.7. Her point becomes even clearer if one thinks of such decisions as involving "economic behavior," rather than the Court's linguistically narrower concept of "economic activity." Justice Ginsburg's approach, though clearly broader than the Chief Justice's, would surely not convert all private decisions into economic ones so as to thereby "enable the Federal Government to regulate all private conduct. . . ." Id. at 2643 (Scalia, J., et al., dissenting).

The opinions of the Chief Justice and the joint dissenters might be seen as an attempt to place a clear outer limit on the reach of Congress's power under the Commerce Clause. These Justices repeatedly expressed fear that if the Affordable Care Act were upheld under the Commerce Clause, the effect would be "to extend federal power to virtually all human activity." Id. at 2643 (Scalia, J., et al, dissenting). While Justice Ginsburg sought to allay these concerns by citing cases like *United States v. Lopez* and *United States v. Morrison*, where the Court did in fact draw a line, see §5.3.4, Justice Ginsburg ultimately invoked what she described as "a formidable check on congressional power: the democratic process." 132 S. Ct. at 2624. In the end, what may have separated the majority and the dissent as to the need for a bright-line limit on the reach of the Commerce Clause were the Justices' respective levels of confidence in the ability of the people to operate as an effective check on congressional abuses of the commerce power.

Despite its dramatic quality, the effect of the decision in *Sebelius* is likely to be quite narrow, for the case was literally unique. It represented the first — and for a while, at least, probably the last — time Congress sought to use the commerce power to force individuals to engage in market activity that they would otherwise have refrained from. The decision should therefore have no impact on Congress's ability to regulate those who have affirmatively chosen to engage in economic activity.

After ruling that the "individual mandate" provision of the Affordable Health Care Act exceeded Congress's authority under the Commerce and Necessary and Proper Clauses, the *Sebelius* Court then went on to uphold the provision as being a proper "tax" that fell within Congress's Article I, §8, cl. 1 power to tax. See §5.4.1.

Example 5-1

Partly due to ignorance on their part, many people in the United States do not eat a balanced diet; as a consequence, they experience significantly increased health care costs. It has been estimated that for the country as a whole, the annual medical burden of malnutrition and obesity accounts for nearly 10 percent of total medical spending. As a result of having to provide medical care to these individuals, everyone's medical premiums have risen because those with unhealthy eating habits pay only a fraction of the medical costs associated with their behavior. Congress is considering several means of addressing this problem. First, individuals would be prohibited from bringing "junk food," as defined by statute, aboard any train, plane or boat traveling in interstate commerce. Second, any company that sells or otherwise provides food to its employees would be barred from selling or providing them with junk food if any of the food has traveled in interstate commerce. Third, every individual would be required to eat a federally mandated minimum amount of vegetables each day. Are these three provisions within Congress's power under the Commerce Clause?

Explanation

First, the ban on bringing junk food aboard any train, plane, or boat traveling in interstate commerce would be valid as a regulation of the channels of interstate commerce. Second, the ban on selling or providing junk food to company employees might be justified under the Commerce and Necessary and Proper Clauses, at least as applied to food that has traveled in interstate commerce. Because Congress could entirely ban such foods from interstate commerce, reducing its consumption would be an indirect but necessary and proper means of lessening that flow. As to junk food that did not travel in interstate commerce but was instead grown, sold, and consumed locally, this still involves a class of economic or commercial activity that is subject to federal regulation under the principle of *Wickard v. Filburn*. Third, the requirement that individuals consume a federally prescribed minimum amount of vegetables each day would cross the line drawn in *Sebelius* between regulating commerce and compelling it. Indeed, Chief Justice Robert's opinion in *Sebelius* used "ordering everyone to buy vegetables" as an example of something Congress could not do under the Commerce Clause. *National Federation of Independent Business v. Sebelius*, supra, 132 S. Ct. at 2588.

§5.4 THE POWER TO TAX AND SPEND

Article I, §8, cl. 1 provides that Congress may "lay and collect Taxes, Duties, Imposts and Excises, to pay the Debts and provide for the common Defence and general Welfare of the United States. . . ." This language confers on Congress a power to tax and spend. That means that any purported exercise of the power must be in the form of a tax or an expenditure, the definitions of which we will examine below. Moreover, given the language of the clause, the ends to which the power may be applied are at least theoretically confined to those ends specifically described in the text — the debts, common defense, and general welfare of the nation. But to the extent these terms have been interpreted, they have been construed broadly to vest Congress with an almost unreviewable discretion to define the ends to which the power to tax and spend may be applied. See *Helvering v. Davis*, 301 U.S. 619, 640-641 (1937) (the discretion to define the general welfare belongs first to Congress); *South Dakota v. Dole*, 483 U.S. 203, 207 n.2 (1987) (the term "general welfare" may not be a judicially enforceable restriction). In short, the power conferred by Article I, §8, cl. 1 vests Congress with the authority to impose taxes and to make expenditures whenever doing so will, in the perception of Congress, be beneficial to the common defense or general welfare of the nation.

Most important, in *United States v. Butler*, 297 U.S. 1, 65-67 (1936), the Court held that the power to tax and spend is a distinct constitutional power, fully effective without reference to other granted powers. There is no need, therefore, to demonstrate that a taxing or spending measure is directed toward interstate commerce, naturalization, the establishment of post offices, or any other granted power. Thus although Congress may not be able to regulate a local activity that does not substantially affect interstate commerce, Congress may nonetheless tax that activity, or spend money to encourage it, as long as in doing so Congress is promoting the general welfare. See, e.g., *National Federation of Independent Business v. Sebelius*, 132 S. Ct. 2566 (2012) (though Congress under the commerce power could not force individuals to buy health care insurance, it could impose a tax on those individuals as a means of encouraging them to do so). In short, the power to tax and spend stands on its own and may be exercised whenever doing so comes within the terms of the grant and does not exceed applicable limitations.

Example 5-J

The Federal Disaster Relief Act provides federal money to communities and individuals who have suffered losses caused by natural disasters such as floods, earthquakes, and hurricanes. The relief is available without any need to show a connection to interstate commerce or to any other national concern. Is the act within the scope of the general welfare power?

Explanation

Yes. Regardless of the purely "local" nature of the catastrophes such that they would very likely fall beyond the scope of Congress's regulatory powers, the presumed congressional judgment that these expenditures are for the general welfare of the nation will be upheld as well within the discretion of Congress.

Like all constitutional powers, the power to tax and spend is subject to the Bill of Rights as well as to other generally applicable constitutional limitations. See, e.g., *Marchetti v. United States*, 390 U.S. 39 (1968) (Fifth Amendment Self-Incrimination Clause limits the power to tax). In addition, there are three specific textual limitations on the power to tax: (1) taxes must be uniform throughout the United States (Art. I, §8, cl. 1); (2) any direct tax must be proportional to the population of the states (Art. I, §9, cl. 4); and (3) no tax or duty may be laid on exports (Art. I, §9, cl. 5). Before examining these limitations, we first consider what constitutes a tax.

§5.4.1 What Constitutes a Tax for Purposes of the Taxing Power?

In deciding whether a measure qualifies as a tax for purposes of Article I, §8, cl. 1, the label employed by Congress is not dispositive. Instead, the Court has adopted a functional approach under which deciding whether a particular measure can be fairly characterized as a tax for these purposes depends on the resolution of two preliminary questions. First, does the measure operate as a tax — i.e., does it raise some revenue? *National Federation of Independent Business v. Sebelius*, supra, 132 S. Ct. at 2594 ("the essential feature of any tax [is that] it produces at least some revenue for the Government"). If it does, it is presumptively a tax, even if the amount raised is minimal. *Sonzinsky v. United States*, 300 U.S. 506, 512-514 & n.1 (1937). If it does not raise "some" revenue, then the measure is not a tax and is valid only if authorized by some other granted authority. Second, even if the measure raises some revenue, does it function in a fashion that is more properly characterized as prohibitory or penal? In other words, is what purports to be a tax actually a disguised regulation? If so, the measure cannot be validated as an exercise of the power to tax, but must be validated, if at all, by reference to some other granted power, typically the commerce power. These principles apply even to a measure which Congress may have labeled as a penalty or regulation; i.e., under the Court's functional approach, such a measure may still be deemed to be a tax for purposes of Article I, §8. *Sebelius*, supra, 132 S. Ct. at 2596-2597 ("what is called a 'penalty' here may be viewed as a tax" for "labels should not control").

The "Some Revenue" Test

The *Sonzinsky* case provides a good example of the low threshold imposed by the "some revenue" test. In that case, a firearms dealer challenged the constitutionality of the National Firearms Act of 1934, which required every such dealer to register with the Commissioner of Internal Revenue and to pay a special excise tax of $200 per year. The term "firearm" was defined as "a shotgun or a rifle having a barrel less than 18 inches in length, or any other weapon, except a pistol or revolver, from which a shot is discharged by an explosive, if capable of being concealed on the person, or a machine gun, and includes a muffler or silencer for any firearm." 300 U.S. at 511-512. The excise tax had been paid by 27 dealers in 1934 and by 22 dealers in the subsequent year. Thus the revenue generated by this measure — $9,800 — was at best minimal and quite likely less than the cost of administering the law. Yet this minimal amount was sufficient to classify the measure as a tax. Id. at 514 & n.1. See *United States v. Kahriger*, 345 U.S. 22, 28 n.4 (1953) (listing other applications of the "some revenue" standard). In essence, the "some revenue" test creates a very low threshold that is easily crossed if any measurable amount of revenue is generated by the law at issue.

Of course, if a purported tax raises no revenue whatsoever, it will fail the "some revenue" test and as a consequence cannot be classified as a tax. Yet the instances in which this will occur are rare if not nonexistent. Suppose, however, that Congress enacted a statute that imposed a $100,000 per transaction tax on any liquor retailer who knowingly sells alcoholic beverages to minors. If the effect of the measure was to eliminate such transactions completely, quite obviously no revenue would be generated. As a consequence, the measure is not a tax but rather a prohibitory regulation. Its constitutionality must, as a consequence, be assessed under the standards of the commerce power.

Is the Law Penal or Prohibitory?

Even if a purported tax raises some revenue (which is usually if not universally the case), the measure still may be more properly characterized as penal or prohibitory and therefore not a true tax. If so, the General Welfare Clause cannot be used to validate the measure. Yet once it has been established that a purported tax raises some revenue, the presumption that the measure is a true tax is difficult to overcome. For one thing, the mere presence of a regulatory effect is inadequate to rebut the presumption. As the Court has observed, "Every tax is in some measure regulatory. To some extent it interposes an economic impediment to the activity taxed as compared with others not taxed. But a tax is not any the less a tax because it has a regulatory effect. . . ." *Sonzinsky*, supra, 300 U.S. at 513. Moreover, the Court has expressed its unwillingness to inquire into the "hidden motives" of Congress in an effort to determine if a tax is in reality an attempt to exercise a power not granted by the Constitution. Id. at 513-514.

The difficulty of rebutting the presumption is demonstrated by the decision in *Sonzinsky*. The defendant there argued that the $200 annual levy on his business as a firearms dealer was "not a true tax, but a penalty imposed for the purpose of suppressing traffic" in firearms. Id. at 512. He explained that this levy was part of a broader scheme under which cumulative levies were imposed on firearms transactions in a manner designed to penalize or prohibit such transactions:

> The cumulative effect on the distribution of a limited class of firearms, of relatively small value, by the successive imposition of different taxes, one on the business of the importer or manufacturer, another on that of the dealer, and a third on the transfer to a buyer [was] prohibitive in effect and [disclosed] unmistakably the legislative purpose to regulate rather than to tax.

Id. at 512-513. The Court was unpersuaded. On its face, the measure was a tax, and consistent with that characterization the levy raised some revenue. The presumptive validity having been established, neither the regulatory effect of the overall scheme nor the plausible motive of Congress to prohibit firearms transactions was sufficient to rebut that presumption. Id. at 513-514. Indeed, as the Court has noted, "taxes that seek to influence conduct are nothing new." *Sebelius*, supra, 132 S. Ct. at 2596. Even when it is clear that Congress's purpose in adopting a tax measure was to "shape decisions" and "affect individual conduct," this "does not mean that it cannot be a valid exercise of the taxing power." Id.

The presumption that a revenue-generating measure is a tax is not, however, absolutely irrebuttable. For example, in the *Child Labor Tax Case*, 259 U.S. 20 (1922), the Court held that a revenue-generating measure that purported to be a tax — the Child Labor Tax Law — was indeed a disguised regulation and not a proper exercise of the power to tax. The statute at issue in that case created a detailed set of standards limiting the circumstances under which children could be employed in certain industries. A knowing failure to comply with any of the standards triggered imposition of a 10 percent excise tax on the employer's annual net profits. After surveying the various standards imposed by the act and the circumstances under which a "tax" would be imposed, the Court observed, "In the light of these features of the act, a court must be blind not to see that the so-called tax is imposed to stop the employment of children within the age limits prescribed. Its prohibitory and regulatory effect and purpose are palpable. All others can see and understand this. How can we properly shut our minds to it?" Id. at 37. In essence, the so-called tax was a penalty to enforce compliance with the regulatory standards of the act. It could not, therefore, be validated as an exercise of the taxing power.

A similar result was achieved in United States v. Constantine, 296 U.S. 287 (1935). The measure challenged in that case, the Revenue Act of 1926, imposed an annual $1,000 tax on retail liquor dealers who operated in violation of state law. This tax was in addition to a $25 annual tax imposed on all retail liquor dealers regardless of the legality of their business. The Court concluded that the $1,000 tax was a penalty and therefore not a true tax:

> The condition of the imposition is the commission of a crime. This, together with the amount of the tax, is again significant of penal and prohibitory intent rather than the gathering of revenue. Where, in addition to the normal and ordinary tax fixed by law, an additional sum is to be collected by reason of conduct of the taxpayer violative of the law, and this additional sum is grossly disproportionate to the amount of the normal tax, the conclusion must be that the purpose is to impose a penalty as a deterrent and punishment of unlawful conduct.

Id. at 295.

Both Constantine and the Child Labor Tax Case represent relatively limited opportunities to challenge the legitimacy of purported taxes. This is true for two reasons. First, the statutes challenged in each case illustrate blatant regulatory patterns that do not frequently recur. In this sense, the law sustained in Sonzinsky represents a more typical excise tax, lacking both the detailed specifications of behavior of the Child Labor Tax Law, and the criminal trigger of the Revenue Act. Sonzinsky, 300 U.S. at 513 (distinguishing Child Labor Tax Case and Constantine on these grounds). Second, both cases were decided during an era when the Court, under the enclave theory, was prone to interpret the regulatory powers of Congress in a relatively narrow fashion. In fact, the Court in the Child Labor Tax Case held that its earlier decision in Hammer v. Dagenhart was controlling on the issue of congressional power to regulate matters reserved to the states. In essence, the Child Labor Tax Law was perceived as an attempt by Congress to make an end run around the Hammer decision. Again, Sonzinsky, authored by Justice Stone, who was also the author of United States v. Darby, presents the more typical modern judicial response to exercises of the power to tax. See also Helvering v. Davis, 301 U.S. 619 (1937) (upholding taxes imposed by Social Security Act); Steward Machine Co. v. Davis, 301 U.S. 548 (1937) (same).

In applying the Tax Clause, the current Court has reaffirmed its reluctance "to closely examine the regulatory motive or effect of revenue-raising measures." Sebelius, supra, 132 S. Ct. at 2599. Indeed, when Congress enacted the Patient Protection and Affordable Care Act of 2010, it did not even pretend to be imposing a tax. Instead, Congress imposed a financial "penalty" on those who failed to acquire health insurance. After ruling that this seemingly regulatory measure could not be upheld under the commerce power, the Court then found that the "financial penalty . . . may reasonably be characterized as a tax." Id. at 2600. The Court then went on to find that because the "tax" was neither penal nor prohibitory, it was a proper exercise of Congress's taxing power.

While the Court has read the taxing power generously — even in cases where Congress did not rely on it and where Congress would otherwise have lacked the authority to act — the Court has cautioned that "Congress's ability to use its taxing power to influence conduct is not without limits." Sebelius, supra, 132 S. Ct. at 2599. The line between a permissible and impermissible tax is thus one that the Court is still seemingly prepared to draw, should the right case come along. If under its functional approach the Court were to find a tax to be penal or prohibitory, the most likely result would be that the regulatory tax would then be upheld as an exercise of the commerce power. However, given the Court's recent decisions in United States v. Lopez, United States v. Morrison, and National Federation of Independent Business v. Sebelius, all narrowing the reach of the commerce power, that "likely" result is not the only possibility. See §5.3.4, §5.3.5.

Example 5-K

Recall that in United States v. Lopez, the Court struck down the Gun-Free School Zones Act (GFSZA). Suppose that in response to that decision, Congress enacted the Gun-Free School Zones Tax Act (the Tax Act). The only difference between the Tax Act and the GFSZA is that instead of a criminal penalty, the Tax Act imposes a $10,000 tax on any person who possesses a firearm in a school zone. Suppose also that on facts similar to those presented in Lopez, an individual assessed with this tax challenges the constitutionality of the Tax Act. Assuming the Tax Act raises some revenue, is it a proper exercise of the power to tax? In other words, is the tax imposed penal or prohibitory and therefore a regulation rather than a true tax?

Explanation

In a general sense, the Tax Act is quite similar to the Child Labor Tax Law. Both were adopted as attempted end runs around Supreme Court decisions striking down legislation under the Commerce Clause. Both also prescribe a particular course of conduct that must be followed to avoid the tax — don't bring guns into a school zone; don't employ children under certain specified conditions. The tax imposed by each, therefore, can be seen as a mechanism to enforce compliance with a regulatory scheme. The Tax Act, however, does not contain anything like the detailed regulations provided by the Child

Labor Tax Law. Its complete focus is on a single act, namely, possession of a gun in a school zone. Perhaps this makes the Tax Act more like the National Firearms Act at issue in *Sonzinsky*, where the trigger of the law was also premised on a more general description of the taxable activity. Ultimately, whether this lack of detail is sufficient to distinguish the Tax Act from the Child Labor Tax Law depends on one's judgment as to the degree of deference due Congress. In the context of the commerce power, the Court has certainly suggested that total deference is no longer the appropriate standard. Yet how that judgment will be applied in the context of a tax case remains an open question. In short, the Tax Act is similar to the Child Labor Tax Law because it attempts to regulate local behavior through a tax and effects an end run around a Supreme Court decision, but dissimilar because it does not impose a "detailed" regulatory scheme with which one must comply to avoid the tax.

The Tax Act also invites comparison with the tax struck down in *Constantine*. There, imposition of the tax was triggered by the taxpayer's criminal activity. Yet under the Tax Act, although possession of a firearm in a school zone may be criminal under state law, nothing in the federal act limits its application to possessions that are independently criminal. On the other hand, the size of the tax (like the tax in *Constantine*) is at least indicative of an intent to penalize rather than to generate revenue, and if one couples that with the fact that the tax is being imposed as an alternative to the criminal sanction struck down in *Lopez*, a reasonable case for application of *Constantine* might be made. Yet the Court's recent acknowledgment in *Sebelius* that the regulatory motive or effect of a revenue-raising measure usually plays little role in the analysis suggests that *Constantine* is unlikely to be controlling in this case.

§5.4.2 Specific Limitations on the Power to Tax

As noted above, the body of the Constitution contains three specific limitations on the power to tax. Taxes must be uniform throughout the United States; direct taxes must be in proportion to the population of the states; and no tax or duty may be laid on exports. We will discuss each of these limitations in turn.

The Requirement of Uniformity

Article I, §8, cl. 1 provides that "all Duties, Imposts, and Excises shall be uniform throughout the United States." This mean that taxes must be *geographically* uniform throughout the United States in the sense that the tax must operate "with the same force and effect in every place where the subject of it is found." *Head Money Cases*, 112 U.S. 580, 594 (1884). Thus if Congress imposes an excise tax on oil production, that tax must apply and must be levied in all regions of the United States in which such production occurs. This does not mean that equal revenue must be generated from all states or even that oil production must occur in all states. For example, suppose no oil production takes place in the state of Hawaii. The tax would find no "subject" in that state and would therefore generate no revenue from that state. Nonetheless, the federal tax remains uniform since it applies wherever its subject occurs.

Suppose, however, the federal excise tax described above expressly excludes from its coverage the production of oil in the Arctic Circle region of Alaska. Does this geographic exclusion violate the principle of uniformity? The answer depends on the purpose behind the exclusion. If the purpose is to treat equally circumstanced oil production differently simply because of the region in which that production occurs, then the uniformity principle is violated. If, however, there is something distinct about the production of oil in the Arctic Circle that warrants differential treatment — e.g., the relative difficulty and expense of oil exploration in that region — the uniformity principle is not violated. Thus, the subject of the tax is narrowly defined to exclude the special circumstances related to Arctic Circle oil production. See *United States v. Ptasynski*, 462 U.S. 74, 84-86 (1983) (holding that similar tax exemption for Alaskan oil did not violate the Uniformity Clause).

Direct Taxes and Proportionality

Article I, §9, cl. 4 provides that "No Capitation, or other direct, Tax shall be laid, unless in Proportion to the Census or Enumeration herein before directed to be taken." A *capitation* (or head tax) is a tax paid by every person without regard to property, profession, or any other circumstance; a *direct tax* is a tax imposed on the ownership of real or personal property. By way of comparison, an excise tax, sometimes referred to as an indirect tax, is a tax imposed on an activity or the exercise of a privilege. The proportionality requirement means that the state-by-state revenue generated by either a capitation or a direct tax must be apportioned among the states according to the population of each state. In other words, the tax would have to generate the same revenue per person in every state of the union, as measured by the previous census, even though per capita wealth varies considerably from state to state. An excise tax is not subject to this limitation.

At one time it was thought that a tax on income was a direct tax subject to the proportionality requirement. See *Pollock v. Farmers' Loan & Trust Co.*, 158 U.S. 601 (1895). However, the adoption of the Sixteenth Amendment ended the controversy over the constitutionality of nonapportioned income taxes by providing Congress with the "power to lay and collect taxes on incomes, from whatever source derived, without apportionment among the several States, and without regard to any census or enumeration."

From a modern perspective, the proportionality limitation is relatively unimportant since Congress in the twentieth century has not imposed a capitation or true direct tax other than perhaps an income tax. In *National Federation of Independent Business v. Sebelius*, the Court rejected arguments that the federal "tax" imposed on those who failed to obtain health insurance was a capitation or direct tax that had to be apportioned among the states on a per capita basis — something Congress had made no effort to do. The tax was not a capitation for it was not imposed on everyone, but rather only on those earning more than a certain income and who had not obtained health insurance. Nor was it a direct tax because it was not imposed on the ownership of land or personal property. 132 S. Ct. at 2598-2599.

Prohibition on Taxes or Duties Laid on Exports

Article I, §9, cl. 5 provides that "No Tax or Duty shall be laid on Articles exported from any State." The word "export" signifies goods in transit to a foreign country. The prohibition prevents Congress from taxing either goods in export transit or services that are related to that transit. For example, a federal tax imposed on premiums paid for insurance to cover the shipment of goods to foreign countries is a tax on a service related to goods in export transit and hence is in violation of the Export Clause. *United States v. International Business Machines Corp.*, 517 U.S. 843 (1996). Congress may, however, impose taxes on goods not in transit but intended for export, as long as the tax is nondiscriminatory vis-à-vis the potential export status of the goods — i.e., as long as the tax is not imposed *because* the goods are intended for export. Thus a nondiscriminatory tax that applies to all tobacco products regardless of their potential export status may be applied to tobacco products that are not yet in export transit even though those products are ultimately intended for export.

§5.4.3 What Constitutes an Expenditure for Purposes of the Spending Power?

Turning now from the taxing power to the spending power, we begin with a simple proposition. For purposes of the spending power, an expenditure is an outlay of money by the federal government — i.e., an expenditure occurs whenever the federal government spends money. Such money may be provided to private individuals and entities, or to state and/or local governments. If the spending is directed toward the common defense or the general welfare, then it falls within the authority granted by the power to tax and spend. Note that Congress may also spend money incident to its other powers, without relying on the spending power. For example, as part of a regulation of interstate commerce Congress may spend money to establish a federal administrative agency to enforce statutory standards. As was true of the power to tax, the Court's review of exercises of the spending power is quite deferential. Thus although the Court has frequently observed that any expenditure must be for the "general welfare," in practice the Court has left it to Congress to determine the scope of that term, noting that "[t]he level of deference to the congressional decision [to spend] is such that the Court has more recently questioned whether 'general welfare' is a judicially enforceable restriction at all." *South Dakota v. Dole*, 483 U.S. 203, 207, n.2 (1987) (citing *Buckley v. Valeo*, 424 U.S. 1, 90-91 (1976) (*per curiam*)).

Regulatory Spending

The Court's deference is not, however, absolute. If the Court concludes that a spending measure is actually a disguised regulation, the measure will not pass muster as an exercise of the spending power. The circumstances under which this will occur are rare, but the potential for such judicial intervention nonetheless remains a possibility. One of the leading cases is *United States v. Butler*, 297 U.S. 1 (1936). At issue in *Butler* was a provision of the Agricultural Adjustment Act of 1933 (AAA), which empowered the federal government to enter contracts with farmers under which the government purchased the farmers' agreement to submit to a federal regulatory scheme designed to reduce the production of particular crops. The Court concluded that this spending program was a disguised effort to regulate production. Two reasons were given. First, the program was not truly voluntary. A farmer who refused to accept the government's offer would be placed at a substantial competitive disadvantage compared to those farmers who entered the program, subjecting the former to potential financial ruin. Thus the coercive nature of the program left farmers with no real "power of choice." Id. at 70-71. In essence, the regulatory scheme was imposed on them. Second, *Butler* was decided while the Court still adhered to the enclave theory under which the regulation of production was insulated from the regulatory powers of Congress. Hence the contracts entered under the AAA bound the farmers to a federal regulatory scheme that could not otherwise have been applied to them. Id. at 74-78.

The force of the *Butler* decision has been somewhat eroded by subsequent decisions and jurisprudential developments. Certainly, as a general matter, the Court today is more deferential toward congressional exercises of power than it was when *Butler* was decided. And as has been noted several times, the Court no longer follows the enclave theory. Thus if *Butler* were decided today, even if "coercive" or "regulatory" spending were found, that spending would likely be validated as an exercise of the commerce power. The argument is straightforward. Farming for profit is economic activity that substantially affects interstate commerce. Indeed, one would expect that *most* coercive spending measures would satisfy the current Commerce Clause standards. But even under modern jurisprudence, it does not necessarily follow that *all* coercive spending can be validated by reference to the commerce power. Moreover, even if a coercive spending measure can be upheld under the Commerce Clause, it may still run afoul of some other constitutional limitation on the exercise of federal power, such as the principle of state sovereignty embodied in the Tenth Amendment.

Example 5-L

The Aid to Families Act (AFA) is a federal statute that provides food stamps to families with a demonstrated need for welfare assistance. Under the AFA as originally enacted, a single mother with demonstrated need and one dependent child was entitled to a monthly allotment of $250 in food stamps. An incremental increase of $50 in food stamps was provided for each additional child. As part of a welfare reform package, however, Congress amended the AFA to provide that any single mother receiving food stamps under the act who has two or more dependent children and who bears an additional child will, instead of receiving an increase in benefits, lose half of the AFA benefits for which she was previously eligible. This means that a single mother of two would have her $300 monthly allotment reduced to $150 on the birth of a third child. Can this measure be validated as an exercise of the spending power?

Explanation

The provision of food stamps certainly involves an expenditure of federal money, and Congress could reasonably conclude that providing food stamps to needy families advances the general welfare of the nation. The amendment, however, may well be coercive and therefore valid only if it comes within the regulatory powers of Congress. Because food stamps are distributed on the basis of need, it would seem that this drastic cut in benefits, both in design and operation, coerces indigent single mothers into compliance with what can be fairly characterized as a federal regulation of family size and family living arrangements. In essence, the "power of choice" to determine both the size of her family and which of her children will live with her as dependents, is taken from the single mother just as the "power of choice" was taken from the farmers who were financially coerced into compliance with the congressional crop reduction plan in *Butler*. Either you comply with the federal plan or you will be subjected to severe economic consequences. (Consider whether the coercive spending label would attach had the AFA amendment merely provided that birth of an additional child would generate no increase in the family's food stamp allotment.)

Assuming the AFA amendment is coercive, can it be validated under the Commerce Clause? In other words, could Congress pursuant to the commerce power regulate the size of "welfare" families? Probably not. Bearing children, although fraught with economic ramifications, is not commonly understood as economic activity. Given *United States v. Lopez* and *United States*

v. *Morrison*, this in itself may preclude reliance on the commerce power. But even if such noneconomic activity can be regulated under the commerce power, given the further reasoning in *Lopez*, the government would face a difficult task in establishing that welfare family size "substantially affects" interstate commerce. Presumably the government's argument would be premised on a causal chain that begins with welfare family size and ends with interstate commerce: Increased family size leads to a lack of discipline, which leads to poor education, which leads to unemployment and economic dislocation, which may lead to crime, which affects local businesses, which ultimately affects interstate businesses, etc., etc. Yet it was precisely this type of "inference piled upon inference" that the Court rejected in *Lopez*. Thus despite the demise of the enclave theory, *United States v. Butler* when coupled with *Lopez* and *Morrison* may, under limited circumstances, provide an effective basis for challenging the constitutionality of purported spending measures. Note that this hypothetical provision may also violate principles of substantive due process because of its infringement on a mother's liberty interests in bearing children and in her family living arrangements. See Allan Ides and Christopher N. May, *Constitutional Law: Individual Rights* §2.5.2 (6th ed. 2013).

One should not take *Butler* or the foregoing example to suggest that the modern Court will readily find that the enticement provided by an offer of federal money to private entities and individuals is the equivalent of coercion. In fact, just the opposite is true. Yet given the moderate resurgence of Commerce Clause scrutiny, additional judicial scrutiny of spending measures is not beyond the realm of possibility.

Unconstitutional Conditions

Even if a particular spending measure is not deemed to be coercive or regulatory and thus falls within Congress's Art. I, §8, cl. 1 spending power, it may still run into possible constitutional difficulties if receipt of the federal funds is conditioned upon the recipient's agreeing to surrender certain constitutional rights. Under the *unconstitutional conditions doctrine*, the government may not deny a benefit to a person on a basis that infringes his or her constitutionally protected rights, even if he or she has no absolute entitlement to the benefit in question. *United States v. American Library Association, Inc.*, 539 U.S. 194, 210-211 (2003). The doctrine is based on the principle that the government should not be able to use its largesse to in effect buy up a person's constitutional rights by dangling a carrot in front of them, for a person may have no real choice in the matter. While the Supreme Court has continued to recognize this potential limitation on the government's use of its spending power, the modern Court has viewed the doctrine as applying only to First Amendment rights, and as being triggered only if the conditions go beyond what amounts to a "reasonable choice." Otherwise, if the conditions are "reasonable and unambiguous," and ones that a recipient is "not obligated to accept," the doctrine will not come into play. *Grove City College v. Bell*, 465 U.S. 555, 575-576 (1984) (recognizing doctrine but finding that it was not violated because even if the funding conditions violated the First Amendment, the recipient educational institutions were not obligated to accept them). See also *Rumsfeld v. Forum for Academic and Institutional Rights, Inc.*, 547 U.S. 47, 59-61 (2006) (recognizing doctrine but finding it inapplicable where the funding conditions involved were ones the government could constitutionally have imposed directly).

Spending Directed Toward the States

Just as federal money may be used to entice private action, the federal government sometimes uses the "carrot" of federal expenditures to lure states into participating in federal programs. Congress may thus condition grants to the states upon the states' taking certain actions "that Congress could not require them to take." *National Federation of Independent Business v. Sebelius*, supra, 132 S. Ct. at 2659. For example, the federal government may condition the receipt of federal highway funds on a state's willingness to enforce a particular speed limit. Or it may condition the receipt of federal education funds on a state's implementing a school lunch program or a program for regularly assessing the quality of public school teachers. The possibilities for such conditional spending measures are almost endless given the elastic nature of the general welfare concept. But as with spending directed toward private parties, conditional spending directed toward the states must come within the confines of the granted federal authority.

In assessing the constitutionality of conditional spending measures directed toward the states, the Court considers three factors, beyond the threshold requirement that the expenditure be for the general welfare: (1) whether the condition imposed on the receipt of federal funds is stated unambiguously so that a state accepting the funds is fully aware of the consequences of that acceptance; (2) whether the condition imposed is related to the expenditure; and (3) whether the financial inducement to which the condition attaches is so strong that it passes the point where pressure turns into compulsion, in which case the spending measure must be upheld, if at all, as a regulation. *South Dakota v. Dole*, 483 U.S. at 207-212. These considerations reflect the idea that Spending Clause measures are "'much in the nature of a *contract*.' The legitimacy of Congress's exercise of the spending power 'thus rests on whether the State voluntarily and knowingly accepts the terms of the 'contract.'" *Sebelius*, supra, 132 S. Ct. at 2602.

The first two factors are almost self-explanatory. When a state accepts federal funds, it is entitled to know the consequences of its acceptance. In other words, Congress must tell the state precisely what it must do in order

263

to receive and continue receiving the federal money. As the Supreme Court recently explained, " 'legislation enacted pursuant to the spending power is much in the nature of a contract,' and therefore, to be bound by 'federally imposed conditions,' recipients of federal funds must accept them 'voluntarily and knowingly.' States cannot knowingly accept conditions of which they are 'unaware' or which they are 'unable to ascertain.' " *Arlington Central School District Board of Education v. Murphy*, 548 U.S. 291, 296 (2006). Satisfaction of this requirement is determined by reference to the appropriate statutory language. If the relevant statutory language is ambiguous, a court can rely upon prior judicial decisions or administrative agency regulations that may have clarified the language, in determining whether a recipient received adequate notice as to what the applicable funding conditions were. In *Jackson v. Birmingham Board of Education*, 544 U.S. 167 (2005), the Court on this basis held that Title IX of the Education Amendments of 1972, which on its face bars sex discrimination by recipients of federal funds, also prohibits retaliation against those who have complained of Title IX violations, even though Title IX itself is silent on the matter of such retaliatory measures. See also *Forest Grove School Dist. v. T.A.*, 557 U.S. 230, 246 (2009) (applying unambiguous statement rule).

Second, the condition must be germane to the particular expenditure involved. This is essentially a rational relationship test. In *South Dakota v. Dole*, for example, the requirement was easily satisfied by a condition imposed on the disbursal of federal highway funds that required any state accepting the funds to make the possession of alcoholic beverages illegal for persons under 21 years of age. The condition was, in the Court's words, "directly related to one of the main purposes for which highway funds are expended — safe interstate travel," the theory being that states with lower drinking ages invited increased interstate travel (and accidents) by underage drinkers. 483 U.S. at 208-209. The result would likely be different were the government to condition the receipt of *other* federal funds, such as monies the state receives under a federal housing assistance program, on the state's raising its drinking age to 21.

The third factor essentially parallels the problem of coercion addressed in *Butler*. When the carrot of a federal expenditure turns into the stick of federal coercion, the proper framework of analysis is no longer the spending power. As the Court stated in *Dole*, "Our decisions have recognized that in some circumstances the financial inducement offered by Congress might be so coercive as to pass the point at which 'pressure turns into compulsion.'" Id. at 211 (quoting *Steward Machine Co. v. Davis*, 301 U.S. 548, 590 (1937)). Yet, in contrast to spending measures directed at individuals, this principle has only rarely been applied to void a conditional spending measure designed to entice state compliance with federal standards or state participation in a federal program. The reason for this is that "[i]n the typical case we look to the States to defend their prerogatives by adopting 'the simple expedient of not yielding' to federal blandishments when they do not want to embrace the federal policies as their own." *Sebelius*, supra, 132 S. Ct. at 2603. Thus, in *Dole*, the Court held that the threat of a 5 percent reduction in the amount of the state's federal highway funds for failure to adhere to the mandated drinking age was not coercive, for the money represented less than half of 1 percent of South Dakota's state budget. Perhaps coercion would have been found if Congress had threatened to completely eliminate a state's share in federal highway funds. And, of course, even if a particular conditional spending measure were found to be coercive, it might still, depending on the circumstances, be upheld as a valid regulation under the commerce power.

Example 5-M

The 2010 Affordable Care Act significantly expanded the federal Medicaid program under which federal funds are given to the states on the condition that they provide specified medical care to the needy. The earlier Medicaid program required coverage only for certain categories of needy individuals, with no mandatory coverage for most childless adults, and with flexibility as to the parents of needy families. Under the 2010 amendments, states by 2014 must expand their Medicaid programs to cover all individuals under the age of 65 whose income is below 133 percent of the federal poverty guideline. The federal government will initially pay 100 percent of the cost of covering these newly eligible individuals, with that percentage gradually dropping to 90 percent. A state that refuses to adopt the expansion will lose the funds associated with the expansion, as well as its existing Medicaid funds. Medicaid spending accounts for about 20 percent of the average state's total budget, and federal funds cover roughly 50 to 80 percent of this amount. States that decline to adopt the Medicaid expansion will thus lose federal funds that account for between 10 and 16 percent of their total state budget. Is this conditional spending program a valid exercise of Congress's spending power?

Explanation

Under the first *Dole* factor, the question is whether the expanded coverage condition imposed on the receipt of federal funds was stated so clearly and unambiguously that a state accepting federal funds was aware of the consequences of that acceptance. When states signed onto the Medicaid program, they surely knew that Congress might from time to time amend the program. But the question here is whether the significant expansion effected by the 2010 act was something states could be expected to have anticipated when they agreed to participate in Medicaid. Here, a good argument can be made that the expansion is beyond what a state could reasonably have anticipated when it first signed on to the program. The expansion can be seen as creating an entirely new universal health care program, quite distinct from the original program that was limited to certain recognized categories of the needy. The fact that the Affordable Care Act created a separate funding provision to cover the costs of those made newly eligible further strengthens this argument.

As to the second *Dole* factor, whether the condition imposed is related to the federal expenditure at stake, this hinges on whether we view the original Medicaid program and the Affordable Care Act expansion as involving different programs, or whether the latter is better characterized as simply a modification of the earlier program. If these are viewed as different programs for the reasons suggested above, then this factor is not met because the government would be using a state's failure to adopt the Affordable Care program as a reason to terminate its funding for the distinct and preexisting Medicaid program.

Finally, a strong argument can be made that this is one of those rare instances when the federal government in its relations with the states has crossed the line between persuasion and coercion. The amount of money at stake here is substantial. In the *Dole* case, if South Dakota refused the federal invitation to raise the state's minimum driving age to 21, the state would lose only 5 percent of its federal highway funds, representing less than half of 1 percent of the state's budget. Here, by contrast, a nonparticipating state would lose 100 percent of its federal Medicaid funds. Depending on the wealth of the state, this would amount to anywhere from 10 to 16 percent of the total state budget. If this spending program were thus deemed to be penal or regulatory, it could be upheld only if Congress has the power to regulate the states in this manner. Such power does not exist, however, for the Court has held that under principles of federalism, Congress cannot compel the states (as opposed to merely giving them an incentive) to enforce a federal regulatory scheme. See §5.6.

In *National Federation of Independent Business v. Sebelius*, 132 S. Ct. 2566 (2012), the Court held that Congress in this case exceeded its power under the Spending Clause. First, the change effected by the Affordable Care Act was "a shift in kind, not merely degree." Id. at 2605. "A State could hardly anticipate that Congress's reservation of the right to 'alter' or 'amend' the Medicaid program included the power to transform it so dramatically." Id. at 2606. Second, the penalty for failure to adopt the new condition, loss of all Medicaid funds, went beyond what the germaneness requirement permits. "[W]hile Congress may have styled the expansion a mere alteration of existing Medicaid, it recognized it was enlisting the States in a new health care program." Id. at 2606. It would have been different were noncomplying states merely denied the separate Affordable Care funding. Finally, "the financial 'inducement' Congress has chosen . . . is a gun to the head." Id. at 2604. "The threatened loss of over 10 percent of a State's overall budget . . . is economic dragooning that leaves the States with no real option but to acquiesce in the Medicaid expansion." Id. at 2605. The Court went on to hold that the act could still be implemented as long as nonparticipating states would lose only the additional Affordable Care funds without also being stripped of their separate Medicaid funding. Id. at 2607.

Regulatory Authority Over Third Parties

The spending measures we have considered so far were all of a conditional nature — i.e., the recipient (whether a private party or a state governmental entity) agreed, in exchange for receiving the funds, to abide by certain federally imposed requirements. In these settings, any regulatory authority the government obtained through use of its spending power was exercised directly over the recipient of the federal funds. However, there are situations where the government may use its spending power to obtain regulatory authority over third parties, not themselves recipients of federal funds, whose conduct may nonetheless impair the integrity of the spending program. *Sabri v. United States*, 541 U.S. 600 (2004), involved a federal statute that criminalizes the bribery of state, local, or tribal officials of entities that receive over $10,000 per year in federal funds. The defendant in that case was a real estate developer who allegedly bribed a city councilor in a city that received $29 million in federal funds that year. While the federal spending itself clearly fell within the scope of the spending power, the question was whether Congress could rely on that spending to then criminalize the conduct of a private party, even though there was no proven connection between the bribery conduct and the federal funds. In upholding the statute, the Court explained that "Congress has authority under the Spending Clause to appropriate federal monies to promote the general welfare . . . and it has corresponding authority under the Necessary and Proper Clause . . . to see to it that taxpayer dollars appropriated under that power are spent for the general welfare." Id. at 605. Since "[m]oney is fungible," said the Court, "money can be drained off here because a federal grant is pouring in there." Id. at 606. Thus, "Congress was within its prerogative to protect spending objects from the menace of local administrators on the take. The power to keep a watchful eye on expenditures and on the reliability of those who use public money is bound up with the congressional authority to spend in the first place. . . ." Id. at 608. The Necessary and Proper Clause therefore allowed Congress to criminalize the conduct of those not themselves the recipients of federal funds but whose conduct threatened indirectly to impair the integrity of a federal spending program.

§5.5 THE POWER OVER FOREIGN AFFAIRS

The power over foreign affairs is composed of specific textual grants such as the power to regulate foreign commerce (Art. I, §8, cl. 3) and the treaty power (Art. II, §2, cl. 2), coupled with the implied authority of the United States to exercise those powers inherent in the concept of nationhood and sovereignty.

United States v. Curtiss-Wright Export Corp., 299 U.S. 304, 318 (1936). Essentially this means that the United States possesses the full range of international powers conducive to participation in international affairs, including the power to enter alliances, the power to establish principles of international law in concert with other nations, and the power to engage in hostilities up to and including war. In terms of the allocation of these powers as between Congress and the President, except where the Constitution provides specifically for a congressional role (e.g., only Congress may declare war, and presidential treaties are subject to Senate ratification), primary authority in the field of foreign affairs rests with the President. As the Supreme Court noted in *American Insurance Association v. Garamendi*, 539 U.S. 396, 414 (2003):

> Although the source of the President's power to act in foreign affairs does not enjoy any textual detail, the historical gloss on "executive Power" vested in Article II of the Constitution has recognized the President's "vast share of responsibility for the conduct of our foreign relations." While Congress holds express authority to regulate public and private dealings with other nations in its war and foreign commerce powers, in foreign affairs the President has a degree of independent authority to act.

While the exercise of these powers, whether by Congress or the President, must conform to the text and principles of the Constitution, one can expect the judiciary to be quite deferential in examining whether any exercise of the power over foreign affairs exceeds the scope of constitutionally vested authority or transgresses constitutional limitations.

§5.5.1 The Foreign Commerce Power

The power to regulate commerce with foreign nations is granted in the same clause that grants Congress the power to regulate interstate commerce: "Congress shall have Power . . . To regulate Commerce with foreign Nations, and among the several States. . . ." Art. I, §8, cl. 3. In examining exercises of this power, the Court has consistently deferred to the judgment of Congress. Thus while the interstate commerce power has, from time to time, been the subject of close judicial scrutiny, the foreign commerce power has not. This is true in part because the foreign commerce power has not often been used in a manner that implicates the states' police powers and in part because of a judicial tendency to be more deferential toward exercises of national power touching on foreign relations. See *Japan Line v. County of Los Angeles*, 441 U.S. 434, 448 (1979) (suggesting that the scope of the foreign commerce power is greater than that of the interstate commerce power). The net result is that under the foreign commerce power, Congress possesses a plenary power to regulate freely in the broad sphere of commerce with foreign nations. That power may be exercised to impose embargoes and protective tariffs on goods shipped from foreign nations, to ban the importation of certain goods, and, in general, to establish the standards under which commerce with foreign nations may take place. The test is one of rationality. So long as Congress could rationally conclude that the regulated matter either is foreign commerce or affects foreign commerce, the measure will be sustained. Thus, while Congress could not use the foreign commerce power to regulate the possession of guns in or near schools, there being no rational connection with foreign commerce, it probably could use that power to regulate the possession of *imported* guns in or near schools.

§5.5.2 The Treaty Power

A treaty, for purposes of the Constitution, is a compact between the United States and a foreign nation that conforms to the advice and consent requirements of Article II, §2, cl. 2. That clause grants the President the "Power, by and with the Advice and Consent of the Senate, to make Treaties, provided two thirds of the Senators present concur." A treaty so made is of equal authority with statutes approved by both houses of Congress and signed by the President. Like those laws, a treaty constitutes the "supreme Law of the Land," preempting all state laws inconsistent with the terms of the treaty. U.S. Const. Art. VI (the Supremacy Clause). See §7.5.2 (discussing treaties and executive agreements). Where a treaty creates rights or obligations that are judicially enforceable by state or federal courts, the treaty's meaning for domestic purposes is ultimately determined by the United States Supreme Court, as part of its "duty 'to say what the law is,' *Marbury v. Madison,* 5 U.S. (1 Cranch) 137, 177 (1803)," rather than by any international tribunal such as the World Court. *Sanchez-Llamas v. Oregon,* 548 U.S. 331, 353-354 (2006). Thus, while the Supreme Court will give "respectful consideration" to such a tribunal's interpretations of a treaty (id. at 355), the Court ultimately is not bound by them.

There are two types of treaties: self-executing and non-self-executing. A self-executing treaty is one that establishes enforceable domestic law without any further action by Congress. A non-self-executing treaty is one that requires legislative implementation before its provisions can be of any effect as domestic law. Whether a treaty is self-executing or non-self-executing is a question of interpretation. See *Medellín v. Texas,* 552 U.S. 491, 505-516 (2008). For example, a treaty between the United States and a foreign nation that provides that the citizens of each shall be free to engage in business within the territory of the other on a nondiscriminatory basis appears to require no further implementation by Congress. The treaty establishes the right and is therefore immediately enforceable as domestic law. A conflicting state law would be automatically preempted, as would a previously enacted federal law that was in conflict with the treaty. If, on the other hand, the treaty merely established international standards for the nondiscriminatory treatment of foreign businesses and called upon the signatory states to implement those standards through domestic legislation, the treaty would be non-self-executing. As a general matter, treaties that require an appropriation of money or the criminalization of specified conduct are deemed to be non-self-executing. See also *Hamdan v. Rumsfeld*, 548 U.S. 557, 625-628 (2006) (Court avoids deciding whether the 1949 Geneva Convention, dealing with the treatment of prisoners of war, constituted a self-executing treaty, for an act of Congress made compliance with "the law of war," of which the Geneva Convention is a part, applicable to the military proceedings involved).

As the next example suggests, the inquiry as to whether a treaty is self-executing or non-self-executing can be quite challenging.

Example 5-N

In 1969, the United States, upon the advice and consent of the Senate, ratified the Vienna Convention on Consular Relations (Vienna Convention) and the Optional Protocol to that convention. The Vienna Convention provides that if a person detained by a foreign nation so requests, the foreign nation "shall inform" the consular post of that person's nation of citizenship of such detention, and "shall inform" the person of his right to request assistance from the consul of his own nation. The Optional Protocol provides that disputes arising under the Vienna Convention "shall lie within the compulsory jurisdiction" of the International Court of Justice (ICJ), the principal judicial organ of the United Nations. By ratifying the Optional Protocol to the Vienna Convention, the United States consented to the jurisdiction of the ICJ with respect to claims arising out of the Vienna Convention. In terms of the enforceability of ICJ judgments, Article 94(1) of the United Nations Charter (also a treaty ratified by the United States) provides that "[e]ach Member of the United Nations undertakes to comply with the decision of the [ICJ] in any case to which it is a party."

In 2004, the ICJ, in the *Avena* case, held that, based on violations of the Vienna Convention, 51 named Mexican nationals, incarcerated in various states of the United States, were entitled to review and reconsideration of their state-court convictions and sentences. This was so regardless of any forfeiture of the individual's right to raise Vienna Convention claims because of a failure to comply with generally applicable state rules governing challenges to criminal convictions. In other words, conflicting state laws were trumped by the supreme law of the land embodied in these treaties. One of those Mexican nationals, Medellín, who had been convicted and sentenced under the laws of the state of Texas, sought relief from his conviction and sentence, arguing that the United Nations Charter, the Vienna Convention, and the Optional Protocol were self-executing treaties that required Texas to comply with the judgment of the ICJ in the *Avena* case. Is he correct?

Explanation

Clearly, the "shall inform" language of the Vienna Convention creates an international law duty of compliance with its mandate; yet whether that duty is enforceable as a matter of domestic law is a separate question. The U.S. ratification of the Optional Protocol does, however, establish consent to the jurisdiction of the ICJ in disputes arising under the Vienna Convention. If one were to construe that consent to jurisdiction as a consent to the enforceability of ICJ judgments, the case in favor of "self-execution" would be a strong one, for there would appear to be no additional steps required — i.e., no further legislation required — with respect to the domestic enforceability of those judgments. On the other hand, the consent in the Optional Protocol speaks only to jurisdiction; that being the case, the domestic enforceability of ICJ judgments may well require implementing legislation. Article 94(1) of the United Nations Charter does speak to the question of enforceability when it provides that "[e]ach Member of the United Nations undertakes to comply" with judgments of the ICJ. One could construe this language as establishing an obligation of domestic enforceability; however, it does not quite say that. The "undertakes to comply" directive can be read as an obligation to pursue some unspecified future action at the discretion of the nation involved. In *Medellín v. Texas*, supra, 552 U.S. at 505-514, the Court majority concluded that the above combination of treaties were not self-executing and that the judgment of the ICJ in the *Avena* case was therefore not automatically enforceable as domestic law — i.e., it was not the supreme law of the land. In dissent, Justice Breyer, speaking for two other Justices, argued that the treaties at issue were self-executing and that the United States had consented to the domestic enforceability of ICJ judgments. Id. at 541-562 (Breyer, J., dissenting). While the majority adopted a position that was premised on a presumption in favor of non-self-execution, the dissent entertained no such presumption.

The making of a treaty requires a coordinated effort between the executive branch and the Senate. By tradition, treaty formation and negotiation is the responsibility of the executive branch. Once the terms of a potential treaty are established, the Senate reviews those terms and may either enter its consent (by a two-thirds vote of a quorum), decline to consent, or suggest amendments. Only if the Senate enters its consent may the President ratify the treaty, at which time the treaty becomes a binding international agreement and, if self-executing, a law of the United States.

The subjects to which a treaty may address itself are as diverse as the problems confronting the international community. Importantly, the treaty power, like the power to tax and spend, is a distinct constitutional power that may be exercised without reference to other constitutional grants of power. In essence, the constitutional power to make treaties puts the United States on an equal footing with other nations, empowering it to enter compacts with those nations on any matter of international concern. And although some commentators have suggested that the treaty power cannot be used to address purely internal matters, the Court has never enforced this principle, leaving it to the President and the Senate to determine if a matter is of sufficient international concern to warrant resort to a treaty. Once a treaty is ratified, Congress, pursuant to the Necessary and Proper Clause, may enact legislation to implement provisions of the treaty, even if in the absence of the treaty Congress would not have had the power to do so.

The classic case applying these principles is *Missouri v. Holland*, 252 U.S. 416 (1920). In that case, the United States entered into a treaty with Great Britain that was designed to protect the annual migration of certain bird species that traversed parts of Canada and the United States. The birds, which provided both a food resource and an important form of pest control, were in danger of extinction. The 1916 treaty called for closed hunting seasons and certain other protections. In addition, the signatories agreed to seek implementing legislation in their respective lawmaking bodies. In response, Congress enacted the 1918 Migratory Bird Treaty Act (MBTA), which empowered the secretary of agriculture to impose regulations designed to implement the provisions of the treaty. The state of Missouri filed suit challenging the regulations on the ground that the MBTA operated as "an unconstitutional interference with the rights reserved to the States by the Tenth Amendment." Id. at 431.

The Court assumed that in the absence of a treaty Congress would have lacked the power to pass the MBTA. Indeed, the Court noted that a 1913 federal migratory bird act, adopted several years prior to the treaty with Great Britain, had been held unconstitutional by two federal district courts as exceeding Congress's lawmaking powers. Id. at 432. Yet even if this were the case, the Court held that the MBTA was still constitutional under Art. I, §8, cl. 18 as a *necessary and proper* means to implement the treaty, as long as the treaty itself passed constitutional muster. Nor would the Tenth Amendment bar implementation of the treaty, for as the Court explained it, the Tenth Amendment reserved to the states only those powers not delegated to the United States. The treaty power, and the power to enact legislation necessary and proper to carrying out treaties, were both delegated to the United States. Therefore, a valid exercise of the treaty power could not, by definition, transgress the limits of the Tenth Amendment. Note the similarity between this interpretation of the Tenth Amendment and Chief Justice Stone's description of the Tenth Amendment as stating a "truism" in *United States v. Darby* (see §5.3.2).

The Court in *Missouri v. Holland* did not create a specific test for measuring the validity of a treaty but made it clear that the treaty power vested the United States with a broad authority to enter into compacts with foreign nations on matters that might otherwise not be within the constitutional competence of Congress. In the Court's words,

> It is obvious that there may be matters of the sharpest exigency for the national well being that an act of Congress could not deal with but that a treaty followed by such an act could, and it is not lightly to be assumed that, in matters requiring national action, "a power which must belong to and somewhere reside in every civilized government" is not to be found.

252 U.S. at 433. The migratory bird treaty easily came within that authority since it addressed "a national interest of very nearly the first magnitude." Id. at 435. Moreover, in the Court's view, given the transitory nature of birds, that interest could be protected "only by national action in concert with that of another power. . . . But for the treaty and the statute there soon might be no birds for any powers to deal with. We see nothing in the Constitution that compels the Government to sit by while a food supply is cut off and the protectors of our forests and our crops are destroyed." Id.

Although the *Missouri v. Holland* Court did not state that the President and the Senate had unfettered freedom to determine the subjects to which a treaty could be applied, nothing in the opinion endorses an active judicial scrutiny of such determinations. In fact, the tone of the opinion suggests just the opposite. The President and the Senate will be afforded broad leeway in determining whether a matter is of sufficient national interest and international concern to warrant a treaty on the subject. Significantly, the Court has never held a treaty invalid on the ground that it addressed a subject matter beyond the competence of the treaty power. Of course, it does not necessarily follow that the Court will never do so. But the realm of that possibility is, as a practical matter, quite limited.

Example 5-O

Recall Example 5-H in which we discussed the constitutionality of the Violence Against Women Act (VAWA) in the context of the commerce power. The act created a federal cause of action against any person who commits a crime of violence motivated by the gender of the victim. Included were such crimes as rape and spousal abuse. In *United States v. Morrison*, the Court struck down VAWA as beyond the commerce power. See §5.3.4. Suppose that after that ruling the President, with the advice and consent of the Senate, two-thirds of the Senators concurring, entered a multinational treaty under which all signatories agreed to take efforts to end violence against women. As part of the treaty the signatories agreed to seek implementing legislation within their respective countries, including the adoption of civil and criminal laws designed to deter and punish perpetrators of such violence. Pursuant to that aspect of the treaty, Congress reenacted VAWA. Is VAWA now constitutional?

Explanation

Under the Necessary and Proper Clause, Congress has power to implement the provisions of a treaty through legislation even when there is no independent congressional power to pass such legislation. *Missouri v. Holland.* Therefore, if the treaty is valid, the fact that Congress otherwise lacked the power to enact VAWA is irrelevant. With respect to the validity of the treaty, given that the President made the treaty with the advice and consent of the Senate, the only question is whether violence against women is a proper subject matter for a treaty. In other words, is violence against women a matter of international concern?

A negative answer to this question is premised on the idea that violence against women is a purely internal matter and therefore solely the business of the nation in which it occurs. As such it is of no concern to the family of nations and therefore beyond the scope of the treaty power. Of course, this answer also assumes a willingness by the judiciary to second-guess the President and the Senate as to the appropriateness of any particular subject matter for a treaty. A positive answer focuses on the potential international ramifications of violence against women. If one accepts the proposition that the freedom from gender-motivated violence is a basic part of human rights, any nation seeking leadership among the family of nations has an interest in actively eradicating such violence worldwide. Moreover, it may well be that nations in which such violence is commonplace and culturally acceptable need the assistance of the international community to address the problem effectively, including the good example of its international partners. Moreover, such a treaty might well provide an effective means to avoid sanctions and boycotts against offending nations as well as the resulting international economic dislocations associated with such devices. In any event, the President and the Senate could rationally conclude that violence against women is of sufficient international concern to warrant the making of a treaty. And given the generally deferential review afforded treaties, it seems likely the Court would accept this judgment. If so, the reenactment of VAWA would be constitutional as a necessary and proper means of implementing the treaty.

Missouri v. Holland does not, however, stand for the proposition that a treaty may violate or ignore the Constitution. Indeed, the *Missouri v. Holland* Court observed, "The treaty in question does not contravene any prohibitory words to be found in the Constitution." 252 U.S. at 433. In fact, although no case has specifically so held (because the Court has never been squarely confronted with the issue), the proposition that a treaty must conform to constitutional restraint is generally, if not universally, accepted. See *Reid v. Covert*, 354 U.S. 1, 16-17 (1957) (plurality); *Geofroy v. Riggs*, 133 U.S. 258, 267 (1890). The basic theory is that a treaty, although a law of the United States, is inferior to the Constitution in the same manner and to the same extent as are those laws adopted through the process of bicameralism and presentment. As such, a treaty must conform to constitutional limitations. Thus, for example, a treaty may not impose a duty on exports since doing so would violate the limitations imposed by Article I, §9, cl. 5. Nor, generally speaking, may a treaty violate or alter any other provision of the Constitution, including those found in the Bill of Rights.

We have already noted that a valid treaty preempts conflicting state law. This is so because a treaty is superior to such law according to the Supremacy Clause of Article VI. On the other hand, a treaty and a federal statute are on an equal footing. Neither is inherently superior to the other. As sometimes happens, however, a treaty and a federal law may conflict with one another. If so, the most recently adopted will prevail over the other. *Whitney v. Robertson*, 124 U.S. 190, 194 (1888). Thus a treaty can trump a previously enacted statute and a statute can trump a previously made treaty. Of course, courts will attempt to avoid any such conflict by interpreting the treaty and statute in a manner that permits both to coexist. But if the conflict is real and unavoidable, then the later in time must prevail.

The power to terminate treaties is discussed in Chapter 7 ("The Separation of Powers"). See §7.5.2.

§5.5.3 Executive Agreements

The treaty power is not the exclusive means through which the United States enters into agreements with foreign nations. Since the administration of President George Washington, the executive branch has entered into thousands of international compacts or agreements that do not satisfy the advice and consent requirements of Article II, §2, cl. 2. *American Insurance Association v. Garamendi*, 539 U.S. 396, 414 (2003). The authority to enter into these compacts is deemed inherent in the concept of nationhood, an important exception to the normal rule that the powers of the national government are enumerated in the Constitution. *United States v. Curtiss-Wright Export Corp.*, 299

U.S. 304, 318 (1936). These non-treaty international compacts are known as executive agreements.

There are three types of executive agreements: (1) those that are congressionally authorized by either a prior statutory delegation or subsequent statutory implementation; (2) those that are authorized by the provisions of a preexisting treaty; and (3) those that are undertaken under the independent constitutional authority of the executive branch. All three forms are considered complete constitutional alternatives to treaties (with one caveat noted below). This means that an executive agreement can be used to address the same subject matters as would a treaty. The choice of whether to use an executive agreement or a treaty is essentially a political judgment to be made by the executive branch.

In terms of constitutional power, the validity of an executive agreement depends, at least in theory, on the scope of the granted power pursuant to which the agreement was made. For example, if Congress exercises its power to regulate foreign commerce and in so doing delegates to the President the authority to enter a mutual trade agreement with a foreign state, the constitutionality of any resulting executive agreement would be measured against the scope of the foreign commerce power. Similarly, if a treaty serves as the sole basis for an executive agreement, the constitutional power to make the agreement is derivative of the constitutionality of the treaty. Finally, if the President makes an executive agreement based on an independent executive power, such as the power to recognize foreign sovereigns or the power to act as commander-in-chief, the constitutionality of that agreement depends on whether it falls within the scope of the power exercised. These limits are, however, largely theoretical since the Supreme Court has never held an executive agreement invalid on grounds that it exceeded the powers granted to the national government. Moreover, given the elastic nature of the inherent power over foreign affairs, the likelihood of the Supreme Court ever doing so is slim at best. Assuming that it falls within the scope of the President's powers, an executive agreement is valid so long as it does not violate "the Constitution's guarantees of individual rights." *American Insurance Association v. Garamendi*, supra, 539 U.S. at 416 n.9.

Example 5-P

The President, on her own independent authority, has entered into an executive agreement with the newly formed nation of Transylvia under which the President has agreed to recognize the sovereignty of Transylvia in exchange for Transylvia's agreement to grant the United States title to the assets of Transylvian bank accounts located in the United States. The President plans to use these funds to reimburse citizens of the United States who are creditors of Transylvia. May she do so?

Explanation

Yes. This executive agreement falls squarely within the President's independent power to recognize foreign nations. U.S. Const. Art. II, §3, cl. 3. See *United States v. Pink*, 315 U.S. 203 (1942); *United States v. Belmont*, 301 U.S. 324 (1937). The agreement is constitutional so long as it does not violate any constitutional limitations such as those found in the Bill of Rights.

Where they in fact conflict with state law, "valid executive agreements are fit to preempt state law, just as treaties are. . . ." *American Insurance Association v. Garamendi*, 539 U.S. at 416. The same is true if an executive agreement expressly provides that it will preempt state law. Yet even in the absence of an express provision or a direct conflict, state law may be deemed to be preempted because of its "interference with the foreign policy those agreements embody." Id. at 417. Four members of the Court have recently expressed discomfort with the idea that the President can unilaterally displace state laws through the executive agreement route, particularly when the preemptive effect of such an agreement is then merely implied or inferred by the courts. These Justices would therefore limit preemption in the executive agreement context to situations "where the President . . . has spoken clearly to the issue at hand" — i.e., where the express terms of the agreement call for preemption. Id. at 442 (Ginsburg, J., Stevens, J., Scalia, J., and Thomas, J., dissenting). Otherwise, for federal judges to invoke implied preemption makes them "the expositors of the Nation's foreign policy, which is the role they play by acting when the President himself has not taken a clear stand." Id. at 442-443.

When we turn from the ability of an executive agreement to preempt conflicting state law to such an agreement's ability to prevail over a previously adopted federal statute or treaty, the situation becomes slightly more complicated. With respect to executive agreements that are authorized by Congress or by the terms of a valid treaty, the same "later in time" rule that applies to conflicts between statutes and treaties applies to conflicts between executive agreements and statutes or treaties. Thus a congressionally authorized executive agreement that is adopted later in time than a treaty will trump any conflicting terms in that treaty.

The preemptive reach of an executive agreement that relies solely on the authority of the President is more controversial. Although such agreements, when self-executing, clearly preempt contrary state law, some judges and commentators argue that a purely presidential executive agreement cannot alter preexisting federal law in the absence of congressional implementation. See *United States v. Guy W. Capps, Inc.*, 204 F.2d 655 (4th Cir. 1953), *aff'd on other grounds*, 348 U.S. 296 (1955). Others have argued that this position ignores the independent constitutional authority of the President. Thus, if the President enters an executive agreement pursuant to an independent executive power (e.g., the power to recognize foreign nations or the commander-in-chief power), the agreement is valid federal law and is entitled to the same dignity as a statute passed by Congress or a treaty made by the President and the Senate. Under this second approach, the only question is whether the agreement comes within the scope of the executive power. If it does, then it is entitled to the same preemptive reach under the "later in time" rule as a valid statute or treaty. See Louis Henkin, *Foreign Affairs and the Constitution* 184-187 (1972). This controversy has yet to be addressed by the Supreme Court.

§5.5.4 The War Powers

The Constitution vests Congress and the President with the power to engage in war. Article I describes a number of specific war grants to Congress, such as the power to declare war (Art. I, §8, cl. 11), the power to raise and support armies (Art. I, §8, cl. 12), the power to provide and maintain a navy (Art. I, §8, cl. 13), and the power to spend for the common defense (Art. I, §8, cl. 1). Article II grants the President the power to lead the armed forces as commander-in-chief (Art. II, §2, cl. 1). These powers, coupled with the Necessary and Proper Clause as well as with the inherent authority of the United States to conduct foreign affairs, vest the United States with the complete power to make war. Of course, the war power, like all other granted powers, is subject to constitutional limitations, including those found in the Bill of Rights. However, it was not until 1919 that the Supreme Court first firmly established the principle that war powers legislation is subject to judicial review. See Christopher N. May, *In the Name of War: Judicial Review and the War Powers Since 1918* (1989). Moreover, since then, the actuality of war has sometimes had an unfortunate destructive impact on the Court's willingness to in fact apply constitutional limitations with their full force. See *Korematsu v. United States*, 323 U.S. 214 (1944) (deferring to the government's detention of Japanese-Americans during World War II). In this sense, the war power is perhaps the most dangerous of all constitutional powers.

The power to make war is the power to prosecute war successfully. This means that the war power may be used to prepare for the possibility of war, to take action designed to prevent war, to wage war, to end war, and to ameliorate the effects of war after hostilities have ceased. The scope of this power is, as the foregoing litany suggests, broadly encompassing, and rarely will a court second-guess Congress or the President in any of these "war-related" contexts. Moreover, exercises of the war powers are not limited to precise military or battlefield scenarios. The war powers may be exercised domestically. Thus in preparation for the possibility of war, Congress might establish a student loan program that would ensure the nation an ample supply of scientists and engineers, some of whom might work in the defense industry. Or during a war, Congress might freeze wages and prices as a measure to stabilize an economy buffeted by the effects of war. Finally, during the postwar period Congress might provide educational benefits to veterans to promote educational opportunities and to prevent saturation of the postwar job market. All of these exercises of the war powers come well within the authority of Congress.

The domestic scope of the war powers was examined in *Woods v. Cloyd W. Miller, Co.*, 333 U.S. 138 (1948). At issue in *Woods* was the Housing and Rent Act of 1947, a statute that limited the amount of rent that could be charged for housing in "defense-rental areas" within the United States. The act was passed after the Presidential Proclamation terminating hostilities in World War II but was designed to ameliorate the lingering effects of those hostilities. The Court sustained the legislation under the war powers. In the Court's words,

> The legislative history of the present Act makes abundantly clear that there has not yet been eliminated the deficit in housing which in considerable measure was caused by the heavy demobilization of veterans and by the cessation or reduction in residential construction during the period of hostilities due to the allocation of building materials to military projects. Since the war effort contributed heavily to that deficit, Congress has the power even after the cessation of hostilities to act to control the forces that a short supply of the needed article created.

Id. at 142-143.

The decision in *Woods* should not be read as abdicating all judicial review of war powers measures. In fact, the *Woods* Court specifically affirmed its authority to review exercises of the war powers. Id. at 144. See also *Chastleton Corp. v. Sinclair*, 264 U.S. 543 (1924) (upholding authority of federal court to determine if emergency giving rise to war powers legislation had ceased to exist during post-armistice period). One can expect, however, that only under rare circumstances will a federal court strike down domestic war powers legislation as beyond the powers of Congress. See *Hamilton v. Kentucky Distilleries Co.*, 251 U.S. 146 (1919) (reviewing but affirming War-Time Prohibition Act as within the power of Congress and not violating the Bill of Rights). Rarer still will be instances in which extraterritorial applications of war powers legislation are successfully challenged.

The Supreme Court has historically shown a much greater willingness to exercise judicial review in the war powers setting where the challenged governmental action was not authorized by federal statute or treaty and where the executive was thus acting on its own. This was seen in the recent case of *Hamdan v. Rumsfeld*, 548 U.S. 557 (2006), where the Supreme Court demonstrated a courageous willingness to undertake judicial review, during wartime, of the government's extraterritorial exercise of its war powers. In *Hamdan*, the Court struck down President Bush's use of his war powers to subject a Yemeni national to trial before a United States military tribunal in Cuba. The Court ruled that the President's actions were in violation of a federal statute (the Uniform Code of Military Justice) and contrary to the provisions of a federal treaty (the 1949 Geneva Convention) that Congress had made applicable to the type of proceedings involved. The Court also made it clear that the result would have been different had the President acted with congressional authorization, thus inviting the President to respect the doctrine of separation of powers. As *Hamdan* demonstrates, the principle that federal exercises of the war powers are subject to judicial review remains very much alive — especially where those powers are exercised by the executive not only without the backing of Congress, but in a manner that is clearly contrary to statutory directives.

Some of the most perplexing war powers questions involve potential conflicts between the powers vested in Congress and those vested in the President. For example, the power to make war is divided between Congress and the President. Congress possesses the power to declare war as well as the power to appropriate money for war-making purposes. The President, on the other hand, is the commander-in-chief of the armed forces. Given this allocation, how does one assess the constitutionality of a unilateral presidential order to invade a foreign nation? Or of a congressional refusal to support such an action? Such separation of powers issues are discussed in Chapter 7. See §7.5.1.

§5.6 THE CONSTITUTIONALLY ENFORCEABLE PRINCIPLE OF FEDERALISM

The powers of the national government may in some instances be limited by the principle of federalism. The principle of federalism posits that the government of this nation is shared between two sets of sovereigns, one national and the other state. Each may operate with full dominion within its assigned sphere. According to the theory of our constitutional system, the national government is a "limited" government in the sense that it may exercise only those powers granted to it by the Constitution, while the states, being governments of "reserved" powers, may exercise those powers that have not been granted to the national government or otherwise denied to them. The Tenth Amendment specifically embodies these ideas: "The powers not delegated to the United States by the Constitution, nor prohibited by it to the States, are reserved to the States respectively, or to the people."

There are essentially two ways in which the principle of federalism can be judicially enforced against the national government. First, the principle may operate as a rule of construction that limits the defined scope of constitutionally granted powers. We saw some resurgence of this role in *United States v. Lopez* (see §5.3.4), where the Court narrowed the reach of the commerce power by putting teeth into the "substantially affects" test. Second, the principle of federalism may function as an independent check on the exercise of a granted power in much the same fashion as do provisions of the Bill of Rights. In other words, just as Congress may not use its commerce power to transgress the First Amendment, it may not use that power to violate the principle of federalism. The focus of this section is on this latter aspect of federalism. In other words, to what extent does federalism trump the otherwise legitimate exercise of national power?

The 1941 decision in *United States v. Darby*, which described the Tenth Amendment as a truism — those powers not granted to the national government are reserved to the individual states or to the people — seemed to have rung the death knell for federalism as a check on the exercise of national power. See §5.3.2. Under *Darby*, when confronted with a congressional exercise of authority validated by a granted power, there was nothing left to the states other than to accede to the national mandate. And in the years following *Darby*, this indeed seemed to be the case. The balance appeared to change with the decision in *National League of Cities v. Usery*, 426 U.S. 833 (1976), where the Court reaffirmed the vitality of federalism as a check on national power. There, in a 5-4 decision, the Court struck down provisions of the Fair Labor Standards Act (FLSA) that required states and their political subdivisions to adhere to federal maximum hour and minimum wage provisions. Although the FLSA clearly fell within the scope of the commerce power, the Court held that the enforced application of the FLSA to the states violated the principle of federalism as embodied in the Tenth Amendment. In essence, the FLSA invaded the realm of state sovereignty.

Unlike the Court in *Darby*, the *National League of Cities* Court did not treat the Tenth Amendment as a truism. Rather, the Court viewed the Tenth Amendment as a reflection of the philosophy of federalism embodied in the structure of the Constitution. Under that philosophy, the states are integral parts of the constitutional structure and as such are immune from direct regulation by the federal government, at least with respect to "integral" government functions. The analysis employed by the Court was quite similar to the structural approach adopted by Chief Justice Marshall in *McCulloch*. Ironically, Marshall's structural approach was used in *National League of Cities* to limit rather than enhance the power of the national government.

The reign of this newly enforceable principle of federalism was short lived. Within a decade, *National League of Cities* was overruled by *Garcia v. San Antonio Metropolitan Transit Authority*, 469 U.S. 528 (1985). In essence, Justice

Blackmun had changed his mind. In *Garcia*, a new 5-4 majority returned the Tenth Amendment to the "truism" model of *Darby*. In *Garcia*, which also involved an application of the hour and wage provisions of the FLSA to state employees, the Court held that the principle of federalism was to be protected, if at all, through the political rather than the judicial process. In other words, Congress, which is composed of representatives from the states, must make the necessary judgments about the scope of any intrusion upon state sovereignty. Post-*Garcia*, from the perspective of the judiciary, neither the principle of federalism nor the text of the Tenth Amendment will trump an otherwise legitimate exercise of national power. See *Watters v. Wachovia Bank, N.A.*, 550 U.S. 1, 22 (2007) (if Constitution grants a power to Congress, Tenth Amendment "disclaims any reservation of that power to the States"). But not to worry. The dissenters in *Garcia* promised that this battle over national power and federalism was far from over.

That promise became a reality in *New York v. United States*, 505 U.S. 144 (1992), a case in which a majority of the Court resurrected a narrow aspect of the *National League of Cities* decision. At issue was the constitutionality of the Low-Level Radioactive Waste Policy Amendments Act of 1985. The underlying purpose of the act was to promote the availability of disposal sites for low-level radioactive waste and to ensure that states in which such waste was generated accepted responsibility for the disposal of that waste. To meet those ends, the act provided the states with a series of incentives, the first of which was monetary. States that complied with the federal plan would be financially rewarded for doing so. The second set of incentives authorized states with federally approved disposal sites to deny access to their sites for waste generated in states that did not conform to the federal guidelines. Finally, the act required that a state that failed to meet the federal standards would be required to "take title" to the waste generated within its borders and to accept liability for any damages caused by that waste.

The Court upheld the monetary incentive, concluding that Congress was free to use federal money to entice states into adopting a federal regulatory program. The Court also noted that under the Commerce Clause, Congress could offer the states a choice between adopting a federally approved regulatory program themselves and being preempted by federal regulation of the private activity at issue. This latter possibility was described as "cooperative federalism." Similarly, the Court upheld that portion of the act that granted the states authority to refuse the importation of waste from nonconforming states. This was, according to the Court, an unremarkable exercise of the commerce power, in essence a permissible delegation of the congressional power over interstate commerce to the states.

However, the third incentive, the take-title provision, was held unconstitutional. The Court interpreted this provision as giving a state two options: A state could either take title to the waste product and risk the attendant liability, or it could regulate according to the congressional scheme. Neither of these alternatives was constitutionally acceptable, for either way, the states were being forced to participate in and implement the federal regulatory scheme. They were being treated as administrative agents of the federal government, "commandeered" into federal service. Such a coercive invasion of state sovereignty violated principles of federalism and the Tenth Amendment. Thus, while Congress could preempt the states from the field by imposing direct federal regulation of the private activity (the disposal of low-level radioactive wastes) or try to entice the states into implementing the federal scheme by offering them monetary incentives to do so, Congress could not simply force a state to administer a federal regulatory scheme.

New York v. United States did not overrule *Garcia*, for the cases dealt with completely different types of federal action. It is therefore important to understand what Congress can do under *Garcia* and what it cannot do under *New York v. United States*. Consistent with *Garcia*, Congress can, for example, directly regulate the states as part of a broader federal regulatory scheme that also regulates similar private conduct. Thus, as in *Garcia*, Congress can extend the wage and hours protections of the FLSA to include state employees. Under *New York v. United States*, however, Congress cannot use the states as an administrative arm for implementing federal regulatory policy. Thus while the states may be required by Congress to pay their own employees a certain minimum wage under the FLSA, the states may not be ordered to have their employees perform certain federally mandated functions such as monitoring private employers' compliance with the FLSA. In short, while Congress may seek to entice states voluntarily to join a federal regulatory program, they simply cannot be forced to do so. The critical distinction is thus between enticement and direct coercion.

Example 5-Q

The Brady Handgun Violence Prevention Act (the Brady Act) regulates certain aspects of the sale of handguns. Among other things the act requires a five-day waiting period before a handgun dealer may transfer a handgun to a buyer. During that waiting period, the act requires that the local "chief law enforcement officer" of the locality where the sale is to take place must determine whether sale of the handgun would violate the law; perform a background check on the buyer; and, if the buyer is eligible to purchase the handgun, destroy the filing papers; but if the buyer is not eligible, provide a statement of reasons within 20 days. Does the Brady Act violate the constitutionally enforceable principle of federalism recognized by the Court in *New York v. United States*?

Explanation

Yes. The Brady Act does precisely what the Court in *New York v. United States* says that Congress cannot do. The act commandeers states into enforcing a federal regulatory scheme by making local law enforcement officers the administrative agents of the federal government.

Had the Brady Act simply offered participating states financial incentives to agree to enforce the provisions of the Brady Act, the constitutionally enforceable principle of federalism would not have been violated unless that offer amounted to coercion. See §5.4.3. As long as the federal government does not engage in coercion, it may use the carrot of federal money to entice state cooperation in a federal regulatory scheme. Nor would the principle of federalism be violated if states had been given a choice between administering the Brady Act themselves or having a federal agency do so, assuming, of course, that the enactment of the Brady Act was otherwise within the power of Congress. As with monetary incentives, such cooperative federalism gives the state a genuine choice, including the option of doing nothing, and the constitutionally enforceable principle of federalism is therefore fully satisfied.

Consistent with the foregoing example, in *Printz v. United States*, 521 U.S. 898 (1997), the Court held that the Brady Act, to the extent it imposed federal administrative duties on local law enforcement officers, violated the constitutionally enforceable principle of federalism. In the Court's view, this aspect of the Brady Act was indistinguishable from the take-title provisions struck down in *New York v. United States*. Both the Brady Act and the take-title provisions regulated the functioning of the state executive branch in a manner that offended the principle of "separate state sovereignty" by forcing the respective states to administer a federal regulatory scheme. As such, each provision compromised the "constitutional system of dual sovereignty" mandated by the principle of federalism. Id. at 935. In *Printz*, the Court made clear that under such circumstances, there would be no balancing of interests. A federal law whose object and effect is to force state participation in a federal regulatory scheme is categorically unconstitutional. Id. See also *National Federation of Independent Business v. Sebelius*, 132 S. Ct. 2566 (2012) (invalidating federal Affordable Care Act insofar as its funding withdrawal provision forced states to implement a federal health care program).

Example 5-R

The federal Drivers' Privacy Protection Act of 1994 (DPPA), which we looked at earlier in Example 5-B, regulates the disclosure of personal information contained in the records of state motor vehicle departments. The DPPA prohibits states from releasing such information without a driver's consent unless the disclosure falls within one of the act's exceptions. A state agency that repeatedly violates the DPPA is subject to a civil penalty imposed by the United States Attorney General of up to $5,000 per day for each day of substantial noncompliance. The DPPA also regulates the disclosure of such information by private parties who receive it from the state under one of the act's exceptions. Private actors who violate the DPPA are subject to criminal fines and may be sued civilly by the driver to whom the information pertains. We saw earlier that the DPPA falls within the scope of Congress's commerce power. Does the act violate the constitutionally enforceable principle of federalism?

Explanation

No. As in *Garcia*, the DPPA regulates the activities of the states themselves, as owners of the databases in question. Like the FLSA hour and wage provisions upheld in *Garcia*, the DPPA is a law of general applicability, for it regulates all suppliers to the market for motor vehicle information, including private parties who obtain this information from the states. And, in contrast to *New York v. United States*, the act does not force the states to enact or implement a federal regulatory policy. Unlike *Printz*, it does not commandeer the states by requiring them to enforce those parts of the act that regulate private parties. Instead, the private-party provisions are enforced either through criminal actions brought by the United States or through civil suits filed by those drivers whose privacy has been violated. See *Reno v. Condon*, 528 U.S. 141, 149 (2000) (holding unanimously that the DPPA does not violate "the principles of federalism contained in the Tenth Amendment").

In addition to sometimes serving as a basis for invalidating a federal law, the principle of federalism also serves as an important tool of statutory construction. The Court will not lightly assume that Congress has determined to directly regulate a state or a political subdivision of a state. To overcome this presumption, Congress must make its intent to do so unambiguously clear. See *Gregory v. Ashcroft*, 501 U.S. 452, 456-467 (1991) (construing Age Discrimination in Employment Act as not being intended to cover state judges).

CHAPTER 6

The Supremacy Clause

§6.1 INTRODUCTION AND OVERVIEW

The Supremacy Clause provides: "This Constitution, and the Laws of the United States which shall be made in Pursuance thereof; and all Treaties made, or which shall be made, under the Authority of the United States, shall be the supreme Law of the Land; and the Judges in every State shall be bound thereby, any Thing in the Constitution or Laws of any State to the contrary notwithstanding." Art. VI, cl. 2. This language translates into a fundamental principle of our constitutional system of government: State law must conform to the dictates of the Constitution, and yield to constitutionally valid federal law whenever a conflict between the two arises. To conclude otherwise would be to permit each individual state to control what the Constitution defines as the business of the nation as a whole.

The judicial foundation for the law of federal supremacy can be traced to two opinions by Chief Justice John Marshall, *McCulloch v. Maryland*, 17 U.S. (4 Wheat.) 316 (1819), and *Gibbons v. Ogden*, 22 U.S. (9 Wheat.) 1 (1824). While neither opinion breaks ground beyond that which should be evident from the text of the Supremacy Clause, both opinions affirm, with confident and enduring rhetoric, the principle of federal supremacy within the sphere of constitutionally granted federal powers. The essence of that principle is that no state may transgress the norms of the Constitution or interfere with the constitutional exercise of federal authority.

At issue in *McCulloch v. Maryland* was the authority of a state to impose a tax on the Second Bank of the United States, a federally chartered institution.

The first part of Marshall's opinion upheld the power of Congress to charter the bank. See §5.2. Given that conclusion, the question was whether a state could nonetheless impose a tax on this constitutionally created institution. Marshall described the basic principles of federal supremacy in the introductory section of his opinion:

> If any one proposition could command the universal assent of mankind, we might expect it would be this: that the government of the Union, though limited in its powers, is supreme within its sphere of action. This would seem to result necessarily from its nature. It is the government of all; its powers are delegated by all; it represents all, and acts for all. Though any one State may be willing to control its operations, no State is willing to allow others to control them. The nation, on those subjects on which it can act, must necessarily bind its component parts. But this question is not left to mere reason: the people have, in express terms, decided it, by saying, "this constitution, and the laws of the United States, which shall be made in pursuance thereof," "shall be the supreme law of the land," and by requiring that the members of the State legislatures, and the officers of the executive and judicial departments of the States, shall take the oath of fidelity to it.

Id. at 405-406. Similarly, later in the opinion Marshall observed:

> [T]he constitution and the laws made in pursuance thereof are supreme; . . . they control the constitution and laws of the respective States, and cannot be controlled by them. From this, which may be almost termed an axiom, other propositions are deduced as corollaries, on the truth or error of which, and on their application to this case, the cause has been supposed to depend. These are, 1. That a power to create implies a power to preserve. 2. That a power to destroy, if wielded by a different hand, is hostile to, and incompatible with these powers to create and to preserve. 3. That where this repugnancy exists, that authority which is supreme must control, not yield to that over which it is supreme.

Id. at 426.

Applying the above axioms and corollaries, Marshall concluded that the state's power to tax could not be exercised against the bank. The power to tax was, in fact, the power to destroy. Therefore to permit a state to exercise that power against an institution created by the federal government would necessarily affirm the authority of an individual state to destroy that institution and to negate the federal government's ability to preserve it. Such a conclusion would be directly contrary to the principle of federal supremacy that was embodied in the nature and text of the Constitution. Indeed, it would posit state rather than federal supremacy. Speaking more generally, Marshall observed, "[T]he States have no power, by taxation or otherwise, to retard, impede, burden, or in any manner control, the operations of the constitutional laws enacted by congress to carry into execution the powers vested in the general government. This is, we think, the unavoidable consequence of that supremacy which the constitution has declared." Id. at 436.

The decision in *Gibbons*, five years later, was to the same effect. There the Court, through Chief Justice Marshall, held that the state of New York could not prevent vessels licensed by the federal government from engaging in the coastal trade on the navigable waters of New York. The state law purporting to do so conflicted with a valid federal law and was therefore void. The Court rejected New York's argument

> that, if a law passed by a State, in the exercise of its acknowledged sovereignty, comes into conflict with a law passed by congress in pursuance of the constitution, they affect the subject, and each other, like equal opposing powers.
>
> But the framers of our constitution foresaw this state of things, and provided for it by declaring the supremacy not only of itself, but of the laws made in pursuance of it. The nullity of any act, inconsistent with the constitution, is produced by the declaration that the constitution is the supreme law. The appropriate application of that part of the clause which confers the same supremacy on laws and treaties, is to such acts of the state legislatures as do not transcend their powers, but, though enacted in the execution of acknowledged state powers, interfere with, or are contrary to the laws of congress, made in pursuance of the constitution, or some treaty made under the authority of the United States. *In every such case, the act of congress, or the treaty, is supreme; and the law of the State, though enacted in the exercise of powers not controverted, must yield to it.*

22 U.S. (Wheat.) at 210-211 (emphasis supplied).

Developed doctrine under the Supremacy Clause can be divided into two closely related categories. Within the first category are those cases in which there exists a potential conflict between federal and state law. In such cases, if a conflict is established, the federal law is said to preempt — i.e., to supplant — the state law. Under these circumstances, the state law is void, just as it would be if it conflicted with a provision of the Constitution. This was the type of problem presented in *Gibbons*. State and federal statutes regarding licensing for the coastal trade conflicted and, as a consequence, the federal law preempted the state law.

The second doctrinal category involves those cases in which a state attempts to tax or regulate the federal government or an instrumentality of the federal government. Again, if the state law disrupts a federal program, the state law must give way to federal law. In essence, the federal government and its instrumentalities are immune from such state-imposed interference. Thus in *McCulloch*, the Second Bank of the United States was immune from Maryland's attempt to impose a tax on it.

One should be able to see the close relationship between these two doctrinal categories. Indeed, in describing *McCulloch*, one could just as easily say that the federal law chartering the bank "preempted" the state's effort to tax the bank. So, too, one could describe the federal licensee in *Gibbons* as immune from the restrictions of state law. In fact, as we discuss further below, the doctrine of immunity is really nothing more than a specialized type of preemption in which the "preemptive" conflict takes the form of a tax or regulation directed at the activities of the federal government. Whether a potential conflict is characterized as triggering preemption or immunity, however, the result is the same: If a true conflict exists, state law must yield to the superior federal authority.

In the sections that follow, we examine both categories of federal supremacy. Keep in mind that an underlying presumption of each is that the federal law must itself be valid under appropriate constitutional standards. If the federal law is not valid, the Supremacy Clause is of no effect. Thus a conflict between a state law and the Gun-Free School Zones Act — the law struck down in *United States v. Lopez*, 514 U.S. 549 (1995), as beyond the commerce power (see §5.3.4) — would not trigger the Supremacy Clause. In essence, a conflict with an unconstitutional federal law is no conflict at all.

The final section of this chapter examines the related problem of state-imposed term limits on federal elective office.

§6.2 THE PREEMPTION DOCTRINE

The preemption doctrine mandates that valid federal law, including statutes, treaties, executive agreements, administrative rules, and common law, supplants or supersedes state law that is inconsistent with the specific terms or overall objectives of the federal law. See *El Al Israel Airlines, Ltd. v. Tseng*, 525 U.S. 155 (1999) (preemptive effect of treaty); *Fidelity Federal Sav. & Loan Assn. v. De La Cuesta*, 458 U.S. 141, 153-154 (1982) (preemptive effect of federal regulations).

§6.2.1 Types of Preemption

There are three circumstances under which federal law preempts state law. The first involves express preemption while the latter two deal with implied preemption. First, when Congress expressly describes the extent to which a federal enactment preempts state law, there is *express preemption* and any state law contrary to that express design will be preempted. *National Meat Association v. Harris*, 132 S. Ct. 965 (2012); *Riegel v. Medtronic, Inc.*, 552 U.S. 312, 321-325 (2008). Note, however, that "when the text of a pre-emption clause is susceptible of more than one plausible reading, courts ordinarily 'accept the reading that disfavors pre-emption.'" *Altria Group, Inc. v. Good*, 555 U.S. 70, 77 (2008) (quoting *Bates v. Dow Agrosciences LLC*, 544 U.S. 431, 449 (2005)).

Second, when state law clashes with federal law by imposing inconsistent obligations on affected parties or by interfering with the objectives of a federal scheme, the state law is subject to *conflict preemption* under which the conflicting provisions of state law will be struck. Finally, if a state law operates within a field of law that Congress intends the federal government to occupy exclusively, the state law will be preempted under a theory of *field preemption*. As we will see, these types of preemption may sometimes overlap.

Whether federal law preempts state law in any particular case depends completely on the intent of Congress. See *Wyeth v. Levine*, 555 U.S. 555, 565 (2009) ("purpose of Congress is the ultimate touchstone in every preemption case"). When the intent is express, the question of preemption is greatly simplified. Suppose, for example, that a federal statute prohibited states from regulating the "price, route, or service of any motor carrier with respect to the transportation of property." A state law that purported to impose route restrictions on such services would be expressly preempted by the text of the federal statute. If the same federal law, however, contained a saving clause providing that its preemptive scope "shall not restrict the safety regulatory authority of a State with respect to motor vehicles," a state law that imposed route restrictions based on genuine safety considerations would not be preempted. See *Columbus v. Ours Garage and Wrecker Service*, 536 U.S. 424 (2002) (construing the preemptive reach of a similar statutory scheme); see also *Egelhoff v. Egelhoff*, 532 U.S. 141 (2001) (ERISA expressly preempts state law pertaining to the designation of beneficiaries under a covered life insurance policy and pension plan). When a federal statute's express preemption provision contains a saving clause, there may still be an issue as to whether a particular state law falls within the scope of that clause. See, e.g., *Chamber of Commerce v. Whiting*, 131 S. Ct. 1968 (2011) (Court dividing 5-3 on question of whether challenged Arizona statute fell within saving clause of a federal statute's preemption provision).

In cases not involving express preemption, however, the intent of Congress must be inferred from the circumstances. In cases of conflict preemption, the intent to preempt is inferred from the direct clash between federal and state law. The inference of intent may be somewhat more difficult to establish in potential cases of implied field preemption; the techniques for doing so will be examined below. The question of implied preemption may arise even in cases that fall within the saving clause of an express preemption provision. In other words, the fact that Congress chose not to *expressly* preempt a particular type of state law does not by itself warrant a conclusion that Congress also meant to shield, from implied preemption, those state laws that are disruptive of the federal scheme in question. *Geier v. American Honda Motor Co., Inc.*, 529 U.S. 861, 869 (2000) ("We . . . conclude that the saving clause (like the express preemption provision) does *not* bar the ordinary working of conflict pre-emption principles"); see also *Chamber of Commerce v. Whiting*, supra, 131 S. Ct. at 1981-1985 (after finding that state law fell within saving clause of a federal statute's express preemption provision, Court went on to consider whether there was implied preemption).

§6.2.2 Conflict Preemption

Conflict preemption comes in two forms. In the first, the conflict between federal and state law is premised on the *physical impossibility* of complying with concurrent federal and state standards. See *Florida Lime & Avocado Growers, Inc. v. Paul*, 373 U.S. 132, 142-143 (1963). This category is relatively easy to spot, but also relatively rare. Suppose a state law *requires* doctors to prescribe marijuana as a painkiller to all cancer patients who request the drug. Suppose also that federal law *prohibits* prescribing marijuana to cancer patients under any circumstances. A doctor confronted with a valid request under state law will find it *physically impossible* to comply with both state and federal law, since compliance with one violates the other. As a consequence of this physical impossibility, the congressional intent to preempt is presumed. Similarly, if federal law requires that generic drugs carry the same safety and efficacy labeling that the federal Food and Drug Administration requires for their brand name counterparts, a state law that required generic drugs to be labeled differently would present drug manufacturers with a physical impossibility. Neither would it matter that the generic manufacturer might try to have the federal law changed, as "[t]he question for impossibility is whether the private party could independently do under federal law what state law requires of it." *PLIVA, Inc. v. Mensing*, 131 S. Ct. 2567, 2579 (2011). In this case as well, a court would thus infer a congressional intent to preempt the conflicting state law.

In order to apply conflict preemption, it is necessary to know the intended meaning and scope of the state law involved. Depending upon how that law is construed by the state courts, preemption may or may not be warranted. If a state law is new, and if it could be interpreted in ways that would reduce or avoid a potential conflict with federal law, it may be appropriate for a federal court to defer ruling on the preemption question until state courts have first had an opportunity to construe their own law. See *Arizona v. United States*, 132 S. Ct. 2492, 2510 (2012). (A state law challenged before it could take effect cannot be deemed preempted where "[t]here is a basic uncertainty about what the law means and how it will be enforced. . . . [W]ithout the benefit of a definitive interpretation from the state courts, it would be inappropriate to assume [that the state law] will be construed in a way that creates a conflict with federal law.")

Example 6-A

Directly injecting the drug Phenergan into a patient's vein (the IV-push method) creates a significant risk of catastrophic consequences. A Vermont jury found that as a matter of state tort law, Pharmo, the manufacturer of the drug, had failed to provide an adequate warning of that risk and awarded damages to Diana whose arm had to be amputated as a result of an IV-push administration of the drug. The warnings on Phenergan's label, which did not mention this danger, had been deemed sufficient by the federal Food and Drug Administration (FDA) when it approved Pharmo's new drug application in 1955 and when the FDA later approved changes in the drug's labeling. Under FDA regulations, a drug manufacturer may not unilaterally change an approved label. There is, however, an exception to that general rule that permits a unilateral change if the change adds or strengthens a warning to improve drug safety. Pharmo claims that it could not simultaneously comply with FDA regulations, which generally prohibit changes to an approved label, and the warning standards imposed by state tort law, which would require the label to have been changed. Is Pharmo correct that it is impossible to comply with both federal and state law and that the former therefore preempts the latter in this case?

Explanation

No. There is no "impossibility" of simultaneous compliance. This problem would have presented an example of conflict preemption had the FDA regulations not included the "adds or strengthens" exception, for then Pharmo would find it impossible to comply with the FDA's "no change" rule and at the same time adhere to the requirements of state law. The exception recognized by the FDA, however, eliminates the impossibility, since a warning regarding the IV-push dangers of Phenergan would seem to fall well within adds-or-strengthens standard of the exception. See *Wyeth v. Levine*, supra, 555 U.S. at 569-573 (so holding under roughly similar facts).

The second form of conflict preemption can be a little more complicated. A state law may conflict with federal law by creating "an obstacle to the accomplishment and execution of the full purposes and objectives of Congress." *Hines v. Davidowitz*, 312 U.S. 52, 67 (1941). The analysis of this type of preemption requires (1) identification of the federal objective and (2) a determination of the extent to which state law interferes, if at all, with the realization of that objective. In cases in which the objective is clear from the face of a statute and in which the interference created by state law is palpable, application of this category is quite simple. For example, suppose that a federal regulation permits auto manufacturers to consider a range of options regarding the installation of passive restraint systems in new cars (e.g., air bags, automatic seat belts, or some other innovative option). The goal is to provide manufacturers a flexible range of options to promote innovation that may lower the costs, overcome technical safety problems, encourage technological development, and, over the long term, establish consumer acceptance of passive restraint systems.

Suppose now that an individual injured in an automobile accident sues the manufacturer under state law for the manufacturer's failure to install an air bag in the vehicle in which she was riding. Assuming state law mandates the installation of air bags, it would not be physically impossible for the manufacturer to comply with both federal and state law. After all, the state law merely requires what the federal law permits. Yet, such a state law might interfere with the federal objectives noted above. By requiring manufacturers to use a particular passive restraint system, the industry might well forgo consideration and development of other options that may be less costly, technically safer, technologically more advanced, and overall more acceptable to the public. If that is so, and that appears to be the theory on which the federal regulation is premised, an intent to preempt would be inferred from this conflict between state law and federal objectives. See *Geier v. American Honda Motor Co., Inc.*, 529 U.S. 861 (2000). If, on the other hand, federal law permits the use of either lap-and-shoulder seat belts or lap-only belts, a state law requiring the former might not be preempted if the federal interest in giving manufacturers a choice between the two is shown to be much weaker. *Williamson v. Mazda Motors of America, Inc.*, 131 S. Ct. 1131 (2011) (so holding in case where federal Department of Transportation had expressed some preference for the lap-and-shoulder belt but where Solicitor General advised Court that in contrast to the state-mandated air bag at issue in *Geier*, the federal-choice provision here was not sufficiently important to warrant preempting state's lap-and-shoulder belt requirement).

The Court followed an approach similar to that of *Geier* in *Buckman Co. v. Plaintiffs' Legal Committee*, 531 U.S. 341 (2001), where the plaintiffs claimed to have been injured by use of a medical device approved by the FDA. They alleged that the approval was procured through fraud engaged in by a consulting company that had assisted the manufacturer in procuring FDA approval. The plaintiffs sought damages against the consulting company under state tort law. The Court held that this "fraud-on-the-FDA" claim was preempted by federal law. In so holding, the Court identified the objective of the federal statutory scheme as vesting the FDA with a broad discretion and flexibility to address such claims of fraud. In the Court's view, "[t]his flexibility is a critical component of the statutory and regulatory framework under which the FDA pursues difficult (and often competing) objectives." Id. at 349. The state-based "fraud-on-the-FDA" claim impermissibly undermined this objective of flexibility and was, therefore, impliedly preempted by federal law. By way of contrast, in *Wyeth v. Levine*, 555 U.S. 555 (2009), the Court found no interference with the congressional objective of consumer safety when a state tort law required safety warnings on drug labels beyond those required by the FDA.

With respect to this form of conflict preemption, the Court has suggested that when a state law is challenged on the ground that it poses an obstacle to achieving a federal objective, there may be a third step in the preemption analysis — i.e., in addition to identifying the federal objective and determining the extent to which the state law would impair its realization. This additional step involves "consider[ing] the strength of the state interest, judged by standards of traditional practice, when deciding how serious a conflict must be shown before declaring the state law preempted." *American Insurance Association v. Garamendi*, 539 U.S. 396, 420 (2003). If a state, when judged "against the backdrop of traditional state legislative subject matter," is deemed to be pursuing ends long regarded to be part of its governmental domain, preemption may thus be more difficult to establish than if the state is seeking to enter new or nontraditional waters. Id. at 425. As the Court noted even more recently, "'because the States are independent sovereigns in our federal system, we have long presumed that Congress does not cavalierly pre-empt state-law causes of action.' In areas of traditional state regulation, we assume that a federal statute has not supplanted state law unless Congress has made such an intention 'clear and manifest.'" *Bates v. Dow Agrosciences LLC*, 544 U.S. 431, 449 (2005).

Example 6-B

A valid federal law specifically allows federally insured lenders to include a "due-on-sale" clause in their loan instruments. Such clauses empower a lender, at its option, to declare the entire amount of a loan immediately due if the property securing the loan is transferred without the prior consent of the lender. The purpose of the federal law is to grant lenders broad flexibility in determining when to call a loan. This flexibility is seen as a means of insuring the overall financial soundness of the "thrift" industry. State law, however, provides that a lender may exercise a due-on-sale clause only if the transfer of property actually impairs the security for the loan. Is the state requirement preempted because it imposes an obstacle to the accomplishment of the federal objective?

Explanation

The answer depends on what one identifies as the federal objective. If the objective is to vest federally insured lenders with unfettered flexibility in determining when to exercise their due-on-sale options, then the state law does create an impediment to achieving that goal. Under state law, the complete discretion created by the federal law becomes a more limited discretion, requiring a showing that the lender's security interest has been impaired. In other words, state law limits the federally created flexibility. On the other hand, if one views the federal objective as insuring the financial stability of the lender, one could argue that the state law is consistent with that objective since it permits a lender to enforce a due-on-sale clause whenever the security for the loan has been impaired.

In *Fidelity Federal Sav. & Loan Assn. v. De La Cuesta*, 458 U.S. 141, 156 (1982), the Court concluded, under similar facts, that the state law operated as "an obstacle to the accomplishment and execution of the full purposes and objectives" of the federal law. The flexibility granted the lender by federal law was seen as essential to the ultimate goal of promoting the financial soundness of the thrift industry. Nor was the Court moved by the fact that "real property law is a matter of special concern to the States." Id. at 153. Although it may make a difference in a close case that the subject under regulation has been a traditional concern of the states, when a state law's conflict with a federal statute's goals is as pronounced as the Court viewed it here, "[t]he relative importance to the State of its own law is not material. . . ." Id. See also *Franklin Natl. Bank v. New York*, 347 U.S. 373 (1954) (federal law that grants national banks the right to provide savings accounts preempts state law that prohibits such banks from using the word "savings" in their advertisements).

Example 6-C

In 1996, the Commonwealth of Massachusetts adopted a law that prohibited the Commonwealth from purchasing goods or services from anyone "doing business" with the nation of Burma. The phrase "doing business" was defined broadly to include a vast array of business activities, including providing financial services to the government of Burma, promoting the importation or sale of certain goods to or from Burma, and providing any goods or services to the government in Burma. The law applied to domestic and foreign corporations. The purpose of the Commonwealth's law was to influence the government in Burma to cease serious abuses of human rights. Shortly thereafter Congress passed a similarly motivated statute imposing a set of mandatory and conditional sanctions on Burma. This statute banned most forms of U.S. financial assistance to Burma, instructed U.S. representatives to international financial institutions to vote against loans to Burma, and banned entry visas for most Burmese government officials. The statute also conditionally authorized the President to impose further sanctions on certain "new investments" in Burma, but that definition expressly *excluded* contracts for the sale or purchase of goods, services, or technology. The President also retained an authority to lift sanctions. In essence, the federal scheme was designed to permit the President to apply increasing and decreasing levels of pressure on the government of Burma depending on the circumstances. Finally, the federal statute directed the President to work to develop "a comprehensive, multilateral strategy to bring democracy to and improve human rights practices and the quality of life in Burma." Is the Commonwealth's law preempted by the federal enactment?

Explanation

The Commonwealth's statutory refusal to purchase goods or services from anyone doing business with Burma may go further than its federal counterpart, but it does not require any party, including the Commonwealth itself, to take any action that would violate or contravene a provision of the federal statute. After all, nothing in the federal statute requires anyone, including the Commonwealth, to purchase goods or services from a company that does business with Burma. Thus no one is subjected to the physical impossibility of complying with contrary statutory directives. Yet, the Commonwealth's law may conflict with the overall objectives of the federal scheme. The federal statute vests a flexible authority in the President to develop a "comprehensive, multilateral strategy." Within that strategy, the potential economic sanctions authorized by Congress represent, in essence, a middle-of-the-road approach. By imposing more severe sanctions over which the President has no ostensible control, the Commonwealth's law interferes with the middle-of-the-road philosophy and the objective of flexibility. Moreover, the presence of the Commonwealth's sanctions (and potentially those of other states) not only limits the President's ability to deal directly with Burma, but may also undermine the President's ability to gain international cooperation from partners who object to or are adversely affected by the Commonwealth's policy. Finally, while the states have traditionally engaged in purchasing goods and services for governmental purposes, the interest pursued by the Massachusetts law here — expressing disapproval of Burma's human rights record — is not one that falls within the state's traditional sphere and is thus entitled to less weight in the analysis than it might otherwise have received. The Commonwealth's law is, therefore, preempted. See *Crosby v. National Foreign Trade Council*, 530 U.S. 363 (2000) (so holding under similar facts).

Example 6-D

Prior to and during World War II, Germany's Nazi government confiscated the assets of Jews living throughout Europe. Many of those assets, which included the value of insurance policies, were never returned to the Jews or their descendants after the war. Initial efforts by Western allies to force reimbursement were suspended in 1953 by the London Debt Agreement, out of fear that this might economically cripple the new Federal Republic of Germany. While the German government was nevertheless encouraged to see that restitution was made, its efforts were only partially successful. In the mid-1990s, German courts held that the 1953 moratorium on Holocaust claims by foreign nationals was now lifted. This led to the immediate filing of class-action lawsuits in U.S. courts seeking restitution against companies that did business in Germany during the Nazi era. When the German government and insurance companies protested the filing of these suits, President Clinton signed an Executive Agreement with Germany in January 2001, in which Germany agreed to create a foundation to be funded by the German government and by voluntary contributions from German companies. These funds would then be used by the foundation to compensate people "who suffered at the hands of German companies" during the Nazi era, including those with insurance claims. While the agreement stopped short of providing that lawsuits could not be filed against German companies in U.S. courts, the federal government agreed to submit a statement in any such suit, advising the court of the foundation's efforts and urging that "U.S. policy interests favor dismissal on any valid legal ground." The Executive Agreement also provided that the United States would use its best efforts to have state and local governments treat the foundation as the exclusive mechanism for resolving such disputes.

Meanwhile, California enacted the Holocaust Victim Insurance Relief Act of 1999 (HVIRA) on behalf of the 5,600 documented Holocaust survivors then living in the state. HVIRA required every insurer doing business in California to disclose the details of any insurance policies issued to persons in Europe that were in effect between 1920 and 1945, including policies issued by any parent, subsidiary, successor in interest, or affiliate of the insurer. As to each such policy, the insurer was required to disclose the policy's current status; the policyholder's city of origin, domicile, or address; and the names of the beneficiaries. Any insurer failing to comply with HVIRA faced suspension of its license to do business in California and criminal prosecution for any false representations made. Several insurers have brought suit to enjoin California officials from enforcing HVIRA. Does conflict preemption bar the state from enforcing this law?

Explanation

Because executive agreements are a recognized means by which the federal government may conduct its affairs with foreign countries, they, like federal statutes, may preempt conflicting state laws. See §5.5.3. Because the agreement here contains no preemption clause, the question is one of implied rather than express preemption. While a field preemption argument might also be possible, the question here is whether a conflict preemption challenge would succeed. This is not a case of physical impossibility, for nothing in California's enforcement of HVIRA would preclude anyone, including the federal government, from honoring the terms of the 2001 Executive Agreement. Moreover, the purposes of the state and federal provisions are the same, seeking to obtain compensation for Holocaust victims. Yet the means adopted by the two schemes would appear to differ so fundamentally as to render the state law preempted. Through the Executive Agreement, the President has deliberately chosen to encourage voluntary action on the part of European governments and companies rather than adopt a litigation or coercive sanctions route. This voluntary approach was designed to further the federal government's interest in maintaining amicable relationships with its European allies and with the private companies involved. To permit California's law to be enforced would thus undercut the President's diplomatic discretion and the very deliberate choices that he made in attempting to resolve a controversial matter. Moreover, the area in which the state sought to operate here was not one that involves a traditional state matter, nor did the conduct that gave rise to the state's law occur within the state. On these facts, the Supreme Court held that HVIRA was preempted by the President's Executive Agreement, noting that "[t]he basic fact is that California seeks to use an iron fist where the President has consistently chosen kid gloves." *American Insurance Association v. Garamendi*, 539 U.S. 396, 427 (2003).

§6.2.3 Field Preemption

Congress may also preempt state law by "occupying the field" of a particular substantive area and thereby precluding any type of state regulation within that field. Field preemption may be express or implied. Where such preemption is express, it overlaps both the first and third types of preemption. See §6.2.1.

Express Field Preemption

In *Morales v. Trans World Airlines, Inc.*, 504 U.S. 374, 383-391 (1992), as part of a plan to deregulate the airline industry, a federal statute expressly prohibited states from enforcing any law "relating to rates, routes, or services" of any air carrier. The Court held that the field defined by this proscription was broad enough to encompass regulation of fare advertisements since such advertisements "related" to rates. A state law that purported to regulate fare advertisements was, therefore, preempted. This same rule applies even if the state law is consistent with the overall objectives of the federal scheme, for when Congress occupies the field, it supplants *all* state law that operates within that field. See *Chamber of Commerce of the United States v. Brown*, 554 U.S. 60 (2008) (express field preemption of free speech zone pertaining to labor-management relations); *Rowe v. New Hampshire Motor Transport Assn.*, 552 U.S. 364, 367 (2008) (express field preemption of any law "relating to rates, routes, or services" provided by the trucking industry).

Example 6-E

Dedra Shanklin's husband was killed when a train operated by Norfolk Southern collided with his truck at a railroad crossing. At the time of the accident, the crossing was equipped with advance warning X-shaped signs that read, "RAILROAD CROSSING." The signs had been installed pursuant to a federal program under which the federal government provided funds to the state for their purchase and installation. To receive these funds, the state was required to demonstrate that the warning devices to be installed at each railway crossing within the state met federal railway-crossing warning standards promulgated by the secretary of transportation. Ms. Shanklin brought a wrongful death action against Norfolk Southern claiming that it had negligently failed to maintain adequate warning devices at the crossing. The railroad contends that Shanklin's suit is preempted by the Federal Railroad Safety Act, which provides, "Laws, regulations, and orders related to railroad safety shall be nationally uniform to the extent practicable. A State may adopt or continue in force a law, regulation, or order related to railroad safety until the Secretary of Transportation prescribes a regulation or issues an order covering the subject matter of the State requirement." Is the railroad correct?

Explanation

Yes, this would appear to be a case of express field preemption. Although the Federal Railroad Safety Act grants states the option of adopting railroad safety regulations in the absence of controlling federal law, that option expires once the secretary of transportation prescribes regulations covering the subject matter. Here, the secretary has promulgated regulations setting standards for warning devices at railroad crossings, at least when those warning devices are installed pursuant to a federally funded program, as was the case here. Since plaintiff's negligence claim regarding the adequacy of the warning devices arises out of the same subject matter as is addressed by the federal regulations, her claim is preempted. This is essentially the reasoning the Court adopted under similar facts in *Norfolk Southern Railway Co. v. Shanklin*, 529 U.S. 344 (2000). Since we are dealing with express field preemption, it does not matter that the state's tort law may actually advance the federal interest in safety at highway crossings. Compare *Sprietsma v. Mercury Marine*, 537 U.S. 51 (2002) (construing a federal statute that expressly preempts "a [state] law or regulation" as not preempting common law actions).

In the case of express field preemption, the primary difficulty arises in defining the scope of the field. This is essentially a question of statutory construction, the rule of thumb being to define the field as narrowly as the preemptive language permits so as not to limit unduly the police powers of the states. See *Pacific Gas & Elec. Co. v. State Energy Resources Conservation & Dev. Commn.*, 461 U.S. 190, 205-216 (1983) (state's refusal to license proposed nuclear reactor premised on economic concerns not preempted by federal occupation of the field of nuclear safety).

Example 6-F

The Federal Cigarette Labeling and Advertising Act (FCLA) requires cigarette manufacturers to place a warning label on all packages of cigarettes sold in this country. FCLA also includes a preemption provision. Subsection (a) of that provision provides that "[n]o statement relating to smoking and health, other than the statement required by [this statute], shall be required on any cigarette package." In addition, subsection (b) provides that "[n]o requirement or prohibition based on smoking and health shall be imposed under State law with respect to the advertising or promotion of any cigarettes the packages of which are labeled in conformity with the provisions of this chapter." The state of Massachusetts has adopted a law that prohibits the outdoor display of cigarette advertisements, regardless of content, within 1,000 feet of a school or playground. The purpose of the ban is to prevent children from being enticed by such ads. Is the Massachusetts law preempted by FCLA?

Explanation

The answer depends on how one interprets the preemptive language employed by FCLA. Clearly, the state law does not transgress the ban imposed by subsection (a), because it does not pertain to the content of the information that must be placed on a cigarette package. The outdoor advertising ban does, however, impose a "prohibition" on the "advertising" of cigarettes sold in conformity with FCLA. Moreover, the ban appears to be motivated by concerns pertaining to "smoking and health," namely, the health implications derived from children's developing an interest in smoking. As such, the state advertising ban would seem to fall squarely within the text of subsection (b). See *Lorillard Tobacco Co. v. Reilly*, 533 U.S. 525 (2001) (so holding on similar facts). One could argue, however, that subsection (b) was meant only as a supplement to the preemptive reach of subsection (a) by insuring a unitary, nationwide "warning" requirement, regardless of where that warning appeared — i.e., whether on cigarette packages or on billboards. In this sense, the preemptive reach of subsection (b) would be limited to those state laws that required cigarette advertisers to include a particular type of content within their advertisements, namely, one that conveyed a health message endorsed by the state. It would not, however, preempt a state from banning cigarette advertising in particular locations. This was the view adopted by the dissent in *Lorillard Tobacco Co. v. Reilly*, 533 U.S. at 590 (Stevens, J., dissenting). The basic thesis of the dissent was that subsections (a) and (b), when read together, were designed solely to protect cigarette companies from a multiplicity of warning requirements that might vary from state to state.

Example 6-G

For the past 15 years, Good smoked "light" cigarettes manufactured by Philip Morris (PM). He has sued PM in Maine state court, claiming that PM violated the Maine Unfair Trade Practices Act (MUTPA) by engaging in deceptive advertising. Specifically, he alleges that PM fraudulently advertised its "light" cigarettes as delivering less tar and nicotine than regular brands despite PM's knowledge that the message was untrue. PM has filed a motion for summary judgment arguing that Good's MUTPA claim is preempted by subsection (b) of the Federal Cigarette Labeling and Advertising Act (FCLA), which provides that "[n]o requirement or prohibition based on smoking and health shall be imposed under State law with respect to the advertising or promotion of any cigarettes the packages of which are labeled in conformity with the provisions of this chapter." In response, Good argues that unlike the state law at issue in Example 6-F, the MUTPA is not "based on smoking and health," but is directed toward the prevention of fraudulent deception. How should the court rule on PM's motion?

Explanation

The court should deny the motion. The text of subsection (b) is directed at "prohibitions based on smoking and health." MUTPA, on the other hand, prohibits deceptive advertising regardless of health or smoking concerns. This difference fully distinguishes this problem from the one described in Example 6-F and should be sufficient to rebut PM's motion for summary judgment. Moreover, even if subsection (b) could be broadly interpreted to embrace a deceptive advertising statute, which it does not seem to do, the policy favoring the least preemptive interpretation of an ambiguous statute would also preclude a finding of preemption. On similar facts and similar reasoning, the Supreme Court held that the MUTPA was not preempted by subsection (b) of the FCLA. See *Altria Group, Inc. v. Good*, 555 U.S. 70, 81-87 (2008).

Implied Field Preemption

Even when Congress has not expressly stated its intent to occupy a field, a court may be willing to infer such intent under the proper circumstances. The somewhat flexible and subjective standards for determining that intent were described in the following, often-quoted passage:

> Congress legislated here in a field which the States have traditionally occupied. . . . So we start with the assumption that the historic police powers of the States were not to be superseded by the Federal Act unless that was the clear and

manifest purpose of Congress. . . . Such a purpose may be evidenced in several
ways. The scheme of federal regulation may be so pervasive as to make reasonable the inference that Congress left no room for the States to supplement
it. . . . Or the Act of Congress may touch a field in which the federal interest is
so dominant that the federal system will be assumed to preclude enforcement
of state laws on the same subject. . . . Likewise, the object sought to be
obtained by the federal law and the character of obligations imposed by it
may reveal the same purpose.

Rice v. Santa Fe Elevator Corp., 331 U.S. 218, 230 (1947). In addition, the
legislative history of the federal law may disclose evidence of an intent to
preempt the field.

The Court applied the *Rice* standards for implied field preemption in *City
of Burbank v. Lockheed Air Terminal*, 411 U.S. 624 (1973). At issue in *Burbank* was
the constitutionality of a city noise-abatement ordinance that placed an 11
P.M. to 7 A.M. curfew on jet flights from the Hollywood-Burbank Airport.
The plaintiffs challenging the ordinance argued that the pervasive presence
of federal regulation established an inference that Congress intended to
occupy the field. In agreeing with this conclusion, the Court described in
detail the federal regulation of the airways and airport noise. Id. at 626-639.
Additionally, the Court described the congressionally imposed duty on the
Federal Aviation Administration (FAA) to promote safety in the airways and
to regulate air traffic flow throughout the nation. Id. at 638-639. In the
Court's view, if individual communities were empowered to control the
number and time of flights, the ripple effect throughout the nation would
disable the FAA from carrying out these duties. The Court did recognize that
noise abatement was traditionally within the police powers of the states, but
any presumption against preemption was overcome by a combination of the
pervasiveness of the federal scheme and the potential to undermine that
scheme if states were allowed to impose curfews on jet flights.

The Supreme Court has suggested that it may be inappropriate to
address the question of field preemption unless other possible bases for
finding preemption have failed. In *American Insurance Association v. Garamendi*,
539 U.S. 396, 418 (2003), a case involving a state law that required
insurance companies to disclose information about policies they issued in
Europe during the Holocaust era, the Court thus noted that there was some
authority for the proposition that "state action with more than incidental
effect on foreign affairs is preempted, even absent any affirmative federal
activity in the subject area of the state law, and hence without any showing
of conflict." The Court explained, however, that "the question requires no
answer here" because the state law being challenged failed under the narrower conflict preemption approach. Id. at 419-420. At the same time, the
Court agreed that it may be proper to invoke "field preemption . . . without
reference to the degree of any conflict" were a state "simply to take a

position on a matter of foreign policy with no serious claim to be addressing a traditional state responsibility. . . ." Id. at 420 n.11. Thus, while the Court has suggested that field preemption should usually be invoked as a matter of last resort, it has stopped short of making this a firm categorical rule.

Example 6-H

Under federal law, an alien who is in this country more than 30 days must apply for federal registration, must be fingerprinted, and must carry proof of federal registration. Failure to comply with any of these provisions is a misdemeanor punishable by a fine, imprisonment, or a sentence of probation. The federal government has discretion to refrain from prosecution or enforcement in individual cases where prosecution might frustrate other federal policies, undermine relationships with foreign countries, or be inequitable to the individuals involved. Federal law also imposes numerous strict requirements on aliens regarding their health, education, integrity, character, and length of residence here.

In 2010, undocumented aliens composed roughly 6 percent of Arizona's population. The state responded by enacting S.B. 1070, §3 of which makes failure to comply with the federal government's alien registration requirements a state criminal misdemeanor, punishable by fine or imprisonment; probation is not a sentencing option. The avowed purpose of the Arizona law is to discourage and deter undocumented aliens from living in the state. No provision of federal law expressly preempts such state alien registration statutes. Is the Arizona law preempted by federal law?

Explanation

As the facts indicate, the federal alien registration scheme is pervasive, providing detailed regulations applicable to resident aliens throughout the country. This pervasiveness supports an inference that Congress intended to occupy the field of alien registration. The federal interest in immigration and naturalization under Article I, §8, cl. 4 is paramount within our federal system, further suggesting the preemptive breadth of the federal law. Similarly, the treaty power, which is at least collaterally implicated by these facts, is exclusively within the domain of the federal government. Conversely, the regulation and registration of aliens has not been traditionally left to the states. Taking these considerations together, it would seem fair to infer that Congress intended to occupy this field. As such, §3 of the Arizona law would be preempted on the basis of implied field preemption. See *Arizona v. United States*, 132 S. Ct. 2492, 2502 (2012) (holding on these facts that "the Federal Government has occupied the field of alien registration. . . . Where Congress occupies an entire field, as it has in the field of alien registration, even complementary state regulation is impermissible. Field preemption reflects a congressional decision to fore-close any state regulation in the area, even if it is parallel to federal standards.").

The *Arizona v. United States* Court might also have relied on the first form of implied preemption — conflict preemption — for Arizona's law would seem to operate as an obstacle to accomplishing the purposes and objectives of Congress. It is clear that Congress intended there to be flexibility in enforcing the federal alien registration requirements, a flexibility that would be lost if states were free to criminally prosecute an alien against whom the federal government had decided not to enforce the identical federal provision. In a case like this, the choice between implied field pre-emption and implied conflict preemption may turn on the purpose of the state law. If, as here, that purpose is identical to the federal law's purpose, i.e., to punish and deter undocumented alien entry into the state, field preemption may be the preferred option, for the state is treading into a domain that is exclusively federal. If, on the other hand, the state's purpose is one that falls within the scope of its traditional police power, e.g., health and safety, the Court may be more deferential and find the state law pre-empted only if it can be shown that it seriously undermines the federal scheme. See *American Insurance Association v. Garamendi*, 539 U.S. 396, 419 n.11 (2003) (suggesting this basis for choosing between implied field and implied conflict preemption in cases where state law touches on matters of foreign policy). See also *Pennsylvania v. Nelson*, 350 U.S. 497 (1956) (apply-ing field preemption reasoning in holding that federal sedition act preempted a state sedition act to the extent the latter sought to punish seditious acts aimed at the United States).

Example 6-1

Pursuant to the Public Service Health Act (PSHA), the federal government has promulgated a comprehensive set of regulations establishing standards for the collection of blood plasma by blood plasma centers. The regulations provide detailed rules covering such matters as safety, purity, and potency, essentially regulating all aspects of the collection and distribution of plasma. Nothing in the PSHA expressly preempts state law regulating the collection of blood plasma; nor does the legislative history of the PSHA address this issue.

The town of Hillsborough has adopted ordinances requiring that blood donors be tested for hepatitis and blood-alcohol content, and that they donate at only one plasma center. The Hillsborough ordinances do not conflict within any federal regulations, but rather operate in addition to those regulations. Are the Hillsborough ordinances nonetheless preempted under a theory of implied field preemption?

Explanation

Probably not. Under *Rice v. Santa Fe Elevator Corp.*, supra, one factor to consider in attempting to discover an implied intent to occupy the field is the pervasiveness of the federal scheme. Here the scope of the federal regulations covers the seemingly broad range of issues confronted in the collection of blood plasma. The adjective "pervasive" seems more than apropos. But this alone is not enough. *Rice* further instructs that "we start with the assumption that the historic police powers of the States [are] not to be superseded by [federal law] unless that was the clear and manifest purpose of Congress." 331 U.S. at 230. The Hillsborough ordinances regulate health and safety matters and therefore fall squarely within the state's traditional police powers. As a consequence, despite the pervasive nature of the federal scheme, the argument for field preemption is relatively weak, especially in the absence of legislative history supporting a congressional intent to occupy the field. See *Hillsborough County v. Automated Medical Laboratories, Inc.*, 471 U.S. 707, 712-723 (1985) (finding no preemption under similar facts).

§6.3 FEDERAL IMMUNITY FROM STATE REGULATION

The principle that the federal government and its instrumentalities are immune from state regulation represents a specialized application of the preemption doctrine. Recall that the second form of conflict preemption precludes the states from enacting legislation that creates "an obstacle to the accomplishment and execution of the full purposes and objectives of Congress." *Hines v. Davidowitz*, supra, 312 U.S. at 67. So, too, states may not regulate the operations of the federal government in a manner that impairs or interferes with the "full purposes and objectives" of the federal program at issue. Any such "obstacle" created by state regulation will be struck down under the Supremacy Clause.

Example 6-J

Driving without a valid driver's license is a misdemeanor in the state of Montana. Lester, a resident of Montana, delivers mail on a rural route for the United States Postal Service, an instrumentality of the federal government. He does not have a valid driver's license. If Lester continues to drive his mail truck as part of his postal service duties, may he be punished by the state for driving without a license?

Explanation

No. The state may not require Lester to obtain a driver's license as a prerequisite to driving for the United States Postal Service. To conclude otherwise would be to accept the authority of a state to regulate the employment practices of a federal instrumentality. In precisely such a case, the Court explained, "the immunity of the instruments of the United States from state control in the performance of their duties extends to a requirement that they desist from performance until they satisfy a state officer upon examination that they are competent for a necessary part of them. . . ." *Johnson v. Maryland*, 254 U.S. 51, 55 (1920) (state may not convict postal worker for driving without a license in the course of his employment); see also *Leslie Miller, Inc. v. Arkansas*, 352 U.S. 187 (1956) (contractor working for federal government immune from state licensing requirement).

The principle applied in Example 6-J does not mean that federal employees are completely immune from state law while performing their federal duties. The immunity extends only to those state laws that actually prevent or significantly impair the performance of federal duties. For example, suppose that while performing his duties with the Postal Service, Lester ran a stop sign. May the state cite Lester for this traffic violation? Probably. Unless the federal government has specifically immunized postal drivers from such liability, a state may impose general rules of local law that only incidentally affect "the mode of carrying out the employment." *Johnson v. Maryland*, supra, 254 U.S. at 56. Lester's traffic citation would seem to fall into this category. Requiring Lester to comply with local traffic regulations in no way impairs his ability to carry out his federally assigned tasks. On the other hand, if Lester had been an FBI agent in hot pursuit of a suspect, the state's traffic laws would not be allowed to interfere with the agent's federal mandate to pursue that suspect. The question to ask in any particular case is whether the state law at issue actually interferes with the federal instrumentality's ability to achieve its federally assigned tasks.

A state regulation that otherwise violates the principle of federal immunity from state regulation will be upheld if there is a "clear congressional mandate" to authorize the state regulation. *Hancock v. Train*, 426 U.S. 167, 179 (1976). Thus, in Example 6-J, Congress could expressly require drivers for the Postal Service to possess a valid state driver's license, though in the absence of such a requirement postal workers may perform their duties free from the constraints of the state licensing law.

§6.4 FEDERAL IMMUNITY FROM STATE TAXATION

Although the principle of federal immunity from state taxation described in *McCulloch v. Maryland* could be interpreted as establishing a blanket immunity covering any and all state taxes with a measurable effect on the federal government, the modern doctrine of federal tax immunity is substantially less encompassing. Under the modern doctrine, a state may not impose a tax on the federal government, its property, or on any federal instrumentality that is so closely tied to the federal government that the two cannot realistically be viewed as separate entities. To violate this principle, the *legal incidence of the tax* must fall on the federal government or its instrumentality; in other words, it is not enough that the *economic burden of the tax* is passed on to the federal government. Thus, for example, a state is free to impose a tax on the income of persons employed by the federal government since the legal incidence of that tax falls on the employee and not on the government. See *Arizona Dept. of Revenue v. Blaze Construction Co.*, 526 U.S. 32 (1999) (private contractor not immune from state tax on gross receipts for work done on federal project on Indian reservation).

The immunity doctrine also forecloses states from imposing taxes that discriminate against the federal government, its instrumentalities, agents, or employees. A state could not, therefore, tax the income of federal employees if it did not impose a similar tax on the income of individuals employed by the state or in the private sector.

In general, courts apply the principles of federal tax immunity sparingly to preserve the legitimate taxing authority of the states. Of course, if Congress wishes to extend federal tax immunity beyond these judicially created boundaries, it may do so pursuant to its enumerated powers by expressly preempting certain state taxes.

Example 6-K

The Zandra Company, a privately owned enterprise, has a contract with the federal government under which Zandra manages federally owned atomic laboratories in New Mexico. As part of its management duties, Zandra purchases goods from vendors for use in the laboratories. The purchases are made in Zandra's name, without prior approval by the federal government. Nor is the vendor notified that the purchases are for the federal government or that Zandra is a purchasing agent for the federal government; indeed, the federal government denies that Zandra is its purchasing agent. Although Zandra is liable to the vendor for the purchase price of the goods, title to the goods passes directly to the federal government. The latter reimburses Zandra for the cost of the goods, including any sales taxes. The state of New Mexico imposes a sales tax on all goods sold within the state. The legal incidence of the tax falls on the purchaser. May this tax be imposed on sales to Zandra of goods to be used at the federal laboratory?

Explanation

Yes. The legal incidence of this nondiscriminatory tax does not fall on the federal government, but rather on Zandra as the purchaser. The fact that the economic burden of the taxes will be passed on to the United States is of no relevance. Since the legal incidence of the tax does not technically fall on the United States, the tax will be subject to federal immunity only if it can be said that Zandra and the federal government are so closely tied that they cannot realistically be viewed as separate entities. Given the independence under which Zandra operates, a court is likely to conclude that Zandra and the federal government are separate entities. That being the case, the state may impose this sales tax on the purchases made by Zandra. See *United States v. New Mexico*, 455 U.S. 720, 741-743 (1982) (same conclusion under similar facts).

Suppose, however, that Zandra correctly described itself as a federal procurement agent when it made its purchases; that title to the purchased goods passed directly to the federal government; that the purchase orders declared the purchase to be made by the federal government; and that Zandra was in no manner liable for the purchases. These changed facts might well lead a court to conclude that the purchaser of the goods was the United States, rather than Zandra. Under such circumstances, the legal incidence of the tax would fall on the federal government and the tax would, therefore, be invalid. See *Kern-Limerick Inc. v. Scurlock*, 347 U.S. 110, 114-121 (1954) (same conclusion under similar facts).

Example 6-L

Employees of the United States Forest Service (USFS) are required to live in houses owned by the USFS and located within national forests. The housing is considered a part of the employees' compensation and the government deducts a specified amount from the each employee's salary as "rent" for the housing. The county of Fresno, consistent with the principles of federal tax immunity, does not impose its general property tax on national forest land within the county since the legal incidence of such a tax would fall on the United States itself as the property owner. However, the county does impose an annual use tax on possessory interests in tax-exempt land, including the possessory interests of the USFS employees. Does the use tax as applied to USFS employees violate the principle of federal immunity from state taxation?

Explanation

No. While a state or a subdivision of a state may not impose a tax on the property of the federal government, it may impose a use tax on private persons who are granted the possession or use of that property. This is so because unlike a property tax imposed on federally owned property, the legal incidence of the use tax falls on the person using the property rather than on the federal government. In the immediate case, the legal incidence of the use tax falls on the USFS employees. The principle of federal immunity, therefore, is not violated.

Nor is this tax discriminatory even though it only applies to renters of tax-exempt property. Since the county does impose its general property tax on nonexempt property, the practical effect of the use tax is to place all renters of property on an equal economic footing, for owners of nonexempt property can be expected to pass the economic burden of the tax on to their lessees. See *United States v. County of Fresno*, 429 U.S. 452, 464-468 (1977) (same conclusion under similar facts).

When examining a state tax for a potential violation of the tax immunity principle, be sure to also consider the potential regulatory effects of the tax. For even if a tax does not violate the tax immunity principle, it may violate the regulatory immunity principle if the effect of the tax is to impose an obstacle to the full purposes and objectives of the federal program. While merely increasing the economic costs of a program is not, standing alone, sufficient to trigger the principle of regulatory immunity, such immunity may attach if the increase in cost is so great as to be prohibitive.

§6.5 STATE-IMPOSED LIMITS ON ELECTION TO FEDERAL OFFICE

During the 1980s and 1990s, individual states began to impose limits on the number of terms a person could serve in either the United States House of Representatives or the United States Senate. These states claimed to be acting pursuant to the Elections Clause, Art. I, §4, cl. 1, which grants the states the power to regulate the "Times, Places and Manner of holding Elections for Senators and Representatives. . . ." In *U.S. Term Limits, Inc. v. Thornton*, 514 U.S. 779 (1995), the Court rejected this reading of the Elections Clause, concluding instead that the scope of the clause was constrained by other constitutional principles and provisions. To begin with, in the Court's view, state-imposed term limits on elective federal office violated the "'fundamental principle of our representative democracy,' embodied in the Constitution, 'that the people should choose whom they please to govern them.'" Id. at 783 (quoting *Powell v. McCormack*, 395 U.S. 486, 547 (1969)). The Court further held that state-imposed term limits transgressed specific clauses in the Constitution that defined what the Court perceived to be the *exclusive* qualifications for those federal offices, namely, age, residence, and citizenship. Art. I, §2, cl. 2 (qualifications for House of Representatives); Art. I, §3, cl. 3 (qualifications for Senate). As a consequence, relying on a combination of constitutional text, Framers' intent, and democratic theory, a five-person majority of the Court concluded that the states possessed no power to add to the qualifications for federal office described in the Qualifications Clauses. 514 U.S. at 797-827. See also *Powell v. McCormack*, supra, 395 U.S. at 548 (Congress lacks authority to impose qualifications beyond those described in the Qualifications Clauses).

The state statute at issue in *Thornton* did not actually disqualify anyone from running for federal office. Rather, it denied *ballot access* to candidates who had served more than a specified number of terms. A candidate subject to these restrictions could still be elected through write-in ballots. Despite this theoretical possibility, the Court concluded that the operation of the state's ballot restriction was, in effect, to impose a term-limit qualification since, realistically, few if any candidates would be elected by reliance on write-in votes. 514 U.S. at 828-838. The Court's treatment of this issue further underscored the majority's complete constitutional antipathy for state-imposed term limits on federal elective office. Thus, after *Thornton*, the only way to impose term limits is by amending the U.S. Constitution.

Example 6-M

State X law requires that all state X candidates for the United States House of Representatives must reside in the congressional district they seek to represent in Congress at the time they are elected. Is this law constitutional?

Explanation

Probably not. According to the Court's decision in *U.S. Term Limits, Inc. v. Thornton*, supra, Art. I, §2, cl. 2 of the Constitution establishes the exclusive qualifications for membership in the House of Representatives: "No Person shall be a Representative who shall not have attained to the Age of twenty five Years, and been seven Years a Citizen of the United States, and who shall not, when elected, be an Inhabitant of that State in which he shall be chosen." Since Art. I, §2, cl. 2 does not mention a district residency requirement, a state may not impose one. See *Texas Democratic Party v. Benkiser*, 459 F.3d 582 (5th Cir. 2006) (under Qualifications Clause, state may not require candidates for House of Representatives to be residents of state prior to date of the election); *Campbell v. Davidson*, 233 F.3d 1229 (10th Cir. 2000), *cert. denied*, 532 U.S. 973 (2001) (state may not require candidates for House of Representatives to reside in the particular district in which they seek election); *Schaefer v. Townsend*, 215 F.3d 1031 (9th Cir. 2000), *cert. denied*, 532 U.S. 904 (2001) (under Qualifications Clause state may not require candidates for House of Representatives to be a resident of the state at the time of filing nomination papers as distinguished from the date of election).

In response to the Court's decision in Thornton, the voters of Missouri amended their state constitution to "instruct" all members of the state's congressional delegation to work toward the adoption of an amendment to the United States Constitution that would impose term limits on congressional office. If an incumbent member of Congress failed to take any one of eight specified legislative acts in support of the proposed term-limits amendment, the statement "disregarded voters' instructions on term limits" would be placed next to that candidate's name on the ballot in subsequent primaries and general elections. Similarly, a nonincumbent for congressional office who failed to endorse term limits would be labeled on the ballot as "declined to pledge to support term limits." When the measure was challenged in court, the state defended it as an exercise of the state's power under the Elections Clause. The Supreme Court held, however, that the provision exceeded the state's power under the Elections Clause and instead represented an unconstitutional interference with a federal election by attempting to dictate its outcome. *Cook v. Gralike*, 531 U.S. 510, 524-526 (2001). As to the scope of the Elections Clause, the Court explained:

> To be sure, the Elections Clause grants to the States "broad power" to prescribe the procedural mechanisms for holding congressional elections. Nevertheless, [this state provision] falls outside of that grant of authority. As we made clear in *U.S. Term Limits*, "the Framers understood the Elections Clause as a grant of authority to issue procedural regulations, and not as a source of power to dictate electoral outcomes, to favor or disfavor a class of candidates, or to evade important constitutional restraints." [Missouri's constitutional provision] is not a procedural regulation. It does not regulate the time of elections; it does not regulate the place of elections; nor, we believe, does it regulate the manner of elections. As to the last point, [the provision] bears no relation to the "manner" of elections as we understand it, for in our commonsense view that term encompasses matters like "notices, registration, supervision of voting, protection of voters, prevention of fraud and corrupt practices, counting of votes, duties of inspectors and canvassers, and making and publication of election returns."

531 U.S. at 523-524 (internal citations omitted).

CHAPTER 7

The Separation of Powers

§7.1 INTRODUCTION AND OVERVIEW

The Constitution of the United States is the instrument by which "We the People" created a new national government. One of our great fears as a people, however, was that the authority of this new government might be abused by those who would handle the reins of power. The Founders therefore sought to structure the national government in such a way that no one person or group would be able to exercise too much authority. To this end, the Constitution apportions or divides the powers of the national government among three different branches — the legislative (Congress), the executive (the President and those appointed to assist him or her), and the judicial (the federal courts). This is the principle of separation of powers.

Separation of powers issues arise when it is claimed that one branch of government has usurped or encroached upon the functions of another branch. For example, if the President were to initiate a war without the approval of Congress, the executive's unilateral action might be challenged on separation of powers grounds since Article I, §8 states that the power to declare war belongs to Congress. A separation of powers argument would also arise if Congress sought to bar the President from entering into treaty negotiations without the prior consent of Congress, for such a requirement would encroach upon the executive's authority to conduct foreign affairs. In this chapter we examine a number of the principal areas in which separation of powers issues have arisen.

While the doctrine of separation of powers protects each branch of the government against unwarranted encroachment by the other branches, these limitations exist not for the benefit of each branch as such, but as a means of safeguarding the rights of individuals. *Boumediene v. Bush*, 553 U.S. 723, 742 (2008) (separation of powers "serves . . . to secure individual liberty"). When separation of powers comes up in court, the principle is more often being invoked by individuals than by the injured federal branch. *Bond v. United States*, 131 S. Ct. 2355, 2365 (2011) ("[i]n the precedents of this Court, the claims of individuals — not of Government departments — have been the principal source of judicial decisions concerning separation of powers and checks and balances."). Separation of powers violations therefore cannot be waived by the branch whose powers may have been impaired. For this reason, when the judiciary reviews a law challenged on separation of powers grounds, it is irrelevant that the branch whose authority has been usurped may have consented to the intrusion. "The Constitution's division of power among the three Branches is violated where one Branch invades the territory of another, whether or not the encroached-upon Branch approves the encroachment." *New York v. United States*, 505 U.S. 144, 182 (1992). See, e.g., *Immigration and Naturalization Service v. Chadha*, 462 U.S. 919 (1983) (invalidating, on separation of powers grounds, legislative veto provision impairing President's role in lawmaking process, even though statute containing veto provision had been signed by President); *Myers v. United States*, 272 U.S. 52 (1926) (invalidating, on separation of powers grounds, statute limiting President's power to fire postmaster, even though statute had been signed by President).

§7.2 "CHECKS AND BALANCES" AND THE COMMINGLING OF POWERS

Although the term *separation of powers* does not appear in the Constitution, the separation of powers principle is reflected in the very structure of the federal Constitution. Article I enumerates the "legislative Powers," Article II discusses the "executive Power," and Article III defines the "judicial Power." We have already discussed the legislative power (see Chapter 5) and the judicial power (see Chapters 1-4).

As far as the executive power is concerned, Article II, §2, cl. 1, states that "[t]he executive Power shall be vested in a President of the United States. . . ." The nature of this power is partly enumerated by Article II, §2, which provides that the President shall be commander in chief of the armed forces and that he shall have certain powers, including the power to grant pardons and reprieves, to make treaties, and to appoint judges and other federal officers. Article II, §3 adds that the President shall recommend measures to Congress, receive ambassadors, and take care that the laws be faithfully executed. In addition to these enumerated executive powers, the President is sometimes said to possess other powers that are deemed inherent in the "executive Power" that is "vested" in him by Article II, §1. While this notion of inherent executive power is hotly debated, the Court has at times suggested that it includes the authority to remove individuals from federal office (see *Myers v. United States*, 272 U.S. 52 (1926)), certain powers with respect to foreign affairs (see *United States v. Curtiss-Wright Corp.*, 299 U.S. 304 (1936)), and the power to protect federal officials and federal property (see *In re Neagle*, 135 U.S. 1 (1890); *In re Debs*, 158 U.S. 564 (1895)).

Though the Constitution assigns the legislative, executive, and judicial powers of the federal government to three distinct branches, the Founders did not expect the separation of powers to be airtight. Thus, as a further safeguard against the abuse of power, the Constitution incorporates a system of checks and balances through which the branches of government often share or participate in functions that are principally assigned to a coordinate branch. As the Court said in *Mistretta v. United States*, 488 U.S. 361, 381 (1989), "the greatest security against tyranny — the accumulation of excessive authority in a single Branch — lies not in a hermetic division among the Branches, but in a carefully crafted system of checked and balanced power within each Branch."

This blending or commingling of power to create areas of overlapping responsibility is reflected in many parts of the Constitution. Thus, while the lawmaking authority is assigned to the legislative branch, the executive may participate in this process through the President's power to recommend (Art. II, §3) and to veto (Art. I, §7) legislation. Similarly, though the duty to carry out the laws is conferred upon the executive, the legislature may influence the exercise of this authority by its power to impeach executive officials (Art. I, §§2–3; Art. II, §4), and through the Senate's right to reject the President's nominees for executive office (Art. II, §2). Even the judicial power of the federal courts is shared with the other branches in the sense that the President and the Senate select the judges of these courts (Art. II, §2), and Congress may remove them by impeachment (Art. I, §§2-3; Art. II, §4; Art. III, §1); in addition, Congress has the authority to narrow the jurisdiction both of the lower federal courts and of the Supreme Court in its appellate capacity (Art. I, §8; Art. III, §§1-2) (see Chapter 2). Finally, the federal courts frequently involve themselves in the functions of the legislative and executive branches through the exercise of judicial review. See Chapter 1.

By allocating the powers of the federal government among three branches, and yet at the same time commingling those powers so that many governmental functions require cooperation among the branches, the Founders deliberately created a system in which there is inherent tension between the three branches. It is inevitable that this scheme of government will give rise to boundary disputes in which it is claimed that one branch has aggrandized itself by usurping authority that belongs to another branch, or that one branch has encroached upon the independence, authority, or integrity of a coordinate branch.

These so-called interbranch disputes are often handled by the competing branches themselves through the give and take of the political process. There are several reasons for this. First, as we saw in Chapter 3, separation of powers issues often pose special problems of standing and ripeness; they may also trigger application of the political question doctrine. Second, even when separation of powers matters are justiciable, it may take many years before an issue actually reaches the courts. For example, the legislative veto device, first adopted by Congress in 1932 and opposed by a host of Presidents, was not held to be unconstitutional until half a century later. See *Immigration and Naturalization Service v. Chadha*, 462 U.S. 919 (1983) (§7.4.2).

The fact that the federal judiciary may not yet have resolved a particular separation of powers issue does not diminish the issue's importance. Rather, it simply means that with respect to such questions, the "law" of separation of powers will, for long periods of time and perhaps forever, be determined by the day-to-day practices of the political branches, rather than by a definitive pronouncement from the Supreme Court.

§7.3 TEXTUAL VERSUS STRUCTURAL OR FUNCTIONAL ARGUMENTS

There are two different but related types of arguments that may be used to address a separation of powers problem. The first involves a textual approach while the second employs a structural or functional approach. At times, the line between the two types of argument may vanish.

§7.3.1 Textual Separation of Powers Arguments

A textual separation of powers argument is based on a specific clause of the Constitution. Numerous constitutional provisions are designed to promote the separation of powers by assigning certain powers, duties, or functions to a particular branch. The war power, for example, is divided between two branches: The power to *declare* war is given to Congress (Art. I, §8, cl. 11), while the power to *conduct* war is given to the President (Art. II, §2). If the President were to declare war without the approval of Congress, this action could be challenged by making the *textual* separation of powers argument that the President has violated Article I, §8 by usurping power that the Constitution has assigned to Congress.

Other textual provisions seek to insure the separation of powers by protecting each branch from outside interference. For example, Congress is shielded from executive encroachment in a number of ways: Members of Congress cannot be arrested while attending legislative sessions and may not be prosecuted for any speech or debate undertaken as part of the legislative process (Art. I, §6); the President cannot compromise the independence of Congress by appointing its members to other offices (Art. I, §6); and the President may adjourn Congress only if the House and Senate are unable to agree on a date of adjournment (Art. II, §3). A *textual* separation of powers argument would arise if any of these provisions were violated.

§7.3.2 Structural Separation of Powers Arguments

The second approach to separation of powers problems is through a structural or functional argument. Even where no specific textual provision of the Constitution has been violated, the action of one branch may nonetheless run afoul of separation of powers because it threatens the tripartite structure of our federal government by altering the balance of power among the branches. This type of argument is structural in that it draws upon "inference from the structures and relationships created by the constitution. . . ." Charles Black, *Structure and Relationship in Constitutional Law* 7 (1969). At the same time, the argument is also functional in that it involves a pragmatic assessment of the impact a challenged action may have on the ability of the three branches to function effectively in a system based on checks and balances.

A structural threat may arise if one branch aggrandizes itself by encroaching upon or usurping functions that are more appropriately performed by a coordinate branch. Aggrandizement and encroachment typically go hand in hand: By aggrandizing its own powers the offending branch usually encroaches upon the authority of another branch. For example, if Congress passes a law barring the President from dismissing certain executive officials without the approval of the Senate, Congress has aggrandized its own powers while at the same time encroaching on the President's authority to administer the executive branch. However, a structural separation of powers argument might also arise where one branch, though not aggrandizing its own powers, nonetheless encroaches on another branch's legitimate sphere of authority. This might occur, for example, if Congress were to prohibit the President from nominating any person for a federal district court judgeship without the consent of the governor of the state.

In some cases it may be appropriate to make both a *textual* and a *structural* separation of powers argument because of the fact that the text of the Constitution is ambiguous.

Example 7-A

Suppose that Congress required the President to recognize and establish diplomatic relations with a new foreign state such as those that emerged after the collapse of the Soviet Union. Congress's action might be attacked on separation of powers grounds using the textual argument that Article II, §3, which states that the President "shall receive Ambassadors and other public Ministers," implicitly gives the President the authority to recognize foreign governments. If a court were to reject this textual separation of powers claim on the ground that Article II, §3 does not expressly address the issue of recognition, how else might the President challenge Congress's action?

Explanation

Congress's action might still be challenged by making the structural or functional separation of powers argument that the power to recognize foreign governments is indispensable to the President's ability to conduct foreign affairs, and that Congress has therefore encroached upon the President's domain and sought to aggrandize its own power by usurping authority that should be exercised by the executive alone.

As we will see below, to the extent that courts in separation of powers cases do not read the relevant textual provisions rigidly and literally, but instead construe them in terms of their underlying goal or function of promoting a separation of powers, the distinction between textual and structural arguments vanishes. If a court, in deciding whether a specific textual provision has been violated, approaches the question in terms of aggrandizement or encroachment, the textual and structural approaches to separation of powers problems thus collapse into one.

§7.3.3 Analyzing Separation of Powers Problems

To analyze a separation of powers problem from a textual as well as a structural or functional perspective, you might pose the following questions:

1. Has one branch of government exercised a power or performed a function that a *specific clause* of the Constitution requires to be performed by, or only in conjunction with, another body or branch?
2. Has one branch of government *aggrandized* its authority by *usurping* power that more appropriately belongs to a coordinate branch?
3. Has one branch of government *encroached* upon the functions of a coordinate branch so as to undermine that branch's integrity or independence?

If any of these questions is answered in the affirmative, a court will likely find that there has been a violation of separation of powers.

The discussion of separation of powers issues that follows is divided into two areas, the first involving the domestic arena and the second dealing with war and foreign affairs.

§7.4 THE DOMESTIC ARENA

Within the domestic sphere, separation of powers issues have arisen among all three branches of the federal government. As we shall see, many of these disputes have pitted Congress and the executive against one another. Yet it would be a mistake to think of separation of powers as a principle that merely governs relations between the two political branches. The Court has relied on the doctrine of separation of powers to prevent congressional and executive encroachment upon the judicial branch. See, e.g., *Hayburn's Case*, 2 U.S. (2 Dall.) 409 (1792) (separation of powers bars Congress from subjecting federal judges' decisions on Revolutionary War pension claims to review and revision by other branches). The Court has also held that separation of powers protects the executive branch against unwarranted interference from the judiciary. See, e.g., *United States v. Nixon*, 418 U.S. 683 (1974) (separation of powers affords President a qualified privilege against compelled judicial disclosure of confidential communications).

§7.4.1 Presidential Exercise of Lawmaking Power

Article I, §1 of the Constitution states in unequivocal terms that "[a]ll legislative Powers herein granted shall be vested in a Congress of the United States. . . ." The use of the word "all" would seem to exclude any exercise of the legislative or lawmaking power by any other branch, except as expressly provided by the Constitution. As we noted earlier, the President is expressly authorized to participate in the lawmaking process by recommending new legislation and by vetoing measures that have been approved by Congress. Beyond this, however, to what extent may the executive engage in lawmaking?

Example 7-B

Suppose that a study has shown that the average American worker puts in four hours of overtime per week, often at the employer's insistence. One effect of this practice is to reduce the number of available jobs and to thus increase the nation's unemployment rate. To combat this practice, the

President issues an executive order barring employers from forcing workers to put in any overtime. The executive order authorizes the Justice Department to enforce the order by obtaining a court injunction against any employer who violates the order. Is the executive order valid?

Explanation

Assuming there is no federal statute imposing such a ban on employers, the President's action constitutes a clear exercise of lawmaking power. The President has in effect made a law governing overtime work. Had such a measure been enacted by Congress, the executive's Article II, §3 duty to "take Care that the Laws be faithfully executed" would have fully justified the President's instructions to the Justice Department. In the absence of a congressional statute, however, the President has assumed the dual role of lawmaker and law enforcer, thereby violating separation of powers.

One could analyze this problem in either textual or structural/functional terms. A textual argument would urge that by vesting "all" legislative power in the Congress, Article I precludes the exercise of the lawmaking power by the executive. A structural or functional approach would argue that the President has sought to aggrandize the executive branch by usurping power that should more appropriately be exercised by the legislature. One of the fundamental principles of separation of powers is that "[t]here can be no liberty where the legislative and executive powers are united in the same person, or body of magistrates. . . ." *The Federalist No. 47*, at 302 (Madison, quoting Montesquieu) (Clinton Rossiter ed., 1961).

In *Youngstown Sheet & Tube Co. v. Sawyer*, 343 U.S. 579 (1952), the Court confronted a similar exercise of executive lawmaking when President Truman, to avert a wartime steel strike, directed the secretary of commerce to seize and operate the nation's steel mills. Though no act of Congress authorized the executive to deal with a threatened strike in this manner, the President contended that he had the "inherent power" to do so. The Court rejected this claim. In an opinion by Justice Black, the Court agreed with the steel companies that "the President's order amounts to lawmaking, a legislative function which the Constitution has expressly confided to the Congress and not to the President." Id. at 582.

Youngstown arguably left open the question of whether the President may exercise lawmaking power in a national emergency to deal with contingencies Congress has not had an opportunity to address. In *Youngstown*, the Court noted that Congress had earlier considered and rejected the option of allowing the President to seize industries in order to avoid major shutdowns. The President was therefore unable to claim that he was exercising lawmaking power on an interim basis until Congress could deal with the situation.

A number of Justices suggested that had the emergency arisen in a setting where Congress had not already spoken, President Truman might have been justified in acting on a temporary basis. Instead, the President's power was, in Justice Jackson's words, "at its lowest ebb," for Truman's course of action was "incompatible with the expressed or implied will of Congress. . . ." Id. at 637. See also *New York Times Co. v. United States*, 403 U.S. 713 (1971) (President lacked authority to seek a judicial prior restraint against publication of classified information where Congress, in creating a system for the classification of documents, had declined to give the executive this remedy).

Example 7-C

Example 5-N, supra, addressed the question of whether a certain group of treaties — the Vienna Convention on Consular Relations, the Optional Protocol to that convention, and the United Nations Charter — were "self-executing," thus making a judgment of the International Court of Justice (ICJ) arising out of the Vienna Convention enforceable as a matter of domestic law in the United States. The Supreme Court held that these treaties were not self-executing. Hence, the ICJ judgment, which pertained to 51 Mexican nationals convicted and sentenced under state law, was not enforceable in the absence of implementing legislation. Suppose, however, that the President issued the following order pertaining to the judgment of the ICJ:

> I have determined, pursuant to the authority vested in me as President by the Constitution and the laws of the United States of America, that the United States will discharge its international obligations under the decision of the International Court of Justice in [*Avena*], by having State courts give effect to the decision in accordance with general principles of comity in cases filed by the 51 Mexican nationals addressed in that decision.

In short, the President's action appears to implement the treaties by declaring their enforceability within the several states. Does the President have the power to do so?

Explanation

No. The order is a form of lawmaking, even more clearly so than President Truman's action in *Youngstown*. By making an unenforceable treaty enforceable, the order transforms that which is not law, namely, a non-self-executing treaty with no domestic enforcement mechanism, into a legal principle enforceable against the states as the supreme law of the land. So held the Supreme Court in *Medellín v. Texas*, 552 U.S. 491, 525-526 (2008). As the Court explained, "Once a treaty is ratified without provisions clearly according it domestic effect, . . . whether the treaty will ever have such effect is governed by the fundamental constitutional principle that '[t]he power to make the necessary laws is in Congress; the power to execute in the President.'" Id. at 526 (quoting *Hamdan v. Rumsfeld*, 548 U.S. 557, 591 (2006)). And turning to *Youngstown*, the *Medellín* Court observed, " 'the President's power to see that the laws are faithfully executed refutes the idea that he is to be a lawmaker.'" 552 U.S. at 526-527 (quoting *Youngstown*, 343 U.S., at 587).

The Nondelegation Doctrine

Youngstown involved a case where the President exercised lawmaking authority in a manner that was contrary to the intent of Congress. What if Congress has instead expressly authorized the President or an executive branch agency to promulgate rules or standards to govern a particular area: Would the executive's exercise of lawmaking authority still be unconstitutional?

The Supreme Court has often said that because Article I, §1 vests "all" legislative power in the Congress, Congress may not constitutionally delegate its lawmaking power to another branch of government. However, this so-called nondelegation doctrine is a fiction. Congress may — and often does — authorize the other branches to establish rules or standards for a particular area. The Court will uphold such delegations of the lawmaking power as long as Congress by statute sets forth "an intelligible principle to which the person or body authorized to [act] is directed to conform. . . ." *Touby v. United States*, 500 U.S. 160, 165 (1991) (quoting *J. W. Hampton, Jr. & Co. v. United States*, 276 U.S. 394, 409 (1928)); see also *F.C.C. v. Fox Television Stations, Inc.*, 556 U.S. 502, 535-537 (2009) (Kennedy, J., concurring).

The intelligible principle test is extraordinarily easy to meet. It has been deemed satisfied where the only guidance provided by Congress was that the standards in question be "fair and equitable" or in the "public interest." With the exception of two cases decided in 1935 involving statutes, "one of which provided literally no guidance for the exercise of discretion, and the other of which conferred authority to regulate the entire economy on the basis of no more precise a standard than stimulating the economy by assuring 'fair competition'" (*Whitman v. American Trucking Associations*, 531 U.S. 457, 474 (2001)), the Court has never invalidated a federal statute on the ground that Congress improperly delegated its lawmaking power to another branch. Instead, the Justices have routinely upheld statutes that confer lawmaking authority on the executive branch, and even on the federal judiciary. As to the former, see *Whitman*, 531 U.S. at 472-476 (upholding law authorizing the Environmental Protection Agency to set air quality standards "requisite to protect the public health" with "an adequate margin of safety"); as to the latter, see *Mistretta v. United States*, 488 U.S. 361 (1989) (upholding law authorizing Sentencing Commission, an independent entity within the judicial branch, to promulgate sentencing guidelines for the federal courts).

The Court's tolerant attitude toward delegation of lawmaking authority reflects a flexible and pragmatic view of separation of powers. Congress often lacks the time and expertise to develop intricate rules and regulations for many areas covered by federal legislation. Through delegation Congress is able to enlist the assistance of its coordinate branches. Moreover, virtually every statute involves a certain degree of delegation, for no matter how carefully a law is written, some policy judgments "must be left to the officers executing the law and to the judges applying it. . . ." *Mistretta v. United States*, supra, 488 U.S. at 415 (1989) (Scalia, J., dissenting). Whether or not delegation is unconstitutional is thus a question of degree and the Supreme Court has "almost never felt qualified to second-guess Congress regarding the permissible degree of policy judgment that can be left to those executing or applying the law." Id. at 416.

Example 7-D

In Example 7-B above, suppose that the executive order prohibiting employers from requiring overtime work was issued pursuant to a statute that authorized the executive to regulate employee overtime in any manner the President believes necessary to promote the public welfare. Would the executive order violate separation of powers?

Explanation

Taking a strict textual approach to the question, one might argue that because Article I, §1 vests "all" legislative power in Congress, the statute authorizing the President to regulate overtime and the executive order issued pursuant to it are both invalid, for Congress has attempted to delegate lawmaking authority to another branch.

However, the Court has not construed Article I, §1 literally, but has instead adopted a functional approach that recognizes the practical necessity for Congress to share its lawmaking authority with other branches. The Court would uphold the executive order here as long as the statute gave the executive an intelligible principle to guide its action. The requirement that the overtime regulations promote the public interest satisfies this requirement. See *National Broadcasting Co. v. United States*, 319 U.S. 190, 215, 225-226 (1943) (upholding statute authorizing Federal Communications Commission to regulate broadcast licensing "as public interest, convenience, or necessity" require).

The Item Veto

In 1996, Congress enacted the Line Item Veto Act. The act gave the President the authority unilaterally to "cancel" certain provisions contained in bills that had been signed into law. This so-called item veto could be exercised by the President to cancel items of new spending, to rescind any dollar amount of discretionary budget authority, and to cancel any new limited tax benefits. In contrast to the veto power conferred on the President by Article I,

§7, cl. 2, the statutory item veto allowed the President to reject *selected portions* of a law rather than having to approve or reject the measure *as a whole*. Moreover, it allowed the veto to be exercised *after* the measure had been enacted into law, rather than when it was first presented to the President for his approval or rejection. If the President exercised this line item veto authority, the cancellation took effect immediately. A cancellation would thereafter become "null and void" if Congress subsequently approved and the President signed a "disapproval bill" with respect to a particular cancellation. If the President vetoed the disapproval bill using his Article I, §7 veto power, the disapproval bill would become effective only if Congress overrode the President's veto by a two-thirds vote of both Houses.

In *Clinton v. City of New York*, 524 U.S. 417 (1998), the Supreme Court declared the Line Item Veto Act unconstitutional because it gave the President the practical and legal authority to amend acts of Congress by unilaterally repealing portions thereof. This, said the Court, violated the "finely wrought" lawmaking procedure spelled out in Article I, §7 of the Constitution, which requires that *before* a law may be enacted, amended, or repealed, it must be approved by both Houses of Congress and either signed by the President or repassed over his veto. Id. at 447. Contrary to these constitutional requirements, the Line Item Veto Act gave "the President the unilateral power to change the text of duly enacted statutes." Id. Its effect was to "authorize the President to create a different law — one whose text was not voted on by either House of Congress or presented to the President for signature." Id. at 448. As Justice Kennedy noted in a concurring opinion, the item veto violated separation of powers not only because it was unauthorized by the text of the Constitution but because it "enhances the President's powers beyond what the Framers would have endorsed." Id. at 451. The Court concluded by observing that if the President is to possess such authority — which is enjoyed by many state governors — "such change must come not by legislation but through the amendment procedures set forth in Article V of the Constitution." Id. at 449.

§7.4.2 The Legislative Veto

While the Court has taken a very liberal attitude toward congressional delegation of lawmaking authority to the other branches, when Congress exercises legislative power itself the Court has insisted that Congress adhere strictly to the letter of the Constitution. This means that any legislative action on the part of Congress must meet the requirements of bicameralism and presentment set forth in Article I, §7. *Bicameralism* mandates that a legislative act of Congress must be approved by both the House and the Senate. *Presentment* requires that before any measure approved by the House and Senate can become law, it must be presented for approval to the President; if the President vetoes the measure it may become law only if it is repassed by a two-thirds majority in each House of Congress. A so-called "legislative veto" provision, which allows either or both Houses of Congress to disapprove action taken by the executive branch, will normally violate one or both of these requirements. These are the same "finely wrought" lawmaking requirements that doomed the presidential item veto in *Clinton v. City of New York.*

The bicameralism and presentment requirements apply only to "legislative action" on the part of Congress. In *Immigration and Naturalization Service v. Chadha,* 462 U.S. 919, 952 (1983), the Court, in an opinion by Chief Justice Burger, defined legislative action as that which has the "purpose and effect of altering the legal rights, duties, and relations of persons . . . outside the Legislative Branch." In that case, the House of Representatives had passed a resolution blocking the attorney general's decision to suspend the deportation of an alien. The attorney general acted pursuant to a statute authorizing such suspension in cases where deportation would result in extreme hardship; the same statute authorized either House of Congress to then override the attorney general's decision. The *Chadha* Court held that this "one-House legislative veto" amounted to legislative action because it affected the rights and duties of both the alien and the attorney general — i.e., Chadha was deprived of the right to remain in the United States and the attorney general was placed under a duty to deport him. The House's action was therefore unconstitutional since it did not satisfy either the bicameralism or the presentment requirement of Article I. By contrast, the *Chadha* majority would not find legislative action to be involved if the House were to adopt a resolution appointing a special committee, taking up a bill out of order, or recessing until Wednesday morning — for none of these actions affect the rights or duties of persons outside of Congress.

Example 7-E

Suppose that a federal statute authorizes the Interstate Commerce Commission (ICC), in the interest of safety, to issue regulations restricting the use of billboards along interstate highways. According to the statute, Congress may by concurrent resolution disapprove any such regulations. A *concurrent resolution* requires the approval of the House and Senate but does not need to be approved by the President. Pursuant to this statute, Congress adopts a concurrent resolution blocking an ICC regulation that would have banned all billboards along Interstate Highway 80. Is the concurrent resolution valid under the principles announced in *Chadha?*

Explanation

The concurrent resolution is unconstitutional. It involves legislative action since its purpose and effect are to alter the rights and duties of persons outside the legislative branch, including advertisers and ICC officials. Bicameralism does not pose a problem. In contrast to the one-House veto struck down in *Chadha*, the concurrent resolution involves a two-House legislative veto since it had to be approved by both the House and the Senate. Presentment, however, was not met because a concurrent resolution is not submitted for approval to the President.

The Court's reasoning in *Chadha* has been widely criticized. As Justice Powell wrote in a concurring opinion, the action taken by the House in that case might more properly have been characterized as being judicial rather than legislative in nature. Instead of adopting a general rule, the House had "made its own determination that [Chadha] did not comply with certain statutory criteria." 462 U.S. at 964-965. This type of action, in which an existing statutory rule is applied to the facts of a particular case, involves an adjudicatory function traditionally performed by the courts or by administrative agencies within the executive branch. The House's action was therefore unconstitutional, said Powell, not because it violated the Bicameralism and Presentment Clauses, but on structural grounds: Congress had impermissibly sought to aggrandize itself by "assum[ing] a judicial function in violation of the principle of separation of powers." Id. at 960. As Powell went on to explain, this usurpation "raises the very danger the Framers sought to avoid—the exercise of unchecked power" at the expense of individual rights, for Congress is not "subject to the procedural safeguards, such as the right to counsel and a hearing before an impartial tribunal, that are present when a court or an agency adjudicates individual rights." Id. at 966. And, unlike trial courts and executive agencies whose adjudicatory activities are ordinarily subject to judicial review, this exercise of judicial power by Congress was totally unchecked, for it was subject neither to review by the courts nor to a veto by the President.

In a dissenting opinion, Justice White likewise approached *Chadha* in structural or functional terms. However, he rejected Justice Powell's characterization of Congress's action as being judicial in nature, and instead seemed to agree with the majority that the legislative veto was employed here as part of Congress's lawmaking power. Yet in contrast to the majority, White did not find the text of Article I dispositive. While under Article I, no bill, order, or resolution may become law unless it has met bicameralism and presentment, it is not clear from the text that congressional action taken *pursuant to a properly enacted law*—as was the case with the House's "veto" in *Chadha*—must again satisfy these requirements. In White's view, since the Constitution "does not directly authorize or prohibit the legislative veto," it

326

was necessary to approach the question in functional terms, asking "whether the legislative veto is consistent with the purposes of Article I and the principles of separation of powers which are reflected in that Article and throughout the Constitution." 462 U.S. at 977-978. In White's eyes, the legislative veto was not inconsistent with the goal of the Bicameralism and Presentment Clauses, which was to "limit[] the methods for enacting *new* legislation," not to "restrain the scope of congressional authority pursuant to duly enacted law." 462 U.S. at 982 (emphasis supplied).

At the same time, Justice White acknowledged that under the principle of separation of powers, a legislative veto would be invalid in circumstances where it usurped or encroached upon the inherent functions of another branch. Though he did not regard this as being a problem in *Chadha*, he suggested that Congress could not use the legislative veto to impose "[a] legislative check on an inherently executive function, for example, that of initiating prosecutions. . . ." Id. at 1002. For similar reasons, Congress presumably could not use the legislative veto to prevent the judiciary from deciding a particular case. On the other hand, if the legislative veto were invoked to control the executive's or the judiciary's exercise of rulemaking authority delegated to it by Congress, Justice White would have found no separation of powers violation, for the function being interfered with was one that belonged to Congress in the first place. Thus, in Example 7-E above, White's functional separation of powers analysis would have allowed Congress to block the ICC's billboard regulations by concurrent resolution. The ICC's action constituted an exercise of legislative authority delegated to it by Congress rather than the performance of an inherently executive function.

This discussion highlights the markedly different results that may flow from a textual, as opposed to a structural or functional, approach to separation of powers. The former approach, adopted by the majority in *Chadha*, had the effect of invalidating all uses of the legislative veto, while the latter approach, at least as employed by Justice White, would have permitted Congress to use the device as a means of controlling the other branches' exercise of lawmaking authority delegated to them by Congress.

§7.4.3 The Administrative State

Many of the separation of powers issues that have reached the courts have involved the federal administrative state — i.e., the numerous agencies and commissions that Congress has created within the executive branch. Separation of powers questions have been triggered by the scope of authority given to these entities, and by congressional efforts to restrict the President's control over some executive agencies and commissions.

While the Constitution created the presidency and the vice-presidency, it did not establish any additional offices within the executive branch. That task has fallen to Congress, which, over the years, has used its enumerated powers to create a myriad of departments, commissions, offices, bureaus, and agencies within the executive branch, each charged with implementing or executing certain federal laws or programs.

These administrative agencies have frequently been endowed with both legislative and judicial authority. Though such a commingling of functions raises separation of powers concerns, we saw earlier that the Court has generally turned a blind eye toward Congress's delegation of its lawmaking authority to other branches, including the executive (see §7.4.1). The Court has likewise upheld federal statutes that permit executive branch agencies and commissions to exercise judicial power. In *Commodity Futures Trading Commission v. Schor*, 478 U.S. 833 (1986), the Court held that Congress could permit an executive commission to adjudicate federal and state law claims between commodities brokers and their clients even though the claims also fell within the Article III jurisdiction of the federal courts.

Separation of powers issues concerning the administrative state have likewise been triggered by congressional attempts to curtail the President's control over executive branch agencies. As the nation's chief executive, the President in theory oversees the hundreds of agencies that make up the federal bureaucracy. Yet Congress has from time to time sought to insulate certain executive branch agencies — i.e., so-called independent agencies — from presidential influence and control, either by limiting the President's role in the appointment process, or by restricting the President's ability to remove agency personnel from office. We turn now to a consideration of these appointment and removal issues.

§7.4.4 The Appointment of Federal Officers

Other than the President, the Vice-President, and members of Congress, all of whom are elected, everyone who works for the federal government is by one means or another appointed to his or her position. The question sometimes arises as to whether or not a particular official was appointed in a proper manner. The answer will hinge largely on how the position is classified. For these purposes, every nonelected federal official is deemed to be (1) a principal officer of the United States; (2) an inferior officer of the United States; or (3) a mere employee.

The Appointments Clause of Article II, §2, cl. 2 provides that *principal officers* must be appointed by the President "with the Advice and Consent of the Senate. . . ." However, the clause gives Congress a menu containing four options for the appointment of *inferior officers*. Congress may decide that inferior officers shall be appointed in the same way as principal officers — i.e., nominated by the President with confirmation by the Senate. Or, Congress may elect to "vest the Appointment of such inferior Officers, as they think proper,

in the President alone, in the Courts of Law, or in the Heads of Departments."
The Appointments Clause does not address or restrict the manner of appointing mere employees, sometimes also referred to as nonofficers.

Classifying Particular Government Positions

Since the permissible appointment options available to Congress depend on
whether the position involves a principal officer, an inferior officer, or a
mere employee, it is critical how the position in question is classified. The
Court has held that the term "officer" of the United States includes "any
appointee exercising significant authority pursuant to the laws of the United
States," *Buckley v. Valeo*, 424 U.S. 1, 127 (1976). The term "employee" covers
those "lesser functionaries" who are "subordinate to officers of the United
States. . . ." Id. at 126 n.162. These definitions, however, are so general that
they offer little guidance; they also do not address the difference between
principal and inferior officers. Indeed, the Justices have conceded that "[t]he
line between 'inferior' and 'principal' officers is one that is far from
clear. . . ." *Morrison v. Olson*, 487 U.S. 654, 671 (1988). The same is true
of the line that separates inferior officers from mere employees.

Ultimately, the difference between principal officers, inferior officers, and
employees turns on an assessment of the amount of authority attaching to the
position in question. While this is a difficult attribute to measure, the Court has
suggested that a number of factors may go into the assessment, including (1)
the nature and extent of the official's duties, and whether or not they include
policymaking functions; (2) the amount of independence and source of supervision — e.g., whether the official answers directly to the President, to a
principal officer, or to someone lower in the government hierarchy — and
(3) the position's tenure in terms of whether it is continuing, temporary, or
intermittent, and the circumstances under which the official may be removed.

The classification of government positions is relatively easy at the
extreme ends of the spectrum. For example, cabinet members like the attorney general and the secretary of state who head major departments of the
federal government and who answer solely to the President are clearly
principal officers. Not only do they exercise enormous power and have a
great deal of policymaking authority, but they are supervised directly by the
President. While cabinet members serve at the will and pleasure of the
President rather than for a fixed term, the insecurity of their tenure is
overshadowed by the importance of their duties and the fact that they are
not supervised by any other executive officer besides the President.

At the opposite extreme, those who work for the government in positions such as mail carriers, prison guards, and computer programmers are
mere employees. Those holding these jobs do not exercise significant
authority. They implement rather than make policy, and are ordinarily
supervised by persons far down in the executive hierarchy. Though these
positions are often permanent and subject to termination only for cause,

thus satisfying the third factor noted above, the lack of significant authority is dispositive. In a close case, however, the fact that a position is only temporary may be critical in placing it on the employee side of the line. See, e.g., *United States v. Germaine*, 99 U.S. 508, 511–512 (1879) (surgeon who was appointed by commissioner of pensions to examine pension applicants, and who was compensated at rate of $2 per exam, was employee rather than inferior officer since duties were not continuing and permanent).

In the middle ranges of the spectrum, the task of distinguishing between officers and inferior officers is often difficult. In these cases, the second factor may be critical. As the Court has observed, "the term 'inferior officer' connotes a relationship with some higher ranking officer or officers below the President: whether one is an 'inferior' officer depends on whether he has a superior" who is a principal officer. *Edmond v. United States*, 520 U.S. 651, 662 (1997). "'[I]nferior officers' are officers whose work is directed and supervised at some level by others who were appointed by presidential nomination with the advice and consent of the Senate." Id. at 663. In *Edmond*, the Court thus found that judges of the Coast Guard Court of Criminal Appeals, who are supervised by the judge advocate general and by the Court of Appeals for the Armed Forces, were inferior rather than principal officers because they "have no power to render a final decision on behalf of the United States unless permitted to do so by other executive officers." Id. at 665.

While the extent and source of supervision is of major importance in distinguishing between officers and inferior officers, the tenure factor may also play a decisive role, allowing someone who would otherwise be an officer to be deemed an inferior officer on account of the temporary nature of his or her position. See *United States v. Eaton*, 169 U.S. 331 (1898) (vice-consul appointed to perform functions of consul on temporary basis was inferior rather than principal officer even though Article II, §2 refers to "consuls" as being principal officers).

Example 7-F

Following a scandal in which U.S. customs agents were found to have accepted bribes from drug smugglers, a federal statute created the office of customs prosecutor. The customs prosecutor is authorized to investigate the U.S. Customs Service and to bring criminal proceedings against any customs agent found to have accepted a bribe. The statute provides that the customs prosecutor is to be appointed by the attorney general. Once appointed, the customs prosecutor is to continue in office until the attorney general certifies that the investigation and all related prosecutions have been completed. The customs prosecutor may be removed from office by the attorney general but only for cause. Is the appointment provision valid?

Explanation

If the customs prosecutor is a principal officer of the United States, the appointment provision is invalid since Article II, §2 specifies that principal officers must be nominated by the President and confirmed by the Senate; no other appointment option is available. On the other hand, if the customs prosecutor is an inferior officer, Congress had the right to vest the appointment in the attorney general, as head of the Justice Department. The appointment would likewise be valid if the customs prosecutor were a mere employee since the Constitution does not specify the means of appointing employees or nonofficers.

The duties of this position are far too significant to classify its holder as an employee. The question is thus whether the customs prosecutor is an officer, or an inferior officer. The power to investigate and prosecute crimes is considerable and involves a great deal of discretion. The customs prosecutor is appointed by the attorney general, a principal officer, but it is unclear whether the attorney general has authority to supervise the customs prosecutor's work. If such authority is lacking, it would appear that the customs prosecutor is not "inferior" to any executive branch officer. While the attorney general has the power to remove the customs prosecutor, this does not give the attorney general any real control over the office since removal may occur only for good cause.

On the other hand, the customs prosecutor is charged with investigating and prosecuting only a narrow range of crimes. Moreover, the position is not permanent and must terminate as soon as the task for which it was created has been accomplished. While this is a close case, the Court might conclude that because of the temporary nature of the position, the customs prosecutor is an inferior rather than a principal officer, and that the method of appointment selected by Congress was therefore valid. See *Morrison v. Olson*, 487 U.S. 654 (1988) (holding that an independent counsel was an inferior officer); *United States v. Nixon*, 418 U.S. 683, 694 (1974) (intimating that a special prosecutor was an inferior officer).

In the preceding example, if the position of customs prosecutor were permanent rather than temporary, there is a better chance that the customs prosecutor would qualify as a principal officer. In close cases like this, the tenure and permanence of the position may be determinative.

While there have not been many decisions addressing the question of whether a particular governmental official is a principal rather than an inferior officer, the Court has tended to resolve those disputes that have arisen by finding that the position in question falls into the inferior category. The Court has thus held that supervisors of elections, U.S. commissioners, postmasters first class, special prosecutors, and independent counsel are inferior rather than principal officers. The effect of these rulings is to give Congress expanded leeway in selecting the method of appointing such officers. In particular, it allows Congress to limit the President's powers by divesting the chief executive of any direct role in the appointment process. While Congress may, of course, choose to vest the appointment of an inferior officer in the President (with or without participation of the Senate), Congress can also bypass the President entirely and vest the appointment in a department head or in the federal courts. By selecting either of these latter options, Congress may seek to ensure that the position is filled by someone who is not beholden to the President and who will therefore enjoy a greater degree of independence from presidential influence and control. As we will see in §7.4.5, Congress may also promote such independence by placing restrictions on the President's ability to remove a particular officer.

Even if a government position, such as that of a federal judgeship, qualifies as being that of a principal officer, the President may be able to fill the position on a temporary basis, without Senate consent, by making a "recess appointment." Article II, §2, cl. 3 thus states that "the President shall have Power to fill up all Vacancies that may happen during the Recess of the Senate, by granting Commissions which shall expire at the End of their next Session." This power is one a President may seek to invoke to appoint someone for whom he has been unable to obtain Senate confirmation. Such recess appointments may last for as long as two years, depending on when the next Senate session ends. In 2004, President Bush invoked this power to unilaterally appoint a U.S. Court of Appeals judge for the Eleventh Circuit during an 11-day *intrasession* Senate break. A divided U.S. Court of Appeals upheld the President's action even though it was not an *intersession* appointment made during the break between the Senate's two-year sessions, the vacancy arose before the break in question, and the Senate had previously blocked that particular appointee's confirmation. *Evans v. Stephens*, 387 F.3d 1220 (11th Cir. 2004) (en banc), *cert. denied*, 544 U.S. 942 (2005).

Interbranch Appointments

If Congress wishes to use its control over the appointment process to create executive branch agencies that are truly independent of presidential control, it can bypass the President as well as the heads of departments and vest the appointment of inferior officers in the judicial branch. Since federal judges enjoy life tenure and may be removed only through impeachment — a process in which the President plays no role — such interbranch appointments are totally insulated from executive influence. Congress has resorted to this device on only a few occasions. Though interbranch appointments have been challenged on the ground that Congress may not authorize the courts to make appointments outside the judicial branch, the Supreme Court has rejected such objections on the ground that no such limitation appears in the Appointments Clause.

Nevertheless, the Court has suggested that the judicial appointment of inferior executive officers might be invalid if it would impair the constitutional functions of either branch, or if there is an "inherent incongruity" because the officer is to be appointed in a field where judges have no special knowledge or expertise. Thus, while the Court has upheld statutes providing for the judicial appointment of election supervisors, *Ex parte Siebold*, 100 U.S. 371 (1880), and prosecutors, *Morrison v. Olson*, 487 U.S. 654 (1988), the Court has suggested that there might be an incongruity problem if Congress permitted the federal courts to appoint officials in the Department of Agriculture or the Federal Energy Regulatory Commission, areas with which judges are likely to be unfamiliar. Id. at 676 & n.13.

Before leaving the subject of interbranch appointments, it is important to note that sometimes the executive appoints employees of other branches. For example, Article II, §2 specifies that "judges of the supreme Court" must be appointed by the President, with the advice and consent of the Senate. Moreover, Congress has occasionally authorized the President, either alone or with the approval of the Senate, to appoint officials deemed to be part of the legislative branch, including the comptroller general, the librarian of Congress, the architect of the capitol, and the public printer. See *Bowsher v. Synar*, 478 U.S. 714, 746 n.9 (1986) (Stevens, J., concurring).

Appointments Made by Congress

The Court's willingness to uphold interbranch appointments applies only to appointments that are made by the judiciary or the executive. Congress can not reserve for itself the authority to appoint officers of the United States. This conclusion flows directly from the language of the Appointments Clause. The menu of options contained in Article II, §2 simply does not include vesting the appointment of principal or inferior officers in Congress or in any of its members. The Founders were understandably unwilling to give Congress the power to both create new federal positions and then fill them with persons of Congress's own choosing. For Congress to so participate in the appointment of officers would violate separation of powers. Congress would be aggrandizing itself by usurping functions that the Constitution carefully assigned to the other branches.

Example 7-G

Suppose that a federal statute created the federal Commission on Smuggling. The commission is authorized to develop regulations governing the conduct of U.S. customs agents, and to impose sanctions upon any agents it finds to have been derelict in their duties. The commission consists of six members appointed as follows: (a) two are appointed by the President with the approval of both Houses of Congress; (b) two are appointed by the Speaker of the House of Representatives with the approval of both Houses of

Congress; and (c) two are appointed by the President pro tempore of the Senate with the approval of both Houses of Congress. The commission members serve a term of six years, during which time they may be removed from office only by impeachment. Are the appointment provisions valid?

Explanation

Given the substantial quasi-legislative and quasi-adjudicative duties of the commission, its members are clearly officers of the United States within the meaning of Article II, §2. There is a good argument that the commissioners are principal officers; in addition to possessing broad rulemaking and adjudicative authority, they do not appear to be subject to supervision or removal by any higher executive officials.

Yet, whether the commissioners are principal or merely inferior officers, none of the appointment modes is valid. Part (a) is improper because Article II, §2 allows presidential nominations to be approved only by the Senate; here, the House has improperly insinuated itself into the confirmation process. Parts (b) and (c) are also flawed, for even if the commissioners are inferior officers, none of the Article II, §2 menu options allows appointment by the President pro tempore of the Senate or by the Speaker of the House; any claim that the President pro tempore and the Speaker qualify as "heads of departments" would be unavailing, for, as the Court held in *United States v. Germaine*, 99 U.S. 508 (1879), this term refers to the heads of the major *executive branch* departments. This example is based upon *Buckley v. Valeo*, 424 U.S. 1 (1976) (invalidating appointment procedures for federal Election Commission).

The only time Congress may directly participate in the appointment process is if the position is a purely legislative one in the sense that it involves only the performance of investigatory, informative, or other tasks for Congress. In such a case, the appointee is not an officer of the United States, but rather an agent or employee of Congress. However, if such persons perform any duties of officers of the United States, their appointment would have to conform to Article II, §2.

It should be noted that Congress does not necessarily violate the Appointments Clause if it merely assigns additional duties to those who have already been properly appointed as officers of the United States. For example, Congress frequently creates councils and commissions, some or all of whose members are persons who currently hold other government positions. If the designated members are officers who were appointed to their existing positions in accordance with Article II, §2, there is no constitutional infirmity if Congress later gives them the additional duty of sitting on another council or commission. However, a person who was appointed as an inferior officer by the President alone, by the head of a department, or by the courts could not be named by Congress to a position whose duties involve those of a principal officer; any appointment as a principal officer may be made only by the President with the advice and consent of the Senate.

Setting Qualifications for Office

While Congress may not itself participate in the appointment of federal officers, Congress often specifies the qualifications of those who are eligible to hold a particular office, thereby limiting the discretion of the appointing authority. Congress might insist, for example, that a nine-member commission consist of no more than five persons from the same political party, that three members be licensed attorneys, that at least four members be women, and that one member be a state governor. Lest this example seem far-fetched, when Congress authorized the President to appoint the seven members of the United States Sentencing Commission with the advice and consent of the Senate, Congress required that at least three commissioners be federal judges selected after the President had considered a list of six judges recommended by the Judicial Conference of the United States, and that no more than four commissioners could belong to the same political party. *Mistretta v. United States*, 488 U.S. 361, 368 (1989). The Supreme Court upheld the constitutionality of this appointment procedure but without specifically addressing the limitations placed on the President's discretion. It is arguable that at some point, Congress might so circumscribe the discretion of the appointing authority that the appointment would for all practical purposes be one made by Congress itself, in violation of Article II. The Court has yet to address such a case.

§7.4.5 The Removal of Federal Officers

In contrast to the appointment process that is addressed in some detail by the Appointments Clause, the Constitution is almost completely silent on the question of who possesses the authority to remove federal officials from office. The extreme remedy of impeachment is covered by Articles I and II (see §7.6), but the Constitution nowhere addresses the process of removing officials under less egregious circumstances. While this issue might have been resolved by insisting that officers be removed in the same manner by which they were appointed — e.g., an official nominated by the President and confirmed by the Senate could be dismissed only by the President with the Senate's consent — the Court has never demanded such symmetry. In fact, under the developed case law, the attempt to use a symmetrical removal procedure would often be unconstitutional.

Because no textual provision of the Constitution addresses the question of removal other than in the impeachment context, the limitations that the Court has developed in this area involve structural or functional, rather than textual, applications of the principle of separation of powers.

Most of the issues involving the removal process have arisen out of efforts by Congress to restrict the President's power to dismiss executive branch officials. Without the ability to limit the President's removal authority it would be impossible for Congress to create independent agencies that operate free of partisan influence and executive control. While politics is a desirable ingredient in many areas of government activity, this is not always the case. For example, politics should normally play no role in the process of adjudication since a person's rights or duties under the law should not hinge on partisan considerations. To the extent that adjudicatory functions are performed by agencies within the executive branch, as they often are, it may therefore be critical that those who perform these duties not serve at the whim and pleasure of the President. Even when executive agencies exercise legislative power under rulemaking authority delegated by Congress, it may still be important to ensure the agencies' independence so as to prevent an excessive concentration of lawmaking power in the President.

Some have urged that placing limitations on the President's ability to remove officials within the executive branch violates separation of powers because it destroys the concept of a unitary executive in which "*all of the executive power*" resides in the hands of the President. See, e.g., *Morrison v. Olson*, 487 U.S. 654, 703-715 (1988) (Scalia, J., dissenting). However, the Court has rejected such an approach. Instead, it has sometimes allowed Congress to vest the removal power in persons or bodies other than the President, and has permitted Congress to limit the circumstances under which certain executive officials may be removed. Yet not all restrictions on the President's removal authority are valid.

Congressional Participation in the Removal Process

Congress has at times sought to reserve for itself a role in the removal of executive branch officials. The Court has flatly rejected these efforts, holding that it violates separation of powers for Congress to "draw to itself," other than through impeachment, "the power to remove or the right to participate in the exercise of that power." *Myers v. United States*, 272 U.S. 52, 161 (1926). If Congress were allowed to participate in the removal process, this "would, in practical terms, reserve in Congress control over the execution of the laws," for the officer in question might feel a need to comply with Congress's wishes, in effect giving Congress a veto power over executive action. *Bowsher v. Synar*, 478 U.S. 714, 726 (1986).

Example 7-H

Assume that, in Example 7-G above, Congress amended the law creating the federal Commission on Smuggling to provide that the commissioners shall be appointed by the President and confirmed by the Senate. During their six-year term of office, commissioners may be removed only by impeachment or by joint resolution of Congress. Are the appointment and removal provisions constitutional?

Explanation

The appointment provision is valid. Whether the commissioners are principal or merely inferior officers, Article II, §2 permits nomination by the President with confirmation by the Senate. The removal provision is invalid, however, insofar as it allows removal by joint resolution of Congress. A *joint resolution* requires approval by the House, the Senate, and the President. Congress has thus improperly reserved a role for itself in the removal process. See *Bowsher v. Synar*, supra (Congress may not reserve right to remove comptroller general by joint resolution, for comptroller general is an officer performing executive functions).

Separation of powers problems do not arise where Congress insists upon participating directly in the removal of legislative branch officials and agents. Either House of Congress or both Houses together may dismiss committee counsel, investigators, pages, and staff members who assist Congress in performing its legislative duties. Separation of powers concerns arise only when Congress attempts to participate in the removal of officials who perform executive or judicial functions, thereby creating a risk that Congress will usurp authority that belongs to another branch.

Other Interbranch Removals

While Congress is categorically barred from participating in the removal of officials located outside the legislative branch, the Court has sometimes upheld interbranch removal authority in other contexts where there is no realistic danger of usurpation or encroachment. In *Mistretta v. United States*, 488 U.S. 361 (1989), the Court thus ruled that separation of powers was not violated by a statute allowing the President to remove members of the U.S. Sentencing Commission for cause. Even though the commission is part of the judicial branch and some of its members are federal judges, since the commission does not perform any judicial duties, giving removal authority to the executive did not upset the balance of power among the branches by allowing the President to coerce judges in adjudicating cases.

Assigning Removal Authority to an Executive Official Other than the President

While Congress cannot participate directly in the removal of executive or judicial officers other than through impeachment, Congress can in other ways curtail the President's ability to remove executive officers. One possibility is to vest the authority to remove a particular official in some executive branch official other than the President. For example, federal law provides that "[e]ach assistant United States attorney is subject to removal by the Attorney General." 28 U.S.C. §542(b). If the President wanted to fire an assistant U.S. attorney, she could not dismiss that officer herself but would have to go through the attorney general. If the attorney general refused to comply with the President's wishes, the President would have to dismiss the attorney general and name a successor willing to carry out the President's wishes. By thus shielding front-line federal prosecutors from direct removal by the President, Congress has to a limited degree insulated federal law enforcement operations from executive or political control.

However, in certain situations it would violate separation of powers for Congress to deprive the President of the authority to dismiss a subordinate. The Court has recognized that some executive branch officials work so closely with the President that she must be able to terminate their services at will. *Morrison v. Olson*, 487 U.S. 654, 691 (1988). Any congressional interference with a President's ability to dismiss such officials would impermissibly encroach upon the integrity and independence of the executive branch. For example, it would probably be unconstitutional for Congress to prescribe that the President could dismiss the secretary of state only with the approval of the Vice-President.

Limiting the Executive's Grounds for Removal

Another avenue utilized by Congress to limit the President's removal power is to provide that a particular executive branch official may be removed only for cause. Restrictions of this type are often used in conjunction with the vesting of removal authority in someone other than the President. For example, the federal statute authorizing the appointment of independent counsel provides that "[a]n independent counsel . . . may be removed from office, other than by impeachment and conviction, only by the personal action of the Attorney General and only for good cause, physical or mental disability . . . , or any other condition that substantially impairs the performance of such independent counsel's duties." 28 U.S.C. §596(a)(1).

The Supreme Court has held that congressionally imposed restrictions on the grounds for removing executive officers are valid unless the nature of the position makes it "essential to the President's proper execution of his Article II powers" that the officer be "removable at will." *Morrison v. Olson*, supra, 487 U.S. at 691. At one time the Court suggested that "good cause"-type limitations on removal were valid only with respect to officers who perform quasi-legislative or quasi-judicial functions, as opposed to purely executive functions. However, in *Morrison*, the Court held that Congress could likewise restrict the grounds for removing independent counsel who perform the purely executive function of enforcing the criminal law. The critical question, said the Court, is not whether an office is characterized as "purely executive," but whether the "good cause" removal provision will "interfere with the President's exercise of the 'executive power' and his constitutionally appointed duty to 'take care that the laws be faithfully executed.' . . ." Id. at 689-690. As long as there are legitimate reasons for immunizing even a purely executive office from political influence, Congress may insist that the official be removable only for cause. Moreover, Congress may seek to ensure that the "good cause" limitation is not flouted by the executive, by providing for judicial review of the removal decision. Id. at 693 n.33.

Multiple Layers and Limited Grounds

In our previous examples, Congress acted to constrain the President's authority to remove an executive officer *either* by assigning removal authority to an executive official (whom the President could remove at will), or by leaving removal authority in the President's hands but limiting the grounds on which he could effect removal. Each of these mechanisms imposes only one level of protection against the President's removal authority, i.e., either a "good cause" restraint on what the President may do, or a "good cause" restraint on what someone other than the President may do, but over whom the President has unfettered dismissal authority. Thus, if the President believed there was good cause for removing an executive officer, the President, depending on the congressional constraint, could either terminate the individual himself, or unilaterally remove the subordinate who possessed the removal authority but refused to invoke it, replacing that subordinate with someone who would effect the removal. Under either of these scenarios, "only one level of protected tenure separated the President from an officer exercising executive power. It was the President — or a subordinate he could remove at will — who decided whether the officer's conduct merited removal under the good-cause standard." *Free Enterprise Fund v. Public Company Accounting Oversight Board*, 130 S. Ct. 3138, 3153 (2010).

Suppose that Congress now decides to combine these two mechanisms by first providing that members of an executive branch agency may be removed only for good cause, and second, by vesting removal authority in an executive agency whose members are removable by the President but only for specified good cause. This is what Congress did in creating the Public Company Accounting Oversight Board. Its members could be removed by the Securities and Exchange Commission, and only for good cause, while Commission members could be removed by the President, but again only for good cause. As a result, even if the President disagreed with the Commission's determination to terminate (or not terminate) a Board member, "he is powerless to intervene — unless that determination is so unreasonable as to constitute 'inefficiency, neglect of duty, or malfeasance in office'" on the Commission's part. Id. at 3154.

In *Free Enterprise Fund*, the Court held that use of this "dual for-cause standard" was unconstitutional, for it unduly impaired the President's authority as head of the executive branch. "By granting the Board executive power without the Executive's oversight, this Act subverts the President's ability to ensure that the laws are faithfully executed — as well as the public's ability to pass judgment on his efforts. The Act's restrictions are incompatible with the Constitution's separation of powers." Id. at 3155.

Prohibiting Removal Except by Impeachment

The most drastic step Congress might take to restrict the President's removal power would be to provide that an executive official shall remain in office for a specified period, during which time removal may occur only by impeachment. Congress might seek to accomplish the same thing in a less explicit way by failing to include any provision for the officer's removal. In either case, no one in the executive branch could remove the officer, even where good cause existed. If the President were unhappy with the officer's performance and the officer was unwilling to resign, the President's only option would be to ask Congress to effect the removal through impeachment. See §7.6.

The Supreme Court has not directly addressed the issue of whether Congress could strip the President and his subordinates of authority to remove an executive branch official for cause. In *Wiener v. United States*, 357 U.S. 349 (1958), the Court held that the President lacked the authority to remove members of the federal War Claims Commission when Congress had made no provision for their removal. President Eisenhower had removed the incumbent commissioners "for no reason other than that he preferred to have on that Commission men of his own choosing." Id. at 356. In declaring the removals improper, the Court held that a President has no constitutional right "to remove a member of an adjudicatory body like the War Claims Commission merely because he wanted his own appointees on such a Commission. . . ." Id. at 356. However, the Court was careful to note that this was not a case where the President had sought to remove the commissioners "for cause involving the rectitude of a member. . . ." Id. at 356. More recently, in Morrison v. Olson, 487 U.S. 654 (1988), the Court again implied that separation of powers might be violated if Congress sought to strip the President and his subordinates of the ability to remove executive officers even for cause. In Morrison, while Congress had barred the President from removing an independent counsel, the Court emphasized that because removal for "good cause" could still be effected by the Attorney General, "[t]his is not a case in which the power to remove an executive official has been completely stripped from the President, thus providing no means for the President to ensure the 'faithful execution' of the laws. . . . [T]he Executive, through the Attorney General, retains ample authority to ensure that the counsel is competently performing his or her statutory responsibilities in a manner that comports with the provisions of the Act." Id. at 692.

Example 7-I

Congress created the Disaster Claims Board to adjudicate claims for compensation filed by persons injured in a recent southern California earthquake. Members of the Board are appointed to three-year terms by the President with the advice and consent of the Senate. The statute makes no provision for removing members during their terms of office. May a newly inaugurated President nevertheless remove the Board members before their terms have expired?

Explanation

The failure of Congress to make any provision for removal may, under the circumstances, be inferred to mean that it did not want the President to be able to remove the Board members at will. The adjudicatory nature of the Board's functions suggests that it was intended to operate with impartiality, free of presidential influence and control. Therefore, if the President's only reason for wishing to dismiss the Board members was a desire to name appointees of his own, the President's action would be unconstitutional.

However, if Congress's silence were construed to bar the President from removing a Board member even for good cause, the limitation would probably be unconstitutional as an unwarranted encroachment on the President's Article II, §3 duty to "take Care that the Laws be faithfully executed." Thus, if the President's reason for removing the Board members was that they had been derelict in performing their duties, the President could constitutionally remove them from office.

Example 7-J

In Example 7-I, suppose that the statute creating the Disaster Claims Board had provided that Board members could be removed only for "good cause" and only by the local assistant U.S. Attorney. An assistant U.S. Attorney is removable by the Attorney General at will. Would this provision governing the removal of Disaster Claims Board members be constitutional?

Explanation

Congress may vest removal authority in an executive official other than the President so long as this does not unduly impair the President's executive authority. The provision here vests authority to remove Board members in an assistant U.S. Attorney and at the same time limits the grounds on which such a removal can be effected. However, because the assistant U.S. Attorney is removable at will by the Attorney General, who is in turn removable at will by the President, this case is less problematic than that presented by *Free Enterprise Fund*. There, even if the President believed there was good cause to terminate a Board member, if the Commission refused to do so, the President's hands were tied absent a separate showing of good cause for terminating the Commissioners. Here, by contrast, if a President firmly believes there is good cause to terminate a Board member, and the assistant U.S. Attorney refuses to do so, the President could ask his Attorney General to terminate the noncooperating assistant U.S. Attorney. If the Attorney General refused, the President could then replace that Attorney General by someone who was willing to carry out the President's wishes. Thus, the President in the end would not be forced to retain an executive official whom he believed there was good cause to dismiss, even though the process for effecting such a removal would be cumbersome and perhaps practically infeasible. A Court that was strongly protective of executive power might therefore strike down this scheme on the basis that it impermissibly interferes with the President's ability to execute the laws.

Appointment, Removal, and the Unitary Executive

In several recent decisions, the Court has signaled that it may take a much harder look at congressional restrictions on the President's ability to appoint and remove officials who perform federal executive functions. Specifically, the Court has suggested that Congress may violate separation of powers if it vests the duty of executing or enforcing federal laws in persons who are not subject to appointment and removal by the President. In *Printz v. United States*, 521 U.S. 898 (1997), the Court thus ruled that the Brady Handgun Violence Prevention Act unconstitutionally assigned to state and local law enforcement officials the task of conducting background checks on new gun buyers. The Brady Act not only violated principles of federalism by commandeering state officials to implement a federal regulatory program (see §5.6), but it also violated separation of powers by impairing the President's Article II, §3 duty to "take Care that the Laws" of the United States be executed. The Court said that because the Framers insisted upon "unity in the Federal Executive," federal laws must be executed by the President personally or by those over whom there is "meaningful Presidential control. . . ." Id. at 922. In an aside, the Court questioned whether such control "is possible without the power to appoint and remove" (id.), powers that the President of course lacks with respect to state and local officials.

A similar suggestion appeared a few years later in *Vermont Agency of Natural Resources v. United States ex rel. Stevens*, 529 U.S. 765 (2000), a case involving the federal False Claims Act (FCA). The FCA authorizes a private party — known as a "relator" — to bring a civil lawsuit on behalf of the United States against anyone who knowingly submits a false or fraudulent claim for payment to the federal government. If the relator wins, he or she receives a bounty consisting of a percentage of the amount recovered on behalf of the United States. The United States may, but is not required to, intervene as a plaintiff in the action. By authorizing these so-called qui tam suits, Congress in effect assigned private plaintiffs the responsibility for enforcing certain laws of the United States. In *Vermont Agency*, the Court held that the FCA did not authorize the specific suit that was involved there. However, the Court went out of its way to note that if the FCA had authorized the suit, there would then arise "the question of whether *qui tam* suits violate Article II, in particular the Appointments Clause of §2 and the 'take Care' Clause of §3." Id. at 788 n.8. Like the Brady Act struck down in *Printz*, the FCA assigns responsibility for executing certain federal laws to persons outside the executive branch over whom the President lacks the power of appointment or removal. Justice Stevens's dissent in *Vermont Agency* disputed the suggestion that *qui tam* actions violate Article II, based on the fact that they were commonplace at the time of the Founding and thus not incompatible with the Framers' understanding of the President's executive power. Id. at 801.

Printz and *Vermont Agency* thus cast doubt on congressional attempts to assign the duty of enforcing federal laws to persons outside the federal executive branch. In addition, however, they also raise doubt as to the constitutionality of the many independent agencies that Congress has created within the executive branch (see §7.4.3). These independent agencies are, by definition, insulated from any "meaningful Presidential control" since the President typically lacks the power either to appoint or to freely remove their members. It remains to be seen whether *Printz* and the less overt suggestion in *Vermont Agency* will be used by the Court to require that Congress place these agencies under more direct presidential control. Such a judicial ruling would greatly strengthen the power of the President vis-à-vis that of Congress.

§7.4.6 Congressional Exercise of Executive Power

One of the core principles of separation of powers, closely related to that which we have just discussed, is that Congress may not give to itself, its members, or its agents a role in the execution of the laws. In *The Federalist*, Madison repeated Montesquieu's warning that "[w]hen the legislative and executive powers are united in the same person or body . . . there can be no liberty, because apprehensions may arise lest *the same* monarch or senate should *enact* tyrannical laws to *execute* them in a tyrannical manner." *The Federalist No. 47*, at 303 (Clinton Rossiter ed., 1961).

We have already encountered this issue in a number of different settings. The principle was violated when Congress sought to appoint certain federal officers (see Example 7-G). It was likewise violated when Congress sought to participate in the removal of executive officers (see *Myers v. United States*, 272 U.S. 52 (1926), §7.4.5), for as the Court has said, "[t]o permit the execution of the laws to be vested in an officer answerable only to Congress would, in practical terms, reserve in Congress control over the execution of the laws." *Bowsher v. Synar*, 478 U.S. 714, 726 (1986). The same principle formed the basis for Justice Powell's objection to the legislative veto exercised in the *Chadha* case, for as Powell viewed the matter, the House was seeking to perform an adjudicatory function usually performed by executive agencies (or by the courts). *Immigration and Naturalization Service v. Chadha*, 462 U.S. 919, 959-967 (1983); see §7.4.2.

Congress has violated this separation of powers principle in other contexts as well. It has on occasion insisted that members or agents of Congress participate directly in executing the laws. Such efforts by Congress are unconstitutional, for they represent a legislative usurpation of authority that the Constitution has assigned to the executive branch. Thus, in *Bowsher v. Synar*, supra, the Court held that since the comptroller general is an officer of Congress, separation of powers precludes Congress from giving this officer a role in implementing the Balanced Budget and Emergency Deficit Control Act of 1985.

Example 7-K

Suppose that a federal statute authorizes the government to transfer operating control of the national parks to the states in which the parks are located. For the transfer to occur, the state must agree to administer the parks through a five-person National Park Commission, appointed by the governor; at least two of the five commissioners must be United States senators or representatives from the state. Is the statute valid?

Explanation

The statute is invalid because it permits members of Congress to help implement the federal law transferring control of the national parks to the states. The fact that the members of Congress who perform these duties are selected by state governors does not alter the critical fact that Congress is seeking to vest its members with a role in executing a federal law. If it is important that the states' management of the national parks be subject to federal oversight, the Constitution requires that this function be assigned to the federal executive branch, not to Congress. See *Metropolitan Washington Airport Authority v. Citizens for the Abatement of Aircraft Noise, Inc.*, 501 U.S. 252 (1991) (Congress could not transfer control over national airports to the states, subject to oversight by a board consisting of members of Congress, in part because Congress may not participate in the exercise of executive power).

Direct congressional involvement in the implementation or enforcement of federal laws may also violate the Incompatibility Clause of Article I, §6, cl. 2, which provides that "no Person holding any Office under the United States, shall be a Member of either House during his Continuance in Office." This clause would not pose an obstacle in Example 7-K, above, since the National Park Commission appointed by the governor involves a state rather than a federal office. However, the Incompatibility Clause would pose a problem if Congress insisted that one or more of its members be appointed to a *federal* executive office.

Example 7-L

Suppose that Congress passed the China-United States Friendship Act creating a China-United States Friendship Commission to administer scholarly, cultural, and artistic exchanges between the two countries. The statute provides that the commission shall be composed of eleven members appointed by the President, including two members of the Senate and two members of the House of Representatives. Is the commission constitutionally composed?

Explanation

The presence of four members of Congress on the commission poses several constitutional problems. First, the fact that Congress, through its members, is seeking to participate in implementing the China-United States Friendship Act violates structural principles of separation of powers, for this represents a legislative usurpation of and encroachment on the executive's assigned duty to execute the law.

In addition, there are textual separation of powers problems. Since the commissioners are probably inferior officers rather than mere employees, the appointment mechanism itself is proper, for the Appointments Clause allows Congress to vest the appointment of inferior officers in the President alone. The Incompatibility Clause, however, bars Congress from insisting that the President appoint four members of Congress to serve as inferior officers. See *Public Papers of the Presidents, Gerald R. Ford, 1975*, at 1718-1719 (1977) (stating that because of the Incompatibility Clause, members of Congress may serve only in an advisory capacity as nonvoting members of the Japan-United States Friendship Commission).

§7.4.7 Separation of Powers and the Judiciary

The principle of separation of powers is as applicable to the judicial branch as it is to the legislative and executive branches. We have already encountered several separation of powers issues that implicated the federal courts, including interbranch appointments (see §7.4.4) and interbranch removals (see §7.4.5). There are two other separation of powers concerns that are especially pertinent to the federal courts: (1) the judicial branch may not be assigned or allowed to perform tasks that are more appropriately undertaken by the other branches; and (2) Congress may not interfere with final judgments of the federal courts. We will briefly consider both of these issues.

Assigning Nonjudicial Duties to Federal Judges

The Supreme Court has held that federal judges may not be assigned executive or administrative duties of a nonjudicial nature if this would threaten the independence and integrity of the federal judiciary, or aggrandize it at the expense of the other branches. The Court has thus held that Congress may not authorize federal courts to review private claims against the government where the courts' decisions are then subject to review by executive officials, for the performance of such duties on behalf of the executive impairs the integrity of the judiciary as an independent branch. See *United States v. Ferreira*, 54 U.S. (13 How.) 40 (1852) (federal judicial power could not extend to adjudication of claims under 1819 treaty with Spain where Court's decision was subject to final review by secretary of treasury); *Hayburn's Case*, 2 U.S. (2 Dall.) 409 (1792) (suggesting that federal courts could not determine pensions for Revolutionary War veterans if those determinations were reviewable by secretary of war). The Court has likewise suggested that it would violate separation of powers to permit federal judges to dismiss a prosecutor from office while an investigation or court proceeding is underway, for the judicial performance of this administrative function would aggrandize the judiciary and encroach upon the executive's domain. See *Morrison v. Olson*, 487 U.S. 654, 682-683 (1988).

However, in keeping with its pragmatic, flexible approach to separation of powers issues, the modern Court has sustained federal laws that assign rulemaking or administrative duties to the federal courts. In *Mistretta v. United States*, 488 U.S. 361 (1989), the Justices held that Congress did not violate separation of powers when it created the U.S. Sentencing Commission within the judicial branch and gave the commission, some of whose members were federal judges, the duty of issuing federal sentencing guidelines. Similarly, in *Morrison v. Olson*, 487 U.S. 654 (1988), the Court rejected a separation of powers challenge to the Ethics in Government Act, which authorized a panel of federal judges to appoint, partially supervise, and terminate the office of the independent counsel when the duties of counsel are substantially complete. In both cases, the Court concluded that despite the nonjudicial nature of the duties assigned to federal judges, the judiciary had not upset the balance of power by usurping or encroaching on the authority of the other branches.

Interfering with Federal Court Judgments

The doctrine of separation of powers prohibits Congress from encroaching on the integrity of the judicial branch by retroactively commanding federal courts to reopen or reconsider final judgments already rendered. A critical attribute of the independent federal judiciary created by Article III is "the power, not merely to rule on cases, but to *decide* them, subject to review only by superior courts in the Article III hierarchy. . . ." *Plaut v. Spendthrift Farm, Inc.,* 514 U.S. 211, 218-219 (1995). Just as the decisions of Article III courts may not be made subject to review by officials of the executive branch (see *Hayburn's Case*), Congress is proscribed from expressing its disapproval of final federal court judgments by directing that they be set aside or reopened. Such a practice, which was once widespread among state legislatures in the years following the break with England, was expressly rejected by the Framers of the federal Constitution.

Example 7-M

Joe Smith filed suit under the federal Civil Rights Act against the Meechum Valve Company, alleging that the company had fired him because of his sexual orientation. The federal district court dismissed the action on the ground that the Civil Rights Act did not bar discrimination on the basis of sexual orientation. Two months after the case was dismissed, Congress amended the act to expressly bar discrimination based on sexual orientation; in doing so, Congress stated that the amendment was to apply to all pending lawsuits and to any suits that had been dismissed within the previous six months. Can Smith take advantage of the new amendment to the Civil Rights Act?

Explanation

If Smith had filed a timely appeal of the district court's judgment of dismissal so that his case was pending in the U.S. court of appeals at the time the Civil Rights Act was amended, Congress would not violate separation of powers by insisting that the amended statute be applied to Smith's suit even if this means reversing the judgment of the district court. Since no final judgment had yet been rendered, the court of appeals may constitutionally be required to decide the case according to the then-existing laws.

On the other hand, if Smith had opted not to appeal the district court's judgment of dismissal within the 30 days permitted by the federal rules, the judgment in his case would have become final by the time Congress amended the Civil Rights Act. It would then be unconstitutional to let Smith reopen the case, for this would amount to a congressional reversal of the final judgment of a federal court. Such a step would violate separation of powers; not only would Congress have aggrandized its own power vis-à-vis the judiciary, but Congress would also have trespassed significantly into the judicial domain. See *Plaut v. Spendthrift Farm, Inc.,* 514 U.S. 211 (1995).

Example 7-N

The federal Prison Litigation Reform Act (PLRA) established new standards for federal court injunctions in civil actions challenging prison conditions. Under the new standards, a federal court may issue prospective injunctive relief in such cases only if it finds that the relief "is narrowly drawn, extends no further than necessary to correct the violation of a [prisoner's] Federal right, and is the least intrusive means necessary to correct the violation. . . ." The same criteria apply to existing injunctive decrees. If an interested party moves to terminate an existing decree, the motion must be granted unless the court makes (or has made) findings that the relief meets the new standards set forth by PLRA. If the court does not rule on the motion within 90 days after it is filed, the existing injunction is automatically stayed until the court enters a final order ruling on the motion. Does this automatic stay provision of PLRA violate separation of powers principles?

Explanation

No. When a court grants prospective injunctive relief, it retains continuing supervisory jurisdiction over the case, allowing the court to modify the injunction at any time to reflect a change in circumstances, whether of law or of fact. Unlike a judgment awarding or denying monetary relief, a judgment granting injunctive relief is thus never "final" in the *Plaut* sense. PLRA's automatic stay provision reflects the changed legal circumstances governing prospective relief in the prison setting. Once a court has had 90 days to consider application of the new standards, the existing decree is no longer enforceable unless and until the court determines that injunctive relief is warranted by the new legal standards established by PLRA. Since the automatic stay provision does not reopen or interfere with a final judgment of an Article III court, it does not violate separation of powers. See *Miller v. French*, 530 U.S. 327 (2000) (upholding automatic stay provision of PLRA).

The Court in *Miller* noted that a distinct separation of powers issue might be raised if a congressionally imposed time constraint on judicial action were so severe as to impair the independence of the judiciary. Id. at 349. However, the Court had no occasion to decide this question because the lower courts did not address the sufficiency of the statutorily allotted time period. See id. at 352-353 & n.4 (Justices Souter and Ginsburg, concurring).

As we saw earlier, in Chapter 2, Congress is also prohibited from using its control over the jurisdiction of Article III courts to interfere with the judiciary's authority to decide cases that are otherwise properly before them. In *United States v. Klein*, 80 U.S. (13 Wall.) 128 (1872), Congress was found to have violated this principle by requiring the federal courts to dismiss any pending suits for the recovery of property seized during the Civil War where the claimant was shown to have been pardoned for participation in the rebellion. At the time this statute was passed, Klein had already won a judgment in the court of claims and the government's appeal was pending in the Supreme Court. The statute was unconstitutional both because it sought to tell the Supreme Court how to decide the case (i.e., against Klein), and because it sought to set aside a judgment that the court of claims had previously rendered in Klein's favor. See §2.2.2.

§7.5 WAR AND FOREIGN AFFAIRS

The fields of war and of foreign affairs have generated numerous separation of powers disputes between Congress and the President. This stems partly from the fact, noted in Chapter 5, that the Constitution is relatively inarticulate in defining the foreign affairs powers of the national government, thereby creating doubt as to where specific authority resides. In addition, some of the war and foreign affairs powers that are expressly delineated are shared jointly by Congress and the President, with the result that each branch may be in a position to claim that the particular authority belongs to it.

As we noted in §7.2, some of these separation of powers disputes touching on war and foreign relations have never been presented to the courts; others have been the basis for litigation but have not yet been definitely resolved. In this section we will consider some of the major disputes that have arisen between Congress and the President over which branch possesses certain powers in the war and foreign relations fields.

§7.5.1 Declaring War and Initiating Hostilities

Theory versus Practice

Article I, §8, cl. 11 of the Constitution states that "Congress shall have Power . . . To declare War. . . ." It was no accident that the Founders conferred this power on Congress rather than on the President. One of the familiar lessons of English history was the ease with which the Crown could lead the nation into war without the consent of Parliament. While the Constitution provides that "[t]he President shall be Commander in Chief of the Army and Navy of the United States," Art. II, §2, cl. 1, the power to declare war was deliberately assigned to Congress. As a further safeguard against the executive's being able to engage in war without the consent of the people, the Founders provided that no appropriation made by Congress "[t]o raise and support Armies . . . shall be for a longer Term than two

Years." Art. I, §8, cl. 12. This two-year limitation, which is unique to military appropriations, ensures that the President will have only a limited "war chest." In addition, it forces each new Congress to reassess the wisdom of continuing hostilities that may have been approved by a prior legislature.

While the Founders clearly envisioned that the decision to initiate war would rest solely with Congress, they also realized that there might be emergency situations requiring an immediate response that could not await congressional action. An early draft of Article I, §8 had proposed giving Congress the power to "*make* war"; Madison's notes on the federal Convention show that this was changed to "*declare* war" so as to "leav[e] to the Executive the power to repel sudden attacks." II *The Records of the Federal Convention of 1787*, at 318 (Max Farrand ed., 1966). The Founders thus contemplated that the decision to *initiate* war or hostilities was to be made by Congress; however, the President in an emergency could take action to *defend* the nation without having to obtain the prior approval of Congress.

This original understanding concerning the war power is reflected in the Supreme Court's decision in *The Prize Cases*, 67 U.S. (2 Black) 635 (1863), upholding President Lincoln's decision to declare a blockade of southern ports without a formal declaration of war from Congress. The Court explained that "[b]y the Constitution, Congress alone has the power to declare a national or foreign war," but "[i]f a war be made by invasion of a foreign nation, the President is not only authorized but bound to resist force by force. He does not initiate the war, but is bound to accept the challenge without waiting for any special legislative authority." Id. at 668.

During the nineteenth and twentieth centuries, this understanding of the respective authority of Congress and the President concerning the war power became more and more obscured. With increasing frequency, Presidents sent the armed forces into hostilities solely on their own initiative, even where there was no pretext of defending the United States against sudden attack. A 1967 Senate Foreign Relations Committee study found that "[t]he use of the armed forces against sovereign nations without authorization by Congress became common practice in the 20th century." *National Commitments*, S. Rep. No. 797, 90th Cong., 1st Sess. 12 (1967).

The War Powers Resolution

In 1973, Congress responded to this pattern of unilateral executive action by adopting the War Powers Resolution, 50 U.S.C. §§1541-1548. This joint resolution was enacted over President Nixon's veto. It declares that except in "a national emergency created by attack upon the United States, its territories or possessions, or its armed forces," American troops may be introduced into hostilities or situations where hostilities are imminent only pursuant to a declaration of war or other authorization from Congress. The War Powers

Resolution requires that "in every possible instance," the President must consult with Congress *before* sending troops into such hostile situations, and that he in any event notify Congress within 48 hours *after* troops have been introduced "into the territory, airspace, or waters of a foreign nation, while equipped for combat," unless the deployment is merely a "supply, replacement, repair, or training" operation. If troops have been sent into a hostile situation, the President is obligated to terminate their use within 60 to 90 days, unless Congress in the interim has declared war, specifically authorized the use of troops, or extended the 60-day period. By concurrent resolution — i.e., a two-House veto — Congress may direct the President to remove the troops even more quickly.

In vetoing the War Powers Resolution, President Nixon raised several constitutional objections to the measure. First, he charged that Congress could not "take away, by a mere legislative act, authorities which the President has properly exercised under the Constitution for almost 200 years." Second, Nixon claimed that the provision allowing Congress, by concurrent resolution, to direct the withdrawal of armed forces from hostile situations violated the Presentment Clause. *Public Papers of the Presidents, Richard M. Nixon, 1973,* at 893-895 (1975). In light of the Court's subsequent ruling in *Immigration and Naturalization Service v. Chadha,* 462 U.S. 919 (1983), striking down the legislative veto (see §7.4.2), Nixon's second objection to the War Powers Resolution was well taken. His first objection, however, was more dubious, for the Supreme Court has noted that separation of powers violations cannot be waived even if the branch whose authority was encroached upon may have acquiesced in the intrusion. See §7.1. Thus, even if over the years Congress had permitted the President to usurp the power to declare war, this would not permit the executive to claim that the power now belongs to the President. On the other hand, a longstanding practice may serve to aid the Court in defining the acceptable boundaries of congressional and executive authority.

Example 7-O

On March 1, at the request of the prime minister of France, the President of the United States sent armed forces to a French island in the Pacific that was under attack by Cuban military forces. The President gave Congress no advance warning of his decision to employ U.S. troops. The President later defended the decision on the ground that an 1882 treaty between the United States and France bound each nation to assist the other in repelling an attack upon its territory or possessions. Was the President's action constitutional?

Explanation

The President's unilateral decision to initiate hostilities with Cuban military forces in the Pacific would appear to have usurped Congress's authority to decide whether or not the United States should engage in war. Even if the Cuban attack on the French island was sudden and unexpected, it did not constitute a sudden attack on the United States, its territories, or armed forces. The situation therefore does not fall within the emergency exception contemplated by the Founders and recognized by the Court in *The Prize Cases*.

The President's reliance on the treaty with France is misplaced. If a treaty purported to give the President the authority unilaterally to commit the United States to war, the treaty would be unconstitutional. Article I, §8, cl. 11 assigns the power to declare war to Congress — i.e., to the House and the Senate. A treaty confirmed by the Senate alone cannot take the place of a congressional declaration of war. Many U.S. mutual defense treaties respect this fact. For example, the Southeast Asia Collective Defense Treaty, September 8, 1954, Art. 4, 6 U.S.T. 81, 83, committed the United States to respond to an attack upon one of the signatories "in accordance with its constitutional processes."

Under the War Powers Resolution, the President was required to notify Congress by March 3 that he had sent U.S. troops into hostilities. Moreover, whether or not he gave such notice, the 60-day clock for withdrawal began to run on that date. The President, therefore, had to remove the troops by May 2, unless "unavoidable military necessity" required an extra 30 days to effect a safe withdrawal, in which case U.S. armed forces would have had to be removed within 90 days — i.e., by June 1 — unless Congress in the interim had authorized the President's action or extended the period during which troops could remain there.

The Situation Today

Example 7-O assumed that the situation was to be handled according to the terms of the 1973 War Powers Resolution. However, the War Powers Resolution is a statutory, not a constitutional, regulation of executive power. Virtually every President since Richard Nixon has adopted Nixon's view that the War Powers Resolution is unconstitutional. As a result, the resolution has failed to end the dispute between Congress and the executive as to which branch possesses the power to declare war. All Presidents since President Nixon have denied that they were under any obligation either to notify Congress or to obtain a declaration of war before sending American troops into hostilities. As we noted in Chapter 3, efforts to challenge such presidential action in federal court have usually been rebuffed under the doctrines of standing, ripeness, or political question.

So long as the federal courts decline to become involved in cases challenging the President's unilateral introduction of armed forces into hostilities, this separation of powers dispute between the legislative and executive branches as to the locus of the power to initiate hostilities will continue to be resolved by the political branches themselves. As Justice Jackson wrote concerning presidential usurpation of congressional authority, "there was worldly wisdom in the maxim attributed to Napoleon that '[t]he tools belong to the man who can use them.' We may say that power . . . belongs in the hands of Congress, but only Congress itself can prevent power from slipping through its fingers." *Youngstown Sheet & Tube Co. v. Sawyer*, 343 U.S. 579, 654 (1952).

A Congress determined to protect the authority given to it under Article I, §8 has the means of doing so through its control over the purse strings. Congress may — as it did toward the end of the Vietnam War — refuse to appropriate new funds to support a "presidential war"; Congress may also bar the further expenditure of funds that have already been appropriated. Should a President flout these restrictions, a resolute Congress could invoke its ultimate power of impeachment.

§7.5.2 Treaties and Executive Agreements

The President may enter into international compacts either through treaties or executive agreements. See §§5.5.2, 5.5.3. As we have previously noted, a treaty requires the advice and consent of the Senate, while an executive agreement does not. A number of separation of powers issues may arise concerning treaties and executive agreements.

The Permissible Subject Matter of Treaties

If a President enjoys strong support in the Senate but lacks a majority in the House, the President may be inclined to use a treaty to accomplish a particular objective rather than seek legislation from Congress. This raises the question of to what extent a treaty may serve as a substitute for a statute.

Example 7-P

Suppose that federal law imposes a quota on the number of Canadian immigrants who may apply for United States citizenship each year. If the President wishes to increase this quota, she could seek legislation to this effect from Congress. However, if a majority of the House of Representatives is opposed to the President's plan, a bill to increase the Canadian quota would fail. Could the President instead accomplish her objective by invoking the treaty power?

Explanation

If the President has the support of two thirds of the Senate, a treaty with Canada increasing the quota would win Senate ratification. Yet should the President decide to proceed by treaty, rather than by seeking new legislation from Congress, the House of Representatives will have been completely shut out of the process. This is troubling in light of the fact that Article I, §8, cl. 4 gives *Congress* the power "[to] establish an uniform Rule of Naturalization"; by depriving the House of any role whatsoever in changing this law, the President has arguably violated the principle of separation of powers.

As intuitively appealing as this argument may be, it will likely fail. If the argument were sound, a great many treaties would be invalid, for they deal with matters that also fall within the scope of Congress's legislative powers under Article I. The fact is that treaties frequently operate as a substitute for congressional legislation. This overlap in subject matter is suggested by the fact that, on occasion, after a President has failed to win ratification of a treaty from the requisite two thirds of the Senate, the executive has achieved the same goal through a statute or joint resolution that needs only a simple majority in each House. The potential overlap is also evident from the fact that treaties and statutes sometimes conflict with one another, a phenomenon that could not occur if the two operated in mutually exclusive realms. The Court has never held that a treaty is invalid simply because it governs an area that Congress could have regulated under one of its enumerated powers. See *Edwards v. Carter*, 580 F.2d 1055 (D.C. Cir.), *cert. denied*, 436 U.S. 907 (1978) (treaty transferring property to Panama was valid even though Article IV, §3 expressly gives Congress the power to dispose of property belonging to the United States).

Yet a good argument can be made that some functions that the Constitution has assigned to Congress cannot be performed by treaty, at least in the absence of congressional authorization. For example, Article I, §9, cl. 7 states that "[n]o money shall be drawn from the Treasury, but in Consequence of Appropriations made by Law"; a treaty that sought to appropriate funds without an appropriation by Congress would likely violate this textual limitation. Similarly, a treaty that purported to make certain conduct a crime would probably violate the Due Process Clause of the Fifth Amendment; that clause was intended to incorporate the Magna Carta's prohibition against the Crown's depriving a person of life, liberty, or property except according to the common law or pursuant to an act of Parliament. See *Davidson v. New Orleans*, 96 U.S. 97, 101-102 (1878). It has likewise been argued that a treaty may not substitute for a congressional declaration of war, for this particular power — unlike the power over naturalization considered in Example 7-P — was given to Congress in order to prevent the President from taking the nation into war without the people's consent. To permit the President and the Senate alone to declare war would circumvent a vital check on the war power.

Abrogating Treaties

Once a treaty has been formally made, the question has sometimes arisen as to which of the political branches has the power to terminate the treaty. May the President terminate a treaty unilaterally, or is the consent of the Senate and perhaps the House also required?

Example 7-Q

In 1978, when President Carter recognized the People's Republic of China (Peking) as the sole government of China, he announced that he was terminating the 1954 Mutual Defense Treaty between the United States and the Republic of China (Taiwan). Members of Congress filed suit in federal court challenging the President's action, claiming that a President may abrogate a treaty only with the consent of two thirds of the Senate or a majority of both Houses of Congress. Was the President's action constitutional?

Explanation

Though Article II, §2, cl. 2 defines the procedure for making treaties, the Constitution is silent on the question of how a treaty may be terminated. One might contend that the procedure employed to abrogate a treaty should mirror that used to enter into a treaty. On the other hand, it is arguable that the Constitution's failure to require any Senate or congressional approval for the abrogation of a treaty means that this authority rests with the President, as part of the executive power. Historically, the United States has terminated treaties in a variety of ways, including by statute directing the President to send notice of termination; by statute without separate presidential notice; by the President with the approval of both Houses of Congress; by the President with the consent of the Senate; and by the President alone.

In *Goldwater v. Carter*, 444 U.S. 996 (1979), the Supreme Court dismissed a challenge to President Carter's unilateral termination of the 1954 treaty with Taiwan, ruling that the case was not justiciable. Of the six Justices who voted to dismiss the case, four concluded that the issue of how a treaty may be abrogated poses a political question, another Justice found that the challenge was not ripe, and the sixth Justice did not disclose his reasoning. The issue thus remains an open one, to be resolved by the political branches themselves until such time as the Court may choose to resolve it.

A related issue, which should not be confused with that of formally terminating a treaty, arises when a statute enacted by Congress conflicts with a prior treaty. The Supremacy Clause of Article VI provides that treaties and acts of Congress are both "the supreme Law of the Land." See §5.5.2. If the federal government passes a statute that is contrary to the terms of an earlier treaty, is the treaty still binding?

Example 7-R

In our prior Example 7-Q, suppose that while the 1954 Mutual Defense Treaty with the Republic of China (Taiwan) was still in effect, Congress approved and the President signed a bill providing that under no circumstances may the United States use its armed forces to defend Taiwan. Is the law valid in light of the fact that the 1954 treaty committed the United States to protect the Republic of China in the event of attack?

Explanation

Since under the Supremacy Clause treaties enjoy the same status as acts of Congress, the principle that applies when two acts of Congress conflict with one another also governs where an act of Congress conflicts with a treaty — i.e., "the last expression of the sovereign will must control." *Chinese Exclusion Case*, 130 U.S. 581, 600 (1889). See §5.5.2. It was on this basis that in Example 7-P the treaty increasing the quota for Canadian immigrants prevailed over the prior act of Congress.

Here, the statute barring use of American troops to defend Taiwan did not formally terminate the 1954 treaty, but to the extent that the two conflict, the statute, as the more recent enactment, will prevail. While the act of Congress thus trumps the treaty for domestic purposes, this de facto repudiation of the treaty may have repercussions for the United States under international law.

By the same reasoning, if a treaty conflicts with a prior act of Congress — as was the case in Example 7-P — the treaty will control.

Executive Agreements as a Substitute for Treaties

We noted earlier that the President can reach international accords either by treaty or by executive agreement. This very choice raises a separation of powers issue concerning the extent to which the White House is free to employ executive agreements instead of treaties as a means of excluding the Senate from the process. Since a treaty is effective only if ratified by two thirds of the Senate, whereas an executive agreement does not need the approval of anyone in the legislative branch, Presidents may prefer executive agreements over treaties for a number of reasons. First, executive agreements can take effect even in the face of Senate opposition that would doom a treaty. Second, even where adequate Senate support may exist, executive agreements can take effect immediately without the long delay that sometimes accompanies ratification of a treaty. Yet, to the extent that the Framers viewed the Senate as a critical check against excessive foreign entanglements, and not merely as a procedural hurdle to be circumvented, the President's use of executive agreements to bypass the Senate may raise serious separation of powers concerns.

This constitutional issue does not arise as frequently as one might expect. There are practical considerations that discourage Presidents from using executive agreements wholly to ignore Congress. For one thing, if the accord is one that will need to be implemented through legislation or that will require the appropriation of funds, the President risks alienating Congress by excluding the Senate from the process. In addition, by ignoring the House and Senate, a President takes the risk that Congress will respond by passing a law that overrides the executive agreement or requires that it be renegotiated. See *Dames & Moore v. Regan*, 453 U.S. 654, 688 n.13 (1981) (noting Congress's rejection of an executive agreement with Czechoslovakia).

These practical deterrents to executive agreements do not operate in all cases. Nor will use of such an agreement always trigger separation of powers concerns. If an executive agreement is employed as a means of exercising powers that the President independently possesses under Article II, constitutional difficulties are unlikely to arise. For where the power is one that the Constitution has assigned to the President, the decision to exercise that authority without involving the Senate neither encroaches on the Senate's power nor aggrandizes the executive domain.

Example 7-S

May the President enter into an executive agreement with France to conduct joint naval exercises in the Pacific or to designate the location of a U.S. consulate in France?

Explanation

Since Article II, §2 designates the President as "Commander in Chief of the Army and Navy," she possesses the independent power to arrange for naval exercises. The President is accordingly free to exercise this power through an executive agreement rather than through a treaty that would give the Senate the ability to block her action. The President has neither usurped the Senate's authority nor aggrandized the executive sphere.

The President would likewise be justified in using an executive agreement rather than a treaty to designate the location of a U.S. embassy abroad. The authority to recognize foreign governments and establish diplomatic relations with them is included in the President's Article II, §3 power to "receive Ambassadors and other public Ministers. . . ." The executive thus has discretion to decide whether or not this authority will be exercised in a manner that gives the Senate a consenting role.

For similar reasons, executive agreements that implement federal statutes or treaties seldom present separation of powers problems. It is the President's Article II duty to execute the laws and treaties of the United States. In such cases, if the President elects to implement a statute or treaty through an executive agreement, there is no danger of usurping the Senate's authority, for the Senate has already played its constitutional role in this process by having approved the statute or treaty being implemented. Some statutes and treaties expressly state that they may be implemented through an executive agreement. Even where such authorization is lacking, the use of an executive agreement may be appropriate. Thus, if Congress passes a law giving the President authority to set postal rates with foreign countries, the President could legitimately employ an executive agreement for these purposes whether or not the law specified the manner of implementation.

Executive agreements are most likely to raise separation of powers concerns when they neither represent an exercise of one of the President's Article II powers nor involve the implementation of a specific statute or treaty. In these cases, there is a danger that the President is using the executive agreement route to usurp Congress's role in the lawmaking process or the Senate's role in approving treaties. Executive agreements of this type, especially if they have a major domestic impact, may be invalid unless Congress has expressly or impliedly authorized their use. With such authorization, however, the use of the executive agreement route is valid as an exercise of lawmaking authority delegated to the President by Congress.

Example 7-T

The President entered into an executive agreement with Mexico that allows fruits and vegetables grown in Mexico to be imported into the United States and sold here, even if they do not meet pesticide standards set by state law. If a wholesale fruit seller in Arizona is prosecuted for selling Mexican-grown tomatoes that do not comply with an Arizona pesticide law, may the seller defend the action on the ground that the President's executive agreement bars enforcement of the state law?

Explanation

Since a valid executive agreement preempts conflicting state law, *United States v. Pink*, 315 U.S. 203 (1942) (see §5.5.3), the question is whether this executive agreement is valid. The state might argue that the agreement exceeded the President's constitutional authority. The agreement in effect regulates interstate and foreign commerce, an area that Article I, §8, cl. 3 assigns to Congress, not the President. The state thus has a good argument that the executive agreement violates separation of powers by encroaching on Congress's sphere of authority. As such, the executive agreement is invalid and cannot displace state law.

The outcome would be different if the agreement had been made to carry out a federal statute or treaty, or if Congress had authorized the President to enter into such agreements. For example, if the Senate had previously ratified a treaty with Mexico under which each country agreed to encourage the exchange of agricultural produce, the agreement would likely have been a valid exercise of the President's Article II duty to implement the laws and treaties of the United States. Without such a treaty, however, and absent an act of Congress authorizing the President to enter into the accord, the agreement is probably unconstitutional.

The probable invalidity of the executive agreement described in Example 7-T is supported by the decision in *Dames & Moore v. Regan*, 453 U.S. 654 (1981). The Court there upheld an executive agreement by which President Carter, to settle the Iran hostage crisis, suspended all lawsuits against Iran that were pending in American courts and nullified all pending attachments of Iranian assets. While the Iranian accord resolved a major international crisis, it also had the severe domestic impact of totally displacing contract, tort, and other state law claims that private parties had against Iran. In upholding the agreement, the Court stated that "crucial to our decision" was the fact that Congress had expressly or impliedly approved and acquiesced in the domestic aspects of the accord. Id. at 680, 688. This strongly suggests that absent such legislative approval, the agreement with Iran would have violated separation of powers.

The *Dames & Moore* Court acknowledged that "the President does have some measure of power to enter into executive agreements without obtaining the advice and consent of the Senate." Id. at 682 (citing *United States v. Pink*, 315 U.S. 203 (1942)). However, as the Court noted, the executive agreement in *Pink* settling certain claims with Soviet Russia was made in conjunction with the President's formal "recognition of the Soviet Government, [and] the establishment of diplomatic relations with it." 315 U.S. at 223. The agreement with Russia thus involved an exercise of the President's Article II, §3 recognition power, and therefore did not need to be founded

359

on a delegation of authority from Congress. No similar executive power could be invoked to sustain the agreement with Iran, nor could it be defended on the basis that it was implementing a statute or treaty. It was therefore critical that Congress had expressed its approval for the Iran hostage agreement.

The *Dames & Moore* decision helps to resolve the anomaly that executive agreements trump conflicting state law even though such agreements are not mentioned in the Supremacy Clause. The Framers were certainly aware of the fact that international accords did not always take the form of treaties. This is evident from Article I, §10, which bars states from entering into "any Treaty, Alliance, or Confederation," but allows them to enter into an "Agreement or Compact . . . with a foreign Power" if Congress consents. Since the federal government is presumably allowed to enter into any of these various accords, why were only treaties mentioned in the Supremacy Clause? A possible explanation for this omission is that the Framers perhaps did not expect executive agreements to be used in ways that would displace state law. In other words, they may have thought that such agreements would be limited to diplomatic and overseas matters, and that any accord having a significant domestic impact would take the form of a treaty. If this surmise is correct, *Dames & Moore*'s reluctance to recognize a blanket power to use executive agreements in lieu of treaties squares with the Framers' intent. In other words, except in those limited situations where an executive agreement can be defended as an exercise of one of the President's Article II powers, international accords that will conflict with state law may be valid only if they are made pursuant to authority delegated by Congress. See *American Insurance Association v. Garamendi*, 539 U.S. 396 (2003) (holding that President Clinton's Executive Agreement with Germany preempted a conflicting California statute where the agreement fell squarely within President's Article II power to conduct foreign relations).

§7.6 IMPEACHMENT

Congress's power of impeachment is probably the strongest weapon possessed by any branch of the federal government for checking and restraining the actions of a coordinate branch. Through the impeachment process, Congress can force the removal from office of the President, the Vice-President, Justices of the Supreme Court, lower federal court judges, and any other officer of the United States. Yet, the impeachment weapon, for all its power, has been used sparingly. During the first 200 years of the nation's history, no President, Vice-President, cabinet official, or Supreme Court Justice was ever removed from office by impeachment. In all, fewer than a dozen removals have occurred, all involving lower federal court judges.

The impeachment process is described at several places in the Constitution. Article II, §4 states that "The President, Vice President and all civil Officers of the United States, shall be removed from Office on Impeachment for, and Conviction of, Treason, Bribery, or other high Crimes and Misdemeanors." It is important to distinguish between impeachment and conviction; only the latter results in an official being removed from office. Presidents Andrew Johnson and Bill Clinton, and Associate Justice Samuel Chase, were all impeached by the House of Representatives, but none were removed from office because the Senate failed to convict them of the charges brought by the House. Article I, §2 provides that "The House of Representatives . . . shall have the sole Power of Impeachment." If the House votes out articles of impeachment against an official, the official will be tried by the Senate. The officer will be removed from office only if two thirds of the Senators vote to convict. Art. I, §3, cl. 6. In the impeachment process, the House plays a role similar to that of the grand jury in a criminal case, while the Senate sits as the equivalent of a petit jury. During the Senate trial, members of the House serve as prosecutors. If the President of the United States is being tried, the Chief Justice presides over the trial; otherwise, the impeachment process rests entirely in the hands of Congress.

It is generally accepted that the Framers did not intend impeachable offenses to be limited to conduct that is criminally punishable. In 1804, Associate Justice Chase was impeached for engaging in intemperate and partisan criticism of the Republican Party while on the bench, conduct that was surely not criminal. On the other hand, not every crime would necessarily constitute a basis for impeachment. The "high Crimes and Misdemeanors" for which impeachment may occur involve conduct that entails an abuse of power or a serious breach of trust, or that in some other way demonstrates an official's unsuitability for office — whether or not the conduct is criminal. The goal of impeachment is not punishment but "removal from Office." If the conduct that led to an impeachment conviction happens also to be criminal, Article I, §3 makes clear that the official may be criminally prosecuted: "the Party convicted shall nevertheless be liable and subject to Indictment, Trial, Judgment and Punishment, according to Law." Still, the wrongs that may be a basis for impeachment will not always overlap with those wrongs that are punishable as crimes.

The Constitution fails to answer many questions concerning the impeachment process. There is no textual definition of "high Crimes and Misdemeanors." Nor does the Constitution specify exactly what procedures the House and the Senate are to follow in conducting an impeachment proceeding. However, these questions are unlikely to be resolved by the courts. In *Nixon v. United States*, 506 U.S. 224 (1993), the Supreme Court strongly suggested that issues arising out of the impeachment process involve political questions that are to be resolved by Congress rather than by the judiciary.

The *Nixon* case involved a suit brought by U.S. District Judge Walter Nixon after he was impeached by the House, convicted by the Senate, and removed from office. Nixon objected that the procedure followed by the Senate was unconstitutional. Under Senate Rule XI, Nixon was tried by a Senate committee rather than by the full Senate. A transcript of the committee hearing and a committee report were presented to the full Senate, which, after hearing oral argument, voted to convict Nixon. Nixon claimed that the trial should have taken place before the full Senate. He based his argument on Article I, §3, cl. 6, which states that "[t]he *Senate* shall have the *sole* Power to try all Impeachments" (emphasis supplied). The highlighted words in this clause, said Nixon, require a trial before the full Senate. The Supreme Court rejected the challenge on the ground that the question was a political one.

Though the issue presented in *Nixon* was the narrow one of whether an impeachment trial may be conducted before a Senate committee instead of the full Senate, the Court's rejection of the challenge was couched in broad terms that suggest that any challenge to the impeachment process will meet a similar fate. Chief Justice Rehnquist's opinion for the Court stated that "[t]he parties do not offer evidence of a single word in the history of the Constitutional Convention or in contemporary commentary that even alludes to the possibility of judicial review in the context of the impeachment powers." 506 U.S. at 233. The Chief Justice also noted that the Framers had rejected the idea of placing the impeachment power in the federal judiciary out of fear that the Court lacked the fortitude, the credibility, and the numbers to exercise such "awful discretion." Id. at 234. In addition, said Rehnquist, "lack of finality and the difficulty of fashioning relief counsel against justiciability," id. at 236; for once the Senate has removed an official and a successor has been chosen, it will often be difficult for a court to order reinstatement. These objections to judicial intervention apply to every impeachment challenge, not just to the objection raised by Judge Nixon. It is therefore not surprising that Justices White and Blackmun, in their concurring opinion, characterized the majority as having ruled that the impeachment power is "one of the very few areas of legislative authority immune from any judicial review." Id. at 244.

§7.7 THE SPEECH OR DEBATE CLAUSE

The Speech or Debate Clause of Article I, §6, cl. 1 shields Senators and Representatives from criminal and civil liability by providing that "for any Speech or Debate in either House, they shall not be questioned in any other Place." This clause mirrors a nearly identical guarantee found in the English Bill of Rights of 1689. As the Supreme Court has noted,

"Behind these simple phrases lies a history of conflict between the Commons and the Tudor and Stuart monarchs during which successive monarchs utilized the criminal and civil law to suppress and intimidate critical legislators." *Johnson v. United States*, 383 U.S. 169, 178 (1966). The Speech or Debate Clause protects members of Congress, as well as their aides and employees, from civil and criminal actions and from proceedings instituted before executive branch agencies. The privilege extends to proceedings brought by private parties as well as by government officials. When the clause applies, it confers an absolute privilege — i.e., it protects members even if they acted with malice or under circumstances where it may have been clear that their conduct was unlawful.

While the privilege conferred by the Speech or Debate Clause is absolute, it does not apply to all actions taken by Senators and Representatives. Because the purpose of the clause is to insure the independence and integrity of the legislative branch, members of Congress are shielded only for so-called legislative acts — i.e., actions that are an essential part of the legislative process. In addition to speeches and debates on the floor of Congress, other legislative acts shielded by the clause include introducing bills, voting in Congress or in committee, utterances made in committee hearings and reports, and statements printed in the *Congressional Record*. However, other conduct may not be protected.

Example 7-U

Senator Fitzgerald has been indicted for bribery and income tax evasion by the Justice Department. The Senator is charged with receiving and failing to report a $25,000 payment from Tim Clancy, an Irish immigrant, in exchange for the Senator's promise to introduce a bill granting Clancy U.S. citizenship. The senator has moved to quash the indictment on the ground that the Speech or Debate Clause bars the government from prosecuting him. Should the motion be granted?

Explanation

Introducing a bill in Congress is a legislative act that is immunized by the Speech or Debate Clause. To the extent that the government's suit depends on proving such conduct on the senator's part, the indictment would have to be quashed. However, if the government can prove its case without relying on any legislative acts, the suit may continue. Thus, on the bribery count, the government may need to prove no more than that the senator *promised* to introduce a bill on Clancy's behalf; the promise, as opposed to the act of introducing a bill, is not a legislative act, and is therefore not shielded by the clause. On the income tax evasion count, there appears to be no need for the government to prove any legislative acts on the senator's part. The government's case could be proved by simply showing that the senator received $25,000 from Clancy and that the payment was not reported on the senator's federal income tax return. See *United States v. Helstoski*, 442 U.S. 477 (1979); *United States v. Brewster*, 408 U.S. 501 (1972).

As this example suggests, the Court has tended to read the Speech or Debate Clause narrowly. Thus, while the clause would shield a member from a libel suit based on statements made in Congress and/or printed in the *Congressional Record*, a libel action may be brought against the member of Congress if those statements are then reprinted and circulated in a newsletter. The publication of a newsletter is not a legislative act shielded by the Speech or Debate Clause. *Hutchinson v. Proxmire*, 443 U.S. 111 (1979).

If members of Congress are shielded from lawsuits involving legislative acts on their part, how is it possible to bring an action challenging the constitutionality of an act of Congress? The Speech or Debate Clause would bar a suit against a senator or representative to enjoin him or her from voting for an allegedly unconstitutional measure, or to collect damages for his or her having already adopted such a law. However, to challenge the validity of a federal statute it is unnecessary to sue a member of Congress. Rather, suit is brought against the executive branch official charged with implementing the particular law; that official may be sued for injunctive relief and may also be liable for damages (see §7.8.1).

The Speech or Debate Clause poses a more serious obstacle where one seeks to challenge some action by Congress other than the enactment of a statute. Assuming the action in question is taken by Congress without the participation of anyone from the executive branch, it may be more difficult to get around the bar of the Speech or Debate Clause. Yet creative litigants have sometimes managed to do so.

Example 7-V

Adam Clayton Powell was reelected to the U.S. House of Representatives from New York but the House voted under Article I, §5, cl. 1 to exclude him, charging that he had committed various improprieties while previously a member of Congress. Powell sued in federal court to enjoin the House from denying him his seat. Named as defendants were five members of the House, and three House employees — the clerk, the sergeant-at-arms, and the doorkeeper; the employees were sued for having refused to extend to Powell the services and pay to which he was entitled as a duly elected congressman. Is the suit barred by the Speech or Debate Clause?

Explanation

The members of Congress must probably be dismissed from the suit because voting on whether to exclude a member likely qualifies as a legislative act that is shielded by the Speech or Debate Clause. The three House employees are protected by the clause only to the extent that they, too, were performing a legislative act. However, unlike the defendant House members, the House employees are not being sued for having engaged in the legislative act of voting. Instead, the suit against them arises from their having implemented the House's exclusion action through refusing to provide services and pay to Powell. This conduct on their part does not involve a legislative act, anymore than it would if a member of Congress had refused to extend these services to Powell. As a result, the suit against the three House employees is not barred by the Speech or Debate Clause. If Powell wins his suit against them, an injunction will allow him to take his seat and collect his pay, thereby effectively nullifying the House's decision to exclude him. See *Powell v. McCormack*, 395 U.S. 486 (1969) (even if suit for wrongful exclusion may not be brought against House members, suit may proceed against House employees when their conduct does not involve a legislative act); *Gravel v. United States*, 408 U.S. 606, 616-621 (1972) (explaining *Powell*).

§7.8 EXECUTIVE IMMUNITY AND EXECUTIVE PRIVILEGE

There is no textual provision comparable to the Speech or Debate Clause that protects the executive branch against direct intrusions from the other branches. However, the Supreme Court has nonetheless recognized the existence of such a shield for executive branch officials as being implicit in the structure of the Constitution. Without some insulation from interference by the coordinate branches, the executive might not be able to perform its assigned functions in an independent and competent manner. These judicially created protections are of two types:

- Immunity from suit; and
- Privilege against compelled disclosure of information.

§7.8.1 Executive Immunity from Suit

No Immunity from Criminal Actions

The President, Vice-President, and other executive branch officials enjoy no immunity from criminal actions. This is clear from Article I, §3, cl. 7, which states that an officer who has been impeached may still be subject to criminal prosecution (see §7.6). In this respect, the immunity possessed by executive officials is narrower than that enjoyed by members of Congress under the Speech or Debate Clause, for the latter serves as a shield even against criminal prosecution based on the performance of legislative acts.

It has been suggested that an executive official cannot be criminally prosecuted while still in office, on the theory that if the official were convicted and sentenced to prison this would in effect remove the defendant from office and thereby constitute a judicial usurpation of Congress's impeachment power. Even if this argument has some merit, it should not bar an officer from being prosecuted, convicted, and sentenced, as long as any sentence of imprisonment is stayed until the defendant is out of office. In practice, the federal government and the states have brought criminal actions against high-ranking executive branch officials (and federal judges) who were still in office, without encroaching on Congress's exclusive power of impeachment. Spiro Agnew was thus indicted for federal income tax evasion and bribery while Vice-President of the United States; Agnew later resigned from office.

Qualified Immunity from Civil Damages Actions

Federal executive branch officials and employees generally enjoy a qualified immunity from civil damages actions based on their having violated a person's constitutional or statutory rights. In *Bivens v. Six Unknown Named Federal Narcotics Agents*, 403 U.S. 388 (1971), the Court created a common law cause of action that may allow federal officials who violate a person's constitutional rights to be sued for legal and equitable relief. See §4.2.7. However, the executive's ability to function would be severely impaired if federal officers knew that any action on their part that was later determined to have been unlawful would expose them to personal damages liability. Not only would such a rule be unjust, but "the threat of such liability would deter [an official's] willingness to execute his office with the decisiveness and the judgment required by the public good." *Butz v. Economou*, 438 U.S. 478, 497 (1978) (quoting *Scheuer v. Rhodes*, 416 U.S. 232, 240 (1974)). More important, wholly apart from the issue of monetary liability, the burden of having to defend against such lawsuits could jeopardize the ability of government officials to perform their jobs. While Congress could address these problems by entirely barring damages actions against federal officials or by providing that officials be reimbursed by the government, in the absence of such statutory protections (which the legislative branch might be unwilling to adopt) the Court has fashioned its own common law immunity doctrine for federal executive officials.

As at the state level, this immunity is absolute rather than qualified for federal executive officials and employees to the extent they are performing prosecutorial (as distinct from investigative or administrative) functions. *Buckley v. Fitzsimmons*, 509 U.S. 259, 268-271 (1993). Otherwise, federal officials have only a qualified immunity from civil damages actions which is virtually identical to that enjoyed by state and local officials sued under 42 U.S.C. §1983 based on their performance of executive functions. See §§4.2.6 ("Holding Officials Personally Liable in Damages"). While the privilege is not absolute, it is nevertheless very protective of government officials, allowing them to avoid liability if at the time they acted there were *objectively reasonable* grounds to believe their conduct was lawful. The use of an objective rather than a subjective standard is designed to make the actor's state of mind irrelevant, thus allowing the question of immunity to be disposed of as a matter of law early in the litigation — e.g., by motion for summary judgment. Under the qualified immunity standard, officials and employees will be immune from civil damages liability if the rights they violated were not "clearly established at the time an action occurred. If the law at that time was not clearly established, an official could not reasonably be expected to anticipate subsequent legal developments. . . ." *Harlow v. Fitzgerald*, 457 U.S. 800, 818 (1982). "In other words," as the Court explained recently, "'existing precedent must have placed the statutory or constitutional question beyond debate.'" *Reichle v. Howards*, 132 S. Ct. 2088, 2093 (2012) (quoting *Ashcroft v. al-Kidd*, 131 S. Ct. 2074, 2083 (2011)). Four Justices have suggested that qualified immunity should be even stronger for federal officers like the U.S. Attorney General who perform their duties on a national rather than a more localized basis since the applicable constitutional principles, as articulated by different state and federal courts, may be much less clear than they are for officials who operate in a single state or single federal circuit. *Ashcroft v. al-Kidd*, supra, 131 S. Ct. at 2086-2087 (Kennedy, J., concurring).

In *Saucier v. Katz*, 533 U.S. 194 (2001), the Court addressed the process through which a trial court must assess a qualified immunity defense. First, the determination should be made as soon as possible after the suit is filed. "Where the defendant seeks qualified immunity, a ruling on that issue should be made early in the proceedings so that the costs and expenses of trial are avoided where the defense is dispositive." Id. at 200. Next, the Court specified a two-step process to be followed by a trial court in resolving the qualified immunity defense. As a first step, the court must determine whether the facts viewed in a light most favorable to the plaintiff establish a constitutional or statutory violation. If not, the case must be dismissed. Second, if the alleged facts do support the plaintiff's claim, the court must determine whether the right asserted by the plaintiff "was clearly established." Id. at 201. See §4.2.6 (discussing the level of specificity at which a right must be "clearly established"). The Court has recently held that *Saucier's* two-step approach, while often beneficial in the development of constitutional precedent, is not mandatory. Rather, lower courts have discretion to alter the sequence when doing so will preserve scarce judicial resources. *Pearson v. Callahan*, 555 U.S. 223, 236-243 (2009). By addressing the qualified immunity issue first, if a court finds that immunity in fact exists, it can then avoid devoting further time and resources to what may be a complex constitutional or statutory question whose resolution would have no effect in the case at hand.

Example 7-W

Paula has worked as a doctor for the U.S. Veterans Administration (VA) since 1985. In 1995 she learned that throughout this period, the women's restrooms at the VA facility where she works were under secret observation by supervisors using one-way mirrors. Assume that in 1991, Congress adopted the Federal Employees Privacy Act (FEPA), which requires all federal facilities to respect the privacy rights of employees. Though FEPA did not specify that restroom surveillance falls within the scope of the act, in 1993 the U.S. Court of Appeals for the D.C. Circuit concluded that FEPA prohibits such activity.

In 1995 Paula sued three VA supervisors, alleging that they had violated her privacy rights under the Constitution and under FEPA. She sought an injunction against further surveillance of the women's restrooms, and damages. The trial court found that the defendants violated Paula's privacy rights under the Constitution and under FEPA. Will the doctrine of qualified immunity bar Paula from obtaining injunctive relief and damages against the defendants?

Explanation

The doctrine of qualified immunity has no bearing on claims for injunctive relief; the court may therefore enjoin the defendants from continuing to engage in such activity. However, the doctrine of qualified immunity will shield the defendants from damages liability if a reasonable person in their shoes would not have known that the conduct was illegal at the time it was undertaken. Once the U.S. Court of Appeals ruled in 1993 that FEPA prohibits restroom surveillance, most courts would agree that a reasonable person should have known that such conduct was illegal. Paula can therefore probably collect damages for the period after 1993.

For the years before 1993, defendants' ability to invoke qualified immunity will hinge on how clear the law of privacy was at the time. Since the Constitution does not specifically identify a right of privacy and since FEPA was not specific on this point either, Paula will be able to recover damages for the pre-1993 period only if case law had clearly established that government workers have a constitutional right to be free of restroom surveillance. If the law on this point was not clearly established until later, Paula will be unable to collect damages for the years between 1985 and 1993.

Absolute Civil Damages Immunity for the President

While most executive branch officials and employees enjoy only a qualified immunity from civil damages actions, a different rule applies in the case of the President of the United States. "In view of the special nature of the President's constitutional office and functions, we think it appropriate to recognize absolute Presidential immunity from damages liability for acts within the 'outer perimeter' of his official responsibility." Nixon v. Fitzgerald, 457 U.S. 731, 756 (1982). The Court in Fitzgerald held that the President's absolute immunity from civil damages is "rooted in the constitutional tradition of the separation of powers. . . ." Id. at 749. Although the Court purported to leave open the possibility that Congress could abrogate this absolute immunity by expressly creating a damages action against the President, the Court's repeated emphasis of the fact that the President's absolute immunity derives from separation of powers concerns strongly suggests that any such effort on Congress's part would be unconstitutional. As Chief Justice Burger wrote in a separate opinion, "once it is established that the Constitution confers absolute immunity, as the Court holds today, legislative action cannot alter that result." Id. at 763 n.7 (Burger, C.J., concurring).

The President's absolute immunity from damages liability for acts within the "outer perimeter" of his official duties does not extend to lawsuits arising from conduct that occurred before the President took office. Nor is the chief executive entitled to a temporary constitutional immunity from such suits until after he or she leaves the White House. In Clinton v. Jones, 520 U.S. 681 (1997), the Court held that the Constitution did not entitle President Clinton to either dismissal or stay of a civil damages action brought against him in federal court on the basis of events that occurred while he was governor of Arkansas. Since the suit did not involve any of Clinton's official duties as President, the primary rationale for the immunity doctrine — i.e., "to avoid rendering the President 'unduly cautious in the discharge of his official duties'" (id. at 693-694) — did not come into play.

Clinton urged that allowing the suit to proceed would nonetheless violate separation of powers by imposing "an unacceptable burden on the President's time and energy, and thereby impair the effective performance of his office." Id. at 701-702. The Court rejected the argument, noting that any such interference was "highly unlikely" given the district court's ability to manage the case. Id. at 702. More important, said the Court, even if the litigation were quite burdensome, the separation of powers doctrine does not shield a President from the judicial process, whether in connection with judicial review of his official actions or from suits involving his unofficial conduct. Id. at 703-706. While a district court has the inherent discretion to stay the trial or discovery in such a suit against the President, neither is mandated by the Constitution. In Clinton's case, the Court concluded that the trial court abused its discretion by deferring the trial until after Clinton left office, for, given the danger of prejudice to the plaintiff, the President had not made an adequate showing of need. Id. at 706-708.

Though the President has an absolute immunity from civil damages actions for official actions, the President's aides generally enjoy only the same qualified immunity possessed by other executive branch officials. *Harlow v. Fitzgerald,* 457 U.S. 800 (1982). The Court has suggested that under very limited circumstances, a presidential aide might be able to establish entitlement to absolute immunity, but the aide would have to "show that the responsibilities of his office embraced a function so sensitive as to require a total shield from liability." Id. at 813. The difficulty of making this showing is suggested by *Mitchell v. Forsyth,* 472 U.S. 511 (1985), in which the Court rejected the attorney general's claim that he should enjoy absolute immunity for having authorized a warrantless wiretap on national security grounds.

§7.8.2 Executive Privilege for Presidential Communications

In addition to enjoying an absolute immunity from damages liability for official actions, the President possesses an executive privilege against compelled disclosure of presidential and other high-level executive branch communications. This constitutionally based privilege for presidential conversations and correspondence reflects the reality that without some assurance of confidentiality, those who advise the President may feel a need to "temper candor with a concern for appearances and for their own interests to the detriment of the decisionmaking process." *United States v. Nixon,* 418 U.S. 683, 705 (1974). The privilege is rooted in the doctrine of separation of powers, for it seeks to protect "the independence of the Executive Branch within its own sphere. . . ." Id. at 706.

The executive privilege for presidential communications is qualified rather than absolute. It is a presumptive privilege that may, under certain circumstances, be overcome by the need for disclosure. If a President invokes the privilege, the court will apply a balancing test to determine whether the privilege prevails. To preserve secrecy while the issue of privilege is being weighed, the federal court may review the material *in camera.* On the executive's side of the scales the Court will consider the basis on which the President claims the privilege and the degree of disclosure sought. When the privilege rests on the need to protect military or diplomatic secrets, it is almost certain to prevail. By contrast, if the President bases the privilege merely on the general interest in confidentiality, the privilege may have to yield. On the other side of the balance, the Court will examine the purpose for which the information is sought. If disclosure is sought in connection with a pending criminal trial, the privilege is more likely to yield than if the information is desired as evidence in a civil case. See *Nixon v. Fitzgerald*, 457 U.S. 731, 754 n.37 (1982) ("there is a lesser public interest in actions for civil damages than, for example, in criminal prosecutions"). In *United States v. Nixon*, supra, the Court employed this balancing test in rejecting President Nixon's claim of executive privilege with respect to White House tapes and papers that had been subpoenaed for use in a federal criminal prosecution. The Court held that the President's presumptive privilege, which was "based only on the generalized interest in confidentiality, . . . cannot prevail over the fundamental demands of due process of law in the fair administration of criminal justice." 418 U.S. at 713.

Executive privilege issues have also arisen in noncriminal settings. In *Nixon v. Administrator of General Services*, 433 U.S. 425 (1977), the Court upheld a federal statute that gave the National Archives custody over presidential tapes and records compiled during the Nixon Administration. President Nixon, who claimed that the right to control the fate of these materials belonged exclusively to him, challenged the statute partly on the ground that transfer of the tapes and records to the National Archives would violate the executive privilege for presidential communications. In rejecting this contention, the Court observed that Nixon's assertion of privilege rested solely on a general interest in promoting "candid communication of views by Presidential advisors," id. at 451, and that the statute caused only a limited disclosure since the archivists were part of the executive branch. In addition, two of Nixon's successors — Presidents Ford and Carter — supported the transfer because it would ensure the availability of the materials to future administrations. Thus, the general interest in executive secrecy upon which Nixon relied was counterbalanced by other needs of the presidency itself. The Court concluded that given the "minimal nature of the intrusion into the confidentiality of the Presidency, . . . the claims of Presidential privilege clearly must yield to the important congressional purposes of preserving the materials and maintaining access to them for lawful governmental and historical purposes." Id. at 454. The same balancing approach was later employed to reject Nixon's challenge to National Archive regulations that allowed for public access to these materials. *Nixon v. Freeman*, 670 F.2d 346, 355-359 (D.C. Cir.), *cert. denied sub nom. Nixon v. Carmen*, 459 U.S. 1035 (1982).

Another setting in which the issue of executive privilege has arisen involved a civil suit against the Vice-President and other senior executive branch officials, seeking to force them to make certain public disclosures allegedly required by the Federal Advisory Committee Act. *Cheney v. U.S. District Court for the District of Columbia*, 542 U.S. 367 (2004). While the defendants did not invoke executive privilege as such, they did object on separation of powers grounds to a district court order allowing the plaintiffs to engage in wide-ranging discovery through the compelled production of documents. Even though there had been no formal invocation of executive privilege, the Supreme Court held that the same principles underlying that doctrine may also limit a court's authority to compel discovery in a civil case. Applying the balancing test, the Court distinguished *United States v. Nixon* as a case where information was being sought in a criminal rather than, as here, a civil setting. As the Court explained, "The need for information for use in civil cases, while far from negligible, does not share the urgency or significance of the criminal subpoena requests in *Nixon*." *Id.* at 384. On the other side of the balance, this was a case in which "[t]he Executive Branch, at its highest level, is seeking the aid of the courts to protect its constitutional prerogatives." *Id.* at 385. Moreover, in contrast to *Nixon*, where the subpoena orders were narrow and very specific, the discovery order here was broad and far reaching. On balance, this was thus a far stronger case than *Nixon* for honoring the executive interest in protecting confidential information. While the Supreme Court remanded the case for further proceedings, it admonished that "all courts should be mindful of the burdens imposed on the Executive Branch in any future proceedings." *Id.* at 391.

The Dormant Commerce Clause

CHAPTER 8

---

§8.1 INTRODUCTION AND OVERVIEW

On its face, the Commerce Clause, Article I, §8, cl. 3, is merely an affirmative grant of legislative power to Congress, authorizing it "[t]o regulate Commerce with foreign Nations, and among the several States, and with the Indian Tribes." In Chapter 5, we examine the extent to which Congress may legislate under this clause. One of the first Commerce Clause issues to confront the Supreme Court, however, was whether this affirmative grant of power to Congress also carried with it the negative inference that the states are thereby precluded from regulating interstate and foreign commerce.

The Court has in fact construed the Commerce Clause both as a grant of power to the national government and as a limitation on the power of the states. Where Congress has exercised its affirmative power under the Commerce Clause by enacting federal legislation, any conflicting state laws will be struck down under the Supremacy Clause and principles of preemption. See §6.2. Yet even where Congress has not legislated under the Commerce Clause and the clause thus remains dormant, state laws that burden or discriminate against interstate or foreign commerce may still be invalidated on the ground that they violate the dormant or negative Commerce Clause. The Commerce Clause thus serves "as a negative and preventive provision against injustice among the States themselves. . . ." *West Lynn Creamery, Inc. v. Healy*, 512 U.S. 186, 193 n.9 (1994). In its dormant or negative aspect, the clause "reflect[s] a central concern of the Framers that . . . in order to succeed, the new Union would have to avoid the tendencies toward economic Balkanization that had plagued relations among the Colonies and later among the States under the Articles of Confederation." *Hughes v. Oklahoma*, 441 U.S. 322, 325-326 (1979).

Suppose, for example, that state C passes a law requiring that all crates of apples sold or shipped into the state be labeled with either the applicable U.S. Department of Agriculture (USDA) grade, or no grade at all. Many of the apples sold in state C are grown elsewhere. Until passage of the law, out-of-state apples were often labeled in accordance with special grading systems that were superior to the USDA grades. Out-of-state sellers must now abandon their use of special grades if they are to have continued access to state C's market. Could an out-of-state apple dealer challenge the state C law on the ground that it violates the dormant Commerce Clause? See *Hunt v. Washington Apple Advertising Commission*, 432 U.S. 333 (1977) (upholding such a challenge under the dormant Commerce Clause). In this chapter, we will consider this and other problems as we examine the circumstances under which the dormant Commerce Clause may be used to strike down state regulatory or tax measures.

Before proceeding, however, it should be noted that not all members of the modern Court have subscribed to the notion that there should be a "dormant" or "negative" aspect to the Commerce Clause. In a 1997 decision, Justice Thomas, joined by Chief Justice Rehnquist and Justice Scalia, argued that there is no valid textual or other justification for the Court's dormant Commerce Clause jurisprudence, and urged that the clause should at most be used to strike down discriminatory state taxes on interstate or foreign commerce; beyond that, they said, the task of protecting interstate commerce from state interference should be left exclusively to Congress. *Camps Newfound/Owatonna v. Town of Harrison*, 520 U.S. 564, 610-620 (1997) (Thomas, J., Scalia, J., and Rehnquist, C.J., dissenting). Justices Thomas and Scalia then added that the so-called dormant Commerce Clause should not play a role even when states impose discriminatory taxes on interstate or foreign commerce; instead, the Court in such cases should rely on the Import-Export Clause of Art. I, §10, cl. 2. Id. at 621-637. And see *South Central Bell Telephone Co. v. Alabama*, 526 U.S. 160, 171 (1999) (declining to address the state's argument that the Court should "'formally reconsider' and 'abandon' its negative Commerce Clause jurisprudence" because the state did not present the argument in a timely manner). Needless to say, if these views were to be adopted by a majority of the Court, our understanding of the dormant Commerce Clause — not to mention the length of this chapter! — would be radically altered.

§8.2 EARLY DEVELOPMENTS

In *Cooley v. Board of Wardens*, 53 U.S. (12 How.) 299 (1851), the Supreme Court held that whether a state law violates the dormant Commerce Clause depends on the nature of the activity being regulated. If the subject is one that by its very nature requires a uniform national rule, the power to regulate belongs exclusively to the federal government, and any state regulation of the activity is barred. If, on the other hand, the activity is one that does not demand a uniform system of control, the states are free to regulate the area until such time as Congress chooses to do so itself.

Cooley in effect divided the map of interstate and foreign commerce into two areas: an exclusive zone and a concurrent zone. In the first area, the federal government possesses the sole and exclusive power to regulate. State laws that regulate subjects falling in the exclusive zone violate the Commerce Clause, even in the absence of any conflicting federal legislation. In the second zone, the states possess a concurrent power to regulate, and may do so as long as the federal commerce power remains dormant. However, if Congress decides to regulate the area itself, any conflicting state laws will be struck down under the Supremacy Clause and principles of preemption. See §6.2.

The problem with the *Cooley* doctrine was that it offered no clear way to determine which activities require a uniform national rule and thus fall within the exclusive zone, and which lie within the concurrent zone where state regulation is at least temporarily allowed. Perhaps because of this difficulty the Court eventually abandoned the test and adopted a "direct/indirect" test to decide when state laws violated the dormant Commerce Clause. Laws that placed a direct burden on interstate commerce were invalidated, while those that only indirectly burdened commerce were upheld. However, the distinction between laws that directly burdened interstate commerce and laws that placed only an indirect burden on such commerce proved as elusive as the *Cooley* doctrine. The Court eventually abandoned this test as well, although from time to time the Court will use the direct/indirect language in a purely descriptive sense.

The modern Court has developed a more sophisticated approach to the dormant Commerce Clause. The Court no longer asks whether the nature of the activity involved is such that it requires a uniform national rule; nor will the Court automatically uphold a state law that only indirectly affects commerce. Yet the Court in a sense still plays the *Cooley* game, albeit with a new and more complex set of rules. The issue in dormant Commerce Clause cases today remains the same as that addressed in *Cooley* — i.e., has the state sought to regulate or tax interstate commerce in a manner that would be better left to Congress?

§8.3 THE MODERN TEST: AN OVERVIEW

There are essentially three types of state laws that potentially run afoul of the dormant Commerce Clause under the modern Court's approach:

- Laws whose purpose is to regulate interstate commerce, or whose effect is to control out-of-state transactions;
- Laws that discriminate against interstate commerce; and
- Laws that do not discriminate against, but nonetheless burden interstate commerce.

These categories may be thought of as representing a spectrum of possibilities, all of which are premised on the policy against state protectionism. That policy is most clearly threatened by laws falling in the first category, and is least likely to be impaired by laws that fall only in the final category.

Yet one cannot simply plug a problem into one of these categories and hope to discover the correct result. It is often far from apparent in which category or categories a law belongs. The most effective approach is therefore to examine every potential dormant Commerce Clause problem in a way that illuminates the possible relevance of each category. To this end, the modern Court's approach to the dormant Commerce Clause can be thought of as comprising five inquiries designed to test whether a state law violates the principles of the clause. These inquiries are triggered whenever a state law appears to affect interstate or international economic transactions.

The five inquiries are as follows:

1. Is the law rationally related to a legitimate state purpose?
2. Does the law have the practical effect of regulating out-of-state transactions?
3. If the law discriminates against interstate or foreign commerce, does it represent the least discriminatory means for the state to achieve its purpose?
4. Are the burdens the law places on interstate or foreign commerce clearly excessive in relation to the benefits which the law affords the state?
5. Does the law represent the least burdensome means for the state to achieve its goal?

The exploration of these inquiries will provide a basis on which to judge the constitutionality of a state law under the dormant Commerce Clause. Do not expect to see each of these five factors discussed in every dormant Commerce Clause decision. Since any one of these questions can prove dispositive in a particular case, courts will often focus on only those questions that are controlling.

§8.4 RATIONAL RELATIONSHIP TO A LEGITIMATE STATE PURPOSE

The requirement that a state law be rationally related to a legitimate purpose consists of two distinct elements: First, the law must have a legitimate purpose or goal, and second, the means chosen by the state must be reasonably adapted to attaining that end. This element of the dormant Commerce Clause analysis is very similar to the so-called rational basis test that the Court often uses under the Due Process Clause to decide whether the government has impermissibly interfered with a person's nonfundamental liberty interests or property rights. See Allan Ides and Christopher N. May, *Constitutional Law: Individual Rights*, §2.2.3 (6th ed. 2013).

§8.4.1 Legitimate State Purpose

A state law that affects interstate or foreign commerce must have been enacted for a purpose or goal that falls within the state's so-called police powers. Under their police powers the states may regulate and tax for the health, safety, morals, and general welfare of the public. This power is extraordinarily broad in its scope. It would be impossible to catalog all of the specific ends that it may legitimately embrace. Suffice it to say that these ends are as varied and as plentiful as the problems state and local governments must confront on a day-to-day basis. The state's police powers are constrained only by the federal and state constitutions and by preemptive federal law.

To make things more intriguing, when a state enacts a law, it will not always identify the measure's purpose or goal. The statute itself may be silent on this point, and the legislative history, assuming there is any, may be equally unenlightening. While the question of a statute's purpose is in theory one of fact, in a dormant Commerce Clause case, courts usually permit the defender of a law to advance a purpose even in the absence of any evidence that the legislature actually had that purpose in mind. Under the rational basis test, it is enough that the suggested purpose be one that the legislature *might* have been pursuing. Because of this extreme judicial deference and because of the breadth of permissible state goals, it is usually quite rare that a law challenged under the dormant Commerce Clause is overturned on the ground that it lacked a legitimate purpose.

There are, however, two purposes that a state may not pursue consistent with the dormant Commerce Clause. If a court finds that either of these was the actual purpose of the law, the law will be struck down even though other purposes might have saved the measure. First, a state may not enact a law for the purpose of regulating interstate or foreign commerce, as that is an end that the Commerce Clause has assigned to the federal government. For example, while a state may limit the number of common carriers that operate on certain routes in order to protect public safety (see *Bradley v. Public Utilities Commission*, 289 U.S. 92 (1933)), it may not do so simply because it believes there is already enough interstate commerce occurring between two points (see *Buck v. Kuykendall*, 267 U.S. 307 (1925)). The circumstances under which a state will violate this principle are quite rare. Notice, for example, that by presenting the safety rationale of *Bradley*, a state can easily circumvent the difficulties it would face had it relied on the illegitimate interstate commerce purpose advanced in *Buck*. Second, a state may not enact a law for the purpose of shielding local interests from the effects of interstate competition; such laws involve the illegitimate goal of "economic protectionism" and are discussed in the next section.

§8.4.2 Economic Protectionism

While a state may pursue a broad array of goals under its police power, the dormant Commerce Clause bars a state from seeking to benefit its people by shielding them from the economic consequences of free trade among the states. As we noted earlier, one of the primary purposes of the Commerce Clause was to guard against the "tendencies toward economic Balkanization that had plagued relations among the Colonies and later among the States under the Articles of Confederation." *Hughes v. Oklahoma*, 441 U.S. 322, 325-326 (1979). Laws aimed at insulating the state from interstate competition involve what the Court has called simple economic protectionism. Such laws are invalid per se under the dormant Commerce Clause. As Justice Cardozo wrote in *Baldwin v. G.A.F. Seelig, Inc.*, 294 U.S. 511, 523 (1935), "The Constitution was framed under the dominion of a political philosophy . . . that the peoples of the several states must sink or swim together, and that in the long run prosperity and salvation are in union and not division."

A law will be deemed to be economic protectionist if it was enacted because of the fact that it will shield locals from the effects of out-of-state competition. In our apple problem (see §8.1), state C's labeling law would be deemed economic protectionist if it were shown that it was passed at the behest of the local apple industry to make it more difficult for growers in other states to sell their fruit in state C. In the case on which our apple problem is based, plaintiffs in fact argued that state C had adopted its labeling law for just such protectionist reasons. However, while the Court agreed that there were "some indications in the record to that effect," it stopped short of finding that there was "an economic protection motive" behind the law. *Hunt v. Washington Apple Advertising Commission*, 432 U.S. 333, 352 (1977).

A situation involving economic protectionism as a law's ultimate goal was presented in *South-Central Timber Development, Inc. v. Wunnicke*, 467 U.S. 82 (1984). There, an Alaska statute required that timber taken from state lands be processed in Alaska before being shipped out of state. Because the admitted purpose of the law was to shield Alaska's infant timber processing industry from the effects of interstate and foreign competition, the measure was held to be invalid per se.

Economic protectionism is equally fatal if it is merely a means, a stepping stone, or an intermediate goal toward the attainment of a legitimate end. Thus, in the *Baldwin* case noted above, New York adopted a health measure designed to ensure that residents would have an adequate supply of local milk. This goal was accomplished through a milk-pricing law designed to make it virtually impossible for out-of-state suppliers to compete in the New York market. By thus shielding local dairy farmers from interstate competition, the statute sought to ensure a dependable supply of local milk even in times of general shortage. While New York's ultimate goal was the valid one of protecting public health, it was achieved by the economic protectionist means of shielding local farmers from interstate competition. Even though economic protectionism was only an intermediate goal or stepping stone toward a legitimate end, the law was still held to be unconstitutional per se.

Whether a statute's mediate or ultimate purpose involves economic protectionism is a question of fact. The key is whether the measure was adopted because of—rather than in spite of—its competition-shielding effects.

Example 8-A

A state statute bars the importation of baitfish from other states. The effect of the law is to shield local baitfish suppliers from the competition posed by out-of-state suppliers. Is the law economic protectionist and therefore invalid per se?

Explanation

The answer depends on why the state banned the importation of baitfish. If the law was adopted because of the fact that it would protect the state's own baitfish sellers from their out-of-state competitors, then it constitutes simple economic protectionism. If, on the other hand, the measure was enacted to safeguard the state's fish population from parasites thought to be carried by imported baitfish, the law is not economic protectionist, for it can no longer be said that it was adopted because of the fact that it will shield local baitfish suppliers from interstate competition. While local baitfish suppliers no doubt welcomed the ban and perhaps even lobbied for it, the measure was adopted in spite of — rather than because of — its competition-shielding effects.

Example 8-A is based on *Maine v. Taylor*, 477 U.S. 131 (1986), where the Court rejected an argument that the State of Maine was guilty of economic protectionism in banning importation of live baitfish. The Court found that Maine had adopted its ban for environmental reasons, rather than to shield the local baitfish suppliers from out-of-state competition. The decision in *Maine v. Taylor* should be contrasted with the decision in *Baldwin v. G.A.F. Seelig* noted earlier. In *Baldwin*, the state chose a means specifically designed to insulate local farmers from out-of-state competition, while in *Maine* the state adopted a means that merely had the effect of protecting local baitfish producers from out-of-state competition. Only in *Baldwin* was the per se rule of invalidity invoked since only in that case did the state purposefully engage in economic protectionism.

Thus, not all laws that halt the flow of interstate commerce at a state's borders are necessarily economic protectionist. If such measures are enacted for reasons other than shielding local interests from the effects of interstate trade, they are not invalid per se. For example, a genuine quarantine law that bans the importation of diseased crops or animals is not economic protectionist if it was adopted for health reasons, even though it has the incidental effect of shielding local sellers from out-of-state competition. Quarantine laws, while not per se invalid, may of course be struck down because they fail to meet one of the other requirements of the dormant Commerce Clause analysis.

Since a finding of economic protectionism is fatal, courts are often reluctant, as in *Hunt*, to conclude that a statute is tainted by the evils of protectionism. However, even if a court stops short of finding that a law was motivated by protectionism, the measure will still be subject to very strict scrutiny because of the fact that allegedly protectionist laws always involve discrimination against interstate commerce. As such, they are frequently struck down on the ground that the state has failed to use the least discriminatory means of achieving its goal. See §8.6.2.

§8.4.3 Rational Relationship

Once it is found that a state law has a legitimate purpose untainted by the evils of economic protectionism, it must be determined whether the law is rationally related to its goal. Courts are extraordinarily deferential in making this determination. Under the rational basis test it is assumed that facts were known to the legislature that would make the challenged law a reasonable way of achieving the state's ends. Even if it might be shown that the measure does not in fact further its goal, or that it actually tends to defeat its alleged goal, the Court is still unlikely to find that the statute lacks a rational basis. The question is not whether the challenged law in fact furthers its purpose, but whether a reasonable legislator might have thought the law would achieve the desired end. After all, even rational, reasonable people sometimes make mistakes.

Thus, in our apple hypothetical, state C might argue that requiring use of the USDA grade or no grade at all is a rational way to protect consumers against fraud and deception. A court would be unlikely to reject this argument even if it were shown that by allowing apples to be sold without displaying any grade, the law increased rather than reduced the incidence of consumer fraud.

There is one caveat to these observations. If a court is unwilling to find that a particular statute is protectionist in design, evidence of protectionism may occasionally cause the court to apply the rational basis test with somewhat less deference than is normally accorded the legislative judgment.

The extraordinary deference that the Court normally accords the states in applying the rational relationship requirement is suggested by *Minnesota v. Clover Leaf Creamery Co.*, 449 U.S. 456 (1981). *Clover Leaf* involved a state statute that banned the sale of milk in nonreturnable, nonrefillable plastic containers, but permitted such sales in paperboard milk cartons. Although there were some indications of an economic protectionist purpose, the Court concluded that the principal purpose of the law was to advance legitimate environmental concerns. Yet there was substantial evidence that the legislature's judgment was wrong in this regard, and that the banned plastic containers were in fact more environmentally sound than the protected paperboard containers. The Court nonetheless held that the statute survived the rational basis test since the question was "at least debatable. . . ." Id. at 469. In short, once a legitimate purpose is identified, it is highly improbable that the measure will be struck down on the basis that it is not reasonably adapted to that end.

§8.5 EXTRATERRITORIAL REGULATORY EFFECTS

A state law that is rationally related to a legitimate goal may still be invalidated under the dormant Commerce Clause if the law, in its practical effect, regulates commerce that occurs *wholly* outside the state's borders. Such a law is unconstitutional per se, whether or not its extraterritorial regulatory effect was intended by the legislature. This in some ways resembles the requirement, discussed in §8.4.1, that a state law must not have been adopted with the purpose of regulating interstate commerce. Here, it is the regulatory effect, rather than the purpose, that is critical. However, to fall within the per se rule, the law must have a regulatory effect — as opposed to simply an economic effect—on wholly out-of-state activities. This means that the law must prohibit or mandate certain out-of-state behavior such that a failure to comply will result in the imposition of legal sanctions. The mere fact that a law may create an economic incentive to comply with its provisions with respect to out-of-state activities will not suffice. In addition, the extraterritorial regulatory effect of the law must be proven and may not be merely speculative.

In *Brown-Forman Distillers Corp. v. New York State Liquor Authority*, 476 U.S. 573 (1986), the Court invalidated a New York statute that had the effect of regulating the price at which liquor could be sold in other states. The statute at issue required liquor distillers to post monthly wholesale prices for sales within New York, and to affirm that these prices were no higher than the lowest price charged to wholesalers in other states. Once the New York posted price took effect, distillers were barred from reducing either their New York price or their out-of-state prices, without permission from New York officials. The statute thus regulated the price at which liquor could be sold outside New York by forbidding the reduction of those prices below the New York posted price. The only way the distillers could avoid this regulation of their out-of-state prices was by abandoning the New York market, something New York could not force them to do. The Court held that because of the statute's extraterritorial regulatory effect, it was subject to a per se rule of invalidity under the dormant Commerce Clause.

The same rule was applied in *Healy v. The Beer Institute*, 491 U.S. 324 (1989). There, the Court invalidated a Connecticut law that required out-of-state brewers to affirm that the prices they charged to Connecticut wholesalers were no higher than the prices they charged in neighboring states. While the statute in *Healy* did not literally prohibit brewers from lowering their out-of-state prices, its practical effect, when read in conjunction with the laws of other states, was to make it legally impossible for them to do so. A brewer could avoid this extraterritorial regulation only by ceasing to do business in Connecticut. The statute was held to violate the extraterritoriality principle since, as a practical matter, it regulated sales transactions that took place wholly outside the state.

Read carefully, *Brown-Forman* and *Healy* suggest that for a state law to be per se invalid as a forbidden extraterritorial regulation, it must meet two requirements. First, the state law must be such that it in fact prohibits, mandates, or controls certain out-of-state behavior through the threat of legal sanctions rather than merely influencing that behavior for economic reasons. Second, the legal impact of the law must fall on a transaction that occurs wholly outside the state, as opposed to a transaction that is partly related to the state. Accord *Pharmaceutical Research and Manufacturers of America v. Walsh*, 538 U.S. 644, 668-670 (2003) (state law that does not regulate out-of-state transactions does not violate extraterritoriality principle).

There is language in *Brown-Forman* and *Healy* that might seem to support the view that simply causing an effect on out-of-state transactions, rather than actually regulating them, will suffice to render a law per se invalid. Yet the extraterritoriality principle has not been and is not likely to be applied in so extensive a fashion. There are many types of state laws that have the practical effect of influencing behavior in other states. For example, state tort law, which establishes particular standards of care for manufacturers and assemblers of goods, will as a practical matter shape the conduct of out-of-state producers of goods, for if they fail to comply with these standards and their products then cause injury to someone in the state, they will be held liable in damages. The same is true of state laws that require certain safety features or disclosures on products; the practical effect of such statutes is to compel out-of-state manufacturers to comply with their terms if they wish to participate in the market there. In neither of these examples, however, is the extraterritorial effect regulatory in the sense that the law mandates specific extraterritorial behavior; rather, the extraterritorial behavior is induced by economic incentives. Thus, unless the per se rule of *Brown-Forman* and *Healy* is applied very carefully, a vast array of state statutory and common law provisions would be struck down under the extraterritoriality principle.

Example 8-B

A new state X law provides that no vegetables may be sold in the state unless they are certified by the state agricultural commissioner as having been grown without the use of certain pesticides. No other state bans the use of these specific pesticides. Growers who do not comply with the law are barred from selling their produce in state X. Smith grows vegetables in state Y and sells most of his crop in state X. Because of the state X law, Smith must now cease using these pesticides on his fields in state Y if he wishes to continue participating in the state X market. May Smith successfully argue that the state X law is per se invalid because of its proven extraterritorial effects?

Explanation

No. With respect to the first requirement, the state X law does have the effect of legally controlling Smith's crop-raising activity in state Y. If Smith wishes to sell his produce in state X, he has no choice but to comply with state X's pesticide rules when growing his crop in state Y. If he fails to comply with these rules, he will be sanctioned by being barred from the state X market.

Though the first requirement of *Brown-Forman* is met, Smith's challenge will fail under the second requirement. In contrast to the liquor laws in *Brown-Forman* and *Healy*, state X is not regulating an activity or transaction that is wholly unconnected with the state. Instead, state X's pesticide law applies only to those out-of-state crops that will later be sold in state X. Vegetables to be sold in other states need not be grown in compliance with the state X rules.

Example 8-C

Suppose that in the previous example Smith could have shown that it is not feasible to segregate his crops on the basis of the state where they will later be sold. As a result, the practical effect of state X's law is to bar him from using the designated pesticides on any of his crops, including those that will never be marketed in state X. Would the state X law then be per se invalid because of its demonstrated extraterritorial effects?

Explanation

No. As to the vegetables that will be sold in other states, the second Brown-Forman requirement is satisfied, for the out-of-state production of crops to be sold in other states constitutes wholly extraterritorial activity as far as state X is concerned.

Yet as to these crops, the first Brown-Forman requirement is not met because state X law does not mandate that crops destined for other states be grown without pesticides. The extraterritorial effect that state X's law has on these crops is economic rather than legal. Smith decided for reasons of cost that instead of growing crops intended for state X in a separate area where none of the prohibited pesticides would be used, he would instead extend the reach of state X's law beyond the sphere of activity dictated by the law itself. While such economic considerations may be extremely powerful, they are analytically distinct from requirements imposed by law. State X's law would thus not be per se invalid under the Brown-Forman rule.

The result, of course, would have been different if state X had *required* that farmers selling produce in state X not use certain pesticides on *any* of their crops, including crops not destined for the state X market. In that case, both of the Brown-Forman requirements would be met. The law would be per se invalid insofar as it sought to regulate such wholly extraterritorial activity.

In terms of the potential reach of Brown-Forman and Healy, it may be significant that in both cases, the challenged laws were designed to eliminate any competitive advantage enjoyed by dealers in other states, thereby discouraging local residents from shopping outside the state. This is, of course, a form of economic protectionism, as each state was seeking to shield its local sellers from the competition posed by dealers in other states. It is therefore possible that the Court might in the future limit the extraterritoriality principle to situations in which economic protectionism is also present.

§8.6 DISCRIMINATION AGAINST INTERSTATE COMMERCE

State laws that are rationally related to a legitimate purpose but that involve discrimination against interstate commerce will be invalidated under the dormant Commerce Clause if the state has less discriminatory ways to accomplish its purpose. While one sometimes sees statements to the effect that laws discriminating against interstate commerce are invalid per se, this is true only if the purpose of the discriminatory measure is also economic protectionist—i.e., if it is designed to shield local interests from out-of-state competition. Otherwise, instead of an absolute per se rule, the state will be given a chance to show that there are no less discriminatory alternatives for attaining its goal. As the Court explained in *C & A Carbone, Inc. v. Town of Clarkstown*, 511 U.S. 383, 392 (1994), "Discrimination against interstate commerce in favor of local business or investment is per se invalid, save in a narrow class of cases in which the [state] can demonstrate, under rigorous scrutiny, that it has no other means to advance a legitimate local interest." This critical aspect of the dormant Commerce Clause is deeply rooted in our history. In addition to reflecting hostility toward the economic Balkanization that plagued the states prior to the adoption of the Constitution (see §8.1), the antidiscrimination rule "follows also from the principle that States should not be compelled to negotiate with each other regarding favored or disfavored status for their own citizens. . . . Rivalries among the States are thus kept to a minimum, and a proliferation of trade zones is prevented." *Granholm v. Heald*, 544 U.S. 460, 472 (2005).

§8.6.1 What Constitutes Discrimination?

It is important to bear in mind that the only type of discrimination relevant under the dormant Commerce Clause is discrimination against interstate or foreign commerce. The dormant Commerce Clause is not concerned with other types of discrimination—such as that between long trucks and short trucks, or between apples and other fruits, or between milk containers and other containers. These other types of discrimination must be challenged, if at all, under the Equal Protection Clause of the Fourteenth Amendment. See Allan Ides and Christopher N. May, *Constitutional Law: Individual Rights*, ch. 6 (6th ed. 2013).

A law may be discriminatory against interstate commerce in any of three ways: on its face; by its disproportionate impact on out-of-state economic interests; or as applied. Of course a law might also be discriminatory by design, in the sense that it was enacted to benefit local economic interests at the expense of competitors in other states. Such a law would most likely violate the principle against economic protectionism and thus be subject to the per se rule of invalidity.

Discrimination against interstate or foreign commerce may be apparent from the face of a statute — i.e., from the way it is written. Facial discrimination would be presented by a law that barred the importation of baitfish, by a law requiring shrimp taken in state waters to be processed in the state, by a law requiring natural gas suppliers to favor in-state buyers in times of shortage, or by a law mandating that only apples grown in other states be labeled in a certain way. In each of these cases, the law by its very terms favors local over out-of-state interests.

Yet a law that appears to be discriminatory on its face may not actually discriminate against interstate commerce when other statutes are taken into account. In *Sporhase v. Nebraska*, 458 U.S. 941 (1982), the Court upheld a Nebraska law that barred the shipment of ground water out of state if the water was needed locally. On its face, the statute discriminated against interstate commerce since it preferred Nebraska buyers of water at the expense of buyers in other states. However, another Nebraska law strictly limited the use and transfer of ground water within the state, thus placing equally heavy burdens on intrastate commerce in water. As the Court concluded, "a State that imposes severe withdrawal and use restrictions on its own citizens is not discriminating against interstate commerce when it seeks to prevent the uncontrolled transfer of water out of the State." 458 U.S. at 955-956.

Discrimination may also be present in a law that is facially neutral but whose practical effect is to place greater burdens on out-of-state economic interests than it places on their local competitors. In our apple problem (see §8.1), state C's law requiring that apple crates be marked with either the USDA grade or no grade at all was facially neutral, for it applied to all apples sold in the state. Yet the law would discriminate against interstate commerce if it were shown that prior to passage of the law, the state's own growers used the USDA grade or no grade at all, while special grading systems were used extensively by out-of-state growers. The measure would then be discriminatory because of the disproportionate burden imposed on out-of-state sellers who would have to change their practices while their local competitors could continue to do business as usual. However, as we will see in §8.6.2, such a law is not necessarily unconstitutional, for it may represent the least discriminatory means of achieving a legitimate state purpose.

A law is not discriminatory against interstate commerce, however, simply because the industry or group that it burdens is more heavily concentrated outside the state. As long as the law treats similarly situated in-state and out-of-state members of the industry or group the same in terms of the burdens that are imposed on them, it will not be deemed discriminatory just because more out-of-staters than in-staters are adversely affected by the measure. In addition, a law that favors a state-created public benefit corporation over an out-of-state private business entity is not discriminatory against interstate commerce so long as that state-created entity does not itself discriminate against interstate or foreign commerce. See *United Haulers Assn., Inc. v. Oneida-Herkimer Solid Waste Management*, 550 U.S. 330, 334 (2007) (flow control ordinance that forced haulers to deliver all in-state waste to a state-created processing facility did not discriminate against interstate commerce since all private businesses — including waste haulers and waste processors — were treated the same, whether they were in-state or out-of-state entities).

Example 8-D

A state Z corporate takeover law regulates stock tender offers by entities that seek to acquire control of corporations having their principal place of business in state Z. The act regulates such tender offers regardless of where the entity making the tender offer is located. However, it is undisputed that, because of state Z's small size, most of the tender offers that are subject to the act will be made by out-of-state entities. Does state Z's law discriminate against interstate commerce?

Explanation

No. The act is facially neutral, applying to all tender offers regardless of the location of the entity that launched the offer. While the burden of the law will fall more heavily on out-of-state rather than in-state companies, this is merely the result of the fact that there are more entities launching such tender offers outside the state than there are inside the state. In contrast to our earlier apple problem, the burden that the act places on those in-staters and out-of-staters to whom it applies is, both facially and as a practical matter, exactly the same. "Because nothing in the . . . Act imposes a greater burden on out-of-state offerors than it does on similarly situated [state Z] offerors, we reject the contention that the Act discriminates against interstate commerce." *CTS Corp. v. Dynamics Corp. of America*, 481 U.S. 69, 88 (1987).

For the same reason, a Montana severance tax on coal mined in the state did not discriminate against interstate commerce where 90 percent of the coal was shipped to consumers in other states. Though out-of-staters bore 90 percent of the tax burden, the tax did not distinguish between in-state and out-of-state consumers, all of whom were taxed the same amount on the coal they consumed. *Commonwealth Edison Co. v. Montana*, 453 U.S. 609, 619 (1981).

However, a statute that is neutral on its face and that would not disproportionately burden interstate commerce if it were enforced as written may be nonetheless be discriminatory because of the way it is applied or enforced by state or local officials.

Example 8-E

State X passes a law limiting all trucks operating within the state to no more than 90 inches in width. Might the law discriminate against interstate commerce?

Explanation

The law is facially neutral since it applies to all trucks. It does not disproportionately burden interstate commerce as long as there are many in-state and out-of-state trucks that exceed the 90-inch limit. Yet the law would be discriminatory as applied if it were shown that state officials seldom enforce the measure against local trucks, with the result that its burdens fall only or disproportionately on out-of-state trucking interests.

A law may be found to discriminate against interstate commerce even if some of its burdens fall on local interests. Thus, in *Dean Milk Co. v. City of Madison*, 340 U.S. 349 (1951), a Madison, Wisconsin, ordinance prohibited the sale of milk not pasteurized within five miles of the city. Even though both intrastate and interstate commerce were burdened by the law, the Court ruled that it discriminated against interstate commerce since the burdens were disproportionate. While all out-of-state pasteurized milk was barred from the city, only some Wisconsin milk was affected. To put it differently, all pasteurized milk sold in the city had to have been pasteurized in Wisconsin and none of it could have been pasteurized outside the state.

Finally, for a law to be deemed discriminatory against interstate commerce, the out-of-state interests allegedly discriminated against must be competitors in the same market as the supposedly favored local interests. If the in-state and out-of-state interests deal in different products or services, they are not similarly situated for constitutional purposes. Unless there is actual or potential competition between them, eliminating the allegedly discriminatory state law will not further the Commerce Clause objective of "preserving a national market for competition undisturbed by preferential advantages conferred by a State upon its residents or resident competitors." *General Motors Corp. v. Tracy*, 519 U.S. 278, 298-303 (1997). In *General Motors*, the Court rejected a claim that Ohio had discriminated against interstate commerce by giving a tax exemption to regulated natural gas production companies, all of which were local entities, while denying the exemption to gas marketers or suppliers, all of which were out-of-state entities. The Court found no discrimination because the two sets of entities sold different products and thus operated in distinct markets. As a result, "competition would not be served by eliminating any tax differential" between them. Id. at 303.

§8.6.2 Less Discriminatory Alternatives

If a state law is found to discriminate against interstate commerce, it will be invalidated under the dormant Commerce Clause unless there are no less discriminatory ways for the state to achieve its goal. As a practical matter, it is up to the party challenging the law to suggest that there are less discriminatory alternatives. If the law's defender cannot then show that these alternatives would be less effective in achieving the state's ends, the statute will be held unconstitutional. See, e.g., *South Dakota Farm Bureau, Inc. v. Hazeltine*, 340 F.3d 583, 596-597 (8th Cir. 2003), *cert. denied*, 541 U.S. 1037 (2004) (state law that had a discriminatory purpose violated dormant Commerce Clause, despite lack of "certainty that any alternative will ultimately succeed in meeting the goals" of the law, since defendant state officials had "the burden of proving that no non-discriminatory alternative exists").

Thus, in our apple hypothetical (see §8.1), a plaintiff might argue that a less discriminatory but equally effective alternative to state C's law would be to require that all apples bear the USDA grade along with any other grade the seller wished to employ. The burden of the law would then fall on both in-state and out-of-state sellers who did not previously use the USDA grade. At the same time, out-of-state dealers would not have to abandon their use of special grades. Besides being less discriminatory, this alternative would seem to be at least as effective in preventing consumer fraud as state C's statute, which allowed apples to be sold without any grade whatsoever.

Example 8-F

To conserve its limited supply of minnows, a state makes it illegal to ship minnows taken from state waters for sale outside the state. Is the law unconstitutional because it discriminates against interstate commerce?

Explanation

The law discriminates against interstate commerce by favoring local minnow buyers over buyers in other states. Instead of placing the full burden of conservation on interstate commerce, less discriminatory means of attaining the state's conservation goal might involve simply limiting the number of minnows that can be taken from state waters, or by also restricting the disposal of minnows within its borders. Unless the state could prove that these alternatives would be less effective than the challenged statute in conserving the state's minnow supply, the law would be struck down under the dormant Commerce Clause. See *Hughes v. Oklahoma*, 441 U.S. 322 (1979).

Example 8-G

A state bans the importation of baitfish in order to protect its fisheries from parasites. The law, which is facially discriminatory against interstate commerce, is challenged on the ground that there are less discriminatory ways to achieve the state's ecological goals. Is the statute unconstitutional?

Explanation

If it could be shown that the state's native fish carried the same parasites as out-of-state baitfish and that the state had taken no steps to control its local parasite problem, then a less discriminatory alternative would be to impose restrictions on the sale of native fish as well as imported fish. Yet even if there were no local parasite problem, if it were possible to protect local fisheries from parasites carried by imported fish through means less drastic than a total ban on importation, such as use of screening or sampling techniques, the existence of these alternatives might be enough to invalidate the ban. But if the state could show that these procedures were not yet developed to the point where they were as effective in protecting local fisheries as a total ban on importation, the importation ban would constitute the least discriminatory means available for achieving the state's goals. See *Maine v. Taylor*, 477 U.S. 131 (1986).

Since every law that is economic protectionist is also, by definition, discriminatory against interstate commerce, the least-discriminatory-means requirement gives courts an indirect way to invalidate possibly economic protectionist laws without having to invoke the strong medicine of the per se rule, and without needing to accuse the state of disguising its true purposes. See §8.4.2. For if a state cannot meet the heightened scrutiny accorded to discriminatory laws, it is fairly likely that the state was in fact engaged in economic protectionism but with a police powers pretext. In *Philadelphia v. New Jersey*, 437 U.S. 617 (1978), the Court struck down a New Jersey law that barred the importation of most waste that was generated outside the state. Plaintiffs urged that the law was economic protectionist and thus invalid per se because it was designed to shield local residents from the competition for scarce landfill sites posed by out-of-state waste suppliers. New Jersey, on the other hand, claimed that the law was passed for the valid goals of reducing pollution and protecting open space. While the Court seemed to agree that the state's motives may have been protectionist, it refrained from declaring the statute invalid per se. Instead, the Court suggested that even accepting the state's asserted conservation goal, New Jersey could have adopted the less discriminatory alternative of "slowing the flow of *all* waste into the State's remaining landfills," rather than "impos[ing] on out-of-state commercial interests the full burden of conserving the State's remaining landfill space." Id. at 626, 628. The least-discriminatory-means test is thus a useful device for getting at the evils of protectionism in cases in which there may be doubt as to the state's true purposes or a reluctance on the Court's part to invoke the per se rule of invalidity.

§8.7 BALANCING BURDENS AND BENEFITS

A state law that is rationally related to a legitimate goal and that does not discriminate against interstate commerce may still be invalidated under the dormant Commerce Clause if the burdens it places on interstate or foreign commerce heavily outweigh whatever benefits the measure affords the state. To perform this balancing test, it is necessary to have first identified the purpose of the regulation in question, for benefits are measured in terms of the law's goal. In our apple problem (see §8.1), for example, if state C's labeling requirement was defended as being a rational consumer protection measure, then in weighing burdens against benefits, benefits would be measured in terms of the extent to which the law actually protects consumers.

§8.7.1 Burdens Must Clearly Outweigh Benefits

Courts tend to use the balancing test to strike down a law only if it imposes considerable burdens on interstate commerce and the benefits to the state are slim or nonexistent. If both the burdens and the benefits are significant, there is no precise way of comparing them, and the balancing test is of little use. In such cases, courts may not even weigh burdens and benefits and will instead focus on other elements of the dormant Commerce Clause analysis.

For example, in *Dean Milk Co. v. City of Madison*, 340 U.S. 349 (1951), an ordinance requiring all milk sold in the city to have been pasteurized at a plant within a radius of five miles was defended as a health measure on the basis that the city's two inspectors could not cover a larger geographic area. The law imposed a tremendous burden on interstate commerce since its effect was to exclude from the Madison market all milk processed in other states. Yet the health benefits to the city were also considerable since the law ensured that only safe milk would be sold there. In such a case, the balancing test was inconclusive and the Court, not surprisingly, made no mention of it, instead invalidating the ordinance on other grounds.

On the other hand, in cases where the benefits from a law are clearly insignificant, the Court has not hesitated to invoke the balancing test. In *Southern Pacific Co. v. Arizona*, 325 U.S. 761 (1945), an Arizona law limited the length of trains that could operate in the state. The statute placed a heavy burden on interstate commerce since trains had to be broken up into shorter ones well before entering Arizona. At the same time, the record showed that even though the law was adopted as a safety measure, it increased rather than reduced the number of accidents because of the fact that a larger number of trains operated in the state when train lengths were reduced. The Court had no difficulty in concluding that the burdens the Arizona law imposed on interstate commerce clearly outweighed any benefits it conferred on the state. The same result might occur in our apple problem, for the burdens which the state C law imposes on interstate commerce are quite heavy, while the benefits to the state in terms of consumer protection are probably quite low since sellers do not have to disclose anything about the quality of their products.

§8.7.2 Relevance of Other Statutes

In measuring burdens and benefits, it may be necessary to take into account the existence of other legislation. On the burdens side, for example, when Illinois required all trucks operating in the state to be equipped with a special contour mudflap, the impact of this requirement on interstate commerce depended on the laws of other states. If every other state also required such mudflaps, the Illinois law's burden on interstate commerce would have been de minimis. In fact, however, since no other state required contour mud-flaps and one state barred their use, the burden on interstate commerce was substantial. See *Bibb v. Navajo Freight Lines, Inc.*, 359 U.S. 520 (1959).

The benefits a state receives from a particular law may likewise depend on what other legislation is already in place. If most or all of the benefits said to derive from the disputed statute are already conferred by other laws, a court may conclude that the incremental benefits from the statute are min-imal, with the result that the measure may be invalidated under the balancing test. This was the fate of the Illinois Business Takeover Act, which imposed heavy burdens on interstate commerce to protect Illinois share-holders. Most of the benefits allegedly flowing from the act were already afforded by federal law. Since the Illinois law was largely superfluous, the Court was able to invalidate the statute under the dormant Commerce Clause, using the balancing test. See *Edgar v. MITE Corporation*, 457 U.S. 624 (1982).

§8.7.3 Cases in Which Balancing May Be Inappropriate

In recent years, some members of the Court have expressed discomfort with using the balancing test in dormant Commerce Clause cases. Justice Scalia has flatly rejected the approach on the basis that because the interests being compared are not commensurate, balancing burdens and benefits is like "judging whether a particular line is longer than a particular rock is heavy." *Bendix Autolite Corp. v. Midwesco Enterprises, Inc.*, 486 U.S. 888, 897 (1988). Earlier, in *Kassel v. Consolidated Freightways Corp.*, 450 U.S. 662, 681 n.1, 691 (1981), five Justices rejected balancing in health and safety cases, as long as the benefits to the state are not trivial or illusory; however, none of the five remains on the Court. Yet, even if today's Court were to totally reject balancing in genuine health and safety cases, this would simply mirror the Court's longstanding reluctance to invalidate laws under the balancing test in situations where the benefits to the state are not de minimis. In short, the Court appears unwilling to use the balancing test in any case where the challenged law confers actual benefits to the state.

§8.8 USING THE LEAST BURDENSOME ALTERNATIVE

Suppose that a state law passes muster under the first three steps of our dormant Commerce Clause analysis — i.e., the measure is rationally related to a legitimate state goal, it does not discriminate against interstate commerce, and the burdens it imposes on interstate commerce do not clearly outweigh the benefits the state receives from the law. The Court has suggested that such a law might still be unconstitutional if "the local interest . . . could be promoted as well with a lesser impact on interstate activities." *Pike v. Bruce Church, Inc.*, 397 U.S. 137, 142 (1970).

§8.8.1 Less Burdensome Alternatives

To require that a state use the least burdensome alternative for accomplish-ing its aims represents a very strict standard of judicial review, for courts are in effect second-guessing state legislatures by insisting that of the various means available for accomplishing a particular purpose, the state must choose that alternative which places the least possible burden on interstate or foreign commerce. The Supreme Court condemned this approach in *South Carolina State Highway Department v. Barnwell Brothers, Inc.*, 303 U.S. 177 (1938), where the lower court had invalidated the state's 90-inch width limit for trucks because a 96-inch limit would have been just as effective in achieving the state's goals. According to the Supreme Court in that case,

> Since the adoption of one weight or width regulation, rather than another, is a legislative, not a judicial, choice, its constitutionality is not to be determined by weighing in the judicial scales the merits of the legislative choice and rejecting it if the weight of evidence presented in court appears to favor a different standard.

Id. at 191. The Court's more recent statement in *Pike*, however, suggests that it may now be possible to challenge a law under the dormant Commerce Clause by showing that the state could have achieved its purposes equally well through alternative measures that would have placed fewer burdens on interstate or foreign commerce.

A plurality of the Court employed this approach in *Kassel v. Consolidated Freightways Corp.*, 450 U.S. 662 (1981), to strike down an Iowa law that barred trucks longer than 55 feet from using the state's highways. A trucking company challenging the Iowa statute proved that 65-foot trucks, which were permitted in many surrounding states, were as safe as 55-foot trucks. As a result, a 65-foot limit would have given Iowa the same safety benefits as the 55-foot limit while substantially reducing the burdens on interstate commerce. The plurality, in an opinion by Justice Powell, ruled that because Iowa derived no more benefit from a 55-foot limit than it would have derived from a 65-foot limit, the 55-foot limit violated the dormant Commerce Clause. Though the plurality did not couch its decision in terms of Iowa's having failed to use the least burdensome alternative, its approach was in fact indistinguishable from that of the lower court in *Barnwell Brothers*. The lower federal courts have read *Pike* as incorporating a least-burdensome-alternative requirement into the dormant Commerce Clause analysis. See, e.g., *R & M Oil & Supply, Inc. v. Saunders*, 307 F.3d 731 (8th Cir. 2002) (Missouri law that regulated the storage of propane gas violated the dormant Commerce Clause where less burdensome means of achieving the state's interests were available at the time the law was enacted); *Hyde Park Partners, L.P. v. Connolly*, 839 F.2d 837, 847-848 (1st Cir. 1988) (penalty provision in state law requiring certain disclosures in takeover bids likely violated dormant Commerce Clause where lesser penalties "would be adequate to enforce the disclosure requirement").

The least-burdensome-alternative requirement does not force a state to sacrifice benefits to reduce the burden on interstate commerce. If the state can demonstrate that any less burdensome alternatives are also less effective in achieving the state's ends, its regulation will not be invalidated under this step of the dormant Commerce Clause analysis. Thus, in *Minnesota v. Clover Leaf Creamery Co.*, 449 U.S. 456 (1981), the Court sustained a Minnesota statute that outlawed the sale of milk in nonreturnable, nonrefillable plastic containers. It was urged that Minnesota had less burdensome ways to attain its ecological goals, but the Court rejected this challenge, finding that "these alternatives are either more burdensome on commerce than the Act . . . or less likely to be effective. . . ." Id. at 473.

§8.8.2 Less Burdensome and Less Discriminatory Alternatives

It might appear that the requirement that a state use the least burdensome means of achieving its goal is the same as the requirement, discussed in §8.6.2, that the state also use the least discriminatory alternative available. While in some cases these requirements may amount to the same thing, they are often quite distinct.

A law that discriminates against interstate commerce by definition places heavier burdens on out-of-state interests than it does on local residents. In theory, the state could cure this discrimination in either of two ways: It could increase the burdens on local commerce, or it could reduce the burdens on interstate commerce. While in both cases the state's discrimination against interstate commerce would be reduced or eliminated, only the second approach also reduces the law's burden on interstate commerce. Thus, depending on which of the two approaches is taken, a less discriminatory alternative may or may not be a less burdensome alternative.

Example 8-H

A state prohibits out-of-state trucks from exceeding 10 tons in weight; no weight limit is imposed on in-state trucks. The limit was adopted for the purpose of protecting the state's highways. Because surrounding states have a 12-ton weight limit, the law places a heavy burden on interstate commerce. On what bases might the law be challenged under the dormant Commerce Clause?

Explanation

This law might be challenged on the ground that it discriminates against interstate commerce and that there is a less discriminatory alternative that would achieve the state's goal equally well or better: Apply the 10-ton weight limit to all trucks, including those with in-state plates. This alternative equalizes the burdens placed on intrastate and interstate commerce. Yet, while it is less discriminatory against interstate commerce, it in no way reduces the burdens placed on that commerce.

The 10-ton weight limit might also be attacked on the ground that there are less burdensome ways of achieving the state's goal equally well. If it could be shown that the 12-ton weight limit used by surrounding states is as effective as a 10-ton limit in protecting highways, the 10-ton limit would violate the dormant Commerce Clause requirement that states use the least burdensome means available to accomplish their goals.

In this hypothetical situation, the less burdensome alternative of raising the limit to 12 tons is quite different from the less discriminatory alternative of extending the 10-ton limit to in-state trucks. Redressing the discrimination problem by expanding the law to cover in-state trucks does not cure the fact that the law may be more burdensome than necessary on interstate commerce. Nor, conversely, would solving the burden problem by raising the weight limit for out-of-state trucks to 12 tons in and of itself cure the fact that the statute is discriminatory.

This example may be contrasted with *Dean Milk v. City of Madison*, 340 U.S. 349 (1951). In *Dean Milk*, a city ordinance discriminated against interstate commerce by making it illegal to sell milk that was not pasteurized within five miles of the city, thus barring the sale of milk pasteurized in other states. The Court identified two less discriminatory alternatives: The city could either accept inspections performed in other states, or it could hire additional personnel to inspect pasteurization plants located beyond the five-mile radius. Here, besides being less discriminatory, both of the alternatives — since they involved reducing the burdens on interstate commerce rather than increasing the burdens on local business — were also less burdensome. The less discriminatory alternatives and the less burdensome alternatives amounted to the same thing.

§8.9 STATE REGULATION OF ALCOHOL

State laws that deal with alcoholic beverages are potentially immune from challenge under the dormant Commerce Clause by virtue of the

Twenty-First Amendment. Ratified in 1933, that Amendment repealed nationwide prohibition and provided that in the future, "[t]he transportation or importation into any State . . . for delivery or use therein of intoxicating liquors" would be governed by state law. In some of its early cases construing the Twenty-First Amendment, the Supreme Court suggested that the Amendment's effect was to completely immunize the states from dormant Commerce Clause restraints insofar as alcoholic beverages were concerned. In more recent years, however, the Court has rejected the contention that "the Twenty-first Amendment somehow operated to 'repeal' the Commerce Clause for alcoholic beverages. . . ." *Granholm v. Heald*, 544 U.S. 460, 487 (2005). Instead, while the Amendment does allow states to regulate or prohibit the sale, use, and importation of alcohol on an evenhanded basis, it does not allow them to do so in ways that favor local industry over out-of-state goods. Thus, notwithstanding the Twenty-First Amendment, "state regulation of alcohol is limited by the nondiscrimination principle of the Commerce Clause." Id. The *Granholm* Court on this basis struck down Michigan and New York laws that discriminated against interstate commerce by making it harder for out-of-state wineries to sell directly to consumers in those states than it was for in-state wineries to do so.

§8.10 STATE LAWS THAT AFFECT FOREIGN COMMERCE

State laws that affect commerce with other nations are subject to more searching scrutiny under the dormant Commerce Clause than are state laws that affect only interstate commerce. As the Court stated in *South-Central Timber Development, Inc. v. Wunnicke*, 467 U.S. 82, 100 (1984), "It is a well-accepted rule that state restrictions burdening foreign commerce are subjected to a more rigorous and searching scrutiny. It is crucial to the efficient execution of the Nation's foreign policy that 'the Federal Government . . . speak with one voice when regulating commercial relations with foreign governments.'" Id. at 100 (quoting *Michelin Tire Corp. v. Wages*, 423 U.S. 276, 285 (1976)). While the Court tends to use the same general approach to both types of state regulation, all else being equal it is more difficult for a state to justify laws that burden or discriminate against international trade. This more demanding standard of review would be triggered in our apple problem (see §8.1), for example, if some apples sold in state C were imported from Japan rather than just from other states.

§8.11 CONGRESSIONAL CONSENT OR AUTHORIZATION

If a state law would otherwise violate the dormant Commerce Clause because it fails to meet one of our five requirements, the state may be able to show that its conduct is excused, either because the action was authorized by Congress, or because the state was acting as a market participant. In this section we consider the issue of congressional authorization. Section 8.12 discusses the market participant exemption.

As noted earlier, the Commerce Clause on its face is merely a grant of power to the federal government; it says nothing about the states being barred from regulating commerce. However, as the Court suggested in *Cooley v. Board of Wardens*, 53 U.S. (12 How.) 299 (1851), some areas of commerce are reserved for Congress even in the absence of federal legislation. These areas are protected from state encroachment by the judiciary through its application of the dormant Commerce Clause. In this manner, the federal courts keep certain areas of interstate and foreign commerce free of burdensome state regulations until such time as Congress has a chance to decide how it wishes the particular area to be governed. However, it is Congress rather than the Court that has the last word.

In theory, Congress might perform this watchdog function itself. If it detected an objectionable state law or practice, Congress might invoke its commerce power by passing a federal law on the subject, thereby trumping the state law by virtue of the Supremacy Clause. This occasionally happens. In 1983, Congress expressed its disapproval of state laws restricting the size of trucks. It did so by adopting a federal statute that requires the states to permit the operation of trucks that do not exceed specified length and width limits. See 49 U.S.C. §§31111, 31113 (2000). As a practical matter, however, Congress cannot perform this monitoring task on a comprehensive basis, for the workload would be extraordinary. Instead, the federal courts have assumed this function by invoking the dormant Commerce Clause to protect certain aspects of interstate and foreign commerce from state encroachment until Congress has a chance to deal with the matter.

Since the judiciary's role is essentially one of holding the fort for Congress, if the Court initially strikes down a state law under the dormant Commerce Clause because the Justices believe the matter must be regulated if at all by the federal government, Congress is free to respond by saying, "Thanks, but no thanks!" and may pass legislation that restores the states' ability to regulate the matter in question. Thus, in our apple hypothetical (see §8.1), Congress could authorize the states to regulate the labeling of apples even if state labeling requirements were previously invalidated by the Court. Similarly, even in advance of a judicial ruling, Congress may authorize or consent to state laws that would otherwise violate the dormant Commerce Clause. See, e.g., *New York v. United States*, 505 U.S. 144 (1992) (upholding provisions of the Low-Level Radioactive Waste Policy Amendments Act of 1985 that authorized states with federally approved waste sites to discriminate against interstate commerce by rejecting waste from states that had not conformed with the act's guidelines) (see §5.6).

Any such congressional consent or authorization must be clear and unambiguous. If there is any doubt as to whether Congress has given its permission, a state's conduct will be subject to the normal strictures of the dormant Commerce Clause. In *South-Central Timber Development, Inc. v. Wunnicke*, 467 U.S. 82, 91 (1984) (see §8.4.2), the Court thus rejected Alaska's claim that Congress had authorized it to engage in economic protectionism, explaining that "for a state regulation to be removed from the reach of the dormant Commerce Clause, congressional intent must be unmistakably clear." Similarly, in our apple problem, even if the U.S. Department of Agriculture, pursuant to federal law, had urged states to protect consumers against deceptive labeling practices, this would not be evidence that Congress had authorized the states to do so in ways that might violate the dormant Commerce Clause.

It should be emphasized that while Congress may authorize state conduct that would otherwise violate the dormant Commerce Clause, it has no similar power with respect to other provisions of the Constitution. Thus, when Mississippi argued that its policy of excluding men from a state nursing college was sanctioned by Congress and therefore did not violate the Equal Protection Clause, the Court responded that "neither Congress nor a State can validate a law that denies the rights guaranteed by the Fourteenth Amendment." *Mississippi University for Women v. Hogan*, 458 U.S. 718, 732-733 (1982). See also *Metropolitan Life Ins. Co. v. Ward*, 470 U.S. 869 (1985) (state taxes on insurance companies may be challenged under Equal Protection Clause even though Congress exempted states from restrictions of Commerce Clause). In the context of the dormant Commerce Clause, the Court is merely protecting Congress's options, while in the context of individual liberties the Court is charged with the ultimate task of defining the scope of those rights.

§8.12 THE MARKET PARTICIPANT DOCTRINE

The second way a state may be able to justify conduct that would otherwise violate the dormant Commerce Clause is by showing that the state was acting as a market participant. The dormant Commerce Clause applies to the states only when they tax or regulate private trade in the national marketplace. If a state instead enters the marketplace as a participant, its actions are treated as being like those of a private party, and the state is exempt from the restraints of the dormant Commerce Clause. The Court has justified the market participant exemption on the ground that the Founders did not intend to restrict the states' ability to operate freely in the market, and on the basis of state sovereignty. In addition, less judicial interference may be necessary in market participant cases to the extent that market forces will constrain a state's tendency to act in an economically irrational way by favoring its own citizens.

§8.12.1 The State as Buyer or Seller

The market participant doctrine applies to the state when it engages in the buying, selling, or dispensing of goods or services. Thus, in *Reeves, Inc. v. Stake*, 447 U.S. 429 (1980), South Dakota was a market participant when, in selling cement from a state-owned cement plant, it restricted sales to residents of South Dakota. While such discrimination against out-of-state buyers would normally have triggered close if not fatal scrutiny under the dormant Commerce Clause, because the state was acting as a seller of goods the clause did not come into play. South Dakota would likewise have been exempt from the Commerce Clause if its cement plant employed only South Dakota residents, if it bought raw materials only from South Dakota companies, or if it gave free cement only to South Dakota charities. The same principle applies with respect to the distribution of state-owned services. The dormant Commerce Clause would therefore pose no obstacle where admission to a public university was restricted to state residents.

Yet the fact that a state is buying or selling goods or services does not always ensure that it will be exempt from the dormant Commerce Clause. If the state — whether by statute, regulation, or contract — attempts to exercise control over the actions of private parties beyond the market in which it is a participant, the state will no longer be treated as a market participant and the dormant Commerce Clause will be triggered.

Example 8-1

South Dakota wishes to build a cement plant that will be owned and operated by the state. State law provides that bids for constructing the plant may be submitted only by South Dakota contractors and that the entire work force, including those hired by subcontractors, must consist only of South Dakota residents unless qualified residents are not available. The South Dakota law is challenged by contractors, subcontractors, and workers in neighboring states who claim that it discriminates against interstate commerce. Is the state exempt from the dormant Commerce Clause by virtue of the market participant exemption?

Explanation

To the extent that the state itself will hire only a South Dakota contractor, it is a market participant since it is entering the market as a buyer of services. However, by seeking also to control the hiring practices of the contractor and subcontractors, the state is placing "downstream" restrictions on the conduct of its trading partners. Yet these restrictions are still exempt from the dormant Commerce Clause since they do not operate outside the market in which the state itself is a participant — i.e., the market for construction of a state cement plant. See *White v. Massachusetts Council of Construction Employers, Inc.*, 460 U.S. 204 (1983) (finding that the City of Boston was a market participant when it imposed similar restrictions in contracting for the construction of public buildings).

As this example suggests, the key to whether a state qualifies as a market participant lies in how broadly or narrowly the relevant market is defined. The Court has said that in applying the market participant doctrine, it will define markets narrowly so as to keep the doctrine from "swallowing up the rule that States may not impose substantial burdens on interstate commerce. . . ." *South-Central Timber Development, Inc. v. Wunnicke*, supra, 467 U.S. at 98. As a result, in most cases where states have sought to impose restrictions on their trading partners, the Court has found the downstream (or upstream) restrictions to involve the regulation of a different market from the one in which the state was a participant, with the consequence that the state was subject to the dormant Commerce Clause.

Example 8-J

A state law provides that anyone who buys cement from a state-owned cement plant may in turn sell the cement only to state residents. Is the statute open to challenge on the ground that it discriminates against interstate commerce, or can the state claim immunity as a market participant?

Explanation

The state here is probably a market participant only to the extent that it decides to whom it will sell the cement. Once the state sells the cement to a private party, it becomes a privately owned article of commerce, and any controls the state then seeks to place on what the owner does with the cement involve regulations that are subject to the dormant Commerce Clause. "In contrast to the situation in *White*, this restriction on private economic activity takes place after the completion of the parties' direct commercial obligations, rather than during the course of an ongoing commercial relationship in which the [state] retained a continuing proprietary interest in the subject of the contract." *South-Central Timber Development, Inc. v. Wunnicke*, supra, 467 U.S. at 99. In terms of markets, a court inclined to define markets narrowly might conclude that the state, as a participant in the *cement production* market, was seeking to impose downstream restrictions in the *cement distribution* market, rendering the state's actions subject to the dormant Commerce Clause.

This example is similar to *South-Central Timber Development, Inc. v. Wunnicke*, where the Court held that Alaska, though a participant in the timber market, lost its market participant status to the extent that it sought to require those buying timber from the state to then process it in Alaska before it was shipped out of state. The state's downstream regulation of the timber processing market was therefore subject to the dormant Commerce Clause. The example also resembles *Hughes v. Oklahoma*, 441 U.S. 322 (1979), where Oklahoma was found to have violated the dormant Commerce Clause by barring the out-of-state sale of minnows taken from state waters. While the state might, with impunity, have allowed only state residents to take minnows from state waters, its market participant immunity was lost when it then sought "to prevent privately owned articles of trade from being shipped and sold in interstate commerce." *Reeves, Inc. v. Stake*, 447 U.S. 429, 433 n.4 (1980) (distinguishing *Hughes*).

In deciding whether or not a state that participates in one market is attempting to regulate another market, it makes no difference whether the downstream (or upstream) restrictions are being imposed by statute or by contract. In *South-Central Timber Development, Inc. v. Wunnicke*, supra, where the state used its bargaining power in selling timber to impose downstream regulations in the timber processing market, the Court said it was irrelevant that the processing restrictions were incorporated into the timber sales contract, rather than imposed by state law. The state's contractual attempt to control private activity outside the market in which it was a participant was still subject to the dormant Commerce Clause.

§8.12.2 State Subsidies

In addition to qualifying as a market participant when it buys or sells goods and services, states may also be able to claim market participant status when they distribute subsidies. When states subsidize certain activities, they in effect enter the market with money that is distributed on a selective basis. Though the Court has not squarely addressed the issue, it has on several occasions assumed that subsidies may qualify for market participant treatment. See, e.g., *Camps Newfound/Owatonna v. Town of Harrison*, 520 U.S. 564, 582 n.16, 589 (1997); *New Energy Co. of Indiana v. Limbach*, 486 U.S. 269, 278 (1988). Thus, in our familiar apple hypothetical (see §8.1), if state C decided to support its local apple industry by giving funds only to local apple growers, the state, as a market participant, would probably not be open to a dormant Commerce Clause challenge that it is discriminating against interstate commerce.

The treatment of subsidies becomes slightly more complex, however, if we focus on the source of the money involved. If the subsidy is funded from general tax revenues, there is probably no dormant Commerce Clause problem, for while the state is aiding local businesses, it is doing so without imposing any burdens on interstate commerce. However, if the subsidy is funded by a special tax that is paid by both local and out-of-state businesses, and the revenue from the tax is then returned exclusively to local interests in the form of a subsidy, the subsidy is in effect a tax rebate or a tax exemption that discriminates against interstate commerce. When a state exercises its taxing power, it is not a market participant. State tax laws may therefore be challenged under the dormant Commerce Clause, particularly where, as here, they discriminate against interstate commerce. See §8.13.3.

Example 8-K

A state pays an annual subsidy to local dairy farmers. The subsidy is funded by a special tax on the sale of milk. The tax applies to all milk, whether it was produced in state or out of state. While the subsidy discriminates against interstate commerce, the state claims it is a market participant and therefore exempt from the dormant Commerce Clause. Will the state prevail on this argument?

Explanation

The state's argument will fail. By taxing the sale of all milk and then using that revenue to pay a subsidy only to local milk producers, the state in effect exempts locally produced milk from the special sales tax. The tax and subsidy together operate like a tariff on milk imported from other states. The state does not qualify as a market participant and the tax-subsidy scheme may be challenged under the dormant Commerce Clause. This example is based on *West Lynn Creamery, Inc. v. Healy*, 512 U.S. 186 (1994). Cf. *Pharmaceutical Research and Manufacturers of America v. Walsh*, 538 U.S. 644, 669-670 (2003) (principle of *West Lynn* does not apply when "tax" is distributed to in-state consumers rather than to the out-of-state business's local competitors).

In this same example, if the state had not imposed a special sales tax on milk and had instead simply paid an annual subsidy to local dairy farmers funded out of general state revenues, the state would then have been acting as a market participant; as such, the subsidy would likely have been exempt from challenge under the dormant Commerce Clause. See *Hughes v. Alexandria Scrap Corp.*, 426 U.S. 794 (1976).

§8.12.3 State Tax Credits and Tax Exemptions

It is important to distinguish between subsidies, which will sometimes qualify for the market participant exemption, and tax credits or tax exemptions, which are never eligible for such treatment. Though state tax credits and tax exemptions may have the same financial effect as a cash subsidy to the benefited entity, they are nonetheless treated differently. When the state grants tax credits or tax exemptions, it is not directly involved in the market as a buyer or a seller, but instead acts in a sovereign capacity. Indeed, the "assessment and computation of taxes" is "a primeval governmental activity." *New Energy Co. of Indiana v. Limbach*, 486 U.S. 269, 277 (1988) (invalidating Ohio tax credit that discriminated against out-of-state companies). If the Court were to treat tax credits and tax exemptions as the equivalent of subsidies, this could result in "a dramatic expansion of the 'market participant' exception," given the breadth of activity to which they could be applied. *Camps Newfound/Owatonna v. Town of Harrison*, 520 U.S. 564, 593-594 (1997) (holding state tax exemption ineligible for market participant exception).

§8.13 STATE TAXES AND THE DORMANT COMMERCE CLAUSE

We have been considering the dormant Commerce Clause as it applies to the state when it acts to regulate private activity. The clause also applies to the state when it exercises its power of taxation. While the Court has long recognized that interstate and foreign commerce must carry their fair share of the state tax burden, state taxes may nonetheless run afoul of the dormant Commerce Clause.

In determining whether a state tax violates the dormant Commerce Clause, the Court frequently uses a different analysis than that used to evaluate state regulations. Instead of the regular approach, it may employ a four-factor test that derives from *Complete Auto Transit, Inc. v. Brady*, 430 U.S. 274 (1977). Under the *Complete Auto* test, a state tax will be found to violate the dormant Commerce Clause if the taxpayer shows that the tax (1) applies to an activity that lacks a substantial nexus to the taxing state, (2) is not fairly apportioned, (3) discriminates against interstate or foreign commerce, or (4) is not fairly related to services provided by the state. If the only dormant

Commerce Clause issue is whether a tax impermissibly discriminates against interstate commerce, the Court may not mention *Complete Auto* as such, but rather simply apply the same discrimination analysis that is used in other dormant Commerce Clause cases. See, e.g., *Camps Newfound/Owatonna v. Town of Harrison*, 520 U.S. 564 (1997) (invalidating state tax law on the basis that it was discriminatory but without using *Complete Auto* analysis). We will examine each part of the *Complete Auto* test in turn.

§8.13.1 Substantial Nexus to the Taxing State

The first part of the *Complete Auto* test requires that the subject of a tax — i.e., the activity that gives rise to liability for the tax — must bear a substantial nexus to the taxing state. This requirement is met for example in the case of a real property tax whose subject is the ownership of real property located in the taxing state. The requirement is likewise satisfied by a sales tax, whose subject is the purchase of goods in the taxing state.

By contrast, the substantial nexus test would not be met if a state sought to impose its sales tax on a sale that occurred in another state. Nor would the nexus requirement be met if a state imposed its ad valorem property tax on property that happened to be in transit through the state on "tax day" but which otherwise was not used there. See *Braniff Airways, Inc. v. Nebraska State Board of Equalization*, 347 U.S. 590 (1954).

The nexus criterion of *Complete Auto* is similar to, but distinct from, the Due Process Clause limitation that a state may take judicial jurisdiction over a defendant only if the defendant has certain minimum contacts with the forum state. See *International Shoe Co. v. Washington*, 326 U.S. 310 (1945). Whereas the Due Process Clause is concerned with assuring fundamental fairness to defendants, the dormant Commerce Clause seeks to ensure that interstate commerce is not unduly burdened. Because the purposes of the two clauses are different, activity that may suffice to allow the exercise of jurisdiction will not necessarily suffice to permit the entity to be taxed. Thus, in *Quill Corporation v. North Dakota*, 504 U.S. 298 (1992), the Court held that while an out-of-state seller who had no physical presence in North Dakota could be subjected to personal jurisdiction there, the seller lacked a sufficient nexus with the state for North Dakota to impose a duty on the seller to collect use taxes for sales made to residents of the state.

§8.13.2 Fairly Apportioned

One of the principal dangers faced by companies that do business on an interstate basis is that they will be subject to "multiple taxation" in the sense that because of their interstate character, they will be forced to pay more taxes than would a comparable intrastate business. Consider an example.

Example 8-L

Acme, Inc., manufactures and sells bowling balls in states X, Y, and Z. Acme's gross annual income is $10 million. Zephyr, Inc., also earns gross annual income of $10 million from the manufacture and sale of bowling balls, but all of its operations are confined to state X. States X, Y, and Z each levy a 10 percent tax on the gross annual income of any corporation that does business in the state. Does Acme face multiple taxation?

Explanation

Under this scheme, Acme will pay annual taxes of $1 million (10% × $10 million) to states X, Y, and Z, for a total tax bill of $3 million. By contrast, Zephyr, whose gross income was identical to Acme's, will pay only $1 million in taxes, to state X. Because Acme is an interstate business, it will pay three times the taxes of Zephyr, a company set up on a purely intrastate basis. In this example, Acme has been subjected to multiple (i.e., triple) taxation.

The second part of the *Complete Auto* test is designed to reduce the risk of multiple taxation by insisting that if a state taxes an activity that could also be taxed by other states, the tax must be fairly apportioned so that the state taxes only its fair share of the interstate transaction or activity in question. In this way, interstate commerce will not be put at a competitive disadvantage vis-à-vis purely intrastate commerce.

The apportionment rule applies when a tax is such that other states could impose a similar or identical tax, with the result that interstate commerce would be subject to greater tax burdens than those placed on intrastate commerce. In our apple problem (see §8.1), if the state imposed a franchise tax on every company that does business in the state, the tax, as applied to an out-of-state apple dealer, would have to be apportioned to reach only a portion of the company's income, for a similar tax could be imposed by every other state in which the company operates.

Example 8-M

State X imposes an annual property tax on all trucks present there on "tax day." Does the state have to apportion this tax, or may it impose the tax on the full value of the trucks present there on "tax day"?

Explanation

Even if the trucks have a sufficient nexus with state X to allow them to be taxed, a similar property tax could be levied on the same trucks by other states that use a different "tax day." To ensure that trucks used in interstate commerce are not subject to multiple taxation, as compared with taxes paid by trucks used solely in one state, the tax would have to be apportioned. This might be accomplished by taxing only a percentage of a truck's value; the percentage might be based on the number of days during the year the truck was in state X, or on the portion of the truck's annual mileage that was driven in state X.

Some taxes are, by their nature, such that they need not be apportioned because no other state could impose a similar tax on the same subject or activity. For example, real property taxes may be levied only by the state where the property is located; if another state were to impose such a tax, it would fail the nexus prong of the *Complete Auto* test. Real estate taxes thus need not be apportioned even if they are applied to property owned by an interstate business.

Similarly, a sales tax does not have to be apportioned, for the subject of the tax, the sale of goods, is deemed to occur only in the state where title or ownership to the goods passes to the buyer. See *McLeod v. J. E. Dilworth Co.*, 322 U.S. 327 (1944). Since there is only one state that can impose a sales tax on any particular transaction, there is no risk of multiple taxation of sales that involve parties in different states.

The Subject of a Tax

Whether a tax must be apportioned depends on its subject, for it is the subject of a tax that determines whether other states are in a position to impose a similar tax on the same taxpayer so as to create a risk of multiple taxation. Taxes having the same measure — i.e., taxes that are computed in the same way — may differ in terms of whether they must be apportioned, depending on whether or not they have different subjects.

Example 8-N

The Delta Company manufactures valves at its plant in state X. All of the valves are sold to a buyer in state Y whose purchases last year totaled $100,000. State Y imposes a franchise tax on the privilege of doing business in the state. The measure of the tax is 2 percent of gross receipts. State Y claims that Delta owes it a tax of $2,000 (2% × $100,000). May state Y collect the tax?

Explanation

The subject of state Y's tax — the privilege of doing business in the state — is one that state X could also tax since Delta does business there as well. Without apportionment, an interstate business like Delta would face the risk of multiple taxation, while a company that operated solely in state X or state Y would be taxed only once. State Y therefore cannot apply its 2 percent franchise tax to Delta's entire $100,000 income. Instead, the tax must be apportioned so that state Y taxes only its fair share of Delta's gross receipts.

Example 8-O

In our prior example, assume that instead of a franchise tax, state Y imposes a 2 percent sales tax on goods sold in the state. (Note: While liability for a sales tax — i.e., its legal incidence — technically falls on the buyer, the duty to collect and remit the tax is imposed on the seller.) Can state Y collect $2,000 (2% × $100,000) in sales taxes from Delta?

Explanation

The subject of this tax — the sale of goods — is such that there is no risk of multiple taxation. Because all of the Delta sales being taxed are deemed to have occurred only in state Y, no other state could levy a sales tax on the same sales. State Y could therefore collect the full $2,000 in sales taxes from Delta without having to apportion the tax.

In the previous two examples, though the franchise tax and the sales tax were both measured in the same way (2 percent of sales receipts), because they had different subjects, only the franchise tax created a risk of multiple taxation so as to require that it be apportioned.

Methods of Apportionment

Where apportionment is required because of the risk of multiple taxation, states employ a variety of approaches to ensure that they tax only their fair share of the pie. The approach taken depends partly on the type of tax involved. Consider an ad valorem property tax, whose subject is the ownership of property and whose measure is a percentage of the property's value. If such a tax is imposed on personal property that is in the state only part of the year, it might be apportioned by calculating the percentage of the year the property was present in the state, and then taxing only that portion of the property's value.

To apportion income taxes, franchise taxes, and other taxes measured by a taxpayer's gross or net income, states often use a three-factor formula to determine what share of the income is fairly attributable to a taxpayer's operations in the state. Under the typical version of the formula, the state will tax a portion of the taxpayer's total income calculated by averaging the percentage of payroll, the percentage of property, and the percentage of sales located in the state. Thus, if an entity had 35 percent of its payroll, 10 percent of its property, and 15 percent of its sales in the taxing state, the state would tax 20 percent of the entity's total income (35% + 10% + 15%) / 3 = 20%.

In determining an entity's total income against which this formula percentage is applied, some states use geographical or transactional accounting, which focuses only on those transactions that occurred within the taxing state. However, many states use the unitary business method, which takes into account the total income earned by all of the corporate entities that are part of the same unitary business enterprise as the entity being taxed, including income earned outside the taxing state. See *MeadWestvaco Corp. ex rel. Mead Corp. v. Illinois Dept. of Revenue*, 553 U.S. 16, 30 (2008) (hallmarks of a unitary relationship are "functional integration, centralized management, and economies of scale"). Thus, in *Barclays Bank v. Franchise Tax Board*, 512 U.S. 298 (1994), California, in applying the three-factor formula to determine the locally taxable income of two British corporations doing business in the state, employed the unitary business method to include the worldwide income of the Barclays Group, a unitary business composed of more than 220 corporations operating in 60 countries. Some states limit the unitary business method to the United States' "water's edge" so as to include the income of only those entities in the unitary business group that operate in the United States. However, even under the unitary business method, a state may not seek to tax income received by an out-of-state corporation from an "unrelated business activity" that constitutes a "discrete business enterprise." For the state to attempt to reach such "nonunitary" income would violate the substantial nexus requirement of the Due Process and Commerce Clauses where there is no connection between the taxing state and the nonunitary income. See *Hunt-Wesson, Inc. v. California Franchise Tax Board*, 528 U.S. 458 (2000) (invalidating California's unitary business tax to the extent that it reached nonunitary income that lacked a "minimal connection" to California).

While the states' use of apportionment formulas mitigates the risk of multiple taxation, it does not eliminate it entirely. This results partly from the fact that states using the same formula may apply it differently. Moreover, the states do not all employ the same formula. Some states use formulas that weight the three factors unequally, while others use less than three factors. These variations may produce multiple taxation; i.e., the states, between them, may end up taxing more than 100 percent of a particular taxpayer's income.

Example 8-P

Suppose that a corporation does business only in states X and Y. The corporation's payroll, property, and sales are divided between the two states as follows:

	State X	State Y
Payroll:	10%	90%
Property:	40%	60%
Sales:	70%	30%

What percentage of the corporation's income may each state tax?

Explanation

If state X and state Y each applied the typical three-factor formula and weighted the factors equally, multiple taxation would not occur, for state X would tax 40 percent of the corporation's income [(10% + 40% + 70%) / 3 = 40%], while state Y would tax the remaining 60 percent [(90% + 60% + 30%) / 3 = 60%]. However, if only state X used this formula, and state Y used a single-factor formula based solely on payroll, state X would still tax 40 percent of the income but state Y would now tax 90 percent, for a combined total of 130 percent—i.e., almost a third of the corporation's income would be taxed twice.

———————————

Yet the mere fact that a state uses something other than the typical three-factor formula does not guarantee that multiple taxation will occur. In Example 8-P, if state X and state Y had both used a single-factor formula based on payroll, exactly 100 percent of the taxpayer's income would have been taxed. Multiple taxation will occur only if the states in which a taxpayer operates use different apportionment formulas, or if they use the same formula but apply it differently.

The states enjoy broad leeway in choosing among various methods of apportionment. The Supreme Court has refused to insist that the states all use the same method, as this "would require a policy decision based on political and economic considerations that vary from state to state. The Constitution, however, is neutral with respect to the content of any uniform rule." *Moorman Manufacturing Co. v. Bair*, 437 U.S. 267, 279 (1978).

Since the states approach apportionment in quite different ways, it is easy for an interstate business to allege that it faces a risk of multiple taxation. However, even if it can be shown that a taxpayer is subject to possible or actual multiple taxation, the Court will rarely strike down an apportioned tax on the ground that the apportionment is not fair. If a state has made no attempt whatsoever to apportion its tax, the tax may well be declared unconstitutional. But if the state has adopted some means of apportionment, the tax will most likely be upheld even if it is out of line with the approaches used by other states, and even if it produces actual multiple taxation.

In rare instances the Court has invalidated an apportioned tax, but only as applied to that particular taxpayer. To prevail in such a challenge, the taxpayer "must demonstrate that there is no rational relationship between the income attributed to the State and the intrastate values of the enterprise. . . ." *Amerada Hess Corp. v. Director, Division of Taxation*, 490 U.S. 66, 75 (1989). This is a very difficult showing to make.

§8.13.3 Discrimination Against Interstate Commerce

The third part of the *Complete Auto* test provides that a state tax may not discriminate against interstate or foreign commerce. A tax that does so, either facially or by design, is unconstitutional unless the state can show that there was no less discriminatory way to achieve a legitimate state interest. If the state's only justification is that it was seeking to protect or encourage local business activity, the Court will reject the discriminatory tax as being a forbidden scheme of economic protectionism. See *Bacchus Imports Ltd. v. Dias*, 468 U.S. 263 (1984). Note, however, that a state may provide favorable tax treatment for state-issued bonds without running afoul of this principle. See *Department of Revenue of Kentucky v. Davis*, 553 U.S. 328, 341-343 (2008) (no discrimination when a state exempts from state income tax the interest on bonds issued by it or its subdivisions, while taxing interest income on bonds issued by other states and their subdivisions).

In addition, a facially neutral tax that is applied evenhandedly may nonetheless be challenged as discriminatory if, when considered in light of similar taxes imposed by other states, its effect is to burden those engaged in interstate or foreign commerce more heavily than it burdens similarly situated local interests. This so-called internal consistency test in effect asks, "What would happen if all States did the same?" *American Trucking Associations, Inc. v. Michigan Public Service Commn.*, 545 U.S. 429, 437 (2005).

Example 8-Q

A state imposes an annual tax of $36 per axle on all trucks that use the state's highways. Does the tax discriminate against interstate commerce?

Explanation

Though the state's own tax is facially nondiscriminatory since it applies to both in-state and out-of-state trucks, its practical effect is to discriminate against interstate commerce if trucks operating interstate must pay similar taxes to other states, while purely intrastate trucks pay the tax only once. The net effect is to increase the cost per mile of interstate trucking in favor of wholly intrastate commerce. See *American Trucking Associations, Inc. v. Scheiner*, 483 U.S. 266 (1987).

Example 8-R

State X imposes a flat $100 annual fee on all trucks that engage in intrastate commerce — i.e., on trucks that undertake any point-to-point hauls between cities within the state. A state Y trucking company that engages in both interstate and intrastate hauling in state X has objected to the $100 annual fee on the basis that it discriminates against interstate commerce. How should the court rule on this objection?

Explanation

The $100 annual fee does not on its face discriminate against — much less even apply to — interstate commerce since it only covers those making point-to-point deliveries within the state. The state Y trucking company may argue that the fee should be deemed to be discriminatory because if a similar fee were imposed by every other state in which the company makes any intrastate deliveries, an interstate trucking company would be forced to pay the tax many times over, while a purely intrastate company would pay it only once. However, unlike the previous problem, the $100 fee here is imposed only on companies that engage in purely intrastate commerce. It is not the fact that the company engages in interstate commerce that results in its being subject to multiple taxation; rather, it is the fact that, besides engaging in interstate commerce (for which it would not have to pay the $100 annual fee), the company has also chosen to engage in some purely intrastate commerce. In the latter capacity, the out-of-state company cannot claim any special constitutional protection since its interstate activities are not being taxed at all, and insofar as its purely intrastate business is concerned, it is treated exactly the same as other local companies. See *American Trucking Associations, Inc. v. Michigan Public Service Commn.*, 545 U.S. 429 (2005).

A tax that discriminates against interstate commerce will nonetheless be upheld if it is shown to be a compensatory tax in the sense that it is "designed simply to make interstate commerce bear a burden already borne by intrastate commerce." *Fulton Corp. v. Faulkner,* 516 U.S. 325 (1996). For example, if a state imposes a sales tax on goods bought in the state, residents will have an economic incentive to purchase the item in another state whose sales tax is lower than that in the buyer's home state. To eliminate this incentive, a state that imposes a sales tax will also usually impose a compensatory use tax on the privilege of using goods in the state that were purchased elsewhere. The use tax and the sales tax are set at the same rate, and the buyer receives a credit against the use tax for any sales tax already paid on the item. On its face, a use tax does discriminate against interstate commerce, for it applies only to purchases made outside the state. Yet when viewed in a broader perspective, the combined effect of the sales and use taxes is to place intrastate and interstate purchases on an equal footing. See *Henneford v. Silas Mason Co.,* 300 U.S. 577 (1937) (upholding compensatory use tax under dormant Commerce Clause).

The Court has articulated a three-part test to determine whether a tax that is facially discriminatory against interstate commerce may be upheld as a valid compensatory tax:

1. The state must identify the intrastate tax for which the discriminatory tax is designed to compensate, and must show that the purpose for which the intrastate tax is imposed is one that also justifies placing a burden on interstate commerce;
2. The tax on interstate commerce must roughly approximate — and in no event exceed — the amount of the tax on intrastate commerce; and
3. The events on which the interstate and intrastate taxes are imposed must be substantially equivalent so that one tax can fairly be deemed a proxy for the other.

This test is satisfied by a compensatory use tax. First, the use tax is designed to compensate for the state's sales tax; like the sales tax, its purpose is to raise revenue by taxing the process of selling goods where the sale or first use of the good occurs in the taxing state. Second, because the use tax and sales tax are set at the same rate, and because a credit is given against the use tax for any sales tax paid on the same item, interstate and intrastate purchases are taxed at exactly the same rates. Finally, the events taxed are substantial equivalents of one another since both taxes fall on the buyer, who is taxed either for purchasing the good or for using it, but not for both.

While the Court has framed the compensatory tax test in general terms, it has noted that "use taxes on products purchased out of state are the only taxes we have upheld in recent memory under the compensatory tax doctrine." *Oregon Waste Systems, Inc. v. Department of Envtl. Quality*, 511 U.S. 93, 105 (1994). In virtually all other settings, the Court has rejected this defense where taxes discriminate against interstate commerce. See, e.g., *Fulton Corp. v. Faulkner*, 516 U.S. 325 (1996) (invalidating "intangibles tax" on value of corporate stock where tax discriminated against interstate commerce by taxing shares issued by companies that did not do business in North Carolina at higher rate than shares issued by domestic corporations); *South Central Bell Telephone Co. v. Alabama*, 526 U.S. 160 (1999) (rejecting argument that a discriminatory corporate franchise tax was a valid compensatory tax that offset the burden that a domestic shares tax imposed on domestic corporations).

§8.13.4 Fairly Related to State Services

The final prong of the *Complete Auto* test is that the state tax must be fairly related to services provided by the state. This might suggest that a tax may be struck down if the *amount* of the tax exceeds the value of the benefits the state has afforded the taxpayer. However, the Court has expressly rejected such a requirement. Instead, the test is simply "that the *measure* of the tax must be reasonably related to the extent of the . . . activities or presence of the taxpayer in the State. . . ." *Commonwealth Edison Co. v. Montana*, 453 U.S. 609, 626 (1981) (emphasis supplied). On this basis, the *Commonwealth Edison* Court held that a Montana tax on the mining of coal, measured in terms of the value of coal extracted, satisfied *Complete Auto*'s fourth prong since the taxpayer's liability varied in proportion to the extent of its activity in the state. The Court refused to consider the taxpayer's claim that the amount of tax it was forced to pay far exceeded the benefits it had received from the state.

It appears that the only taxes open to challenge under this part of the *Complete Auto* test are flat taxes whose measure is in no way tied to the extent of a taxpayer's presence in the state. For example, suppose that Montana imposed a flat tax of $100,000 per year on every company that mines coal in the state. Yet even then, a taxpayer would probably have to prove that the amount of the tax bears no relation to benefits conferred by the state. Since the Court has made it clear that indirect as well as direct benefits are to be taken into account, this prong of *Complete Auto* would seem to be a dead letter.

§8.13.5 Taxation of Foreign Commerce

We saw earlier that state regulations that affect commerce with other nations are held to a higher standard of review under the dormant Commerce Clause. See §8.10. The same is true of state taxes. If a state tax affects foreign commerce, in addition to applying the four-part *Complete Auto* analysis, the

Court will consider two additional concerns: (1) the enhanced risk of multiple taxation and (2) the possible need for federal uniformity.

The enhanced risk of multiple taxation in the international setting stems from the fact that while the federal judiciary can ensure that individual states fairly apply and apportion their taxes, there is no comparable tribunal at the international level to impose this obligation on other nations. As a result, an entity engaged in foreign commerce may be subjected to both a fairly apportioned state tax and an unapportioned foreign tax, leading to possible multiple taxation. In our apple hypothetical (see §8.1), for example, a Japanese apple exporter would face multiple taxation if state C levied a sales tax — which ordinarily does not need to be apportioned — on all apples sold in the state, while under Japanese law the company was also required to pay a sales tax to Japan on its sales in state C.

Example 8-S

A state imposes its ad valorem property tax on shipping containers that are owned by a Japanese shipping company and that are present in the state on "tax day." The tax is apportioned based on the number of days of the year that the containers are used in the state. The same containers are subject to an unapportioned property tax in Japan — i.e., the tax is in no way based on the amount of time the container is in Japan. May the company challenge the state's tax on the ground that it violates the dormant Commerce Clause?

Explanation

The state tax satisfies the nexus test, the first part of *Complete Auto*, because the containers are used periodically in the state. It also satisfies the second and third parts of *Complete Auto* since the tax is fairly apportioned and does not discriminate against interstate or foreign commerce. Nor does it violate the fourth or "fairly related" part of *Complete Auto* for it is not a flat tax but instead varies with the value of the containers. Yet the tax is probably unconstitutional because it results in multiple taxation of an entity engaged in foreign commerce because of the fact that the company must also pay Japan a property tax based on the full value of the same containers. See *Japan Line, Ltd. v. County of Los Angeles*, 441 U.S. 434 (1979).

The Court has held that in the context of income taxation as opposed to property taxation, even actual multiple taxation of an entity engaged in foreign commerce will not necessarily invalidate an apportioned state tax. Instead, to strike down an apportioned state income tax, it must be shown that the tax will inevitably produce multiple taxation without regard to the facts of an individual case, and that the state has available to it reasonable alternatives that will eliminate the risk of multiple taxation. The Court on this basis has rejected challenges to California's unitary business tax, as applied to the worldwide income of entities engaged in foreign commerce, even though the state's tax has at times resulted in multiple taxation. See *Barclays Bank v. Franchise Tax Board*, 512 U.S. 298 (1994); *Container Corporation of America v. Franchise Tax Board*, 463 U.S. 159 (1983).

The second additional concern that is triggered when a state tax impacts on foreign commerce focuses on whether the tax impairs federal uniformity in an area where it is essential that the nation speak with one voice. However, the Court will hold a state tax barred by the need for national uniformity only if there are specific indications of a congressional intent to preempt the state's action. In the absence of such evidence of federal preemption, a state tax on an entity engaged in foreign commerce will be found to satisfy this requirement. The preemption doctrine is discussed in §6.2.

The Privileges and Immunities Clause of Article IV

§9.1 INTRODUCTION AND OVERVIEW

The Privileges and Immunities Clause of Article IV, §2 provides that "[t]he Citizens of each State shall be entitled to all Privileges and Immunities of Citizens in the several States." Despite its rather awkward phrasing, the clause prohibits states from engaging in certain types of discrimination against citizens of other states. The clause was modeled after the Fourth Article of the Articles of Confederation, ratified in 1781, which declared,

> The better to secure and perpetuate mutual friendship and intercourse among the people of the different States in this Union, the free inhabitants of each of these States, paupers, vagabonds, and fugitives from Justice excepted, shall be entitled to all the privileges and immunities of free citizens in the several States; and the people of each State shall have free ingress and regress to and from any other State, and shall enjoy therein all the privileges of trade and commerce, subject to the same duties, impositions, and restrictions as the inhabitants thereof respectively. . . .

The Privileges and Immunities Clause was vital to creating a federal system of government. Its purpose "was to help fuse into one Nation a collection of independent, sovereign States. It was designed to insure to a citizen of state A who ventures into state B the same privileges which the citizens of state B enjoy." *Toomer v. Witsell*, 334 U.S. 385, 395 (1948). "Indeed, without some provision of the kind removing from the citizens of each State the disabilities of alienage in the other States, and giving them equality of privilege with citizens of those States, the Republic would have constituted little more than a league of States; it would not have constituted the Union which now exists." *Paul v. Virginia*, 75 U.S. (8 Wall.) 168, 180 (1869). The clause thus protects a citizen's "right to be treated as a welcome visitor rather than an unfriendly alien when temporarily present in [another] State. . . ." *Saenz v. Roe*, 526 U.S. 489, 501 (1999).

The Privileges and Immunities Clause does not bar all forms of discrimination against citizens of other states. Rather, the clause is triggered only if the discrimination affects an interest or right that is deemed to be "fundamental." Even then, the discrimination will be upheld if the state can demonstrate that there is a "substantial reason" for treating out-of-staters differently.

In analyzing a problem under the Privileges and Immunities Clause of Article IV you should proceed by asking three questions:

1. Does the challenged law affect a "fundamental" right, privilege, or immunity that falls within the purview of the clause?
2. Is the law's discrimination of a type that is prohibited by the clause?
3. Does the state have a "substantial reason" that justifies its discrimination against citizens of other states?

We examine each of these three issues in turn.

§9.2 FUNDAMENTAL RIGHTS

The Privileges and Immunities Clause is triggered only if a state discriminates against citizens of other states with respect to interests that are sufficiently "fundamental" to come within the purview of the clause. In *Corfield v. Coryell*, 6 F. Cas. 546, 552 (C.C.E.D. Pa. 1823) (No. 3230), the first case to construe Article IV's Privileges and Immunities Clause, the U.S. circuit court stated that the privileges and immunities protected by the clause include (1) the right to "pass through" or travel in a state; (2) the right to "reside in" a state for business or other purposes; (3) the right to do business there, whether it involves "trade, agriculture, professional pursuits, or otherwise"; (4) the right "to take, hold and dispose of property, either real or personal"; and (5) "an exemption from higher taxes or impositions than are paid by the other citizens of the state." In addition, the Court has emphasized that, to fall within the purview of the clause,

> the activity in question must be "sufficiently basic to the livelihood of the Nation." . . . For it is "[o]nly with respect to those 'privileges' and

'immunities' bearing on the vitality of the Nation as a single entity" that a State must accord residents and nonresidents equal treatment.

Supreme Court of Virginia v. Friedman, 487 U.S. 59, 64-65 (1988).

While the Supreme Court has endorsed the list of fundamental rights articulated in *Corfield*, it has only occasionally added to that list. In *Doe v. Bolton*, 410 U.S. 179, 200 (1973), the Court expanded on *Corfield* by holding that one of the privileges and immunities protected by Article IV is the right to enter a state "seeking the medical services that are available there." A state therefore may not "limit to its own residents the general medical care available within its borders." Id. The law struck down in *Bolton* prohibited out-of-staters from obtaining abortions in Georgia. As we will see in §9.4.2, while a state may be allowed to discriminate against citizens of other states where access to public resources is concerned, because the Georgia law discriminated against out-of-staters with respect to all medical facilities, both public and private, it ran afoul of the Privileges and Immunities Clause.

Example 9-A

State B requires anyone who enters a bicycle race in the state to have a bike racing license. The license fee is $25 per year for citizens of state B and $50 per year for all others. Mack is a citizen of state A who wishes to enter a bike race in state B. He objects to paying a fee that is double that paid by state B residents. Can Mack invoke the Article IV Privileges and Immunities Clause to challenge the discriminatory fee schedule?

Explanation

The Privileges and Immunities Clause will come into play only if the state is discriminating against citizens of other states with respect to a fundamental right. The state will argue that the interest in bike racing does not involve an interest that is protected by the clause because it is purely recreational in nature. In *Baldwin v. Montana Fish & Game Commn.*, 436 U.S. 371 (1978), the Court held that Montana's discriminatory license fees for elk-hunting licenses did not implicate the Privileges and Immunities Clause since elk hunting was a recreational rather than a commercial pursuit and thus did not involve a fundamental right under Article IV, §2.

Mack might reply that even if bike racing, like elk hunting, is purely recreational, the state still violated his fundamental right to "exemption from higher taxes or impositions than are paid by the other citizens of the state," *Corfield*, supra, 6 F. Cas. at 552, an argument that the *Baldwin* Court did not address. Mack might also be able to show that he depends for all or part of his livelihood on bike racing, in which case the Privileges and Immunities Clause would be triggered, for "one of the privileges which the clause guarantees to citizens of State A is that of doing business in State B on terms of substantial equality with the citizens of that State." *Toomer v. Witsell,* 334 U.S. 385, 396 (1948).

Many of the cases that have arisen under the Privileges and Immunities Clause have involved the interest of out-of-staters in "doing business . . . on terms of substantial equality with the citizens of that State." Id. at 396. Indeed, the Court has observed that "the pursuit of a common calling is one of the most fundamental of those privileges protected by the Clause." *United Building & Construction Trades Council v. Mayor & Council of Camden,* 465 U.S. 208, 219 (1984). Yet the Court has suggested that this Article IV privilege is limited to private sector employment and that discrimination against out-of-staters with respect to public employment does not fall within the purview of the clause. Id. at 219. At least one lower federal court has taken the hint and held that government employment is not a privilege or immunity protected by Article IV, §2. *Salem Blue Collar Workers Assn. v. City of Salem,* 33 F.3d 265, 268-270 (3d Cir. 1994), *cert. denied,* 513 U.S. 1152 (1995).

It is important to note that the list of "fundamental rights" under the Privileges and Immunities Clause of Article IV is not the same as the definition of "fundamental rights" for purposes of the Due Process and Equal Protection Clauses. As a consequence, interests like pursuing a livelihood that are fundamental for purposes of Article IV, §2 are not deemed to be fundamental under the due process or equal protection provisions of the Fifth and Fourteenth Amendments.

---

§9.3 DISCRIMINATION AGAINST CITIZENS OF OTHER STATES

§9.3.1 The Requirement of Discrimination

Corfield v. Coryell *and Natural Law*

Early on it was suggested that the Privileges and Immunities Clause of Article IV embodies certain natural law rights that a state may not deny to anyone, including its own citizens. This interpretation was adopted in 1823 by the U.S. circuit court in *Corfield v. Coryell,* supra. There, Justice Bushrod Washington, George Washington's nephew, declared that the rights protected by the clause consist of "those privileges and immunities which are, in their nature, fundamental; which belong, of right, to the citizens of all free governments; and which have, at all times, been enjoyed by the citizens of the several states. . . ." 6 F. Cas. at 551. Under this reading, a state could not deny these rights to anyone. Whether or not there was discrimination against out-of-staters was irrelevant; any denial of one of these "fundamental" privileges and immunities would be invalid, either as a matter of natural law or as a violation of Article IV.

The Rejection of Corfield

Corfield's construction of the Privileges and Immunities Clause would have given absolute protection to certain natural law rights. However, this view was ultimately rejected by the Supreme Court. The Court in 1869 held that the clause is addressed only to the *discriminatory* denial of rights. Its purpose is merely "to place the citizens of each State upon the same footing with citizens of other States. . . . It relieves them from the disabilities of alienage in other States; it inhibits discriminating legislation against them by other States. . . ." *Paul v. Virginia,* supra, 75 U.S. (8 Wall.) at 180. Four years later, in the *Slaughter-House Cases,* 83 U.S. (16 Wall.) 36 (1873), the Court stressed that the clause thus gives no rights to citizens against their own state:

> [It] did not create those rights, which it called privileges and immunities of citizens of the States. . . . Nor did it profess to control the power of the State governments over the rights of its own citizens.
>
> Its sole purpose was to declare to the several States, that whatever those rights, as you grant or establish them to your own citizens, or as you limit or qualify, or impose restrictions on their exercise, the same, neither more nor less, shall be the measure of the rights of citizens of other States within your jurisdiction.

Id. at 77.

Example 9-B

State X recently passed a law barring anyone from working as a licensed plumber unless he or she passes the state plumbing exam (SPE) and serves three years as an apprentice to a licensed state X plumber. Paul is a citizen of state Y. He has been a plumber for many years and has done a great deal of plumbing work in state X. However, Paul can no longer work as a plumber in state X because he has neither passed the SPE nor been apprenticed to a licensed state X plumber. May Paul challenge the new state X law on the ground that it violates his rights under the Privileges and Immunities Clause of Article IV?

Explanation

Since pursuing a trade is a fundamental right under Article IV, §2, the law affects an interest that falls within the purview of the clause. State X will argue that its law does not discriminate against citizens of other states; rather, it requires everyone, including its own citizens, to meet the statutory requirements before they may work as a licensed plumber. On this basis the state would urge that the Privileges and Immunities Clause is not triggered here.

Paul might respond that, while the law is facially neutral, the apprenticeship requirement should be subject to scrutiny under the clause because it has the practical effect of discriminating against out-of-staters like himself. Citizens of other states are far less likely than state X citizens to have been apprenticed to a plumber licensed by state X. It is unclear whether the Court would find such non-facial discrimination enough to trigger the Privileges and Immunities Clause. In *Hillside Dairy Inc. v. Lyons*, 539 U.S. 59, 67 (2003), the Court noted that while "the absence of an express statement . . . identifying out-of-state citizenship as a basis for disparate treatment is not a sufficient basis for rejecting" a claim made under the Privileges and Immunities Clause, it remains an open question whether the clause applies only to "classifications that are but proxies for differential treatment of out-of-state residents" or whether it should also be deemed to reach "classifications with the practical effect of discriminating against such residents. . . ." Thus, Paul might be required to prove that the discrimination was intentional — i.e., that state X adopted the apprenticeship rule because of its discriminatory effect on out-of-staters; otherwise, the law's unintended discriminatory effect might not suffice to bring the clause into play. If Paul can persuade the Court that the apprenticeship rule is discriminatory within the meaning of the clause, the rule will be invalidated unless the state can show that there is a substantial reason for the discrimination. See §9.4.

The Fourteenth Amendment Privileges or Immunities Clause

The requirement that there be discrimination against out-of-staters in order to trigger the Privileges and Immunities Clause of Article IV was not eliminated by the adoption of the Fourteenth Amendment in 1868. In the *Slaughter-House Cases*, the Court rejected a contention that the Fourteenth Amendment in effect removed the discrimination requirement from Article IV. That contention was based on the fact that §1 of the Fourteenth Amendment contains a Privileges or Immunities Clause phrased in absolute terms: "No State shall make or enforce any law which shall abridge the privileges or immunities of citizens of the United States. . . ." Unlike Article IV, the Fourteenth Amendment prohibits *any* abridgment of a citizen's privileges or immunities, whether or not there is discrimination against citizens of other states. However, the Court in the *Slaughter-House Cases* held that the privileges and immunities given absolute protection by the Fourteenth Amendment involve a completely different set or list of rights than those protected by Article IV. Article IV protects the privileges and immunities of *state citizenship*, whereas the Fourteenth Amendment protects the privileges and immunities of *national citizenship*. As a result, the Fourteenth Amendment did not give "any additional protection" to the privileges and immunities of state citizenship by in effect eliminating the discrimination requirement from Article IV. 83 U.S. (16 Wall.) at 73-80.

There is a marked difference between the privileges and immunities of Article IV and those that are protected by the Fourteenth Amendment. With respect to Article IV, the *Slaughter-House* Court endorsed *Corfield's* list of the privileges and immunities of state citizenship, including the rights to pursue a trade or occupation, to own property, and to travel freely in the state, and taxation—all on an equal basis with a state's own citizens. On the other hand, the privileges or immunities of national citizenship, which receive absolute protection under the Fourteenth Amendment, embrace such interests as the right to travel throughout the United States, the right to protection of the federal government while at sea or abroad, the right to petition the national government, the right to habeas corpus, and the right to the protection of federal treaties. Id. at 79-80. However, because most of these rights are protected against state violation by other parts of the Constitution, the Fourteenth Amendment Privileges or Immunities Clause as construed by the Court in the *Slaughter-House Cases* has been rarely used.

Example 9-C

A Louisiana law gives one corporation a monopoly over all slaughtering and butchering operations in the City of New Orleans, thereby preventing other butchers from pursuing their trade in that city. Does this law violate the rights of independent butchers under the Privileges and/or Immunities Clauses of either Article IV or the Fourteenth Amendment?

Explanation

The Louisiana law offends neither clause. While the right to pursue one's trade is a privilege of state citizenship protected under Article IV, §2, this clause is not triggered here because Louisiana has not discriminated against citizens of other states; the monopoly law affects all independent butchers regardless of their state of citizenship. Nor is the Privileges or Immunities Clause of the Fourteenth Amendment offended by this law since the interest in pursuing a trade is not one of the privileges or immunities of national citizenship that is protected by the Amendment. See *Slaughter-House Cases*, 83 U.S. (16 Wall.) 36 (1873) (holding that Louisiana butcher monopoly statute did not violate the Privileges and/or Immunities Clauses of Article IV or the Fourteenth Amendment).

The Court's decision in *Saenz v. Roe*, 526 U.S. 489 (1999), may have breathed some life into the Fourteenth Amendment's Privileges or Immunities Clause. At issue in *Saenz* was a California welfare provision that discriminated against newly arrived state residents by limiting the amount of welfare they could receive during their first 12 months in California to the amount they would have received in their former states of residence — an amount that was often substantially less than the California benefits for which they were otherwise eligible. As citizens of California, albeit relatively new ones, the plaintiffs could not invoke Article IV, §2, which is designed to protect the interests of citizens of *other* states. However, the plaintiffs were in a position to invoke the Fourteenth Amendment, whose Privileges or Immunities Clause protects the interests of all persons, including those who are citizens of the state in question. The Court in *Saenz* concluded that the California scheme implicated "the right of a newly arrived citizen to the same privileges and immunities enjoyed by other citizens of the same State. That right is protected not only by the new arrival's status as a state citizen, but also by her status as a citizen of the United States." Id. at 502. The Court pegged this right of equal treatment squarely on the Fourteenth Amendment's Privileges or Immunities Clause. Id. at 503. Moreover, any potential violation of this right would be subjected to exacting scrutiny. Id. at 504.

In defense of its law, California explained that its sole purpose in adopting the measure was to save approximately $11 million per year in welfare costs. The Court recognized this interest as legitimate, but found that it could have been accomplished in a nondiscriminatory fashion by a minuscule across-the-board reduction in monthly welfare benefits. As a consequence, "the State's legitimate interest in saving money provide[d] no justification for its decision to discriminate among equally eligible citizens." Id. at 507. The discriminatory provisions of the California law were, therefore, unconstitutional.

The full impact of the *Saenz* decision cannot be judged at this point. The basic principle, however, appears to be that one of the Fourteenth Amendment privileges of U.S. citizenship is the right of every American citizen to change his or her state of citizenship by establishing domicile or residence in a new state and to then be treated by that state on an equal basis with its other citizens. Consider potential violations of this principle whenever a state keys eligibility for any state benefit on the length of time one has been a citizen of the state. See Allan Ides and Christopher N. May, *Constitutional Law: Individual Rights*, §7.4 (6th ed. 2013). There are, however, two caveats to the foregoing. First, there was no dispute in *Saenz* as to the legitimacy of the plaintiffs' claim of California citizenship. The Court's ruling, therefore, has no bearing on situations in which a relatively short duration of residence within the state calls into question the legitimacy of the claim to state citizenship. *Saenz v. Roe*, supra, 526 U.S. at 505. In other words, the underlying presumption of *Saenz* is that the party challenging the discriminatory law is in fact a bona fide citizen of the state. Second, the *Saenz* Court distinguished cases involving "portable" benefits like divorce or a college education that, once acquired by a new citizen while in the state, can then — unlike, say, the right to vote — still be enjoyed once the putative citizen returns to his or her original domicile. Id. While it remains to be seen whether states will be able to impose stricter restrictions on newcomers' receipt of such portable benefits, the underlying theory of *Saenz* would appear to embrace such benefits as well.

§9.3.2 Who Qualify as "Citizens" of Other States?

The Privileges and Immunities Clause of Article IV protects citizens of *other states* against state laws that discriminate in favor of a state's own citizens. To invoke this clause, a litigant must therefore establish that he or she is a citizen of some other state. Without such a showing, the litigant will lack standing in federal court since he or she would be seeking to assert the constitutional rights of others. See §3.4.5.

The Court has long held that corporations are not "citizens" of a state within the meaning of Article IV, §2, even though they qualify as state citizens under Article III's diversity of citizenship provision for federal court jurisdiction. See *Bank of Augusta v. Earle*, 38 U.S. (13 Pet.) 519, 586-587 (1839); *Paul v. Virginia*, 75 U.S. (8 Wall.) at 177-180. Laws that specifically discriminate against out-of-state corporations are therefore not subject to scrutiny under the Privileges and Immunities Clause (though they can be challenged under other constitutional provisions such as the dormant Commerce Clause or the Equal Protection Clause). Nor would out-of-state corporations have standing under the Privileges and Immunities Clause to challenge a state law that discriminates generally against out-of-staters in favor of a state's own citizens.

Example 9-D

The State of South Dakota operates its own cement plant. The state has a policy of favoring local buyers of cement over out-of-state buyers during periods of cement shortages. Under this policy, the state refused to sell cement to Reeves, Inc., a Wyoming corporation, on the ground that Reeves was an out-of-state entity. Can Reeves challenge South Dakota's policy under the Article IV Privileges and Immunities Clause?

Explanation

No. As a corporation, Reeves is not protected by the clause. Although South Dakota is discriminating against out-of-staters with respect to the fundamental right to do business (i.e., buy cement) in the state, Reeves lacks standing to invoke the Privileges and Immunities Clause since it would be invoking the constitutional rights of third parties rather than its own rights. See §3.4.5. Reeves might challenge the policy under other constitutional provisions, and a Wyoming individual or partnership could challenge it under Article IV, §2; however, as we will see in §9.4.2, since a state-owned good is involved, the South Dakota policy would probably not violate the Privileges and Immunities Clause. Cf. *Reeves, Inc. v. Stake*, 447 U.S. 429 (1980) (Wyoming corporation unsuccessfully challenged South Dakota cement policy under the dormant Commerce Clause but did not invoke the Privileges and Immunities Clause).

Natural persons are protected by Article IV, §2 if they are "citizens" of another state. Under Article IV, a natural person qualifies as a "citizen" of a particular state if he or she is (1) a United States citizen and (2) a bona fide resident of that state. *Slaughter-House Cases*, supra, 83 U.S. (16 Wall.) at 73-74; *Blake v. McClung*, 172 U.S. 239, 246-247 (1898). This definition of state citizenship tracks §1 of the Fourteenth Amendment, which specifies that "[a]ll persons born or naturalized in the United States . . . are citizens of the United States and of the State wherein they reside."

The fact that a U.S. citizen resides in a particular state does not necessarily make him or her a citizen of that state. To be a citizen of a state, a person must be a domiciliary or bona fide resident of that state. This means that one must have taken up residence there with the intent to remain indefinitely — as opposed to moving to a state with the intention of living there only for a fixed or temporary period. Once a person establishes a domicile or bona fide residency in a state, that status is not lost until he or she establishes a new domicile somewhere else.

Example 9-E

In Example 9-D, suppose that South Dakota also refused to sell cement to Saul because he does not live in the state. Saul was born and raised in South Dakota but moved to Wyoming a few years ago to attend college. During the summers he operates his own small construction business in Wyoming. When Saul moved to Wyoming his plan was to attend college there and then move to a warmer climate such as Florida. Can Saul claim that South Dakota's refusal to sell him cement violated Article IV, §2?

Explanation

No. While South Dakota interfered with Saul's fundamental right to do business in the state, he can challenge the cement policy under Article IV only if he is a citizen of some other state. That he now lives in Wyoming is not enough to make him a Wyoming citizen for purposes of Article IV. Since he was born and raised in South Dakota, Saul is a United States citizen and was at least originally a citizen of South Dakota. To change his state citizenship and become a Wyoming citizen, he must establish his domicile or bona fide residence there. Yet Saul did not take up residence in Wyoming with the intention to remain there indefinitely. His intent was rather to stay in Wyoming only until he graduated and to then move to Florida. Thus Saul is not a citizen of Wyoming. Nor is he a citizen of Florida, for he has not yet taken up residence there. Instead, he is still a citizen of South Dakota and therefore cannot use the Privileges and Immunities Clause to challenge actions taken by his own state.

The Court has often said that "the terms 'citizen' and 'resident' are 'essentially interchangeable,'... for purposes of analysis of most cases under the Privileges and Immunities Clause." *United Building & Construction Trades Council*, supra, 465 U.S. at 216. While this may be "essentially" true in "most cases," we have seen that residency alone is not enough to ascertain a person's state of citizenship for purposes of Article IV. It is also necessary to determine whether the person is a U.S. citizen and whether he or she is a bona fide as opposed to just a temporary resident of the state.

Nevertheless, the Court's rough equation of "citizenship" and "residency" is useful in detecting possible Privileges and Immunities Clause problems. Laws that limit certain rights or privileges to "residents," "permanent residents," or "bona fide residents" of a state discriminate against out-of-state citizens in much the same manner as laws that specifically favor "citizens" of the state. For by disadvantaging those who are not "residents," a state discriminates against citizens of other states, few of whom are residents of the state, in favor of the state's own citizens, most of whom are residents of the state. Thus, in terms of spotting Article IV, §2 issues, it may be helpful to think of the terms "citizen" and "resident" as being essentially interchangeable.

§9.3.3 Discrimination Based on Municipal Residence

Thus far we have considered the Privileges and Immunities Clause as a means of challenging laws that discriminate against out-of-staters. The clause may also be invoked against laws that discriminate against people who do not reside in a particular city, county, or other political subdivision of the state.

Laws that favor residents of a city necessarily discriminate against citizens of other states. While a city's residents may include some people who are citizens of other states, municipal residency requirements necessarily disadvantage the vast majority of citizens of other states who do not live there. "A person who is not residing in a given State is *ipso facto* not residing in a city within that State. Thus, whether the exercise of a privilege is conditioned on state residency or on municipal residency he will just as surely be excluded." *United Building & Construction Trades Council*, supra, 465 U.S. at 216-217.

Even though municipal residency laws also burden those of the state's own citizens who live outside the city in question, these laws still discriminate against citizens of other states by favoring in-staters at the expense of nearly all out-of-staters. And, if every city in the state were to adopt a similar law, the net effect would be to benefit all of the state's citizens at the expense of nearly all out-of-staters. Moreover, to the extent that municipal residency requirements burden other citizens of the state, these in-staters are in a position to obtain redress through the political process by securing passage of a state law prohibiting such local favoritism. The disadvantaged citizens of other states have no similar remedy since they are not permitted to vote in the state where the discrimination has occurred.

Example 9-F

To alleviate a severe unemployment problem, the city of Hampton adopted an ordinance requiring every business in the city to have a work force composed of at least 40 percent city residents. As a result of this ordinance, Ruby, who does not live in Hampton, was dismissed from her job as a teller with a private bank in Hampton. May Ruby challenge the ordinance as violating her rights under the Privileges and Immunities Clause of Article IV?

Explanation

If Ruby is a citizen of the state in which Hampton is located, she cannot invoke Article IV, §2, for the clause only protects citizens of other states. However, if Ruby lives in a neighboring state and commuted to work in Hampton, she has standing to invoke the Privileges and Immunities Clause.

The interest in pursuing a trade or occupation is a fundamental right that falls within the purview of the clause. Though the Hampton ordinance discriminates on the basis of municipal rather than state citizenship, it favors those state residents who live in Hampton, at the expense of nearly all out-of-state citizens. The Privileges and Immunities Clause is therefore triggered and the ordinance will be struck down unless the city can show that there is a substantial reason for discriminating against out-of-state residents like Ruby.

§9.4 THE SUBSTANTIAL REASON TEST

If a state or local law discriminates against citizens of other states with respect to a fundamental right falling within the purview of the Privileges and Immunities Clause, the law is not automatically invalid. Instead, the defender of the law will be given an opportunity to justify the measure by showing that "there is a 'substantial reason' for the difference in treatment." *United Building & Construction Trades Council,* supra, 465 U.S. at 222. However, if a state or local law discriminates with respect to publicly owned goods or resources, the Court will apply a relaxed version of the substantial reason test under which the discrimination is likely to be upheld.

§9.4.1 The General Test

Laws that discriminate against citizens of other states with respect to a fundamental right are normally unconstitutional if "there is no substantial reason for the discrimination beyond the mere fact that they are citizens of other States." *Toomer v. Witsell,* supra, 334 U.S. at 396. Under the Court's substantial reason test, such a law will be upheld only if it is shown that,

1. There is a substantial reason for the difference in treatment — i.e., noncitizens constitute a unique or peculiar source of the evil at which the law is aimed — and
2. The discrimination is closely related to the state's objectives, taking into account whether there are feasible less discriminatory or less restrictive ways of achieving the state's goals.

See *Supreme Court of Virginia v. Friedman,* supra, 487 U.S at 64-65 and *Supreme Court of New Hampshire v. Piper,* 470 U.S. 274, 284-288 (1985) (using this test to invalidate state laws that limited admission to the bar to lawyers who were bona fide residents of the state). While the substantial reason test entails a fairly strict standard of judicial review, it is arguably not as exacting as that used under the dormant Commerce Clause to review state laws that discriminate against interstate commerce. See §8.6. Thus, as one court has noted,

> A statute will survive a Privileges and Immunities analysis if a State can demonstrate a "substantial" interest that is . . . "reasonably," "substantially," or "closely" related to the discriminatory means employed. By contrast, under the Dormant Commerce Clause, "discrimination against interstate commerce in favor of local business or investment is *per se* invalid, save in a narrow class of

cases in which the [state] can demonstrate, under rigorous scrutiny, that it has no other means to advance a legitimate local interest."

Bach v. Pataki, 408 F.3d 75, 89 n.27 (2d Cir. 2005), *cert. denied*, 546 U.S. 1174 (2006).

Example 9-G

South Carolina imposes a license fee on commercial shrimp boats. The fee is $25 for boats owned by state residents, and $2,500 for boats owned by nonresidents. Moe operates a commercial shrimp boat in South Carolina waters. Because he is a citizen of Florida, he had to pay South Carolina a fee of $2,500. Can Moe successfully challenge South Carolina's fee structure as violating Article IV's Privileges and Immunities Clause?

Explanation

The fee statute affects two fundamental rights that are within the purview of the Privileges and Immunities Clause, for it impairs Moe's right to do business in the state and his right to "an exemption from higher taxes or impositions than are paid by the other citizens of the state. . . ." *Corfield v. Coryell*, supra, 6 F. Cas. at 552. Moreover, the law clearly discriminates against citizens of other states who must pay a fee 100 times larger than that paid by South Carolina citizens. The fee statute will thus be struck down unless it passes the substantial reason test.

The state must first prove that nonresidents pose a special problem that warrants charging them a higher fee than the state charges its own citizens. The state might argue that its goal is to conserve the supply of shrimp by discouraging nonresidents who use larger fishing boats and thus take a disproportionate number of shrimp from state waters. Or the state might claim it is more difficult to enforce its fishing regulations against nonresidents because they live outside the jurisdiction. For either of these arguments to succeed, the state must prove that nonresidents in fact pose the unique evils attributed to them. If, for example, large boats are sometimes also used by residents, the "larger boats" rationale will not provide a valid reason for treating noncitizens differently. Alternatively, the state would have to prove that noncitizens are actually more likely to ignore its fishing regulations or that there are demonstrable extra costs entailed in enforcing the state's fishing regulations against them.

Even if South Carolina shows that citizens of other states pose either or both of the peculiar evils ascribed to them, the state must also prove that it chose the least discriminatory and least restrictive feasible means of achieving its goals. With respect to conservation, a less discriminatory and less burdensome alternative would be to charge *all* boat owners (resident and nonresident) a graduated fee based on the size of a particular vessel. As to the enforcement goal, a less restrictive means would be to charge nonresidents a higher fee designed merely to compensate the state for the added costs of enforcement; it is unlikely that the extra enforcement costs would justify a fee 100 times greater than that charged locals. See *Toomer v. Witsell*, 334 U.S. 385 (1948) (invalidating similar South Carolina shrimp boat license fee schedule).

In some situations, discriminatory taxes or fees imposed on citizens of other states may be defended under the substantial reason test by showing that the apparent discrimination merely places out-of-staters on an equal footing with state residents.

Example 9-H

In Example 9-A, we saw that the Privileges and Immunities Clause would likely be triggered if Mack were a professional bike racer. State B's law charging out-of-staters a $50 bike racing fee while in-staters paid only $25 would then be invalid unless the state could satisfy the substantial reason test. Could the state do so here?

Explanation

State B might contend that the fee is designed to compensate state and local authorities for police and traffic-diversion costs incurred in connection with bike races. The state might argue that out-of-state racers like Mack pose a unique evil because state B citizens have already paid a portion of these expenses in the form of a $25 annual bicycle *license fee*. If this were in fact the case, charging in-staters a *racing fee* of $25 and out-of-staters a fee of $50 puts everyone on a par, for everyone pays $50 per year to bike race in state B, regardless of his or her state of citizenship.

However, Mack might be able to show that the fee schedule is more discriminatory than necessary to place citizens and noncitizens of state B on an equal footing. Perhaps only $10 of the $25 license fee paid by state B bike owners is used to defray the cost of bike races. In this event, to charge out-of-state bike racers an extra $25 (rather than an extra $10) forces them to pay more than their fair share of these expenses. To put it differently, the state B law is more discriminatory and more burdensome than is required to compensate for the unique evils posed by out-of-state racers.

Example 9-1

New York law prohibits anyone from carrying a handgun in the state unless he or she has a New York firearms license. The only persons eligible for such a license are permanent residents of the state or those whose principal employment is there. Even then, licenses are not automatically granted. Applicants are closely screened and investigated before a license will be issued. Thereafter, the state closely monitors licensees and reserves the right to revoke a license *sua sponte* if at any time it appears a licensee is no longer wholly reliable. Bach, who lives in Virginia where he is licensed to carry a weapon under that state's law, regularly drives to New York to visit his parents. He wishes to take his pistol with him on these trips because the route to their home goes through some high-crime areas. However, because Bach does not live or work in New York, his application for a handgun license was denied. Can he successfully challenge the New York firearms law under Article IV's Privileges and Immunities Clause?

Explanation

Bach would first have to establish that the right to carry firearms falls within the purview of the Privileges and Immunities Clause. While the right is not one the Supreme Court has recognized for these purposes, Bach might be able to persuade a court to extend the reach of the clause to cover such a right, even though the Court has not done this often. If carrying a firearm is deemed to be a protected privilege or immunity, the clause is triggered here since New York is discriminating against nonresidents of the state. The state would have to show that it has a substantial reason for doing so. Nonresidents would seem to present a particularized evil in terms of the state's ability to screen applicants and to monitor their behavior after a license has been granted, since it is more difficult to obtain the requisite information from other states. Whether the degree of discrimination is closely related to the state's objectives and whether feasible, less discriminatory alternatives are available, are closer questions. While the information the state requires is in theory available for persons living in other states, as a practical matter it would be more difficult if not impossible for New York to obtain such information, particularly if other states have no real incentive to cooperate with New York officials. The latter might be the case if those states have their own gun licensing schemes and would hence gain little if anything from the additional expense of cooperating with New York. See *Bach v. Pataki*, 408 F.3d 75 (2d Cir. 2005), *cert. denied*, 546 U.S. 1174 (2006) (holding that New York's firearm possession law did not violate the Privileges and Immunities Clause).

§9.4.2 State-Owned Goods or Resources

Where a state discriminates against citizens of other states with respect to goods or resources that belong to the state, the Privileges and Immunities Clause applies with relaxed strength. Unlike the dormant Commerce Clause, which is wholly inapplicable when the state acts as a market participant (see §8.12), the Privileges and Immunities Clause continues to play a role in such settings, albeit a diminished one. The difference in approaches is explained by the fact that while the dormant Commerce Clause is concerned with potential conflicts between "state *regulation* and federal regulatory authority," the Privileges and Immunities Clause seeks to preserve "interstate harmony," a concern that "cuts across the market regulator-market participant distinction that is crucial under the Commerce Clause." *United Building & Construction Trades Council*, supra, 465 U.S. at 220. Thus, "[r]ather than placing a statute completely beyond the [Privileges and Immunities] Clause, a state's ownership of the property with which the statute is concerned is a factor — although often the crucial factor — to be considered in evaluating whether the statute's discrimination against noncitizens violates the Clause." *Hicklin v. Orbeck*, 437 U.S. 518, 529 (1978).

This relaxed standard of review applies when the state sells state-owned property such as timber or oil from public lands, when it dispenses services like health care or education, and when it spends or distributes public monies. In each of these areas, the Privileges and Immunities Clause allows state and local governments to favor citizens of the state over out-of-staters — as long as the breadth of the discrimination is not excessive. There is no bright line marking the point at which the state will be held to have run afoul of the Privileges and Immunities Clause. However, an important consideration is the extent to which the state has attempted to impose discriminatory conditions on private transactions in which the state itself is not directly involved. The broader the scope of such discrimination, the greater the chance that the state will be found to have violated the Privileges and Immunities Clause.

Example 9-J

When Alaska decided to sell oil and gas from state-owned lands, it passed a law requiring that any company directly or indirectly benefiting from the state's decision to sell its oil and gas must adopt an employment policy that favors Alaskans over citizens of other states. Under this "Alaska Hire" law, the resident hiring preference applies not only to contractors and subcontractors who pump, transport, or refine the state's oil and gas, but to every company that supplies goods or services to any of these contractors or subcontractors. Leila is a citizen of Montana who works six months a year for an Alaska accounting firm. As a result of Alaska Hire, she was fired from her job because the firm for which she worked provides accounting services to an Alaska firm that services trucks used by a catering service that sells food to workers building the Alaska pipeline. May Leila successfully challenge the Alaska Hire law on the ground that it violates the Privileges and Immunities Clause?

Explanation

If Alaska had merely imposed its resident hiring preference on the contractors with whom the state deals and on their immediate subcontractors, there might be no Privileges and Immunities Clause problem. However, the state has gone far beyond these contractual layers to reach purely private transactions that are many stages removed from the state's decision to sell its oil and gas. The breadth of Alaska's discrimination is so far-reaching as to bring the Privileges and Immunities Clause and the substantial reason test into play at full strength. Compare *Hicklin v. Orbeck*, supra, 437 U.S. at 534 (invalidating similar Alaska law under Privileges and Immunities Clause on basis that "the breadth of the discrimination mandated by Alaska Hire goes far beyond the degree of resident bias Alaska's ownership of the oil and gas can justifiably support"), with *United Building & Construction Trades Council*, supra, 465 U.S. at 220-223 (intimating that city did not violate Privileges and Immunities Clause by imposing a resident hiring preference that was limited to those contractors and subcontractors who worked directly on city-funded public works projects).

§9.5 OTHER MEANS OF CHALLENGING DISCRIMINATION AGAINST OUT-OF-STATERS

Article IV's Privileges and Immunities Clause provides a useful means of attacking many state and local laws that discriminate against out-of-staters. Yet, as we have seen, the clause does not reach all forms of discrimination against persons or entities from other states. First, corporations are not protected by the Article IV Privileges and Immunities Clause. Second, the clause only protects those interests that are deemed to be "fundamental"; lesser interests, such as those of a recreational nature, do not fall within the purview of the clause. Third, the clause does not come into play if a state discriminates against people who were *formerly* citizens of another state but who are now citizens of the discriminating state—e.g., laws that discriminate against newer residents of the state.

Even though the Privileges and Immunities Clause of Article IV does not reach these forms of discrimination, there may be other means of challenging them under the Constitution. These alternative avenues of attack are addressed elsewhere in the Constitutional Law course. However, it is useful to consider them briefly so that you do not confuse the role of the Privileges and Immunities Clause with that played by other clauses of the Constitution.

§9.5.1 Discrimination Against Out-of-State Corporations

If a state discriminates against corporations created under the laws of another state — i.e., foreign corporations — those out-of-state corporations lack standing to invoke the Article IV Privileges and Immunities Clause. Since corporations are not "citizens" within the meaning of the clause, for them to invoke the clause would involve asserting the rights of third parties. See §§3.4.5, 9.3.2.

An out-of-state corporation will nonetheless be able to challenge the discriminatory state law under the dormant Commerce Clause. See §8.6. State and local laws that discriminate against businesses from other states or against interstate commerce are often challenged on this basis by corporate plaintiffs, even though that plaintiff is barred from invoking the Privileges and Immunities Clause. See, e.g., *Dean Milk Co. v. City of Madison*, 340 U.S. 349 (1951) (successful challenge by Illinois corporation to Madison, Wisconsin, milk ordinance that discriminated against out-of-state milk producers); *Lewis v. BT Investment Managers, Inc.*, 447 U.S. 27 (1980) (successful challenge by New York corporation to Florida law that discriminated against out-of-state financial institutions). This dormant Commerce Clause line of attack is, of course, also available to out-of-state individuals and noncorporate entities, in addition to any argument they might make under the Privileges and Immunities Clause.

Out-of-state corporations and individuals may also be able to challenge state laws that discriminate against them by invoking the Fourteenth Amendment Equal Protection Clause. This clause provides that no state shall "deny to any person within its jurisdiction the equal protection of the laws." While corporations are not "citizens" for purposes of Article IV, §2's Privileges and Immunities Clause, they are "persons" within the meaning of the Fourteenth Amendment §1. Even though only a low-level, rational basis standard of review will be called for in most cases where out-of-state corporations invoke the Equal Protection Clause, the clause will sometimes work to overturn discriminatory state legislation. See *Metropolitan Life Ins. Co. v. Ward*, 470 U.S. 869 (1985) (applying Equal Protection Clause to invalidate Alabama law taxing out-of-state insurance companies at higher rate than domestic companies).

§9.5.2 Discrimination Against Citizens of Other States Where No "Fundamental" Right Is Involved

Natural persons, unlike corporations, are protected by the Privileges and Immunities Clause, but only with respect to interests that are sufficiently fundamental to come within the clause's protection. In those instances where discrimination against citizens of other states does not fall within the purview of Article IV, the individual might still raise a challenge under the Fourteenth Amendment Equal Protection Clause. However, these challenges will typically trigger only a rational basis standard of review and therefore will not often succeed. See *Baldwin v. Montana Fish & Game Commn.*, supra, 436 U.S. at 388-391 (state's discriminatory fee schedule for recreational elk hunting did not trigger the Privileges and Immunities Clause and was found not to violate the Equal Protection Clause).

§9.5.3 Discrimination Against Former Citizens of Other States

The Privileges and Immunities Clause comes into play only when a state is discriminating against people who are citizens of other states. If a state discriminates against those of its *own citizens* who moved to the state relatively recently, but who are now domiciliaries of the state, the Privileges and Immunities Clause is not applicable.

One example of such discrimination against newcomers is the so-called durational residency requirement or waiting period. This bars new residents from receiving certain benefits until they have lived in the state for a specified length of time. Discrimination against former residents of other states may also take the form of so-called fixed-point or fixed-date residency requirements; these provide that persons are eligible for some state benefit only if they lived in the state either at a certain point in their lives (e.g., birth, graduation from high school) or at a certain date (e.g., on January 1, 1990).

All of these forms of discrimination against former citizens of other states are subject to challenge under the Equal Protection Clause and the Privileges or Immunities Clause of the Fourteenth Amendment. If the benefit or privilege that the state is denying to the newcomer is sufficiently vital and important, the discrimination will be subject to strict scrutiny under the Equal Protection Clause because it penalizes people for exercising the fundamental right to migrate or travel from one state to another. See, e.g., *Shapiro v. Thompson*, 394 U.S. 618 (1969) (one-year durational residency requirement for receipt of welfare assistance violates Equal Protection Clause); *Attorney General of New York v. Soto-Lopez*, 476 U.S. 898 (1986) (limiting civil service employment preference to those resident veterans who lived in the state at the time they entered military service violates Equal Protection Clause).

Even if the discrimination against newcomers does not involve a benefit sufficiently vital to burden the fundamental right to travel and is thus not subject to strict scrutiny under the Equal Protection Clause, it might still be subject to strict scrutiny under the Privileges or Immunities Clause of the Fourteenth Amendment. See §9.3.1. Moreover, the discrimination might not even pass muster under the Equal Protection Clause. See, e.g., *Zobel v. Williams*, 457 U.S. 55 (1982) (Alaska statute that paid annual dividends to state residents based on length of time they had lived in the state violated Equal Protection Clause); *Williams v. Vermont*, 472 U.S. 14 (1985) (state auto registration tax that discriminated against newcomers to state violated Equal Protection Clause). See Allan Ides and Christopher N. May, *Constitutional Law: Individual Rights*, §7.4 (6th ed. 2013).

Table of Cases

Table of Cases

Table of Cases

448

Index